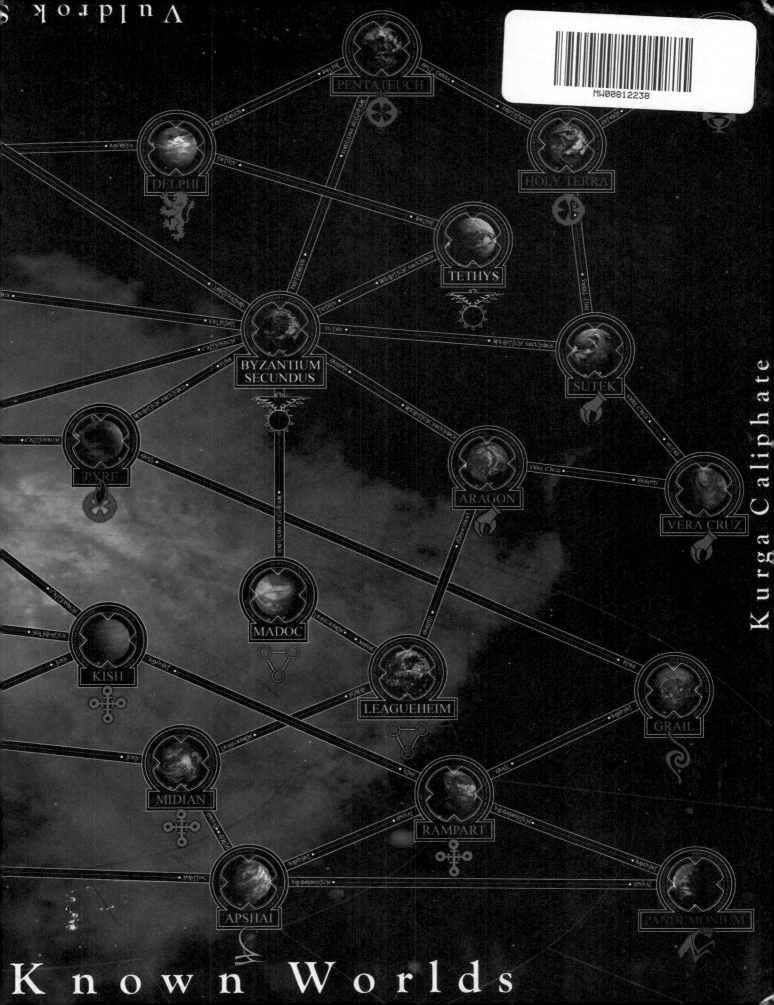

Science Fiction Roleplaying

by Bill Bridges & Andrew Greenberg

FADING SUNS Second Edition

Credits

Game design: Bill Bridges and Andrew Greenberg

Additional design: John Bridges, Ken Lightner, Ed Pike

Development and typesetting: Bill Bridges

Writing: Bill Bridges, Brian Campbell, Andrew Greenberg, Robert Hatch, Jennifer Hartshorn, Chris Howard, Sam Inabinet, Ian Lemke, Jim Moore, Rustin Quaide

Editing and proofreading: Bill Bridges, Andrew Greenberg, Jennifer Hartshorn (first edition)

Art direction: John Bridges

Art: John Bridges, Mitch Byrd, Darryl Elliott, Jason Felix, Sam Inabinet, Mark Jackson, Jack Keefer, Andrew Kudelka, Brian LeBlanc, Larry MacDougall, Alex Sheikman, Ron Spencer, Joshua Gabriel Timbrook

Cover art, Jumpweb map and logo: Rob Dixon

3D starship models: David Sweet, Jeff Toney

Jumpgate sculpture: Jay and Dave Marsh

Jumpgate photography: Karl Hawk

Thanks to all the first and second edition playtesters: Emrey Barnes, Forest Black, Milo Blue, John Bridges, Bernie Clark, Ian Cooke, Neal Sainte Crosse, Suzanne Sainte Crosse, Gary Deariso, Rick Denning, Brad Freeman, Amelia G, Stephen Gilliam, Garner Halloran, Andy Harmon, Jennifer Hartshorn, Debbie Hoppe, Chris Howard, Daniel Landers, Ian Lemke, Ken Lightner, Jim Miller, James Moore, Bonnie Moore, Matt Moses, Bryce Nakagawa, Dave Parrish, Ed Pike, Todd Shaughnessy, Stephen E. Smith, Joshua Gabriel Timbrook, Chris Wiese.

Special thanks to Andy Harmon and everyone on the **Fading Suns** electronic mailing list for their ongoing input and critiques!

www.holistic-design.com

Holistic Design Inc.
5295 Hwy 78, D-337
Stone Mountain, GA 30087

Contents

Prologue:
Alustro's Quest

To: Archbishop Marcus Aurelius Palamon, Cathedral of Saint Maya, Holy City, Galatea, Byzantium Secundus

Dearest Uncle,

It has been long since I last wrote you. I apologize for not doing so sooner, but the dangers involved were too great. I'm sure you will scoff at such a remark, but I tell you it is true. How dangerous, I hear you ask, to write to the Archbishop of Byzantium Secundus? No one would dare delay delivery of such a missive, and none would dare break its seal to read it.

As you know, trusts and confidences can be betrayed under intact seals. My liege, Erian Li Halan, has many enemies, not the least of which is her brother, a hateful man bent on destroying her. To that end, he has enflamed many of his allies against her, some of whom are involved in the highest levels of information gathering. I could not risk even a letter to you, lest it reveal our whereabouts before we had moved on.

Such cloak and dagger lives disgust you, I know. I wish I could live otherwise. I yearn for the life of simple contemplation I left behind on Midian when I eagerly joined Erian on her mission to the stars. My hunger for new sites and experiences could not be sated, and the cold walls of the monastery seemed a prison. Ironic that it now seems a warm den of rest and safety, after so many years on the roads between the stars.

But I am not writing for pity or justification. I simply explain my situation so that you understand the long years between correspondence. I wish so much to speak with you in person, to walk the corridors of your great cathedral and hear you orate the virtues of the Prophet's disciples again, in your commanding voice that was once a pillar of faith for me. It matters little that I betrayed your own faith by joining the Eskatonic Order rather than the Orthodoxy — the words of the Prophet are shared by both our sects.

I digress. I must put aside reflection and state the matter about which I write. My liege readies to travel again, this time on a new path, one full of possibility and danger. I am to go with her, for our fates are one. I am her confessor, and spiritual guide besides. No longer is this role just in her service, however — it is also in mine, for I have been gifted with dreams and visions leading me toward an uncertain but important future.

I wrote of the Gargoyle of Nowhere in my last letter, that monolithic relic left behind by the Anunnaki, they who wrought the jumpgates and tamed the heavens before our kind was raised from the muck by the hand of the Pancreator. The vision it gifted us then — the maddeningly vague clues which lead us from world to world in search of ever more clues — only now begins to take shape.

To explain this shape, I must first explain where we have been and what we have seen. The Known Worlds are huge, sprawling across the nightscape of the dimming stars forty worlds strong. While this is a paltrey sum compared to the hundreds of worlds once known to the Second Republic, it is still a testament to humankind's unity that even so many worlds as these have stayed together, connected through the jumpweb now under the rule of Emperor Alexius.

I have been to many of these worlds — nearly all of them, in fact. How many people can claim that? Most never leave their hovels, let alone their provinces — and to leave one's very planet is a momentous step indeed. From there to travel to more than three worlds is a jaunt even most Charioteer star-pilots never achieve. But to travel like Erian and her entourage — unimaginable.

And yet we have done so. We have broken all bonds of place and come and go from hither to yon as birds migrate through the seasons or as leaves travel the aether or float along the stream. What's more — we are not alone. More and more people of brave will and good constitution awaken from a long night of captivity on their homeworlds to escape gravity and go outwards, to worlds once known only to their grandparents or more distant ancestors in the past. The Emperor Wars kept everyone penned in, trapped behind

enemy lines in their own homes.

But that dark time is over at last. Alexius is ascendant and the jumproads are open once more. The cage is broken and the beasts have slipped through the bars.

Yes, I mean beasts. For every man and woman of good heart and purpose who now travel between the worlds of the Empire, two or three scoundrels of black heart and base desire also go forth. For this reason, only a fool travels alone, and those of good intent are best served by their own kind. I do not follow Erian because feudal duties alone decree it — I do so because in her service I am among others of good heart, some with strong arm and hand to defend us bodily from the harm others intend. I can attempt to sooth a soul with words of scripture, or even seal a wound with prayer, but I can do little to prevent injury in the face of evil.

Cardanzo, Erian's bodyguard, is a capable man and goodly tactician. Of even greater might is Onggangarak, our Vorox friend who has elected us members of his *angerak* — his blood pack. No better soldiers could one ask in the quest for right.

And no better pilot than Julia Abrams. Although her demeanor is caustic, her heart is strong and deeply tied to ours. She is the engine of our escape and a hearty companion on the road — a true follower of the first disciple, Paulus the Traveler, he who guided the Prophet on his sojourns.

In your response to my last letter, you warned me against associating too closely with the Ur-Ukar aliens, whom you, like many, distrust for their seemingly primitive, clannish ways. I have learned to look beyond the expected, and seen the truth that lies in people's hearts. Sanjuk oj Kaval is a woman of supreme courage. Her travails on her harsh homeworld of Kordeth, in the subterranean caverns of her clan, have only strengthened her bravery. While she is as yet largely ignorant of scripture, I have made a pact with her — for every legend she tells me of Ukari culture, I read to her verse from the Omega Gospels. In such a way does understanding between two different peoples grow. It is just such an interchange that must take place on a galactic scale, to overcome the centuries of ignorance and hate fostered between fiefs and territories.

The Church teaches us of the good in our souls, and yet acts as if people are mean and evil unless taught otherwise. The rod of rulership must fall heavily on humanity and its alien brethren lest they rise up to do evil. Or so the widespread belief — justification — goes. I know otherwise. I know that even the most oppressed men will share their only foodstores with suffering strangers, even if such strangers be from strange locales and other worlds. Yes, distrust and suspicion is rampant, and some are more likely to be greeted by a lynch mob than an invitation to dinner, but this is by no means as universal as we are all taught.

Perhaps during the Emperor Wars and its aftermath,

distrust was the lot of humankind. But with each new starship that comes from afar bringing goods undreamed of before; with each new person who comes bearing news of distant and long-forgotten family on other worlds; with each new knight that comes from the Emperor bringing law to the lawless regions, understanding and hope grows.

When men have hope, they begin to cherish their dreams once more. No matter how dark the suns may fade, the light of hope cannot be fully extinguished.

The fading suns. I have tried often to forget them, for their dimming light fails to show the way forward, only the way back. I no longer want to look back. I want only to go forward, to solve the dilemma of our impending ruin, to reignite the stars that have for so long only portended our doom. Heresy? To hope to change what the Pancreator has wrought? But you yourself preach that it is not the Pancreator that darkens the day, but the demons who haunt us and hover before the light, casting their mournful shadows over our stars.

Why not act against them? Why simply sit and wait for the end, assured that judgment will come swift to all. What if that judgement depends on our acting? If we fail in this, how will we be judged then?

Go back to the Prophet's words and read them afresh. I believe with the deepest sincerity that he was not speaking for the people then, but for now. He spoke of a "dark between the stars," and the demons that dwell therein. He spoke of the evil which would descend on us and the ways that we might fight it. Yet when he said these things, were not the stars shining bright? Did not humankind have its greatest moments yet before it, in the founding of the Second Republic that was to come?

Then why was he so ill at ease and dark of heart? Why in an Age of Miracles did he alone see danger? I tell you he did not see with the eyes of the present but with the future — to our present, to our time and its rising darkness. He set down words which we would need now to survive against the chill end of time.

All his deeds, all his acts and words that enriched us, did so in the hope that we would not simply look to them as artifacts of a better past, but as examples of a greater future. It is for us now to become as his disciples and follow their steps toward the stars, to Quest, Defend the Faith, Right Wrongs, Seek Justice, Heal the Injured, Aid the Needy, Seek Wisdom and Look Within.

If Paulus could do so, why not we? If Mantius and Lextius, Maya, Amalthea, Hombor, Horace and Ven Lohji — why not we?

I know your answer. Heresy. We are not saints, and we dare not elect ourselves so. I agree. I am no saint. But I can try to be. I can muster all my will and faith toward walking as one who can make a difference, one who can change fate

for the better.

Worry not that the Inquisition will hunt us for such hubris; they already have. I have dodged more flameguns and brown-robed fanatics over the past years than I thought could possibly exist. There are so very many who desire to punish others for reaping benefits they themselves fear to ask for.

We have surely sinned in that we travel in a starship. Is not this the sort of technology they spew sermons against? I am not ignorant of the dangers of such tech, for the Second Republic proved what science without faith can produce, and its mewling horrors are not easily forgotten. But I will not stand against all technology because some of it was misused.

I digress again. I meant to tell you of our travels, of the sights I have seen since last I wrote. I have sent you in separate letters copies of my journals of the past three years. While they tell of my deepest thoughts and our entourage's trials on many worlds, I want here to tell of the things I could not enter into those journals, because the hectic pace of our lives prevented it. I want to impress upon you what I found, how things are not as we are told, and why I seek to go even farther.

My thoughts first turn to Malignatius, that frozen hell of a world, gulag for so many suffering under the whim of House Decados. No better served were the people, however, when House Li Halan ruled the world before the Emperor Wars. I know the Li Halan well, having lived in their service all my life, and I believe I can thus see their faults clearly. Never are the common folk under them allowed to rise, no matter how they prove themselves otherwise. But the virtue of the Li Halan is that neither do they mistreat their charges, unlike the Decados. While surely even the lowliest Decados peasant may rise to better status for committing any number of heinous deeds that please their lords, most are trampled under foot.

This world is renowned for its religious schisms and the many charismatics who have risen to guide people onto often bizarre spiritual paths. Such loud men and women have branded the world fanatic, and this is surely how the Orthodoxy sees it. But what if I were to tell you that, hidden in the ice caves under the surface, there are many monks of astonishing enlightenment? I met one, a Friar Ged, who treated me to such a dialogue of scriptural questioning that I had not had since my first exposure to Magister Tarsus, my Eskatonic examiner. I came to realize that no matter the political situation in a place or the tenure of its people as a whole, there are always unique individuals worthy of encountering.

And there are wonders, too, visions of beauty and natural awe. I can never forget my undersea swim on the world of Madoc, a planet whose surface is mainly ocean and achepeligo. Using breathing suits provided us by a wealthy guildswoman — technology of which I'm sure many in the Church disaprove — our entourage swam deep down to examine the ruins of that planet's previous culture, a civiliza-

tion that had fallen even before humans left Holy Terra.

Off in the far distance, fearful to come near us, I saw shadowy figures flit in and out of the coral ruins, watching us with their large eyes. One wore sparkling armor of sea shells and another bore a luminous staff — these were no simple sea creatures. They were Oro'ym, the fabled amphibian sentients of that world. I wished so much to approach them and speak with them, hoping they knew our language, but they fled whenever I drew near.

Even more enigmatic than the Oro'ym, however, were the Vau. Ah, I wish I could see the look of shock and indignation on your face when I tell you that I have met a Vau. I even shook its hand, although it seemed bemused by the gesture. It was on Manitou, that border world where the Church itself treads only lightly for fear of raising the ire of the Vau rulers. Here many of the outlaw dregs of humanity have collected — not its pirates and murderers so much as its thought criminals, those who follow different gods or indulge in pastimes harmful only to themselves but which are punishable by death in the courts of the Known Worlds.

I will not tell you why we were there, for you would greatly disapprove. I will simply say that, while wandering the agora and marveling at the wealth of black market goods, an emissary from the local Vau mandarin approached us. He appeared to be of their worker caste, a lowly position among his kind but still far and away more prestigious than our serf class. He seemed curious about us, but afraid to show it. Nonetheless, he came up to Erian and smiled, a gesture alien to his kind but one which he had obviously practised for our sake. She greeted him, unsure what to say or do, and I offered my hand. He took it. And then he left, as if he had already gone further than he was allowed.

I still don't understand the matter, but I am impressed nonetheless. Perhaps my leige is destined for greatness, and the Vau somehow know of this. It is said that they have machines that foretell that future, and ancient prophecies given to them by the Anunnaki. Who can say for sure? They remain removed from humankind, protected by their superior technology.

The Ur-Obun also seemed to favor my leige, and believe she is destined for something, although Julia opines that they were simply "sucking up" to a human noble. Our stay on Velisimil was short, but most relaxing. While Erian made alliance with many Umo'rin members, I spent a meditation retreat in a humble Voavenlohjun temple. I was the only human, but they welcomed me as if I were one of their own. They do not separate involvement in the Church into sects as we do; all who follow the Prophet's teachings are sacred to them. Of course, they see all religious system as sacred in a way, although they certainly do not honor them equally. They recognize prereflective faith and postreflective grace, fear not.

I will shock you again with an admission concerning the Ur-Ukar — I have sat in a cavedark ceremony on Istakhr. It was not a true cave like on Kordeth, but a deep basement. Nonetheless, it was pitchblack. I joined the others, Sanjuk and her family, in reading the deed carvings of their ancestors on the wall. I only know a little Ukarish, and missed much of what was written, but Sanjuk's recitation aided me.

A barbaric practice? How so? It brought them together and united them in blood and a shared past. That Sanjuk allowed me to join in was a great honor and a sign that she considers me as trustworthy as family — a powerful trust for an Ukari.

What I found most enlightening about the reading, however, was the history of the Ukari gods. While Sanjuk sneers when I mention the common human belief about the truth of their gods, I still believe it so. How can any deny, after hearing the legends of the Ur-Obun and Ur-Ukar, that their deities were any other than the ancient Anunnaki? That this powerful race grandfathered these younger races in their early days hints that perhaps they did the same for us, on old Urth.

The xenoarchaeologists of the Second Republic thought so. Is this not why they named the Anunnaki after the old gods of Urth? What if these gods of our prereflective ancestors were from the stars? And what if they took our ancestors with them on their journeys? What would have become of such humans? Do they still exist among the stars?

These questions are impossible to answer as yet. I hope to do so one day, however.

But let me not leave out opinions on the Merchant League and noble class. You'd surely be most disgruntled at my omission — if you've bothered to read this far. I know you have been to Leagueheim, for your disproval of its "Republican sympathies" was most apparent to me even at a young age. But even you were somewhat awed at its spires and cities, one of the few worlds that still resembles the Second Republic at its height. I have walked those spires, and ambled the sky lanes from building to building, traveling leagues without ever touching ground.

As I walked, flitters would hover near me with guildsmembers offering me rides, confused that I would willingly choose to walk when I could ride for free. But I knew their kind offers were not truly free, for I would surely be subject to a sales pitch of one kind or another should I choose to ride in their gravity-defying chariots. It is indeed true that everything is for sale on Leagueheim, including allegiances.

How refreshing then, to meet those for whom allegiance is a matter of honor, not firebirds. I mean the Hazat — those nobles of a most martial bent whose hot-headed fury has shaken up the Empire on many occassions. Erian has allies in the house, and we have visited them often. On one

occassion, on Aragon, we were witness to that most famous of noble pastimes: the duel.

Erian was to be Baron Allejandro Campeiro Justin de Justus's second in a fight. This means that, while she would not fight herself, she would hand him his weapon and watch for treachery from the baron's opponent. We all gathered to watch, and I was ready to mend any wounds taken by either side.

It was a short but vicious fight, with terms of surrender alone. Whomever gave in first would be the loser. Such a duel between Hazat nobles is usually to the death, but the baron's opponent was an al-Malik dandy, Sir Jacob Saladin al-Malik, whom we all doubted would choose death before honor. He was an expert swordsman, though, and had first blood on the baron in mere seconds. But our friend ran him through moments later, thanks only to a malfunction in Sir Jacob's energy shield.

Nobles rely on these shields to protect them from the worst harm, although they don't stop relatively harmless blows from landing. It is these small wounds which add up over the course of a duel, however. In this case, the shield failed, and a mortal wound was delivered — or would have been mortal if not for the miracles of faith. My Eskatonic training allowed me to call upon the Pancreator's mercy to heal his wound, thus saving his life.

Instead of triumph, the baron was mortified, for he had no intention of winning a duel in such a way. Sir Jacob, who had been his enemy at the start of the day, became his friend by the end, for so gracious and generous was Baron Allejandro to his wronged opponent that he spared no expense in making things right. He invited the lord to recuperate at his mansion, in as much opulance as he could withstand. For his part, Sir Jacob was more than relieved at being brought back from death's door, and he pledged to tithe heavily to my order when next the chance arose.

I tell this tale not to impress you that I move in the company of nobles, but to mention the odd sense of honor they display. Sometimes, that is; not everywhere universally. There are nobles who are far from honorable, those who shame their very class by becoming tyrants. I speak of Duke Granzil Hassan Keddah, a lord on Grail who mistreats his people terribly. Even the Etyri of his fiefs have fled, flown on to other territories in high eeries rather than suffer his decrees, even though it is illegal for them to have done so. He has called a hunt on these avian sentients, but one which has been thankfully ignored by fellow nobles of his house, who have denied these hunters entry onto their fiefs.

And so I come, through long digression, back to the heart of the matter: the shape of my destiny in Erian's company. My lady has taken a great step forward and allied herself to the greatest power in the Known Worlds: she has taken pledge as a Questing Knight, in fealty to the Emperor himself. She now places his needs over those of her own house, although we both pray they never come into conflict. By this act of fealty, she is empowered to Quest.

To such happy news I add this: I, too, have taken an oath, one which places me in even greater fealty to her and her lord. I have become an Imperial Cohort, the new office opened by Alexius for those who wish to aid the Questing Knights but for whom such rank is closed themselves. Since I am not of noble blood or landed rank, this chance to aid my lady with the full support of her lord is a welcome opportunity. Cardanzo, Julia and Onggangarak have also pledged themselves as Cohorts, and so we all form a knightly company now in Alexius's service. We, too, can now Quest with the full support of a great lord — our destiny nears completion. The riddles posed years ago the Ur can begin to be answered.

I hope that this act of mine pleases you more than my previous decisions. My refusal of orthodoxy hurt you, but perhaps my new fealty to the shining star of your diocese on Byzantium Secundus will assure that my deeds will from now forwards be in the name of universal justice and law.

I know that you did not fully approve of the emperor at first, but his regular appearance in your cathedral for services has warmed you to him. I know this because I saw it myself. You and he, his Imperial Eminance, chatting together like old friends after the service, surrounded by bodyguards on all sides.

Yes, I saw this, for I was in your cathedral yesterday, witnessing your service from the high balcony. I so wanted to come down and greet you, to pray in the first pews before you. But I did not dare. Too many eyes are upon you, and your reaction to my presence would have alerted Erian's enemies, even if word took time to reach them.

My lady prepares a mission of great import and I go with her, as always. I know not where or what our pledge leads us toward, for it is not yet revealed to us. We leave, however, tonight. I had hoped to visit you in your personal quarters, far from prying eyes, but it is too late. I delayed too long, and duty pulls me away to another world, perhaps even to barbarian space, for many Questing Knights have been dispatched there of late.

I will see you again, uncle. I will kiss your hand in recognition of your high station and because you are my mother's brother. Fear not for me or my liege. If I should die on the reaches far from home, the Pancreator's light will still find me and guide me back, as it will all of good heart and right hand.

Farewell.

Your nephew,

Provost Guissepe Alustro

Introduction

Once the suns shone brightly, beacons in the vast night of space, calling humanity onward. The stars symbolized humanity's vast potential, a purpose and destiny revealed in progress, inciting an exodus of unlimited growth to the distant stars. Once people looked to the heavens with hope and longing in their eyes.

Then the suns — and hope — began to fade.

It is the beginning of the sixth millennium and history has come to an end. Humanity's greatest civilization has fallen, leaving ignorance and fear scattered among the ruins of many worlds. A new Dark Age is upon humanity and few believe in renewal and progress anymore. Now there is only waiting. Waiting for a slow death as the age-old stars fade to cinders and the souls of the sinful are called to Final Judgment.

But not all believe in this destiny. A leader has arisen, an emperor sworn to unite the worlds of Human Space together again under one banner. To ignite hope once more in their hearts.

It is a monumental task, for most people have already given up and fallen into the ways of the past, playing serfs to feudal lords. What is hope to them now but a falsehood which leads to pain? Better to leave the hard decisions to their masters and let the Church console their souls.

There are enemies everywhere, those who seek to selfishly profit from humanity's demise: vain nobles ruling far-flung worlds, power-hungry priests who seek dominion over the lives of men, the greedy merchant guilds growing rich from bartering humanity's needs and wants. They are not alone. Others are out there among the darkening stars, alien races angry with humankind for age-old slavery, and enigmatic alien empires with agendas too paradoxical to fathom.

It is in such a universe that individual men and women must live. Only a few of them will question. Fewer still will act on their questions and seek answers, ways to break the grip of custom and law. To free themselves and once more seize the stars — and their destiny.

Roleplaying Explained

If you're new to this artform and hobby, this book may seem strange to you. Don't worry; it will make more sense the further you read. **Fading Suns** is a roleplaying game, a highly imaginative activity which can provide hours of fun and a means of creative expression.

The hobby of roleplaying began in the early 1970s, growing out of miniature wargaming. People got a bit bored with sending historical armies against each other's forces; they wanted to mix it up with elves, orcs and wizards. Fantasy gaming was born. Then, some people stretched the boundaries further, by playing individual heroes rather than whole armies. Wargaming turned into roleplaying, where players not only fought enemies, but acted out the roles of their characters, creating dialogue for them and histories detailing the character's birthplace, upbringing and what her goals in life were.

The players of the games collaborated in creating whole worlds, environments for their characters to adventure in, usually inspired by the works of J.R.R. Tolkien and Robert E. Howard. Roleplaying game publishers provided premade worlds for gamers to use, and new supplements for the most popular of these worlds were eagerly awaited by avid gamers. Eventually, gamers began experimenting with new genres, such as science fiction, post-apocalypse, superheroes, horror and even Westerns.

The hobby has grown over the years to encompass a wide variety of gaming methods, from hack-and-slash com-

bat with detailed rules for combat resolution, to intensive storytelling with broad rules designed to help move a story forward rather than slow it down with dice rolling. Different people prefer different methods.

Fading Suns is primarily a game about heroes and the dramatic conflicts they encounter, from palace intrigues to cliffhanging combats. It provides a framework for players to create games from any perspective they desire. If they want to play soldiers who fight evil with guns and fists, the rules are here. If they want to play merchants who prefer diplomacy to violence, or priests wrestling with a metaphysical crisis, rules and helpful dramatic hints are also provided. **Fading Suns** is whatever the players want it to be.

How To Roleplay

Just how do you play a roleplaying game, anyway? First, you get your friends together, because roleplaying games are rarely played alone (it is possible, but requires special rules for solo gaming). It takes at least two people, but is usually best with three to six players, including one special player: the gamemaster.

One person takes on the task of the gamemaster, devising dramas and challenges for the player characters to overcome. The gamemaster plays all the people the characters meet and introduces the plots that go on around the characters, drawing them into dramatic conflict. The gamemaster is like a playwright, an author and a movie director rolled into one. He is the "Greek chorus" when necessary, telling the players what's going on as a narrator reveals a story element. He is also an actor, playing the wheedling informant the players' characters hook up with on the black market, the vain baron who seeks the characters' aid in rescuing his daughter, or the jolly innkeeper who is kind enough to extend the characters credit, because he likes their faces.

The gamemaster creates the plots that move the story forward, but it is the players who decide how their characters will react to the people and machinations active around them. Each player is like an actor taking on a role, but she is also a co-author of the drama, along with the gamemaster and the other characters. She decides who her character is and how that character reacts to the story.

Unlike a novel or film, a roleplaying game is a truly interactive experience, created from an interplay between the gamemaster and the players. The gamemaster introduces a conflict, the players react to it as they see fit (within the guidelines of their character concepts and characters' knowledge), and the gamemaster, taking the players' reactions into account, adjusts his plot as needed and introduces the next conflict. Players speak their characters' dialogue, all spontaneously in reaction to the gamemaster's plot. Roleplaying is even more interactive than computer games touted for their interactivity; no computer can yet match the sheer variability introduced into roleplaying games by clever players. It's an adage that you can never guess what a player will do in a roleplaying game, and it's a true one.

One important rule to remember is that roleplaying games are not won or lost like traditional board or video games. There are no scores to tally up. Regardless of whether the characters win or lose their struggles, it is the playing of the game itself — the flow of imagination and interaction — that determines whether or not a game succeeds.

The first step in learning to play **Fading Suns** is reading this book. Each chapter reveals more information about the setting and the rules of the game. The Example of Play provided at the end of Chapter 6 shows how the rules are used by gamemasters and players to run a **Fading Suns** roleplaying drama.

Tools

All you need to play **Fading Suns** is one 20-sided die, at least one six-sided die (although more are helpful), paper, pencils or pens, and — most importantly — imagination. The 20-sided die can be found in most hobby gaming stores that sell roleplaying games.

A Futuristic Passion Play

Fading Suns is primarily a science fiction game, which means that there are starships, blasters, powered armor, alien races, and weird science. But there are also many elements of traditional fantasy gaming: heroic characters and struggles, a feudal sociopolitical structure (noble lords, high priests and headstrong merchants), powerful artifacts and great mysteries. And there is horror: monsters and maddening discoveries revealing terrifying metaphysical truths.

In short, **Fading Suns** is a game which has everything a roleplaying universe needs in order tell stories of such varied and exotic themes as can be found anywhere — in our very own world here and now. Why should our created universes be more restrictive than the real world? By making them so, we only rob ourselves of the enriching heritage of stories left to us by previous generations from all corners of the earth. We owe it to ourselves to make our worlds as rich, vivid and complex (even maddeningly so) as that outside our doors.

Like all games, **Fading Suns** should be entertaining and fun to play. But roleplaying games can be more than mere pastimes. The players can strive for the same artistic goals as the author of a novel, a film or a play. **Fading Suns** is a passion play of sorts, a story about the triumphs and even tragedies of its characters that takes place in an imagined future. Many possible stories can be told here, from galaxy-spanning epics to the most personal of tales.

Like medieval passion plays, **Fading Suns** deals with grand themes universal to human experience. Its main theme is the Seeking. This is the mythological role all heroes play: the knight on quest, seeking power to vanquish his enemies or the secrets of self-discovery. Success or failure on this quest is not as important as the insights learned while on it.

The atmosphere of the dramas played out in **Fading Suns** is one of tragic ignorance. Civilization is in decline, and superstition and fear are everywhere. New ideas and frontiers are spurned by a nervous populace, fearful of change for the harm it brings. But it is just this sort of willful ignorance that keeps civilization from rising again. It is such fear that keeps hope buried and great challenges from being met. The player characters represent the heroes who can break the bonds of this ignorance and bring something new and great to their culture, to reawaken and invigorate life.

Without further ado, we give you a glimpse into the tumultuous fate of humankind four millennia from now....

Chapter 1: The Universe

History

The chronicle of humanity's history among the stars is a long one, stretching over two millennia. It is not a quiet story. From the greedy planet-grabbing of early colonists to the bloody battles of the Emperor Wars, humans have rarely slept peacefully in the void. They have prospered, suffered defeat, and dared to hope again. And they have not traveled down the paths of history alone; aliens walk among them, with long histories and destinies of their own to complete. To understand where humanity now stands, one must look to the beginning…

Prehistory

Humans know little of interstellar history before they reached space. What they do know comes from the histories of the Ur-Obun, Ur-Ukar and amphibian Oro'ym alien races, along with theories suggested by Second Republic archaeologists and a smattering of phrases from the enigmatic Vau, who may know much they are not telling.

These tales and the evidence cobbled from terraforming digs shows that there were once at least one, although possible two, previously extant though now extinct alien races of incredibly high advancement. One of these presumed races left the jumpgates behind. Little is known about them. Gargoylelike figures — both demonic and angelic in appearance — can be found in many ancient ruins and on the jumpgates.

Together, these two races are called the Anunnaki, or the Preadamites. They are also known as the Ur (proto-race), which is also a prefix used to identify their relics. Scholars believe one of these races — those presumed to have built the jumpgates — is older than the other. This race is called by various names: Jumpmasters, Gatekeepers, Inceptors,

Architects, and many more. The presumed younger race is known as the Successors, or Marauders. This latter name comes from alien legends, for their myths speak of two races of gods or elder beings who often warred against each other. One race protected mortals, while the other harassed them. Scholars believe that these "gods" were not mere metaphors, but memories of the Ur.

The idea of a mythical prehistorical war between elder races has some physical evidence to support it. Different digs have revealed ruins of extreme age with architectural motifs resembling those found on certain jumpgates. These ruins were not simply abandoned; they were destroyed in a war. Planetary cataclysms and upheavals cannot explain the devastation clearly wrought by high-tech weaponry, perhaps fusion guns and bombs. This great war was surely the cause for the disappearance of these two races, who leave the stage of history, abandoning their caretaking or harassment of the Children of the Ur some time around 100 AD.

The Children of the Ur are not the only races to have been touched by these precursors. Their mark is found in every system that bears a jumpgate, not only in the gate itself, but on nearly every planet in the system. While some of their remains may be only survey markers, others are more extant, from small cities to whispers of their behavior in the mythologies of most sentient races. Indeed, most races, including humans, believe that they were visited and affected by the Ur at some point early in their development. For what purpose, none can say.

The Anunnaki's only seeming legacy is their technology. The jumpgates opened space for humans, the Children of the Ur and the Vau. But they also left a mystery behind. People still gaze in wonder at the enigmatic Gargoyles jutting from ancient ruins or from the edge of jumpgates.

The First Republic

Humanity's dream of a united, one-world government was finally realized by the beginning of the twenty-second century. Decades of strife and war by extremist but minority political factions left the mass of world citizenry desperate for peace. The price of this peace was freedom, and the people, exhausted after years of global violence, gladly paid it.

The First Republic, also called the Human Combine Age by Second Republic historians, was created by a conglomeration of mercantile leaders, ardent capitalists made rich from years of war who had come to realize that overt war (and increasing anarchy) was hurting profits and growth. Banding together to back a world government initiative begun by the United Nations, these "zaibatsu" soon ruled the Republic. Representatives, originally elected by UN member nations, were nothing more than shills for the most powerful zaibatsu, international corporations whose money kept these troubled nations alive. Eventually, even the illusion of elected representation was dissolved, and the duly enfranchised leaders of the Republic were overtly made of up of corporate heads. Corporate policy became government policy. The hallmark of united and stable government was built on a foundation of vast police powers and conditional civil rights. Nonetheless, the First Republic took humanity to the stars.

Certain visionaries within the government recognized that a new frontier was required to channel the energies and aggressions of the populace and to garner new resources to make up for the dwindling resources of the overdeveloped Earth. Corporations turned their eyes to space. The first project was the moon, and a moonbase was quickly established. Next came Mars. After initial disasters, humanity finally landed on the red planet and found it relatively hospitable. Colonization followed, along with massive resource extraction industries. The rest of the solar system followed in the following centuries.

The lure of yet more distant stars initiated an ambitious long-term program: the launching of "slow ships." These starships traveled below the speed of light and would take generations to reach even the closest star system, but people lined up anyway to volunteer for these expeditions outward to new horizons. There were two types of slow ships, the Generation Ships (where the crew lives awake for their journey, sealed inside a Dyson sphere) and Deep Sleep Ships (where the crew is frozen to be thawed on arrival). Relatives bid their loved ones goodbye, knowing they would probably never see them again, but hopeful that their descendants would one day meet on distant worlds. The ships were sealed and launched, and began their journey through the void toward distant lights.

Then, soon after the turn of the twenty-fourth century, the jumpgate was discovered. Floating at the edge of the solar system, past Pluto, was an amazing alien artifact from a race long gone.

The Jumpgate

The jumpgate was a monumental curiosity. It was the first sign of alien life and technology yet encountered by humanity (excepting the controversial remains left on Mars, long covered up and unknown to the public). And it was baffling. Long "powered down," the gate showed no sign of activity. Its function was hotly debated. Finally, a team of scientists working long shifts triggered the power and activated the gate. The space inside the hoop of the gate warped as light was bent in an inward spiral — and then opened onto alien vistas, a view of a distant star system.

This was the first sure sign humanity had of the Anunnaki and their works. The realization that humans were not the only race to reach the stars was a humbling experience, but one which many frontier-minded humans quickly got over. The zaibatsu saw opportunity where others saw awe.

Data was quickly retrieved from the powered-up gate and translation began. Soon, enough theoretical knowledge about the gate's technology existed to allow manufacture of a proto-jump engine. It was bulky and huge. Attached to an unmanned probe, the Republic prepared to launch it into the new infinity. This was a major unifying event, bringing people all over the world together in rapt expectation as the probe's retros fired and sent it hurtling into the gate. In a flash, it was gone. Now, the waiting commenced.

Three months later, the gate activated and the probe floated back into Earth's solar system, transmitting its image data collected in Unknown Space. A solar system waited, with a habitable planet similar to Earth. It wasn't long before the First Republic had volunteers lining up across the globe to be the first to see another world. A crew was selected, trained over long months and finally readied for launch.

Again, the world gathered to see it. The intrepid crew took off, shooting through the fiery glow of the alien jumpgate — and no one expected what came next. Each astronaut experienced a sublime moment of ecstasy and profound remembering of some deep truth once known and since lost. When they arrived on the other side, the memories again faded, but their afterglow remained. A religion was born, named after the word left on the lips of all the astronauts: Sathra.

The new world had no sentient life, and was ripe for colonization. It was called Sathra's Boon (since renamed Sutek). Soon, the exodus — and the conflicts — began. Internal, covert war ignited among the zaibatsu, as corporations fought for control of space's new riches. Most citizens were unaware of the conflicts exploding in the corridors of power on Earth, Mars and on Sathra's Boon.

Timeline

Date	Event
BC 40,000	Date for oldest known Anunnaki ruin
AD 100	Anunnaki disappear from history as they abandon the Ur-Obun and Ur-Ukar
1800	Vau reach space
2100	First Republic, solar system developed
2305	Humans discover the jumpgates
2500	First Republic collapses, nobility rises up
2500-3500	Diaspora
2700	First Contact with the Shantor
2723	Prophet sees Holy Flame; Age of Miracles
2730	Shantor Revolt leads to creation of alien reservation system
2845	First Contact with the Vau
2849	Death of the Prophet; Age of Miracles ends
2855	Ukar War. The Church unites humanity against invading Ur-Ukar
3500-4000	Merchant interests combine forces to create Second Republic with capital at New Istanbul (later Byzantium Secundus), massive terraforming
4000	Mass unemployment, intensified by fading suns phenomenon and increased religious millennialism, leads to collapse of Second Republic. Nobility leaps in, seizes Byzantium Secundus, and ensures that the Republic cannot be saved
4000-4986	Dark Ages
4525	Barbarian Invasions. Human star-nations unaligned to nobles, Church or League ally to plunder Known Worlds and are beaten back after many casualties on both sides
4540	Vladimir begins uniting stars through his campaign against the barbarians
4550	Vladimir I is crowned emperor and is assassinated. A regent, elected every 10 years by electors (composed of major houses, the Church and the League), stands in the emperor's stead
4900	Symbiot Wars begin. Symbiots attack outlying worlds. Parasitic forces convert many planets, forcing the human populations to evacuate. They are halted at Stigmata
4956-4995	The Emperor Wars
4992	Kurga Conflict on Hazat border begins
4993	Alexius Hawkwood crowned emperor
4995	All five Royal Houses finally concede victory to Emperor Alexius
4999	Game begins in the period of Consolidation as Emperor Alexius cements his gains

The First Republic found the religion of Sathraism to be an annoyance. Pilots who had "found God" were harder to control. In addition, the pilots sought to undergo more jumps than were necessary, risking their health (and thus their ships). Sathraism was outlawed, but to little effect. Only when the Republic managed to design a force field buffer preventing the Sathra experience did the religion suffer a serious setback. Ships were built with integral buffers; any attempt to dismantle the buffer disabled the engines. The mystical visions were over; without communion, many pilots could not maintain their zeal and lapsed from their mystical convictions, so easily forgotten anyway, like a dim dream. Many Sathraists tried to build their own ships, and still received their visions for many years. But the Republic was ruthless in hunting down rogue ships and destroying them. Within a matter of years, Sathraism was forgotten, an underground religion with few converts (although it would briefly surface again in the coming age of exodus).

Progress and expansion pushed on. Further study of the jumpgate revealed new routes to yet more worlds. The wagon train was on. With people spreading so far so fast, and with the zaibatsu busy attacking and defending their own, the discontents and idealists slipped away into the night and seized the stars for themselves. The First Republic's New Frontier had become the means to its own end. The Diaspora, and the fall of the First Republic, had begun.

Diaspora

The first colonists were mainly workers from the many corporations involved in resource extraction, but among them were those seeking escape from the corporate control and centralization which had so long strangled Earth. The First Republic had become an oppressive institution serving the best interests of a top elite, deaf to the pleas of the common man. But once the jumpgate allowed entry to other worlds, each with new jumproutes leading to a staggering array of still other worlds, the First Republic could no longer control their citizenry. They were free among the stars.

An age of Balkanization and independence began, as tight-knit special interest communities took off on ships of their own (the jumpgate engine technology was "leaked" by a cabal of anarchists). Many of the worlds they landed on saw new experiments in government; the early homogeneity of these colony worlds ensured that some of these experiments worked. Where hostile conditions or hostile colonists would not allow it, worlds fell into survivalist barbarism, as the First Republic refused their pleas for aid, too busy itself fighting to maintain control over Earth's solar system. On many of these worlds, governments grew up around strong individualist leaders who left the reins of power with their progeny, creating royal lineages. These noble houses become the main means of the zaibatsu's

downfall, as they began small wars, seizing First Republic resources here and there, whittling down the dwindling Republic.

The untrammeled richness of some of the worlds allowed the colonists to create mini-mercantile empires of their own, while other places saw colonists fight bitter and violent wars for poor resources. But everyone wanted a piece of the action, a world they could call their own.

The Prophet and His Church

Amid this exuberant chaos, the Prophet began his sermons. Traveling from world to world, this powerful religious figure single-handedly created a new monotheism.

The discovery of greatly advanced alien races (the Ur jumpgate makers) changed everything humanity had ever assumed about its own origins and spiritual destiny — humans were no longer unique for their intelligence and tool-using capability. In light of irrevocable proof of intelligent life in outer space, the leaders of the major religions of Earth were too backward looking to advance their churches into the new era of space travel. As humans left for the stars, they left their gods behind to search for new ones.

During the Diaspora, human colonies fractured their ties to central government, society and religion. Ancient Earth religions long dead, many of them polytheist and pagan, were resurrected by colonists desperate to escape the materialistic technocracy which they believed was strangling their destiny. A new age of spiritual diversity began, bringing with it tribalism, dogma and fanaticism.

But old religions and archaic forms of worship rang hollow amid the stars. Something new was required. Something which would address both hope and grief, as did all the great religions. Into this void of belief came the Prophet. Much has been said or written about him since, and many divergent beliefs are professed by different peoples as gospel, as is the way with all true prophets.

His name was Zebulon, a Catholic or Orthodox Christian priest (argument continues as to which) fascinated with the new potential opened up by the jumpgates. He went to the stars in search of more evidence of their makers. He found something greater by far. All laymembers know the litany: "In 2723, the Prophet saw the Holy Flame." On a frontier world (lost now amid the fading stars), Zebulon was gifted by God with a mystical vision of the Holy Flame residing in the Empyrean. God gave the Prophet new words for his children, to take them into the new age of space exploration. But he was also given a vision of hell, revealing that demons lurked in the "dark between the stars" seeking to snuff the Holy Flame. Church heads say that the suns grow cold as the demons and the sins they awaken in humanity block the light of the Holy Flame from the universe.

Zebulon began to preach his vision throughout the fron-

tier, creating a new religious movement. He spoke of evil hidden among the stars, demons whose shadows blocked the light of the Holy Flame. He spoke of the need to expand outward and explore, gathering the marvels that were found into cathedrals. He spoke out against the soulessness of machines and the nihilistic effect they had on humanity, in defiance of the reigning technofetishism among Diasporans.

Zebulon searched holy texts and teachings from Earth and elsewhere for wisdom, realizing that only by uniting all of humankind's wisdom could humanity's faith thrive under the pressures of their star sojourn. As the Prophet revised his teachings, he introduced ideas from a variety of religions. He called God the Pancreator and revealed that this was the same God spoken of in all religions, and that only now, once humans had reached the stars, could the creator of the universe — of all the worlds and creatures therein — reveal him/her/itself in full glory. The suns were not only potent symbols of the Pancreator's divine light, they were material manifestations of divine spirit, of the Holy Flame which quickens all life.

The Prophet gathered many faithful under his banner, but there were seven special disciples honored by the Prophet above others. These have become saintlike figures by the time of Emperor Alexius, with many legendary parables and powers attributed to them. There was actually an eighth disciple, an Ur-Obun, but she has been ignored by the Church and is recognized only by a few, although she created an Ur-Obun sect of the Church which still thrives on Obun.

During the Prophet's time, Sathraism experienced a silent resurgence as engineers dismantled the field buffers which prevented jump ecstasy. With no Republic to stop them, pilots again began their communions. But the Prophet stood against them, opposing the hallucinatory ecstasy of unfettered jumps. As the Universal Church gained power, Sathraism again went into decline. Soon, ship owners, often devout Church members, forbade anyone to shut down the Sathra dampers on their ships. Eventually, all ships were again fitted with dampers from their factories, and Sathraism was dead.

The Prophet died in a jumpgate accident while trying to plead for peace with the Vau, who were enacting punishment for violation of their space. His Church blamed the Vau for years, although many have realized that the Prophet's final mission to them was for peace and have since sought conciliation. The symbol of the Church is still a modified jumpgate, the sign of the Prophet's death and his message of questing.

The exceptionally long life of the Prophet is a source of awe for the faithful, who attribute his near-immortality to faith, while others believe it a testament to longevity drugs. Regardless, the years of his life are seen as an Age of Miracles by post-Fall humanity, a time when any person of faith could

The Virtuous Disciples

Eight disciples gathered about the Prophet one-by-one during his early Questing; actions they displayed during this sojourn became the basis of their saintly purviews in the post-Fall Church. Each saint oversees and protects a particular virtue of the Church; a pilgrim involved in one of these activities usually asks the saint to look down upon him from the Empyrean and aid him in his task. There are also lesser saints, usually deceased patriarchs of the Church, each with a virtue or activity to oversee. Tightknit families or groups often seek to declare their loyalty to one another under the patronage of a saint, sealed with a theurgic rite called the Oath to the Saints (see in Chapter 5: Occult).

The major virtues of the Church, as supremely displayed by the Disciples, are:

Virtue	Disciple
Questing	Paulus the Traveler
Loyalty	Lextius the Knight
Compassion	Amalthea the Healer
Protection	Mantius the Soldier
Justice (Retribution)	Maya the Scorned Woman
Wisdom	Horace the Learned Man
Humility	Hombor the Beggar
Discipline	Ven Lohji the Ur-Obun

There are also certain sins which were abhorred by the Prophet above all others. Sin darkens the light of the Holy Flame and causes the suns to fade. The major sins are Pride, Greed, Lust, Envy, Sloth, Wrath, and Oathbreaking. There are other sins which have since been proclaimed by the Church but were not mentioned by the Prophet: Usury (moneylending) and Invention (the Pancreator's creation is fixed — who are we to add to it? That was the sin of the Second Republic).

work wonders. It is said that the first theurgic rituals were codified then, although their practice waned during the Second Republic such that the existence of such magic was considered a hoax by some. Its return in the Dark Ages, however, has renewed the simple folks' faith in miracles.

After the Prophet's death, his core teachings were collected into one book titled the Omega Gospels. Church theologians argue that there are two phases to his teachings, the early Omega Gospels, teaching about warding evil and cultivating the virtues, and the later Compassionate Truths, mystical teachings about understanding and love. Over the millennia since the Prophet walked the stars, the Church has grown and developed its own answers to theological questions raised in the Prophet's teachings. By the time of Emperor Alexius, theology is a thorny and many-sided is-

sue argued over by many different sects and orders.

The Universal Church was formalized after the Prophet's death by one of the Prophet's followers, Palamedes, a son of House Alecto. Palamedes gathered the disparate faithful together against the threat of the Vau and the Ur-Ukar, cementing the burgeoning religion into a political force. It was Palamedes' place in Church history that later helped Vladimir I gain the Church's help in his bid for empire. The creation of the Church was by no means sudden and clear. Other followers of the Prophet went off in their own directions with their own ideas for a Church. But in the end, Palamedes' religion won out, although with certain exceptions (the sects and orders).

Palamedes declared himself patriarch, the spiritual and temporal head of the Church, and set forth guidelines on how future patriarchs were to be chosen (by a college of archbishops). Since then, the Church has been led by a long list of venerable men and women (women can hold the office of patriarch, and may elect to be called matriarch if they wish). The Church guided humanity through the Fall (although they aided in engineering its start) and now holds a steady front against evil from within and without.

First Contact: The Shantor

Amid the territorial struggles of the Diaspora, humanity encountered its first sentient race. The Shantor of Shaprut were an equinelike race who had achieved a degree of civilization despite their limited tool-using capabilities. Living on the vast grass plains of Shaprut, they celebrated a culture which valued strong family ties and romantic relationships, although this also enforced a fierce tribalism which often led to conflicts with other tribes. Indeed, clan warfare was common and good soldiers were the most honored members of a tribe. However, no soldier was long respected if he did not revere his family or play out the elaborate rites of courtship with his spouse. The Shantor also practiced a religion akin to sun worship.

But their world was rich in minerals, and their indigenous cultures stood in the way of extraction. In the Diaspora, interplanetary supremacy depended on resources. The feeling of the Shaprut colonists was that if they did not take the bounty, someone else would. In addition, the Shantor could not communicate with humans without technical assistance, such as computer voiceboxes. All too often, they were viewed as little more than smart animals. For these reasons, most humans did not feel responsible for displacing the Shantor. They even saw themselves as a necessary civilizing influence on the horselike race, providing them with jobs in the mines, although with often grueling, laborious tasks.

Many Shantor revolted. Those who still lived on the plains led assaults on colony mining operations. The large and clever Shantor are dangerous when riled, and the loss of life and property they caused summoned the wrath of the colony leaders. Armies descended onto Shaprut to put the unruly rebels down. A guerrilla war ensued, but the result was never in question. The broken Shantor rebels were herded up and shipped off-world, scattered onto reservations throughout human space, sometimes onto worlds hostile to their way of life. Families were separated, their members never to see each other again.

The great shame of humanity's first contact has haunted many humans for centuries. The Prophet was only beginning his questing as the Shantor's culture was dismantled, but he spoke out against the tragedy. However, he had too few followers then, and no power to change the course of history as yet. Restitution has yet to be made to the surviving Shantor. Certain people believe that if the Prophet had not died such an untimely death in Vau Space, the fate of the Shantor and other sentients to follow them might have been different. But Palamedes, first Patriarch of the formalized Universal Church of Celestial Sun, concerned himself little with the injustices committed against politically impotent alien races.

And so the fate of most sentient races encountered by humanity followed that of the Shantor. Regardless of their tenacity and degree of technology, they soon came under human rule. While some live in peaceful coexistence with humans, such as the Ur-Obun, Vorox and Gannok, others resisted human encroachment bitterly. The programs of forced relocation and land grabbing were to cause centuries of bad relations with the most advanced power in the known universe: the Vau.

The Vau

A newly discovered jumpgate delivered humanity onto a small but lush world they called New Monaco (now called Apshai). It was the home of the G'nesh, a quiet, insectoid alien race who spent most of their time making elaborate and beautiful plant and tree sculptures linked by organic webbing. They ignored the new colonists at first, but when the colonists forced some G'nesh from their gardens and claimed the land for themselves, the G'nesh became quite indignant. All they would say was, "It is not allowed. Please leave." Of course, the colonists scoffed. These weak gardeners offered no threat to them.

But their patrons did.

A massive starship appeared through the jumpgate, a ship whose like had never been seen before. Harnessing a great ball of raging plasma energy, this dreadnought destroyed the human fleet placed around New Monaco. Small ships disengaged from its hull and went hurtling to the planet below, there dropping off vicious cargo: Vau soldiers.

These soldiers systematically began wiping out all the human colonists encountered. The minor house officials in charge of the planet desperately tried to surrender before the greater and technologically superior forces, but their cries

went unheeded. The Vau killed everyone.

Afterwards, they boarded their ships and left. The G'nesh went back to gardening. The only thing the Vau left behind was a message: "Leave this planet alone. It is the property of the Vau Hegemony. Do not follow the jumproads from this gate further."

Of course, humanity did go further, seeking retribution for their loss. What they found were more Vau worlds, worlds of vastly superior technology. Few returned to tell the tale; those that did were "allowed" to return. Finally, the Vau accepted a human diplomat, Benjamin Verden of House Justinian. Benjamin returned from his first sojourn overwhelmed by the superiority of the Vau. He was thankful for one thing he had become convinced of on his trip: The Vau were non-expansionist. Their very political structure sought and upheld stability over all other virtues. Their empire and way of life had changed little in the last few centuries, following the dictates of their first space emperor.

Benjamin discovered that the G'nesh were a conquered race. The Vau dealt with their subjects in very different ways than humans. The G'nesh put up a valiant fight against the invading Vau. Upon surrender, the general of the G'nesh, having learned Vau culture well, demanded the Vau give him "face" before he could stop the war. This is an important concept to the Vau: Honor and dignity come before life itself. For the general to willingly suffer such a shame as defeat the Vau had to also sacrifice something: They gave the G'nesh long life and peace in return for submission. In other words, the G'nesh live under a socialized retirement granted by their conquerors, all because their general had understood the Vau social system.

This insight was to help humanity well in dealing with the Vau in centuries to come, but for now, the Vau made it clear that they had no interest in the "pollutant" that was humanity. Relations were distant and formal for centuries. It was clear that, while the Vau did not want foreign ideas to infect their society, they also did not want humanity to get too close a look at their technology.

The encounter with the Vau bolstered the power of the Church, especially after the death of the Prophet in a jumpgate accident in Vau Space. Humanity trembled before the threat of a technologically superior (though non-expansionist) alien race. Palamedes' Church drew them together and bolstered their confidence. Humanity was, after all, chosen for the stars. It was its destiny. To turn back now would be to fail the Pancreator. The urgings of the priests gave humanity a unifying creed, a universal doctrine of excellence with which to move forward in the face of defeat. It is ironic that it was the Church which gave humans the prod to reach so high; the same Church which centuries later would admonish them for such a sin.

The event which would finally cement the power of the

burgeoning Church arrived before word of the Prophet's death had spread to all the worlds.

The Ukar War

The Ur-Ukar had struggled through centuries of internal conflict on their hostile and subterranean world of Kordeth before finally reaching the stars. They colonized three planets near their system, Okh'cha and Kradle (later called Aylon and Istakhr), and Ustar (now a Lost World), and were ready to expand still further when they encountered humans on Criticorum. It was hate at first sight. The vain Ukari saw a world for conquering and a race to enthrall. They attacked with little warning and took the main capital on Criticorum. Human response was swift. Noble families on Shaprut and New Istanbul formed a fleet to re-take the planet. A long and bitter war ensued, taking place on almost every planet or moon in the system.

The revolt spread as Ukari slipped onto other planets and began guerrilla assaults. Soon, humans on nearly a dozen worlds had suffered from the aliens. The Ur-Obun, who had been encountered soon after the Shantor, quickly recognized their ancient brethren and spoke out against them, joining the humans in condemnation of the Ukari tactics. The Obun's anti-Ukar speeches helped gain them the greater sovereignty status they still enjoy in Emperor Alexius' time.

Then, an Ukar on Shaprut used his psychic powers to force the Shantor to revolt. The Shantor broke from their reservation and stormed across the villages and towns which sat on the Shantor's once-open plains. The retribution was fierce and decisive; nearly a quarter of the Shantor were killed before the remainder surrendered. When it was discovered that Ukari psionics had been responsible, Patriarch Palamedes raised the fist of the newly formed Universal Church.

Psychic powers had developed strongly in humanity after the first sojourn through the jumpgate, and the practice slowly grew, with new powers being developed as the years and generations passed. With the suppression of Sathraism, the advent of new psychic powers slowed. Rarely during any of this time, however, were psychics viewed as particularly dangerous. Rather, humanity was fascinated with the new potentials revealed. All that changed when the Ukari arrived.

The Ukari were advanced psychics from birth, but they had little compunction governing the use of their powers. When they employed mind tricks against the Shantor, humans began to fear them and no longer sought a peaceful end to the Criticorum conflict. Humanity could not rest until these mind controllers were in chains.

Patriarch Palamedes used these assaults to preach against alien dangers and the need for humans to unite. The words of the Prophet seemed eerily designed for such

effect, with their talk of demons and evil among the stars. The presence of an Ur-Obun among the disciples was conveniently overlooked. New converts to the Church grew every day, especially after each Ukar terrorist maneuver. Finally, Palamedes gathered together the leaders of those worlds harmed by the Ukari and sent them to take retribution from the Ukari first-hand.

Using information gathered from some unknown source, Palamedes sent the fleet to the Ukari homeworld of Kordeth, whose location had been previously unknown. Spiraling out of the jumpgate, the fleet split up and began hitting any ship they came across. The surprised the Ukari — the ill-prepared system defenders retreated and formed a phalanx around their homeworld. A standoff began.

On the planet below, panic broke out and old Ukari clan rivalries ignited. Kept in check by the powerful Overlord and his expansionist campaign, enemies of the ruling family rose up and sabotaged the planetary defense. Pilots loyal to the minor clans heeded the calls and broke off from the phalanx, leaving the planet defenseless against the assault. The human fleet rushed in and began bombing the surface of the planet, unaware that most Ukar cities were deep underground.

The fleet sent in a landing party to seize the surface capital, home of the Overlord. The Overlord surrendered while his rivals hid in the caverns below, knowing that they would inherit the planet once the humans had gone. Their plan did not go as well as they had wished. The humans did not leave, but only came in greater numbers until all Ukari resistance was squashed. Nobles and merchant leaders of numerous worlds came to ensure that the Ukari would not rise again. Ukari colony worlds were seized and eventually sold to noble families, while Kordeth itself was sold to powerful mercantile consortiums.

In the later times of the Second Republic, the Ukari would sue for greater freedom from the domination they suffered for their mistaken acts, and they would be given such freedom, but for now, they were a kept people.

Palamedes' victory ensured the safety of Human Space, or so the Church preached. The bold event was trumpeted to people on worlds far from Kordeth who had suffered little from the war, but it still had an effect. The fear of alien invasion was imminent everywhere, and a Church which had proven itself effective against such enemies was a beacon shining in the night.

Order From Chaos

New technology progressed quickly, as scientists made amazing discoveries by observing phenomena on other worlds, or by taking lore from alien races (occasionally sharing it). Incredible advances were made, but they were not spread equally among the commonwealth of humanity. There was no central unity by which the whole of humanity could

prosper from the work of the many worlds.

As some worlds prospered (most often those with strong, hereditary leadership: the nobles), they subsumed others under them, and soon many star-faring, interplanetary governments flourished. The heart of all these operations, however, was commerce. Some planets had certain resources in abundance while lacking others. Trade was necessary for the betterment of life everywhere. The greedy, overarching attitude of the zaibatsu and the new royalty could not long maintain a foothold in the new sprawl of worlds, where another choice always existed. Eventually, the worlds did come together again. A new mercantile alliance was formed with great democratic ideals, temporarily silencing the resentful royalty by strength of numbers. The Second Republic was born.

It is again ironic that it was the Church's teachings of a humane and ethical philosophy that gave rise to an institution which was to eclipse the Church's role. Indeed, under the Republic, humanity's yearning for spiritual answers was drowned by the array of material comfort and sensual stimuli available to every citizen. The Church would soon revise its previous philosophy and adapt one much harsher to human luxury.

Second Republic

Some thinkers at the close of the twentieth century believed that liberal democracies were the ultimate progression of government, that, after such a form of governing becomes universal, no further progress is possible. Perfection of governance will have been achieved. Many citizens of the Empire believe these thinkers were right. But hindsight, as they say, is 20/20.

Humanity reached its pinnacle in the form of the Second Republic, a time of quick progress and amazing changes. The standard of living for the average citizen was raised on all worlds. Technology knew no limits. With the vast resources of other worlds and a unity of purpose, nothing was impossible. All was to be achieved.

It was a time of genetic engineering, curing many diseases and deformities but often leading to the creation of freakish, near-human races. A time when terraforming was all the rage, when almost every world in humanspace was "fixed" to be more Earthlike, to make better homes for humanity (wiping out native ecosystems in the process, along with the natural habitats of many alien races). A time when the threat of physical danger was a myth, and accidental death a nearly-forgotten idea. Sports of extreme danger were practiced readily, for a personal energy shield or MedPac was always around to protect or revive the victim of even fatal accidents.

The citizenry soon forgot the traumas and triumphs that had forged their way of life. Existing in an unbroken bubble

of prosperity, they forgot what it was to be human, to strive, to love and to sacrifice. And to hate.

The bubble soon burst from within. The Republic had grown too far and too fast in technological mastery. Many of its wonders were introduced with no consideration for their effect on the wider populace. Most technology displaced workers, and soon there was no need for work. But the economy did not keep up with these changes, and people still needed money to live. But where to get it? The welfare system of the Republic was grand but not built to uphold the sheer number of citizens displaced from their livelihoods by technology (or cheap alien labor). As this reality was sinking in, unknown terrorists managed to sabotage the central computer net controlling welfare information. Anarchy ensued on many worlds as citizens were denied money. Riots began.

Divestiture

The nobility of many worlds, weak but still extant, saw their chance. They began orchestrating deals with the overextended central Republic government for more local power to crush riots in return for increased tax revenues, all the while refusing to pay out welfare money. This begins a period later historians term Divestiture, for as the Republic ceded out power, it lost more and more control over the bureaucratic beast the government had become. Finally, massive corruption in the central government, along with the increased tax burden, caused outlying worlds to secede. These Rogue Worlds, typically under the power of noble families, were too powerful to put down; the Republic was forced to deal with them on their own terms.

Then the stars began to darken. Only after three suns with populated planets noticeably dimmed did people begin to realize that the fading suns phenomenon was not going away. But what was causing it? Many disgruntled and discontented people had their own answers: "The Republic is to blame; some damn experiment gone wrong!" "The scientists are responsible; their technology's doing this!" "It's the aliens' fault, some sort of cruel revenge."

The Universal Church began to preach, explaining why the suns were fading: Humans were sinful and had, in their pride, overreached, claiming the powers of the Pancreator for themselves. The Pancreator chose to take their power from them by taking the very light of the worlds away. This message hit the right nerves, and a vicious millennialism was born. People needed reasons to hate, and a target to direct it toward. While the Church fathers were genuinely concerned with the souls of a largely unspiritual populace, they could not help falling into old habits. They took humanity's discontent and directed it at the Republic, the source of the Church's own problems.

In an attempt to recapture support, the Republican president made a deal with the Orthodox sect of the Church. In return for the Church's open acceptance of the Republic's secular authority, the Republic would declare Orthodoxy the official and only recognized sect of the Church. This ignited religious wars as breakaway sects — and religions wholly unaligned to the Universal Church — fought for their rights.

It is during this time that the legendary Saint Rasmussen spoke his famous lament: "Oh that my head were water, and mine eyes a fountain of tears, that I might weep day and night for lost humanity! Tremble, ye sinners, for the long night is upon us and the suns themselves are seen to fade. Repent, and know salvation. Repent, or die!" He was torn apart by a rioting crowd of zealots as the words left his lips.

The nadir of this conflict came when certain Rogue Worlds, with the support of alien races, arrived through Byzantium Secundus' jumpgate to seize control of the government. This surprise assault took the Republic off-guard, and Byzantium fell to the rebels. As word spread to the worlds of the Republic, utter chaos ensued. The major noble houses knew their chance had come at last, that all they had worked toward over the years had finally come to fruition.

Ten houses banded together and sent a fleet to retake Byzantium Secundus. With their now-vast military might, gathered through the years of Divestiture, they retook the capitol with little resistance. As the smoke in the presidential palace cleared, the Ten Houses raised their own banner.

The Fall of the Second Republic was complete. Progress died. History worked its way toward a peak and then reversed itself. As the Church proclaimed, humanity now suffered the humiliation of reliving its past failures over again, in a grand lesson of hubris for a fallen race.

But many remember the humanism and ideals of the Republic and hold them close to their hearts. The Merchant League refuses to relinquish them, even in the face of Inquisitorial censure from the Church or military might from the houses. An ideal is not reality, however, but a guiding light. Many have been lost in the darkness even while standing in the light. So it was with the citizenry of the Second Republic. The lights were dimmed. The New Dark Ages had begun.

The New Dark Ages

The ten triumphant noble houses soon gained the backing of the Church, for they supported (for political purposes) the Republic's recognition of Orthodoxy. They also officially accepted the tenet that humanity was sinful and that the Church had righteous power over the lives of the sinful. In return, the Orthodox patriarch backed the houses, finding many lines in scripture to prove the nobles' case against the godless Republican senators. Besides, the Rogue World rebels had many sectarian leaders among them; they could not be allowed to build a new government on Byzantium Secundus

which might defuse the new power of the Orthodoxy.

The Church moved quickly to stamp its doctrine on all it could. Its main tenet was that technology was evil. It had caused the downfall of humanity, and so humans must not respect or practice it. The noble houses agreed, seeing a method by which their new populace could be kept in line. They, of course, sought an exception to the anti-technology creed. The Church resisted, and thus began decades of squabbling between the noble houses and the Church. The Church would excommunicate a house member for technological practice, while a house would seize a Church world, destroying a cathedral as a "casualty of war."

Both sides finally came to a necessary agreement. The Church needed some measure of tech for itself, and had to concede some to the houses. So, the nobility was conceived to be in a form of "extreme penance," "to compassionately take on sinful tasks to save the common man from such stain." Thus, use of technology (and the powers of rulership) were seen as necessary evils, and nobles were martyrs seeking to save humanity from again staining itself (sins for the few, saving grace for the masses). The Church also claimed a saintly role in this, decreeing it to be the duty of priests to guard the commoners from tech. For this purpose, the priests must be knowledgeable in recognizing tech, but if they were penitent enough, their souls would remain pure on Judgment Day.

But this sharing of power between the two forces was not complete. The guildsmen who possessed what technological knowledge remained made their bid for power. They formed the Merchant League from the remaining Republic senators and corporate heads and refused to hand down their knowledge of technology. Without them, starships could not long run; military battle armor and weapons could not long operate. And Church communications would be cut.

The houses began a reign of terror, hunting down and imprisoning anyone who claimed to be a guildsman. The Church began excommunicating the leaders of the League, forcing the loyal to refuse them succor. To no avail. The League had too many starships and worlds of its own. And they had trade. Without their jumpmaps and know-how, the supply of many necessary materials to Church and house worlds would be cut off. Indeed, many worlds had already purposefully sealed their jumpgates, and disappeared into the long night of history. The priests and nobility were forced to give the League a cut of the action.

And so formed the triune government of the Dark Ages, an uneasy and fractured alliance which often broke out into open conflict between the parties, causing much suffering among the common human and alien. The Ten elected one among them as council leader, but these leaders always had enemies, and rarely ruled for long. In addition, membership among the Ten was fluid; houses rose and fell over the years, with only the strongest or craftiest maintaining their positions for long. The Church patriarch continually tried to cement political power in the hopes of building a theocracy to replace the sorry government that ruled in place of the Second Republic, but there were always too many heresies and sectarian conflicts to squash instead. The guilds of the League sought to claim restless worlds or recapture the Rogue Worlds, but they were often outmaneuvered by the nobles.

Into this fractious universe came the barbarians.

Barbarian Invasions

After the Fall, the borders of the Known Worlds shrank. Some worlds deliberately cut themselves off from jumptravel by blockading their gates and attacking anyone who tried to enter their systems. Others lost their ability to reach space as civil wars destroyed starships and the factories to repair them. Most worlds were too busy to aid the small backworlds and, after years of dealing with their own struggles, they often forgot about these worlds or had lost the jump coordinates to reach them in the massive data purges of the Church Inquisitors.

Certain worlds "sealed" their jumpgates, cutting themselves off from the madness going on around them for an unknown amount of time. Those with the technical know-how and a detailed understanding of jumpgates can seal a gate — that is, shut down all travel from one or more directions. However, once this is done, no one can control when the gate to those directions can be opened again. The seal may last a week or it may last for centuries; no one knows. The time is governed by an internal mechanism in the gate which is too arcane to be understood. Some of the worlds which sealed themselves off during the Fall have yet to reappear.

Untold numbers of planets were cut off from humanity's central civilization, some to be rediscovered later, others to disappear from history forever. Who knows how many lost planets in the depths of space still support human life? In addition to the worlds of the Second Republic — worlds reached only by jumpgate — there are thousands of star systems without jumpgates, with unknown residents. Some of these stars — those nearest to Earth in light years — were the targets of First Republic slow ships. But these generation ships were forgotten after the jumpgates were discovered, and none has ever reached the Known Worlds. Indeed, few people in the Empire pay attention to stellar distances such as light years; such details became unnecessary after the jumpgates, as travel across vast distances became possible in the blink of an eye.

In this environment of fractured roadways, not all worlds were claimed by the houses, Church or League. Many forgotten planets began independent governments of their own. Most of these governments remained hostile to their neighbors, fighting centuries-long feuds, and some looked upon

the riches of the Known Worlds and lusted for them. Cut off from the center of the Republic, many of these worlds slowly lost technology, devolving into Diaspora-level conditions or worse.

A few leaders of such forlorn worlds who still had starships were able to form a coalition and raid the Known Worlds, targeting those worlds that they could sweep onto, pillage and escape from before aid could arrive. The barbarians were no longer at the gate — they were through it and plundering.

Delphi, House Hawkwood's homeworld, suffered the worst of these assaults. House Hawkwood was able to gather troops with the aid of its minor house allies, and after a bloody battle, fended off the assaults to their homeworld. However, it was no major military victory, for the bulk of the barbarian army had already left with its loot.

The Ten knew that the raiders' success would soon cause more barbarians to break through. But its internal squabbling prevented it from forming a united front against the invaders.

The barbarians, as expected, did return, and this time in greater numbers. Two large star-nations united to lay claim to outlying worlds. They succeeded. Years of simmering battle began, whereby the noble houses would reclaim their worlds for a few months, and the barbarians would seize them yet again.

A disunited, selfish nation cannot long survive such outside pressure. One person was needed to unite it and send its enemies running.

Vladimir Unites the Stars

The problem of a united front against the barbarians was keenly felt by Vladimir Alecto, the recently elected leader of the Ten. Vladimir saw that the far-flung and fractured commonwealth of humanity would soon crumble before the might of its enemies if someone did not act to bring the Known Worlds together. His primary aim, of course, was power. The welfare of humanity may have been secondary, but important nonetheless, for it was the fuel which drove him (or so he told himself).

Pledging to lead the Known Worlds to victory and reclaim the embattled worlds, Vladimir began gathering allies. A military genius, he had a strong following among all the minor noble houses and five of the Ten. (The Ten at that time were Alecto, Justinian, Gesar, Van Gelder, Windsor, the Hazat, al-Malik, Li Halan, Hawkwood, and the tenth, the Decados.) He also gained the support of the Church and the League. He won these allies easily, for commerce was threatened by the barbarians, souls were in danger, and he promised the owners of the worlds that he would return the planets to their power rather than claiming them for himself.

After years of battle, the barbarian invaders were bro-

ken and forced back to their own worlds. The jumproads connecting entry into the Known Worlds were often sealed or hidden to prevent future sorties. But Vladimir did not keep his promises in full. For those major houses who had not fully supported him, he claimed their worlds for himself. Civil war erupted.

The Gesar, Windsors, Van Gelder, Decados and certain minor houses were turned against him, along with many sects and guilds. But the rest of the Known Worlds were behind him. The war was bloody. Years after it had begun, Vladimir accepted the surrender of the rebel houses and declared himself Emperor. He introduced the Great Charter, instituting the office of the electors, those who could vote on his successor. Each elector was given a scepter — a vote rod — as proof of office, and Vladimir distributed these scepters to all his allies in the houses, Church and League.

A great coronation ceremony was held on Byzantium Secundus when Vladimir arrived to take the throne. But as he placed the crown upon his head, fire erupted from his eyes and he fell dead to the floor. Years of hard-won victory ended in seconds. The assassin behind the deed has never been revealed, and many whisper that demons were at work.

Vladimir had no blood successor. A race was on to claim the throne after him. House Alecto, weak from the expenditure of its resources during Vladimir's campaigns, fell to the status of a minor house. Unfortunate deaths and assassinations soon destroyed the remainder of its royal line, and the house became extinct ten years after Vladimir's death.

The Gesar and Windsors also became extinct, too weak from their recent surrender to carry on. They had all lost too many sons and daughters to Vladimir's war and soon lost those few who remained. Van Gelder held onto their power and became a minor house only by allying with the Decados. With this extra power, the weak Decados, using blackmail to influence other minor houses and even the League, maintained its royal status and entered the race for the Imperial Throne. The Ten now became the Five, composed of Hawkwood, Decados, the Hazat, Li Halan and al-Malik.

But the electors could come to no accord. Instead of an Emperor, they elected a temporary regent to rule for 10 years until an Emperor was chosen. The office of regent lasted longer than anybody had planned, for when the 10 years had passed, a new regent was elected. And 10 years later, yet another one. It would be centuries until a new Emperor would again ascend the throne.

Symbiot Wars

The Second Republic had its secrets and at least one of these came back to haunt the Known Worlds. Not all citizens of the Republic appreciated the massive terraforming program whereby all worlds were slowly transformed into human (Earthlike) environments, with the subsequent upheaval of native alien races and the disappearance of unique flora and fauna. The Republic suffered its share of ecoactivists and terrorists.

One such cabal of ecoterrorists eked out a precarious existence in the jungles of Chernobog, harassing the Second Republic terraforming engineers. After a particularly successful sabotage of machinery, they retreated into unexplored jungle to avoid the authorities' intensive search. There, they disturbed a previously unknown alien race. The Xolotl awakened from hibernation and began parasitically infesting the humans in an attempt to breed. Two of the terrorists had occult powers (psi and theurgy), and the result was explosive: A new race of beings, neither Xolotl or human but something unique— a Symbiot.

Transformed in body and mind, infused with an almost instinctual hate for humans, the two quickly bred, creating Symbiot progeny from their non-psychic fellows, and from the plant and animals native to Chernobog. After gathering strength and practicing their newfound powers, they assaulted the human capital with fury. Unable to withstand — or even comprehend — the weaponry of the Symbiots, the Second Republic retreated from Chernobog and sealed the jumpgate so that no one could get onto or off the contaminated world. The Republic then worked to hide news of the event from the citizenry; the last thing they wanted was an alien threat to cause more chaos (those who argued that such a threat was exactly what was needed to unify the fractious Republic were laughed at). They managed to hide the secret so well that the planet of Chernobog and its alien residents were entirely forgotten. The Known Worlds entered the Dark Ages blissfully unaware of the terrible threat waiting beyond their borders.

Nearly a millennium after the Fall, the Symbiots returned. Sometime in the intervening years, they had attained jump capability in their organic ships, although even now no human understands how this is possible. Unable at first to break through the sealed jumpgate to Stigmata, the Symbiots had expanded out and away from the Known Worlds. The Imperial Eye is still unsure how many worlds they hold in the space past Chernobog.

It was only a matter of time until they came back to their point of origin. A Symbiot ship passed through the jumpgate at Absolution and landed in an outlying city. Its crew began slaughtering the residents without warning. The Symbiot's organic tech was astonishing — living ships, battle armor and even guns. The very thought of these things repulsed the human defenders even as they died fighting against them. The Symbiots did not capture the world — that was never their intent. But they left the resource extraction industry in shambles and the human population decimated. The attack was a warning. More would follow.

Daishan and Stigmata, other worlds on the borders of Human Space, became wary and ready for attack. But the

Symbiot forces did not arrive in fleets. They moved in mysterious ways, attacking through the least expected avenue: the very flora and fauna of the planets turned on the human "colonists." The Symbiots planned their assaults for years, having finally broken the jumpcodes to these worlds earlier. They secretly converted whole ecosystems under the very noses of the ignorant colonists. Humans found it hard to fight off whole forests or herds of predatory beasts working in teams to devour scout units.

The humans, as expected, resorted to firebombing and ecodestruction to eliminate their opposition. But even this did not destroy the Symbiots; their seeds lay deep in the organic structure of their chosen planets. The new growth over the charred forests strangely grew more quickly than it should have, and this time stronger, more resilient to fire damage. The Symbiot planet forces learned from their failures and grew defenses against them. The colonists of Daishan were forced to evacuate the planet, giving it over entirely to the Symbiots.

It was clear that the Symbiots were masters of guerrilla warfare against a technologically superior force. While they could not immediately seize the worlds for themselves, they could ensure the humans a costly defense and an eventual route. But not without a final gesture — the human fleet defending the retreat bombed the planet from orbit with all its might, leaving the world a scorched, uninhabitable rock.

The regent moved quickly to defend Stigmata, the system the Symbiots would have to pass through to reach the rest of the Known Worlds. The Imperial Fleet was dispatched and the battles began. Things did not go well for the Imperial forces. While they had more advanced weaponry than the Symbiots, the parasites were tenacious. While the Symbiots made few advances, neither could they be easily beaten back. The regent formed a new office to handle what was turning into a long-term situation, that of the Stigmata Garrison Commander, in charge of a vast amount of Imperial military resources.

Finally, in one area, surprisingly and for no apparent reason, the tide was turned and the Symbiot forces pushed back. Upon investigation, it was discovered that two people were largely responsible: Friar Berthold of the then-heretical Eskatonic Order and Damiana, a Charioteer trader. These two were unusual in that they were both practicing occultists: Berthold was a theurgist and Damiana a powerful psychic. They were residents of the planet before the Symbiots had arrived, joined together in a secret coven. They had gathered other local residents together to mount a guerrilla defense against the Symbiot invaders, a rebellion which went on unnoticed by the Imperial fleet. The friar's litanies and Damiana's psionics succeeded where military might failed.

They had discovered the key to fighting the Symbiots on something close to even terms. However, psychic powers, once the high science of the Republic, were outlawed by the Church. Covert deals had to be made before occult powers would be accepted. The Church had to be brought in and given credit for the affair. The Eskatonic Order had to be accepted into the fold. It would later become one of the major sects vying with the Orthodoxy for control of Church resources.

Once all was agreed upon, the Church unleashed other Eskatonic Order priests and rogue psychics (promised absolution for their service) onto Stigmata. They were contracted Inquisitors given the power to cleanse the taint in any way they saw fit. It worked. Where science could not clean out the parasites, psychics and theurgists did. From then on, the Eskatonic Order heralded theurgy as the replacement of science. Only here could man look to see wonders, they claimed, but only the holiest and most penitent of priests could work such magic.

Centuries after it had begun, the Symbiot War was brought to an uneasy standstill. The Symbiots still held some territory, but gained little new ground. The long, protracted guerrilla battle on the frontier was at an end, and an uneasy silence descended upon the front.

Magic had gained a foothold on human consciousness again, one which the houses, Church and League soon found hard to control. Covens, underground organizations of psychics, began to operate openly, with agendas in conflict with the powers that be. Individuals seeking power turned to forbidden paths, asking aid of invisible entities whose names were whispered in occult circles. These Antinomists risked their souls and those of their fellow humans in their bids for power, and not the least of them were members of the Five Houses who sought imperishable power against their enemies.

The Emperor Wars

The office of regent could not last forever without some challenge. While individuals had tried short-lived bids for the title of Emperor at various times during the Dark Ages, none had come close to succeeding.

Fifty years after the Symbiot Wars had calmed, leaving a tense and fearful populace waiting for the next alien expansion, House Hawkwood made its bid for power. Darius Erik Hawkwood made overt offers to the Church and League electors for increased power in return for their votes. This set off a flurry of counter-offers from the other houses, each fighting to gain scepters. Decades of political, military and social struggle began, a struggle which oftentimes threatened the borders of the Empire.

The houses were not the only forces seeking the Imperial Throne. The patriarch, fearful of giving the nobility too much power, moved to gain worlds of his own, pursuing the Church's ancient desire for a theocracy. He was largely un-

successful, but powerful enough to force certain noble houses in the race to recognize the superiority of the Church.

The Merchant League sought a chance for increased power amid the chaos. Years of war among the nobility had turned the populace against the families. The League sought to use this hatred to kick the royals out. They sought to gain enough worlds to secede and declare a Third Republic. They, like the Church, were unsuccessful, for a popular figure arose to appease all the quarreling forces.

A master diplomat and military tactician, Alexius of House Hawkwood had taken up where Darius, his uncle, had left off. He eventually claimed enough hold on a number of worlds to meet the final challenge. With the grudging backing of the patriarch (who finally saw which way the wind was blowing) and the hesitant backing of the Leaguemeister, Alexius Hawkwood claimed the Imperial Throne. A short, quick battle broke out at the Imperial Palace on Byzantium Secundus, but Alexius was prepared. Hidden Hawkwood forces and mercenary fleets moved in and stifled all opposition. The opposing houses were forced to retreat. On that very day, Alexius was crowned Emperor of the Known Worlds, and no assassin's trick could stop him.

At first, only House Hawkwood, the Li Halan and the al-Malik conceded (the latter were Alexius' main allies in the war; the Church and the League respectively, had already recognized the Emperor, and they could do little but follow), but the Decados and the Hazat both refused to recognize the claim. Years of fighting ensued, this time more vicious than before.

The Decados gave in sooner than anyone expected, surprising all and causing people to wonder whether they had seen the writing on the wall or were plotting some as-yet-unrevealed scheme. A barbarian border war on the Hazat's borders weakened that family's forces enough that, following the Decados' recognition of Alexius' claim, it was also forced to capitulate. It claims that it willingly recognized Alexius in return for his aid in the war and his recognition of their claim to the barbarian world.

The Emperor Wars were finally at an end, although they had lasted far too long. Almost two generations of open conflict had taken its toll on the Empire. Planets were ravaged and many starships lost beyond repair. While the borders remained steady (at great cost), the lives of Imperial citizens were the worse for wear.

But where there was conflict, there is now stability. An Emperor sits upon the throne, and what he decrees is so. No more arguing, no more stalling. Maybe now, say the citizens, things will get done.

Consolidation

Six years after his coronation, Alexius is the undisputed Emperor of the Known Worlds. He has done an astonishing job of consolidating power under his rule, and has brought a stability to the Empire unknown for centuries. While his work is not complete, for many factions still vie against him in hidden, shadowy ways — and some even openly — most recognize that even death may not topple his throne. Although he has no heir as yet, should he produce one, that son or daughter will surely assume his rule (especially with the five vote scepters set aside for him or her — as many as the noble houses combined).

Nonetheless, his popularity — while stronger than it was even three years ago — is not universal. The wars still haunt many who lived through them. The bloody battle for the throne left many people landless or without families; they bear deep grudges against the man they consider to be a tyrant. And peace is not fully assured yet — new conflicts constantly threaten.

The Hazat fight a war against the barbarian Kurga Caliphate over ownership of a Lost World called Hira, a war which threatens to draw in more factions if the Hazat are successful in petitioning the patriarch to declare their cause a Holy War. The Kurgans are alleged to follow a heretical version of the Prophet's teachings, scripture which the Orthodoxy does not want tainting the souls of Known Worlders.

The barbarian Vuldrok Star-Nation has increased its raiding of Hawkwood worlds of late, and seems to be itching for a confrontation with Alexius — whether to test his mettle and resolve or to provoke a full-fledged war is unknown.

The Symbiots, however, seem to have retreated from the frontlines on Stigmata. They have withdrawn into their territories for now, although the meaning of this move — uncharacteristic for the chaotic shapeshifters — is hotly debated. Are they building their strength for a greater assault? Or have they recognized defeat? Rumors persist of high-level contact between supposedly sentient Symbiot leaders and Imperial Eye agents hinting at peace initiatives, but most doubt such fables. How can there be peace with mindless animals?

And what of the Vau? Distant and aloof for years, their requests for diplomatic visits have increased of late, although their dialogues are seemingly meaningless, consisting of elaborate discussions of the weather or gardening tips. Some pundits whisper that the enigmatic aliens are sizing the Empire up, prepared either for a new expansion or new trade.

But border conflicts and high-level intrigues matter little to the common man. Most people are once again proud. Under Alexius, their destiny again seems assured. The jumproutes have opened to an unprecedented degree, reuniting worlds long sundered by war and factionalism. Interstellar trade is strong again, and with it an increasing network of news and gossip. Even here the Emperor has displayed power, using guilds of canny marketers to careful control his image.

Alexius has declared a new age of discovery and offers rich rewards or even peerages (or more powerful titles) to those who can reopen the paths to the Lost Worlds and riches of the Second Republic. He has instituted the Order of the Phoenix — the Questing Knights — to spread word of his rule and law to outlying regions and even into barbarian space. Their ranks are swelling, causing grumbling among the elite of the houses as second and younger sons and daughters — fearing to inherit little glory and wealth from their own families — seek to win it from the Emperor through adventure.

In addition, Alexius has opened the ranks to the guilds and sects, creating the role of Imperial Cohort, aide and companion to his knights. Cohorts are promised a share in the spoils of Imperial adventures — the chance for wealth and fame or the ability to spread the good word. This gesture to the League and Church is yet more proof to many that Alexius understands the multi-faceted nature of power in the Known Worlds.

The Church, however, frowns on Alexius' emphasis on questing and rediscovery of the past's riches, seeing once again the march of humanity's folly. The Orthodoxy suspects that the Questing Knights' true mission into barbarian space is an elaborate land-grab for the Empire, a way to give Alexius more worlds than the other houses combined. Of course, no crusade against barbarian powers could succeed without noble and Church support, but the question of fair division of spoils already worries the patriarch.

The Merchant League, however, sees opportunity in the opening of new jumproutes and the consolidation of existing routes (and even the hope of deposing Alexius and declaring the Third Republic on top of his reforms).

Never since the Fall has there been such opportunity for advancement and power by the common man. Rarely has human destiny stood in such balance: to fall back or go forward.

Society

There are two main social classes in the Known Worlds: freeman and serf. Seventy-five percent of the Known Worlds populace are serfs, the common folk working the fields on far-flung planets. Their lives are regimented and unchanging; few ever leave their home village. Of the twenty-five percent of freemen, eighteen percent are yeomen, folk of low class but more socially mobile than serfs. They do not necessarily owe allegiance to anyone, and if they do, it is usually through a willing contract of service. Artisans, learned scribes and rural officials make up this class. The remaining seven percent of the populace are nobles, Churchmen and Leaguemembers.

Player characters in **Fading Suns** are usually freemen. They are not forced by birthright into an unwilling servi-

Time

Time is a tricky issue in the Known Worlds. Each world has its own method of measuring time; the terraforming efforts of the Second Republic failed to change the rotational inconsistencies of all the planets. Some worlds have longer days than others, while some have longer nights. Each world also has its own native system of marking months, although such local chronological systems were spurned by the Second Republic, who relied instead on perfect nuclear clocks. Most starships (and noble mansions and merchant agoras) are equipped with nuclear clocks set at the same second as the central clock on Holy Terra. Thus, although time is relative, clocks are not.

The Empire uses a central calendar based on Holy Terra's solar and lunar cycles. Citizens of the Empire keep two times: their local time and Empire time. But most peasants live solely by the local seasonal cycles on their homeworlds. They measure time in spans — the time it takes for a celestial body (the sun or moon) to traverse the sky by the length of an adult hand held up to it. This might seem to make for a highly subjective judgment except that there is usually a central sun dial or water clock to declare the exact number of spans in a day or night; the peasant matches his own internal clock to the local, official clock.

tude to a noble lord, a Church sect or a guild. Instead, they can choose their own destiny — as far as they are willing to fight for it. Most of the power struggles within the Known Worlds are played out by freemen, especially that seven percent of especially privileged nobles, priests and merchants. These are the movers and shakers, those who can leave their homeworlds to visit other peoples and places.

Life Among the Fading Suns

The average person born in the Known Worlds is a peasant or yeoman. Unfortunate enough to have been birthed after the Fall of the Second Republic — the pinnacle of human civilization — all that is left to her are the crumbs of previous progress. Her world is in decline, not just technologically, but spiritually. Regardless of the rise to power of a Universal Church, the energetic and invigorating spirit of questing and questioning which marks healthy spirituality is largely absent. Instead, there exists a concern that the soul be "in order," ready for judgment (and probably found wanting). There is no place for risk-taking; all things belong in their place, and to overreach is folly, risking not only an individual soul but the entire commonwealth of lost hu-

manity. To the peasant: the fields. The yeoman: the work-shops. The guildsman: the agora. The priest: the chapel. The noble: the palace. And to the Emperor: the stars.

The loss of a scientific method or point-of-view among the common populace has helped to keep technology in decline, creating a scavenger mentality for the things of the glorious past. In addition, the nobles want the commoners to stay in their place; to question is to invite revolt. The Church blames technology and science for humanity's predicament, and thus represses the very basis of science: questioning. And the Merchant League wishes to keep what secrets it has for itself, sharing only with those willing to give their money or their service to the guilds. These forces together help to keep civilization from rising.

While the rebirth of civilization is sought by many in **Fading Suns**, civilization in and of itself is not valuable. It is what people do with it that makes it worthwhile. A false civilization's "worth" can be seen in the weary eyes of the enslaved and subjugated alien races, whose cultures have been outlawed and dismantled by the empire of humanity.

The Nobility

Erian Li Halan sighed, looking back over the past, over moments of past betrayal. Well she remembered the day her father died, bequeathing all to her hated older brother, leav-

ing nothing for her, not even a manor or other minor holding. He had not cared for her ideas — too radical for the Li Halan aristocracy.

Rather than accept the shame and unbearable charity of living off her brother — who would make each day of her existence a living Gehenne — she chose to forge her own life, far from the place she once considered home. With her had come her most cherished friends: her bodyguard Cardanzo, confessor Brother Guisseppe Alustro of the Order Eskatonic, and her old childhood friend, Julia Abrams, now a pilot with the Charioteers.

None of them were safe on Midian, not with her brother as baron — he could use the resources of the house to enact his hatred against her and her entourage. So they had rocketed into the darkening sky for distant stars and sights untold.

Her destiny had been revealed countless times since, in occult prophecies from Ur artifacts, dreams or strange coincidences. They led her farther and farther from home. But her brother followed. He would not allow Erian to gain honor and prestige at his expense. He unleashed countless assassins and Inquisitors upon her, but she always managed to stay a step ahead.

One day, however, there would be a showdown, and they would then see whose royal blood won out...

31

The Houses

Today's Royal Houses are the descendants of the nobles who rose up to claim planets during the last years of the First Republic and who reigned supreme on these worlds during the Diaspora. The Second Republic never succeeded in completely eliminating them, and when it collapsed, the nobles seized control of their planets, ensuring that the Republic would be unable to bring events back under control. As the Republic spiraled out of control, the nobles claimed more and more authority, and the disenfranchised masses fervently supported them in exchange for food and work.

A few of the noble families managed to lay claim to more than one planet or jumpgate. Based upon spurious claims of descent from earlier royalty, they began to call themselves Royal Houses. When the Republic lay in its death throes, they began jockeying for position among one another, and dozens rose and fell during that time. Ten houses claimed the most worlds, and formed an alliance of convenience. They called themselves the Ten, and most minor houses were forced to ally with one or more of them to maintain their own claims.

Five of these houses fell or became extinct during Vladimir's rise to power. Now five remain in power as the major houses, though many more remain as minor ones. The big five — Hawkwood, Decados, the Hazat, Li Halan and al-Malik — rule, in one way or another, almost all the Known Worlds. The Emperor controls a few other planets, and the Church and the League have theirs. Other than those, the Royal Houses own the stars.

Hawkwood

During its history, House Hawkwood has seen more ups and downs than a prostitute in zero-g. In its earliest days it was the leading house, and the one everybody expected would declare itself emperor. Then a consortium of other houses, led by the Decados, combined forces to bring it crashing down. It collapsed almost to the point of extinction, but one member managed to revive its fortunes and rebuild it. Within generations it had again become one of the greatest houses... before the first barbarian invasion broke through at Delphi and devastated the house's holdings. Other catastrophes have come and gone, but House Hawkwood has survived them all.

House Hawkwood is once again on an upswing, much to the delight of both the family and its subjects. The house has long relied on the goodwill of its people, rewarding them well during the good times and protecting them during the bad. However, family members have had the house's past drummed into their heads, and go to extremes to live up to the standards they believe their ancestors set.

Right now the house is at a crossroads. Its leader has just become emperor, but he is distancing himself from the very force that brought him to power. The new head of the house, Victoria Hawkwood, has made no comment on this, but lower-level leaders seem to find this detachment galling. A number of landed Hawkwood barons have become especially vocal in their complaints, noting that despite their sacrifices during the Emperor Wars, the Emperor has not split the rewards of empire with them. They have not received additional lands or even a break in their taxes since he became emperor.

On the other hand, a number of landless Hawkwood knights have found a place under the Emperor as Questing Knights. They have flocked to his banner and serve in a number of capacities, not all of them militaristic. They help administer the Empire, explore its darkest boundaries and bring back crucial information.

Leading Hawkwoods: Emperor Alexius, Princess Victoria Hawkwood (current house leader), Baroness Morgein Hawkwood (famed diplomat and adventurer), Duke Alvarex Hawkwood (Alexius' brother, often at odds).

Roleplaying Notes: Starting the moment a new Hawkwood is born, the house surrounds her with evidence of her inevitable destiny. By the time she turns five she can rattle off the deeds of leading Hawkwoods from centuries past. By the time she's 12, she realizes just how critical House Hawkwood has been in humanity's progress. By the time she reaches 16 years old, she has no doubt but that every action she takes will have critical importance to everyone in the Known Worlds.

Yes, some Hawkwoods rebel against or break under the strain the family puts them under, but these weren't true Hawkwoods anyway. Real Hawkwoods can deal with anything. Real Hawkwoods never doubt themselves. Real Hawkwoods know that their blood makes them able to face any enemy, overcome any obstacle. Real Hawkwoods know that failure of any kind is not acceptable. And most Hawkwoods often find themselves doubting that they are real Hawkwoods.

Stereotypes

While most outsiders know that each house has its own distinct character, they often fail to see the diversity within each one. Not all Hawkwood are honorable while some (few) Decados are. Some al-Malik are very religious, while some Li Halan have become heretics. The roleplaying hints in each section provide a brief guide for both players and gamemasters who want to add these nobles to a game, but they should not feel forced to follow these guidelines. Create characters who do what you want them to do regardless of anyone else's preconceived notions.

Still, this background enforces a certain air of superiority. Hawkwood nobles can be vain, headstrong and bigoted, but they can be equally courageous, charitable and progressive. Having a Hawkwood in charge means it is just as likely that he will be extremely capable as there is that he will be oblivious to his many faults.

This background also means that Hawkwood nobles are extremely conscious of honor, and house leaders readily voice their approval of dueling. Backing down from a challenge is not acceptable, but finding an equitable solution to the dispute (other than fighting) is. Emperor Alexius certainly became famous for his ability to compromise, but not all Hawkwoods have developed this talent.

Character Stereotypes: Explorer (Captain Sir Richard Francis Burton), military officer, populist leader, duelist, diplomat, heir to greatness, second(+) child out to prove him/herself, inbred prince/princess, spoiled brat.

The Decados

House Decados was the last of the Royal Houses to join the alliance against the Republic, known as the Ten (they were the tenth). However, it claims to be one of the oldest royal houses, long existing incognito. Its founders claimed descent from the Russian czars through Princess Anastasia. Such claims have often been denounced, in part because the first members of the house came from the intelligence services of a number of different planets and initially had no familial ties. Only after several generations of interbreeding could most of the Decados legitimately claim to be related to one another.

This interbreeding has continued through the years, and no one will deny that House Decados is an odd group of people. The Decados claim that this eccentricity is the prerogative of those destined to rule, while their detractors say it is the sign of sick and deranged minds. Whatever the case, their parties are the subject of much gossip for months afterward (though this is not always a good thing).

Still, House Decados has always been one of the most influential, if least trusted, Royal Houses. Its role in finally overthrowing the Republic is well-documented, though scholars still argue just how extensive it was. In any case, House Decados has long been an insurmountable barrier to anyone with democratic ideals.

It has also proven a barrier to other houses, and is a fierce and intractable foe. Its spies and assassins roam the Known Worlds, and Decados leaders have an uncanny knack for knowing everything about their foes — even things the enemy is unaware of. Additionally, the Decados have mastered the arts of body manipulation and alteration. Their Jakovian Agency spies are said to pass as anyone they desire, and even change appearances numerous times while on a single assignment.

That they lost the Emperor Wars despite this advantage surprised a number of observers. Indeed, the Decados seemed to have the upper hand until a stunning series of Hawkwood advances carried the day. That the Decados were unable to predict the Hawkwood maneuvers has struck many people as odd. The additional fact that the Decados have been, of all things, good losers has struck them as even odder. Rumors abound as to what the house's motivation may be, but no one seems to know for sure.

Leading Decados: Prince Hyram Decados (house head), Duchess Salandra Decados (second-in-command, alleged sometime paramour of Alexius), Baron Nicolai Decados (lost final battle against Alexius, not seen since).

Roleplaying Notes: Think of decadent Renaissance Italian nobles, such as the Borgias, and add an element of Oriental exoticism. Decados are classic two-faces, with an act they put on for everybody else, but a secret, true face they hide underneath. The real skill in dealing with Decados machinations is discerning this hidden face (the most dangerous Decados are those who can project many layers of masks).

Decados, like Hawkwoods, enjoy dueling, but they tend to cheat. Of course, that goes for everything the Decados do. All's fair in love, war and everything else. Poisoned stilettos, fencing foils that project false images of where they are, shield dampers, psychic attacks — anything they can get into the dueling arena will do. Any advantage they can get in any other arena will also be taken.

On top of all the stories about Decados decadence is the rumor that the Decados are secretly Antinomists, making pacts with demons to gain the emperor's throne. But then, every vile rumor that could be made about the Decados has been made, much to the house's enjoyment.

Character Stereotypes: Cruel overlord, oily spy, determined Machiavellian prince/princess, decadent caliph, disgraced son/daughter (disgraced for trying to reform the house), fallen noble, curious investigator, cruel duelist, vain ambassador.

The Hazat

Once the advisors to the now-extinct Chauki Royal House, the Hazat overthrew their masters, ejecting the last Chauki from an airlock, and soon helped to engineer the Fall. Since then the Hazat have tried to spread their influence, and have been repeatedly stymied.

The Hazat have always relied on force of arms, and defeated House Chauki by turning the army against it. In the process the Hazat found themselves forced to promise the army a significant role in ruling their domain — a role that has only grown over time.

This deal means that the Hazat couldn't curtail their military buildup even if they wanted to. It also means that

almost all young Hazat go through extensive military training throughout their childhood. Of course, even when the Hazat begin their military training at around five, they are trained for a command position. During the Emperor Wars, it was not uncommon for 12-year-old Hazat knights to lead forces of hardened veterans.

By the same token, the Hazat go to great extremes to prove their courage and ability. Just tell a Hazat that no one has ever successfully wrestled the great tusked otter of Leminkainen, and the Hazat will be on the next space ship out. The al-Malik used this fact to great effect during the Emperor Wars when they spread a rumor that a newly opened planet featured an unbeatable type of wild bull. The house captured a dozen Hazat who rushed into space to be the first to fight these animals.

While jokes about Hazat intelligence are therefore relatively common, no one can deny their ability in the field — or the effect they have on their soldiers. While the Hazat may be even more condescending to serfs than anyone else, they empathize with their soldiers and do everything they can for them. Retired soldiers in Hazat society occupy a place of honor, and have even been known to veto actions by the local Hazat ruler. Distinguished service by freemen within the Hazat military is often rewarded with money. Serfs may even become freemen, and freemen may get grants of land.

Despite this, word has gotten out about at least one insurrection within the Hazat army since the Emperor Wars ended. Hazat nobles express both surprise and indignation at the very idea that such a thing could have occurred, but the rumors persist nonetheless. Still, no one is able to advance a good reason as to why the Hazat army of all armies would mutiny.

Leading Hazat: Prince Juan Jacobi Nelson Eduardo de Aragon (head of the family), Duke Jose Alfonso Louis Eduardo de Aragon (Hazat ambassador on Byzantium Secundus, one of the most respected diplomats in the Known Worlds), Baroness Lucinda Dulcinea (current Stigmata Garrison Commander).

Roleplaying Notes: Members of the Hazat pride themselves on their honor and ability, and a slight to either will not be forgiven. By the same token, these are the traits they most value in others, and anyone they see with these qualities will quickly earn their respect. While sons and daughters of the Hazat all train in leadership and military skills, they also admire people who have developed other skills, like diplomacy, theology and such. Still, the surest way to a Hazat's heart is through skill at combat.

Despite this, the Hazat do not go for the dueling fad as much as the other houses — too many nobles hide behind their shields. A Hazat duel is fought shieldless and with heavier weapons.

Character Stereotypes: Military officer, second (or later) son/daughter, soldier of fortune, bodyguard (attendant to the royal house, trained as a Hazat), commando, peacekeeper, Sheriff of Nottingham.

Li Halan

House Li Halan is an old and distinguished one, but its current prestige belies its sordid past. Once renowned for its extreme debauchery and callous disregard for its subjects, modern historians agree that its bacchanals put those of House Decados to shame. Rumors of traffic with demons were among the milder accusations.

Then, during the Barbarian Invasions, House Li Halan found the Pancreator. The entire family converted in a single night, and several prominent members were immediately sent off to monasteries, never to be seen again. Since then the family has been the height of orthodoxy, battling heresies and even blocking attempts at change within the Church itself.

While the Li Halan actively tried to make one of their own, Flavius Li Halan, emperor, the House expressed no regret at losing the Emperor Wars. Part of Emperor Alexius' concessions at the end of the Wars was to back an Orthodox Patriarch, thus at least temporarily blocking the aspirations of the other sects. While the patriarch has not actively opposed the Emperor in any dealings, he is known to take much of his advice from the Li Halan.

The family's orthodoxy carries into all other areas of life as well. The Li Halan are the strictest adherents to the nobles' code of etiquette, and proselytize on these areas just as much as they do on religion. The house itself is rigidly structured, with each member of the family having no question as to where her place is. Observers have a more difficult time uncovering internal dissent within this family than in any other, rumors of occasional internal purges notwithstanding.

The planets of the Li Halan have also become far more structured. It is almost unheard of for a serf on a Li Halan planet to become a freeman, and freemen find it extremely difficult to obtain land. On the other hand, serfs and freemen rarely complain about their lot, for the house provides far more services to its people than does any other (with the possible exception of the Hawkwoods). Of course, priests on Li Halan planets stress the need for people to stay in the niches which the Pancreator has ordained for them, and tradition has caused Li Halan society to begin resembling an extremely intricate caste system. To do any work other than what ones parents did, or to marry outside of that occupation, is becoming rarer and rarer.

Leading Li Halan: Flavius Li Halan (family head, resides on Kish), Cardinal Fang Li Halan (main advisor to the Patriarch), Duchess Fatima Li Halan (has land holdings second only to the Emperor).

Roleplaying Notes: Li Halan nobles are usually strict adherents to orthodoxy in all its forms. Royals have high Faith, and for this reason, few have good Tech. They, like the Church, do not approve of dueling, but this has not stopped a Li Halan or two from becoming renowned duelists, much like Aramis of *The Three Musketeers*. House leaders deny this, of course.

Of course, just because the Li Halan maintain firm beliefs does not mean they are dogmatic and stupid. They have more in common with Joan of Arc, Thomas á Becket, or any number of noble saints than televangelists. Additionally, no few Li Halan have explored the mystical teachings of the Prophet and delved into theurgy.

Character Stereotypes: Crusader, pious knight or musketeer, saint, martyr (give up all worldly goods and family position), incognito friar (posing as common man), Fisher King, sectarian rebel (non-orthodox), secret pagan priest or demonist (Gile deRais).

al-Malik

This house is easily the least accessible and most rarely encountered. Its members live apart from the people they rule, keeping an air of distance about them even on those rare occasions when they tour their domains. During these times, they even speak in elegant metaphors that only fellow al-Malik understand. It seems the only time an al-Malik family member feels comfortable is when she is meeting with the members of the Merchant League, the house's historical allies.

House al-Malik has always been tied to the guilds, and some historians have hypothesized that it bought its position as a Royal House using money from banking and trade, and might still be involved in these endeavors. House al-Malik actively discourages such speculation, however, and its trained enforcers are more than capable of squelching such rumors.

House al-Malik can almost always count on League support, and al-Malik mansions are almost always filled with technological wonders. An al-Malik's shield is sure to be in working order, her rapier may well vibrate when it hits an opponent's flesh, and some even carry personal think machines (which the al-Malik cryptically call "computers").

The al-Malik do not appear to have any special deals with any individual guilds. In fact, the guilds lay less exclusive claim to al-Malik planets than they do to those of other houses. The Criticorum and Istakhr markets are second only to that on Leagueheim itself. Everything is for sale at these places, and there is a buyer for everything. Of course, there are parts of the bazaars where pious visitors do not go.

These connections between the al-Malik and the guilds have attracted no small amount of Inquisition attention. In-

deed, the al-Malik are undoubtedly the most investigated of the royal houses. However, aside from a few reprimands for low-level nobles, the house has never been officially accused of anything. The al-Malik often joke about paying their tithe directly to the Inquisition.

Leading al-Malik: Duke Hakim al-Malik (head of house), Duchess Yusara al-Malik (Duke Hakim's wife, leading patroness of the arts), Baronet Salome ab-Rashman (famed explorer).

Roleplaying Notes: Many nobles consider the al-Malik to be the most passionate of the houses. They throw vibrant parties, like good times and own the most interesting devices. Members of this house have a good deal of substance to back up their flash and glitter, however. An al-Malik is likely far better educated than other nobles even if she has less combat training. The al-Malik have no common opinion on dueling; some like it, some don't.

Additionally, despite their reputation, the al-Malik do not dislike the common people. If anything, they like them too much. They tend to hearken to latter-day Second Republic socialist philosophies, even though they are ardent capitalists. Their wealth affords them the dilettante pastimes of imagining a better world, a Utopian Third Republic — heresy, of course, so they deny such rumors. But the house's enemies whisper that it has teamed up with the League in building for such a future. Others argue that the al-Malik love commoners because they rarely see them up close.

Character Stereotypes: Patron to adventurers, adventurer, Third Republic architect, historian, beloved (or hated) dictator (Castro or Stalin), political reformer, webspinning spy (building network of loyal non-royal contacts).

The Minor Houses

A number of other houses have risen and fallen through the years, some never expanding beyond one planet, while others almost named one of their own Emperor before fading away. Most of these still have descendants in positions of power, though some, such as the Alecto, Gesar and Windsors, are believed to be completely extinct.

In fact, almost all the Known Worlds had their own unique ruling family at one point or another. Some of these families managed to extend their reach, taking over one or two other planets, marrying into other families and getting planets through dowries and inheritance, or allying with another family to share a planet. Others never left their homeworld and have slowly become less and less a factor. Almost every planet has several minor houses with interests and representatives on it.

Some of the minor houses that still exist, like the Sacrananka, have descended to the point of complete insignificance, their last survivors living in squalor or reverting to serfdom. Others, like the Keddah of Grail, remain the pri-

mary power on their own planet, above and beyond the Royal Houses or the Emperor.

Almost all of the remaining minor houses owe fealty to one of the five Royal Houses, though these chains of command are often intricate to the point of incomprehensibility. For instance, long before the Emperor Wars, House Torenson gave one of its planets to House Keddah in exchange for the Keddah pledging fealty in the event of war with the al-Malik. Before this pledge could be fulfilled, House Dextrite forced the Torensons to pledge fealty to them. Then the Dextrite were in turn subsumed by the Masseri. When the al-Malik declared war on the Masseri, the Masseri had the power to force House Keddah (by then a minor house) to abide by its centuries-old pledge to the almost-extinct house Torenson. The war severely weakened the Masseri, but before the war could be concluded, the Decados conquered the Masseri and have never allowed the Masseri/al-Malik war to end. In this way they have kept the remnants of House Keddah bound to them for almost a century.

Still, not all of the minor houses are on the decline. Several came into being in the last few centuries, and one, House Shelit, made its appearance recently when the Hazat discovered a jump route to its world (Hira, currently the source of the Kurga Conflict). Since then House Shelit and the Hazat have maintained close ties, but Shelit nobles have spread their influence and wealth around the Known Worlds. House Shelit also has access to some lost think machine technology, and has jealously guarded its knowledge.

Despite their subservient role, the minor houses play an important part in the Known Worlds. The Royal Houses do not have enough members to oversee every part of their domains, and the minor houses still appear to rule in a num-

---

Inside the Noble Mind

In **Fading Suns**, nobles are the biggest celebrities, the richest moguls, the most powerful politicians and the greatest sports stars all rolled into one. Whether a noble has ever done anything worthwhile or not, he expects to be treated as if the suns only shine at his sufferance. And, for most of his life, that is how he has been treated.

Seeing everyone fall to their knees at his approach does something to him. Having peasants wet themselves when he addresses them cannot help but affect his mind. He becomes sure of his superiority, and everything around him reinforces this belief. The best nobles use this to bolster their parental feelings toward others and feel that they must act to help the less fortunate. Baser nobles see these events as confirming their own unaccountability and their right to do as they please.

ber of places. On other planets they often own much of the land and industry, and house members are both the cultural and civic leaders.

Indeed, were all the minor houses to unite, they might very well be able to overthrow the Royal Houses. The likelihood of this is infinitesimally small, but it does provide extra impetus for the Royal Houses to keep the minor ones in their collective place. While members of some of the minor houses have managed to make names for themselves, the Royal Houses have prevented the complete resurrection of any of the minor ones. As long as the minor houses are busy carrying out the Royal Houses' wishes, they will never be free to plan their own rise. What follow are some of the more prominent minor houses.

Minor Houses

Juandaastas (long-standing ties to alien races, especially the Ur-Obun)

Justinian (once major, lost badly when Vladimir died)

Keddah (rulers of the planet Grail, bound to Decados by treaty, warring with al-Malik)

Masseri (conquered by Decados and on decline)

Shelit (newly discovered house with odd technological ties)

Thana (supported psychic research many years ago)

Torenson (strong proponents of rigid rules of etiquette)

Trusnikron (renowned beast tamers, strict adherents to their own code of honor)

Van Gelder (once major, now allied to Decados for survival)

Xanthippes (an ancient matriarchy with strict control over its own territory)

Extinct Houses

Alecto (Vladimir I's house, lost last sons in first Emperor War, a number died in odd accidents)

Chauki (overthrown by the Hazat)

Gesar (allied to Vladimir, lost last sons in first Emperor War)

Windsors (allied to Vladimir, lost last sons in first Emperor War)

The Entourage

Nobles do not spend all their time cloistered away in dark, dank castles, scheming and brooding. They often take their scheming and brooding on the road. They tour their domains, visit other nobles of their own or other houses, look for mates, try and expand their holdings and sometimes even seek to help their subjects. Of course, no noble would be so foolish as to travel alone. Not only is such a practice unsafe, but a noble caught without an entourage would be immediately suspect or a laughingstock.

Common hangers on for nobles include bodyguards (usually battle-hardened veterans but sometimes also members of military orders), religious advisors or confessors, intelligence advisors (actually called spies or assassins if they work for the Decados), a dueling partner, pilot or chauffeur, and hangers-on who give the noble additional prestige — paramours, aliens, entertainers, scholars, noted explorers, sycophants, etc.

One of the odder situations is when two (or more) nobles from different houses travel together. Either they will each bring their full entourage in an effort to intimidate each other or else, for the sake of their mutual sanity, will pare it down to just the essentials — a single bodyguard, trusted servant or valued confidant.

Traveling groups composed of nobles from different houses are not at all rare. The peasantry might be amazed to see a Decados and a Hawkwood strolling along arm in arm, but other nobles would not give it a second thought. In fact, many older nobles encourage the practice, hoping that their progeny will form lasting alliances and perhaps bring back important information. At the very least, the nobles will get to know their future enemies.

Noble Etiquette

Intricate rules of conduct affect all aspects of noble and royal society, governing everything from the clothes they wear to what they say when they kill one another. These rules have grown out of centuries of custom and practice, and the nobles rigidly enforce their code. Those who violate these policies do so at risk of condemnation, ostracism and even death. Still, some cynics insist that the only reason to have these laws is so the nobles will have something to break.

Most non-nobles think of these rules mainly in regard to hospitality and courtly love. These are certainly the two best-known areas, for the bards sing of both — courtly love (for the great songs it inspires) and hospitality (for the great meals it gets them). These two areas are certainly important aspects of noble etiquette, but they are by no means the only ones. Dueling is illustrated as an example of another area of etiquette.

Of course, these rules only apply to how nobles deal with each other. No noble would ever allow any rules to limit how she can treat her social inferiors. Peasants murdered, priests ridden down and traders plundered — all these are fair play for a noble. On the other hand, addressing a planet's governor as "my lord" when a duke of the owning house is present is a most unpardonable sin.

While each house has its own take on these conventions, time has codified enough of them to give all nobles a firm set of guidelines. The punishment for etiquette violations is nowhere nearly as rigid, being at least partially determined by how important the offending noble is, but no one — not even the prince of a Royal House — can get away with one. In extreme cases, the violator will find herself chal-

lenged to a series of duels. At the very least, an offender will be ignored at parties. Fellow nobles who used to spend hours in conversation with her barely spend five minutes. Others who would have said hello ignore her completely.

If the offending noble is not crucially important, then other nobles will stop involving her in social functions entirely. No more invitations to tea parties, no more alien hunts, and no more masquerade balls. This social ostracism can be bad enough, even driving some nobles to suicide, but that is not the worst punishment. The noble is cut off from her main source of gossip, and for nobles, information is second in importance only to status. Not knowing who is hating whom and, more importantly, who is hating *that* noble, can be maddening.

Nobles who have violated social decorum may never be fully accepted back into proper society. No matter what they do, that element of suspicion can linger forever, coloring everything they accomplish. Only the greatest of exploits, the strictest adherence to etiquette, or the most stunning social endeavors can wipe the slate clean again.

Courtly Love

The official rules for love and marriage within the nobility have nothing to do with one another. Arranged marriages, weddings of convenience, mandatory divorces — all are part and parcel of being a noble. The structure surrounding marriage is rigid, and only rarely do these lead to satisfying monogamous partnerships with committed participants. Far more common is the joining of two people who could care less about each other, grow to hate each other, and carry on constantly with other people.

The bards have noticed this and turned it into a central facet of noble life; probably the only facet of which all nobles are proud. For a man or woman to commit totally and completely to another person is an important moment, one which has inspired more songs than any other subject.

Not all sexual relationships between nobles involve courtly love. In fact, courtly love is somewhat rare despite all the great songs devoted to it. Nobles are as susceptible to momentary infatuation as anyone else, and dalliances are a common occurrence. Those involving courtly love, however, are far more interesting.

Tabitha al-Malik is often held up as a model of courtly love. Tabitha, who lived centuries ago, married Lars Hawkwood while engaged to Juan Alecto while wooing Justine Decados. In one year she provided the bards with more material than most nobles can inspire in a lifetime.

As Tabitha taught, the wooing process begins slowly and carefully, no matter how smitten the suitor might be. Rushing this point of the relationship cannot help but ruin the courtier's chances. The process differs only slightly if one (or both) of the participants are married to someone else. Then the romance begins a little more quietly, but then

nobles generally try to begin these as subtly as possible, for fear that word of rejection might cause them to be laughed at by their peers.

The initial overtures include the traditional flowers, poems and gifts, all carried by intermediaries and seconds. Public meetings between the two romantics should be calm and subdued, giving little hint to those unfamiliar with the relationship that anything is out of the ordinary. Of course, those wise to the ways of etiquette will immediately notice the feigned coolness and understand the true situation.

Private meetings between the paramours should be both tense and exciting. Their conversation will be laden with innuendo and laced with hidden meaning. At this point, physical contact is discouraged, but often happens nonetheless. Its presence is a sure sign that the first stage is over.

Once both parties are sure of the other's interest, their relationship becomes a matter of public record. Their dealings become more passionate, more chaotic and, for outsiders, more interesting. Those lovers burdened by the unfortunate baggage of marriage try to act discretely in public, but this requirement is often ignored — much to the bards' delight. Of course, the bards delight even more in the next step — the break up.

Hospitality

Some cynics say that the main reason for the laws of hospitality is to give nobles protection when they kill their guests. Since these laws detail not only a host's obligation to his guests but also the guests' obligation to their host, it is easy to find something that one or the other has violated. This violation can then be punished as the injured party sees fit and can get away with.

There are a great many variables in the rules of hospitality. Was the guest invited? Did she bring an entourage? Was she ever romantically involved with the host? Just how important is she? The fact that each house, and each branch of each house, has its own take on these rules makes hospitality even more complex.

Some things, however, are sacrosanct. Once a guest is invited into a noble's home, no matter what the guest's rank, the host is obligated to protect her from all harm, no matter where it might come from. Additionally, he should go to great ends to ensure that her stay is at least pleasant, if not luxurious. Being known as a generous host is extremely important to almost all nobles.

By the same token, guests may take no actions which might bring scorn upon their host. Should a host ask something of them, they must oblige, unless it would put them at risk. For instance, should a host ask some traveling nobles to escort his daughter to an Imperial ball, they should feel obliged to do so. Of course, if the host just happened to forget to mention that his daughter had recently offended the Ur-Ukar ambassador, then so be it. That shouldn't nec-

essarily lead to trouble.

Other rules of hospitality detail how fine a gift should be given to the host's family based on both the giver and the recipient's social status, how good the hospitality should be for each visitor, and even how long visitors should stay. Commoners are usually completely befuddled by these practices. Just why does a duke have to give a knight a more valuable present than a baron must give a marquis?

Duels

The Church strongly opposes duels as well as the ceremonies and rituals that have grown up around the practice, but this has done little to stem their popularity. Nobles who feel they have been grievously offended and don't have access to an assassin can have their closest friends (or expendable underlings) approach the offender and denounce the crime. The offending noble then draws his sword with a great protestation of innocence and threatens to run the accuser through. At this point the accuser will quickly proclaim that there is someone who has been more severely wronged than he, and that this victim seeks redress. The accused makes a big show of his innocence and says that he will do anything to clear his name. The two then come to agreement about a time and place to "resolve this horrid situation."

At the appointed time and place, both parties will appear with sword in scabbard and dueling shield turned on. There are no such things as dueling pistols; nobles consider it far more honorable to stab an unarmed opponent in the back with a poisoned dagger than to shoot her from 40 paces. The shield requires nobles to use all their skill to do less damage than the shield blocks. After all, nobles do not necessarily feel the need to fight to the death. If an opponent surrenders, the victor will usually not kill him. Indeed, etiquette requires that a duelist allow a disarmed opponent to regain his blade (though most nobles will expect an "accidental" follow up attack while disarmed), let a fallen foe stand up (again, with the possibility of an accidental hit), and hold off if an enemy's shield fails (accidental attacks in this instance are often fatal).

Any violation of the code will not go unnoticed. Duels draw large crowds and are often overseen by priests, despite the Church's opposition to the practice. Each fighter will bring along as many friends and allies as possible, all to ensure that nothing goes awry. Other nobles who have heard about the duel will come just for the fun of it. Local authorities, however, will not attend, finding business as far away as possible. A noble's duel is not open to any inferiors outside of the nobles own entourage.

Note that the duelist's code does not require that the victor accept his adversary's surrender. A noble who gets a

reputation for fighting to the death, however, will make even more enemies and will find it hard to stop a duel he is losing. Additionally, some nobles will make a point of snubbing one of their own who is too violent — at least, one who is too violent to other nobles.

The Emperor

The most powerful individual in the Known Worlds is Emperor Alexius, once the head of House Hawkwood. While he still maintains strong ties with his house, he has renounced its leadership in order to establish the role of emperor free and clear of past entanglements. Alexius's critics say he is merely trying to establish two powerful forces to ensure his rule — one being the armies of the Emperor and the other being his loyal house legions.

Alexius now makes his home on Byzantium Secundus, the historic center of interstellar politics. While he officially rules fewer planets than do any of the houses, his actual powers are exceptional. The most obvious manifestation of this might is the Imperial Guard, some of the best-trained and equipped troops in human history. His other strengths are more subtle — and more powerful.

Emperor Alexius officially controls the empire's tax collection network, its army of scholars and historians busily trying to reconstruct old technologies, its many law enforcement and espionage agencies, and the largest collection of Philosophers Stones (powerful Ur artifacts) in the Known Worlds. All of the Royal Houses have pledged their loyalty and are obligated to provide him assistance whenever he requests it. What form this assistance may take, however, has not been determined.

Alexius is still defining his role as emperor. He has announced plans to consolidate more power in his position and has been laying the groundwork for war against the barbarians — a war he would lead, and whose troops would be beholden to him. The Royal Houses have no intention of giving him permanent control of their troops, so no one knows exactly what will happen. The events of the next few years will have a powerful impact on the balance of power for years to come.

To aid him in this endeavor, the Emperor has put out a call for landless nobles to join him, implying that they may find new territory on unexplored planets. So far his call has mainly attracted his old allies in his family, but some members of other houses have come on board as well. A few members of minor houses have also shown up, hoping for the chance to rebuild their own dynasties under his banner.

There is an underground group of mystics, soldiers and citizens of all classes who see Emperor Alexius as their God-Emperor, their savior and the one who will reignite the dying stars. The emperor is silent on the matter, but the Church has made it clear that such views are heresy; Inquisitors are searching for the leaders of this cult.

The Imperial Eye

Before his assassination, Emperor Vladimir established a fact-finding and intelligence-gathering organization called the Imperial Eye. He brought in nobles from a number of royal and minor houses, gave them extensive budgets to establish the agency, and then died. The Eye lived on, however, serving the stewards and regents who took over after Vladimir's death and before Alexius' rise.

Officially this organization serves Alexius by gathering and analyzing information. It maps out new jumproutes, tracks economic development on the recovering worlds and has one department dedicated to discovering why the stars are fading. During the chaos and confusion of the Emperor Wars, however, the Eye found itself accused of activities outside the scope of its original charter.

Accusations of activities like spying, smuggling and even assassination rarely came to anything, and when an agent was tried, the agency always managed to show that he was acting outside the bounds of the Eye. No evidence ever appeared that the Eye had actually tried to make one of its own patriarch. The leaders of the Eye hold themselves up as selfless servers of humanity. Its detractors (usually the Emperor's enemies) denounce them as self-serving manipulators who plot and scheme against everybody. Whatever the case, the Eye has a reputation among the common folk as an organization to avoid second only to the Inquisition.

The Universal Church of the Celestial Sun

Adept Guisseppe Alustro wiped the sweat from his brow. He drew his cowl closer over his face and clutched his charred book sack tightly to his side as he shoved his way through the filthy, brute-cart laden street. If he could reach the royal berths of the starport before he was sighted again, he might just make it off-planet alive.

"Curse those meddling Avestites!" he thought as his eyes darted about warily, searching for signs of the heavy robes and smoking guns. "When would they accept that Eskatonic priests were God-fearing members of the Church just as they were? But no use griping — sectarian conflict is not what this witchhunt is all about. No, Erian Li Halan's brother has called them against me, attempting to discredit Erian since I am her confessor. If I am deemed heretic for my studies, then she will also be tainted with the charge."

He turned the corner of the final lane and saw the entryway a mere five strides ahead. He pushed forward, shoving artisan hawkers aside — but then halted, staring at the back of the robed woman rushing to reach the gates

before him. Smoke rose up about her torso from the muzzle of the flamegun she slung low.

Alustro shut his eyes for only a moment, sending a silent prayer to the Pancreator, and then ran forward as fast as he could, knocking the Avestite to the manure-stained cobblestones. Then he was past her and running. A yell behind and the sound of air igniting, and Alustro could smell the hairs on the back of his head burning...

Sects and Orders

No single institution has as much impact on day-to-day life in the Known Worlds than does the Church. Despite the Church's many factions and sects, the average peasant sees it as a giant monolith, dedicated to saving humanity from the evil inherent in the universe. As far as commoners can tell, all priests, bishops, archbishops and patriarchs work toward the same goal, hand-in-hand, fighting evil together. Never mind the fact that they call one another heretics; the Church itself is good. The peasants' view only changes when someone tries to replace the sect of their ancestors with a new one.

The Universal Church is not so universal; it is deeply divided by sectarian conflicts. It would have fractured into multiple churches long ago were it not for a string of extremely strong Orthodox patriarchs who held it together—that and a need for unity against the nobility and the merchants.

There are five major sects and dozens of minor ones. Some get along; most don't. A lot of the minor sects are branches from the major ones, but others have alien, local or even historical roots.

Urth Orthodox

Orthodox priests represent the old, authoritarian guard of the Church, maintaining stability while fighting off heresies. They are also those most concerned with temporal power. Traditionally (with few exceptions), the patriarch has been Orthodox.

They believe, following key bulls set out in the New Dark Ages, that grace is achieved through working within the structure set forth by the patriarchs, who follow in the footsteps of the Prophet. The Pancreator works not through inner visions but through real works, duties performed in the material world. He shows his will through sacramental forms: rituals, artifacts, stations of office, etc. Wavering from time-tested doctrine in this time of darkening light is dangerous and foolhardy. One fool can hurt many good people; all must walk the proper path and follow the correct guidelines. Those who don't may damn us all.

Despite their political bent, they are nonetheless fervent believers and moral guardians. They aim to give succor and comfort to all who need it, including serfs. The Or-

Stereotypes

Priests may seem at first to be all of the same stripe. They usually wear the same uniforms (varying somewhat with sect) and preach the same overall beliefs. But this is a mere façade. Looking past the catechisms, robes and rosaries, each priest approaches his or her faith differently. While some try as hard as they can to follow the party line, many do so in the way they best see fit. Not all Avestites are screaming fanatics; some may be calm and introspective, truly compassionately worried about the collective sins of the universe. Likewise, not all Orthodox priests are intolerant to non-doctrinal points of view; some are fascinated with the new ideas and perspectives cropping up on the many worlds of the Pancreator.

Despite the Church's often iron-handed role in politics, the priests who preach at the cathedrals throughout the Known Worlds are, for the most part, truly devout and unconcerned with worldly power. It is the state of the soul they concentrate upon, and the fate of the soul as it leaves its mortal coil. Without the selfless acts and counsel of Church priests, the populace of the Known Worlds would surely be worse off and deeper in despair.

thodoxy is the only large organization in the Known Worlds that cares enough about the livelihood of the commoners to aid them, live among them and even educate them (although they do not seek commoner emancipation). Through these good works, they have nearly seventy-five percent of the Known Worlds populace behind them. The fact that this populace has no legal power does little to quell the noble's fear of riots and uprisings, and thus everyone heeds the Orthodoxy's desires.

Membership in the Orthodox Church is open to all, although applicants for priesthood must undergo years of training in ritual and doctrine.

Leading Orthodox priests: Patriarch Hezekiah the Elder (current head of the Church on Holy Terra), Hierophant Palamon (Archbishop of Byzantium Secundus), Archbishop Sigmund Drual (syneculla — right-hand man — to the patriarch)

Roleplaying Notes: While the Orthodox stance may seem suffocatingly authoritarian in theory, in practice it allows its priests much leeway to choose their own means and even to interpret doctrine in their own way. The Church is built upon the ongoing creation of the Pancreator and humanity's participation in that creation, seen as a sort of passion play. The darkening light of the suns is due to humanity's sins in overreaching their part in the play.

Through humility and good works, humanity can part the curtains which block the light from the stars and again take part in the revealed light of creation. But until that time, humans are on probation and must temper their actions.

Each person can experience his or her role in the Pancreator's creation. It is the duty of the Church to aid in separating right experience from wrong perception. Demons can fool people, and only Church doctrine can guide in seeing past false experience by providing a time-proven guideline. Priests are needed to provide witness to the Church's truth for the Pancreator's creations. However, there are many worlds, each with their own particular problems. Lack of rapid communication prevents direct answers from Holy Terra. The training a priest receives is designed to give him a broad framework with which to interpret any of the myriad trials of life; it is a priest's responsibility to have the courage to make his own interpretations based on experience, with doctrine as guidance. Those priest's whose answers to religious problems are most in line with the current patriarch's beliefs (some say political needs), are those who rise the highest in the Church hierarchy.

Nonetheless, while a priest owes respect and obedience to those above him, she has the duty to rely on her own experiences and convictions (as long as she does not slip too far into mysticism). Creation is ongoing, and the Pancreator reveals himself to his children in different ways at different times. Priests must be ever alert for these omens and be ready to provide the correct interpretation of them for the leity. Others look to the Church for answers; a priest must be prepared to give them boldly.

Character Stereotypes: Confessor (perhaps personal confessor to a noble or a rich merchant), community leader, elder, wiseperson, healer, missionary, monk, pilgrimage guide, penitent, diplomat, exorcist

Brother Battle

Throughout history, monastic battle orders have existed within organized religion: the Knights Templar, Hospitalers, Shaolin priests, Jannisaries, and others. In the Known Worlds, there are the Brothers Battle, said to be the most elite combat corps in history. Fanatically dedicated to defending the Prophet's faith with might and force of arms, the Brothers of this exclusive order are respected — and feared — by most Known Worlders.

The order began early in the New Dark Ages, when the need for hard-line and able defenders of the faith was greatest. They personally defended the life of the patriarch from an assassination attempt on Holy Terra. In return for their service, the patriarch ordained the order, giving it special powers within and without the Church, conceded to by the noble houses, who were trying to cover up their role in the assassination attempt. Since then, the order has grown in skill and influence, building upon martial techniques created by previous Brothers. These techniques are kept secret. Those who have been ousted from the order are not allowed to teach them; if they are caught revealing them to others, the penalty is death.

Brothers adhere to strict discipline and suffer harsh penalties for breaking their vows. Oathbreakers must undertake dangerous penance quests which many do not survive. There is a strong support network from Brother to Brother, although monks are often sent on individual missions across the Known Worlds, spreading their network thin.

The order does not work well with other units in the secular military chain of command. Brothers will not take orders from any but their superiors within the order, so they are rarely used as common soldiers, instead being employed as commandos and special tactics units.

Membership requirements are strict. Only youths under ten years old are accepted, although the order adopts many orphans. There have been very few exceptions to this rule throughout the order's history, although the handful of older individuals who have been accepted provide hope for many petitioners. New members are sent to the monastery on De Moley, there to spend the next ten or more years of their lives in rigorous training and spiritual contemplation. Local peasant mothers on De Moley often leave their newborn children on the monastery's doorstep, hopeful that their offspring will be taken in and be given a better life and opportunity than a peasant's son or daughter would otherwise have. However, the order does not accept every child left on its stoop. Many are left to survive or die outside the gates. Those who live longer than expected are often accepted.

The Brother Battle order wields much power, and many Orthodox patriarchs have felt threatened by their strength. Their piety and military might are needed by the emperor on the Symbiot and Barbarian fronts, and while they have rarely used the political power gained through this, the Orthodoxy anticipates the day they must clash, fearing that Brother Battle will win out. Thus, the order is under increased scrutiny for heresy and any other slip-up that could lead to their dissolution.

Despite the name, women may join, although it is rare.

Leading Brothers: Master Claudius of De Moley (head of the order), Adept Falkner of Stigmata (leader of the Brother Battle unit on the Symbiot front), Adept Aaron of Urth (currently the Brother Battle representative on Holy Terra).

Roleplaying Notes: Supreme martial discipline is the hallmark of a Brother Battle. Exercises are performed religiously, designed to maintain both body and spirit. Once a Brother Battle has been given a holy task, he will ignore all other considerations which impede or distract from that task. For this reason, the brothers are desired as elite guards or commandos by anyone who can afford them — their price, however, is not coin, but glory to the Pancreator. If the task has no religious purpose, it is deemed unworthy of attention. However, their interpretation of religious matters is broad enough to include many things, and any task which aids the Order is deemed worthy.

One of these tasks is to guard the pilgrimage routes from planet to planet. In so doing, they often guard the money and valuables of their charges — for a tithe, of course. This has lead to a growing network of money-exchange which threatens the hegemony of the Reeves guild in such matters and has levied accusations of usury at the Order.

Young brothers, newly ordained, are urged to leave the monastery for an extended pilgrimage through the Known Worlds. Since Brother Battle is in one sense the worldliest of orders, Brothers should know the worlds they may be called on to fight one day. They are also urged to mix with other sects and orders to better understand them, for the order is called to fight for them often. Likewise, personal understanding of nobles, merchants and other freemen is deemed wise. It is common for these wandering Brothers to attach themselves to certain groups as bodyguards or even leaders before eventually returning to their monastery for further duty.

Character Stereotypes: Holy warrior, elite commando, smiter of heathens, kung-fu master, ex-gunfighter (trying to hang up his guns)

Eskatonic Order

An extremely mystical and occult order, the Eskatonics seek to guard the light of the Holy Flame from the impending eschaton, or apocalypse. They are engaged in a personal and individual pursuit of the holy. Unlike the Orthodox Church, they believe there is a spark of the Holy Flame in each person, and that it is the duty of the enlightened (those fully conscious of the Holy Flame within them, made aware through a personal vision) to cultivate this flame and fan it into a fire. Their main means to this end is theurgy.

Their exclusive entry requirements, however, ensure that they have the smallest membership of any order, and thus the smallest support network. But their occult practice tempers each member into a powerful and noteworthy priest. They emphasize inner mysteries and philosophy, with perhaps too little attention to outer reality. They are doom-sayers, believing the worst about humankind's fate. In their view, only a few will recognize the light and escape the Final Darkness. They claim to have personal experience with certain vile demon sultans who they say are to blame for the dimming stars, and believe that only the order's wisdom and magic can avert the final doom (they also claim detailed knowledge of the "bodiless powers of the Empyrean", or angels).

They claim direct lineage from certain of the Prophet's disciples, to whom the Prophet gave secret lore, wisdom

which the early Eskatonics were given the responsibility of safeguarding. They were an underground, secret society of Church priests until the Symbiot Wars, where they were allowed to operate openly only by grace of their own theurgy. Eskatonic magi proved to be one of the few effective weapons against the Symbiots when they attempted to move past Stigmata. The patriarch had to ordain them or risk losing more worlds to the parasitic invasion. Since then, the Eskatonics have been very careful to behave (or at least hide their excesses well) lest they suffer official censure and be forced underground again. But the common populace often fears them, and they are constantly at risk for Inquisitorial searches and heresy declarations.

Rank within the order is built around the slow dissemination of secrets and occult techniques. The order's fathers created a carefully wrought system of study, whereby a student would only be exposed to lore he was capable of understanding. Rank is awarded only to those who have proven themselves mentally and spiritually worthy of it. Then, the secrets of that rank are taught slowly and, once mastered, the student is ready for the next rank.

Humility is all-important during training and ordination. No priest is allowed to rise in rank without first confessing, and those priests who do not undergo confession on a monthly basis are shamed until they learn to do so. The practice of flagellation, the wearing of hair-shirts and other self-inflicted tortures are also encouraged. The order believes that these extreme measures prevent hubris, for the history of the order tells of priests whose pride grew, and whose sins caused whole worlds to perish. While they have managed to keep the truth behind these dead worlds from the populace and the Church at large, there is good reason these magi are feared.

Leading Eskatonics: Magus Moore of Pentateuch (head of the order), Magister Osanto of Manitou (keeps tabs on psychic covens), Philosophus Antonia de Cadiz (Hazat wizard), Provost Alustro (young nephew of Orthodox Hierophant Palamon)

Roleplaying Notes: Eskatonics are the most curious of priests. Most are impatient to learn the secrets hidden in the universe, and since their strict tutelage regimen prevents them from learning whatever they desire, they often leave their cathedrals for pilgrimages across the stars searching for secret lore. This is fully in line with the Prophet's exhortations for questing. Indeed, higher ranking priests often become jealous and protective of their hard-won lore and are loathe to hand it down to students, all the more reason for the student to seek on his own.

But it is a dangerous universe out there, so few Eskatonics go alone. Most attach themselves to a retinue, either a noble entourage, a merchant caravan, or some motley group of people powerful enough to help her search for the lore she seeks.

While the Eskatonics are few in number and sometimes jealous of one another, when they meet among the stars, they are often eager to exchange lore, for they inevitably become lonely for others who can understand the profound thoughts going on in their heads.

Character Stereotypes: Wizard, philosopher, doomsayer, occult investigator, demon-hunter, artifact hound

Temple Avesti (Avestites)

Inquisitors. The fanatic and disciplined Avestites are the hard-liner arm of the Church, often too regressive for even the patriarch's tastes, although he is often thankful for the power to unleash them on victims. While not all Inquisitors come from this sect, most do (the Avestites long ago gained most of the chairs on the Inquisitorial Synod).

Temple Avesti began as a breakaway movement from the Orthodoxy, composed of puritans who felt that the Church was not stern or strong enough in punishing the excesses of its members (to the Avestites, everyone is a member of the Church whether they like it or not). These extremists built their temple in the burning desert on the planet Pyre. Pledged to punish sinners lest they corrupt the faithful, the Avestites embarked from Pyre on expeditions to cleanse other worlds. Their violent and unannounced terrorist attacks on "sinners" angered the often-powerful victims of these attacks: nobles and rich merchants. After too many incidents with no response from the Orthodox Church, royal fleets arrived off Pyre to destroy these uncontrollable zealots. But the patriarch's fleet also arrived and ordered the nobles to halt their assault. The Archbishop of Urth went to Temple Avesti and explained to the sect leader the terms of the sect's surrender to patriarchal authority. If they did not submit, the Church would depart and leave them to their fate before the royal fleet. After short consideration, the temple master relented and threw himself on the mercy of the Church.

Since then, the Avestites are considered penitents, owing duty to the patriarch and his bishops. While they can act on their own, they must also heed the call of the Orthodox priests when they require it. However, the extremes to which Avestites take any task often tempers the frequency of their use by the bishops. They are called on official business only when all other methods have failed.

Hopeful Avestites must petition for membership into the sect, and only those who can prove that they are sinless — or *extremely* repentant — are given entry. Only the ignorant or unlearned are allowed, for education is seen as a burden on the soul which is hard to extinguish. Thus, their membership comes from the poorest peasants, the lowest classes who often seek revenge for their lack of empowerment. Most members never again leave the temple on Pyre; they spend their lives in prayer or hard labor for the temple. Those who

prove their prowess in sniffing out sinners are promoted as pilgrims, those who will deliver punishment to sinners across the Known Worlds. The best pilgrims are granted Inquisitorial seals and eventually become ordained Inquisitors.

Avestites are often bigoted and anti-alien, but can likewise be pillars of nobility and kindness — to those deserving of it. Aliens are allowed in the sect if they can prove their faith like all other applicants. To the sinless, Avestites are perfect gentlemen, having learned the lesson of temperance from the sect's humble downfall. To those they deem sinners, however, no amount of cruelty is enough. They take the Prophet's words about sinners and burning quite literally, and their heavy flame-retardant robes and cowls are instantly recognizable. Their high priests even prefer to carry flameguns to enact a literal punishment on sinners.

Their symbol, the flame, is borne on pendants which, with the flick of a switch, become searing brands with which they mark sinners' foreheads. Those peasants who bear this brand (which takes months to heal for those who cannot afford tissue regenerative serums) are shunned by their fellows, although the upperclasses unfortunate enough to suffer such humiliation often receive pity and commiseration from their friends, though not publicly.

Leading Avestites: Archbishop Dolmen of Pyre (leader of the sect), Bishop Gondo Ortiz de Aragon (head of the Inquisitorial Synod), Canon "Loose" Buchanan of Shaprut (overlord of local cathedral, thought responsible for massacre of refugees from Stigmata)

Roleplaying Notes: Avestites are extremely concerned about the level of sin going on around them and find it hard not to interfere. They are nosy busybodies who believe that everyone's business is their business. To an Avestite, individual values such as privacy are seen as excuses to hide sin. Avestites are allowed little privacy among their own kind, living in common bunkrooms, eating together, working together, praying together. Never (or rarely at best) is there time for private contemplation. Perhaps this is why Avestites are so eager to get off Pyre on lone pilgrimages.

But Avestites are not liked by the common folk. While they are feared, a lone Avestite can still easily find himself ganged up on by a bold mob and dragged into an alley for a vicious beating or worse, hearing cries of: "This is for Uncle Lon (kick), who you burned for supporting Obun rights! And this is for Cousin Jocko (punch), tortured for buying ham on Restday!" For this reason, even lone Avestites will attempt to attach themselves to a retinue, claiming to seek comrades against sin, but in actuality seeking strength in numbers.

Character Stereotypes: Inquisitor, fanatic preacher, cult leader, arson, religious terrorist, political activist (arguing for theocracy), missionary, far missionary (bringing the word and the flame to heathens beyond the borders), border guard (defending the border from aliens and barbarians), renegade cultist (thinks Avestites go too far), spy (disguised as member of other sect/order), bounty hunter

Sanctuary Aeon (Amaltheans)

Sanctuary Aeon is a healing order, seeking to bring grace and mercy to all. While its membership is open to anyone, few people volunteer for this selfless duty. The priests of Sanctuary Aeon may be few in number, but they are beloved by all. The love the common folk bear them for their selfless sacrifices have provided them practically ironclad protection from Inquisitors and heresy police: When Sister Vermidian was accused before a crowd of peasants on Criticorum of consorting with demons, the peasants rose up and tried to hang the Inquisitor as the heretic.

The order was begun by Amalthea, a physician who became one of the Prophet's disciples. After the Prophet's death, she tried to forge his sayings into a Church different from that which Palamedes Alecto was forming. Her Temple of Eternal Sanctuary was almost as popular as Palamedes new Universal Church. But in the end, the Universal Church appealed more to people's need for authority, power, guilt and redemption. However, the Eternal Sanctuary, or Sanctuary Aeon as it eventually became, still had a strong following, especially in the aftermath of harsh wars. The Sanctuary was eventually incorporated into the Church, and today stands as a strong voice for mercy and compassion before the patriarch's often stern bulls.

The order's head monastery is on Artemis, and all initiates must go there for their initial training in healing bodies, minds and spirits. The planet is flooded with the sick and injured who can afford the journey, but there are never enough Amaltheans to help them all. Once ordained, priests are expected to return to their homeworlds and bring their skills to bear in relieving suffering there. Otherwise, they can choose to stay on Artemis or travel as mendicant healers. Some are sent by the order to aid on the war fronts, never as soldiers, but as healers or even diplomats.

Because their numbers are small, they demand penance from those they aid, asking for them to perform tasks to relieve other suffering souls, thus increasing compassionate acts tenfold more than their order could perform alone. While Amaltheans will aid others without a promise of a penance task, they are bid by the order's leaders to enact this promise whenever possible. The nature of the promise is up to the healer enacting it, and there is no set guideline for the difficulty of the task compared to the healing. An Amalthean will generally ask for what she feels is the promiser can achieve, but she is free to enact a harsh task if she feels the sufferer needs it.

The Amaltheans are a rare voice in the Church, preaching the rights of all living beings, sentient or not. They admonish those who seek their aid to never harm an animal or sentient creature even if it threatens them in return; they can defend themselves, but must avoid killing.

Leading Amaltheans: Archbishop Sakhya of Artemis (head of the order), Bishop Deander of Stigmata (physician in charge of war relief), Canon Teras Myrin of the Road (wandering healer, beloved by many), Cardinal Oma of Apshai (ambassador to the Vau)

Roleplaying Notes: Amaltheans fight against their own negative thoughts. Like everyone else, they know anger, hate and fear. Unlike everyone else, they are often punished severely for such thoughts. Instead of giving vent to these emotions, they are taught to suppress them. At the same time, they are compassionate and non-judgmental of other people's failings. This duality has created a lofty martyr complex among many Amaltheans, whereby they believe that their sins are worse tenfold than those of other people, and so they must shut them out (or in) and even hide them from themselves and others. This tends to make hubris even worse for them, as they have no healthy way of confessing their guilt.

Nonetheless, those Amaltheans who have effectively wrestled with their own imperfections have become powerful forces for change in the Known Worlds. It was the unyielding hunger strike of Sister Ananda that finally convinced

Patriarch Jacob to reword his bull concerning the harsh punishment of certain sins against the nobility (a bull believed to have been paid for by the nobility).

But their own sense of deep sin causes many to fear being alone, believing that the presence of others will somehow prevent their committing deeper sins, or at least distract them from themselves. Thus, wandering Amaltheans seek out others travelers, and few people refuse the chance to add a physician to their retinue.

Character Stereotypes: Doctor, counselor, shaman, peace activist, war medic, diplomat, ambassador, iconoclast (resisting militant society), apologist (defending militant society)

Mendicant Monks (Hesychasts)

Some faithful do not involve themselves with the hierarchical orders within the Church and instead become monks, retreating as hermits to the wilderness, as cenobites to the monastery or as mendicant, wandering friars. While these monks do not answer to any direct authority, neither do they partake of the full benefits of a sect or order. They have exchanged the restrictions of ordained membership for freedom to seek the Pancreator in whatever way they will — as long as it does not smack of heresy.

Distanced as they are from the center of the Church,

they rarely have any input or effect on theological or doctrinal issues. But the occasional mystic has come from the wilderness to impress all with his insight, causing a stir and a genuine revival within the Church. But this rarely lasts more than a generation or so, as the Church hierarchy again takes precedence over subjective viewpoints. Some mystics, if popular enough, are enshrined as a saints after death, allowing the Church to claim that it is a living tradition open to new insights from the Pancreator or his chosen prophets.

Hermits usually stake out a territory in the wilderness of a distant planet, one far from Empire and Church politics. They often become the protectors of these wilds, disturbed only rarely by a local peasant seeking a cure for warts or a love philter. Monastery monks rarely leave their chosen abode, instead spending their lives in contemplation or performing scriptorial duties, copying Church documents for posterity. The recent Emperor Wars took a toll on certain monasteries, leaving some in ruins with monks left to wander in search of a new retreat.

Mendicant friars are those who have taken the word of the Prophet on the road, to deliver it to the places furthest from Holy Terra and bring salvation to the ignorant souls who dwell there. Being near penniless, as scripture requires of most monks, they must rely on the kindness of others to get where they are going. This often involves making deals with League merchants for passage in exchange for prayer services, or wheedling into a noble's entourage in exchange for confessional services (although not all monks are necessarily ordained to give confession). Friars tend to be resourceful types, and know that scripture must sometimes be placed aside toward the greater good of getting the word out to the people.

Renowned Hesychasts: Brother Hedrick the Bear (friar tending to the Kurgan border), the Hermit of the Nowhere Wastes (madman believed to be an oracle for angelic beings), Brother Aris of Maelestron Monastery (renowned mystic and philosopher whose works are becoming highly influential among young Orthodox priests)

Roleplaying Notes: Hesychasts want nothing of the squabbling going on back on Holy Terra, with all the abstract arguments over the inheritance of the Holy Flame in the soul or the proper way to sit at morning prayer. To them, it is direct experience of the Pancreator's creation — whether in raw nature or among the peasantry — which reveals best the *skopos*, or purpose, of creation. Monasteries can help weed out the useless chatter of the world and reveal the true light.

Character Stereotypes: Mad hermit, quiet monk, enlightened mystic, jolly friar, lazy ex-priest, iconoclast, detective (Sean Connery in "The Name of the Rose," or Brother Cadfael)

Sectarian Conflicts

The Church was very involved in the Emperor Wars. The patriarch tried to institute a theocracy to replace the Empire, but he received too little support. After long negotiations with the five Royal Houses, he eventually declared the Church's support for Alexius Hawkwood, giving him much needed popular approval in his bid for the seat of the Empire.

However, the political struggles the bishops and priests involved themselves in caused a backlash of disillusionment against the Church among the populace at large. People looked to new sects or orders and turned away from their traditional (sometimes many generations-long) allegiances to their previous sects. The Orthodoxy suffered a decline in membership as other sects swelled, setting the stage for a behind-the-scenes conflict throughout all levels of the Church, from the grand cathedrals to tiny shrines in backworld hamlets — the struggle to save the souls of Human Space has heated up.

But this cross-sectarian shift is caused not only by the bishops' nasty political dealings: growing apocalyptic fear has caused many to desert the past and throw their lot in with any who can promise instant salvation before the suns die out. Fear of final judgment is in the back of everyone's minds, and those who can most readily address this fear — with more fear and guilt or by compassion and understanding — benefit the most.

More information on Church theology and cosmology can be found in Chapter Five: Occult.

The Inquisition

The Inquisition is perhaps the most feared organization in the Known Worlds. Even the Emperor's mighty legions, as deadly as they are, do not stir the fears of the populace as much as a single Inquisitor knocking at the door.

The Inquisition is empowered to scour the universe for anything which might pose a danger to the souls of humanity, as decided upon by the Church. Such things include proscribed technology, demon-worship, psychic powers, pagan cults, strange alien goings-on, and people who pose a political danger to the Church.

Yet despite what peasants and sinners believe, the Inquisition is not everywhere. It takes a special meeting of the Inquisitorial Synod (council of priests) to award an Inquisitorial Seal to a priest (or group of priests), and each seal usually has a specific mission attached to it; the performance of unassociated missions does not necessarily have the backing of the Church. With Church backing, Inquisitors are nigh-immune to punishment for any action they undertake while inquisiting. Without such backing, disgruntled or insulted nobles or merchants can handle the transgressor however they see fit — within the limits of the law, of course.

A seal can be stripped from its bearer by the synod, the patriarch or the council of archbishops. If a seal was awarded by a lesser synod (a meeting of local synod members, not comprising the full council), it can be nullified by the planet's archbishop. Such lessor synods are often convened to try local affairs not important enough to summon the whole council. Calling the full synod together takes time, for the members must travel from their various worlds to the synod chambers at Holy Terra. Only grave and long-term threats suffer from full synod scrutiny.

Inquisitorial seals can be awarded to anyone the synod deems worthy, not only priests but nobles or any freeman. However, such privilege and power is rarely handed to those who have not proven themselves loyal to whatever political cause the synod pursues.

Then there are full-time Inquisitors, those who have been given broad seals with lifetime durations. These dangerous enforcers have an extreme degree of power, able to cruise the universe at will dispensing justice however they see fit. While they are officially immune from any but Church prosecution, some of the more overzealous or impolitic Inquisitors have suffered tragic but unexplained "accidents."

The Merchant League

Julia Abrams cursed up a storm and steered the starship towards the jumpgate. The radio buzzed and a voice came through:

"You have more lives than a shazzle, Abrams. I don't care how long it takes, but I'll get paybacks for all you done to me! Those lousy, fake Obun prayer bowls made me the laughing stock before the Vau! You can't understand what it's like to have a Vau sneer at you! By the Pancreator's blue ba—"

Julia cut off the transmission. She couldn't help it if the bowls weren't genuine. They were sold to her as the real deal, and her Ukari shipmate even confirmed it. She slapped her own forehead then at the stupidity of it all, and then turned on the loudspeakers throughout the ship.

"Hey, Sanjuk, you lousy Ukar!" she screamed into the voicebox. "You knew those bowls were fake!"

A voice came through from the engine room: "You trust an Ukari to identity an Obun toy? Who's the fool here? The merchant or the buyer?"

Julia fumed. She had to be more careful with her sources. Another deal gone bad would ruin her rep in the Li Halan fiefs and make her a laughing stock among her fellow Charioteers. She grimaced; she'd always been more pilot than merchant anyway, but in her guild, you often had to play both roles to get anywhere.

The Guilds

All that remains of the massive conglomerates that once ruled the Second Republic are the merchant guilds, grudgingly united in the Merchant League. Five guilds have risen to prominence, but none of them has enough authority alone to control the entire League. In fact, despite their prestige, even if they worked together (an unlikely event) they would have a hard time forcing the League to do anything if all the lesser guilds were united against them.

The five leading guilds are the Charioteers, the Engineers, the Scravers, the Muster and the Reeves. They have each established their own specialties and defend them vigorously. However, none of them hold a complete monopoly in any of their areas. All guild members understand that their success lasts as long as they can make it last and not a moment longer. Guild members constantly seek out ways to expand their reach, and if that means undermining their brothers and sisters, then so be it.

The main guilds have carved out their own hegemonies, be they in territory, product or service. On some planets a number of different guilds get along fine, each catering to their own customers and engaging in friendly rivalries. On other planets, the same guilds fight it out tooth and nail, using every weapon in their arsenal to destroy the competition.

Still, no matter how fiercely they compete with one another, they all understand that they have common enemies. Should nobles or Church leaders attempt to take advantage of the League's internal squabblings, the guilds will do their best to put up a united front. By the same token, if a League member is being unjustly threatened by outsiders, other guild members may act to protect her. Of course, if they feel they have nothing to gain and everything to lose, they will abandon her without a second thought and only slight regret.

Guild leaders, called deans, try to maintain some sort of order within the league, but trying to get this many strong-minded and competing individuals to agree on anything is a task. Each Leaguemeister, the official head of all the guilds, comes to power with a pledge to lead all the guilds in harmony, but somehow this never seems to work out.

Charioteers

The Charioteers hold the most prominent position among the guilds because they control the roads to the stars. Any citizen who wants passage on a ship must go through the Charioteers (or Travelers Guild, as they are also called). They own most of the jumproutes and maps, and woe be to those who muscle in on their territory. The Charioteers are what most common folk think of when they talk about the guilds.

Most common merchants are members of this guild or its subsidiaries. They are the most well-known traders, and their traveling "medicine shows" and bazaars are a popular

seasonal feature on many worlds. The Charioteers began as a star pilots guild. Many Second Republic citizens owned and flew their own ships and began their own trading businesses between the worlds (one of the more popular start-ups at the time); many of them sought entry into the guild. This transformed the Charioteers into a more active merchants guild.

The leadership of the guild is perhaps the most active in the Known Worlds. Even its oldest deans continue to cruise the trade routes, buying low and selling high. Most people have seen at least one of its members, dressed in clothes which could only have been designed to attract as much attention as possible, standing in a town square, making the guild's clarion call, "You want it, I got it!"

People friendly with the Charioteers can buy almost anything from them, and its guild members have access to one of the greatest information networks in existence, allowing them to sell knowledge as well as goods. However, its members are renowned for giving lip service to whatever religion will get them the most sales that day, and often attract unwanted attention from the clergy.

Some nobles seem to believe that the Charioteers support the creation of the Third Republic and are secretly building it. While no evidence has yet been uncovered, merchants of the Charioteers are often watched carefully. On the other hand, commerce between the stars would stop completely if anything happened to this guild. They own far more ships than any other single group, and while they may not have as many warships as the Hawkwoods or the Decados, their small merchant vessels are sometimes surprisingly well-armed.

Leading Charioteers: Dean Zale Gailbreath (head of guild, rumored advocate of Republican ideals), Consul Kris Chartash (renowned trader, head of one of the largest shipping organizations), Consul Lillian Staggs (well-known explorer, now runs the extremely famous passenger service called Stagg Lines — "We'll Take You Anywhere").

Roleplaying Notes: Other guilds like to jokingly refer to the Charioteers' split personalities. On the one hand, they are the most friendly, outgoing traders in the universe. They seem sure that everyone is their friend, that everything is wonderful and that the only thing that can make life better is for you to buy their merchandise. On the other hand, don't even think about crossing them on their own spaceships. These are the taciturn, no-nonsense pilots who care much more for their machines than any human.

This perception is partly the result of a growing split within the guild between its best traders and its best pilots. While in the past the Charioteers' leaders have been talented in both areas, its consuls have become more and more specialized of late. The same is becoming true of the rank and file. Dean Gailbreath has only recently begun battling

Stereotypes

The guilds got where they are today by attracting a certain type of members, but that membership has become more varied as time has passed. The roleplaying hints in each section provide a brief guide for both players and gamemasters who want to add these guild members to a game, but they should not feel forced to follow these guidelines. Create characters who do what you want them to do regardless of anyone else's preconceived notions.

this trend, and has tried to promote more members skilled in both areas.

Character Stereotypes: Pilots or vehicle operators of any type, merchants, archaeologists or artifact dealers, wandering teachers, carny attractions (traveling freak show owners or participants).

The Supreme Order of Engineers

High technology is at a premium in the Known Worlds, for those who understand it are few. Many of them are members of this guild. When a starship needs to be constructed or repaired, when a personal shield has burnt out and needs fixing, when an arm has been blown off and needs replacing, an Engineer is the only one to summon.

This is one of the least-known guilds, for it makes no effort to sell product to the peasantry. Instead it has concentrated its efforts on developing new technologies and ensuring that no one else makes the same discoveries. Its hidden labs and concealed factories have churned out extraordinary innovations in cybernetics, genetic engineering, explosives, space flight, medicine and other areas. The Engineers have in turn made the results of these breakthroughs available to the rich and powerful, for only the wealthiest can afford them. Additionally, the Engineers have gone to great lengths to ensure that their customers do not try to duplicate the technical innovations.

For this reason, there are many who refuse to deal with the Engineers — or at least that's what they say. Others note that the Engineers appear to be their own best customers, and that is extremely unnerving to many. It is rare to meet an Engineer who has not used his own body altering technology on himself, giving himself cybernetic implants, physical modifications or strange cosmetic additions. A first meeting with an Engineer is guaranteed to be at least unnerving, if not downright petrifying.

An additionally upsetting aspect of the Supreme Order of Engineers is its connection to the Church. No one, either in the Church or in the order, will deny that almost 1000

years ago the Engineers were once either a holy order or part of a holy order. Whatever happened in those ancient times remains a mystery today, but Church leaders have done little to either discipline this group or bring it back into the flock. Some guild members worry that the Engineers have maintained their ties to the Church. Some Church officials worry about the same thing and whisper that the holy order the Engineers broke away from still exists in secret.

Their worries are heightened by the fact that the Supreme Order of Engineers is also one of the most secretive guilds. Getting information from the Engineers is next to impossible, and even other League members find it difficult to communicate with them. The Engineers have structured their guild in such a way that new members know almost nothing, and discretion is a key component to advancement.

Leading Engineers: Master Malifice Hereditus (head of guild, never seen but rumored to be far more machine than human), Crafter Wavefinder Luceta (Expert with thinking machines, unnaturally beautiful), Crafter Philius Mordela (former priest, guild ambassador to Holy Terra).

Roleplaying Notes: While Engineers are renowned for their standoffishness, this in no way diminishes their value to others. Many nobles consider it a point of prestige to have an Engineer in their entourage, and even priests recognize their occasional usefulness. Still, many Engineers are more than a little inhuman and can disquiet even their best friends.

Most Engineers seem driven to advance within the guild. The two quickest routes are through service or invention. Protecting guild secrets can be as valuable to promotion as creating new innovations. Guild leaders do seem to have their own criteria, however, and most low-level members do not know exactly what will bring them favor, so they do their best at both.

Character Stereotypes: Starship engineers, inventors, scientists of all types (including mad scientists), repairmen, weaponsmiths, crafters, cyberfetishists

Scravers

Scravers hide behind a veneer of "respectability" in the form of a scavengers guild. They make their mark by recovering and refitting derelict spacecraft, patching together Second Republic artifacts everyone else deemed beyond redemption, and by finding artifacts where no one thought any could be. But this is only one part of their interstellar enterprise.

Anything the Charioteers or Engineers can't sell legitimately somehow ends up in the Scravers' hands and passes through their vast network with no questions asked. When casinos appear on a planet, they are probably owned by the Scravers'. If a brothel appears protected from both the law and the Church, it probably belongs to the Scravers. If peasants begin organizing and demanding better wages, nobles blame the Scravers. The Scravers have mastered the art of finding income everyone else has passed on.

They tend to hide behind the cover of various sub-guilds and are master spies. They have dirt on just about every major political figure imaginable, and are ready to use it if the nobles, priest, etc. try to squash them. The occasional crime clean-up effort is allowed, but no real attempt to destroy this guild is tolerated. They operate an underground network of spies and assassins for hire to the royal houses.

Most citizens really don't link the scavengers to the mob, since high-profile crime trials have cleared the scavengers guild of wrongdoing (sure, there are always stories about rigged trials, but most peasants trust the law because they're medieval innocents, not postmodern deconstructionists). The Scravers have their hands in most of the usual guild businesses, but they continue to specialize in repairing and re-selling old and (usually) abandoned equipment. Buying from a Scraver means paying a cheap price but getting what you pay for.

Scravers also have strong investments in gambling facilities, and some of their largest rehabilitated ships have become their interstellar casinos. In space they escape the scrutiny of the antigambling sects, and this also allows them to pick up high rollers from every planet. Of course, their gambling ties also mean that they are constantly accused of having ties to every organized crime figure in the Known Worlds — a charge they only half-heartedly deny.

The Scravers are made up of many small local groups paying fealty to deans, but each claiming a lot of autonomy. They must pledge their loyalty both to their local organization but also to the umbrella group. This is a blood oath; joining one branch is for life, and a hidden tattoo is required as a mark of loyalty. Thus Scravers can find welcome everywhere, albeit a suspicious one.

Leading Scravers: Dean Benita "The Fox" Ivankov (head of guild, only dean of a major guild who does not live on Leagueheim), Consul Carlos "Two-Time" Ong (head of the Leagueheim Bazaar), Consul Oliver Lords (uncovered Second Republic military depot and sold it to Hawkwoods; now League ambassador to Emperor).

Roleplaying Notes: "Anything for a Bird" could be the motto of this guild. While its members are fiercely protective of their own operations, they have no compunctions about muscling in on other people's projects. They can also find innovative ways to make money from someone else's job. If an Engineer runs a spaceship repair station, he's probably paying a Scraver for parts. If a Charioteer needs a warehouse, he's probably paying a Scraver to have his goods loaded and unloaded.

By the same token, Scravers are famous for the risks they take in search of profit. They are more than willing to put their own lives (or anyone else's) on the line. Rumor of a cache of Second Republic vases will send them scurrying

into the heart of an unexplored jungle. Tell them that the head-hunting Vorox guarding the vases like to gamble will send them there twice as fast.

Character Stereotypes: Smugglers, archeologists, gangsters, scavengers, assassins, information brokers, hit men, gamblers, extortionists (Royal Houses are dangerous but rewarding targets), pirates.

The Muster (Chainers)

While most guilds make their money off of goods and services, the Chainers make theirs off living beings. Their ships ferry mercenaries, technicians, animals, foodstuffs and, some say, slaves to their many customers. People who buy from them find themselves constantly able to acquire skilled help for almost any situation. They may also find themselves shanghaied or facing the wrath of those who miss the skilled help.

The Muster is the freeperson's labor guild, providing trained (but union-regulated) labor for freepersons to various contractors. Since skilled and trained talent is not easy to find since the Fall, if you want a job done right, you must go through the Muster. The guild was begun long ago as a soldier's rights group for mercenaries; in the centuries since the Fall, it has become the union for all laborers.

However, this does not mean they are liberal watchdogs looking out for human rights; the only rights sacred to them are those of guild members (only freepersons can apply). It is one of the hardest guilds in which to gain membership, because members (skilled labor) get good benefits and security for the rest of their lives. The Muster drives hard bargains for its skills.

For most Muster contracts, the work force is made up of "temps" hired by the guild, with the sweet, managerial positions going to Muster guildmembers. This is usually a good place for characters to find a job when all else fails. However, the Muster prefers not to pay its labor base at all, and for that reason it acquires slaves. This has given it the nickname "Chainers." Slaves rarely provide more than grunt labor, but there's a lot of that needed in the wide universe. Chainers are well-known among the peasantry for kidnapping people on small worlds and shipping them off far away where they'll never be recognized. The Church frowns on this and punishes it when discovered.

Chainers tend to wear armor and armorlike clothing, and most carry weapons wherever they go (even today, the high-ups in the guild are usually ex-mercenaries). They often travel in packs and rarely pass up an opportunity to raid for slaves. They are also thought to dabble in psychological conditioning, and to have modified their merchandise accordingly.

Leading Chainers: Dean Kryanida Halostro Sekimen (head of guild, master military strategist), Consul Erwin

Gerhardt (leader of the famous Desert Tigers armored legion and teacher of tactics at the League Academy), Consul Tereza Solace (rumored to be both psychic and head of the guild's slave operations; sometime called the cruelest person in the universe).

Roleplaying Notes: Members of the Muster are extremely proud of their skills and abilities, about the records of Muster mercenary units and artisans, and about the variety of contracts they can fulfill. They are much less willing to talk about the slaves who make much of what they do possible. They may enjoy the fear their reputation causes, but it often seems they would prefer not to have that reputation at all.

This has made the Muster extremely League conscious. Muster leaders reinforce the guilds' unity at every opportunity. No member of a guild is to be injured if it is at all avoidable. Other guilds get huge discounts on Muster services. No guild member will be enslaved. Of course, if someone takes untoward advantage of the Muster's good nature….

Character Stereotypes: Professional mercenaries, ex-soldiers looking for work, freelance jack-of-all-trades, artifact hunters, adventurers for hire, ex-slave given membership for saving owner's life, slavers (human hunters, "most dangerous game"), professional tradesman (yeomen of all types), psychologists.

The Reeves (Gray Faces)

The Reeves hold the reins of commerce and economy. They are the Known World's bankers. They also govern higher learning and education, producing lawyers and philosophers. Many non-papal courts require a Reeve to preside. In addition, the current Leaguemeister is a Reeve (as was the last one).

The Reeves also provide some of the most talented advocates for helping decide important matters. Church leaders will usually accept a Reeve to defend a heretic when they would accept no one else. Nobles caught up in disputes with one another are happy to have a Reeve hear their disagreement, but would prefer to have one on their side. Of course, in a League dispute, any guild would like to have a Reeve advocate on its side.

The Reeves do not engage in trade nearly as extensively as the other families do, but they are recognized as one of the leading guilds primarily for their incredibly extensive money-lending operations. Long ago their ancestors crafted special agreements between themselves and some of the Royal Houses to ensure that the houses would borrow from no one but them. While most of these houses have since faded to irrelevance, the Reeves have grown in prominence, often ending up with most of the houses' possessions when they fail to pay off their loans. Those allied with the Reeves do not receive much in the way of trade benefits, but they get their loans at extremely low rates. However, the Reeves are very quick to mobilize the League Fleets or other enforcers at the first sign of someone going into default.

Of course, money is not the only thing Reeves demand in exchange for their loans. They have been known to delay or even cancel required payments, but then get the debtor to do certain favors for them. These favors have ranged from simple labor to obtaining party invitations to attacking enemies to obtaining noble titles to, as the story goes, influencing the vote that made Alexius emperor.

Publicly the Reeve leaders appear to be the most conservative of the League leaders, but more than one has gotten into trouble with the various sects for acts considered extremely unorthodox. Usually the Reeves manage to get these incidents covered up, and do their best to maintain a staid and discreet appearance. Never expect a Gray Face to wear the gaudy cloaks of the Charioteers or the ominous robes of the Engineers.

By the same token, the Reeves have gone to great lengths to suppress stories that would cast doubt on their legitimacy. The one which gains the greatest credence, and which seems to drive Reeve leaders into fits of indignation, is that the earliest Reeves made their money as pirates and their first loans were in fact ransoms. No one can prove that this was the case, but neither can the Reeves disprove that ships under their protection are the least likely to be attacked by corsairs.

Leading Reeves: Leaguemeister Tyrus Spear (head of the League, renowned jurist and advocate), Dean Melissa Winters (leading banker, one of the richest people in the Known Worlds), Consul Carmichael Yoster (Admiral of the League Fleet, of questionable military ability).

Roleplaying Notes: There are many stories as to how the Reeves acquired the nickname Gray Faces, but the most common one has to do with how fervently they strive to avoid controversy. They have a reputation for composing arguments and opinions with so many exceptions that they can mean anything. Even when you hire one of the famed Reeve advocates you have no way of knowing that he will support you the next time this issue comes up.

A growing number of Reeves are fighting this old caricature, however. They have become more active in League politics and in affairs outside the guilds, seeing it as their duty to show people how to better resolve their differences. Leaguemeister Spear has not officially endorsed their activities, but younger Reeves say he supports them. Older Reeves, however, mutter about this unseemly behavior and meet behind closed doors.

Character Stereotypes: Wealthy adventurer, lawgiver (sheriff, deputy for hire), philosopher, gentry wanna-be (seeks landed title, such as baronet, laird, etc.), Third Republic architect, loan enforcer, statesman, royal chamber-

lain, seneschal, crusading advocate, ardent capitalist (hires other characters to help out with get rich quick schemes)

The Lesser Guilds

Nobody knows just how many guilds exist throughout the Known Worlds. At least two hundred are part of the League, and many more have no official sanction. Many of these only exist on one planet, and often only in one city on that planet. Still, any activity a freeman might want to engage in probably has a guild to support him.

Some of the better known of these lesser guilds cater to artists and entertainers. Musicians and troubadours have two extremely influential alliances — the Masque and the Carnivalers — allegations of psychic training not withstanding. They, and several other guilds, have forced the renowned League Academy to provide facilities for its members. Even the court jesters have a small but venerable guild, and one of its finest members is on the Academy faculty.

Lesser guilds have made their mark on the League in a number of ways. For instance, a printers guild has done much to preserve non-religious books, though it has been careful not to disseminate anything of which the Church might disapprove (Church criticism, information on technological developments or accurate histories). Not all of the printers' work is in print, however. They have also begun transcribing old documents kept in an electronic format.

Some of these guilds provide a wide variety of functions but limit their activities to a small area. For instance, the Morticus Guild of Tethys originally began as a family bakery several hundred years ago. Its members became wealthy enough (and their liege impoverished enough) that they were able to buy their freedom. Now they control a number of different trades on Tethys, including labor on new buildings, hauling goods between its two main cities, providing workers for artifact recovery and overseeing all transactions between the planet's human and native alien populations.

A few guilds limit their activities to Leagueheim itself. Since Leagueheim's population is made up primarily of freemen, most of its people have joined guilds. Thus the Courtesan Guild, Ancient Society of Sacred Alchemists and the Purloiners Guild may have branches elsewhere, but they usually deny it. They can be found on Leagueheim, however, displaying their goods and services proudly.

Independents

Not all freemen belong to a guild. Some have either lost their guild affiliation or never had one to begin with. These independent agents often work for the guilds, but sacrifice the protection and stability such an organization offers for freedom and autonomy. They cannot call on back up when they are in trouble, but they also do not have to submit to someone else's commands. This arrangement is far from the norm in the Fading Suns, for almost everyone is beholden to someone else. Independent agents are the only people without a liege of some kind (though even they must profess allegiance to the emperor).

While the guilds provide these independent agents with most of their work, they are not the only customers who take advantage of these unique arrangements. Nobles will seek them out, especially when they do not want the guilds to become aware of certain tasks or if they want to be able to deny any involvement. The Church supports the feudal order even more fiercely than the nobles do, but it uses free agents in its fight against heresy. After all, better that someone living on the outskirts of society risk her soul than someone at its heart.

A player interested in taking on the role of an independent agent should determine not only what skills his character has developed, but why he has become an independent agent. If one of the guilds kicked him out, then does he maintain any ties to the League? If a noble recently made him a freeman, then why, and what obligations does he still have to that noble? If the character ran away from his previous obligations, be they to a noble or to the Church, then does his previous master still pursue him?

An independent agent takes a great deal of risk in making his way through the Known Worlds. These characters are best suited for life on the outskirts of civilization, perhaps near the barbarian worlds or on newly rediscovered planets. The closer an independent gets to the heart of civilization, the more pressures he will feel to commit to a master.

Guild Territoriality

While most people know better than to trust a trader, few understand just how deep the League's involvement throughout the Empire goes. Most people only see guildmembers visiting a planet, setting up a small shop and selling their wares. The guilds actively try to maintain this view of their operations, concealing their massive installations and armies of mercenaries. Those in the know believe the Merchant League has committed itself to bringing about a new republic. Others point to guild involvement in sabotaging technical research and restricting planetary production as signs of a more sinister goal.

Most of the guilds have a monopoly on at least one resource or device. They guard these areas zealously, going to extremes to ensure their continued mastery. For instance, the Engineers have long been the sole provider of Lypee-55, a key ingredient in longevity serums. Rumor has it that at one point House Li Halan began synthesizing the liquid in their labs on Manitou. The Engineers uncovered what the house was up to and offered the Li Halan a huge sum of money for it to stop. When the Li Halan made it clear that they would do no such thing, the Engineers offered them a

Guild Safe Houses

The Merchant League has no illusions about its popularity in the Known Worlds. Nobles tax almost everything it does, peasants look for every opportunity to steal from its shops and the Church condemns its very existence. So the League makes friends the only way it knows how — it buys them.

Almost every planet has at least one non-League person who, at guild expense, will take care of League members or goods. Most planets have one in every major city. This person usually keeps his ties to the League secret, but provides essential services. He will store guild merchandise, hide people on the run, arrange clandestine meetings, and help guild members in trouble.

Sometimes one guild pays his expenses and other times a number contribute to the pot, but either way, that person will usually do what the League needs done. The trouble comes in finding this person. No registry of these agents exists. If the Charioteers have paid for someone on Cadavus to look after their interests, then they are unlikely to tell other guilds about it.

A problem the League often faces with these agents is that they often believe that the League will sanction their activities, no matter what they might be. At least one of these safe houses turned out to be home to a coven of warlocks, and the League has since tried to be more careful about who it pays off. Of course, there is no way for the League to ever be completely confident.

Philosophers Stone. When that didn't work, a number of Manitou's power plants malfunctioned and exploded. Only one was nuclear, but it took out the main laboratory complex — and the neighboring city of 100,000 people. The Li Halan have made no further study of Lypee-55.

Additionally, individual guilds often battle each other, both militarily and financially. Alliances within the League seem to shift with the solar winds, and today's ally becomes tomorrow's stepping stone. While most of the guilds have staked out the area they claim as their own, providing a variety of goods and services within that region, the boundaries are rarely fixed. It is not uncommon for a Royal House to "request" that a guild set up shop in territory previously controlled by another guild. This creates competition within that territory, driving down prices and stimulating the local economy. It can also have the unintended effect of creating violent competition, wrecking the local economy and killing scores of innocent bystanders.

The guilds usually hire outside agents to handle these matters, preferring to keep their most loyal forces engaged against non-merchant opponents. Freelancers can earn a

great deal raiding enemy guild warehouses, stealing their secrets and assassinating key people. These same freelancers are often the first ones sacrificed when the guilds make up or need to cover their tracks.

Academy Interatta

Despite the incessant battles between the guilds, when they have worked together they have accomplished some incredible feats. One of these is the mighty League Starfleet. Another, and perhaps more important, achievement is the Academy Interatta, the only major educational facility not under the Church's control. Located on Leagueheim, the Academy is the one place where guildmembers can meet peacefully, getting to know each other before learning how to stab one another in the back.

While this is the view most people have of the Academy Interatta, others tell a darker story. No research is forbidden at the Academy, they say, and its teachers and students have delved into the darkest areas of knowledge. Of course, the guild dismisses such stories as Church propaganda, but the legends persist. Tales of researchers whose hair turned white overnight, professors who went mad after viewing vile videotexts in its famous library and students sacrificed to dark gods abound.

Other people say that these reports grew out of the constant politics that go on between and within the Academy's many departments. Professors and department heads have accused each other of everything from body odor to plagiarism to pederasty to murder to genocide. Sometimes the accusations are true; usually they are just additional weapons in the battle for Academy funding and prestige.

While the politicking within the Academy is usually related to the different departments and not the different guilds, individual guilds certainly make their presence felt. The Muster has ensured that the Academy fund a military affairs department with ties to the League Starfleet. The Engineers influence much of the technical research carried out at the Academy. Even the Courtesans Guild had amazingly little difficulty in adding one of its members to the faculty.

The Academy itself is a sprawling entity, with classes and research taking place all over Leagueheim and even at a few locations off planet. Students and guilds pay the professors directly, and the professors pool much of their income in order to maintain and upgrade the facilities. Much of the Academy's best features have been donated directly by one guild or another.

Indeed, the entire League backs the Academy Interatta to an extreme degree. Many League leaders spent at least some time as students at the Academy, and most of these have fond memories of their time there. They also recognize its need as a central storehouse for knowledge. One of the Academy's strongest departments, as well as the one which appears most free of guild meddling, is the Reclamation Department. This agency is dedicated to finding and recovering lost wisdom, and it receives incredible amounts of funding for this purpose. While it usually pays for lost data, it has been known to send heavily armed mercenary teams to recover ancient records and old spaceship logs. Since these operations tend to upset priests and nobles wherever the mercenaries go, the Reclamation Department only resorts to such efforts when it feels the need is greatest — or when it can get away with it.

Piracy

None of the powers in the Fading Suns officially condones piracy, but it continues nonetheless. Nobles blame the guilds, the guilds blame the nobles and everyone casts a worried eye at some of the more fervent sects. No one can deny that the problem grew during the Emperor Wars and continues at high levels. The Emperor has said he will bring it under control but has committed most of his resources to his new efforts against the barbarians. What little he has sent against the pirates has not met with much success.

The League would seem to have the most to lose from the pirates, but has done little more than the Emperor. Aside from some highly publicized attacks on freelance pirates, the guilds seem to prefer paying ransoms to mounting pirate-hunting expeditions. This does nothing to quell tales of

guild-financed pirates or ambushes carried out by one guild on an enemy within the League.

Of course, everybody tries to pass the blame off on barbarians and aliens. In fact, both barbarians and aliens have been captured raiding merchant vessels. Some of the most extreme alien-independence organizations have even attempted to license privateers or raid shipping on their own. These have raised an immediate hue and cry from the nobles and guilds, who combined forces to drive these pirates from the stars.

Contrary to popular belief, the pirates' general strategy is not to attack a merchant ship with blaster cannons blazing. This creates far too much risk of losing valuable cargo. Pirates infinitely prefer fast ships to heavily armed ones, and they close with their targets as quickly as possible, broadcasting threats of what they will do to anyone who resists them.

Most ships have only minimal crews anyway, most of whom have little to lose if pirates take the ship. Pirates rarely kill ship crews, only punishing them if they resist. Most crew members prefer to surrender at once or after putting up only a token resistance. The pirates board at will, take the cargo (and the ship if they have enough men) and set the crew adrift in lifecraft.

There are exceptions to this rule. Mad Carnegie Jones gained a reputation for torturing and killing the crews of the

ships he captured, jettisoning their bodies off into space. His career ended shortly before the Emperor Wars when a merchant ship resisted and ended up ramming his craft. The attack destroyed both ships, and Jones was left to die in space.

Searching out space pirates is especially difficult. Since merchants tend to fly certain predetermined routes designed to make space travel as fast and inexpensive as possible, pirates have little problem ambushing a suitable target. Additionally, pirates who operate in certain areas seem to have excellent contacts in the nearby space ports. These can tell them about tempting targets as well as possible threats. Pirate hunters rarely have these luxuries. They have to try to discover where pirates make their bases, disguise themselves and sail the trade routes, or capture space port informants. Then they have to defeat the pirates in battle.

Aliens

Onganggorak smiled, a gentle gesture but one which appeared vicious and gruesome to the poor serf who had stumbled upon the giant Vorox by the woodland stream.

"Aaah! No eat! No eat!" the serf cried, dropping his walking staff and holding his palms out to show he was unarmed. He knew better than to try an outrun a Vorox.

Ong's brow wrinkled in consternation and he shook his head, disappointed in the human. "I have no intention of eating you. I'm simply gathering water for my Lady Erian Li Halan and her entourage."

The serf looked puzzled. "So you're tame, then?"

Ong's eyes rolled and a grunt escaped his throat. "Tame?! Is that what you call it when a Vorox acts civilized?!"

The serf took a step back, but realized that the Vorox had no intention of harming him. "But... most Vorox are... feral. Aren't they?"

The Vorox nodded his head as he stood, his height truly startling the peasant again. "There are those on Ungavorox who have yet to learn the benefits of civilization. I am not one of them. Now, good day to you, human."

"Wait!" the serf cried. Ong stopped and looked expectantly at the man. "Uh... is that one that's been killin' babies in the next village feral, then?"

Ong simply sighed and walked away. It was a worn-out routine to blame Vorox for every disaster to strike from the wilds. Surely some local predator had claimed the small prey instead.

The serf persisted, following behind. "You know, the one they say calls himself Adanga Unga?"

Ong spun around and stared at the peasant, as if his stare could root out a lie. Adanga Unga here? On Grail? How did that villain get so far from Ungavorox? Ong snarled; he would have to investigate now. He couldn't let his old

rival run free to ruin the Known Worlds, Ong's adopted home...

Known Worlds Races

There are a number of sentient races living in the Known Worlds. Almost all of them have suffered some indignity at the hands of humans. For most, it was the claiming of their homeworld by human colonists, and the resulting terraforming which utterly changed their ancestral home. Many of these races became homeless refugees, herded onto reservations a mere fraction of the size of their previous homes — or worse, onto different worlds entirely. For others, it was the wars which decimated their populations, leaving the survivors to eke out a living from human charity, carefully watched for any sign of rebellion. Most of these poor souls yearn to escape Human Space, even if it means leaving their natural environments behind, and aliens are in the forefront of new space exploration.

Not all are unhappy, however. There are more than a few cases in which aliens have benefited from human intervention. The Etyri of Grail were in danger of dying out due to the predation of vicious beasts before they could develop sufficient tech to save themselves from their hunters. But humans arrived, recognized the Etyri's sentience, and built safe reservations for them, also providing weapons which more than evened the odds against their predators. (The fact that their predators might also have been sentient did nothing to stop humans from aiding their extinction.)

Three other major races claim some political, economic or military power, and are granted certain concessions from the Empire, giving them more rights and freedoms on their homeworlds than most aliens enjoy. While they have all been under human rule since the Diaspora (Second Republic at the latest), they accept this for the most part, although there are those individuals who chaff under such "bondage." These three races are detailed below.

The Children of the Ur

The Ur races (also known as the Anunnaki) are the oldest known races. They disappeared before humans reached the stars, leaving behind many powerful artifacts, including the jumpgates which make star travel possible. Their purpose is a mystery, as is the nature of their legacy: What happened to them? Did they intentionally leave the jumpgates for the younger races to use? Too many questions remain unanswered.

The Ur are known to have interfered with certain races before these races achieved solar system or star travel, and many believe that they directly helped the Vau to reach the stars. Humans argue about their secret influence in ancient human affairs, although there is no definitive proof of this. Their influence in the Known Worlds can most clearly be seen in the cousin races, the Obun and the Ukar. These young

races are called the Children of the Ur, or more simply, the Ur-Obun and the Ur-Ukar.

While these Ur Children know very little of the Anunnaki, their myths and legends tell of godlike beings who shaped their cultures, weaving the fates of Obun and Ukar alike for good or ill in a sort of cosmic chess match. One pantheon of gods is believed to have won out over their rivals, with the result that the rivals' pawns were removed from their homeworld and placed in a vicious, adversarial environment to rebuild their tattered and displaced culture: the Ukar. The Obun, pawns of the victorious gods, enjoyed a golden age of peace, learning and spiritual study.

Then, the gods withdrew from the lives of mortals, leaving the Obun and the Ukar to develop on their own. That was many millennia ago, and the two races have traveled down radically different paths since. During this time, the Obun fell back into barbarism, but regained their civilization through a renewal in spiritual doctrines and discipline. The Ukari have had a warlike and aggressive culture ever since the gods betrayed them.

Regardless of the vast amount of time which passed during their separation, the Obun and Ukar language has remained similar enough that fluent speakers of one tongue can sometimes understand the other. The appearance and design of their tech shows obvious Ur influence, but is rarely more advanced than current Known Worlds standards.

Ur-Obun

The Obun had not explored beyond their solar system before the Second Republic arrived to usher them into the commonwealth of Known Space. They were treated better than most alien races due to their obvious link to the Ur, but they were no longer the masters of their own destiny.

One of the first Obun to explore the stars was Ven Lohji, who became one of the Prophet's eight disciples, and returned to Obun after the Prophet's death to preach her message, creating what would become the Obun sect of the Universal Church (Voavenlohji in the Obun language). However, an unfortunate incident during the Dark Ages involving an Ur-Obun priest and a Church bishop resulted in a religious war which wiped out a large part of the Ur-Obun population. Most of them still live on their homeworld of Velisimil, under the watchful auspice of House Hawkwood.

Obun have few strictly defined family units. They honor their mother and father, but the task of raising a child is taken up by every Obun. An uncle or aunt will often take charge of a child's schooling, but all Obun have a responsibility to the child. When an Obun goes bad (becomes a criminal or murderer), those Obun involved in his upbringing blame themselves and usually retreat from their worldly duties for spiritual contemplation or pilgrimage, pondering what they did wrong.

The Obun have a government composed of an elected Ruling Council called the Umo'rin. Candidates must volunteer for public duty, and must pass the "Ordeal": a rigorous test of the applicant's physical, mental and spiritual capabilities. Once the candidate has passed this test (most do not), his or her seat on the council is rarely contested. They are one of the very few races in the Known Worlds who do not have a noble, although there are levels of rank in the Ruling Council which are somewhat equivalent.

Appearance: Most Obun are brown-skinned, as if deeply tanned, although racial divisions exist: bronze, red and yellow-skinned Obun are known. Their hair is usually black and their eyes are black and pupilless. They tend to be thinner than the average human, but they are generally more nimble.

Leading Ur-Obun: Soleel HanSeer (head of the Ruling Council), Bishop Forsti HanKavak (head of the Obun Church), Bran Botan vo Karm (Emperor Alexius' left-hand counsel).

Roleplaying notes: The Ur-Obun are sought out as third party diplomats and peacemakers, but they can be vicious if they turn their minds to it. Their culture values learning and philosophy over all other pursuits, and Obun have a knack at answering questions which have long plagued others. While their culture differs from that of humans in the Known Worlds, they have lived among humans long enough to mix well (picking up as many bad influences as good, some Obun say). An Obun can expect a respectful (if somewhat cold) reaction from most humans he meets.

Most Ur-Obun are born with advanced occult abilities (either Psi or Theurgy), and have a well-developed, moral belief structure to support their powers. For this reason, they are often more trusted as psychics than are human psychics.

Character Stereotypes: Diplomat, mystic, priest, pilgrim, curious merchant, archaeologist, angry iconoclast (looked upon as deranged by Obun society)

Ur-Ukar

The Ur-Ukar obviously did not belong on the planet from which they began their star-faring. The surface of Kordeth is hostile to life and the Ukari are forced to live beneath the surface in a network of tunnels circling the globe. Their legends speak of a great wrong done by one of their kind in "heaven," and they were banished by the gods to this hell in retribution.

The Ukar achieved space travel before their cousins, the Obun, but were blocked by the Second Republic after colonizing only three other systems. A blockade war against the Ukari homeworld lasted for decades, with the Ukari finally suing for peace and accepting reservations on their claimed worlds while the Republic took over the governance of these planets.

Traditional natives of the Ukari homeworld live the first five years of their lives in near or total darkness. At age six,

they are "brought to the light," or slowly acclimated to light and surface living. Due to their lightless beginnings, touch is more important to them than sight, although their sight has never become atrophied. They carve their bodies with raised tattoos or carvings (called *baa'mon*) spelling out their names (on their faces) and their deeds (on their chests, arms and legs). Ukarish as a written language is a sort of short-form Braille, meant to be "read" off someone's skin (although the language has been adopted for books).

Ukar from reservations on other worlds have similar traditions, but they often live in light since birth and usually do not read Ukar tattoos as easily. There is often a low-level but mutual disdain between homeworlders and "rez" Ukari.

They come from strong family clans and wage feuds against rival clans. These feuds began when the early Ukari fought over limited resources, but resentment has been handed down generationally even in times of abundant resources. Certain clans hold leadership positions over other clans because they were able to convince human noble houses to recognize them over other clans, although they do not seem well-liked by the "lesser" clans.

Appearance: Ukari resemble the Obun in overall physical characteristics, except that they are extremely pale, usually with white or light blond hair. Their eyes are always black and pupilless.

Leading Ur-Ukar: Torquil oj Borduk (chief of ruling clan, recognized by the empire as leader of the Ur-Ukar), Baal oj Ak (infamous psychic terrorist), Domina "Many-Scars" Corduvan (leader of FAR)

Roleplaying notes: The Ur-Ukar are a violent but crafty race, more worldly than their spiritual cousins. They are often secretly sought out by houses or guilds to provide certain "services" that their subterranean origins allow them to perform well: thievery and assassination.

Their sense of hearing and touch are better than a human's, and they find it easy to move quickly and fight in enclosed spaces. The harsh necessities their race faced early on caused them to develop a better sense of technology than their cousins or even most humans.

Like the Obun, they are born with advanced occult abilities (always Psi), but have little morality guiding its use. Lacking societal guidance, most suffer from an overactive Urge.

Character Stereotypes: Thief, assassin, repair technician (the grimiest work in the tightest spaces), terrorist, bitter diplomat, optimistic leader (fighting against ingrained resentment and tribalism)

Vorox

Multi-limbed monstrosities. The ultimate predators on their homeworld, the Vorox should never have achieved sentience. All the known rules about natural selection deny it.

But they did, and with seemingly no coaxing from without. Certainly, it is a crude and unsophisticated sentience, but this may simply be due to the limitations of their crude culture. Critics debate: Are Vorox the equal of human intelligence? Evidence suggests not, but those few who have escaped the bonds of their violent culture have proven otherwise.

They have colored fur and are immune to many poisons (a by-product of their very toxic, nasty evolutionary environment) and they can't eat vegetables. They can walk on two legs (leaving four arms free), four legs (leaving two free), or six legs for the best speed.

There are two types of Vorox: feral and civilized. Feral Vorox are not unintelligent; they simply do not have the benefits of a technological society. They are not allowed off-planet, for they are considered brutal and dangerous. Civilized Vorox are those who have had their claws cut, and are thus "tamed." This cutting usually takes place at puberty and the Vorox is then educated in what culture and learning exists in their crude society. Civilized Vorox are allowed off-world and perform a variety of functions for Known World governments. The de-clawing ceremony began as a ritual imposed on Vorox culture by humans, but eventually became a source of pride for the civilized Vorox, a sign that they had evolved past their brutal cousins of the jungle. They have an odd religion (although no theurgy) which guarantees a soul only to those Vorox who have accepted civilization — the rest are believed to be feral animals trapped in a cycle of meaningless eating and being eaten.

The royal caste of Vorox are allowed to keep one claw, which secretes a poison deadly to humans and Vorox. This potent symbol of their rule has often gotten them in trouble off-world.

Appearance: Large, fur-bearing mammals with six limbs, four of which can double for arms or legs (each hand has opposable thumbs). Their growl is loud and grating, ending with a note not audible to humans but jarring nonetheless.

Leading Vorox: Kummanga (king of ruling caste), Urgumantangu (shaman of Vorox church), Arng-arng-arng (warrioress famed for Symbiot kills)

Roleplaying notes: Vorox are like hyperactive teenagers in puberty — they are passionate, quick to anger or play, rowdy and wide-eyed. Most Vorox find this whole culture thing, with its rules and regulations, to be a burden, but some find it a challenge.

They seem to have an instinctual respect for power and an urge for clannishness (feral Vorox hunt in packs — called *angerak* — for their planet's other predator are more than a match for a single Vorox), which helps to uphold their ruling families and leaves them somewhat in awe of upper-class Known Worlders. They seem to crave respect and want desperately to be considered members in good standing of whatever group they join. Many a Church patriarch has upheld Vorox as pillars of loyalty, one of the Prophet's primary virtues. Indeed, Vorox are fiercely loyal to their friends, family or group (guild, house, sect, etc.). But there are no set guidelines for resolving conflicts between allegiances, and many Vorox have gone mad trying to decide which takes precedence when these groups are at odds. Passionate tragedies have been written about noble Vorox raised to civilization against harsh odds brought low when forced to choose between royal family and chosen friends, or friends and sect loyalties.

Vorox are highly sought by humans as shock troops or guerrilla warriors. They were gleefully dropped on Stigmata during the Symbiot War, but when converted Vorox returned with Symbiot abilities, they wreaked more havoc than could be imagined. They aren't allowed near Symbiots anymore.

Character Stereotypes: Warrior, bodyguard, gladiator, jungle guide, explorer, League stevedore, fanatic priest, incognito feral, cultured orator (trying to break down anti-Vorox stereotypes), famed athlete, traveling companion

Other Races

There are numerous other sentient races in the Known Worlds. Almost every planet with a jumpgate seems to host an intelligent race in varying degrees of advancement, although only the Children of the Ur (and perhaps the Oro'ym) had achieved space travel by the time humans encountered them. Some of these races were dislocated from their homeworlds by landgrabbing humans, but most still have a reservation or two on their planet of genesis. Below are some of the more well-known aliens, even though they are rarely met away from their homelands. (Details on these races can be found in the **Fading Suns Players Companion** sourcebook.)

Gannok: These squat, monkeylike beings are from Bannockburn, near the Symbiot frontier. Bannockburn hosts some of the strangest Ur ruins known; the Gannok lived among these ancient monoliths, building odd devices from the leftover technology. Scholars believe the Gannok are somewhat new to sentience, since little evidence of previous cultures exist on their world. They have little native tech of their own, but they are clever tool-users, with an amazing inclination for invention. For this reason, they are prized as starship engineers, as their physiques (including short, prehensile tails) allow them to crawl into cramped spaces. The outer layer of skin on their arms, legs and back exudes an oily substance similar to tissue regenerative serum, giving them remarkable immune systems and healing faculties. However, they also have a prankster's way about them, but little common sense.

Shantor: An ungulate race from Shaprut. The passion-

ate Shantor were victims of humanity's First Contact; they now live on reservations scattered across the Known Worlds and are few in number. They have a warrior culture that highly values family ties and worships a solar deity, although they believe this deity resides in their homeworld's sun. They cannot speak Urthish, and their spokesmen wear specially made voiceboxes (called *dolomei*) which allow them to simulate human vocal cords.

Ascorbites: Bloodsuckers from Severus. The carapaced but humanoid Ascorbites had little time to develop a civilization of their own before humans arrived and relegated them to the status of primitives and savages. They have since lived up to these designations, refusing to live in cities and running wild in the jungles of Severus. Some claim, however, that they have villages deep in the wilderness, and have developed strange psychic powers, plotting to use these against humans.

Hironem: The reptilian Hironem are from Cadiz, although a reservation is all they have left of the continent they once ruled. Scholars believe that the Hironem were within a century of space-travel when they were encountered by Diaspora colonists, as they had already sent manned ships to investigate their moon. Little of their native tech is left, however, as human tech quickly became the norm on colonized Cadiz. Their reservation is built around their former capital city, where sits the throne of their God-King. Some believe that their culture was influenced early on by the Vau, as they have a similar caste-system. Many study Hironem culture hoping to get some insight into the Vau.

Etyri: An avian race from Grail. The flying Etyri survived fierce competition against their land-based predators only with the aid of human technology. One of the least populous sentient races, the Etyri are highly religious, deeply concerned about the afterlife and what form it takes. Few Etyri leave their homeworld, and those who do are often considered insane by their brethren. But they are sometimes deemed heroes, questing for the secrets waiting beyond death to pave the way for Etyri to come.

Oro'ym: An amphibian race from Madoc, the Oro'ym were simply a myth for most of the Dark Ages before they revealed their hidden, underwater colonies to humankind.

The seabed of their homeworld contains numerous ruins pointing to a once-glorious past millennia ago, and their legends imply that Oro'ym once traveled the stars serving the Anunnaki. They are mere primitive now, however, happy for what human tech they can barter for. Primitive does not mean stupid — they are crafty and highly intelligent, and their underwater abilities make them highly prized sailors or artifact hunters.

Xenophobia

For most people living on the worlds of the **Fading Suns**, anyone different is immediately suspect. This includes those who manifest psionics, cybernetics, magic, genetic alterations, odd languages, odd knowledges, or is a member of an alien race. People stare at them in the streets, avoid them, refuse to deal with them, report them to authorities or even attack them.

Most people, be they peasants, artisans, serfs, nobility, clergy or merchants, live in the same place their entire lives. Traveling to another city, much less another planet, is a significant event. Those who stand out, or who travel regularly, tend to stand apart from the rest of the population and, at the same time, gravitate to one another.

Alien races are treated with suspicion and even outright fear by the peasants of the Known Worlds. Aliens receive a more enlightened reception among freemen and the educated class, but there is suspicion even there, for fear or guilt over human treatment of aliens and the simmering bitterness displayed by these second-class citizens often leads to a separatist mentality.

Most aliens have suffered under humanity's rule. Some suffer in silence, but others take every opportunity they can to reclaim their lost heritage or take some measure of revenge against the race that so dominates their lives. There are a number of aboveground alien rights groups, and even more alien independence and supremacy organizations. By the same token, there are a number of secretive human groups which seem intent on suppressing or even destroying non-human races as well as those derived from humans.

The best-known alien organization is the Frontier for Alien Rights (FAR), which works with several guilds to make aliens the legal, political and economic equals of humans. FAR's opponents waver between calling it a pawn of the League and an organization dedicated to destroying humanity, but most people see it as a well-meaning but impotent group. Those in the know point to its constant success in rescuing and relocating refugees as proof that it either has strong allies or more power than it admits.

The Sargonites used to be a powerful organization dedicated to driving indigenous races off planets where humans wanted to live, but was believed destroyed during the Second Republic. Recent assassinations and harassment of lead-

Racism

Fading Suns does not condone racism. The appearance of racist or bigoted characters or policies by human or alien governments is meant to reflect and address issues of bigotry which take place in the real world. It is a method of introducing dramatic issues into the passion play of the game universe, to be used or discarded in stories as the gamemaster and players see fit.

ing alien activists by people claiming to be Sargonites has led to concerns that this cult might have reappeared — or might never have been destroyed at all. It has been most active in areas under Hazat control, but word of its activities has begun to come from across the Known Worlds.

Alliances

For aliens traveling off their homeworlds, it is a practical necessity to join or ally with a powerful group. In the fractured world of the **Fading Suns**, the person who stands alone often suffers for it, either from the machinations of rivals and their allies or because he has no one to stand beside him against the angry mob.

Members of noble houses often seek out aliens to join their entourage, either hoping to add some exotica to their stable or out of a genuine desire for a new perspective. The League needs aliens for much the same reasons, although increased profit is also a motive: aliens have a higher success rate selling goods to their own kind than do human merchants. In addition, an alien bonded to the League seems safer to the yokels coming out for a Charioteer medicine show, although most aliens have no desire to be paraded around as freaks from foreign lands. Most Church sects see the admittance of aliens as a victory for the Church, a proof of its universal nature, and are eager to ordain them. However, most human peasants don't want an alien preaching at them, which leaves alien priests to either preach to their own, join a monastery or seek their calling among the stars.

Even for those who are members of a power group, it always helps to have friends to guard one's back. Tight-knit gangs or bands of chosen friends are common in the Known Worlds and aliens far from home need them more than most. Few do not benefit from an alien bandmate: Vorox are renowned for their loyalty no matter how badly they are treated (although trust is another matter entirely); Ur-Obun are well-respected for their wisdom and always seem to have some insight unavailable from other sources; and Ur-Ukar have bad temperaments and are hard to win over, but once won, they value friendships highly, especially because they are so hard to achieve in this conflictive world.

When traveling the worlds of the **Fading Suns**, only a fool goes alone.

Beyond the Borders

There are two major alien races outside of Human Space: the Vau and the Symbiots. The Vau are the oldest and most advanced race yet encountered (the Ur are older, but a living Ur has never been met, and nobody even knows what they looked like). The Symbiots are the newest star-faring race, born from a melding of human and Xolotl (a parasitic entity), although they have "converted" other races since their genesis and seem intent on claiming many worlds within humanspace.

The Vau

(pronounced Vow, heavily nasal at the end)

The Vau are an ancient race who first achieved star travel in the 1800s (human time). Very little is known about their ways, and they purposefully keep it that way. The Vau actively guard their borders against human intrusion, but they rarely enter Human Space themselves. They seem to view Known Worlders as unwelcome children, although they are rarely overtly hostile to them. The philosophy seems to be, "As long as they stay on their side of the fence, we'll get along fine."

They have a caste society, with a peasant class on the bottom, a soldier class above, an artisan class above that, and a mandarin class (including priests) at the top. Little detail of the intricacies of Vau culture is understood, for few humans have been firsthand witness to it. The mandarins are not the leaders, but they are the only diplomats humans are allowed to meet. They seem to be bureaucrats for the most part, ferrying messages back and forth from the true Vau leaders, who have yet to be encountered.

There are three worlds along the borders of Known Space where Vau maintain some form of presence, although humans are rarely allowed to see too deeply into their activities there. The fact that the Vau eventually allowed humans to colonize these worlds caused many to believe that the Vau were finally beginning to accept humans, but more cynical people (the colonists among them) claim that colonies were only allowed because the Vau want to scrutinize humans for weaknesses.

Appearance: The Vau are tall (averaging seven feet in height) and thin. Their skin is somewhat wrinkled, and they have nostrils in place of protruding noses. Their eyes are pupilless, although they vary in color, unlike those of the Children of the Ur. They dress in different fashions depending on their caste status: Soldiers invariably wear segmented and lacquered armor with an energy pike while mandarins wear long and ornate robes with elegant shoulder and headpieces.

Tech: Vautech is elegant and aesthetic, with graceful curving lines and seductive sigils. Most devices involve energy of some sort, even simple tools. Their technology was superior to humanity's during the Diaspora, but the Second Republic exceeded it in some areas. However, since the fall of the Republic, the Vau are again in the lead. They do not have a progressive society, and their technology has changed little since before the Second Republic. The basis of their tech, like their religion, medicine and culture, is energy. They are masters of forces. Energy shields were created from stolen Vautech; if you want a first-class shield, a Vau engineer is where you go to get it. However, since the Vau are forbidden to trade technology to humans, this is a secretive black market.

Symbiots

Shapeshifters. Parasites. Godless beasts who turn friends into foes. These are some of the various facts and/or beliefs humans have about Symbiots, but little is really understood about this new race and great threat to human hegemony over the Known Worlds.

The Symbiots claim to perceive a "lifeweb" stretching across space, knitting and weaving deeply into planets and across the stars. They are apparently out to claim supreme hunting rights over their food chain, or are protecting it from harm. Each Symbiot is a unique creature, and finds it hard to confederate with fellow Symbiots. Nonetheless, tribes or clans have developed among them, but nothing is known by humans about these family groups. They breed among themselves, creating bloodlines by selecting strong genetic traits, but also by parasitically "converting" other races (human, Ur-Obun or Ukar, Vorox). They claim the conversion is voluntary once the target has seen the Lifeweb, but Known Worlders don't believe this claim for a moment — they've seen firsthand what happens when friends and family have been converted: they turn into bestial killing machines or seductive parasites.

Symbiots have a "motherform," the base shape that they are most in tune with, and this is usually tied to a particular species of flora or fauna, such as an oak or a bear. They are molecularly amorphous (shapeshifters) and claim to have a special, mystical relationship with the universe. Some claim that they have awakened their cellular consciousness and exist in more than one dimension.

The Xolotl, the race which co-created the Symbiots, are believed to be extinct; those encountered on Chernobog are thought to have been the remnants of a previously extant star-faring race, or the "pets" of an extinct star-faring race who seeded them throughout many worlds (fossil remnants have been discovered). No Xolotl has been encountered since the initial Symbiot conversion, although the Imperial Eye is said to be desperate to find one that they can study, hoping to glean a weakness with which to attack the Symbiots.

Appearance: A Symbiot's motherform is an organic blend of human/animal or human/plant, with a definite emphasis on the human side. A human Symbiot can pass among other humans as long as no one gets a real good look at him, but he will often be revealed if seen naked in full light. Some feature always betrays his true race, be it fur, carapace, fangs, claws, cat-eyes, leaves and branches, horns, tail, etc. But they are shapeshifters, and can take on different shapes as needed. Alien Symbiots, such as Ur-Obun or Vorox, look like representatives of their race with animal or plant feature exceptions.

Tech: Symbiot technology is organic and alive: living guns and bullets, swords and Krinth-flesh armor, acid-spit-ting Shexeez snakes, etc.. They grow this nonsentient equipment from plants or raise them as animals. Each tribe has its own methods and special organic technology. Even their spaceships are organic (though few people have seen their weird, insectlike hulks).

Myths and Legends

In an atmosphere of superstition, many myths and legends have arisen. The interpretation of strange and alien phenomena by authority figures is often considered more important than the phenomena itself. Fact is rarely separated from opinion, for the perceptions of the qualified observer (i.e., an Inquisitor) are considered part of the truth. The question becomes not whose facts are right or wrong, but whose are more valuable, worthwhile or "safe." The Church is the near-universally acknowledged leader in this arena. Non-Church approved interpretation of phenomena can be dangerous, and those spreading it may find themselves sought by the Inquisition.

Below are some of the more prevalent mythologies of the people who populate the Known Worlds.

The Fading Suns

It is a true and universally acknowledged fact that the suns are fading. Even the Vau recognize this. But why? There are as many answers as there are opinions. The Church is undecided, and many sects battle over interpretation. In general, however, a consensus emerges: The suns are dying because history is over. The passion play is coming to an end. Man's time in the universe is nearly done, and what he has done with it will be tallied at the end and judged for good or ill. Many fear it will add up to more ill than good. Thus, humanity must unite to save itself, to show a united front of penance — hence, the importance of the Universal Church.

But different voices whisper other meanings when the Inquisition's collective back is turned. Some say the Vau or Symbiots are causing the suns to fade, and that their secrets should be wrested from them. Others dare to say it is the jumpgates that are at fault, that with every jump a star loses its vital energy and begins to die.

The Reborn Sun

A heresy is at work among the people, spread by a mysterious and mystical sect. It dares to bring hope to the people — but a hope, says the Church, clothed in dreams of Imperium and totalitarian rule. For this heresy says that, upon the day of the Emperor's coronation, a distant star was reborn. A sign of renewal amid the dying of suns, this star has become a symbol of rebellion for many disgruntled people.

Fierce arguments can be heard across the Known Worlds: This supposed star is small and insignificant. Some say it

did not exist before, and that its birth was only happenstance. Others, using ancient lore to back them up, claim that the star's distance belies any direct involvement, for its birth/rebirth would have happened many years ago, its light only now reaching the Known Worlds. Others, also claiming ancient lore, say that all things are interconnected in non-linear time, and that events today could influence events of yesterday. Star maps are consulted proving the star did not exist before, while other maps clearly show it did. Some maps show that the star has always been as bright as it is now, while some records note its dimming.

The birth of this "new sun" remains a confusing and as-yet unprovable issue. Whichever side one stands on, one is sure to make enemies.

Warlocks

Strangers are rarely welcome in most villages in the Known Worlds. Peasants are often violently superstitious, and all-too-ready to punish a stranger for some freak misfortune or turn of luck, from earthquakes to a string of gambling losses. Those strangers who betray psychic powers or even theurgy are especially feared. They are blamed for nearly all the evil which occurs in the lives of the unfortunate. When a famine lasts too long or a child dies, a warlock is surely at work. When a cow gives bad milk, it's a sure sign that a warlock has been prowling around the farm.

Those individuals who are blessed with occult powers — whether psychic abilities or divine magic — bear a sign which usually betrays their status as "different". These signs vary, and can be anything from an odd birthmark to religious stigmata. How the local peasantry reacts to such signs depends on how good or bad their fates have been of late, but it usually ranges from cold to hateful.

Those occultists accused of bad deeds are called warlocks, witches, sorcerers or black magicians. Even worse are those accused of demon worship, dubbed Antinomists by the Church. To be declared any of these terms is to be reviled and chased out of town — or worse. Most towns have hanging trees or burning poles for the punishment of such people.

In such an atmosphere, the development of psychic powers, once believed to be the next evolutionary step for humans, is rare. When a person discovers she has psychic powers, it is often cause for horror and shame. Those who seek to develop these powers must do so in secret, usually with the aid of underground covens.

Void Krakens

There are... *things*... in space. Things which are seemingly alive in the void, where no life should exist. Never glimpsed in full and never leaving direct proof, these *things* have nonetheless left their mark on the hulls of battered starships or shown themselves in the sea of floating crew-

men flooding from ruptured hulls, forming a graveyard of unburied dead preserved forever in the chill vacuum.

Perhaps as a result of humankind's reacquaintance with magic, or perhaps merely as a delayed reaction to the Second Republic's vast expansion, these creatures began to appear between the stars in the very void of space soon after Alexius' coronation. Monsters came from out of the inky blackness and devoured starships whole, or left little behind to tell the tale. A new terror descended on humanity; space was no longer safe.

Once the matter had been researched, it was discovered that these mysterious ship destroyers had been around for a long time. Reports of disappearing ships were common during the Diaspora, but the voices of the few witnesses claiming to have seen monsters were unheeded, considered but the prattling of insane minds suffering from oxygen deprivation. The reports soon died down, but they reappeared during the Second Republic's frontier search and terraforming craze. Again, the crazed eyewitness accounts were unheeded. Instead, Vau were believed to be the culprits, using ships of a new, unknown design. Before the matter was ever resolved, the attacks ceased.

But now, in an age of extreme superstition, the new reports traveled among the populace like wildfire, igniting fears and legends. Some are convinced that these assaults are the work of a mysterious new race from worlds far from Human Space. Their cyclic activity implies that they either leave for long periods or go into hibernation. Whatever the reason, they have either returned or are again awake.

Vau have been questioned (diplomatically, of course), but they know no more than humans. It is clear, however, that they have suffered similar assaults throughout history and have many of the same questions as humanity.

The stars lanes are now deadly paths to tread.

The Final Act

Big changes are at hand for the Known Worlds. Emperor Alexius has declared a new adventure, a search for the Lost Worlds of the Second Republic. A search for hope and a new beginning. He offers great rewards for those few who are bold enough to seize destiny. On the new frontier, humans and aliens face challenges never before seen. Noble or priest, guildsman or alien; all have an equal part to play in the next great act of history. The lights dim, the darkness deepens. The final passion play begins....

Chapter 2: Rules

Lady Erian Li Halan stood at the edge of the wide balcony and stared out over the fields of Veridian, central continent of Byzantium Secundus. The rains had diminished to a mist, refracting into rainbows heralding the setting sun. She fingered the new medallion hanging from her neck — a rising phoenix over a brightening star, emblem of Emperor Alexius' Questing Knights.

There would be great trials soon. Conflicts and intrigue seemed to be the warp and woof of her fate. For a moment, she regretted the bonds that held her entourage to her. In the past three years, they had become far more than traveling companions and aides — they were friends, the closest thing she had to family, now that her own kin had turned against her. She wished she could send them away, far from the troubles to come. But this was impossible; she would need them — their skills were invaluable. As selfish as it seemed, she had a destiny to fulfill, and no noble worthy of the name could fail to live up to it — regardless of the sacrifices called for.

"Let it begin," she said aloud. "Let come what may, I shall be ready."

Fading Suns is a roleplaying game, and as such is largely free from the restrictive rules inherent to games such as chess and football. Literally the entire universe is opened up before the players, and, within the limits of their characters' capabilities and the gamemaster's fiat, anything is possible. Many situations are resolved not by impersonal rules, but by the players' knowledge and cleverness. For example, if the characters are being hotly pursued by the diabolical subterranean Slug Symbiots of Stigmata, and one player has the foresight to realize that the right-hand tunnel immediately ahead leads to an old salt mine, the characters will very likely escape to safety (salt being quite lethal to the slimy Slug Symbiots).

Nevertheless, **Fading Suns** has some simple rules to resolve events whose outcome is uncertain. These rules, and the extrapolations thereof, will enable players and gamemasters to simulate and arbitrate any situation — though the gamemaster's decisions supersede any and all rules in this book.

Interpreting the Rules

Always remember that the purpose of a roleplaying game is to provide as much conflict, drama, passion and sheer fun as possible. Unlike most board and card games, roleplaying games are not about winning or losing, but about playing and having a good time. The gamemaster should always temper his interpretation of the rules with an eye toward character, excitement and entertainment — even at the expense of strict realism.

For example, a character is climbing a 10,000-meter mountain. She reaches a treacherous escarpment, and the gamemaster asks the player to make a Dexterity + Vigor roll to see if the character can navigate the cliff. The character fails the roll.

Theoretically, the gamemaster can tell the player, "Okay, your character slips and falls. She's dead." This is not unreasonable — mountain climbing *is* hazardous, people *do* suddenly slip and fall, and the character *did* fail her roll. Such a result, however, is hardly in the spirit of heroic adventure. It's also liable to irritate the player, and while the players should not dominate the game, their characters shouldn't simply die like gnats.

A better gamemaster might say something like, "As you grope your way up the cliff, the handhold supporting your weight crumbles into powder. You hear a rasping noise, and the entire cliff face disintegrates into a torrent of loose shards. As you begin to plummet to your doom, you flail wildly at

the remaining rock, and your left hand clutches a protrusion, halting your fall. You are now suspended above a 10,000-meter abyss, holding on by one hand... and as you look up at your hand-hold, you see cracks starting to appear in the protrusion as well. What do you do?"

Both the outcomes described above are valid results of a failed roll. Both adhere to the letter of the rules. But the second situation is much more suspenseful and gives the player more control over the ultimate outcome of the character's predicament.

Dice

Fading Suns uses dice to determine the outcome of situations where luck plays a role. Most rolls are resolved using a 20-sided die, but some rolls (damage, armor) use the familiar six-sided dice used in many board games. 20-sided dice can be found in most comic and hobby stores — anywhere that roleplaying games are sold.

Time

Time in Fading Suns is measured in five units, ranging from the smallest to the largest. These are: the turn, the span, the act, the drama and the epic. Note that time in Fading Suns is measured in cycles rather than exact, standard amounts; plot advancement, rather than an exact hour-minute-second count, determines the flow of time.

- **Turn** — The turn is the smallest unit of time in the Fading Suns universe, and the most precise. Generally speaking, a turn equals three seconds. In one turn, a player can attempt one action at no penalty or can attempt multiple actions (up to three actions per turn), though multiple actions impose penalties to the success of those actions. Some actions (defusing a bomb, climbing a building) take longer than one turn.

- **Span** — The next-greatest unit of time is the span. A span is a sequence of events occurring at the same time and in the same place. Think of a span as a scene in a movie or TV show — the events occurring between a fade-in and fade-out. Generally speaking, a span comprises a fairly short and enclosed sequence of events (interrogating a shady merchant prince, attending a Hawkwood banquet, conducting a chase through the slums, fighting a duel, etc.). This is, however, not always the case; events of a span can take place over lengthy time periods or distances, so long as the characters are engaged in a specific task.

For example, characters may spend a grueling week traveling 100 kilometers across the frozen tundra of Malignatius, surviving the vagaries of cold and privation. So long as the characters are primarily involved in journeying to their destination and battling the terrain, this is considered a span. Following their trek, the characters arrive at a hidden bunker where evil cultists are conducting diabolical rites to the

When *Not* to Use the Rules

Character interaction and player cleverness are intrinsic to the play of Fading Suns — much more so than strict adherence to nitpicky rules. In fact, there are several situations in which it is better simply to throw out the rules and let the game flow.

- If characters are doing something easy or routine. If a character is walking along and comes to a six-foot-wide chasm and decides to jump it, and there are no stressful or other extraneous circumstances, let the character jump it. Sure, it's possible that a character could suddenly become incredibly klutzy and twist his ankle or otherwise plummet into the abyss, but the possibility is so minute that it can safely be ignored (and even if such an event occurred, it'd be a stupid, anticlimactic way for a hero to die).

Now, if the jumping character is currently engaged in a back-and-forth duel at the lip of the chasm, or has been poisoned and can barely remain upright, a Dexterity + Vigor roll might well be called for....

- If a player solves a story problem through ingenuity — i.e., if secret documents are hidden in a hollow statue, and the player specifically states that his character breaks

open the statue during his search, there's no need to make a Perception + Search roll to determine whether the character finds the documents. (If the character merely examines the statue, a Perception + Search roll might be called for. And if the character goes nowhere near the statue, the player may not even be allowed the opportunity to make a roll.)

- If a character does something stupid or obnoxiously provocative — i.e., if a character slaps the face and publicly questions the parentage of the eldest scion of House Hawkwood, there's no need to make a Calm roll to determine whether the Hawkwood challenges the upstart to a duel.

- "Deus ex Machina": Certain events spell inevitable doom even for heroes, and this is doubly true in the grim and fatalistic Fading Suns milieu. The gamemaster should use these "acts of God" sparingly — the players are the nexus of the game, and most players dislike being deprived of control over their characters' destinies. But, for example, if the characters are on a planet whose sun goes nova, and they have no way of getting off the planet, there's no need to roll massive numbers of damage dice, etc. The characters die — no ifs, ands or buts.

Void Krakens. The characters enter the one-room bunker and, in a pitched battle, defeat the foul coven. This is also a span. Even though the journey took place over a week's time and 100 kilometers, while the battle lasted 10 minutes and took place inside a 20-meter-square bunker, both advanced the plot by about the same amount.

• **Act** — A series of spans that collectively resolve a major plot point is referred to as an act. The closure of an act often involves a major revelation, a drastic change in time and/or location, or a dramatic shift in character fortunes. For example, the characters, after having learned the whereabouts of their kidnapped comrade, infiltrate the impregnable Muster battle station where their companion is being held. They spend the game session alternately ducking and battling guards, infiltrating the Muster command, and breaking into the maximum-security cell block. Finally, before they can rescue their comrade, the characters' deception is uncovered and they are captured and sentenced to slavery. This entire sequence of events constitutes an act; the next act will hopefully involve the various trials and tribulations of escaping their predicament.

• **Drama** — A drama comprises an entire story. Generally speaking, a drama begins when characters involve themselves (or are involuntarily involved) in a plot and ends only when the characters resolve the plot one way or another. Less happily, a drama can end in defeat, as characters fail to thwart the machinations of the villain, rescue the noble, save the planet, loot the palace or whatever. A drama ends whenever the players and gamemaster can say, for better or for worse, "THE END."

• **Epic** — The largest unit of time in **Fading Suns**, an epic comprises a series of stories, usually involving the same characters or the same overall plotline, such as the Race for the Throne of the Empire or the Rise of House Juandaastas. For example, J.R.R. Tolkien's "The Hobbit" is a drama — a complete story in itself — but is part of the overall epic of Middle Earth, because the events initiated by Bilbo Baggin's discovery of the ring are continued by Frodo and the Fellowship in "The Lord of the Rings." In **Fading Suns**, the chronicle of the player character's lives and adventures together, spanning many stories, is an epic.

Other units of time may prove important during certain acts. For example, if the characters are imprisoned in a noble citadel, and the guards declare that the characters are to be executed in four hours' time, the actions taken during those four hours prove critical.

Distance

Distance in **Fading Suns** is measured in metric units: meters, kilometers, kilograms, etc..

Actions

Players interact with the **Fading Suns** world through the medium of their characters, and these characters affect their environment through actions. Actions in **Fading Suns** are just like actions in the real world. A player describes what she wants her character to say or do, and the gamemaster uses his judgment and these rules to adjudicate the outcome.

Many actions — conversation, routine movement, etc. — can be resolved automatically, without recourse to the rules. Indeed, sometimes an entire act passes in this manner, as characters investigate, bargain and converse with allies and informants. Some actions, however, such as combat, athletic feats and occult invocations, require goal rolls (see below) to determine the characters' success or failure.

Trait Ratings

All **Fading Suns** characters are defined by trait ratings. For human characters, trait ratings generally range from 1 to 10, though aliens and other nonhuman entities can have higher or lower ratings. These 1 to 10 ratings measure characters' innate ability or prowess with their traits, and basically correspond to the classic, informal 1 to 10 scale used to measure athletic performances, product quality, potential significant others' (or innocent bystanders') desirability, etc. Basically, having a 1 in a trait indicates that the character is either naturally inept or a rank beginner, while having a 10 means that the character has achieved near-perfection or total mastery of the trait. So, a character with a 1 in Dexterity is a real klutz (virtually an invalid, in fact), while a character with a 10 is one of the universe's finest athletes. Likewise, a character with a 1 in Xenobiology is a beginning student, while a character with a Xenobiology rating of 10 is a universally respected, Einstein-class savant of alien lore.

Trait ratings are used to determine the outcome of actions. Obviously, the higher a character's trait ratings, the better that character will be at actions corresponding to those traits. A weak character has a chance to budge a heavy trapdoor, but a strong character will have a much better chance and will probably perform the feat in far less time.

Multiple Actions

A character may attempt up to three actions per turn, but additional actions levy a penalty to goal numbers (-4 if attempting two actions, -6 if attempting three). Furthermore, the same action may not be performed multiple times in a turn: a character cannot swing a sword three times, but may swing a sword, dodge the return blow, and kick at his foe's kneecap (all at a -6 penalty).

Firearms are the exception to this: A gun may be fired a number of times equal to the rate of fire. See Chapter Six: Combat for more information on firearms.

Initiative

Sometimes it's crucial to know which character acts first in a given turn, such as when two characters simultaneously dive for a nearby weapon. In such cases, the character with initiative gets to act first. Initiative is determined by comparing competing characters' skill ratings; the character with the highest skill acts first. In cases of ties or in situations in which no skill applies, compare the character's Wits rating; the character with the highest rating acts first. If Wits also tie, the actions are completely simultaneous (in the example above, both characters grab the item and must now make Strength + Vigor actions to attempt to wrest it from the other's grasp).

Goal Roll

Whenever the outcome of an action is in doubt, the gamemaster calls for a goal roll. This roll is made using one 20-sided die. The player (or gamemaster, in the case of gamemaster characters and environmental phenomena) must roll a score on this die that is equal to or less than the assigned goal number.

A player's base goal number is determined by adding the character's relevant characteristic trait rating to his skill trait rating. Thus, if a character wanted to fire a pistol at a foe, and the character had a Dexterity characteristic of 7 and a Shoot skill of 6, the player would need to roll "13" or less on the 20-sided die.

Things aren't always that simple, however. In many cases, the goal roll is adjusted up or down by situational modifiers. Consider the case of the aforementioned pistol shot. All other things being equal, it's easier to hit a dinosaur-sized foe than a rabbit-sized one. Thus, the gamemaster might assign a bonus to the player's goal if his character was trying to shoot a rampaging T. Rex, and might assign a penalty if the character was firing at a speeding jackrabbit.

With practice, gamemasters can easily assign an appropriate difficulty modifier to any action. These modifiers, in conjunction with the characters' traits, allow any situation in the universe to be simulated. Beginning gamemasters should use the example bonuses and penalties in the sidebar as models for assigning difficulties, but should not be afraid to wing it.

Multiple bonuses and penalties may be levied against an action or actions; simply add and subtract until a final result is achieved. For example, a character attempts three simultaneous actions (-6 to goal number), all of which are easy (+4 to goal number). Each action takes a -2 penalty.

Any die roll equal to or less than the goal number indicates a success, but a player whose action succeeds should remember the exact number rolled; this is important for calculating the subsequent effect roll (see below).

Effects of Success

The goal roll, above, determines whether a character's action succeeds or fails. If the action fails, that's that; go on to the next character. If an action succeeds, however, the player must still determine how well the action succeeds. Consider the pistol shot described above. There's a big difference between grazing a foe in the shoulder and blasting fiery doom straight through his left eye to incinerate his brain pan and send the shards of his charbroiled skull spraying hither and yon — even though both results are, technically, successful shots.

The number rolled on the goal roll is the number of successes scored. These successes can be used directly to gauge how poorly or how well a character succeeded in a task: the more successes, the better the character did at the task. However, the number of possible successes (from 1 to 18) leaves a lot of room for interpretation. For some situations, such as rolls to determine weapon damage or how well a complementary skill aided in another person's task, a smaller scale is more useful. To make things a little easier, **Fading Suns** successes translate directly into "victory points," which can be calculated by consulting the Victory Chart (see the sidebar). For most actions, the player can simply consult the Victory Chart to determine the level of success. One victory point is minimal — the character squeaked through by the skin of her teeth. Two victory points indicate a decent job — onlookers will accept the feat as satisfactory, though they certainly won't be awestruck. Five or six victory points indicate a virtuoso performance, and so on.

Victory points are also used when calculating modifiers to others' goal rolls (for example, when using a complementary skill or inciting Passion). Each victory point gained adds a positive modifier of 1 to another's goal roll.

An Example Action

Gorgool the bard is entertaining at a Hawkwood soiree. He begins an improvised epic praising the virtues of his host, and the crowd falls silent. The gamemaster asks Gorgool's player to make a goal roll using his Wits characteristic and his Perform (lute) skill.

Gorgool's Wits rating is 6, and his Perform (lute) rating is 7 (he's a talented boy). Thus, the goal roll would normally be 13. However, the gamemaster gleefully informs Gorgool's player that the task is a Demanding one (-4): Gorgool's doing this off the cuff, he's a little drunk, and the host doesn't have that many virtues to sing about. The goal roll is thus 9.

Gorgool's player grits his teeth and makes the roll. Luckily, he scores an "8" — a success. Consulting the Victory Chart, the player sees that 8 translates into two successes —

Bonuses

Modifier	Task	Example
+2	Natural	Singing a well-known song
+4	Easy	Seducing someone already "in the mood"
+6	Piece of cake	Recognizing a world famous celebrity
+8	Child's play	Walking and chewing gum at the same time, listing the Church's Virtues and Sins
+10	Effortless	Striking a bound and helpless foe

Penalties

Modifier	Task	Example
-2	Hard	Long range for firearm, seeing in moonlit darkness
-4	Demanding	Maximum range for firearm, performing two actions per turn, seeing through fog or smoke
-6	Tough	Performing three actions per turn; hanging onto a speeding, veering vehicle, seeing in near or total darkness
-8	Severe	Climbing a sheer rock face with no equipment
-10	Herculean	Striking a bullseye at 100 yards while blindfolded

Victory Chart

Successes	Victory Points/ Victory Dice*	Accomplishment
1-2	1/+0	Barely satisfactory
3-5	1/+1	Mediocre
6-8	2/+2	Pretty good
9-11	3/+3	Good job
12-14	4/+4	Excellent
15-17	5/+5	Brilliant
18-20	6/+6	Virtuoso performance

* One victory point is gained per *three* successes (rounded down) scored.

okay, but not wonderful. Gorgool's performance will definitely not live in the annals of bardic history, but the gamemaster tells the player that Gorgool entertains the crowd, receives a small bag of coin tossed at him by a sentimental old fart of a noble, and catches the eye of a mildly appreciative, moderately attractive maiden.

Effect Dice

Certain feats, such as combat, require a few more variables. These sorts of rolls are resolved with "effect dice," which can represent a weapon's damage or a suit of armor's protective value. Since there are more dice rolled than with the goal roll, effect dice are rolled with six-sided dice — it is easier to roll a lot of six-siders than a bunch of 20-siders. Results of 1, 2, 3 or 4 are successful; results of 5 or 6 are failures. Each successful die generates one point: a "wound" point in the case of damage or an "armor" point in the case of armor.

Wound points are applied against the target's Vitality rating, but only after accounting for any armor or other protection he may be wearing — each armor point subtracts one wound point before damage is applied. The number of dice actually rolled varies with weapon damage or armor value (see the Weapons and Armor Charts in Chapter Six: Combat).

There is another variable to consider with damage dice — the effectiveness of a character's blow. Victory points gained on the attack goal roll are converted into damage dice, called "victory dice." Victory points convert to victory dice on a 1-for-1 basis.

A player does not have to use the entire number of victory dice generated from victory points — she may choose to "pull her punch" by using as few as one die. The weapon dice must still be used in full, however — it's impossible to "be gentle" with a greatsword!

After being hit, a target can roll his armor dice (if any); each successful die equals one armor point. Since no goal roll is made (skill is not involved), victory dice are not added to armor dice. Energy shields are another form of personal protection, but they represent a special case; see *Energy Shields* in Chapter Seven: Technology.

(A effect die roll can also be made using a d20, if no six-sided dice are available. The goal number is 13 or less for each die.)

An Example Combat Action

Gorgool had no idea that the maiden he was flirting with has a jealous and drunken paramour in the crowd. As he exits the hall for a breather, flush with his lute-playing success, the angry fellow suddenly appears and swings his fist at Gorgool.

The attacker makes a goal roll, adding his Dexterity 4 and his Fight 6 to get a result of 10 — he must roll this or less on a 20-sided die. The result is a "7" — a success with two victory points (see the Victory Chart). His fist normally inflicts two dice of damage, but with the victory dice from his attack, he gets to roll four dice (his two victory points convert directly into damage dice). He rolls these dice — six-siders this time — with results of 2, 6, 3 and 4 — three

successful dice, which translates to three wound points.

Gorgool is not wearing armor — it would be uncouth to bring armor to a performance — so he takes the full three points to his Vitality. Gorgool reels backwards, his jaw throbbing in pain. Before the attacker can land another blow, the house guards arrive and drag the belligerent boyfriend away, immune to his pleas for leniency. The maiden, hearing the commotion, rushes out and sees poor Gorgool wiping blood from his chin. She moves to comfort him. While Gorgool will have a bruise in the morning, the evening is not a total loss....

Modifiers to Actions

The system described above, once learned, is fairly simple. Following are rules that the gamemaster can employ to make actions more realistic and interesting, but a little more complex. Beginning players and gamemasters might want to wait a bit before tackling these extra rules.

Critical Success

Beginner's luck. A perfect "10." A magnum opus. A legendary performance. Sometimes everything just clicks into place, and a person performs a feat far beyond what her abilities should allow her to accomplish.

Such a happy event in a **Fading Suns** game is referred to as a critical success. When a character makes a goal roll, and the number scored on the die exactly equals the goal number, that character scores a critical success. A critical success *doubles* the number of victory points. Thus, if a character had a goal number of 9, and rolled a "9" exactly, the critically successful character would garner six victory points (or victory dice) instead of the usual three.

Note that the chance of a critical success is always 5%, no matter how good you are. Scoring a critical success is largely a matter of "being in the right place at the right time," and is thus beyond the player's and character's control. However, characters who are already skilled at a given task will have *better* critical successes — a rank beginner who shoots a three-point free throw from half court will receive disbelieving cheers from his friends, but an accomplished guitarist who performs the concert of a lifetime will garner national acclaim.

If a roll is accented (see Optional Rule: Accents), the accented number is used to determine critical success. Thus, if Lars the axeman has a goal roll of 11, accents the roll by +3, and rolls an 8 with an axe swing, the 8 is treated as 11. Lars scores a critical success.

Critical Failure

The downside of critical successes are critical failures: those situations where a person not only fails, but does so spectacularly (and often in a humiliating, injurious or even lethal fashion). Critical failures, also called "fumbles," far

transcend normal failures: the gunslinger doesn't just miss her foe, she shoots herself in the foot; the would-be Casanova doesn't just get a polite rejection, he gets a slap, a cry of loathing and an antistalking injunction; the actor doesn't just make a bad film, but an utter turkey, one that destroys his reputation and career.

Much to the players' chagrin (and amusement), critical failures can occur to their **Fading Suns** characters. Whenever a player rolls a natural "20" on a goal roll, a critical failure occurs. Not only does the attempt fail, but the gamemaster invents something else — something awful — that happens along with the failure.

Contested Actions

When two people clash — in combat or in a verbal joust at a royal soiree — usually only of them one will come out the winner. This is simulated in **Fading Suns** with contested actions: Both characters' rolls are compared against each other. The lowest successes subtract from the highest successes, and the character left with the most successes wins.

For example, Julia is trying to convince a black market merchant to return her stolen money. Her chosen form of debate is her fists. But the sleazy merchant decides to meet Julia's fists with a knife slipped skillfully from his boot. Julia tries to twist away from the thrusting steel by dodging — a contested action. She rolls her Dexterity (6) + Dodge (7) and gets 6 successes. The merchant rolls his Dexterity (5) + Melee (4) and gets 8 successes. Julia's 6 successes are subtracted from the merchant's 8, leaving the merchant with 2 successes — enough to hit Julia, but at least Julia avoided the full force of the blow.

Contested actions are often signified in the rules by stating that one roll is "versus" another roll.

Complementary Actions

Sometimes a character's expertise in one field will help his performance in a totally different field. For example, a character may have spent his childhood on the "deathworld" of Stigmata, which is inhabited by highly toxic flora and fauna. Later, his partner, a physician, attempts to treat the bite of a deadly Stigmatan marsh eel. The character's knowledge of folk remedies against the marsh eel's bite (Regional Lore) may actually assist the physician's task (Physick).

A complementary action goal roll is resolved per the standard rules, but the number of victory points garnered on the complementary roll instead becomes an addition to the goal number of the primary roll.

Example: In the above situation with the marsh eel, the character rolls a die against a goal number of 8 (his Wits of 4 plus his Regional Lore of 4) and scores a 6. This translates into two victory points, so the physician adds +2 to the goal number of his Physick roll.

Automatic Success and Failure

A natural roll of "1" on a goal roll always succeeds, no matter what the odds are against the character. Conversely, a natural "19" rolled on the die is always a failure, no matter how skilled the character is or how easy the task is. Murphy's Law happens to the best of us. A natural "20" rolled is even worse (see Critical Failure).

Excessive Goal Numbers

It is possible in some circumstances, due to theurgic bonuses or cybernetic enhancements or some other means, for a character's goal number to exceed 20. For every three points over twenty, the character may add one to his victory dice total (see the Extended Victory Chart, below). A goal roll should still be made, even though there is little chance of failure (a "19" always fails, while a "20" is a critical failure). A result of "18" is considered a critical success. A character with a goal number of 24 who rolls an "18" would have 16 victory points (six, plus his two bonus points, multiplied by two for the critical success). However, if he had merely rolled a "7", he would still have four victory points (two, plus his two bonus points).

Extended Victory Chart

Goal	Victory Point bonus
21-23	+1
24-26	+2
27-29	+3
30-32	+4
33-35	+5
etc.	

In order to keep players from trying to take too much of an advantage in combat, the gamemaster should restrict goal numbers over 20 to those which occur either through a character's unmodified characteristics and skills or through supernatural and technological effects, rather than simple bonuses due to the ease of a roll.

Sustained Actions

Certain actions cannot be simulated with one all-or-nothing roll. For example, if two characters are engaged in a desperate struggle, one attempting to push the Planetary Destruct lever to the ACTIVATE position, the other frantically trying to keep the lever from being deployed, this action is rarely accomplished in one turn. Particularly if the two characters are of roughly equal strength, the lever will inch forward, then backward, then forward again, as the two strive to attain their goals inch by precious inch.

Sustained Action Chart

Task	Victory Pts	Condition
Simple	6	Climbing a tree
Complex	9	Researching the weaknesses of a noble
Involved	12	Climbing a sheer cliff
Obscure	18	Deciphering Vautech
Arcane	23+	Repairing Vautech

Such actions are called sustained actions. Sustained actions simulate any feat — a tug-of-war, an arm-wrestling match, the building of a machine — in which success requires a prolonged effort. Sustained actions require goal rolls just like normal actions; however, instead of determining flat-out success or failure, the points of each goal roll are totaled and tallied against a predetermined score (this score is decided by the gamemaster, based on the difficulty of the feat — see the accompanying Sustained Action Chart for guidelines). When the proper amount of "victory points" have been garnered, the feat is accomplished. Failing a roll means that no victory points are garnered that turn. If the character suffers three failures, or one critical failure, the task simply proves impossible.

For example, a priest's land rover sputters to a halt in the middle of the Algol Desert, and a sandstorm whips up on the horizon. Muttering prayers to the enigmatic gods of technology, the character hauls out his tools and gets to work. The gamemaster tells the player that the character must roll his Tech (6) + Mech Redemption (6) to fix the engine. The task is a Hard one (-2 to rolls), and fixing the engine is an Involved feat (there's a lot of funny parts in there), so the priest must score 12 or more victory points to repair the infernal contraption.

Sustained actions can be assisted or resisted. If others are assisting (for example, to lift a heavy sarcophagus cover), simply add all victory points together until success is scored. If someone resists the action (as with the Planetary Destruct Lever example, above), determine the victory point total as usual, but subtract the opponent's victory points from the character's. This can even cause a character to accumulate "negative" victory points, which must be overcome before positives can be garnered.

For example, take the aforementioned tug-of-war for the Planetary Destruct lever. The gamemaster decrees that whichever combatant first garners six victory points pulls the lever to the desired position. On the first turn, Combatant #1 scores two victory points, while Combatant #2 scores four. Combatant #2 is now two points toward invoking planetary devastation, and Combatant #1 is two points in the hole — he must score two points even to bring the lever back to a neutral position.

Second Tries

A character who fails a task may try again. However, the second attempt suffers a -2 penalty in addition to any other modifiers, and the third attempt (for really tenacious or stupid characters) takes a -4 penalty. If, after three failures, the character still can't accomplish a feat, that feat is simply beyond his capabilities — for now. He may, however, try again next span at no penalty.

Final Words

These rules are designed for simplicity and to enhance enjoyment for all participants. Gamemasters: if you find a given rule overly complex, not complex enough or otherwise unsuitable, feel free to replace it with one of your own devising. These rules are yours, to shape, bend or break as you choose.

Optional Rule: Accents

Heroic fiction is full of extreme feats: the fighter pilot screaming down the turret-filled tunnel, concentrating all his skill and training on targeting the photon torpedoes on that tiny chink in the battle station's impregnable armor; or, conversely, the desperate, Hail Mary swing that is the last chance at taking down the villain before he pushes the PLANETARY DESTRUCT button.

Fading Suns simulates these types of endeavors with "accents." Accents simulate extra control or effort applied to an action, at the expense of power or finesse respectively.

A player must announce her intent to accent a goal roll before the roll is made. When accenting a roll, a player declares whether she is adding to or subtracting from the die roll, and announces what amount she chooses to add or subtract. A character may only add or subtract an amount equal to or less than her character's skill (not characteristic).

The amount accented adds to or subtracts from the actual die roll, not the goal number. The goal number remains the same. Thus, a negatively accented goal roll (representing a cautious, precise effort) has a better chance to succeed, but will score fewer successes. Conversely, a positively accented roll (representing a do-or-die, give-it-all-ya-got effort) will score more successes if it succeeds, but has a greater chance to fail.

For example, Thrako punches a thief. He decides to accent the roll by adding 5 (well within his Fight skill range). His Dexterity + Fight equals 12 — he needs to roll 12 or less on the die. He rolls 5, a good roll, but not great. However, he gets to add 5 to his roll (his accent), making the roll a 10 — a hit with 10 successes. If he had rolled 8 or above, he would have missed — his accent would have increased the roll past his goal.

Die rolls indicating automatic successes, automatic failures and critical failures are unaffected by accents. Thus, an unadjusted roll of "1," "19" or "20" is treated normally, as if the accent was never applied. However, rolls that become automatic successes, automatic failures or critical failures by the application of an accent (i.e., a roll of "15", accented by +7 to 22, that effectively becomes a critical failure) are treated as naturally rolled automatic successes, automatic failures or critical failures. It is all too easy for even the best swordsman to injure himself by overextending....

There are a few more rules to keep in mind when accenting:

• **Wyrd Points** — It costs one Wyrd point (see Chapter Three: Traits) to accent an action. If a character has used up all her Wyrd points, she may not accent actions.

• **No Multiple Actions** — A character cannot perform multiple actions within the same turn that she accents. It simply takes too much effort for a character to throw everything she's got into an action (positive accent) or too much time to be cautious with one (negative accent).

• **-3 Initiative Penalty** — An accenting character suffers a -3 penalty to his initiative for the action.

• **Lore skills** — Lore skills or other rolls to access knowledge, research a fact or any similar long-term action may not be accented.

• **Victory Points** — Positively accented actions yield more victory points than usual (along with an increased chance to fail the roll) while negatively accented actions yield less (in return for an increased chance to succeed in the roll). See the modified Victory Charts below:

Positively Accented Rolls

Successes	Victory Points/ Victory Dice*
1-2	1/+0
3-4	1/+1
5-6	2/+2
7-8	3/+3
9-10	4/+4
11-12	5/+5
12-14	6/+6
15-16	7/+7
17-18	8/+8

* One victory point is gained per *two* successes (rounded down) scored.

Negatively Accented Rolls

Successes	Victory Points/ Victory Dice*
1-4	1/+0
5-8	1/+1
9-12	2/+2
13-16	3/+3
17-20	4/+4

* One victory point is gained per *four* successes (rounded down) scored.

Chapter 3: Character Creation

The most important part of **Fading Suns** is the character. Just as characters are crucial to a novel, play or film, so characters (the players' and the gamemaster's) are the driving force behind a **Fading Suns** drama. Players can jump right into the game by choosing one of the premade characters at the end of this chapter. Most, however, will want to create their own.

Because the character is the nexus of the game, the hub around which everything else turns, a player must make some choices when building her character. There are two methods a player can choose from with which to create a character: Character Histories or Custom Creation. Building a Character History is the simplest and quickest method, but also the one with the least choice and variability. It involves taking a character through three stages representing his upbringing, apprenticeship and early career. Afterwards, there are some extra stages that help flesh out the character and even allow him to take some of the stranger abilities available in **Fading Suns**, such as psychic powers, theurgic magic or cybernetic enhancements.

The Custom Creation process provides a player with a number of character points with which to purchase his character's traits: characteristics, skills, weird powers, etc. Though this process of building a character may seem a bit involved and time-consuming at first, it provides players with the maximum amount of choice and character depth. (The Character Histories process uses the same amount of character points; they are spent on previously built templates.)

Character Concept

The most important part of character creation, and the most fun, is determining a character concept. Who and what do you want to be? A player inventing a character concept

bears many similarities to a novelist or playwright creating a character for her literary endeavor, and the process is just as involved (and just as rewarding).

When determining a concept, envision all facets of your character. Is he human or alien? What does she look like? Did he grow up amid the palatial estates of a noble planet, or did he come of age on the savage streets of a megaslum? Is the character an outworld barbarian, utterly unfamiliar with civilization and its trappings? Is the character blunt or subtle? Brutal or sophisticated? Worldly or superstitious? Honest or devious? Does he have any peculiar mannerisms or speech patterns? A favorite object or item of clothing? All these things and many more help to focus your character and set him apart.

Here are some things to consider when formulating your character concept. Ask these questions to yourself, and try to answer as the character would (this can help you find your character's voice).

• **Are you human or alien?** This is, perhaps, the most important decision to be made in terms of concept. Players contemplating running an alien character should be advised that this is a difficult roleplaying challenge. Aliens don't always think like humans do, and often have trouble interacting with the predominantly human Imperial society. Aliens are also often distrusted and ostracized.

• **What was your childhood like? Your adolescence?** The diversity of the **Fading Suns** galaxy allows for a nearly infinite variety of back stories. Were you a spoiled and pampered noble or did you come of age on a backwater serf-world? Were you raised by loving parents, or were they distant and cold? Were you, perhaps, an orphan, taken in by a monastery — or sold to the Muster slavers at an early age?

• **What is your social background?** A character raised as a noble will have a tremendously different outlook on life

than will a character born into serfdom. Do you expect instant obeisance from all or do you feel you have to fight for every shred of property and dignity? Or were you destined for the Church?

• **When did you discover your occult powers?** Some characters manifest powerful occult properties early in life, much to their chagrin if they're stuck on superstitious backwater worlds. If your powers manifested early, were you ostracized? Hunted as a witch? Revered as a god? Did you keep your powers secret, use them to take advantage of others, or try to better your society?

• **What is your profession? Did you ever want to be something else?** How do you earn a living? Are you an illiterate jack-of-all-trades, or have you mastered the secret lore of the guilds? Did you choose your profession, or were you forced into it by circumstance?

• **Are you a believer in superstition or reason?** Do you strive to recover the lore of the Second Republic, or do you feel that certain things are best left buried? Do you shudder when imagining the dark between the stars, or do you seek to discover the secrets spiraling in the galactic abyss?

• **Are you a follower of a religion, or do you have faith only in yourself?** The Church is an all-pervasive entity in the **Fading Suns** universe, and while it does great good, it can also be stiflingly oppressive. Do you place your soul's trust in the Church, or do you scorn the beliefs others hold dear? Perhaps you are a pagan, or even a demon-worshipper (though the latter can be disruptive to the game).

• **How do you feel about technology?** Technology in the **Fading Suns** world is not the user-friendly helpmate it is in the present day. **Fading Suns** residents see technology as mysterious, unreliable, magical and often inimical. Those who work closely with technology are often distrusted and are occasionally branded as magicians.

• **Are you happy with the status quo, or are you a revolutionary? A criminal?** Long live Emperor Alexius — at least that's what everyone says to his face. Perhaps you feel differently. Are you a loyal Imperial citizen (perhaps truly believing that the Empire is acting in humanity's best interests) or would you love to see the Empire fall? Perhaps your family was impoverished or destroyed in the Emperor Wars, driving you to sedition. Or perhaps you have a loved one in an opposite political camp — how does your patriotism affect your relationship?

• **What are your important likes, goals and dislikes? Do you have a loved one? A lost love? A dire enemy?** The little — or not so little — things can be among the most important facets of a character. Does your character like a certain color or type of food? Does he have a certain speech pattern or mannerisms? Does he want to own a merchant line of his own — or do his ambitions run toward dethroning the Emperor?

There are an infinite number of questions to be asked about each character, and the more detailed the conceptual process becomes, the richer and more real the character will seem.

At the heart of **Fading Suns** are the distinctions of class. Leaders aren't made — they're born. One does not get promoted to the nobility; one must be the scion of generations of nobles. Suggested character roles, the social classes that make up the Known Worlds, are given in the Character Histories section. These include the nobles, the priesthood, the merchants, the serfs and the outsiders, be they alien or barbarian.

Character Histories

If the player chooses to use this method to build her character, she must first ponder her character concept, as explained earlier. She chooses which of the main factions she wishes her character to be a member of: a noble house, a Church sect, a League guild or an alien race. Each faction produces characters with unique skills — nobles tend towards dueling and diplomacy, priests towards healing and study, guildsmembers towards technology or thievery, and each alien race's culture is different, producing philosophers or warriors.

Each character builds his history in stages. The three main stages are Upbringing (the character's youth), Apprenticeship (adolescence) and Early Career (the character's first few years in the role that will make her famous — or infamous). In addition, there are some extra stages representing further years in a career or the gaining of weird powers, either occult or cybernetic.

Each stage provides characteristics and skills common to characters of that faction, class and environment. Also, not all stages are alike — there are some choices to be made within each stage: Was the young noble raised at High-Court or in a Rural Estate? Did the priest get his initial training in a city Cathedral or a wilderness Monastery? The player should review each stage and decide which option is best for his character.

Certain stages may provide the character with a skill and/or characteristic he already gained in an earlier stage — all skill and characteristic bonuses are cumulative. For example, if a character learns Remedy 1 during his Appren-

Character Sheet

There is a character sheet provided at the end of this book for use by gamemasters and players. It is pretty self-explanatory (assuming that you've read this chapter), but there are a few things worth pointing out:

• Alliance refers to the character's major associates. A noble would list his house here, a member of the Merchant League his guild, and a priest his Church sect.

• When marking variable point traits such as Vitality and Wyrd, draw a rectangular box around the number of dots equal to the level of the trait (left to right). When those points are lost or spent (due to inflicted damage or the use of occult powers), draw a slash or "x" over the last dot in the box, working from right to left as more points are lost. Since lost points eventually come back (they are healed or replenished), it is best to mark losses with a pencil.

• Remember to underline the character's primary Spirit characteristics.

ticeship, and his Early Career also provides him Remedy 1, he then has the Remedy skill at two levels. If a successive stage provides a character with a language he already speaks or reads, he may use those points (usually 2 per language) elsewhere: either to boost skills he already possesses or learn new ones.

However, characters cannot begin play with any skill or characteristic above 8 levels. If this happens during character history, the player should take the extra levels and redistribute them elsewhere. For example, an al-Malik noble with a Landless Upbringing, a Duelist Apprenticeship and an Early Career as a Duelist will have a Dexterity of 9. The player must take this extra point (lowering the Dexterity score to 8) and put it into another characteristic.

Each faction has a list of suggested Benefices; these are entirely optional — players do not have to purchase these for their characters. They are simply meant to provide an idea of what the average noble, priest, guildsman or alien of that faction/race is likely to have.

Those Who Rule: Nobles

The role of the noble is to be the master of all things: accomplished ruler, skilled warrior, able diplomat, gifted artist, vigorous worker and so on. The reality is often far different, but the goal is still worth striving for. All the houses, whether royal or minor, share certain characteristics, but all are very different.

Suggested Benefices: Nobility, Riches

Hawkwood

The Hawkwoods are proud that one of their own has become emperor, but all believe they are destined for greatness. It is both their privilege and their duty, and they act accordingly.

Decados

The family that many observers believed would win the Emperor Wars, the Decados are praised for their sophistication, wit and charm. They are feared for their malevolence, fury and treachery. To befriend a Decados is to ally with a viper.

The Hazat

A Hazat's pride in her soldiers is only surpassed by her pride in herself. Trained since birth to lead soldiers, she is as at home in an army sleeping bag as in a feather bed. Still, the Hazat are extremely aware of their role in society, and will never let their inferiors forget it.

Li Halan

Once renowned as the most decadent house, House Li Halan is now the most tied to the Church. Li Halan elders give readily to Church charities, and younger members of the house are the first to join crusades and serve in the Orders of Battle. While most nobles owe their loyalty primarily to their own house, the Li Halan owe it only to the Pancreator.

Suggested Benefices: Church Ally (1 -11 pts)

al-Malik

Some observers have suggested that the al-Malik grew out of a Second Republic merchant family, but now the house strives for nobility in all things. Of course, that doesn't keep its members from accumulating some of the best collections of Second Republic artifacts to be found this side of Leagueheim.

Suggested Benefices: Passage Contract (8 pts)

Minor House

In addition to the five Royal Houses, there are innumerable minor ones. Some of these used to be big, some are on their way up, and some have never gotten anywhere and probably never will. Thus, minor houses range from the most virtuous to the most vile, and gamemasters and players should get together to design their own.

Either choose a house in the Character Histories that best fits, or use the Custom Creation method.

Benefice Restriction: Nobility (9 pts maximum)

Questing Knight

Not all nobles have a respectable place in their family's fiefs. Second or third sons and daughters don't have much to inherit and must thus seek out their own opportunities. Many of them look to Emperor Alexius, who has chartered the Company of the Phoenix — the Questing Knights, nobles who swear a term of fealty to the Emperor and travel the realm enacting his new vision — whether it be upholding fealty rights for downtrodden peasants, putting down Republican rebellions, or traveling beyond the Known Worlds into barbarians space, seeking word or evidence of Lost Worlds.

Those nobles wishing to become Questing Knights should take the Questing Knight Tour of Duty (see Extra Stages in Character Histories, below).

Suggested Benefices: Imperial Knight Charter (5 pts), Well-Traveled (5 pts)

Upbringing

This stage represents the noble's youth, generally from birth to eight or ten years of age. During this time, she is molded by her faction's traditions and her family's expectations of her.

High-Court

The youth is raised in a palace, attended to by servants and tutors. She is watched carefully and must ever live up to high expectations. However, she gets to meet foreign visitors and witness famous doings.

Hawkwood: *Characteristics* — Strength +1, Dexterity +1, Wits +1, Extrovert (primary) +2; *Skills* — Melee +1, Etiquette 1, Lore (Heraldry) 1, Read Urthish (2 pts); *Blessing* — Unyielding (+2 Endurance when honor is at stake); *Curse* — Prideful (-2 Calm when insulted)

Decados: *Characteristics* — Dexterity +1, Perception +2, Ego (primary) +2; *Skills* — Etiquette 1, Lore (rival house) 1, Inquiry 1, Read Urthish (2 pts); *Blessing* — Suspicious (+2 Perception when rivals about); *Curse* — Vain (-2 Perception when being flattered)

Hazat: *Characteristics* — Endurance +1, Perception +2, Passion (primary) +2; *Skills* — Impress +1, Melee +1, Etiquette 1, Read Urthish (2 pts); *Blessing* — Disciplined (+2 Calm in combat situations); *Curse* — Vengeful (-2 Calm when honor impinged, will never forget a slight)

Li Halan: *Characteristics* — Wits +1, Extrovert or Introvert +1, Passion or Calm +1, Faith (primary) +2; *Skills* — Etiquette 1, Focus 1, Lore (Theology) 1, Read Latin (2 pts); *Blessing* — Pious (+2 Extrovert among the sinful); *Curse* — Guilty (-2 on all rolls when opposing Church officials)

al-Malik: *Characteristics* — Dexterity +1, Wits +1, Extrovert or Introvert +1, Calm (primary) +2; *Skills* — Etiquette 1, Speak Graceful Tongue (2 pts), Read Urthish (2 pts); *Blessing* — Gracious (+2 Extrovert to guests); *Curse* — Impetuous (-2 Wits when trading)

Rural Estate

The youth is raised in a manor or castle. While it is far from the important doings at high-court, it is still quite a step above the lot of most freemen and peasants. The young noble has tutors, but they must divide their time between teaching and other tasks, leaving the child to find her own way at times.

Hawkwood: *Characteristics* — Strength +2, Dexterity +1, Wits +1, Extrovert (primary) +1; *Skills* — Etiquette 1, Lore (Fief) 1, Read Urthish (2 pts), Ride 1; *Blessing* — Unyielding (+2 Endurance when honor is at stake); *Curse* — Prideful (-2 Calm when insulted)

Decados: *Characteristics* — Dexterity +2, Perception +2, Ego (primary) +1; *Skills* — Etiquette 1, Lore (rival house) 1, Knavery 1, Read Urthish (2 pts); *Blessing* — Suspicious (+2 Perception when rivals about); *Curse* — Vain (-2 Perception when being flattered)

Hazat: *Characteristics* — Endurance +2, Perception +2, Passion (primary) +1; *Skills* — Impress +1, Melee +1, Etiquette 1, Read Urthish (2 pts); *Blessing* — Disciplined (+2 Calm in combat situations); *Curse* — Vengeful (-2 Calm when honor impinged, will never forget a slight)

Li Halan: *Characteristics* — Wits +1, Extrovert or Introvert +1, Passion or Calm +1, Faith (primary) +2; *Skills* — Etiquette 1, Focus 1, Lore (Theology) 1, Read Latin (2 pts); *Blessing* — Pious (+2 Extrovert among the sinful); *Curse* — Guilty (-2 on all rolls when opposing Church officials)

al-Malik: *Characteristics* — Dexterity +2, Wits +1, Extrovert or Introvert +1, Calm (primary) +1; *Skills* — Etiquette 1, Speak Graceful Tongue (2 pts), Read Urthish (2 pts); *Blessing* — Gracious (+2 Extrovert to guests); *Curse* — Impetuous (-2 Wits when trading)

Landless

The youth's family is landless, and must rely on the charity of other nobles for lodgings or fostering. This often means that the youth lives in many homes during her childhood, and must defend against the insults of higher-born children who share the castles.

Hawkwood: *Characteristics* — Strength +1, Dexterity +2, Wits +1, Extrovert (primary) +1; *Skills* — Impress +1, Vigor +1, Melee +2, Ride 1; *Blessing* — Unyielding (+2 Endurance when honor is at stake); *Curse* — Prideful (-2 Calm when insulted)

Decados: *Characteristics* — Dexterity +2, Perception +2, Ego (primary) +1; *Skills* — Melee +1, Observe +1, Sneak +1, Knavery 2; *Blessing* — Suspicious (+2 Perception when rivals about); *Curse* — Vain (-2 Perception when being flattered)

Hazat: *Characteristics* — Endurance +2, Perception +2, Passion (primary) +1; *Skills* — Impress +1, Melee +1, Shoot +1, Vigor +1, Remedy 1; *Blessing* — Disciplined (+2 Calm in combat situations); *Curse* — Vengeful (-2 Calm when honor impinged, will never forget a slight)

Li Halan: *Characteristics* — Wits +1, Extrovert or Introvert +1, Passion or Calm +1, Faith (primary) +2; *Skills* — Melee +1, Observe +1, Focus 1, Lore (Theology) 1, Remedy 1; *Blessing* — Pious (+2 Extrovert among the sinful); *Curse* — Guilty (-2 on all rolls when opposing Church officials)

al-Malik: *Characteristics* — Dexterity +2, Wits +1, Extrovert or Introvert +1, Calm (primary) +1; *Skills* — Melee +1, Inquiry 1, Lore (Trading) 1, Speak Graceful Tongue (2 pts); *Blessing* — Gracious (+2 Extrovert to guests); *Curse* — Impetuous (-2 Wits when trading)

Apprenticeship

Born to privilege, a noble's life is molded from the start — the individual has little choice in his upbringing and career, for it has been planned out by his family. Nonetheless, there are various pastimes and endeavors she can choose to excel at. While most Hawkwood and Hazat gravitate towards military pastimes and al-Malik and Li Halan toward leisure or study, nobles from any house — but especially the Decados — appreciate diplomatic endeavors.

Military

Soldier: *Characteristics* — Strength +2, Dexterity +2, Endurance +1; *Skills* — Fight +1, Shoot +2, Vigor +1, Remedy 1, Social (Leadership) 3, Survival 1, Warfare (Military Tactics) 1

Starman: *Characteristics* — Dexterity +1, Wits +2, Perception +1, Extrovert +1; *Skills* — Impress +1, Melee +1, Shoot +2, Remedy 1, Social (Leadership) 2, Spacesuit 1, Think Machine 1, Warfare (Gunnery) 1

Diplomacy/Intrigue

Characteristics — Wits +2, Perception +1, Extrovert +1, Calm +1; *Skills* — Charm +2, Observe +1, Sneak +1, Arts (Rhetoric) 1, Etiquette 2, Inquiry or Knavery 2, Social (Debate or Oratory) 1

Leisure

Duelist: *Characteristics* — Strength +1, Dexterity +2, Endurance +1, Passion or Calm +1; *Skills* — Dodge or Vigor +1, Melee +2, Fencing Actions (Parry, Thrust, Slash), Remedy 1

Dandy: *Characteristics* — Dexterity +1, Wits +2, Perception +1, Passion or Calm +1; *Skills* — Any skill +2, Charm +1, Observe +1, Shoot +1, Arts (choose a favorite) 1, Drive (Aircraft or Landcraft) 1, Empathy 1, Gambling 1, Ride 1

Study

Characteristics — Wits +2, Introvert +2, Passion or Calm +1; *Skills* — Academia 1, Focus 3, Inquiry 1, Lore or Science (object of study) 3, Read Urthish or Latin (2 pts)

Early Career

Upon her coming-of-age, the young noble chooses the role she will fulfill for her house. She is officially knighted. (Those nobles who do not pass through this stage, but who become priests or guildsmembers instead, do not receive noble rank. While they are still considered royal, they receive none of the benefits or responsibilities of noble station.)

Military Command

Soldier: *Characteristics* — Strength +2, Dexterity +2, Endurance +2, Wits +1, Perception +1, Extrovert +1, Passion or Calm +1; *Skills* — Dodge +1, Fight +1, Impress +1, Observe +1, Melee +1, Shoot +2, Vigor +1, Remedy 1, Social (Leadership) 4, Survival 1, Warfare (Military Tactics) 1; *Benefice* — Rank (Knight)

Starman: *Characteristics* — Dexterity +2, Endurance +2, Wits +2, Perception +1, Extrovert +1, Passion or Calm +2; *Skills* — Impress +1, Melee +1, Shoot +2, Drive Spacecraft 1, Read Urthish (2 pts), Remedy 1, Social (Leadership) 2, Spacesuit (2 pts), Think Machine 1, Warfare (Gunnery) 1, Warfare (Starfleet Tactics) 1; *Benefice* — Rank (Knight)

Court

Duelist: *Characteristics* — Strength +1, Dexterity +2, Endurance +2, Wits +1, Perception +1, Extrovert or Introvert +1, Passion or Calm +2; *Skills* — Dodge +1, Melee +2, Etiquette 1, Fencing Actions (choose basic or advanced below), Remedy 1; *Benefice* — Rank (Knight)

Basic Fencing Actions (for characters who did not experience the Duelist Apprenticeship): Parry, Thrust, Slash, Draw & Strike

Advanced Fencing Actions (only for those who experienced the Duelist Apprenticeship): Draw & Strike, Parry/Riposte — or — Disarm, Feint

Ambassador: *Characteristics* — Dexterity +1, Wits +2, Perception +2, Extrovert +2, Calm +2, Faith or Ego +1; *Skills* — Charm +2, Observe +1, Sneak +1, Arts (Rhetoric) 1, Etiquette 2, Inquiry or Knavery 2, Lore (court rivals) 1, Social (Debate or Oratory) 1, Read Urthish (2 pts), Ride 1; *Benefice* — Rank (Knight)

Questing

Characteristics — Body characteristic (choose one) +2, Body characteristic (choose two) +1 each, Mind characteristic (choose one) +2, Mind characteristic (choose one) +1, Spirit characteristic (choose one) +2, Spirit characteristic (choose one) +1; *Skills* — Charm or Impress +1, Dodge +1, Combat skill (choose Fight, Melee or Shoot as primary) +2, Combat skill (choose secondary) +1, Observe +1, Sneak +1, Vigor +1, Drive (choose craft) 1, Inquiry or Knavery 1, Lore (people and places seen) 1, Remedy 1, Speak (2 pts, choose dialect), Streetwise 1; *Benefice* — Rank (Knight)

Tour of Duty

The noble caps her early career with a tour of duty in either her previous pastime or another — such as duty in the Emperor's Questing Knights. See Extra Stages, below.

Those Who Pray: Priests

No single institution has as much impact on day-to-day life in the Known Worlds than does the Universal Church of the Celestial Sun. Despite the Church's many factions and sects, the average peasant sees it as a giant monolith, dedicated to saving humanity from the evil inherent in the universe. As far as they can tell, all the priests work toward the same goal, hand-in-hand, fighting evil together. Never mind the fact that they call one another heretics; the Church itself is good. The peasants' view only changes when someone tries to replace the sect of their ancestors with a new one.

Suggested Benefices: Ordained (3-13 pts), Vestments (1 pt)
Benefice Restriction: Riches (7 pts maximum)

Urth Orthodox

Orthodox priests spend their time tending to the spiritual needs of their flock and defending the faith from outer and inner evil — whether it be aliens, barbarians or the heresies of other sects.
Suggested Benefices: Noble Ally (1 -11 pts)

Brother Battle

Brother Battle monks spend years training to become the most effective agents of the Pancreator's justice in the sinful universe. Their strict discipline and martial training make them incredibly efficient soldiers, although they rarely heed secular military commands. Despite the order's name, women can become monks.

Eskatonic Order

Eskatonic priests scour the universe for mystical lore to help defend the faithful from evil. Their questing has lead to many new discoveries which may better life for all — or open a Pandora's Box of secrets best left hidden.
Suggested Benefices: Secrets (2 pts), Refuge (6 pts)

Temple Avesti (Avestites)

The heavy robes of these fanatics are instantly recognizable — as are the smoking flameguns they bear to enact a literal punishment on the sinful. This sect long ago gained most of the chairs on the Inquisitorial Synod, much to the regret of its political enemies.

Sanctuary Aeon (Amaltheans)

This healing order was founded by Saint Amalthea after her travels with the Prophet and has continued since then to bring grace and mercy to all. Amaltheans are deeply beloved by the peasants they selflessly aid. See the Sanctuary Aeon Character History for sample traits.
Suggested Benefices: Ally (1-11 pts)

Mendicant Monks (Hesychasts)

Some priests want nothing to do with Church politics and join monasteries far from the centers of Church power — or live in huts in the wilderness seeking mystical visions or quiet lives of contemplation. Some friars take to the road to spread the gospel among the common folk whom the Church has ignored or forsaken.
Either choose a sect in the Character Histories that best fits, or use the Custom Creation method.
Suggested Benefices: Cloistered (+1 pt)
Benefice Restriction: Ordained (9 pts maximum)

Imperial Priest Cohort

Some priests hear the call to more worldly duty, enflamed by the values and vision espoused by Emperor Alexius. To these few is open the role of Imperial Cohort to Alexius's Questing Knights. A priest accepted into this august company gives spiritual succor and advice to a knight, and accompanies him on his travels into dire lands far from the bosom of the Church. He gains the unprecedented opportunity to preach to new converts and provide sterling example to all — even if it costs him the ire of the more politically-ambitious Church priests, ever opposed to Alexius's ascendancy.

Those priests wishing to become Cohorts should take the Imperial Cohort Tour of Duty (see Extra Stages in Character Histories, below).
Suggested Benefices: Cohort Badge (3 pts), Well-Traveled (5 pts)

Upbringing

Most priests or guildsmembers grow up in similar towns or cities; their early experiences often determine whether they gravitate toward the marketplace or the monastery. Unlike nobles, these freemen have not yet chosen their faction (although their families may already be planning a career for them). The two factors to consider here are the character's environment and social status. Exception: Brother Battle monks are chosen at an early age; see below.

Environment

City: *Characteristics* — Wits +2, Perception +2; *Skills* — Observe +1, Inquiry 1, Streetwise 1

Town: *Characteristics* — Wits +1, Perception +1, Extrovert +2; *Skills* — Charm +1, Vigor +1, Inquiry 1

Country: *Characteristics* — Strength +1, Endurance +2, Faith +1; *Skills* — Vigor +1, Beast Lore or Drive Beastcraft 1, Lore (Regional) 1

Class

Wealthy: *Characteristics* — Extrovert +1; *Skills* — Read Urthish (2 pts)

Average: *Characteristics* — Extrovert or Introvert +1; *Skills* — Charm or Impress +1, Lore (Folk or Regional) 1

Poor: *Characteristics* — Faith or Ego +1; *Skills* — Knavery 1, Streetwise or Survival 1

Brother Battle Warrior Monk

A Brother Battle monk's harsh combat training begins early.

Characteristics — Strength +1, Dexterity +2, Endurance +1, Faith +1; *Skills* — Dodge +1, Fight +2, Melee +1, Shoot +2, Vigor +1, Focus 1, Remedy 1, Stoic Body 1; *Blessing* — Disciplined (+2 Calm in combat situations); *Curse* — Clueless (-2 Perception to notice social cues)

Apprenticeship

Note that nobles can join the priesthood at this stage; instead of choosing a noble Apprenticeship, they choose the one appropriate to their sect and environment.

Cathedral

The priest receives his first training in a city cathedral, and is thus close to libraries, learned people and perhaps even high technology.

Orthodoxy: *Characteristics* — Wits +1, Extrovert +1, Calm +1, Faith +2, Charm or Impress +1; *Skills* — Academia 1, Focus 1, Lore (Theology) 1, Physick 1, Social (Oratory) 2, Read Latin (2 pts), Remedy 1; *Blessing* — Pious (+2 Extrovert among the sinful); *Curse* — Austere (-2 Passion before members of the flock)

Eskatonic Order: *Characteristics* — Wits +1, Introvert +2, Faith +2; *Skills* — Observe +1, Academia 1, Alchemy 1, Focus 3, Lore (Occult) 1, Stoic Mind 1, Read Latin (2 pts); *Blessing* — Curious (+2 Extrovert when seeing something new); *Curse* — Subtle (-2 Extrovert when explaining something)

Temple Avesti: *Characteristics* — Endurance +1, Perception +2, Faith +2; *Skills* — Impress +1, Melee +1, Observe +1, Shoot +1, Inquiry 1, Lore (Doctrine) 1, Search 1, Torture 1; *Blessing* — Pious (+2 Extrovert among the sinful); *Curse* — Righteous (-2 Calm when judgment questioned)

Sanctuary Aeon: *Characteristics* — Dexterity +2, Tech +1, Calm +1, Faith +1; *Skills* — Charm +1, Arts (Music) 1, Empathy 1, Lore (Theology) 1, Physick 3, Remedy 2, Stoic Mind 1; *Blessing* — Compassionate (+2 Passion when helping others); *Curse* — Gullible (-2 Wits against attempts to fast-talk)

Parish

The priest begins his career in a country or town parish, a small but perhaps quaint church servicing the locals. It tends to preach to the same flock every week, which gives the priest a familiarity with the region and its people.

Orthodoxy: *Characteristics* — Wits +1, Extrovert +1, Calm +1, Faith +2; *Skills* — Charm or Impress +1, Empathy 1, Focus 1, Lore (Theology) 2, Lore (The Flock) 1, Physick 1, Remedy 1, Social (Oratory) 2; *Blessing* — Pious (+2 Extrovert among the sinful); *Curse* — Austere (-2 Passion before members of the flock)

Eskatonic Order: *Characteristics* — Wits +1, Introvert +2, Faith +2; *Skills* — Observe +1, Alchemy 1, Empathy 1, Focus 3, Lore (Occult) 1, Remedy 1, Stoic Mind 2; *Blessing* — Curious (+2 Extrovert when seeing something new); *Curse* — Subtle (-2 Extrovert when explaining something)

Temple Avesti: See Cathedral, above.

Sanctuary Aeon: *Characteristics* — Dexterity +2, Calm +1, Faith +2; *Skills* — Charm +1, Arts (Music) 1, Empathy 1, Lore (lives of the local people) 1, Physick 3, Remedy 2, Stoic Mind 1; *Blessing* — Compassionate (+2 Passion when helping others); *Curse* — Gullible (-2 Wits against attempts to fast-talk)

Monastery

The priest begins his training in a monastery, a place secluded from outsiders and dedicated completely to the spiritual life. Study and contemplation is favored over preaching and good works.

Orthodoxy: *Characteristics* — Wits +1, Introvert +1, Calm +1, Faith +2; *Skills* — Academia 1, Focus 2, Lore (Theology) 1, Physick 1, Stoic Mind 1, Read Latin (2 pts), Read Urthish (2 pts); *Blessing* — Pious (+2 Extrovert among the sinful); *Curse* — Austere (-2 Passion before members of the flock)

Eskatonic Order: *Characteristics* — Wits +1, Introvert +2, Faith +2; *Skills* — Academia 1, Alchemy 1, Focus 2, Lore (Occult) 1, Stoic Mind 1, Read Latin (2 pts), Read Urthish (2 pts); *Blessing* — Curious (+2 Extrovert when seeing something new); *Curse* — Subtle (-2 Extrovert when explaining something)

Temple Avesti: See Cathedral, above.

Sanctuary Aeon: *Characteristics* — Dexterity +1, Introvert +1, Calm +1, Faith +2; *Skills* — Empathy 1, Lore (Theology) 1, Physick 3, Remedy 2, Stoic Mind 1, Read Urthish (2 pts); *Blessing* — Compassionate (+2 Passion when helping others); *Curse* — Gullible (-2 Wits against attempts to fast-talk)

Brother Battle Warrior Monk

Characteristics — Strength +1, Dexterity +2, Endurance +1, Faith +1; *Skills* — Combat skill (choose Fight or Melee) +1, Shoot +1, Remedy 1, Stoic Body 1

Depending on the combat skill chosen above, choose one of the following:

Mantok Martial Arts: Martial Fist, Martial Kick, Martial Hold

Sword Fencing: Parry, Thrust, Slash

Early Career

The priest is ordained and receives his first posting: to preach and aid the people of a cathedral, church or parish; to live a cloistered life of contemplation in the monastery; or to bring the good word to others as a traveling missionary.

Preacher/Pastor

Characteristics — Wits +2, Perception +1, Extrovert +2, Introvert +1, Passion +2, Faith +2; *Skills* — Charm or Impress +2, Observe +1, Empathy 1, Focus 1, Inquiry 1, Lore (Flock) 1, Physick 1, Read Latin (2 pts), Remedy 1, Social (Oratory) 2, Speak Latin (2 pts); *Benefice* — Rank (Novitiate)

Monk

Characteristics — Body characteristic +1, Wits +2, Perception +1, Introvert +2, Calm +2, Faith +2, Observe +1, Academia 1, Empathy 1, Focus 3, Inquiry 1, Lore (Theology) 1, Lore (area of interest) 2, Physick 1, Read Latin (2 pts), Remedy 1, Stoic Mind 1; *Benefice* — Rank (Novitiate)

Missionary

Characteristics — Endurance +2, Wits +1, Perception +2, Extrovert +2, Passion +2, Faith +1; *Skills* — Charm or Impress +3, Observe +1, Drive Beastcraft 1, Empathy 1, Focus 1, Inquiry 1, Lore (Doctrine) 1, Physick 1, Remedy 1, Ride 1, Social (Oratory) 2, Streetwise 1; *Benefice* — Rank (Novitiate)

Healer

Characteristics — Dexterity +2, Endurance +1, Wits +1, Tech +1, Extrovert +2, Calm +1, Faith +2; *Skills* — Charm +2, Observe +1, Empathy 2, Focus 1, Lore (local populace) 1, Physick 3, Remedy 3, Social (Oratory) 1, Tech Redemption (choose type) 1; *Benefice* — Rank (Novitiate)

Inquisitor

Characteristics — Strength +2, Dexterity +1, Endurance +2, Perception +2, Passion +2, Faith +1; *Skills* — Impress +2, Observe +2, Shoot +2, Sneak +1, Vigor +1, Inquiry 1, Lore (Heresy) 1, Search 1, Stoic Body or Mind 1, Streetwise 1, Tracking 1, Torture 1; *Benefice* — Rank (Novitiate)

Brother Battle Warrior Monk

Characteristics — Strength +3, Dexterity +1, Endurance +3, Passion or Calm +1, Extrovert or Introvert +1, Faith +1; *Skills* — Dodge +1, Combat skill (choose Fight or Melee) +2, Combat skill (choose Fight or Melee) +1, Shoot +2, Physick 1, Focus or Stoic Body 2, Survival 1, Warfare (Military Tactics) 1; *Benefice* — Rank (Apprentice)

Choose one of the following:

Mantok Martial Arts: Claw Fist or Tornado Kick

Sword Fencing: Disarm or Feint

Tours of Duty

The priests completes her early posting by learning on the job with a tour of duty with the Church or as a Cohort to the Emperor's Questing Knights — or with a Theurgic Calling. See Extra Stages, below.

Those Who Trade: Merchants

The guilds may be all that remain of the giant corporations of the Second Republic, but they have carved out an important place in the Empire. While nobles may snub them and priests may call them sinners, the merchants know they provide a necessary service — one neither the houses or the sects could get along without.

Suggested Benefices: Commission, Riches, Passage Contract

Charioteers

Some Charioteers claim that they own the space lanes, and their claim is not far off. Master pilots and master traders both, they fly from star to star with cargo, sometimes illegal, but always highly prized.

Engineers

More than just mechanics, the Engineers recreate old tech, discover their own innovations, and merge them all into their lives and (sometimes) bodies. The Engineers do not offer their services to everyone, and even those they do help often wonder if it was worth the cost.

Scravers

This guild got its start recovering old technology, but the uses it found for these artifacts gave it a whole new role. Now it has casino space stations, slot machines, pharmaceutical labs and more, all protected by some of the best enforcers in the business.

The Muster (Chainers)

The Muster is the kind of bogeyman parents use to scare children: a guild which specializes in the trade of people. While their main role is to act as agent for skilled workers like mercenaries, technicians, engineers, and occasional entertainers, they've also picked up a (well-deserved) reputation as slavers.

Reeves (Gray Faces)

Often acting quietly behind the scenes, the Reeves have a reputation as the richest and most avaricious guild members. It is not a reputation they fight. They do fight anyone who tries to take their money away.

Yeoman (Freelancer)

Since the serfs seem to believe that almost anyone involved in trade is a guild member, a number of freemen have taken advantage of the fact. They may do any kind of work, they may work with the guilds, they may pretend to be full members, but really they are beholden to none.

Either choose a guild in the Character Histories that best fits, or use the Custom Creation method.

Note: Freelancers do not need to hold a Commission to begin play with guild skills. They are assumed to have picked them up while doing work for the League.

Imperial Guild Cohort

It is not only knights and priests to whom Emperor Alexius has extended his call for duty — he also summons guildsmembers to become Imperial Cohorts, to offer aid and assistance and be staunch helpmates to his Questing Knights.

In return for offering their skills and fealty, they reap the rewards of first claim on the merchant routes into newly explored territories. While this may make a guildsmember new enemies, it also brings new opportunities to one's guild.

Those guildsmembers wishing to become Cohorts should take the Cohort Tour of Duty (see Extra Stages in Character Histories, below).

Suggested Benefices: Cohort Badge (3 pts), Well-Traveled (5 pts)

Upbringing

Guildsmembers share the same upbringing as priests (see p. 9).

Apprenticeship

Note that nobles can join a guild at this stage, although it is considered scandalous; instead of choosing a noble apprenticeship, they choose the one appropriate to their guild and environment.

Academy

Each guild maintains a training academy where the most promising new members are enrolled.

Charioteers: *Characteristics* — Dexterity +2, Wits +1, Extrovert +2; *Skills* — Impress +1, Drive (primary specialty) 3, Drive (secondary specialty) 2, Mech Redemption 2, Remedy 1, Spacesuit 1; *Blessing* — Curious (+2 Extrovert when seeing something new); *Curse* — Nosy (-2 Calm when seeing something new)

Engineers: *Characteristics* — Dexterity +1, Wits +1, Tech +3; *Skills* — Inquiry +1, Read Urthtech 1, Tech Redemption (primary specialty) 3, Tech Redemption (secondary specialty) 1, Science (primary specialty) 2, Science (secondary specialty) 1, Think Machine 1; *Blessing* — Innovative (+2 Tech when trying to invent something new); *Curse* — Unnerving (-2 Extrovert when dealing with serfs)

Scravers: *Characteristics* — Strength +2, Perception +2, Ego +1; *Skills* — Impress +1, Combat skill (choose Fight, Melee or Shoot) +1, Sneak +1, Gambling 1, Inquiry 1, Knavery 1, Speak Scraver Cant (2 pts), Streetwise 2; *Blessing* — The Man (+2 Impress when

leading underlings); *Curse* — Possessive (-2 Calm when cut out of the action)

Muster: *Characteristics* — Strength +1, Dexterity +2, Tech +2; *Skills* — Combat skill (choose Fight or Melee) +1, Impress +1, Shoot +2, Drive (choose specialty) 2, Lore (people and places seen) 1, Mech Redemption 1, Remedy 1, Streetwise 1; *Blessing* — Bold (+2 Passion while acting when other hesitate); *Curse* — Callous (-2 Extrovert when asked for aid)

Reeves: *Characteristics* — Wits +2, Perception +2, Introvert +1; *Skills* — Impress +1, Academia 1, Art (Rhetoric) 1, Bureaucracy 1, Etiquette 1, Inquiry 1, Lore (Finance or Law) 1, Read Latin (2 pts), Social (Debate) 1; *Blessing* — Shrewd (+2 Wits against attempts to fast-talk); *Curse* — Mammon (-2 Faith when money involved)

Guildhall

Most guildsmembers and applicants get their training on the job, hanging out at the guild hall and petitioning higher-ranking members for jobs or training.

Charioteers: *Characteristics* — Dexterity +2, Wits +1, Extrovert +2; *Skills* — Impress +1, Drive (primary specialty) 2, Drive (secondary specialty) 1, Empathy 1, Lore (people and places seen) 1, Mech Redemption 1, Remedy 1, Speak (2 pts, local dialect); *Blessing* — Curious (+2 Extrovert when seeing something new); *Curse* — Nosy (-2 Calm when seeing something new)

Engineers: *Characteristics* — Dexterity +1, Wits +1, Tech +3; *Skills* — Shoot +1, Inquiry +1, Read Urthtech 1, Tech Redemption (primary specialty) 2, Tech Redemption (secondary specialty) 1, Science (primary specialty) 2, Science (secondary specialty) 1, Think

Machine 1; *Blessing* — Innovative (+2 Tech when trying to invent something new); *Curse* — Unnerving (-2 Extrovert when dealing with serfs)

Scravers: *Characteristics* — Strength +2, Perception +2, Ego +1; *Skills* — Impress +1, Dodge +1, Combat skill (choose Fight, Melee or Shoot) +1, Sneak +1, Gambling 1, Inquiry 1, Knavery 1, Speak Scraver Cant (2 pts), Streetwise 1; *Blessing* — Lucky at Cards (+2 Gambling when cheating); *Curse* — Possessive (-2 Calm when cut out of the action)

Muster: *Characteristics* — Strength +1, Dexterity +2, Tech +2; *Skills* — Combat skill (choose Fight or Melee) +1, Impress +1, Shoot +1, Drive (choose specialty) 1, Lore (people and places seen) 1, Mech Redemption 1, Remedy 1, Search 1, Streetwise 2; *Blessing* — Bold (+2 Passion while acting when other hesitate); *Curse* — Callous (-2 Extrovert when asked for aid)

Reeves: *Characteristics* — Wits +2, Perception +2, Introvert +1; *Skills* — Impress +1, Observe +1, Academia 1, Bureaucracy 1, Etiquette 1, Inquiry 1, Lore (Finance or Law) 1, Read Latin (2 pts), Social (Debate) 1; *Blessing* — Shrewd (+2 Wits against attempts to fast-talk); *Curse* — Mammon (-2 Faith when money involved)

The Streets

Those who don't have any luck in the academies or guildhalls get their training in the toughest school of all: hard knocks.

Charioteers: *Characteristics* — Dexterity +2, Wits +1, Extrovert +2; *Skills* — Impress +1, Drive (choose specialty) 2, Lore (people and places seen) 1, Knavery 1, Mech Redemption 1, Remedy 1, Speak (2 pts, local dialect), Streetwise 1; *Blessing* — Curious (+2 Extrovert when seeing something new); *Curse* — Nosy (-2 Calm

when seeing something new)

Engineers: *Characteristics* — Dexterity +2, Wits +1, Tech +2; *Skills* — Shoot +1, Inquiry +1, Read Urthtech (2 pts), Tech Redemption (choose specialty) 2, Science (choose specialty) 2, Streetwise 1, Think Machine 1; *Blessing* — Innovative (+2 Tech when trying to invent something new); *Curse* — Unnerving (-2 Extrovert when dealing with serfs)

Scravers: *Characteristics* — Strength +2, Dexterity +1, Perception +2; *Skills* — Impress or Sneak +1, Dodge +1, Combat skill (choose Fight, Melee or Shoot) +2, Gambling 1, Knavery 1, Speak Scraver Cant (2 pts), Streetwise 2; *Blessing* — Lucky at Cards (+2 Gambling when cheating); *Curse* — Possessive (-2 Calm when cut out of the action)

Muster: *Characteristics* — Strength +2, Dexterity +2, Tech +1, Combat skill (choose Fight or Melee) +1, Impress +1, Shoot +1, Drive (choose specialty) 1, Knavery 1, Remedy 1, Search 1, Streetwise 2, Tracking 1; *Blessing* — Bold (+2 Passion while acting when other hesitate); *Curse* — Callous (-2 Extrovert when asked for aid)

Reeves: *Characteristics* — Dexterity +1, Wits +2, Perception +2; *Skills* — Impress +1, Observe +1, Shoot +1, Sneak +1, Academia 1, Etiquette 1, Inquiry 1, Lore (Law) 1, Social (Debate) 1, Streetwise 1; *Blessing* — Shrewd (+2 Wits against attempts to fast-talk); *Curse* — Mammon (-2 Faith when money involved)

Early Career

The guildsmember is officially commissioned into the guild and gets his first job(s).

The Market

The character spends most of her time in marketplaces across the Known Worlds, learning the how to sell to rubes and royals alike.

Characteristics — Dexterity +1, Endurance +1, Wits +2, Perception +2, Extrovert +2, Passion or Calm +2; *Skills* — Charm or Impress +2, Combat skill (choose Fight, Melee or Shoot) +1, Observe +2, Gambling 1, Inquiry 2, Lore (Agora) 1, Speak (2 pts, dialect), Streetwise 1; *Benefice* — Rank (Associate)

Merchant: Sneak +1, Knavery 1, Streetwise 1

Money-Lender (usually a Reeve): Etiquette 1, Lore (Finance) 2

Starship Duty

The character's first jobs are aboard starships. While she gets to see many new places, most of her time is spent in cramped quarters for weeks on end. Still, the money's good.

Characteristics — Dexterity +2, Endurance +1, Wits +2, Perception +1, Tech +1, Extrovert or Introvert +2, Passion or Calm +1; *Skills* — Charm or Impress +1, Combat skill (choose Fight, Melee or Shoot) +2, Drive (Spacecraft) 1, Lore (people and places seen or jumproads) 1, Remedy 1, Science (Sensors) 1, Spacesuit, Tech Redemption (choose one) 1, Think Machine 1, Warfare (Gunnery) 1; *Benefice* — Rank (Associate)

Pilot (usually a Charioteer): Drive (Spacecraft) 2, Science (Sensors) 1

Engineer (usually an Engineer): Tech Redemption (Mech, Volt or High Tech) 2, Science (Engineering) 1

Gunner: Warfare (Gunnery) 2, Gambling 1

Mercenary

The character is a contract soldier. Usually only the Muster guild fields these fighters, but the occasional Scraver bully-boy has been known to hire himself out for war, and the Engineers occasionally provide combat engineers to high bidders.

Soldier: *Characteristics* — Strength +2, Dexterity +3, Endurance +2, Tech +1, Passion or Calm +2; *Skills* — Dodge +1, Fight +2, Impress +1, Melee +2, Shoot +3, Vigor +1, Drive (choose specialty) 1, Mech Redemption 1, Remedy 1, Survival 1, Tracking 1; *Benefice* — Rank (Associate)

Combat Engineer: *Characteristics* — Strength +1, Dexterity +2, Endurance +2, Wits +1, Perception +1, Tech +2, Passion or Calm +1; *Skills* — Combat skill (choose Fight or Melee) +1, Observe +1, Shoot +2, Drive (choose specialty) 2, Remedy 1, Tech Redemption (choose primary) 3, Tech Redemption (choose secondary) 2, Science (Engineering) 1, Warfare (Artillery) 1, Warfare (Demolitions) 1; *Benefice* — Rank (Associate)

Scholar/Scientist

While many nobles seeking scholars and learned men for their entourages turn to the Church, some know that the guilds also produce erudite candidates — in matters of finance or law, there is none better than a Reeve, and few travel guides outside the Charioteers really know what they're talking about. The Engineers, or course, are the only ones to turn to on matters of science.

Scholar: *Characteristics* — Wits +2, Perception +2, Tech +1, Extrovert +2, Introvert +2, Passion or Calm +1; *Skills* — Charm or Impress +1, Observe +1, Academia 1, Etiquette 1, Focus 1, Inquiry 1, Lore or Science (choose a primary topic) 3, Lore or Science (choose a secondary topic) 2, Read Urthish (2 pts), Social (Debate) 1, Think Machine 1; *Benefice* — Rank (Associate)

Scientist: *Characteristics* — Wits +2, Perception +2, Tech +2, Introvert +2, Passion or Calm +1, Faith or Ego +1; *Skills* — Academia 1, Focus 1, Inquiry 1, Lore or Science (choose a primary topic) 3, Lore or Science (choose a secondary topic) 2, Read Urthtech (2 pts), Tech Redemption (choose primary) 3, Tech Redemption (choose secondary) 2, Think Machine 1; *Benefice* — Rank (Associate)

Seedy/Illegal Activities

And then there are the other jobs — those best left unmentioned on one's resume. But don't worry: the best rise to the top of their profession and word gets out to the right people.

Characteristics — Strength +2, Dexterity +2, Endurance +2, Perception +2; *Skills* — Combat skill (choose Fight, Melee or Shoot) +2, Dodge +1, Gambling 1, Inquiry 1, Knavery 2, Lore (local underworld) 1, Streetwise 2; *Benefice* — Rank (Associate)

Thief: *Characteristics* — Passion or Calm +2; *Skills* — Impress +1, Observe +1, Sneak +1, Sleight of Hand 2

Spy: *Characteristics* — Extrovert or Introvert +2; *Skills* — Charm or Impress +2, Observe +2, Sneak +1

Tours of Duty

Once a character gets her rank pins, she seeks her next job, something to polish the skills before cutting out on her own. Or she can seek duty as a Cohort to the Emperor's Questing Knights. See Extra Stages, below.

Those Who Differ: Aliens

There are many sentient alien races in the Known Worlds, but less than a handful have any political power. Three races are strong or numerous enough to have a degree of freedom on their own homeworlds — within limits, of course, for each of these races' homeworlds is owned by one of the royal houses or the League. Enclaves of their original cultures exist on their homeworlds, but most of these aliens live in a human-run universe. Any of them can hold a Commission in the League or Rank in their own noble caste.

Other alien races are detailed in other **Fading Suns** supplements. The gamemaster and players should feel free to create their own alien races and character roles.

Building Alien Characters: A players must spend some of her Extra points on special powers and abilities unique to the character's race — she must pay for a royal Vorox's extra limbs and poison claw. The minimum costs for buying an alien character are listed below. Suggested traits can be found in the Character Histories for each race.

Ur-Obun

The spiritual Ur-Obun are sought out as third party diplomats and peacemakers. Unlike their aggressive brothers, the Ukari, Obun culture values learning and philosophy over all other pursuits, and Obun have a knack at answering questions which have long plagued others. An Obun may be Ordained in the Obun sect of the Church (Voavenlohjun).

Upbringing

Most Obun are raised on their homeworld (Velisamil), but some may come from colonies on other (usually cosmopolitan) worlds.

Characteristics — Strength (max 9), Dexterity (base 4) +1, Endurance (max 9), Wits +1, Extrovert or Introvert +1, Calm +1, Faith +1, Psi or Theurgy 1; *Skills* — Empathy 1, Etiquette 1, Focus or Stoic Mind 1, Speak Obunish, Speak Urthish (2 pts); *Blessing* — Just (+2 Passion when righting a wrong); *Curse* — Condescending (-2 Extrovert among the unenlightened)

Apprenticeship

Obun can instead choose to join a guild or human sect for their Apprenticeship and Early Career stages (especially true of off-world Obun).

Umo'rin Counselor: *Characteristics* — Wits +2, Perception +1, Extrovert or Introvert +2; *Skills* — Charm +2, Observe +1, Empathy 1, Etiquette 1, Focus or Stoic Mind 1, Inquiry 1, Lore (choose topic) 1, Social (Debate or Oratory) 2

Voavenlohjun Priest: *Characteristics* — Wits +2, Introvert +1, Faith +2; *Skills* — Charm +1, Observe +1, Academia 1, Alchemy 1, Focus 2, Lore (Metaphysics) 1, Remedy 1, Stoic Mind 2

Vhem-saahen Champion: *Characteristics* — Strength +1, Dexterity +2, Endurance +1, Passion or Calm +1; *Skills* — Combat skill (choose Fight or Melee) +2, Shoot +2, Vigor +1

Early Career

Umo'rin Counselor: *Characteristics* — Dexterity +1, Wits +2, Perception +1, Extrovert or Introvert +2, Passion or Calm +2, Faith +2; *Skills* — Charm +2, Observe +1, Empathy 1, Etiquette 1, Focus or Stoic Mind 2, Inquiry 2, Lore (choose topic) 2, Social (Debate or Oratory) 2, Read Obunish or Urthish (2 pts); *Benefice* — Rank (Federate)

Voavenlohjun Priest: *Characteristics* — Dexterity +1, Wits +2, Perception +1, Introvert +2, Passion or Calm +2, Faith +2; *Skills* — Charm or Observe +1, Academia or Alchemy 1, Empathy 1, Focus 3, Inquiry 1, Lore (Metaphysics) 1, Physick 1, Remedy 2, Read Obunish (2 pts), Stoic Mind 2; *Benefice* — Rank (Novitiate)

Vhem-saahen Champion: *Characteristics* — Strength +2, Dexterity +2, Endurance +2, Wits +1, Perception +1, Passion or Calm +2; *Skills* — Combat skill (choose Fight or Melee) +2, Shoot +2, Vigor +1, Focus or Stoic Mind 2, Remedy 2; *Benefice* — Ally (3 pts)

Choose one of the following:

Martial Arts: Martial Fist, Martial Kick, Martial Hold

Fencing: Parry, Thrust, Slash

Tours of Duty

Ur-Obun have these modified tours of duty (see Extra Stages, below):

- Their first Tour gives them only 12 pts for skills. (If an Obun wishes to become an Imperial Cohort, he gains only 9 pts for skills.)

- If the character purchases the Natal Psi Psychic Awakening history, he adds the Psi 3 to his current rating.

- If the character purchases the Neophyte Theurgic Calling history, he adds the Theurgy 3 to his current rating.

Ur-Ukar

Cousins to the peaceful Ur-Obun, the Ukari are bitter, violent criminals — or so most Known Worlders believe. They have suffered great oppression, due in part to their war with humanity upon the two races' first contact. The bitter Ur-Ukar fight in internecine clan wars in the subterranean caves of their homeworld. Traditionally-raised Ukari rarely even see light until age three or five. They are thus at home in dark, cramped spaces. Those who escape such blood conflicts by going off-world often hire themselves out as assassins or mercenaries. Their subterranean origins give them an edge in nocturnal activities.

Upbringing

Characteristics — Strength (max 9) +1, Dexterity (base 4) +1, Endurance (max 9), Perception +2, Passion or Calm +1, Tech (base 4), Psi 1, Urge 1; *Skills* — Fight +1, Sneak +1, Knavery 1, Speak Urthish (2 pts), Speak Ukarish, Survival 1; *Blessing* — Sensitive Touch (+2 Perception to discern touched objects); *Curse* — Bitter (-2 Calm when dealing with humans), Ostracism (mild)

Apprenticeship

Many Ukari join a guild instead of learning the traditional clan careers.

Chieftain: *Characteristics* — Dexterity +1, Wits +1, Perception +1, Extrovert +1, Passion or Calm +1; *Skills* — Dodge +1, Combat skill (choose Fight or Melee) +2, Impress +1, Shoot +1, Knavery 2, Lore (Poisons) 1, Stoic Mind 1, Survival 1

Warrior/Outlaw: *Characteristics* — Strength +1, Dexterity +2, Endurance +1, Passion or Calm +1; *Skills* — Dodge +1, Combat skill (choose Fight or Melee) +2, Impress +1, Shoot +1, Knavery 2, Lore (Poisons) 1, Stoic Mind 1, Survival 1

Early Career

Chieftain: *Characteristics* — Strength +1, Dexterity +1, Endurance +1, Wits +1, Perception +1, Extrovert +2, Passion or Calm +2, Faith or Ego +1; *Skills* — Dodge +1, Combat skill (choose Fight or Melee) +2, Impress +1, Shoot +1, Knavery 1, Lore (Poisons) 1, Stoic Mind 1, Survival 1; *Benefice* — Rank (Quan)

Choose one of the following:

Jox Kai Von Boxing: Martial Fist, Martial Kick, Martial Hold
Kraxi Knife Fencing: Parry, Thrust, Slash

Warrior/Outlaw: *Characteristics* — Strength +2, Dexterity +1, Endurance +2, Perception +1, Extrovert or Introvert +1, Passion or Calm +2, Faith or Ego +1; *Skills* — Dodge +1, Combat skill (choose Fight or Melee) +2, Impress +1, Shoot +1, Knavery 1, Lore (Poisons) 1, Stoic Mind 1, Survival 1; *Benefice* — Family Ties (3 pts)

Choose one of the following:

Jox Kai Von Boxing: Martial Fist, Martial Kick, Martial Hold
Kraxi Knife Fencing: Parry, Thrust, Slash

Tours of Duty

Ur-Ukar have these modified tours of duty (see Extra Stages, below):

- If the character purchases the Natal Psi Psychic Awakening history, he adds Psi 3 to his current rating.
- Ur-Ukar can become Imperial Cohorts if they desire.

Vorox

These multi-limbed monstrosities are highly valued as shock troops or guerrilla warriors. Only "civilized" Vorox are allowed to leave their homeworld, for the "feral" kind are too unruly and dangerous. But most Known Worlders are hard-pressed to tell the difference between the two. Civilized Vorox have their poisonous claws removed to prove their commitment to civilization. Noble Vorox are allowed to keep one claw as a sign of their rank.

Upbringing

Chieftain: *Characteristics* — Strength (base 4, max 12) +1, Dexterity +2, Endurance (base 4, max 12) +1, Wits (base 2) +1, Tech (base 1), Passion (always primary); *Skills* — Impress +1, Fight +1, Vigor +1, Speak Urthish (2 pts), Speak Vorox (2 pts), Survival 1, Tracking 1; *Blessings* — Predatory (+2 Perception, -2 Calm when hungry), Giant (+2 Vitality, base 14 meters run), Sensitive Smell (+1 Perception to discern scents); *Curse* — Uncouth (-2 Extrovert in

social situations); *Benefices* — Bite (Dx+Fight, Init -1, 3d DMG), Extra Limbs (total of six limbs usable as arms or legs), Poison Claw (6 pts: Dx + Fight, DMG 3. Vorox poison is a slow-acting paralytic. If the claw inflicts damage, the target is poisoned and suffers a cumulative -1 penalty per turn on all physical actions; when a number of turns equal to the target's Vitality rating is reached, the target is unable to take any physical actions for the rest of the span); *Afflictions* — Ostracized (mild), No Occult (Cannot awaken Psi or Theurgy)

Warrior: *Characteristics* — Strength (base 4, max 12) +1, Dexterity +2, Endurance (base 4, max 12) +1, Wits (base 2), Tech (base 1), Passion (always primary) +1; *Skills* — Dodge +1, Fight +2, Melee +2, Observe +1, Sneak +1, Vigor +1, Remedy 1, Speak Vorox (2 pts), Survival 2, Tracking 2; *Blessings* — Predatory (+2 Perception, -2 Calm when hungry), Giant (+2 Vitality, base 14 meters run), Sensitive Smell (+1 Perception to discern scents); *Curse* — Uncouth (-2 Extrovert in social situations); *Benefices* — Bite (Dx+Fight, Init -1, 3d DMG), Extra Limbs (total of six limbs usable as arms or legs); *Afflictions* — Ostracized (mild), No Occult (Cannot awaken Psi or Theurgy)

Apprenticeship

At this stage, the Vorox is usually "civilized" by humans so that she can move through society in an acceptable manner. Vorox can choose to join a guild instead.

Characteristics — Strength +1, Dexterity +1, Endurance +1, Perception +1, Passion +1; *Skills* — Dodge +1, Fight +2, Impress +1, Melee +1, Observe +1, Sneak +1, Vigor +1, Survival 1, Tracking 1

Early Career

Chieftain: *Characteristics* — Strength +1, Dexterity +1, Endurance +1, Wits +1, Perception +2, Extrovert or Introvert +1, Passion +2, Faith or Ego +1; *Skills* — Dodge +1, Fight +1, Melee +1, Observe +1, Shoot +1, Vigor +1, Tracking 1; *Benefice* — Rank (Knight)

Graa (Vorox Martial Arts): Banga (charge), Drox (Second Hand)

Warrior: *Characteristics* — Strength +1, Dexterity +1, Endurance +1, Wits +1, Perception +2, Extrovert or Introvert +1, Passion +2, Faith or Ego +1; *Skills* — Dodge +1, Fight +1, Melee +1, Observe +1, Shoot +1, Vigor +1, Tracking 1; *Benefice* — Family Ties (3 pts)

Graa (Vorox Martial Arts): Banga (charge), Drox (Second Hand)

Tours of Duty

Vorox can take only ONE additional tour of duty — either the first Tour of Duty, the Imperial Cohort Tour of Duty or the Cybernetic Enhancements; they cannot awaken Psi or Theurgy. Vorox Chieftains can become Questing Knights by taking the Questing Knight Tour of Duty.

Extra Stages

The character can continue his previous career or begin a new one, learn occult powers or implant cybernetic devices in his body. A character may take TWO of the following options. (Exception: Characters who take the Loaded-for-Bear cybernetics can take only that option.) For instance, a noble could continue his career as a military commander (he takes a Tour of Duty) and awaken his psychic powers (he takes Natal Psi) — or he could spend all his time with his career (he takes a Tour of Duty and Another Tour of Duty).

Tour of Duty

Characteristic (choose one) +1, Characteristic (choose another) +1, Skills (choose new ones or add to existing skills) +14

Worldly Benefits

Choose one of the following:

Promotion and rewards: Rise in rank one level, choose Well-Off Riches or Cash (1000 firebirds)

High promotion: Rise in rank two levels, Good Riches or Cash (600 firebirds)

Rich rewards: Wealthy Riches or Cash (2000 firebirds)

Friends: Cash (100 firebirds), choose 6 pts from Ally, Contact, Gossip Network, Retinue, Passage Contract, or Refuge

Promotion and friends: Rise in rank one level, Cash (100 firebirds), and choose 4 pts from Ally, Contact, Gossip Network, Retinue, Passage Contract, or Refuge

Another Tour of Duty

(Must first buy Tour of Duty)

Characteristic (choose one) +1, Characteristic (choose another) +1, Skills (choose new ones or add to existing skills) +10

More Worldly Benefits

Choose one of the following:

Promotion and rewards: Rise in rank one level and gain more Riches or Cash (rise one level)

High promotion: Rise in rank two levels

Rich rewards: Gain more Riches or Cash (rise two levels)

Friends: Choose 4 pts from Ally, Contact, Gossip Network, Retinue, Passage Contract, or Refuge

Imperial Tours

Nobles, priests and guildsmembers can swear fealty to Emperor Alexius and serve a tour of duty in the elite Company of the Phoenix. Nobles become Questing Knights while priests and guildsmembers become Cohorts.

Characters who purchase an occult or cybernetic history can take the Imperial Tour of Duty as their second option. Other characters must take the Imperial Tour in lieu of the standard Tour of Duty; Another Tour of Duty can be taken as their second option, and is considered to be an extension of Imperial service.

Questing Knight Tour of Duty

All bonuses are the same as the standard Tour of Duty, except that the character has only 10 pts for skills. The character does gain an Imperial Charter (see Benefices).

Cohort Tour of Duty

All bonuses are the same as the standard Tour of Duty, except that the character has only 11 pts for skills. The character does gain a Cohort Badge (see Benefices).

Occult Powers

While it is theoretically possible for a character to possess both Psi and Theurgy, it is rare and not condoned by the Church. Beginning characters can purchase either Psi or Theurgy, but not both.

Psychic Awakening

Characters from any faction (except Vorox) can be psychics.

Natal Psi: Psi 3, Wyrd +2, Choose a primary path: Level 1, Level 2, Level 3 powers, +1 skill related to a Psi power

Savant Psi (must first buy Natal Psi): Psi +2, Wyrd +1, Primary path powers: Level 4, Level 5, choose a secondary path: Level 1, Level 2, choose one Worldly Benefit from the regular Tour of Duty

Theurgic Calling

Neophyte Theurge: Theurgy 3 (9 pts), Wyrd +2 (4 pts), Rites: Level 1 (1 pt) Level 2 (2 pts), Level 3 (3 pts), +1 skill related to a rite (1 pt)

Adept Theurge (must first buy Neophyte Theurge): Theurgy +2 (6 pts), Wyrd +1 (2 pts), Rites: Level 4 (4 pts), Level 5 (5 pts), Additional rites: two rites (Level 1 & Level 2) or one Level 3 rite (3 pts), choose one Worldly Benefit from the regular Tour of Duty

Cybernetics

Some people like machines so much they put them in their bodies — a level of intimacy abhorrent to the Church. Nonetheless, people keep doing it, especially if they have noble house or guild membership to keep the Inquisition away.

Tweaked

Spend 20 Extras pts on cybernetic devices or associated characteristics (cost: 3 pts per +1) and/or skills (cost: 1 pt per +1). See Chapter Seven: Technology for a list of devices.

Character History Points

For the curious, here's how character points and Extras were spent using the Character Histories method:

Upbringing (5 pts on characteristics, 5 pts on skills), Apprenticeship (5 pts on characteristics, 10 pts on skills), Early Career (10 pts on characteristics, 15 pts on skills)

Extra points are spent during the extra stages: Tour of Duty (two stages, 20 pts per tour), Psychic Awakening (two stages, 20 pts per stage), Theurgic Calling (two stages, 20 pts per stage), Cybernetic Enhancement (two options: 20 pts stage or 40 pts stage).

The base 10 pts of Benefices were spent on rank at the end of the Early Career stage and the rest were spent on Worldly Benefits during the Extra Stages.

Some exception were made: Vorox spend many of their Extra points during their Upbringing (those beefed up traits are expensive!), allowing them to take only one other Extra Stage instead of two.

Loaded-for-Bear

Note: A character who purchases this option can take no other Extra Stages! Spend 40 Extras pts on cybernetic devices or associated characteristics (cost: 3 pts per +1) and/or skills (cost: 1 pt per +1). See Chapter Seven: Technology for a list of devices. Also choose one Worldly Benefit from the regular Tour of Duty.

Final Touches

Now the player can purchase Curses and Afflictions if he desires, and spend the Extra points they provide. He should also review his Spirit characteristics and declare which of them are primary (see the Spirit Characteristics sidebar) and underline the primary traits on the character sheet. Finally, he should determine his Vitality rating (5 + Endurance) and his Wyrd points (see Wyrd in Chapter Four: Traits).

The character is now ready to enter the tumultuous palaces, bazaars and wilds of the Known Worlds.

Custom Creation

For those who prefer a more detailed and unique touch, there is the Custom Creation method of character building. Players spend points between characteristics, skills and Benefices, using the lists given in Chapter Four: Traits.

Character Points and Extras

Characters are built with a variable number of character points: points that can be spent to buy ratings in various traits. Three categories of traits — characteristics, skills and Benefices — have a fixed number of character points assigned to them; these points can be spent (usually on a 1-for-1 basis) to purchase trait rating increases in the appropriate category.

Additionally, all characters receive 40 Extra points, which can be spent to purchase further trait increases, to buy new traits, or to purchase previously unattainable traits (blessings and occult powers). Unlike assigned points, Extra points are not always spent on a 1-for-1 basis; it costs more Extra points to increase a characteristic than to buy a new skill, for example.

Step One: Formulate Character Concept

Character creation begins by coming up with a character concept, as described above. When selecting a concept, try to come up with something that is interesting, fun, and different from the other players' characters. At the same time, however, choose a concept that can work well with the other characters and within the framework of the gamemaster's setting. A scuzzy space pirate won't fit in very well with a group whose members are all nobles, politicians and courtiers.

Once a character's concept is chosen, you can begin filling out the character sheet. Choose the character's name, race, gender and age. Also, what planet is she from? What is her social class? All characters in **Fading Suns** are assumed to be freemen unless the player chooses otherwise: Benefices allow the character to be serf (worth Extra points) or a noble (this costs points). Finally — and very important — what is her chief alliance? Is she a member of House Hazat, a Muster mercenary, or a priest of the Eskatonic Order? Step Two will help determine a character's alliance.

Step Two: Select Character Role

Once a concept has been established, the player picks one of the 26 character roles most suitable to that concept. Note that a character does not have to choose a compatible character role; great roleplaying opportunities can be had by choosing a role whose stereotypical characteristics are at odds with the character concept and personality. A humble Hawkwood noble or compassionate Muster slaver, for example, can provide unique roleplaying experiences.

Character roles are presented throughout the Character Histories section, with some additional custom roles (Barbarian Outworlders) in the nearby sidebar.

Step Three: Select Characteristics

Characteristics are the innate qualities of a character, the hereditary or otherwise deep-rooted aspects defining the character. Like most traits, characteristics range from 1 to 10, with 1 indicating an extreme deficiency and 10 indicating human perfection.

There are three types of characteristics: Body (physical characteristics), Mind (mental characteristics) and Spirit (psychological and emotional characteristics). Characters may also have occult characteristics, traits relating to a character's interaction with extradimensional forces, but these are bought later in the character creation process. Player characters' Body and Mind characteristics start at a base rating of 3 (invalids or morons are incapable of surviving the travails of the **Fading Suns** universe).

Spirit characteristics are broken into four "trait pairs": Extrovert vs. Introvert, Passion vs. Calm, and Faith vs. Ego. These traits quantify aspects of a character's personality, and are also important when practicing magic and psionics. Each trait in a pair opposes its counterpart. Within each pair, the player selects one trait of the pair to be primary; this trait begins at 3. The opposed trait begins at 1, with the exception of the Other trait. This trait is always secondary and begins at 1 (it represents things normally incomprehensible to the untrained human mind).

A beginning character may not raise a characteristic above 8 (such perfection requires not only innate ability, but also tempering in the fires of experience). The one exception to this rule is a Vorox's Body characteristics, which can be raised to 10 (only experience points, however, can raise them above this).

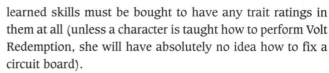

Spirit Characteristics

Unlike other traits, Spirit characteristics represent aspects of personality and are thus a little trickier to rate than, say, Dexterity. The traits are opposed traits, representing polar aspects of a character's psyche, and thus each Spirit trait counterbalances its opposed trait. Most characters will have a higher rating in one characteristic of a pair than in its opposite. The trait with the highest rating is considered primary; the lesser trait is secondary. (Primary characteristics begin with a rating of 3, while secondary characteristics begin at 1. Underline the primary characteristic on the character sheet.)

On the one hand, it is entirely possible to have characters with reasonably strong (or very weak) ratings in both traits of an opposed Spirit pair. For example, a character can be gregarious and friendly (a high Extrovert score), yet still be self-aware (a moderately high Introvert score). Less happily, a character can be neurotic and twitchy (low Calm rating), yet depressive and weak-willed (low Passion score). It is thus possible to raise the primary Spirit trait, the secondary Spirit trait, or both. In fact, a player can raise a character's secondary Spirit trait to a level equal to his primary Spirit trait, representing a balanced character whose "yin and yang are in harmony."

However, the traits are still opposed, and thus one cannot have extremely high levels in both traits. Thus, while Spirit characteristics are rated from 1 to 10 just like other traits, a rating in one lessens the maximum rating of the opposed characteristic. So a character with a Passion rating of 7 can have a Calm rating of no more than 3 (such a zealous character finds it difficult to control her inner fervor no matter what). The same is true for Extrovert vs. Introvert, and Faith vs. Ego.

Take note — even if both traits are equal, the initially chosen primary characteristic is still considered primary and should remain underlined. This distinction becomes important in certain types of psychic combat.

Players receive 20 points to divide among their characteristics. Characteristics are fully described in Chapter Four: Traits.

Step Four: Select Skills

Skills are instinctive and learned aptitudes that characters possess. There are two kinds of skills: natural and learned. Natural skills begin at a base rating of 3 (all characters have some rudimentary ability to fight or sneak), while learned skills must be bought to have any trait ratings in them at all (unless a character is taught how to perform Volt Redemption, she will have absolutely no idea how to fix a circuit board).

Skills are bought as characteristics are. Certain skills are available only to guild professions — the Merchant League has a monopoly on certain high-tech oriented skills (one must belong to a guild or have a guild contract to learn guild skills; see the Guild Contract Benefice).

Players receive 30 points to divide among desired skills. Skills are fully described in Chapter Four: Traits.

Step Five: Select Benefices

Players may now purchase Benefices, those elements defining their birthrights, monies or other societal advantages. Benefices cost a variable amount depending on how much of the benefice a player wants: A character who is filthy rich must spend more Benefice points than someone who only has a small nest egg.

Benefices, more than any other traits, define the character's relationship to the rest of **Fading Suns** society. The player should thus carefully consider her character's concept when choosing benefices.

Characters may also choose Afflictions: negative Benefices. Afflictions are social handicaps (enemies, ostracism, etc.) that actually provide additional Extra points during Step Six of this process.

Players receive 10 points to divide among desired Benefices. Benefices are fully described in Chapter Four: Traits.

Step Six: Spend Extra Points

Now the players receive 40 Extra points to spend as they choose. Extra points are the only way to buy blessings, occult characteristics or powers. The Extra Point Costs chart delineates the cost to purchase new or additional levels in the various trait ratings.

Extra Point Costs

Trait	Cost (to raise by 1)
Characteristic	3
(Body, Mind, Spirit, Occult)	
Wyrd	2
Skill	1
Benefice	1
Blessing	1
Combat Action	1 per level
Occult Power	1 per level

Curses and Afflictions provide additional Extra points.

Learned Skills

Academia	Cybernetics
Acrobatics	Engineering
Alchemy	Genetics
Archery	Geology
Artisan	Meteorology
Arts	Physics
Beast Lore	Terraforming
Bureaucracy	Xeno-Biology
Combat Actions	Search
Fencing	Sleight of Hand
Martial Arts	Social
Crossbow	Acting
Disguise	Debate
Drive	Leadership
Aircraft	Oratory
Beastcraft	Spacesuit (Guild skill)
Landcraft	Speak
Spacecraft (Guild skill)	Barbarian
Watercraft	Graceful Tongue
Empathy	(al-Malik skill)
Etiquette	Dialects
Focus	Latin
Gambling	Scraver Cant
Inquiry	(Scraver skill)
Knavery	Urthish
Lockpicking	Xeno
Lore	Stoic Body
Folk	Stoic Mind
Jumproads	Streetwise
Object	Survival
Regional	Tech Redemption
Xeno	(Guild skill)
Performance	Craft Redemption
Physick	High-Tech Redemption
Read	Mech Redemption
Barbarian	Volt Redemption
Latin	Think Machine (Guild
Urthish	skill)
Urthtech	Throwing
Xeno	Torture
Remedy	Tracking
Ride	Warfare
Science (Guild skill)	Artillery
Anthropology	Demolitions
Archaeology	Gunnery
Astronomy	Military Tactics
Biology	Xeno-Empathy
Chemistry	

Building Alien Characters

A player must spend some of her Extra points on special powers and abilities unique to the character's race — she must pay for a royal Vorox's extra limbs and poison claw. The minimum costs for buying an alien character are listed below. Suggested traits can be found in the Character Histories for each race.

Ur-Obun

Cost: Ur-Obun characters cost two Extras points to play.

Characteristics: Dexterity (base 4; 3 pts), Strength and Endurance (maximum 9; +4 pts), Psi (base 1; 3 pts) or Theurgy (base 1; 3 pts)

Learned Skills: All Obun gain Speak Obunish for free. However, they must spend points to learn Speak Urthish.

Blessings/Curses: Just (2 pts: +2 Passion when righting a wrong), Condescending (+2 pts: -2 Extrovert among the unenlightened),

Suggested Benefices: Refuge (4 pts, any Obun consulate)

Ur-Ukar

Cost: None

Characteristics: Dexterity (base 4; 3 pts), Strength and Endurance (maximum 9; +4 pts), Tech (base 4; 3 pts), Psi (base 1; 3 pts) and Urge (base 1; +3 pts)

Learned Skills: All Ukari gain Speak Ukarish for free. However, they must spend points to learn Speak Urthish.

Blessings/Curses: Sensitive Touch (2 pts: +2 Perception to discern touched objects), Bitter (+2 pts: -2 Calm when dealing with humans)

Affliction: Ostracized (moderate, +2 pts)

Suggested Benefices: Family Ties (3 pts)

Vorox

Cost: 10 Extras points (16 pts for a royal Vorox with poison claw)

Characteristics: Strength and Endurance (base 4, max 12; 10 pts), Wits (base 2; +2 pts), Tech (base 1; +4 pts), Passion (always primary)

Learned Skills: All Vorox gain Speak Voroxish for free. However, they must spend points to learn Speak Urthish.

Racial Traits: Every Vorox character must purchase these racial traits (Blessings and Curses do not count against the total allowed a character).

Blessings: Predatory (0 pts: +2 Perception, -2 Calm when hungry), Giant (5 pts: +2 Vitality, base run: 14 meters, requires Vorox tailored clothing), Sensitive Smell (1 pt: +1 Perception with smell only)

Members of the royal caste may purchase: Poison Claw (6 pts: Dx + Fight, DMG 3. Vorox poison is a slow-acting paralytic. If the claw inflicts damage, the target is poisoned and suffers a cumulative -1 penalty per turn on all physical actions; when a number of turns equal to the target's Vital-

ity rating is reached, the target is unable to take any physical actions for the rest of the span)

Curses: Uncouth (+2 pts: -2 Extrovert in social situations)

Benefices: Bite (3 pts: Dx + Fight, Init -1, DMG 3), Extra Limbs (6 pts: total of six limbs usable as arms or legs)

Afflictions: No Occult (+6 pts: Cannot awaken Psi or Theurgy), Ostracized (mild affliction; +1 pt)

Suggested Benefices: Family Ties (3 pts)

Barbarian Outworlders

Many barbarians from planets outside the Known Worlds come to the empire seeking a new life, allies against rivals at home, secrets, or simply to assuage their wanderlust. Some are escaped prisoners of war from one of the border conflicts.

Kurgan

Barbarians from the Kurga Caliphate are actually quite polite and mannered. Their ways may differ enough to spook a peasant, but they are intelligent and learned, preserving many things from Second Republic culture that was lost to the Known Worlds after the Fall.

Kurgans are best created with the Custom Creation method. Suggested traits are listed below.

Characteristics: Extrovert, Calm

Natural Skills: Charm, Melee, Shoot

Learned Skills: Fencing Actions, Speak and Read Kurgan, Speak Urthish

Blessings/Curses: Gracious (2 pts: + 2 Extrovert to guests), Haughty (+2 pts: -2 Extrovert around serfs)

Suggested Afflictions: Barbarian (+2 pts)

Vuldrok

The Vuldrok Raiders actually live up to the stereotype of the barbarian held by most peasants — they are rude and brutal in their behavior. Used to taking what they want by might, they rarely heed rules of social propriety and tend to get very miffed when reminded of them.

Kurgans are best created with the Custom Creation method. Suggested traits are listed below.

Characteristics: Strength or Endurance, Tech (2)

Natural Skills: Melee, Shoot, Vigor

Learned Skills: Fencing Actions, Speak Vuldrok and Urthish

Blessings/Curses: Bold (2 pts: +2 Passion while acting when others hesitate), Uncouth (+2 pts: -2 Extrovert at society functions)

Suggested Afflictions: Barbarian (+2 pts)

Example of Character Creation

Susan sits down with the **Fading Suns** rulebook in preparation for making a character for next evening's game. Although she is intrigued by the thought of playing an alien, Susan is a devotee of Japanese anime and decides she wants to play someone similar to a gritty manga heroine. Susan wants her character to be sleek, slick and deadly.

Her character, Susan decides, will be the youngest scion of a noble house: trained in the nuances of war and court, but footloose and adventurous. She sees her character as starting near the bottom rung of her noble house and ruthlessly clawing her way up the power structure. At this point, Susan decides the character will be female; most of the other characters in her player group are male, and she sees the potential for some amusing roleplaying.

After skimming the character roles, Susan quickly decides on the Decados noble role; the Decados' ruthless, Machiavellian ways complement her character's nature perfectly. She pencils in "Decados" in the "Alliance" space on the character sheet.

But Susan realizes her character is not content to play the power games within the Decados structure. Her character is a traveler, one who will span the galaxy and make all sorts of interesting allies (pawns?) in pursuit of her goals.

Perhaps, Susan muses, her character was on the losing side of an internecine struggle and was forced into exile. Yes… the more Susan thinks about it, the more she decides that her character really doesn't like her family so much. Her childhood was plagued by unloving parents and cutthroat competition among her siblings, cousins and other relatives.

At this point Susan comes up with a name: Lucretia. It seems appropriate, since it apparently sprang from both the historical Lucretia Borgia and an old Sisters of Mercy song — both of which, Susan feels, are apt influences for her character's personality.

Looking at the map of the Known Worlds, Susan decides that Lucretia is from Severus, the Decados homeworld. Severus is a hotbed of political activity, as nobles step over each other trying to curry favor from the most powerful families. In such a backstabbing environment, it is no wonder the headstrong Lucretia finds it hard to compete. Success on Severus depends not only on personal ability but on personal ties and rank — an ambitious Decados must lick the boots of her superior but be willing to betray that superior should he fall from favor. Lucretia can't wait to get away from Severus — but dreams of the day when she will return with more power than those who kicked her around.

Character History Method

Assuming Susan wants to build her character the quick and easy way, she can choose the Character Histories method. She knows her character is a scion of House Decados, so she looks at the Upbringing options for that house: she decides that Lucretia was raised at High-Court, in the ducal palace on Severus in fact — the highest court on the planet. There, she encountered many of the political allies and rivals she is sure to meet again as she claws her way to the top of her house's pecking order. Susan pencils in the characteristic and skill bonuses on her character sheet — since she may be adding to those traits in later stages, it's best to use a pencil rather than a pen.

Next, she reviews Lucretia's Apprenticeship options and choose Diplomacy/Intrigue. She writes those traits down on the character sheet. For her Early Career, she decides that Lucretia's independent attitude — due perhaps to an enforced social or political exile — is best summed up by the Questing option. She spends a few moments writing these traits down and choosing from the options given. She chooses: Dexterity +2, Strength and Endurance +1 each, Wits +2, Perception +1, Extrovert +2, Passion +1, Charm +1, Dodge +1, Combat skill (Melee) +3, Observe +1, Sneak +1, Vigor +1, Drive (Aircraft) 1, Knavery 1, Lore (people and places seen) 1, Remedy 1, Speak Severus dialect, Streetwise 1, Rank (Knight).

Susan can now polish her character with a Tour of Duty. She chooses: Dexterity +1, Perception +1, Melee +2, Shoot +1, Sneak +1, Fencing Actions (Parry, Thrust, Slash), Knavery +3, Torture 1, Promotion & Rewards (rise in rank to Baronet, 1000 firebirds Cash).

Instead of a second tour, she decides that Lucretia's latent psychic potential has been realized, and she purchases the Natal Psi option. She choose Psyche as Lucretia's path, and Intuit, Emote and MindSight for her powers. She also buys Empathy 1, to aid her with her psychic intuition.

For her occult Stigma, she declares that Lucretia's eyes are nearly colorless — an eerie effect. Susan thinks this will cause Lucretia to seem distant and cold to others. If the eyes are the windows of the soul, then hers surely look upon strange vistas. Susan decides that Lucretia will wear dark glasses when in public.

For the final touches, Susan also takes three points of Afflictions: Black Sheep at 1 (Lucretia doesn't get on so well with the family) and Vendetta at 2 (in fact, someone in her family wants to duel her). This gives her three more Extra points to spend: she buys the psychic Sensitivity power (from the Sixth Sense path) for 1 point, adds 1 level to her Impress skill and 1 level to her Empathy.

With her history pretty well summed up, she can now prioritize her Spirit characteristics: Faith vs. Ego is easy —

members of House Decados usually have Ego as their primary trait. Although she gained more Extrovert levels from her history than Introvert, Susan decides that Lucretia is a rather guarded person. She chooses Introvert as primary, thinking to raise it higher during play with experience points. Finally, Lucretia's icy self-control points towards Calm as primary over Passion. Susan underlines the primary traits on the character sheet.

That's that. Lucretia's Wyrd rating remains at 5 (Introvert 3 + 2 pts with Natal Psi option), and her Vitality rating is 9 (5 + 4 Endurance). Susan is now finished with character creation. Susan decides that Lucretia's vendetta is with one of her brothers, whom she humiliated politically. The brother now heads a major Decados faction and has every intention of putting Lucretia in her place. She is thus forced to avoid Decados worlds and instead recruit allies among the wild frontier.

As far as equipment goes, Lucretia has 1000 firebirds to spend. This is well enough to get her a relatively good rapier (10 firebirds), a knife (2), a leather jerkin (5), a standard energy shield (500), a hooded cloak (negligible), a med. revolver (200) and 30 rounds of ammunition (10), and some coin left over (273 firebirds). She is now ready to carve her legacy among the stars of the **Fading Suns** universe.

Custom Creation Method

Assuming instead that Susan wants to spend time to build her character in-depth and with every option at her disposal, she chooses the Custom Creation method. Having roughly established her character concept, Susan turns to the character sheet and begins fixing the numbers.

First, Susan decides which of Lucretia's Spirit characteristics are primary. Faith vs. Ego is easy — Lucretia's a proud and cynical sort, relying on herself rather than on some disembodied spirit. Ego is declared as primary, so three points are assigned to that characteristic, leaving Faith as the secondary characteristic; one point is assigned to it.

The other four opposed characteristics, Susan realizes, are a little tougher. She contemplates the Extrovert vs. Introvert pair. While Susan sees Lucretia as a smooth, guileful sort, easily gliding through the social whirlpool, she also realizes that Lucretia is distrustful and rarely shows the true feelings behind the facade. After careful consideration, Susan chooses Introvert as primary (and notes that Lucretia is extremely guarded about her true feelings), but decides to raise Extrovert later in the character creation process (Lucretia is perfectly capable of putting on a demure, genteel, gracious or amorous mask).

Likewise with Passion vs. Calm: Lucretia is certainly capable of feeling intense passion, but rarely lets it rule her (she is vindictive, but can wait years to extract her vengeance). Susan decides on Calm as primary, but notes that

the Calm characteristic represents Lucretia's icy self-control rather than any true feeling of inner peace, and decides to raise the Passion characteristic with Extra points later on.

With her base characteristics thus set, Susan spends her 20 characteristic points. The first thing she decides is that Lucretia is *fast*, able to beat just about anyone or anything to the draw. Five points go into Dexterity, raising it to the beginning maximum of 8. Lucretia is also mentally quick and devious (though tempered by youth), so Susan spends four points to raise Lucretia's Wits rating to 7. Lucretia, while tough and wiry, places more emphasis on finesse than on brute force: Susan spends two points each on Lucretia's Strength and Endurance, raising them to 5. As a Decados, Lucretia learned very early on to beware the poisoned cup (or the poisoned word), so Susan spends three points to raise Lucretia's Perception to 6. Susan leaves Lucretia's Tech rating at 3: Lucretia relies on her own abilities, not on arcane gadgets.

Susan still has four characteristic points to spend. She spends two to raise Lucretia's Passion characteristic to 3, making it the equal of Calm. An additional point goes into Extrovert, raising it to 2. Susan spends the last point on Ego, raising it to 4.

Susan has 30 points to spend on Lucretia's skills. Considering Lucretia's concept as a renegade Decados and looking at the skills list, Susan notes several appropriate skills: Knavery, Etiquette, Fencing Actions, and Inquiry. She decides to spend about half of her 30 points improving Lucretia's natural skills, saving the other half for learned skills.

First off, Susan spends three points on Charm (raising the skill to 6) and two points on Impress (raising it to 5): Lucretia, while not a conventional beauty, has a certain dangerous, predatory sensuality. She is also a skilled fencer, having trained under Decados masters of the blade, so Susan places three points each in Melee and Dodge (both are now 6). Finally, Susan spends one point in Observe, Shoot, Sneak and Fight (raising each of these skills to 4).

She has spent 16 of her 30 points on natural talents. Now Susan takes a look at the learned skills list and begins checking off appropriate skills. Inquiry and Knavery are absolute musts; Susan spends eight points here, raising Lucretia's Inquiry and Knavery to 4 each. Because Lucretia is equally comfortable in ballrooms and barrooms, Susan spends three points to raise Streetwise to 2 and Etiquette to 1. Two points are spent on Urthish literacy (Read Urthish). Finally, she spends her one remaining point to purchase a level in Torture (life among the Decados is no bed of roses!). Susan would like to purchase many more skills, but realizes that she'll have to wait for the Extra point stage.

Now comes the purchase of Benefices. Susan has 10 points to spend on Lucretia's societal advantages. Because

Lucretia is a Decados, Lucretia spends five points on Nobility, making Lucretia a Decados baronet (a certain deal of clout in the house, and some leeway among the scum she prefers to associate with anyway). Five more points go into Riches to gain 1000 firebirds in cash. Susan decides that Lucretia had a fair stipend, but spends money recklessly and is always undertaking various disreputable assignments for extra cash.

Because of Lucretia's checkered past, Susan also takes three points of Afflictions: Black Sheep at 1 (she doesn't get on so well with the family) and Vendetta at 2 (in fact, someone in her family wants to duel her).

Now Susan spends her 43 Extra points (40 + 3 for the afflictions). She may purchase traits not heretofore available to her, like Occult traits and blessings. First off, Susan spends two points to take Lucretia's "hereditary" Decados Blessing of Suspicious. This gives her +2 to Perception when rivals are in the area… and Lucretia has many rivals.

Susan turns to the occult characteristics. She doesn't see Lucretia as being particularly heavy in the magic department, but she undoubtedly has a few tricks up her cloak (perhaps learned from a disreputable sorcerer contact). She decides to concentrate on psi, since that power comes from Lucretia's own will. Susan spends nine points to buy Lucretia a Psi rating of 3. This also sets her Wyrd rating: also 3, equal to her Introvert score. Now she buys a few powers: one point buys Sensitivity (from the Sixth Sense path), one point buys Intuit, two points buys Emote, and three points buys MindSight (all from the Psyche path, very useful for a manipulator like Lucretia). She leaves her Wyrd rating at 3: psi for Lucretia is a last-ditch fallback, not a common tool.

For her occult Stigma, she declares that Lucretia's eyes are nearly colorless — an eerie effect. Susan thinks this will cause Lucretia to seem distant and cold to others. If the eyes are the windows of the soul, then hers surely look upon strange vistas. Susan decides that Lucretia will wear dark glasses when in public.

Susan flips back to skills, since that's where Lucretia could use a boost. First, she spends seven points to buy some Fencing Actions: Parry, Thrust and Slash. She spends two more points to raise Lucretia's Melee score to its maximum of 8 (she's real good!). Two more points raise Charm and Impress to 7 and 6 respectively, and three points raise Sneak, Fight and Shoot to 5 each.

With only 11 points left, Susan has to be careful. She increases Lucretia's Knavery to 7 by spending three points, spends two more points to purchase Speak Severus dialect (the local street argot on her homeworld), another two points on Lore (Known Worlds) to help her in her travels, spends another two points to raise Lucretia's Extrovert characteristic to 3, and spends her remaining two points on raising Streetwise to 6.

That's that. Lucretia's Wyrd rating remains at 3, and her Vitality rating is 10 (5 + 5 Endurance). Susan decides that Lucretia's vendetta is with one of her brothers, whom she humiliated politically. The brother now heads a major Decados faction and has every intention of putting Lucretia in her place. She is thus forced to avoid Decados worlds and instead recruit allies among the wild frontier.

As far as equipment goes, Lucretia has 1000 firebirds to spend. This is well enough to get her a relatively good rapier (10 firebirds), a knife (2), a leather jerkin (5), a standard energy shield (500), a hooded cloak (negligible), a med. revolver (200) and 30 rounds of ammunition (10), and some coin left over (273 firebirds). She is now ready to carve her legacy among the stars of the **Fading Suns** universe.

Sample Characters

The following two pages provides two sample characters who can be used by beginning player characters or as NPCs for the gamemaster.

Sir Galen Trevor Hawkwood

The Trevors once ruled a large fief on Criticorum, but lost it all to the al-Malik during the Emperor Wars. Young Galen Hawkwood is barely old enough to remember playing in the family mansion before he was whisked away to a starship and rocketed to distant relatives on Byzantium Secundus. He was an angry lad, always getting into fights with other noble children who taunted him for his lack of fine clothing or land upon which to go riding. Shuffled from relative to relative, Galen eventually found himself under the absentee patronage of his mother's uncle, a inveterate drunk who spent most of his time passed out. Without strong role models, Galen sought friends in the seedy districts nearby, and learned well the ways of thieves and scoundrels.

Upon his day of majority, he left his scattered family behind and pledged fealty to Emperor Alexius — his last hope for fame and glory was with the Questing Knights. One among that company took pity upon him, recognizing in his strong physique and fervor the makings of a good knight. He spoke for the lad, and Galen was inducted soon after.

He has had a number of adventures so far, although they took the form of rescuing rich merchants from bandits or beautiful noble ladies from less-fitting paramours than himself. He yearns for a proper quest, a true calling off-world where he can win riches and fame as a knight of the Empire. He just hopes that his close friends among the seedier guilds, such as Chief Hally Saintsbane, don't come to the notice of his fellow knights…

Chief Hally Saintsbane

Hally's parents were runaway serfs who had found their way into Byzantium Secundus's Holy City and into each others arms — for one night, at least. Hally never met her father, but had dreams throughout childhood that he was actually a master spy or incognito knight who would one day rescue her from a life of poverty and crime. Her mother raised her until she was 10, and then turned her over to the guilds in return for a small pittance of firebirds — enough to live for a year in squalor, though. At least she wouldn't have to work back-breaking labor for the Church anymore. Hally never saw her again.

CHARACTERISTICS

Name: Sir Galan Trevor Hawkwood   Race: Human
Gender: Male   Alliance: Questing Knight
Age: 19   Rank: Knight

Body		Mind	
Strength (3) 7		Wits (3) 5	
Dexterity (3) 8		Perception (3) 6	
Endurance (3) 8		Tech (3)	

Spirit

Extrovert (3) 6	/	(1) Introvert
Passion (3) 4	/	(1) Calm
Faith (3)	/	(1) Ego

NATURAL SKILLS

Charm (3)	
Dodge (3)	6
Fight (3)	5
Impress (3)	5
Melee (3)	8
Observe (3)	4
Shoot (3)	5
Sneak (3)	4
Vigor (3)	5

LEARNED SKILLS

	LVL
Drive Landcraft	1
Inquiry	1
Lore (People & Places)	1
Read Urthish	
Remedy	2
Ride	1
Speak Byz II dialect	
Streetwise	1

BLESSINGS/CURSES

+/-	Trait	Situation
+2	End	Unyielding
-2	Calm	Prideful

BENEFICES/AFFLICTIONS

Type	Pts
Imperial Charter	5
Ally (older knight)	4

880 firebirds cash (after buying; MedPac, knife, fusion torch, 50 rounds ammo and other listed equipment)

OCCULT

Psi	/
Theurgy	/
Powers/Rites	

COMBAT

STR bonus: +1d

Action	Init	Goal	DMG	RNG
Rapier			6d	
Parry	8	18		
Thrust	10	16	6d	
Slash	6	16	7d	
Draw & Strike	6	16	6d	
Disarm	6	15		
Off-Hand				
Hvy Revolver	13		6d	30/40

ARMOR
Leather 4d,
Dueling Shield (5/10)

SHOTS FIRED
(6 /clip)

VICTORY CHART

Successes	Pts
1-2	0
3-5	+1
6-8	+2
9-11	+3
12-14	+4
15-17	+5
18	+6

Critical success = x2

VITALITY O O O O O O O O O O O O O O O O O O O O
Wound penalties: -10 -8 -6 -4 -2

WYRD O O O O O O O O O O O O O O O

Her new parents were the Scravers. Only the toughest or most cunning survive in their field of business, so Hally had to give up daydreams quickly and learn to pull her own weight or be jettisoned. She had a talent for lying and the street savvy to support it, so she was trained as a decoy who would distract merchants or passersby while cutpurses had their way with the person's valuables. Eventually, however, she graduated to break-ins and burglary.

Dissatisfied with mere crime, Hally set about kissing up to the real Scravers whenever she could — the relic hunters and artifact hounds. Her work paid off and she got a promotion and a license to scrounge. Now, she just needs a way off-planet so she can practice her new profession. Maybe that weird knight she knows, the Questing Knight who walks the walks and talks the talk. He seems genuine street, not like a lot of the wannabes from the palaces. Maybe he's got some way out of here…

Oh, and there's one thing she hasn't told her bosses about yet — she's psychic. She gives off mild static electricitylike shocks to anyone close to her when she uses her powers.

Name: Chief Hally Saintsbane
Gender: Female
Age: 16

Race: Human
Alliance: Scravers
Rank: Chief

CHARACTERISTICS

BODY	MIND
Strength (3) 7	Wits (3) 5
Dexterity (3) 7	Perception (3) 8
Endurance (3) 5	Tech (3) 4

SPIRIT

Extrovert (3)	/	(1) Introvert
Passion (1)	/	5 (3) Calm
Faith (1)	/	5 (3) Ego

NATURAL SKILLS

Charm (3)	
Dodge (3)	5
Fight (3)	
Impress (3)	5
Melee (3)	
Observe (3)	8
Shoot (3)	6
Sneak (3)	6
Vigor (3)	

LEARNED SKILLS

	LVL
Focus	2
Gambling	2
Inquiry	3
Knavery	6
Lockpicking	2
Lore (Underworld)	1
Read Urthtech	1
Sleight of Hand	2
Speak Scraver Cant	
Streetwise	6
Tech Redemption (Mech)	2
Think Machine	1

BLESSINGS / CURSES

+/-	Trait	Situation
+2	Gamble	Lucky at cards
-2	Calm	Possessive

BENEFICES / AFFLICTIONS

Type	Pts
78 firebirds cash (after buying	
Mech Tools, Thieves Keys, knife and	
other listed equipment)	

OCCULT

		Urge
Psi	3 /	Hubris
Theurgy	/	

Powers/Rites	Goal
Sensitivity	16
Darksense	13
Subtle Sight	11

COMBAT

STR bonus: ±1d

Action	Init	Goal	DMG	RNG
Blaster pistol		13	7d	10/20
Palm laser		13	3d	5/10

ARMOR Studded leather — 5d

SHOTS FIRED (10 /clip)

VICTORY CHART

Successes	Pts
1-2	0
3-5	+1
6-8	+2
9-11	+3
12-14	+4
15-17	+5
18	+6
Critical success = x2	

VITALITY O O O O O O O O O O O O O O
Wound penalties: -10 -8 -6 -4 -2

WYRD O O O O O O O O O O O O

Chapter 4: Traits

Traits are numbers players and gamemasters use to rate a character's abilities. They come in a variety of categories and levels, and the combination of them makes up a character. Chapter Two: Rules and Chapter Three: Characters give details on how these traits are chosen and used; this chapter expands the rules given there.

Characteristics

Onganggorak's fur bristled, and the Vorox's nostrils flared in response, sniffing for the scent behind his unease. He knew that smell from somewhere in his past. But the overpowering scents of oil, white-hot metal, and chemical flame in the starship repair berth made it impossible to pinpoint it.

"Sniffing for meat like a beast, Ong?" a voice nearby said. "You think you've come far, but you're still the beast I caught in my trap in that hellish jungle you call home."

Onganggorak grumbled low, an uncontrollable rage building in him. He cast his head about, searching for the source of the voice from the past. A man stepped from the shadows of the palettes, a long, thin rapier gleaming in the sparking light of the welding torches across the room.

"Remember, me, beast?" The man said, slowly raising his blade to the ready. "It is I, Baron Cornado. I hear you have been searching for me these many years. Still bear a grudge? How barbaric. If you were of the royal caste, perhaps you would realize that what I did then — what I do to many others even now — is all part of the sport owed my class. The beasts of the fields are there to amuse us when the burden of leadership becomes too heavy. Your capture and beating was but a means to lighten my burden."

A haze of red filled Onganggorak's vision. He could no longer control the anger that erupted, anger waiting years to be freed and quenched with the blood of this man. He roared and charged.

Characteristics represent a character's natural physical, mental and spiritual (also psychological) abilities. Everyone has at least some capability with Body and Mind characteristics and a natural leaning toward certain Spirit characteristics.

Characteristics are rated by levels, each normally ranging from 1 to 10 (although some alien races can possess higher levels, and cybernetic devices can raise certain characteristics above 10). However, no character can begin the game with more than eight levels in any one characteristic (cybernetics are an exception), although characteristics can be raised to their racial maximums during gameplay with experience points.

Each characteristic is detailed below, along with a list of the most common skills often paired with them.

Body

The physical side of a character, representing how strong, nimble or healthy she is. Any physical task a character undertakes will involve a Body characteristic plus an appropriate skill. For instance, when a character lifts a fallen tree to free a comrade trapped beneath it, the roll is Strength + Vigor.

Strength

Muscle power. Strength determines how much weight a character can lift, and helps in athletic tasks like jumping and climbing (see the Vigor skill) or wrestling. Generally, the higher a character's Strength, the bulkier and more muscular she is, but there are exceptions.

A character can lift a certain amount in kilograms over his head per Strength level without needing to make a roll. To lift more than that, he must make a Str + Vigor roll, with

a -1 penalty per Str level required above his own, up to a maximum of that allowed for his Str +3 (a Str 4 person can lift 120 kg max). Others can join together to lift items; simply add their allowances together: three Str 3 people can lift 120 kg without needing to roll.

In addition, stronger characters deliver more damage in melee combat: add one die for every three levels of Strength above three:

Strength	Weight	Damage Bonus
1	10 kg	0
2	20 kg	0
3	40 kg	0
4	60 kg	0
5	80 kg	0
6	100 kg	+1
7	120 kg	+1
8	140 kg	+1
9	160 kg	+2
10	180 kg	+2
11	200 kg	+2
12	220 kg	+3

Dexterity

Agility and motor control. Dexterity determines how nimble a character is, and helps in combat actions or athletic tasks like running (see the Vigor skill). Generally, the higher a character's Dexterity, the slimmer she is, but there are exceptions.

Endurance

Stamina and robust health. Endurance determines a character's staying power and ability to stave off disease. Generally, the higher a character's Endurance, the larger she is, although this is not always true. Besides physical health, Endurance also represents a strong will to live or endure beyond the breaking point. Endurance helps determine a character's base Vitality (Endurance + 5).

Mind

The mental side of a character, representing intelligence, awareness and technical (or scientific) capability in the Dark Age of the **Fading Suns**. Any task involving thought or reason that a character undertakes will involve a Mind characteristic plus an appropriate skill. For instance, when a character unjams an autofeed slug gun, the roll is Tech + Mech Redemption.

Wits

Intelligence and quick-thinking. Wits determines how well a character remembers and understands things, and helps in any task involving learning. The higher a character's Wits, the quicker she is at figuring things out and reacting to events.

Perception

Awareness and alertness. Perception determines how aware a character is of the world around her and how well she notices hidden things. The higher a character's Perception, the more observant she is of things other people only notice unconsciously.

Tech

On the Known Worlds, the scientific method is by no means common, even among the learned. Those who have the knack or training to comprehend and utilize — let alone invent — technology are rare and often find their way into positions of power in a guild. The Tech characteristic represents a character's knack at understanding technology; its levels match those given on the Tech Level Chart (see Chapter 7: Technology). Tech aids in repairing broken equipment and in comprehending high-tech devices and sciences.

Spirit

The psychological side of a character, representing social inclinations, personal emotions, and degree of individuation. Any task involving emotions or inner quandaries that a character undertakes or suffers will involve a Spirit characteristic plus an appropriate skill (although some characteristics can be rolled without adding a skill). In addition, many occult powers use Spirit characteristics. For instance, when a theurgic character attempts to cast the Prophet's Holy Blessing rite, the roll is Faith + Focus.

Each Spirit characteristic is "opposed" by another characteristic, representing the psychological duality of the human (or alien) condition (at least as it exists in **Fading Suns**). These pairs each share the same scale of levels (1 to 10 for most races), and a rating in one characteristic lessens the maximum rating in its opposing characteristic. In most cases, however, these characteristics will not compete; most people have average scores in each (1 to 3).

Example: Julia Abrams has Passion 6; her Calm rating can thus be no more than 4. If her Calm was 5 before her Passion was raised to 6, then it drops to 4. (Characteristics are raised only through an experience purchase system, so Julia's player has the choice to add to her Passion and lose some Calm, or to add to Calm and lose some Passion — or she can spend her points elsewhere and not worry about it).

Whenever a situation calls for the temporary modification of a Spirit characteristic — either to add or subtract from it — the opposing characteristic is unaffected. Only permanent changes in a characteristic will affect its opposite.

It is rumored that certain secret mystical sects teach paths which lead beyond the conflicting duality of the soul, allowing a character to raise her Spirit characteristics without regard to their opposites.

Extrovert vs. Introvert

Extrovert and its opposing characteristic, Introvert, represent two extremes of interpersonal relationships. Each person tends towards one or the other, although it is possible for these two characteristics to be in balance. Extroverts reach out for others, preferring social situations to sitting alone in a room. Introverts are more comfortable by themselves than with others, and tend to avoid social situations they cannot control. Neither characteristic implies social ability: An Extrovert may be a nebbish nobody likes but who keeps on butting into conversations, while an Introvert may be the quiet author everybody tries to flock around but who avoids parties. Interpersonal activities (partying, acting) are resolved using Extrovert; "inner" activities (writing poetry, trying to remember a long-forgotten fact or repressed memory) are resolved using Introvert.

Passion vs. Calm

Passion and its opposing characteristic, Calm, represent two emotional extremes. As with most emotions, they have a tendency to govern a character as much as she governs them. Some people are hotheads (Passion) and find it hard to control their outbursts. Others are laid back (Calm) and may actually find it hard to get very excited about something.

Inciting Passion

Some people's emotions run hot, and they can explode into angry rages or steamy lusts. The energy of these unleashed emotions may be hard to control, but it can provide an unstoppable force: A knight wades undaunted through impossible obstacles to reach his true love, or a vengeful girl's hatred of the man who killed her family drives her for years against all opposition until she can finally drive her blade into his guts.

Sometimes, a character may want to incite his passions to gain some of this indomitable energy. Passion can aid a character in certain tasks or help him to continue when fatigue would otherwise have felled him. But unleashed passions can be hard to control, and they can take over a character, transforming a soldier into a berserk warrior or a priest into a suicidal martyr.

A character must have a focus for his passion before inciting it. This can be a true love, a deeply despised enemy, a liege or religious tenet worth dying for, a personal invention that will change the world, etc. It should be a worthy passion, one fit to stand in great epics, not a measly hatred of a noble who snubbed you at the ball. The gamemaster must decide whether a passion is worthy enough to incite for gain.

To incite the emotional fires, the character spends one Wyrd point and rolls his Passion as the goal number (with-

Inciting Passion Chart

Situation	Passion
Insulted/humiliated before an important audience	+3
Suffering bigotry (class or race based)	+2
Reputation threatened	+1
Freedom threatened	+2
Livelihood threatened	+3
Life threatened	+5
Favored by a lover	+2
Spurned by a lover	+3
Lover threatened	+4
Friends threatened	+1
House/Church/League matter of importance	+2
Rival/foe within presence	+2
Object of vendetta within presence	+3
Crisis of faith	+3
Money involved	+1
Lots of money involved	+2
In combat	+1
Encountering scary place/people	+1
Encountering terrifying place/people (Symbiots)	+2

out pairing to a skill). Add or subtract any applicable modifiers from the Inciting Passion Chart. Each victory point adds one to the goal number for any rolls related to the focus of the character's passion, whether it be climbing a tower to rescue a true love or swinging a sword at a long-hated foe. Or, at the player's choice, each victory point will instead add one die of damage. The player must choose which option to use before making the roll.

This effect generally lasts for one span, but if it is a deep-enough emotion, the gamemaster may allow the benefits to last for hours or days, but no longer than the focus calls for. If the emotional issue is resolved, the effect ends. After the effect wears off, the character will be exhausted, drained of any immediate zeal. All tasks, for an amount of time equal to the time the passion was incited, are treated as if they were Demanding (-4).

If the roll is a critical success, the character is trapped in the throes of his passion, unable to let go of his task or the object of focus until his emotions are resolved: She rescues her prince from the ransoming barbarians; his wooing is successful and she says yes to marriage; the murdering fiend chokes out a death rattle at the end of your pike; the cathedral has finally been completed even though the bandits tried to stop its construction, etc.

Until this resolution, the character is not in full control of his desires — all else is put aside for the passionate task at hand. Even necessary considerations like eating or healing may be forgotten if they stand in the way of an opportunity for resolution. The character may even give up his life

for the cause if it's the quickest or only means to resolution: He takes a bullet for his lover; she ejects her comrades in the escape pod while staying behind to manually set the self-destruct sequence on the Imperial cruiser; he willingly walks into the knives of his enemies, knowing it is the only way to convince the townsfolk of the Pancreator's mercy.

Remaining Calm

There are times when a character cannot control his emotions and must try to check them: A noble who is gravely insulted, an Inquisitor trapped in a den of sinners, a merchant who is cheated out of his life's savings, etc. When the slight is grievous enough, a roll should be made to determine how well a character succeeds in governing his reaction. The gamemaster decides whether or not a situation requires a roll.

Roll Calm plus an appropriate skill. If the character is at a society ball and must maintain his composure, roll Calm + Etiquette. If the character is in a terrifying situation and trying to stay calm against fear, roll Calm + Impress (or Stoic Mind). If a street gang leader threatens the character but he wants to stay cool, roll Calm + Streetwise. In addition, there may be modifiers to the roll depending on the situation; use the standard bonus and penalty chart.

If successful, the character is in control of her actions. If the roll fails, the character succumbs to whatever undesired emotion plagues her: anger, fear, sorrow, lust, etc. This is usually a momentary lapse of reason, lasting for a turn or so, but the results of that lapse may affect the character for a long time afterwards: That Scraver chief did not appreciate you throwing your drink in her face. Your apologies immediately afterwards fell on deaf ears and you can look forward to a small feud for months or even years to come.

A character's passionate reaction should remain in character: A serf insulted by a noble may be humiliated and angry, but she will probably not leap up and knock him from his mount, although a Muster guildmember might, especially if her comrades are there to back her up.

In general, a character's behavior is decided solely by the player. But when a player refuses to play within the boundaries of his or her own character concept, the gamemaster may require the player to make a roll to govern the character's urges. For instance, Jill is playing a hotheaded Hawkwood named Eleanor. Eleanor is insulted terribly at a party by an upstart Hazat boy, who implies that she hands out sexual favors like candy. Jill knows that this character is connected to her rivals and is trying to goad her, but Eleanor does not know this. There is a disparity between player and character knowledge. Nonetheless, Jill says that Eleanor will ignore the Hazat's insults.

The gamemaster thinks this is drastically out of character for Eleanor, so he requires that Jill make a Calm + Etiquette roll for Eleanor not to fly off the handle at the snotty

Hazat. Since Eleanor is a Hawkwood, she suffers from the family pride (the Prideful Curse: -2 Calm), and may fail the roll. This should not be viewed as a penalty, however, but a wonderful opportunity for roleplaying. The gamemaster should never use forced rolls to punish players, only to lead them into intense roleplaying situations they might otherwise miss due to their lack of roleplaying chutzpah.

Steady Hand

Calm can be used to overcome nervous stress and help improve a character's performance in certain situations. The character must declare a focus of his actions, a single purpose towards which he is directing his intent. He then centers himself and goes to it, ignoring stressful distractions. Only relatively immediate tasks can be declared; long-term tasks may require a calm attitude, but they gain no bonus from this short-term burst of concentration (use Focus skill for long-term tasks).

For instance, a guild Engineer must defuse a planet bomb in less than 10 minutes. He tells everybody to shut up, wipes the sweat from his brow, and bends down to concentrate, repeating to himself over and over, "It's just like back at Master Bocor's foundry. Snip the green wire, not the red. The green one, not the red…" Or a Brother Battle priest kneels to pray before charging a line of foes, calming himself with inspirational mantras from masters of the order.

To gain a steady hand for a task, the character spends one Wyrd point and rolls Calm as the goal number (without pairing to a skill). Add or subtract any applicable modifiers from the Passion/Calm Chart. Each victory point adds one to the goal number for any rolls related to the character's focus, whether it be fighting off an angry mob or getting the jumpdrive engine on line before the pirates' guns tear the ship apart.

It takes three turns to center and concentrate before the roll can be made; any less time means the character simply has not reached a steady centeredness. The effect lasts for a short time, only until the task is completed at the longest. During this time, the character must perform actions related only to his focus. If he undertakes any other actions, his concentration is broken and he loses any steadying effects.

If the roll is a critical success, he becomes fully absorbed in his task to the exclusion of all else. He does not notice what's going on around him unless it is directly related to the task. This fugue state ends only when the task is resolved. The resolution does not have to be successful; when it becomes obvious that the task cannot be completed, the character will lose his obsessional state.

Faith vs. Ego

Faith and its opposing characteristic, Ego, represent two extremes of the soul determining identity. Faith is collective, centered outside the self, looking out or upwards to a spiritual deity for inspiration and meaning. Ego is individualistic, centered in the character's own sense of self (the core of the personal pronoun "I"), gaining inspiration and meaning mainly from itself (although this does not prevent the character from believing in a deity). Both faithful and egotistic characters can be stubborn and divisive but strong and enduring at the same time.

Faith and Ego are rarely rolled. They are mainly applied when using occult powers or weird Ur artifacts. Most people go through life without ever having their Faith or Ego tested, but entry into the occult dimension often puts one's identity to task.

Natural Skills

Cardanzo leapt from the roof of the church to the inn next door and dove behind a low brick wall. Bullets sprayed around him. He had just barely seen the Ur-Ukar sneaking up on him in time. Now under cover, he unholstered his blaster and looked for his opponent. Unable to see the alien, he took careful aim at a distant metal weather vane. He fired and the weather vane vaporized. "Throw down your gun or I'll do the same to you," Cardanzo yelled.

Natural skills are the basic talents inherent to almost everyone. The holiest Ur-Obun has some idea of how to whack somebody, while the lowliest serf knows the basics of trying to impress those around her. Every character starts with three levels in each of these and can buy them up to eight at the beginning of play. Only experience, exceptional training or lost technology can raise them to 10.

This section describes each of the skills as well as a few examples of how to use them in play. Gamemasters should feel free to use or ignore these examples as they so desire. They should also expect players to come up with their own variations on these, and accept or reject them based on how fun they make the game.

Charm

This is the ability to get people to like you. It can be used to ingratiate yourself to someone, reduce their hostility to you, enable you to con them or even make them fall in love with you. Characters should use this skill whenever they hope to leave someone else with a better view of them than they started with. This skill usually only works on individuals and small groups; swaying larger groups requires Oratory or Leadership.

Dupe: While conning, swindling or lying generally requires a Knavery roll (see Learned Skills), Charm can be used to complement the roll. After all, someone who likes you is far more willing to overlook inconsistencies in your story. This Extrovert + Charm roll works as any other complementary roll.

Haggling: If a character wants to negotiate a lower price

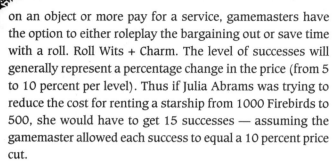

on an object or more pay for a service, gamemasters have the option to either roleplay the bargaining out or save time with a roll. Roll Wits + Charm. The level of successes will generally represent a percentage change in the price (from 5 to 10 percent per level). Thus if Julia Abrams was trying to reduce the cost for renting a starship from 1000 Firebirds to 500, she would have to get 15 successes — assuming the gamemaster allowed each success to equal a 10 percent price cut.

Seduction: One of the more popular uses of Charm, the seduction rules can come into play whether the character is sincere or not. This is almost always a series of Passion + Charm rolls carried out whenever the character and his target are together. Gamemasters might want to set a number of victory points the character must achieve before his feelings are reciprocated. This number is often based on the target's Introvert score or some multiplier thereof.

Dodge

This encompasses all kinds of different ways of avoiding an attack — bobbing and weaving, ducking, leaping over a kick or diving for cover. A successful dodge usually leaves a character about where he was when he made the roll, but players can also specify that their characters end up as far from the attack as possible.

Close Combat: Dodging in hand-to-hand or melee combat is primarily a matter of seeing an attack and getting out of its way. This is almost always a Dexterity + Dodge roll contested against an attacker's roll (the number of successes reduces the number the attacker rolls). Gamemasters may require Perception + Dodge rolls to avoid sneak attacks or Endurance + Dodge during a long fight.

Ranged Combat: Dodging in ranged combat is primarily a matter of seeing an attacker and getting to cover before the bullet, laser or whatever can strike. Throwing oneself flat on the ground can help, but gamemasters should penalize those trying to dodge missile attacks if there is no cover around. This is almost always a Dexterity + Dodge roll contested against an attacker's roll.

Fight

Fight represents a character's ability in unarmed hand-to-hand combat. Low levels generally mean a character rarely gets into fights and, when he does, is little more than a brawler. Higher levels imply that a character has fought a lot, had advanced training in the subject, or both. Extensive training in hand-to-hand combat can also mean having the character learn some martial arts (see Combat Actions, under Learned Skills). More detailed rules on Fight are in Chapter Six: Combat.

Impress

While Charm helps a character make other people like her, Impress can have any number of effects on its target. A character might want to scare someone, gain her respect, browbeat her into submission or just make sure she remembers something. This can be a useful skill for getting information out of people, though that sometimes requires torture.

Dominate: If you want someone to respect you, or just want them to feel inferior to you, roll Extrovert + Impress. These successes generally compare to the target's Ego to see how inferior he feels. Of course, if you are trying to dominate someone in a more romantic manner, roll Passion + Impress and compare the successes to the target's Calm.

Intimidate: This is generally a physical action as the character puffs out her chest, flexes her muscles and glares at her adversary. She rolls Strength + Impress and hopes that the target doesn't have a lot of Ego. This is a good way to get someone she has been beating on to surrender.

Show-Off: Characters will often want to let everyone know how great they are in certain areas. The best way to do this is with the relevant characteristic + Impress. This demonstrates not only the character's talent but also the fact that he can carry it out in an awe-inspiring way. For instance, if Julia Abrams wanted to show an Engineer that she was an authority on cybernetics, she would roll Tech + Impress to dazzle him with her brilliance. If Brother Alustro needs to convince an Inquisitor of his dedication to the Church, he should roll Faith + Impress — or else run really fast (see Vigor, below).

Melee

While Fight deals with unarmed combat, Melee takes into account all the hand-to-hand weapons, be they clubs, energy swords, rapiers or poisoned daggers. The most talented characters generally also learn various fencing actions (see Combat Actions, under Learned Skills). The uses of Melee are more fully explored in Chapter Six: Combat.

Observe

Some people stay constantly aware of the world around them, and others have to work at it — and still remain oblivious to everything else. The Observe skill generally reflects a person's innate sensitivity to the world around him. When she actually tries to see what's going on she should use Inquiry or Search. Thus a sentry would generally need Observe while someone frisking an infiltrator would need Search.

Detection: This is a catch-all category for noticing things that aren't as they should be. For instance, if Cardanzo needs to notice that a cane actually doubles as a laser, he would need to roll Tech + Observe. If Erian Li Halan is around a strange-acting Vorox, she would need to roll Wits + Observe to notice that his low rumblings and stillness mean that something is wrong.

Notice: Things are constantly happening, but that

doesn't mean the character is necessarily aware of them. To hear that assassin sneaking up or to see the scorpion in the weapons locker requires a Perception + Observe roll. The observer needs to roll more successes than the sneaker made on her Dexterity + Sneak roll.

Shoot

Shoot covers any portable missile weapon that doesn't rely on muscle power. This means muskets, lasers, blasters, assault rifles, flamers, stunners and all sorts of weird alien guns. It does not cover such areas as artillery and most ship or vehicle-mounted guns. For more information on using Shoot, see Chapter Six: Combat.

Sneak

Characters do a lot of things that they don't want other people to notice. Sneak takes that into account, and applies to actions like moving quietly, hiding, using camouflage or slipping past sentries. It almost always applies to physical actions, and attempts to sneak into a computer database require science skills, not Sneak.

Camouflage: Concealing oneself is mostly a matter of using the right concealment. Thus characters need to roll Wits + Sneak in order use the materials at hand to best effect.

Hide: Staying still and not being seen is a combination of a number of factors. First it requires that a character fit his body into a suitable hiding place. After that he must stay as still as possible to keep from attracting attention. The first roll is a Dexterity + Sneak roll, but latter rolls require Calm + Sneak.

Move Quietly: Many characters like to skulk around without being noticed. This is an attempt to move without making noise, and generally requires a Dexterity + Sneak roll. The sneaker needs to roll more successes than a listener makes on a Perception + Observe roll.

Vigor

This skill takes into account many of the physical activities in which people engage. Running, jumping, swimming, climbing, and more all fall into this category. Almost everyone has at least some familiarity with these activities, but most people have not had any real training in them. Characters with more extensive training, and who want to make neat rolls and flips, should buy the Acrobatics learned skill.

Some of the rolls listed here give specific details on how far a character can run, jump or swim, but gamemasters should not feel tied to these. For the most part, Vigor rolls are all or nothing affairs. Either the character leapt from the grav car to the galloping horse or else he fell on his face. The distance guidelines are only there for special circumstances.

Climbing: For slow, determined climbing, players should roll Dexterity + Vigor to determine how quickly their characters do it. Getting no successes does not necessarily mean the character falls. Instead she moves neither up nor down, and needs to succeed on a second roll. Characters who are climbing as fast as they can, however, should make a Strength + Vigor roll, illustrating the fact that they are sacrificing safety for speed. Failing this roll could very well cause them to lose their grip. Gamemasters should also feel free to penalize mountain climbers who don't have the appropriate equipment. Gamemasters might also want to penalize characters climbing especially tough mountains but ignore rolls for going up trees.

Holding Your Breath: Endurance + Vigor — and a little luck — determines how long a character can hold his breath before suffocating, or more likely, giving up and gulping for air even when underwater. A character can hold his breath for a number of turns equal to 10 plus his Endurance without having to make a roll. Each turn thereafter, roll Endurance + Vigor. Only one success is necessary, but it gets harder and harder as time passes: the character suffers a -1 penalty each turn after the first in which a roll was made (a character with Endurance 5 does not have to roll until the seventeenth turn; on the eighteenth turn, he suffers -1 to his roll, -2 on the nineteenth, etc.). A critical success will allow the character an extra turn in which he does not have to roll, and Steady Hand (see Calm, below) can be used to offset these penalties. If he rolls a critical failure, he falls unconscious. When a character fails his roll, he can no longer hold his breath.

Jumping: Jumping horizontally or vertically requires a Strength + Vigor roll. A character goes up two feet + one per victory point. With a running start he can leap forward 8 feet + one for every success. From a standing start he can jump forward 4 feet + one for every victory point.

Running: Racing on foot requires a number of different rolls depending on far the character wants to go. Getting a good jump and running fastest over short distances requires a Dexterity + Vigor roll. Longer distances require Endurance + Vigor rolls — often more than one. For gamemasters who need to figure out just how much distance a character has covered in one turn, the average person sprints 10 meters + number of successes on a Dexterity + Vigor roll.

During combat, if a character wants to use one of his multiple actions to run, he may move one meter per point of Vigor. Otherwise, he may move only one meter any direction per action.

Swimming: Swimming is much like running in that short distances require a Dexterity + Vigor roll while longer distances use one or more Endurance + Vigor rolls. Each turn characters can swim one meter per victory point. A character must have at least five levels of Vigor in order to even know how to swim. Four levels is enough to tread water, however.

Learned Skills

Brother Guissepe Alustro sighed and rubbed his eyes. Damn these think machines! he thought. Give me good old Dromli-skin parchment any day. Soothing to the eye and long-lasting. Not like these infernal, glowing glasses precariously preserving words and pictures. Words and images so easily lost with but a misplaced keystroke. Enough complaining! Back to work!

Alustro clicked the button to scroll the words forward to the next paragraph. There was a sharp beep and the screen froze up. A sentence appeared: "System shut-down. File lost."

Alustro's fist hit the table, shaking the think machine screen. The priest sitting nearby looked up and stared at Alustro as if he'd just admitted to the Forlustrian Heresy. Alustro slid his chair back and stood up. He collected his book bag and marched from the cathedral library. He had wasted his time here too long. He would go back to the Engineer and pay his damn fee. At least their think machines worked!

Learned skills may be picked up from books (as is the case with some Lores and Sciences), or learned from others. In fact, most learned skills are difficult to pick up on one's own and require a teacher.

To that end, many people join or ally themselves with guilds (or even certain sects within the Church) for the purpose of learning a particular skill. Of course, many guilds are choosy about whom they will instruct, and a prospective student who does not seem likely to remain with the guild for long will have a hard time finding a guild teacher. It is even rumored that some guilds, such as the Engineers, have been known to resort to extortion, kidnapping and worse to keep their secrets from getting out.

Certain skills, mostly those involving high technology lore, are only taught by the guilds. A Professional Contract (see Benefices) must be purchased before the guild will teach the skill. (The cost of the contract equals the levels learned in the skill.)

Certain skills, such as Social skills, may be learned with a minimum of formal instruction. Others, such as Arts, Sciences and languages require long periods of intense study in order to reach a high level of competency. Teachers who do not belong to a particular guild, noble house or sect are less likely to have access to the latest methods and materials, whereas the student doing an internship with a guild will probably have access to the best training and materials available in the area. Of course, there are exceptions. The independent freelancers have to be among the best in order

to survive, and there is much a student can learn from someone outside the system.

Academia

Roll: Wits + Academia

This skill allows the character to locate information on a particular topic. This includes knowledge of church libraries, guild records and Second Republic lost libraries (although it is harder to use these). Academia is especially useful for those looking for information on lost tech. Academic research of this sort can often take a great deal of time — there is no Dewey decimal system to make all this easy. This skill is much easier for those who can read Latin (especially when using a Church library), Urthish or even Urthtech. To obtain information from people, Inquiry — not Academia — is the relevant skill.

General Research: The first step to locating any information is knowing where to find it. Is the information you're looking for more likely to be found in the Charioteer guildhall's records, or in a Church library? Roll Wits + Academia. Once the best location is determined the character must then sift through the available tomes or records to locate exactly what he is looking for.

Tech Research: To find the needed references, roll Tech + Academia. However, in order to locate technical information the character must have the skill Read Urthtech. Once she has found the manuals or references she needs, she may have to roll Wits + Read Urthtech to comprehend them.

Complementary Skills

• **Lore:** A Lore appropriate to what the character is researching may be used as a complementary skill. A character researching the mating habits of the Ur-Ukar would use the Xeno Lore (specifically Ur-Ukar).

• **Read:** When researching information on a particular race or culture the character may need to have the ability to read the appropriate language. Once the document is located the character may have to roll Wits + Read (appropriate language) to understand it.

• **Sciences:** A Science relating to what the character is researching may be used as a complementary skill. If the character is seeking information on starship drives, the Engineering Science would be useful.

Acrobatics

Roll: Dexterity + Acrobatics

Acrobatics is the study and practice of complex movements of the body, such as flips, cartwheels, etc. This skill also provides a working knowledge of acrobatic actions involving equipment, such as parallel bars and horses. The character also has a superior sense of balance, useful in situations such as tightrope-walking.

Breakfall: The character has practiced falling many times and knows how to land without injuring herself. The

---

Using Complementary Skills

The gamemaster is the final arbiter of which skills may be used as complementary skills to a given roll, and as such should be aware that excessive use of complementary skills can get out of hand if not monitored. Using any complementary skill requires time, usually a turn or more depending on the skill being used. Characters may attempt to use both the primary and complementary skills the same turn, but with the penalties incurred from doing so (-4 to each roll), it is usually more worthwhile to just take the extra time.

The rules for complementary skills can be found in Chapter Two: Rules.

---

victory points on a Dexterity + Acrobatics roll are subtracted from any damage points taken in a fall.

Leaping Dodge: When the character has some room to work with, he can tumble out of harm's way, using his acrobatic skill to complement a Dodge roll. Roll Dexterity + Acrobatics; add the victory points to the Dodge goal roll. Leaping dodges can only be maintained for a number or turns equal to the character's Endurance.

Complementary Skills

• **Stoic Body:** When performing acrobatics while in adverse conditions, such as intense heat or cold, a toughened body may allow the character to ignore or lessen any penalties due to these conditions.

Alchemy

Roll: Faith + Alchemy

The study of alchemy integrates aspects of chemistry, philosophy and physics into the art and science of matter — its different states, and how one type of matter may be changed into another type. Various elixirs and potions may be concocted, and it is said that the most talented among the Eskatonic Order are able to transform water into wine, among other things.

But beware — the Inquisition keeps an eye on known alchemists. They claim that alchemy treads too close to the high science of the Second Republic, and that the hubris of a single alchemist can be dangerous to everyone.

Alchemy involves knowledge and understanding of a substance's spiritual purity and the sympathy it has with other substances — in other words, the spiritual reactions two (or more) substances will have when combined. Alchemists collect catalogs of the correspondences (mystical connections) between substances. They know, for instance, that a toad is impure, and that, when placed near a pure substance, such as a gem, will corrupt that substance, perhaps

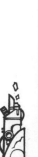

causing the gem to crack. Why this doesn't happen all the time is a matter of great debate among alchemists.

Identify Substance: Given time, a character can identify a substance, determine how pure a substance is, and learn what other substances are present. Are the "jewels" in the box real, or merely cut glass? Is the wine poisoned, or merely lousy wine? Roll Wits + Alchemy.

Complementary Skills

• **Focus:** The ability to concentrate one's energy and attention on the interactions between two substances can aid an Alchemist in understanding their relationship. The Alchemist must focus for at least one turn prior to attempting to learn anything.

• **Science:** Although the Church would be horrified to see base sciences being applied to anything sacred, characters may find that using sciences such as Chemistry to double check their work may be useful.

Archery

Roll: Dexterity + Archery

Archery is the study of marksmanship using a bow. While bows are primarily still used for hunting, they are the ranged weapon of choice on some backwater worlds. Characters skilled at Archery may refer to Chapter Seven: Technology for descriptions of different types of bows which they may specialize in (although use of crossbows falls under the skill of the same name).

Target Shooting: Target shooting is very different from shooting at a moving target. While combat shooting relies mostly on raw Dexterity, target shooting relies more on your ability to weigh a number of factors, including the wind speed and distance from your target, in order to make a perfect shot. Roll Perception + Archery.

Complementary Skills

• **Focus:** A character using Focus as a complementary skill must spend at least one full turn taking aim at his target; no other action may be taken during this turn.

• **Ride:** Ride may be used as a complementary skill to lower the penalty a character would receive when firing a bow while riding a beast. The penalty is reduced based on the number of victory modifiers gained on the Ride roll. See the Ride skill for more details on using weapons from beastback.

Artisan

Roll: Wits + (relevant Artisan skill)

The character is skilled in a particular craft. This skill allows a character to determine the quality of items related to his area of expertise as well as create items. A character must choose a particular specialty, which is his craft of choice, though more than one specialty can be chosen if the skill is purchased separately. The player may invent a craft of his own or choose from the following list: Blacksmith, Carpen-

ter, Cartographer, Cook, Jeweler, Leatherworker, Locksmith, Mason, Potter, Tailor, Weaver.

Evaluate Work: The character may evaluate the work of another craftsman to determine the quality of the work. Roll Perception + (relevant Artisan skill). With a successful roll, the character may determine the approximate value in firebirds as well as any significant flaws.

Arts

Roll: Introvert + (relevant Arts skill)

The character is skilled in one of the arts. This skill is not the actual performance of art, but rather the creation of art — Performance is described under its own skill. There are many arts that the character may be skilled in and, as with Artisan, the character must choose one, though additional arts may be bought as separate skills. The following list details many arts common to humans, though some alien cultures may have arts not defined here, and players should feel free to create their own. The most common arts available to characters are: Calligraphy, Drawing, Embroidery, Illumination, Music Composition, Painting, Poetry, Rhetoric (writing), Sculpting, Stained Glass.

Players must choose one or more Arts as specializations. Skill at various arts can be used for pleasure, as a vocation, or in a variety of other, more "useful" ways.

Evaluate Art: The character can determine the quality and approximate value of an artwork by careful examination. Roll Perception + (relevant Arts skill). More than a cursory glance is required, and the object in question must be carefully examined before the character can attempt to learn anything about it. The character may also be able to identify forgeries.

Determine Artist: In the process of learning a given art, a character learns about other artists in the field, as well the ways people express things through that artform. By carefully examining a work of art the character can attempt to determine who its creator was, though in some cases this may prove impossible. In most cases the character may be reasonably sure as to a piece's creator. Roll Wits + (relevant Arts skill).

Complementary Skills

• **Focus:** Focus may be used as a complementary skill for some arts, particularly Illumination and Calligraphy, though depending upon the nature of the artist it may prove applicable to all arts.

• **Lore:** Certain Lores may be useful as complementary skills when attempting to identify an artist or recognize an art forgery. Knowing the mythology referenced in a tapestry may help immeasurably in determining who may have produced it.

Beast Lore

Roll: Wits + Beast Lore

Beast Lore allows the training of animals and an understanding of how they will react in the wild. Characters skilled at Beast Lore know the ways of animals as well or better than the ways of their own people. Often characters with high scores in Beast Lore are more at home with animals than they are with members of their own race, and are considered uncouth by their peers.

Beast Lore also grants the character skill with training animals. While training domesticated animals (such as ferrets, cats and the gentle shazzles of Vera Cruz) is easier, characters may also work with wild animals. Their understanding of the animal's habits and instincts make it much easier for them to anticipate what the animal is going to do.

Identify Animal: The character can identify an animal's species and may even have particular knowledge of its habits, such as whether or not they consider humans to be a tasty snack. If a character has worked a great deal with a particular animal in the past, she may also be able to tell that animal apart from other seemingly identical animals of the same species by observing its movements and mannerisms. Roll Wits + Beast Lore.

Bureaucracy

Roll: Wits + Bureaucracy

Although it is usually possessed by those who work within "the system", whether the setting is the Church, the merchant guilds or the nobility, knowledge of how to manipulate the network of forms and records can be useful to any character. The ability to cut through red tape — or, conversely, to cover your tracks through an endless maze of paperwork — can be invaluable to anyone seeking to circumvent the establishment.

Document Forgery: Characters with this skill are familiar with the language and layout of typical forms and documents. Roll Wits + Bureaucracy. While forging a tax waiver on Shaprut from the Senior Collector may require additional Regional Lore (and considerable chutzpah), faking a receipt, a will or other common document will be relatively straightforward.

Complementary Skills

• **Lore:** The appropriate area Lore can aid in understanding local customs and rules, especially when it comes to legal documents.

• **Art:** Any character attempting to forge a particular person's signature on a document will also need a relevant Art skill. The result can be well worth it, however.

Combat Actions

Roll: Dexterity + (relevant skill)

Some people spend more time than others training for action, whether it be with foil or fist. Combat Actions are not skills so much as trained maneuvers that provide the character with bonuses or special effects. Combat actions themselves are not rolled, but are instead resolved using Fight, Melee or Shoot skills. They are rated by the level of the relevant skill required to learn them. The more complicated the maneuver, the higher the level. For instance, a sword Parry is only level 1 — a student can perform this feat. But using a dagger in the off-hand without suffering a penalty is level 6 — this requires some practice. For more information and a list of available combat actions, see Chapter Six: Combat.

Fencing: Roll Dexterity + Melee. Fencing in **Fading Suns** is considered to be any melee combat with a lightweight sword, including traditional foils and rapiers as well as extremely rare energy blades. It can also include more obscure fighting methods, such as the Kraxi knife dancing practiced by some Ur-Ukar.

Martial Arts: Roll Dexterity + Fight. Martial Arts may include any formalized school of unarmed combat, such as the noble Shaidan, the crafty Koto, the pious Mantok practiced by Brother Battle, or even the brutal Graa of the Vorox.

Crossbow

Roll: Dexterity + Shoot

Characters skilled with a crossbow are formidable foes, combining the power and range of firearms with a lower, more accessible level of technology. The Crossbow skill is a qualifier on the Shoot skill that allows a character to use a crossbow without a penalty. Without this qualifier, a character subtracts four from his goal roll (in addition to any range penalties) for using a crossbow at long or extreme range. **Note:** This skill has no levels and costs 2 points.

Complementary Skill

• **Focus:** As is the case with Archery, a character may take a turn to focus before shooting.

Disguise

Roll: Perception + Disguise

A useful skill for anyone who wishes to change his identity, Disguise can effectively alter the appearance of a character. This skill is easier against serfs and others outside the group you're trying to impersonate, as many people recognize uniforms moreso than the people behind them.

When making a Disguise roll, keep track of the number of successes. When someone tries to see past a disguise, roll Perception + Observe and compare the successes to the Disguise roll's successes. If the suspicious observer wins,

he sees through the disguise; otherwise, he'll probably take the disguised person on his word.

Alien Disguise: While even the best disguise master will usually not fool someone of an alien race he impersonates, it may be possible to convince humans (or aliens, if the character is an alien impersonating a human) of the veracity of the disguise. Aliens receive a +6 bonus on their Perception + Observe rolls to see through the disguise. Truly clever makeup can help offset this bonus.

Complementary Skills

• **Physick:** Cosmetic surgery can be helpful, or in some cases, necessary to achieve the proper body shape and features, especially when attempting to impersonate someone of a different race.

• **Social (Acting):** The correct body language, accent and mannerisms may all aid a character in her disguise. While people who have never met the person may be taken in with a simple disguise, more involved deceptions require knowledge and execution of personal quirks, dialect and other more personal details.

Drive

Roll: Dexterity + (relevant Drive skill)

Characters who possess the Drive skill are able to drive a given type of vehicle. In addition, this skill includes knowledge of common traffic rules, and the most basic knowledge of how to temporarily repair common problems (such as flat tires on ground vehicles). Anything more complicated will require the Tech Redemption skill. When taking Drive skill, players must choose a particular category of vehicle that the character is familiar with. Furthermore, players may choose, at the gamemaster's option, to specify a particular type of vehicle (i.e.: skimmer) within a category (Landcraft).

Complementary Skill

• **Tech Redemption:** Any character attempting to fix or "soup up" a vehicle will need to know in great detail how it works. Choose an appropriate Tech Redemption skill for the type of vehicle.

Aircraft

Roll Tech + Aircraft. Flitters, suborbitals, jets, helicopters and other air vehicles that remain within the atmosphere. Barring the occasional hot air balloon or flying beastcraft, some form of advanced aircraft is usually found among the upper classes on most worlds, regardless of their Tech Level.

Beastcraft

Roll Extrovert + Beastcraft. Vehicles powered by animals, including horses, giant cockroaches or dolphins. In many outlying areas, Beastcraft is still the dominant form of transportation.

Complementary Skill

• **Beast Lore:** Knowledge of the ways animals will react in a given situation can aid a character using Beastcraft.

Landcraft

Roll Dexterity + Landcraft. Land-based vehicles of all types, including skimmers, bikes, trains and cars. Landcrafts are found in increasing numbers relative to the amount of tech remaining on the planet.

Spacecraft

(Guild skill)

Roll Tech + Spacecraft. All extra-planetary vehicles, from space transport freighters to star fighters. Rare and valuable as one of the most useful types of technology remaining from the Second Republic, obtaining a spacecraft as a non-guild member is nigh-impossible on some worlds.

Complementary Skills

• **Lore (Jumpweb):** Knowledge of the jumpweb of the Known Worlds, including the planetary bodies and satellites to be navigated in each system, is a must for pilots flying regular routes.

• **Science (Astronomy):** Any space pilot attempting to explore uncharted territory will, quite literally, be lost without knowledge of Astronomy to navigate from.

Watercraft

Roll Dexterity + Watercraft. Boats, subs and other vehicles for travel on or under water. In more primitive areas, this may be a conoe or even a simple raft, while more tech-oriented worlds may have speedboats and submarines.

Empathy

Roll: Perception + Empathy

Empathy is the ability to sense what another person is feeling by "reading" him for non-verbal cues. A person's stance, mannerisms and other body language can indicate his emotional state, and may help a character to determine if a subject is lying.

This skill may not be used to read the attitudes of aliens; that requires the Xeno-Empathy skill (see below).

Detect Lie: Although it is not foolproof, characters may attempt to determine if a subject is telling the truth by observing her body language. Like ancient "lie detector" machines, the empath looks for changes in breathing patterns, nervousness and other physical cues. But be warned — the subject may only be uncomfortable about the subject and not actually lying. Roll Perception + Empathy.

Complementary Skills

• **Inquiry:** Knowing the right questions to ask combined with knowledge of how to interpret changes in body language can greatly aid a character attempting to find out information. Does the subject become nervous whenever the duke is mentioned? Is he trying to appear confident — perhaps trying a little *too* hard?

• **Lore (Folk):** Familiarity with a particular culture can be useful in judging emotional and physical reactions.

Etiquette (High Society)

Roll: Wits + Etiquette

Every social group has unwritten rules of behavior, and outsiders unfamiliar with this code are likely to have a correspondingly more difficult time doing anything from getting directions to performing delicate negotiations. Lack of this skill may cause a character to unknowingly commit a dreadful faux pas, causing her ejection from the castle or any number of worse fates.

Presentation: When a character is admitted to noble chambers for an audience, first impressions are everything. If the duke thinks you are a peer (in culture if not rank), then he may be more open and generous with boons. If you come on like a bumpkin, you may wind up being sold to the Chainers simply to prevent you from ever staining the chambers again with your uncouth tongue. Roll Extrovert + Etiquette. If a character is trying to present himself as haughty or above-it-all, he may substitute Introvert for the skill test. But beware — this could wind up insulting the lord if you can't back your attitude up with some royal blood.

Complementary Skills

• **Anthropology or Lore:** Knowledge of a particular culture can help a character to understand the reasons behind social rituals. In addition, different alien races often have customs that are vastly different from those of human society, and thus anyone wishing to fit in needs to learn a very different way of behaving.

• **Charm:** Naturally charismatic individuals will more easily fit in to any given group, including high society.

• **Knavery:** The ability to quickly and skillfully cover up for any faux pas can be invaluable when one is trying to make a good impression.

Focus

Roll: Introvert + Focus

The ability to attain a deep concentration or focus can aid nearly any character, though it is most often possessed by those who are also skilled at prayer or occult powers. Focus is required for meditation, but it may also be used to aid in long or deliberate tasks, such as studying for a test or aiming a sniper rifle. In order to focus for such a task, the character must spend five minutes or more meditating; if less time is taken, use the guidelines under Steady Hand (see the description for the Calm characteristic, earlier in this chapter).

When using Focus as a complementary skill, the amount of modifiers it adds to the primary skill is also the amount subtracted from any Perception rolls that character makes while focused (except for the primary skill).

Complementary Skills

• **Arts or Performance:** Some characters may find that singing, playing an instrument, dancing or sketching may

113

help to focus their minds before beginning a task.

• **Stoic Mind:** Characters who possess the skill Stoic Mind are already adept at a specific type of focus, and thus may apply what they have learned in that respect to other tasks that require similar focus.

Gambling

Roll: Wits + Gambling

Knowledge of the Gambling skill includes rules of play for the most popular games of chance, and usually includes the most common means of cheating at said games. Though characters from nearly any walk of life may understand the basics of gambling, the Scravers are known far and wide for their expertise.

Cheat: The character can cheat at games which involve a certain degree of skill. This includes card and dice games, though not games which are won completely through random chance, such as roulette. Roll Wits + Gambling.

Detect Cheating: Even if a character does not personally cheat, every good gambler learns to recognize when their opponent is trying to pull a fast one. Those who don't learn are usually not very successful gamblers. Roll Perception + Gambling.

Complementary Skills

• **Observe:** Characters attempting to tell if an opponent is cheating will more easily notice things if they are naturally good at observation.

• **Sleight of Hand:** Some games of "chance" may be manipulated by introducing (or removing) certain cards, tiles or game pieces from play. Any character who can do so subtly will subsequently have much better "luck".

Inquiry

Roll: Wits + Inquiry

Inquiry covers the footwork side of investigation, unlike Academia (the paper pusher's version of this skill). The essence of Inquiry is the ability to obtain and correctly interpret information. Any character who engages in any sort of detective work, searching for the tell-tale clues that will indicate what happened at a scene, will find this skill invaluable. Inquiry also includes knowing what questions to ask a suspect, as well as how to interpret what he does — and doesn't — tell you. Inquisitors of Temple Avesti sometimes possess Inquiry, though they often tend to bully their way through the interrogation process rather than using subtlety.

Complementary Skills

• **Observe:** Knowing how to interpret the information isn't much use unless you can get the information first, and this often depends on keen observation skills.

• **Lore (any):** Characters knowledgeable about a particular topic or region will find that their background comes in handy when investigating related subjects ("Ah, this tobacco is the finest quality platinum grade, grown only on the moon of Aragon. Whoever our suspect is, he has considerable resources and contacts within the aristocracy to be spending such an amount on tobacco!").

• **Science (any):** Knowledge of certain sciences may come in handy for more advanced detective work. With the proper tools and knowledge, an entire subject profile may be derived by unraveling the DNA found in a single hair.

Knavery

Roll: Extrovert + Knavery

The art of fast-talking one's way into (or out of) a situation, or simply flat-out lying in a convincing manner. By using a combination of natural charm, verbal misdirection and all-out chutzpah, a character can attempt to bamboozle a target into believing almost anything from "You don't need to see his identification" to "Yes, I really will look younger and sexier if I wear one of these fine hats".

Complementary Skills

• **Charm:** Obviously, a charismatic character will have an advantage when using the Knavery skill.

• **Empathy:** Characters skilled at reading the emotions of others will have much better luck when attempting to tailor their arguments to an individual.

Lockpicking

Roll: Dexterity + Lockpicking

Locks come in a variety of different styles in the Known Worlds, and only a character skilled at manipulating them will have much luck in opening them. While many locks can be circumvented by simply shooting them off, this attracts undue attention and simply is not stylish at all. To pull off a heist quickly and quietly requires that a character be able to utilize more subtle means to achieve her goals. Note that without the proper tools, Lockpicking is far more difficult. Characters who find themselves faced with locks on a regular basis would be well advised to keep their tools on them at all times. Characters who are skilled at manipulating tech locks will find that the necessary tools are often expensive. See Chapter Seven: Technology for more details on locks.

Tech Locks: Occasionally characters will encounter magnetic locks, keypads or even disused Second Republic retinal or palm scanners. In these cases, the character must also be knowledgeable about the technology being used in order to attempt to open the lock. Roll Tech + Lockpicking.

Complementary Skills

• **Artisan (Locksmith):** Characters who understand the construction of a wide variety of locks will have an immediate advantage when trying to figure out how to spring them.

• **Tech Redemption (Mech Redemption):** Knowledge of the way mechanical things work, as well as what can cause them to break, can help a character to determine how a locking mechanism works.

Lore

Lore is a general category, and requires a specialization. Characters skilled at a particular Lore are familiar with the facts, theories and stories associated with it, as well as the particular sub-culture interested in similar things.

Complementary Skill

• **Academics:** Knowledge of where to find information can help any character who needs to research a particular Lore further.

Folk

Roll Wits + Folk Lore. Folk Lore includes the legends and culture of the serfs and commoners in a given area. Although the nobility are not usually as aware of folk beliefs, the legends of an area play an important part in the entire culture.

Jumpweb

Roll Tech + Jumpweb Lore. Knowledge of the jumpweb — the solar systems comprising the Known Worlds — is essential for anyone who wishes to travel between star systems. The Charioteers and Scravers guild comprise the largest groups knowledgeable about the jumpweb of the Known Worlds (and some unknown worlds, rumors say), but independents abound.

Object

Roll Wits + (Object) Lore. Players may choose more specific Lores, such as Rapier Lore (which would grant the character knowledge of the best and worst manufacturers, various styles, etc.).

Regional

Roll Wits + Regional Lore. Characters who have lived in one place for a long time usually possess some amount of Regional Lore. This can include anything from the story of how the city was founded to which ale house serves the best brew.

Xeno

Roll Wits + Xeno Lore. Any character with knowledge of alien races must have Xeno Lore. While information on races such as the Ur-Ukar, Ur-Obun, and Vorox is uncommon, lore on the Anunnaki and Vau is virtually impossible to obtain.

Performance

Roll: Extrovert + (relevant Performance skill)

Characters with the Performance skill are able to dance, perform music or otherwise use Arts skills in a public setting. There's always call for a bard at the local lord's mansion or the tavern. But the bard better be good, or he may wind up contemplating his poor wit in the dungeon or while washing the splattered fruit stains off his tunic. Alliances have begun (and ended) as a result of many such performances. The great Ur-Obun poet Shanor vo Kirn is said to

have caused an Ur-Ukar ambassador to weep — no mean feat — after hearing his moving tribute to those who fell in defense of the HanKavak citadel.

A character can perform many types of arts, such as Lute, Dance, Sing, Storytelling, etc., but each she must buy each one as a separate skill.

The Universal Performance Society (UPS) is active in bringing greater understanding between the disparate groups in the Known Worlds through the arts. This movement was begun by Alicia Decados, who, much to her family's dismay, spent several years training with the famed Vorox dancer Shali-brandor. The reinterpretation of dance that followed was the first of many cultural explosions, bringing a greater understanding between all peoples.

Complementary Skills

• **Arts:** Even if a character has tremendous stage presence and confidence, his performance will be better received if he actually has talent to back up his showmanship.

• **Focus:** Performance is a delicate balance between energy and control, and characters skilled at Focus will be more able to maintain this balance.

Physick

Roll: Wits + Physick

Physick covers anatomy, surgery, diseases and preventative medicine. This may also include the implantation of cybernetic devices, if the character also has that knowledge. Sanctuary Aeon and the Engineers guild are well known for particular specialties.

Characters wishing to use Physick on members of a race other than their own must first make a successful Wits + Xenobiology roll, or they will not be sufficiently familiar with how that particular race's physiology works. Any character likely to encounter aliens in her medical practice would be well advised to bone up on the similarities and differences in biological systems. After all, certain assumptions may lead to the death of the patient.

Surgery: Surgery is a very delicate procedure which involves attempting repair to organs. Only a rare few physicians are skilled surgeons. Roll Dexterity + Physick.

Characters who wish to focus on cosmetic or reconstructive surgery will find that their skills are as much in demand from the Scravers, Chainers and fugitives from justice as they are from the nobility, and that commoners can often come up with as much money as the nobles can when their identity is at stake.

Technical Medicine: The use of certain high-tech tools to aid a physician in her work requires a knowledge of how such things work; while a barbarian may know how to dress a wound to prevent infection, it is unlikely that he will know how to use a laser scalpel. While anyone with Remedy may follow the basic directions for the items commonly found in

a MedPak (such as tissue regenerative salves, stimulants and the like), anything more complex requires a Physick roll. Characters attempting to use medical technology in their work should roll Tech + Physick rather than Wits + Physick, due to the complex nature of the tools being used.

Complementary Skills

• **Remedy:** The ability to quickly and efficiently perform basic first aid without an assistant can greatly speed up and improve the quality of treatment.

• **Science:** A deeper understanding of Biology, Chemistry or even Physics or Cybernetics may be useful for anyone using Physick, depending on the circumstances.

Read

Unless a character possesses the skill Read, it is assumed that she is functionally illiterate. On many worlds this is not uncommon, and may not carry a social stigma in small outlying communities. Even among the nobility literacy is not always a given. Languages players may choose from are listed below. **Note:** This skill has no levels and costs 2 points per language.

Barbarian

Contrary to what many believe, many barbarian tribes, such as the Kurga, do have a written language, often stretching back into the mists of time. The player should specify which particular barbarian tribe's language she is fluent in.

Latin

A nearly forgotten tongue from Holy Terra, Latin is used for all Church rituals, documentation and official communication. Actually, Dark Age Latin is also composed of many Greek and even Sanskrit words — all languages known to have been spoken and written by the Prophet — but consists mainly of classical Latin. Characters who do not have Read Latin will find research in Church libraries all but impossible.

Urthish

The language of Holy Terra and the dominant language in the Known Worlds. It is usually the first language of most humans, and is commonly learned by many alien races as well.

Urthtech

Urthtech is not so much a language as a dialect of Urthish. During the Second Republic, the jargon used by technicians became outrageously specific and self-referential. Since the Fall, understanding of technical terminology (especially odd words coined from forgotten tech) has become increasingly rare. Tech-speak, or Urthtech as it is called, is now practically a separate language, one nearly incomprehensible to people who speak Urthish. Knowledge of Urthtech is necessary for anyone researching lost technology. (Read Urthtech automatically allows someone to speak

it. In other words, he can pepper his conversation with "Tweak the frangewire on the carbcase by three dreks to kick it into chug-chug.")

Xeno

(Ur-Obun, Ur-Ukar, Vorox, etc.)

Each alien race has one (or more) language(s), each of which must be taken as a separate skill.

Remedy

Roll: Wits + Remedy

Although not as all-encompassing as Physick, Remedy provides the all-important first aid that is usually necessary to sustain a character until help arrives. Remedy also includes an understanding of how to administer aid from a MedPak, including the popular tissue regenerative drug, Elixir. Sanctuary Aeon requires that all initiates learn something of Remedy, but many other groups and individuals possess some knowledge to greater or lesser degrees.

Within 10 minutes after a wound has been inflicted, a character can attempt or receive first aid to prevent the wound from worsening. This requires a Wits + Remedy roll; if successful, the injured character heals one Vitality level immediately. If the paramedic rolled a critical success, two levels are healed. (See Vitality, later in this chapter.)

Complementary Skill

• **Physick:** Any character with advanced training in Physick will sometimes be able to apply that knowledge to the more basic skill of Remedy as well.

Ride

Roll: Dexterity + Ride

The Ride skill allows characters to effectively control riding beasts, such as horses, llamas and other genetically similar creatures. To control beasts of burden the Drive skill is normally used.

Jumping: A characters may attempt to get her mount to jump over obstacles such as fences and small streams. This requires precise timing for both mount and rider. Roll Perception + Ride.

Mounted Combat: Not all animals are used to being in combat situations, and to control a mount during a combat can be a challenge even to veterans. A character's combat skill cannot exceed her Ride skill. For example, Erian Li Halan is firing her gun from horseback. Her Shoot skill is 6 and her Ride is 5. Since her Ride is lower, her Shoot skill is only 5.

Complementary Skills

• **Beast Lore:** Understanding the ways of animals and how they will react in different situations can be invaluable in knowing how best to guide them. Will wild horses from Manitou react differently than their more civilized cousins on Aragon, or is the response the same for both?

Science

Guild skill

Roll: Wits (or Tech) + Science

The study of science can be invaluable to characters in a variety of different situations. Because each type of science is a fairly broad category in and of itself, players should choose one or two types of science to specialize in.

Complementary Skills

• **Lores:** Lores may be useful in understanding data obtained from the study of different sciences. How does the information obtained apply to the local culture? What impact would new technology have on the area? What are the local beliefs, and how could new information effect those beliefs?

• **Think Machine:** Characters able to use a think machine to aid them may be able to decrease the amount of time needed to analyze data. Only the most sophisticated machines will be able to draw conclusions from data, but most functional think machines can at least determine trends and anomalies in the data.

Anthropology

Anthropology is used to study and understand other cultures, including alien cultures.

Archaeology

The study of lost civilizations through their artifacts. Characters skilled at archeology might be able to determine what culture or time period a given artifact is from.

Astronomy

The study of the heavens, including stars, planets and other heavenly bodies. Characters proficient at Astronomy will also have some familiarity with the legends and superstitions of their culture regarding the heavens. This can also be used for navigation within star systems.

Biology

The study of organic life, encompassing botany, zoology, anatomy, and a host of other sub sciences. Characters who understand Biology will find that it can be applied in a variety of different situations from Physick to Beast Lore.

Chemistry

The science of matter— its composition and properties, especially on an atomic or molecular scale. The secular cousin of Alchemy, Chemistry differs in that it is based solely upon demonstrable phenomena instead of the spiritual qualities of substances.

Cybernetics

The study of communication and control processes in biological, mechanical and electronic systems. This can include anything from security systems to robotics and biotech.

Engineering

The design and construction of buildings, vehicles, etc.

Genetics

The study of genes, the blueprints for organic life. This science is often coupled with Biology for a more complete understanding of both.

Geology

The study of rocks and planetary bodies. This may also include diverse fields such as metallurgy and plate tectonics, and can be invaluable when constructing underground or stone structures.

Meteorology

The study of the atmosphere, especially weather and weather patterns. Many pilots learn basic Meteorology to aid them in determining routes, and even farmers learn the basics of determining what the weather will be like.

Physics

The study of motion and the transfer of energy. While abstract in theory, the practical applications can be used in a variety of different tasks, from Tech Redemption to Physick and even Artisan skills.

Terraforming

The premier science of the Second Republic, this highly technical craft involves knowledge of many other sciences. A character's Terraforming skill cannot be higher than his Geology, Meteorology and Biology (it cannot be higher than the lowest of these skills). Thus, to learn Terraforming 8, the character must already know Geology 8, Meteorology 8 and Biology 8. Too few folks know this science these days, with bad results for certain planets that are reverting in the absence of technicians to their pre-terraformed (often hostile) states. Legendary are the handful of terraforming architects who remade Byzantium Secundus, Criticorum and Pandemonium. Even more legendary is Doramos, the architect of Pentateuch, who is said to have raised the science to an art form (and an alchemy, say the Eskatonic priests of the planet).

Xeno-Biology

Biology of non-Urthish races and creatures. A must for anyone engaging in Physick upon alien races, inventive characters may apply knowledge of Xeno-Biology to more diverse skills such as Martial Arts — after all, knowing the best place to hit an opponent can be a distinct advantage.

Search

Roll: Perception + Search

This skill allows a character to conduct a methodical search of an area for hidden or concealed objects, doors or compartments. Search can also include frisking someone for concealed weapons or other objects. Characters skilled at Search have a sharp eye for the best hiding places, either from experience at hiding or at finding things. Members of Temple Avesti are known for their unwavering attention to detail when it comes to searching.

Complementary Skills

• **Observe:** Characters who are naturally observant have a much better chance of locating things that are hidden.

• **Sneak:** Characters skilled at not being seen have a natural advantage when searching for hidden things; they simply look in the places *they* would hide something.

Sleight of Hand

Roll: Dexterity + Sleight of Hand

A skill normally associated with charlatans and street entertainers, Sleight of Hand is also useful for anyone wishing to hide small objects, including small weapons. Sleight of Hand does not usually involve actually concealing an object so much as misdirecting the attention of any observers. This skill can also be used to remove small objects from another individual's person.

Conceal: Small objects up to the size of a knife may be concealed from observers. Roll Dexterity + Sleight of Hand. This skill can be invaluable to anyone attempting to smuggle weapons, documents or tools into a secure area.

Pick Pockets: The character can remove objects that are in another person's possession without their knowledge. This includes wallets, rings, small holstered weapons and even necklaces for the truly daring. Objects in pouches simply tied onto belts are much easier to pilfer than things in deep or zippered pockets. Roll Dexterity + Sleight of Hand.

Complementary Skills

• **Knavery:** By supplying a constant patter the character can more easily distract those who are observing her. Knavery can also prove to be invaluable in getting out of the situation should the character get caught.

Social

Each of the following skills are actually separate skills (and must be bought individually) that fall under the Social heading. Though all of these skills are somewhat related in that they deal with social interactions, they are each unique in their approach. For example: a church leader could use Oratory to sway a crowd but could not keep good control over them if she did not have good Leadership skill, once the initial effects of her speech wore off.

All the noble houses have tutors to instruct youngsters on social graces, but the Reeves guild also contains many people who put the average noble to shame.

Each of these sub-skills has its own roll and complementary skills associated with it.

Acting

Roll Extrovert + Acting. Acting may also be used as a Performance skill, but it most often comes into play when a character is attempting to act in a way that is unnatural to

him, such as when impersonating a member of the House Guard.

Complementary Skills

• **Disguise:** A character in a disguise is more likely to be perceived as the individual he is trying to impersonate.

Debate

Roll Wits + Debate. Characters skilled at Debate have learned over time how to present concise, persuasive arguments and to likewise find the flaws in the arguments of others.

Complementary Skills

• **Impress:** Characters who are easily able to impress others will be more likely to sway others to their point of view.

• **Charm:** A character may attempt to use his natural charm when attempting to sway others in a debate. Though use of Charm in a debate can often backfire if those involved in the debate catch on to the fact that they are being bamboozled. In such cases a character's Charm can act as a *penalty* rather than a bonus. This is always at the gamemaster's discretion, of course.

Leadership

Roll Extrovert + Leadership. Few leaders are born that way; most learn through trial and error, as well as observation of those who do it well. Characters skilled at Leadership will have an advantage when trying to organize groups of people. A good leader is skilled at both identifying the skills of others and determining how they can best be put to use.

Complementary Skills

• **Impress:** The ability to impress others can be very important for good leadership. Followers are more likely to listen to someone with a commanding presence and a great deal of self-confidence.

Oratory

Roll Passion + Oratory. This skill is commonly used by politicians and generals alike when attempting to invoke certain emotions in a crowd. Budding revolutionaries will also find this skill useful, as will anyone attempting to plead a case in a court of law. This skill is also common among professional storytellers and bards. Unlike Leadership, Oratory does not have a lasting effect. Also, Oratory differs from Knavery in that it is generally used to incite emotion and passion rather than to out-and-out deceive.

Complementary Skills

• **Empathy:** Understanding the current emotional state of your audience can be an important factor when orating.

• **Lore:** Knowing the familiar stories and parables common to a culture, and using them to illustrate points can involve an audience on a more personal level.

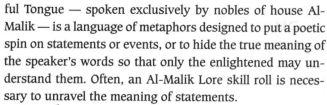

Spacesuit

Guild skill

The ability to function normally while inside a spacesuit or in a zero-gravity environment is not common, and members of the Charioteers guild often get more practice at it than others outside the guild. Many skills which seem straightforward when performed under normal conditions become much more complicated when the character is using a spacesuit or other type of large, bulky armor. The Spacesuit skill offsets any penalties levied for unfamiliarity with spacesuits or zero-g environments. **Note:** This skill has no levels and costs 2 points.

Characters who do not have this skill are not proficient at doing things in spacesuits; all physical actions are considered to be Demanding tasks (-4).

Speak

Speak allows the character fluency in each language chosen. **Note:** This skill has no levels and costs 2 pts per language. Assume that each character can speak her native language.

Each player should choose how and where the language was learned — was it taught to him by a tutor, or did he pick it up from listening to recordings of music? Did she learn the language on the streets, or from a guild trader? While anyone who possesses the Speak skill can communicate in her chosen language, particular dialects and slang can vary greatly, and may add a lot to roleplaying.

How well a character speaks depends on the situation: If he is addressing a crowd, roll Extrovert + Social (Oratory). If performing a dramatic reading, roll Extrovert + Performance. If composing a letter, roll Wits + Arts (Rhetoric). Additionally, understanding the body language of a culture is just as important as understanding the words of the language. Characters able to "get the basic idea" from nonverbal cues will pick up far more nuances of the language than those trying to understand solely by what they hear; roll Perception + Empathy (or Xeno-Empathy when interacting with aliens).

Some characters have compelling voices or speech patterns to aid them when addressing others; see Blessings, later this chapter.

Barbarian

There are two main barbarian tongues: Kurgan (from the Kurga Caliphate outside the Hazat border) or Vuldrok (from the Vuldrok Raiders outside the Hawkwood border). When choosing Speak Barbarian the player should choose a specific dialect.

Graceful Tongue

(Al-Malik noble house skill)

Not so much a language as a mode of speech, the Grace-ful Tongue — spoken exclusively by nobles of house Al-Malik — is a language of metaphors designed to put a poetic spin on statements or events, or to hide the true meaning of the speaker's words so that only the enlightened may understand them. Often, an Al-Malik Lore skill roll is necessary to unravel the meaning of statements.

Dialects

Players may choose different cultural or area dialects to reflect character backgrounds. For instance, the argot spoken in the streets of Pandemonium's Hub is very different than that heard in the Port Authority on Byzantium Secundus.

Latin

An ancient Holy Terra tongue lost for centuries to the rest of the universe, Latin survives as the ritual language of the Church.

Scraver Cant

Scraver guild skill

Based on Urthish but incorporating both alien and invented words, Scravers Cant relies heavily on non-verbal cues and emphasis to give words entirely different meanings.

Urthish

This is the most common language in the Known Worlds, and is possessed by all human characters.

Xeno

(Obun, Ukar, Vorox, Ascorbite, Gannok, Vau, etc.)

As with Barbarian, when choosing Xeno the player must choose a specific language as well.

Stoic Body

Roll: Calm + Stoic Body

The study of Stoic Body is long and arduous, and not for the faint of heart. Still, many believe that the results are well worth the years of training required. Characters skilled at Stoic Body may ignore pain, hunger, sleep deprivation and torture. They can sometimes govern their normally involuntary activities, such as breathing and blinking.

Ignore Wounds: The character can try to ignore the pain of his wounds and continue on while suffering no wound penalties. Roll Calm + Stoic Body; each victory point offsets one wound penalty.

Complementary Skills

• **Focus:** Characters possessing Focus have a greater deal of control over their bodies, especially when dealing with pain. In order to use Focus as a complementary skill the character must have time to clear his mind and meditate, though this can be done before entering a situation in which the character feels he may need it, such as before a battle or before beginning an all-night journey through the desert wastes.

Stoic Mind

Roll: Calm + Stoic Mind

Like Stoic Body, the study of Stoic Mind requires intense training that often takes years of a character's life. It includes the ability to resist occult powers, especially telepathic or empathic intrusion or perusal. It also allows a character to mask her aura, and at higher levels to project an illusory aura. More details can be found under Occult Powers, in Chapter Four.

Complementary Skills

• **Focus:** A character possessing Focus has more control over his mind and is better able to defend against psychic assaults of any sort. As with Stoic Body the character must have time to prepare herself for Focus to be used as a complementary skill.

Streetwise

Roll: Wits + Streetwise

The character is familiar with underworld and criminal activities. Characters with Streetwise often have lived in the "wrong" section of town, and have picked up a number of related skills and knowledges just to get by. This skill may be used to contact the criminal underworld or acquire illegal goods or services, including black-market items. While any character familiar with life on the streets may have Streetwise, it is nearly always found in members of the Scravers and Chainers guilds.

Fencing Goods: The character can attempt to sell goods which have been stolen or are otherwise illegal. Roll Wits + Streetwise. Once a buyer has been located the character will probably be required to negotiate to get the price he desires.

Word on the Street: Characters who know how to get the word on the street know who to talk to — and how to act when talking to them — to get the most valuable information and gossip. Roll Wits + Streetwise. Without skill at Streetwise, characters will have a hard time fitting in or getting the right people to talk to them.

Value Estimation: The character can estimate the value of black-market goods. This varies greatly from place to place and even from day to day, but characters skilled at this are able to second guess the market based on information picked up on the street. Roll Perception + Streetwise.

Complementary Skills

• **Regional Lore:** Characters who are familiar with a particular area are more likely to be able to make contact with members of its underworld, and will often know the best person to contact to get the highest possible price for goods.

• **Speak (Language):** Knowing the language in a place you are seeking illegal goods can be very important. Not only can knowing the native language act as a complementary skill, but gamemasters may decide to give the character significant penalties if she does not.

Survival

Roll: Wits + Survival

The character is skilled at surviving in adverse conditions — generally wild places far from civilization. This includes knowledge of how to improvise makeshift shelters, identify edible plants, trap and fish.

Fire Making: Roll Wits + Survival. Without the proper tools, building a fire in the wild can be a challenge. Knowing where to find dry wood, how to generate enough sparks and how to build a fire for maximum heat (not to mention how to do so without burning down the forest around you) are all essentials for anyone trying to survive in adverse conditions.

Hunting: Roll Perception + Survival. Skilled hunters incorporate knowledge of their prey, their weapon, and the region with patience to produce an effective combination. This may also include the ability to set snares, make decoys or imitate mating calls. Beware, though — if used at the wrong time, this can put the hunter on the business end of a charging blue-striped mountain tiger!

Complementary Skills

• **Beast Lore:** Knowing the habits of local beasts gives a character a distinct advantage when hunting (or being hunted!).

• **Lore (terrain):** The more a character knows about a particular type of terrain, the better chance he has for survival.

• **Shoot or Archery:** Skill with a ranged weapon makes bringing down game considerably easier for the would-be survivalist.

• **Tracking:** Characters who know how to find their prey in the wild will have far better luck than those who simply wait for the prey to come to them.

Tech Redemption

Roll: Tech + (relevant Tech Redemption skill)

Any character who possesses the Tech Redemption skill should choose a specialty, as there are considerable differences between repairing the sole of a shoe and a think machine. In some cases, more than one Tech Redemption skill may be needed to fix a particularly complicated device. While it is most common among the Engineers guild, there are many among the Charioteers and Scravers guilds, as well as some independents, who possess an understanding of Tech Redemption.

Jury-Rig: Roll Wits + (relevant Tech Redemption). This allows the character to effect quick repairs without the proper tools and materials. Such quick-fixes are only temporary and real repairs should be made as soon as possible.

Improve: Roll Tech + (relevant Tech Redemption). The

character can attempt to make improvements on existing devices. Proper tools and materials are always required to make an improvement.

Complementary Skills

• **Artisan:** If a character is attempting to fix a crafted object (a leaking roof, a torn cloak), experience at constructing that type of object from scratch can help the character to produce more finished, long-lasting work.

• **Science:** An understanding of the science behind the construction of an object (particularly Physics) can aid a character to understand the best way to repair an object.

Craft Redemption

Roll Tech + Craft Redemption. This skill can cover the repair of any crafted, non-mechanical/tech item, from a worn scabbard to a cracked plate. Characters may chose to specialize, but anyone skilled at Craft Redemption is considered to be "handy", and able to fix crafted items with a minimum of tools.

High Tech Redemption

(Guild skill)

Roll Tech + High Tech Redemption. With this skill, a character may attempt to fix complex or high-technology devices, such as think machines or starship jumpdrives. Without the proper parts at hand, this can be difficult; however, characters may attempt to jury rig improvised solutions that will work at least temporarily.

Mech Redemption

Guild skill

Roll Tech + Mech Redemption. This skill covers all mechanical devices, from to gas-fueled generators to scissors.

Volt Redemption

Guild skill

Roll Tech + Volt Redemption. This skill allows the character to repair electrical devices, including flashlights, radios, tasers and electronically powered vehicles.

Think Machine

Guild skill

Roll: Tech + Think Machine

One of the great achievements of the Second Republic was the invention of vastly powerful computers and artificial intelligence devices. After the Fall, many of these miraculous fonts of information were destroyed, either by Church inquisitors or peasants fearful and misunderstanding of a machine which thinks. Eventually, guildsmen and wealthy nobles began to build computers again, now called "think machines." In addition, those ancient computers which survived were brought back into use. However, current operating systems (and there are many) differ from Second Republic ones, making it much harder to retrieve ancient data.

The think machine is a contraption largely incompre-

hensible to the average layman. Some have unlocked the mysteries of these ancient computers, and anyone skilled at using them will certainly be looked upon with awe — and more than a little distrust — by those who aren't.

Think Machine skill is a rare ability found most often in members of guilds such as the Engineers and Charioteers, and it allows a character to access and use computers. Accessing information and simple programming are possible. Some members of house Al-Malik are also said to know some of the mysteries of think machines, though they keep whatever knowledge they have secret.

The Vau have their own computers, vastly different from Known World machines. A special skill is required to use them, but it is nigh impossible to find a teacher for this skill.

Complementary Skills

• **Read Urthtech:** Understanding the Urthtech language is often useful for understanding the workings of Think Machines.

• **Sciences (Think Machine):** Knowing the science behind Think Machines can make operating them much easier.

Throwing

Roll: Dexterity + Throwing

Knives, throwing stars, darts and even rocks fall into the category of thrown weapons, and only characters experienced with them will have much luck in hitting their targets. Most folks can fling a rock at someone (roll Dexterity + Vigor), but to throw an object with an edge requires Throwing skill. Otherwise, the target may get hit with the butt of the handle or the flat of the blade, delivering negligible damage.

Some throwing weapons are small enough that a character can fit more than one in his throwing hand (throwing stars, darts, etc.). A character will suffer a -1 penalty to his goal roll for each extra weapon in his hand. See the Weapons Chart in Chapter Six: Combat for further details.

Torture

Roll: Wits + Torture

Considered distasteful by some, a normal business practice by others and an art form by still others, Torture is a means of extracting information from an individual by causing physical or mental pain and discomfiture. Torture is still a commonly used method of obtaining information, particularly by Inquisitors. This means of information extraction is most commonly used on serfs and freemen without alliances to protect them. Temple Avesti, the Muster and the Reeves are among some of the groups most skilled at Torture.

Complementary Skills

• **Empathy:** Using Empathy as a complementary skill allows the torturer to determine what forms of torture would work best on an individual.

• **Physick:** Knowledge of how the body works and of

the location of nerve centers is extremely useful when torturing a subject.

Tracking

Roll: Perception + Tracking

The Tracking skill is often possessed by hunters and rangers, but some bounty hunters and Inquisitors have it as well. Characters skilled at Tracking are able to track their prey through the wilderness by following tell-tale signs of their passing.

Complementary Skills

• **Lore (terrain):** Knowing about the terrain can be useful when attempting to track.

Warfare

Roll: Varies

This skill is a general category which covers several aspects of warfare, from knowledge of tactics to the actual use of engines of war.

Artillery

Roll Perception + Artillery. This skill allows the character to operate and fire ballistae, mortars, cannons, rockets, etc.

Demolitions

Roll Tech + Demolitions. This skill allows the character to plant explosives to achieve a desired effect, such as to blow open a door or collapse a bridge.

Gunnery

Roll Dexterity + Gunnery. This skill allows the character to operate and fire starship weaponry as well as large mounted weapons such as machine guns and laser turrets.

Military Tactics

Roll Wits + Warfare. This skill gives the character general knowledge of military strategy and tactics. Military Tactics is used to know the best method of attack as well as knowledge of how troops will react in combat situations.

Complementary Skills

• **Lore (Xeno):** Know thine enemy. Knowing the habits of an alien culture can often reveal a weakness that can be exploited.

• **Lore (Terrain):** Knowing the terrain you are fighting in can be the first step towards victory. Different types of terrain can have drastic effects on what type of assault or defense should be used.

• **Lore (Regional):** Knowing the layout of a particular region can give a significant advantage in warfare.

Xeno-Empathy

Roll: Perception + Xeno-Empathy

Characters with this skill are able to determine an alien's emotional status by interpreting non-verbal cues. The player must choose to have Empathy with one of the following races,

though this skill may be bought multiple times in order to have Empathy with multiple races. Some of the possible races are: Ur-Obun, Ur-Ukar, Vorox, etc.

Complementary Skills

• **Lore (Xeno):** Having a good background in the history of a race can aid in interpreting their emotions.

Blessings and Curses

Julia Abrams smiled, but then quickly regretted it. Damn it! she thought. When will I learn that droxi is played stonefaced? The Scraver across from her, not betraying a hint of emotion, placed his xyloprene cards on the table. A chon, shek and floon. Julia sank into her chair, knowing that he wouldn't have surrendered his cards if she hadn't shown her own hand. Another round or two and she could have firmed up her chons enough to blow away all his sheks and floons. But she couldn't beat his hand. She didn't have the kind of money she'd just wagered and lost. Her eyes wandered to the door and she wondered how in the world she was going to make it there before they started firing.

Blessings and Curses represent a character's psychological quirks or physical endowments and/or handicaps. Blessings add positive modifiers to a characteristic or skill in a specific situation while Curses subtract from a characteristic or skill. Blessings may raise a characteristic or skill above 10 in certain situations, and Curses can cause a characteristic or skill to have a negative level.

Characters begin with no free Blessings; they must purchase them with Extras. Curses give the character more Extras to spend.

Blessings and Curses have restrictions, or situations which activate their modifiers. If the situation does not come into play, then the character does not receive that modifier. These situations are declared when the Blessing or Curse is bought, and they can be interpreted rather broadly. Situations which occur only rarely or are narrowly interpreted are usually worth more points. Examples are given below. They are meant as guidelines; players can choose to purchase any of them with more or less modifiers than those given below.

No character may purchase more than seven Blessings modifiers or choose more than seven points of Curses. These traits are meant to emphasize a few select character quirks, not to detail every neuroses possessed by the character.

Appearance

These modifiers always apply in situations involving social interaction and are interracial: the beauty or ugliness of the Children of the Ur or the Vorox is generally recognized by humans and vice versa. However, the character's looks may not aid him among those who know him well (gamemaster's discretion).

Blessings

Handsome (1 pt: +1 Charm)
Beautiful (2 pts: +2 Charm)
Angelic (3 pts: +3 Charm)

Curses

Homely (+1 pt: -1 Charm)
Ugly (+2 pts: -2 Charm)
Monstrous (+3 pts: -3 Charm unless seeking pity)

Behavior

Personality quirks can be simulated with Blessings or Curses. For instance, most Hawkwoods are excessively Prideful, and find it hard to turn the other cheek when insulted. Thus, a Hawkwood may have a -3 modifier to her Calm, in case she ever had to roll to maintain her composure — it's important not to lose one's temper at the gala ball.

Blessings

Bold (2 pts: +2 Passion while acting when others hesitate)
Compassionate (2 pts: +2 Passion when helping others)
Curious (2 pts: +2 Extrovert when seeing something new)
Disciplined (2 pts: +2 Calm in combat situations)
Gracious (2 pts: + 2 Extrovert to guests)
Innovative (2 pts: +2 Tech when trying to invent something new)
Just (2 pts: +2 Passion when righting a wrong)
Loyal (2 pts: +2 Passion when following liege)
Pious (2 pts: +2 Extrovert among the sinful)
Shrewd (2 pts: +2 Wits against attempts to fast-talk)
Suspicious (2 pts.: +2 to Perception when rivals about)
Unyielding (2 pts: +2 Endurance when honor is at stake)

Curses

Argumentative (+2 pts: -2 Extrovert in conversation)
Bluster (+2 pts: -2 Extrovert when recounting deeds)
Brainwashed (+2 pts: -2 Wits when confronted with something that disagrees with character's brainwashed belief)
Callous (+2 pts: -2 Passion when asked for aid)
Clueless (+2 pts: -2 Perception to notice social cues)
Condescending (+2 pts: -2 Extrovert among the unenlightened)
Delusional (+2: -2 Perception when confronted with something that disagrees with character's delusional belief)
Disrespectful (+2 pts: -2 Extrovert around authority figures)
Greedy (+2 pts: -2 Calm when money involved)
Guilty (+2 pts: -2 on all rolls when opposing Church officials)

Gullible (+2 pts: -2 Wits against attempts to fast-talk)

Haughty (+2 pts: -2 Extrovert around serfs)

Impetuous (+2 pts: -2 Wits when trading)

Righteous (+2 pts: -2 Calm when judgment questioned)

Mammon (+2 pts: -2 Faith when money is involved)

Nosy (+ 2 pts: -2 Calm when seeing something new)

Phobic (+2 pts: -2 Calm around source of phobia)

Possessive (+2 pts: -2 Calm when cut out of the action)

Prideful (+2 pts: -2 Calm when insulted)

Secretive (+2 pts: -2 Extrovert around strangers)

Subtle (+2 pts: -2 Extrovert when explaining something)

Surly (+2 pts: -2 Extrovert when upset)

Uncouth (+2 pts: -2 Extrovert at society functions)

Unnerving (+2 pts: -2 Extrovert around superstitious people)

Vain (+1 pt: -1 Perception when being flattered)

Vengeful (+3 pts: -3 Calm when honor impinged, will never forget a slight)

Injuries

These traits represent injuries or diseases the character has suffered which impair her functioning.

Curses

Bad Heart (+2 pts: -2 Endurance with athletic tasks)

Bad Liver (+2 pts: -2 Endurance against toxins)

Bad Lungs (+1 pts: -1 Endurance with athletic tasks)

Horrible Scar or Burn (+2 pts: -2 Charm when visible)

Incurable Disease (+3 pts: -1 base Vitality)

Limp (+1 pt: base run = 8 meters)

Missing Arm (+4 pts: -4 Dexterity for tasks requiring two arms)

Missing Eye (+3 pts: -2 Perception due to limited field of vision, -1 Shoot due to poor depth perception)

Missing Leg (+4 pts: -2 Dodge, base run = 2 meters)

Pain Sensitive (+4 pts: -2 to all tasks for two turns after being wounded)

Shaky Hands (+2 pts: -2 Dexterity with fine manipulation)

Knacks

Knacks are those odd abilities which some people seem better at than others. Some are lucky in cards and love, while others seem cursed with bad karma.

Blessings

Ambidextrous (4 pts: +4 to offset the -4 penalty for using an off-hand weapon)

Beastmaster (2 pts: +2 for non-combat interaction with animals)

Born Salesman (2 pts: +2 Extrovert when selling)

Casanova (2 pts: +2 Passion when seducing others)

Compass (2 pts: +2 Wits when figuring out direction or location)

Crack Driver/Pilot (4 pts: +2 to all Drive skills)

Eloquent (2 pts: +2 Extrovert when swaying others through speech)

Fast Draw (2 pts: +2 Initiative drawing and firing a gun in same action)

Grease Monkey (4 pts: +2 with all Tech Redemption skills)

Hacker (2 pts: +2 with all think machine tasks)

Keen Ears (2 pts: +2 Perception with hearing only)

Keen Eyes (2 pts: +2 Perception with sight only)

Lucky at Cards (2 pts: +2 Gambling with cards)

Sensitive Smell (1 pt: +2 Perception with smell only)

Sensitive Touch (1 pt: +2 Perception to discern touched objects)

Sonorous (2 pts: +2 Extro when impressing others through speech)

Thrifty (2 pts: +2 Wits in money matters)

Curses

Bad Hearing (+2 pts: -2 Perception with hearing only)

Bad Vision (+2 pts: -2 Perception with sight only)

Beast Foe (+2 pts: -2 for non-combat interaction with animals)

Clumsy (+2 pts: -2 Dexterity with athletic tasks)

Mechanically Disinclined (+2 pts: -2 with all Tech Redemption skills)

Poor Liar (+2 pts: -2 Wits when lying)

Quasimodo (+2 pts: -2 Passion when seducing others)

Reputation

Most characters, being freemen and adventurers, eventually build a reputation (usually as heroes or thugs). A character's reputation becomes more important the farther up the social ladder she climbs. It is of extreme importance to nobles and is highly valued by priests, and the League often bases promotions on reputation. However, a character's renown can be subjective. While most of the Known Worlders may recognize a character as a hero, there are surely those who see otherwise and may hate the character for whatever deeds caused her to gain such accolades.

Some characters can begin the game with a pre-existing reputation. In addition, it is possible to have more than one reputation, one for the public and another for those who know you best. A Decados may be seen as a cad by the populace, but those in the house may see a cunning motivator. This second, private reputation is worth only half the points as the public reputation.

The character only gains the modifier once she has been recognized.

Blessings

Well-liked (1 pt: +1 Charm)

Charitable (2 pts: +2 Charm)

Honest (2 pts: +2 Extrovert)

Hero (2 pts: +2 Impress)

Curses

Cad (+2 pts: -2 Charm)

Scary (+2 pts: -2 Extrovert)

Liar or known criminal (+2 pts: -2 Knavery)

Tyrant (+2 pts: -2 Charm among peasants)

Size

The following Blessings/Curses apply at all times (unless specified otherwise):

Dwarf (+5 pts: -2 Vitality, base run = 6 meters, requires tailored clothing)

Short (+3 pts: -1 Vitality, base run = 8 meters)

Tall (3 pts: +1 Vitality, base run = 12 meters)

Giant (5 pts: +2 Vitality, base run = 14 meters, requires tailored clothing)

Benefices and Afflictions

Cardanzo waited in the dark corner in the red booth by the back door of the Drunken Amenta. A real dive, but the only place on Rampart he trusted. The whole city was full of scum who couldn't make it on richer worlds like Malignatius. But only on Rampart could he find someone who would know anything about the mysterious Scraver shipments to Pandemonium, the shipments which came through Rampart first. And only in this booth, in this bar, in this miserable part of town would Louis the Teeth agree to meet him. Cardanzo wondered if engaging in such gossip would get him killed one day. That's when the Scraver bully boys walked in with the bats, looking straight at him....

While many people in the Known Worlds prefer to have as little contact with other people as possible, others embrace the worlds around them. They join the clergy, run the guilds, maintain ties with aliens, seek out lost technology, and learn secrets others don't want them to discover. By the same token, mixing with others can cause a person to gain enemies, lose money, acquire obligations or worse. Benefices and Afflictions represent the most important of these. While Blessings and Curses represent features inherent to an individual (directly modifying characteristics or skills), Benefices and Afflictions are based on the individual's place in society. Blessings and Curses will almost never go away, but characters can lose their Benefices and Afflictions, though this should only happen after epic-level adventures.

Characters begin with 5 points of Benefices. They can use Extra points to get more points of Benefices or they can gain Afflictions. Afflictions are negative Benefices; the character has some social problem which gives him additional

Extras to spend on more Benefices or any other trait.

Players should think of these traits as something more than just a way to get more points or powers. The primary reason we include them in the game is as an aid to roleplaying. Choose those that most fit the personality you want your character to have. Really, it doesn't make much sense for a meditative priest to spend the points to get a flux sword. It does make sense for him to take the Cloistered Affliction to represent all those years spent in the monastery — and the way he blushes whenever he talks to a woman.

What follows is only a sample of some of the Benefices and Afflictions a character can have. Players and gamemasters should feel free to come up with their own. They should take care to focus on those that most fit the drama.

Also remember that characters will get some of the effects of Benefices through gameplay. Just because a Scraver doesn't spend the points to buy an energy shield doesn't mean he can't take one from a dead Decados. Of course, that is theft, and if other Decados find out about it (or see the Scraver wearing a shield with the house's crest on it)…

Background

These traits represent events or circumstances of a character's past which affect him to the current day. They include things he knows, things other people know, his history and events from his past.

Benefices

Alien Upbringing (2 pts): Due to some odd series of events, the character was raised by members of another race. It's almost unheard of for humans to care for a Ur-Ukar child or a Vorox to take care of a human infant, but it has happened. A character with this Benefice begins with knowledge of that species' language (the Speak skill) instead of his own. Anyone with a prejudice against non-human races (which includes almost every person in the Known Worlds) will tend to have a special distrust for the character.

Heir (3 pts): The character is next in line for some position of importance. When her parents die, she might become duchess of the al-Malik, inherit a Charioteer spaceship or lead the Vorox, but she has no idea when this will happen. It may never occur or it may be next week — it's all up to the gamemaster. Note that characters who want to be heirs to a noble still need to have the Nobility Benefice (below).

Secrets (1-5 pts): This Benefice is one of the most wide-ranging in the game. The secret the character knows can range from blackmail on a minor noble to the location of a forgotten planet. Gamemasters should work closely with players to ensure their secrets fit into the game he wants to run. What follows are guidelines on how to handle this since

only the gamemaster knows what secrets most influence her campaign.

1 = Blackmail on a minor noble (A Hazat chickened out of a duel)

2 = Discovered a secret coven of psychics

3 = Know the members of the Imperial Eye on your homeworld

4 = Found a cache of Second Republic goods

5 = Location of a forgotten planet (Gamemasters should only allow this kind of secret if they want the characters to go there)

Well-Traveled (3 or 5 pts): The character has been around a bit, and has heard a bit more. The character has the equivalent of Folk Lore 1 for every major planet in his travel radius.

3 = A Royal House's fiefs

5 = The Known Worlds

Afflictions

Addiction (2-4 pts): The character is addicted to some substance, and this addiction makes his life difficult at times.

2 = Basic addiction. Substance is cheap and easily gotten. The character must have at least one dose per week before symptoms of withdrawal begin.

+1 = Stronger addiction: Substance must be had twice weekly before withdrawal symptoms begin.

+1 = Substance is difficult to find (rare or illegal).

Symptoms of withdrawal vary based upon the drug and the withdrawal period. Gamemasters may require Calm rolls, or assign goal penalties as the symptoms get worse — whatever increases the dramatic tension of the moment is appropriate.

Cloistered (1 pt): The character grew up separately from other people, and has never gotten over the fact. Since she has had so few dealings with others, she may well misunderstand them, be nervous around them and have a hard time relating to them. Others are likely to find her odd, especially when she starts using the unique language she developed as a child.

Dark Secret (1-3 pts): Something about the character is so horrible that he will do almost anything to cover it up. Almost no one should know about it at the beginning of the game, but if it does come out, then the player should have a chance to either cover it back up or make up for it.

1 = Embarrassing (So why did you skip out on your wife and kids?)

2 = Dangerous (So, you help run a coven, do you?)

3 = Life-threatening (Don't let anyone find out how you tried to assassinate Emperor Alexius)

Infamous Family (1 pt): The character's family has gained notoriety, and this affects the way people view her. She may come from a family of thieves, heretics or murderers. Note that a character can buy both the Nobility Benefice

127

and this Affliction to represent how certain branches of even the noblest families have their problems.

Lost Worlder (1 pt): The character is from one of the newly rediscovered Lost Worlds. In the millennia between the Fall of the Republic and the rediscovery of the planet, culture has changed greatly. It is a struggle to fit in, and most people are wary of you.

Oath of Fealty (1-3 pts): The character owes an oath of fealty above and beyond his normal obligations. All nobles owe an oath to their prince, all priests to their archbishop, all League members to their dean. This is something in addition to that oath. The object of the oath may call on the character's aid when he/she desires, although there is usually something the character receives in return for this oath (such as a pledge to send soldiers in case the character's fief is under assault).

1 = Serious oath (will aid in major dealings in exchange for same)

2 = Martial oath (will risk life in exchange for a great boon, like land or protection)

3 = Extreme oath (will perform suicide mission in return for something great in case of success, or upkeep of family should task fail)

Obligation (1-3 pts): The character has a duty he cannot avoid. This could be a sacred site he has to keep holy, a Vorox child he must raise, or a payment he must make on a regular basis. This differs from the Oath of Fealty in that the character will not get anything in return for his obligation.

1 = Hindrance (requires the character be on a certain planet for holy days)

2 = Hazardous (puts the character's life at risk)

3 = Extreme (the character has sworn to uncover the heresies of a Brother Battle leader)

Orphan (1 pt): Family ties are the most important ones to the majority of people in **Fading Suns**, but the character doesn't even have these. He lost his family at a very young age and nothing ever replaced it. For him, the Chainers are a very real danger unless he finds some alliance. Note that a character cannot take Nobility or Alien Upbringing with this Affliction, as both of those require a family of some kind.

Stigma (1-4 pts): The character has a stigma of some sort. This is something which, if noticed by the common populace, would cause revulsion, suspicion or fear. When coming up with these, think of what would unnerve a superstitious medieval peasant. (All occultists and cybernetics-bearers have a mild Stigma, although theurgy Stigmas are often seen as holy rather than damning. They do not receive points for this Stigma.)

1 = Mild (wandering eye, hair on palms)

2 = Severe (dwarf, hunchback)

3 = Fearsome (pointed fangs)

4 = Unholy (red eyes, forked tongue)

Vow (varies): Some village priests complain that commoners swear by anything, but some people take their vows seriously. It is not only Church leaders who take vows of celibacy but lay men, nobles and guildmembers as well. Vows generally cover something the character decides to give up, such as material goods, sex or talking. The gamemaster decides how many points it is worth based on the impact the vow has on the game.

Vow of Silence +3

Vow of Poverty +2

Vow of Celibacy +1 (depending on the epic)

Community

Finding someone to trust has its risks in **Fading Suns**, but success has no end of rewards. These Benefices and Afflictions represent how the character relates to specific members of her community. Players do need to be careful how their characters treat these people, however. Today's committed allies may well become tomorrow's sworn enemies.

Benefices

Ally (1-11 pts): The character has a close relationship with someone in a position of power, and that person will go out of his way to help her. The cost of this Benefice is two points less than it would cost the player to buy that same level of status for her character. Thus if the character wants a Duke of House Hawkwood to be his ally, it will cost 11 points, compared to the 13 it would cost the player to have that title. Note that many allies may not have a title, but this should give the gamemaster an idea of how to rank them.

Contact (1 pt): The character has an acquaintance who helps him out in little ways. The contact might provide information, sell good weapons or just be willing to give him a place to stay when he needs it. Players should come up with basic information about the contact, and the gamemaster can flesh her out as he desires.

Family Ties (3 pts): Blood can be thicker than wine, and a character with this Benefice can draw on some exceptionally loyal allies of similar status to himself. Of course, this cuts both ways — if someone kills your father, you will have to hunt him down to the farthest planet.

Gossip Network (1-4 pts): The character has a series of informants who keep her up to date on certain areas of information. These may be cackling old nobles who let her know which lords have committed breaches of etiquette, merchants who will let her know who is buying what, or farmers who will be more than glad to tell her who has gone through their area recently. Their information may not be as good as a contact's, but they are everywhere. Still, the bigger it is, the less reliable the information. The cost varies by size of the network.

1 = City or community

2 = Planetwide

3 = An entire Royal House's holdings

4 = The Known Worlds

Protection (3 pts): Someone (or group of people) is looking out for the character. The character may well owe his protector something in return, but it is always helpful to be a Charioteer with the backing of the local Hawkwoods, even if he does have to fly them wherever they want to go.

Retinue (1-4 pts): If good help is hard to find, then good, loyal help is really going to cost you. You may have any number of servants your wealth can afford, but the really devoted ones cost points.

1 = Unskilled labor (butler, handmaiden)

2 = Noncombat specialist (cook, chauffeur)

3 = Combat able or multitalented (bodyguard, seneschal)

+1 = Fanatically loyal

Afflictions

Dependent (1 pt): Somebody relies a great deal on the character. This may be an elderly family member, a child or an often-in-trouble friend. Whatever the case, the character is likely to have some difficulty ensuring that this person is taken care of.

Vendetta (1-4 pts): Something you, your family or your friends has done have earned you an unyielding enemy. This person (or people) will do everything in his power to make your life difficult.

1 = Satisfied with making character's life miserable.

2 = Wants to kill character

+1 = Group

+2 = Multiple groups

Possessions

Priests may try and get people to look beyond their material condition, but many characters want little more than lots of stuff. While characters may feel that they can buy anything if they have enough money, many items of interest are exceptionally hard to find. Even if the character can find one, the owner might not want to sell it — at least not to someone who's not in his guild or a fellow noble. Characters can begin the game with these objects if they buy them at the start of play as Benefices. Of course, any possession can some day be lost.

Benefices

Jumpkey (2 pts): Usually only Charioteers or high-ranking members of the noble houses and Church have these, since the Charioteers consider it somewhat of a crime for others to carry them. Nonetheless, black market trade in jumpkeys is popular, regardless of the risk of being thrown out of an airlock by a Charioteer protecting his guild's monopoly. Each key holds coordinates for a jumproute between two planets: the departure planet and the destination planet; the key works both ways (coming and going) between these worlds.

Passage contracts (2-10 pts): Thanks to some preexisting arrangement with one of the guilds, the character does not have to worry about booking passage on starships. Of course, the accommodations may not always be the best, and the ship may make a number of stops along the way, but it is a (mostly) sure thing.

2 = Tramp freighter (You ride with the cargo)

4 = Transport (Share a room with nine other passengers)

6 = Stateroom (Made for two, has been known to hold eight or more)

8 = Luxury liner (The best)

10 = Ship is at your command (Whatever you want)

Refuge (2-10 pts): The character has some place he can go where he feels safe. It might be a noble's castle, a hidden monastery, a guild safe house or just a cave he outfitted himself. Whatever the case, it is almost always open to him — unless someone destroys it first. The following costs are only guidelines. Gamemasters should make the player pay for extra protection, comfort or whatever.

2 = Small farm

4 = Guild safe house

6 = Monastery

8 = Castle

10 = Military base

Artifacts and Relics

Characters can begin the game with many different kinds of rare and valuable items. While most equipment is bought with firebirds (see the Riches Benefice, below), some are simply too rare, unique or expensive to put a price tag upon. These include Second Republic weapons (wireblades, flux swords), powered armor, a sentient think machine, occult artifacts and anything else the player can think of. Details for such items can be found in Chapter Seven: Technology.

Ownership of these sort of items can come through family inheritance ("Son, now that you are of age, I bestow upon you *Deathreaper*, the family sword, a wireblade carried by five generations of our family."), lucky scavenging ("Hey, look what I found on that abandoned asteroid base!") or destiny ("Get a load of this: That old monk insisted I carry this rosary; he said the end times will come if I don't.").

Ancient Technology

Advisor (5 pts): The character has a hand-held think machine with an artificial intelligence that can advise him on a number of matters. It is a bit crude, however, and may become more annoying than helpful at times. For more details, see *Think Machines* in Chapter Seven: Technology.

Flux Sword (11 pts): An energy sword, using a more

129

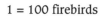

advanced variation on blaster and energy shield tech. While these are still occasionally produced by ingenious weaponsmiths, they are rare.

Mist Sword (13 pts): A flux sword that can be psychically attuned to its wielder — making this a very rare and sought-after artifact by psychic covens.

Neural Disrupter (10 pts): A deadly and banned weapon that harms a victim's brain cells.

Psi Cloak (10 pts): Advanced 2nd Republic tech that provides its wearer defense against psychic attacks and neural disrupters.

Wireblade (12 pts): A monomolecular blade that can easily slice through ceramsteel — or clumsy wielders. These swords are extremely rare and can no longer be made.

Church Relics

Adept Robes (20 pts): The famed armor of the Brother Battle order. A ceramsteel suit powered by fusion; the ultimate in battlefield protection, and thus very expensive. Only Brother Battle characters can begin gameplay with Adept Robes, representing an inheritance from one's master.

Article of Faith (1 pt per +1 bonus): An item that aids a theurge in a particular rite (such as a thorn which adds +3 to an Avestite's Sting of Conscience roll). These come in all shapes and sizes, and not always necessarily obvious to their task.

Saint's Lore (2 pts per rite + 1 per level of the rite): A miraculous item esteemed by all the faithful. A finger bone of Saint Rasmussen might have Avert Evil (Level Three) and Devotion (Level One); the cost would be 8.

Vestments (1 pt): The character has some properly blessed Church equipment — robes, rosaries, miters or others. For more information on vestments, see the Theurgy, in Chapter Five: Occult. These items cannot be bought with money, but must be earned through service to the Church.

Wyrd Tabernacle (2 pts per 1 Wyrd): A holy vessel of spiritual energy. This can take many forms, from a font or a book to a staff or shroud.

Riches

Since each character may come into money in different ways, a variety of methods are described below; players should tailor each option to best fit their characters' histories.

Cash

Through well-earned wages, inheritance, treasure seeking or wise saving, the character begins the game with a goodly sum of firebirds. She may carry it on her person or keep it in a local bank or with trusted friends; regardless, she can access it freely. This money may be spent to equip the character before gameplay. However, unlike Assets, below, this money is all the character has to her name — once it has been spent, it is gone.

1 = 100 firebirds
2 = 300 firebirds
3 = 600 firebirds
5 = 1000 firebirds
7 = 2000 firebirds
9 = 3000 firebirds
11 = 4000 firebirds

Assets

Some characters are lucky enough to have real wealth — not just savings or wages, but land rulership or control of a business. These type of assets provide characters with regular income and are usually tied to a character's rank and station in life. The character does not actually own the business — his house or guild does — but through birthright, luck or hard work, she has gained control over it and thus reaps its benefits (and suffers its responsibilities). She cannot sell the business, but may abdicate her position or temporarily place someone else in charge; during this time, she does not gain the income associated with that asset.

Each form of asset listed below includes a firebird value: how much the asset brings the character in yearly income after paying expenses, barring no disasters or dramatic changes in circumstance for good or ill. When beginning gameplay, a character has access to one-tenth (10%) of his yearly income; he may use this to purchase beginning equipment.

3 = Good (3000 income/ 300 starting cash)
5 = Well-off (5000 income/ 500 starting cash)
7 = Wealthy (10,000 income/ 1000 starting cash)
9 = Rich (15,000 income/ 1500 starting cash)
11 = Filthy Rich (20,000 income/ 2,000 starting cash)

Fief: The character rules or owns a substantial portion of land and the serfs who work that land, creating wealth from its commodities (food, minerals, crafts, etc.) or by taxation. While any freeman can own a plot of land, it is the nobles who own the most valuable land and hold contracts of indenture on serfs. A portion of the land's wealth must go to support these serfs, and bad years where no money is made — or where natural disasters destroyed crops — can cause negative debt to accumulate. Technically, the character does not own the land — his noble house does. Except for the Emperor, a lord always has a lord above him to whom he must answer; misuse of lands is often cause for loss of rank. A lord does not necessarily oversee the daily demands of the fief; usually seneschals or chamberlains undertake this task.

The size of a fief is not the most important factor determining its value; its resources — from raw minerals to manufacturing capability — must also be considered. A small parcel with a single gold mine may be as valuable as an entire province of prime farmland. While there were once rank re-

Sources of Wealth

There are a variety of ways to accumulate wealth in **Fading Suns**. Noble houses get most of their money from the ownership of land and all the resources associated with it — including serfs. The chain of rulership of these lands descends from the head of the house down to dukes, counts, earls and baronets, each of whom may maintain a fief for their family lord. Profits from fiefs are divided in unequal portions throughout this chain. Many minor houses or smaller families within the major houses, divested of their land due to war or debt, maintain their wealth through the ownership of proprietary manufacturing processes or the selling of services.

The Church gains its primary wealth from tithing the faithful, which includes nobles, merchants and freemen. Serfs are also expected to tithe, but the most destitute can instead volunteer labor (with their lords' permission). However, the Church also owns its own lands and indentured service contracts, and maintains these much like noble fiefs. Another method of income is the selling of relics and pilgrimage site entry fees.

Guildsmembers gain their wealth through a number of means, from employment contracts to other guilds, priests or nobles, to the ownership of businesses and the tendering of loans to certain parties. While some may own lands and the resources thereon, they cannot own serfs. They can pay their employees criminal wages such that there is little difference.

Characters can gain money during gameplay by working for their factions in a variety of functions; see *Money*, in Chapter Seven: Technology, for more details.

quirements to rule the most valuable properties, the chaotic land-grabbing of the Emperor Wars has left knights in charge of fiefs once rules by counts while certain dukes now rule lands once considered barely fit for baronets. While such extreme cases are the exceptions, it shows that one's rank is not necessarily a determination of one's wealth. Nonetheless, suggested traditional ranks are listed with each fief size.

In some places, the Church owns and operates fiefs; priests are placed in charge of such assets.

A 3 pt fief might be a shire or village (usually lorded by a baronet), with tenant farms as its resources. 5 pts might be a borough or town (baron) with a silver mine. 7 pts is worthy of a province or city (earl or marquis) hosting prime farmlands. 9 pts is a county or capitol city (count) that derives most of its wealth from taxation. 11 pts is a continent or moon (duke) hosting raw or refined resources (mineral or otherwise).

Business: The character owns a business that creates wealth for her. This usually means that she employs a number of people in a variety of positions to keep the business running, from manual laborers to accountants. Bad business can mean the firing of employees and even loss of assets, or the character must throw all her profits back into the business just to keep it alive — a risky but potentially very good investment. The character does not necessarily oversees the daily operations of the business; she can leave that in the hands of a trusted employee or partner.

A 3 pt business might be a hospital, catering to those who can afford medical care (rather than stand in line with the serfs at the local parish). 5 pts might signify the crafting or manufacture of luxury items. 7 pts could be a weaponscrafter mill that produces firearms or artillery. 9 pts suggests a high-tech manufacturing plant, perhaps a ceramsteel smelter, think machine mill or a fusion generator supplying power to a local grid. 11 pts is usually reserved for the highest profile businesses, such as a starport, shipyards or starbase.

Tariffs/Loans: This covers a variety of ways to gain money on a regular basis, from levying a taxation on all trade in an agora or trade route to loaning money to others in return for a fee upon repayment. At lower levels, the character does not necessarily have to oversee employees (except for the occasional freelance enforcer), but he must monitor his assets regularly, or hire someone to do this for him. This is the most volatile form of Assets, since the character may be cheated out of money or worse: loaners can default and refuse to pay back the loan or merchants can refuse to pay the levied tax, forcing the character to pursue embargoes or even violent methods to recoup her losses.

These sorts of assets are almost always run by members of a guild; the higher the level or the broader the influence, the higher the rank of the "boss."

A 3 pts investment might mean the character owns an agora, and levies taxes and all merchants who place stalls there. 5 pts could represent a number of small loans the character made to prominent locals, such as helping the duke's son with his gambling debts. 7 pts may extend agora taxation continent or planetwide. 9 pts may signify an interstellar trade route monopoly, such as all luxury goods trade between Criticorum and Shaprut. 11 pts may well represent an interstellar banking institution that others regularly turn to for loans.

Afflictions

Indebted (2-6 pts): The character is in debt. He cannot buy more than 3 points of Riches (enough to live on) and must work to assuage this debt, lest his creditor take his land and possessions or sell him to the Chainers.

2 = Minor debt (can eventually work it off)
4 = Major debt (must work very hard to pay off)

6 = Catastrophic debt (risks losing fief and thus rank)
+1 = life at risk (the Scravers are sending over boys with bats)

Spaceships

Starships are among the most expensive things in the Known Worlds. The ability to travel to other worlds at will is not only greatly desired by nearly everybody, it is rare — spacetech is simply not what it used to be. The prohibitive cost of building new ships keeps their commissions exclusive to the highest ranking members of the noble houses, Church and League. Others must maintain older ships; some have been kept running for centuries (thanks to durable Second Republic tech).

It is not recommended that players begin gameplay with spacecraft — they should earn a ship through roleplaying. Even if they can't afford to buy their own ship, they may be able to convince a patron to loan them one in return for missions or duties performed for that patron. For details, see *Starships*, in Chapter Seven: Technology.

Status

Status is one of the most important things a character in **Fading Suns** can have. In the eyes of most people, a person is valued by her rank, not her individual accomplishments. A duchess can get away with almost any vile act, while a commoner had better not even steal a loaf of bread to live.

Benefices

Cohort Badge (3 pts): The character is an Imperial Cohort, an aide de camp to one of the Emperor's Questing Knights. Such status is only granted to members of the Church or Merchant League (characters must also have at least the 3 pt Commissioned or Ordained Benefice). While the knight is allowed the Imperial Charter (see below), his aides also need legal and monetary powers with which to perform their duties. Cohorts gain a small stipend of 100 firebirds per year and free transport on any Imperial Navy ship (a 4 pt Passage Contract). In addition, they can cross feudal boundaries free of taxation and are allowed free counsel in case of legal prosecution.

However, they must uphold a code of behavior and duty. They can never operate against Imperial interests, and they can be called upon at any time to undergo any number of missions for the order or the Emperor (a 3 pt Oath of Fealty).

Note that, while Cohorts are given an emblem to wear, the "badge" is an oath of duty, not a mere symbol. Once a Cohort "turns in his badge," he is no longer bound by its code, but likewise does not receive its benefits.

Commission (3-13 pts): The character is a member of a guild within the Merchant League and can learn guild skills

at the base cost. The higher his degree, the more power (and responsibilities) he has. The degrees are almost always the same for men and women.

	Charioteers	Engineers	Scravers	Muster	Reeves
3 =	Ensign	Apprentice	Associate	Private	Associate
5 =	Lieutenant	Entered	Genin	Sergeant	Chief
7 =	Commander	Fellow	Boss	Lieutenant	Manager
9 =	Captain	Crafter	Jonin	Captain	Director
11 =	Consul	Engineer	Consul	Major	Consul
13 =	Dean	Master	Dean	Colonel	Dean

Coven (2 pts): The character is a member of a psychic coven, such as the Favyana or the Invisible Path (see Chapter Eight: Gamemastering). While participation in coven leadership issues is open only to psychics, non-psychics may also join; they must pledge service (usually as spies or informants in the civilian sector) in return for occasional psychic aid from a coven member. While membership allows psychics the ability to meet with other psychics and petition them for training or aid, it also obligates them to perform missions for the coven. Since membership in a coven is illegal in the eyes of the Church and punishable by imprisonment and even death, these missions can get characters into a lot of trouble.

Householder (1 pt): The character is employed or in some way closely associated with a noble house, merchant guild or Church sect. He might be a minor guardsman, a groundskeeper, cook or masseuse. However, he holds no rank in the organization he works for, but he does gain occasional benefits (the local bartender is careful not to cheat the Decados gate guards).

Imperial Charter (4 pts): Only granted to Questing Knights (who must also have at least the 3 pt Nobility Benefice), this is one of the most powerful knightly order charters. It allows each knight a stipend of 300 firebirds per year and free transport on any Imperial Navy ship (a 4 pt Passage Contract). In addition, knights may inspect public Church or League records (though not private cathedral or guild records). They can cross feudal boundaries free of taxation and are immune from prosecution (all charges are brought before the order's council instead of the ruling body bringing the charge, whether it be noble or Church).

However, they must uphold a code of behavior and duty. They can never operate against Imperial interests, and they can be called upon at any time to undergo any number of missions for the order or the Emperor (a 3 pt Oath of Fealty).

Once a knight leaves the order, she is no longer bound by the charter, but likewise does not receive its benefits.

Nobility (3-13 pts): The character is a member of a noble house. While both royal and minor houses use most of the same titles, a baronet for a minor house generally has less responsibilities and less power than one in a royal house. Note that not only does a character have to buy at least five points of this Benefice to be considered landed, but he must also buy the Riches Benefice in order to get any money from it. If a character wants to be in line to lead a royal house, he must buy both the Duke level of Nobility and the Heir Benefice. The landed titles are the often the same for both men and women (Knight Hillary al-Malik), but the higher ranks often use a gender distinction.

3 =	Knight
5 =	Baronet
7 =	Baron
9 =	Earl/Marquis
11 =	Count
13 =	Duke

Ordained (3-13 pts): The character is an ordained minister of the Universal Church, protector of souls and bringer of light. Men and women have the same titles for the same duties.

	Orthodox/Avesti/Aeon	Brother Battle	Eskatonic
3 =	Novitiate	Apprentice	Novitiate
5 =	Canon	Oblate	Provost
7 =	Deacon	Acolyte	Illuminatus
9 =	Priest	Adept	Philosophus
11 =	Bishop	Master	Magister
13 =	Archbishop	Grand Master	Presbuteros

In addition, there are different duties within the Church each with their own titles. Priests who act as ambassadors to a planet, house or guild are called "legates." Those renowned for theology (and who have been approved by the Patriarch as official theologians) are called "hierophants." A keeper of Church records holds the post of "chartophylax." A deputy to the patriarch is called "syneculla". These duty titles are in addition to the rank titles.

Professional Contract (1-10 pts): This Benefice represents a contract or agreement a character has with a guild in order to learn guild-specific skills. Each point of this Benefice represents how many levels of a guild skill he may buy. One contract might only teach the basics (1-3), while another may be an invite to learn all the secrets (up to 10!). This is usually the only way someone will learn guild skills without joining the League.

Afflictions

Barbarian (2 pts): The character comes from an uncivilized upbringing and must struggle to fit into spacefaring society. Additionally, people from all classes tend to look at her askance and will rarely trust her. She may begin the game with no more than three points in Etiquette.

Bastard (1 pt): The character is a bastard child of a noble. He can still buy a noble title, but he will receive no inheritance.

Black Sheep (1-3 pts): The character is the black sheep of his family and is currently being ostracized by it. The character must have the Nobility Benefice to take this Affliction.

1 = Ostracized (Do not step foot in court, or anywhere the family frequents)

2 = Disinherited (You are cut off from the family fortune, loss of estate)

3 = Disenfranchised (Loss of rank, loss of family name)

Branded (1 pt): Many cultures brand criminals and evil-doers, and the character sports one of these brands. It might be for theft, prostitution, or just speaking bad about the duke, but it is an unerasable feature.

Escaped Serf (2 pts): The character is actually a serf, not a freeman. He must hide this fact or risk being seized by officials for sale to the Chainers — or, worse, be sent back to his original master for punishment.

Escaped Slave (3 pts): The character has escaped from slavery, but now is on the run from everyone. Finding any place of refuge should be next to impossible. This character should have almost no ties to anyone except the other player characters.

Excommunicated (3 pts.): The character has committed some great heresy and repeatedly refused absolution from a priest, forcing the Church to excommunicate him. Orthodox doctrine states that the character is damned, denied the Pancreator's grace. The character is an outcast; any further crimes against Church law or doctrine are punishable by flame.

Fallen from Grace (1-3 pts): This Affliction is similar to the Black Sheep Affliction, but is applied to a sect/order or guild. The character has lost face before his peers and superiors, and will only make up for it after years of penance — if ever. Characters must be Commissioned or Ordained to take this Affliction.

1 = Ostracized (Do not conduct guild business or enter the sect's churches)

2 = Expelled (You have no more guild or church benefits)

+1 = Hunted (You know too much or took something of value with you)

Outlaw (1-4 pts):You broke the law in a big way. Someone, somewhere has put a price on your head, and anyone can collect it. A long jail term is the best you can hope for if you are caught. Guard your back at all times.

1 = Hunted worldwide

2 = Hunted within the domain of one royal house

3 = Hunted throughout the Empire

+1 = Wanted dead or alive

Vitality

Sanjuk oj Kaval clutched the wall-hanging depicting the betrayal of the Ukari gods by the deceitful Obun deities, a well-known tale from the Noddavitya. The hanging was all that kept her from falling as a wave of nausea spread through her. Myth-history was her last care right now — more important was to staunch the bleeding. She removed her hand from the krax wound — so much blood! That damn tlinsada Ukari had coated his blade with Grixi poison.

She yanked the curtain from its rings, and slid open the hidden door in the stone wall. Fingers weak, she fumbled with the MedKit, almost dropping the Elixir injector. She managed to slide it into a vein and gasped at the sudden wave of clarity. Not an opiate high, but a clean cessation of pain. Her stomach wound clotted in seconds.

A footstep in the hall brought her to full attention, her senses reaching out in the dark room, open to even the slightest whiff of displaced air nearby. She slowly drew her blaster from its holster and readied to even the odds with her would-be assassin....

Vitality is the measure of a character's lifeline. It represents how much damage he can take before he is unconscious or dead. The healthier a character is, the more Vitality he has. However, physical size also has a lot to do with it. Vitality is determined by adding a character's Endurance (healthiness) to five (his "vital" levels, generally representing size). Larger or smaller people will have more or less Vitality (see Blessing and Curses).

Vitality is never rolled. Instead, one level is checked off on the character sheet for each point of damage the character suffers. When a character loses all his Endurance levels and only has vital levels left, he begins to suffer penalties to all his activities. When he has lost all but one of his Vitality levels, he must struggle to remain conscious. When he has lost all his Vitality levels, he is dead.

Vital wounds: Each character receives five free Vitality levels; these are considered his vital levels, since impairing them impairs any actions the character undertakes. Once a character has lost his non-vital levels (those provided by Endurance), he suffers a penalty to all tasks he undertakes. This penalty increases with each vital level lost, and matches the standard Penalty Chart given in Chapter Two: Rules. In other words, losing the first vital level means that all tasks become Hard. Losing a second makes all tasks are Demanding, and so on down to Herculean.

Once a character has only one vital level left, he must roll Endurance + Stoic Mind to remain conscious. If he fails, he collapses into unconsciousness and remains so for at least one hour. Once each hour thereafter, the player may roll the character's Endurance + Vigor. If successful, the character awakens. However, unless he has received healing in the interim, he is weak. If he attempts any stressful tasks (any physical task requiring a roll), he must once again struggle to remain conscious.

Healing

Different degrees of wounds heal at different rates. A character heals one vital level per month. After that, further Vitality levels (the non-vital levels gained through Endurance) heal at a rate of one level per week. It thus takes the average Joe, with Vitality 8, about four months and three weeks to heal up from near death. Assuming he lost seven levels (eight would mean death), it takes four months for his four vital levels, and three weeks for his three non-vital levels. If he's only lost three levels (since he has Vitality 8, these are non-vital levels), it would take only three weeks to heal completely.

Loss of a vital level is generally considered major tissue loss (a puncture wound from a sword, a gouge of flesh, etc.), since the vital levels are provided by size and thus take longer to heal.

In **Fading Suns**, there are various methods of accelerating tissue regeneration:

First Aid: Within 10 minutes after a wound has been inflicted, a character can attempt or receive first aid to prevent the wound from worsening. This requires a Wits + Remedy roll; if successful, the injured character heals one Vitality level immediately. If the paramedic rolled a critical success, two levels are healed.

Elixir: Current Known Worlds medical technology is not very good. The rich and powerful can afford the best, which approaches Diaspora or Second Republic level, but the average peasant must rely on medieval — or at best — Victorian style medical help. However, the Second Republic left behind many easy-to-use technologies originally designed for lazy consumers who usually had no technical training of their own. These include MedPacs, personal, hand portable first-aid kits. They still require Remedy skill to use, but they are full of all sorts of goodies, including the popular tissue regenerative drug, Elixir.

This drug requires a Wits + Remedy roll to administer properly. If this roll is successful, roll the drug's potency dice (usually 5d, with a goal number of 13 or less); each successful die heals one wound point. There are more and less powerful batches on the market (and the buyer may not always know which one he's getting). For more details, see *Medical Gear*, in Chapter Seven: Technology.

Wyrd

Wyrd represents a character's spiritual energy, her chi, psychic will, vital force or will to power. Wyrd points are spent for a variety of activities, from activating occult powers (see Chapter Five: Occult), inciting passion or steadying one's hand (see the Passion/Calm characteristics), and ac-

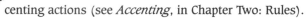

centing actions (see *Accenting*, in Chapter Two: Rules).

A character's beginning Wyrd depends on whether or not she has occult powers, and if so, what kind:

Non-occultists: Beginning Wyrd is equal to Passion or Calm, whichever is primary.

Psi: Beginning Wyrd is equal to Extrovert or Introvert, whichever is primary.

Theurgy: Beginning Wyrd is equal to Faith.

More Wyrd points may be bought with Extras.

Like Vitality, Wyrd is not rolled. Levels are checked off on the character sheet as they are used. Wyrd is regained during game play through meditation, sleep or during certain astrological or religious events.

Meditation: Roll Calm + Focus. One Wyrd point is regained per victory point. One hour must be spent meditating before this roll can be attempted. Once successful, another Wyrd meditation may not be attempted for eight hours.

If the roll fails, a second or third roll may be attempted after one more hour of meditation for each roll. If a third attempt fails, the character is simply unable to reach a meditative state and another roll may not be attempted for twenty four hours.

Sleeping: The character regains one Wyrd point per full hour spent sleeping.

Astrological Events: Stellar happenings have a strange connection to psychic characters. For a psychic, one Wyrd point is regained each night when the moon rises on whatever planet he is on, and he gains an additional point on the first night of a planetary conjunction.

Religious Events: Moments of ceremonial or sacramental importance to a theurge will replenish some lost Wyrd. One Wyrd point is regained at matins (the time of morning prayer) and on religious holidays.

Further details on using Wyrd for occult characters can be found in the Chapter Five: Occult.

Experience

"Ah, Erian Li Halan! A pleasure to have you at my little soiree," the greasy, disgusting al-Malik said, offering Erian a tray of little glasses filled with green wine.

Erian took a glass and nodded. She figured that no response was better than the insults she would surely spit at him if she opened her mouth to speak. She tasted the wine, a wonderful vintage from the count's own vineyards on Istakhr. It really made the head swim. She looked around at the reeling walls, and felt herself slowly falling. The ground slowly rose to meet her.

As she lay on the floor, the glass spilling the remaining poison onto the gleaming tiles, the count bent down to smile in her face. "Don't worry, Erian. You shall not be harmed. I only wish to speak with you at length — on my terms. When you awaken at my villa, we shall have a very long talk."

As she faded into unconsciousness, Erian swore to remember: Never accept a drink from a noble peer unless you see him drink first....

During a **Fading Suns** drama, the characters suffer through many trials and tribulations. It is only fitting that they garner rewards accordingly. Rewards can take many forms: wondrous technological marvels, increased wealth or simple renown.

The truest form of reward, however, is the knowledge, skill and maturity that enable a character to learn from past trials and weather future ones. This increase in learning is reflected in **Fading Suns** by the awarding of experience.

Experience in **Fading Suns** is quantified by points, which the gamemaster awards to the players whose characters participated in an act. Experience points are generally awarded at the end of each act. Players may then spend these points to purchase increases in various traits, as shown by the Experience Increase Chart.

So if a character has an Extrovert rating of 4 and wants to increase it to 5 (and if the gamemaster agreed that the character had indeed been acting more sociable and friendly), the player would have to spend 12 experience points to increase the trait.

The gamemaster may award experience however she wishes, but the following are some reasonable guidelines:

Basic Experience

Basic experience is awarded to all characters who participate in a drama. It is based on the overall success of the characters' endeavors.

- Failure or marginally successful game session   1
- Average game session   2
- Very successful, "over-and-above-goal" session   3

Extra Experience

Individual characters can also earn extra experience over and above the group rate. The following examples provide guidelines for individual experience awards, though the gamemaster is free to invent her own categories.

- **Character performed a great deed: +1**

Fading Suns, despite its grim background, is ultimately a game about heroes. Characters who contribute to the game's drama by performing legendary feats or facing overwhelming odds should be rewarded for their valor and prowess. To qualify for this bonus, however, the deed must not only be impressive in and of itself, but must also be something above and beyond the character's (or any mortal's) capabilities.

For example, a character is a champion swordswoman, and she defeats an opposing house's champion in a thrilling duel. Such a victory may be impressive, and the spectators may laud both combatants' fencing prowess for years to come, but this probably doesn't qualify as a great deed. After all, the character was a champion too, and had an even

Experience Increase Chart

Trait	Cost
Characteristics	
(Body, Mind, Spirit, Occult)	3 x current rating
Learning new skill	2 pts for level 1
Raising skills	2 x current rating
Combat actions, Lore skills	1.5 x level (round up)
Occult powers	2 x current rating
Wyrd	2 x current rating

chance of winning the duel. Now, if the character was an unknown, or had lost an arm just before the battle, or had to face *four* of the rival house's champions, the deed might qualify for extra experience. It's all up to the gamemaster.

• **Player roleplayed very well**: +1

Players who plumb their characters' personalities and thereby add humor, pathos or poignancy to the game session should be rewarded with extra experience. After all, a character who immersed herself in the game's events had a more memorable drama than a character who merely "went along for the ride."

Do not confuse "roleplaying well" with "obnoxiously dominating the game." It's all too easy to design a character with a couple of psychotic quirks and proceed to run roughshod over everyone else's character, performing ludicrous actions and not allowing anyone else to speak or act. A player who designs a character with Tourette's syndrome and uncontrollable pyromania — and then proceeds to interrupt the game every five seconds with strange noises and ignite every flammable object or person — isn't roleplaying well. He's being a disruptive jerk.

• **Character learned something new**: +1 – +3

This is the hallmark of experience: has the character actually changed, grown, gotten wiser or simply wised up? Experience is ultimately about learning, after all, and a character who discovers a heretofore-unrealized truth about his environment and changes his behavior as a result deserves a corresponding increase in his capabilities.

Note that "learning something new" is not necessarily synonymous with "becoming a jaded, tough-as-nails, hard-bitten cynic." A ruthless, worldly Decados assassin who falls in love and learns to trust again is as qualified to receive the bonus as is an outworld ingenue who learns not to believe everything the Scravers tell her.

Spending Experience

Experience is one of the most tangible rewards of **Fading Suns**. However, experience should not be randomly spent in any fashion the player desires. The gamemaster should oversee expenditure, to make sure that characters grow in logical ways based on the events of the drama.

For example, Lucretia (see Chapter Three: Characters) silver-tongues her way through a tension-filled noble summit. Not only does she deftly avoid the attempts of her Decados rivals to incriminate her in the theft of Imperial documents, but she also gains the trust of the Li Halan ambassador, who informs her of a rendezvous between her enemies and the Hawkwood envoy. A successful session all around, and Susan gains three experience points for her pains. Spending the experience on characteristics such as Wits or Perception; skills such as Charm, Impress, Etiquette, Inquiry or Knavery; or even blessings such as Lucretia's innate Suspicious Blessing, is an appropriate means of experience point expenditure. Using the experience to increase Lucretia's Shoot or Dodge ratings, or to buy occult powers, is inappropriate — Lucretia didn't learn anything new about firing a pistol, ducking a blow, or reading minds.

Chapter 5: Occult

"Merciful Pancreator..." was all Erian could say as she stared up at the looming structure. The Gargoyle was poised above her head prepared to leap, frozen in its menacing stance for all eternity. It stood nearly 10 meters tall, carved by the Anunnaki from a metal alloy unknown to even the Engineers, ages before humankind left the cradle of Urth generations upon generations ago.

The wasteland was still. No wind blew, which made the effect even eerier.

She had led her entourage here at great risk to consult the oracle. The Gargoyle of Nowhere was said to give visions of the future to the faithful. Only a few in all of history had been granted such a boon. But her need was dire and her enemies were closing in. She had prayed day and night as their ship exited the jumpgate and made its way to a landing in the crater nearby. She had prayed that her faith was pure enough to be granted a vision.

She glanced at her confessor, Brother Alustro. His eyes were closed and his head bent in prayer. He then looked up and stared intently at the monstrous image from prehistory — and his eyes widened in surprise.

"What do you see, Brother?" Erian asked.

"It... it's looking at me..." he said.

With the fading of the stars, the denizens of the shadows have returned: aliens, monsters, beasties of all shapes and sizes — and magic. The superstitious and miraculous aspects of human consciousness have become real in the **Fading Suns** universe. Like the legends of old, humans can work magic and marshal amazing powers with thought alone... and make pacts with invisible entities best left to themselves.

Is magic just science from another perspective? Or is it something else entirely? Something antithetical to science, with its rational repetitiveness? Is it a thing of chaos, un-tamed? Or is it part of the deep unconscious of humanity's mind, ready to be tamed only by those who are willing to abide by its rules?

Whatever it is, the supernatural is a reality in **Fading Suns**, although one whose main tenant is mystery: the unknown, the unsolvable, the ever-enticing carrot drawing one forward. The occult is not all light and crystals, however; it is more often dark and wild, sparking unforeseen reactions, often terrible to the initiator. This is especially so for Antinomy, which relies on pacts with other entities of mysterious, non-local power. But psychic powers and theurgy can be just as retributive. The mind's powers often reveal that they are greater than the ego which rules them, with wants and desires often at odds with their ruler. Theurgy can cause the initiator to lose grip with his finiteness, his smallness before creation, causing "god complexes" and religious tyranny.

In the end, the measure of an occult power's good (or ill) effects is the person using them. However, unlike most tools, they are not neutral in their use. They enforce an ethical code, and can exact a moral price deeper and more obvious than a common tool. The user must be wary and on guard, lest his power control him.

Powers/Rituals

Powers come in three basic forms: Psychic powers, Theurgy rituals, and Antinomy spells. Only the first two are introduced for player characters in this book. Each of these powers is rated from 1–10. A character may only learn powers equal to or less than his occult characteristic's level. For example, Lucretia has a Psi of 3; she may learn Psi powers of level 3 or less.

Each power requires a roll with a particular characteristic (often a Spirit characteristic, although there are excep-

tions) and skill, as detailed in the power description. Most powers also cost Wyrd points to use; the amount is given in the power description.

Using a psychic power takes one action, unless otherwise noted. Casting a theurgy ritual takes one turn, unless otherwise noted; the theurge cannot perform any other action during that turn. Once cast, however, it usually requires only one action to enforce the rite (to ask a question with Inquisitory Commandment, for example).

If the activation or casting roll fails, the character does not spend any Wyrd points. Only if the roll is successful — or if it is a critical failure — are the listed Wyrd points spent.

Defending Against Occult Powers

Except for occult stigmas (see below), there is no normal way to tell whether someone is or is not using psychic or theurgy powers, unless the power description states otherwise or the occultist himself intentionally betrays it. So, while an oracle consulted by nobles might intentionally reveal her powers, there are no natural signs to reveal whether or not she is faking her omens. Certain powers, such as Wyrd Sight, will reveal the use of occult powers.

Against mental occult powers/rituals (Psyche and Sixth Sense paths, Censure of Guilt rituals, etc.), a target may use his Stoic Mind skill to contest the power (see Contested Actions, in Chapter Two: Rules). Non-occultists defend with Ego or Faith (whichever is higher) + Stoic Mind, while occultists can choose to defend with their Psi or Theurgy characteristic + Stoic Mind. If the target does not have Stoic Mind, he uses only his characteristic for the roll.

If a target realizes he is being psychically manipulated, he can interrupt the power to contest it. Make sure the psychic keeps track of his goal roll successes; compare them against the target's roll. Only if the target beats the psychic's successes is the power canceled; otherwise, it continues for its duration.

A character may ready himself to defend against occult assault with a successful Wits + Focus complementary roll; the victory points are added to the Stoic Mind roll. In this way, someone without the Stoic Mind skill can still defend against occult powers well. "Readying" takes five minutes of meditation and lasts for one span only.

Against physical powers (such as FarHand powers like Crush or Voltage), the target must use Dodge or try to break the grapple normally (using Strength + Vigor).

Gamemasters should be wary of paranoid player characters who are always trying to defend against psychic powers — whether they are being used or not. With experience, certain people can come to suspect when they are being psychically manipulated, but most people have no clue when it comes to occult activity.

Stigma

Each occultist bears an occult stigma, a sign of his or her supernatural differences from common humanity. This stigma does not necessarily have to be connected to the use of her powers, although it is often a metaphor for those powers. For instance, a psychic trained in Sixth Sense may have an odd and uncontrollable tick which makes him blink in one eye when using his powers, or a psychic trained in Psyche powers may uncontrollably whisper when giving psychic commands to his targets, possibly revealing him as the cause of the townsfolk's woes.

Psychic stigmas are somewhat like medieval folk superstitions: A man with hair between his eyebrows or an odd birthmark that happens to resemble a pentagram when looked at from the right angle is surely a werewolf, while a man with hair on his palms and a pale complexion is a vampire (and, of course, the most famous vampire was a noble lord— a revealing clue about peasant superstitions and their intended targets).

Theurgic stigmas, however, tend to be more religious in nature. Those bearing a theurgic stigma are often held in awe by peasants, although fear is also a common response (the theurge may be holy, but trouble tends to follow such chosen ones). Some examples are:

- Lash marks on the arms and back (sympathy with the Prophet's own beating by Diasporan nobles)
- All clothing worn eventually stains red (sympathy with the blood-stained Mantius, the Fourth Disciple, also known as the Soldier)
- Unnaturally long beard which, when cut, grows back to its full length the next day (sympathy with Horace, the Sixth Disciple, also known as the Learned Man) — rarely found among women
- Occasionally speaking in nonsense tongues (sympathy with Hombor, the Seventh Disciple, also known as the Beggar)
- Tears run down the cheeks at inappropriate times (sympathy with Amalthea, the Third Disciple, also known as the Healer)
- Sleepwalking (sympathy with Paulus, the First Disciple, also known as the Traveler).

Players should be allowed to choose their characters' stigmas, but although the gamemaster has to right to veto those he feels are not severe enough, neither should he force crippling stigmas on player characters.

Psi

The existence of psychic powers was a mystery in the twentieth century. During the Second Republic, the mystery was explained: humanity's potential to awaken phenomenal powers with the mind were well-known and documented.

Psychic Powers

Psi powers are listed by the Psi level required to learn the power, the roll required to activate the power (usually a Spirit characteristic + skill), the unmodified range and duration once activated, and the Wyrd point cost to activate the power (the point is spent only if the roll succeeds or is a critical failure). Psychics can modify these powers somewhat by increasing the range or duration of the power or adding additional targets.

Multiple Targets

Unless otherwise specified, powers may be used on only one target at a time. There is one way to adjust this: spending Wyrd points. A character may affect one extra target for each Wyrd point she spends. However, she suffers a -1 to her goal roll for each Wyrd point spent beyond that required to activate the power. Some powers cannot affect more than one target; see the power descriptions.

Range

The base ranges are: touch, sight, sensory (anywhere within a character's direct senses, including hearing; not through live radio or television speakers), and distance. Each power has a range listed. To extend the range, a character must spend Wyrd points. It costs one Wyrd point to extend to the next level (from touch to sight or from sight to sensory, etc.). Once distance is determined, use the chart below:

Distance	Cost
1 kilometer	1 (base for distance ranged powers)
5 kilometers	2
10 kilometers	3
25 kilometers	4
50 kilometers	5
100 kilometers	6
1,000 kilometers	7
planetwide	8
solar system	9
interstellar*	10

* psychics have been known to go mad trying this

The character will suffer a -1 penalty to his goal roll for each Wyrd point spent to extend his range.

Some powers cannot extend their ranges or have an upper limit to how far they may be extended; see power descriptions. Powers with no range listed have no range and cannot be extended.

NOTE: A character watching a distant foe with FarSight must still spend the above distance costs to use Crushing Hand against him; FarSight simply allows him to target the foe.

Time

The duration for many psychic powers is instant, although some last for a span or longer; see the power description. Durations are designated as:

Instant: The power lasts for one turn.

Temporary: The power lasts for 10 turns.

Prolonged: The power lasts for one span.

Perpetual: The power is effectively permanent, although its effects will fade with time and distance from the target and must be reinforced with use. If a year passes without any contact between the psychic and the target, the power's effect ceases.

Each power has its duration listed with it. To extend the duration, a character must spend Wyrd points. It costs one Wyrd point to extend to the next level (from instant to temporary or from temporary to prolonged). Most powers cannot be extended to perpetual; it must be stated in the power description that the power can be perpetual or else no amount of Wyrd will make it so. Instead, to extend a prolonged power, spend 1 Wyrd per additional span. The psychic suffers a -1 to her goal roll for each Wyrd point spent to extend duration.

Wyrd Cost

The symbol W in the power descriptions symbolizes Wyrd. Hence, 1W means 1 Wyrd point.

Penitents

It is an understatement to say that psychics are not well-liked by the Church fathers; loathed and feared are perhaps more accurate. But there are exceptions, such as the Penitents — psychics who have thrown themselves on the mercy of the Church. They are often carted off to distant monasteries far from social centers and trained in moral doctrines and behavioral adjustment. If they respond well to these treatments, they are allowed their freedom — with a proviso. They must wear a symbol of their order so that all the faithful realize that they are reformed psychics and they must always obey the dictates of Orthodox priests of higher rank than they (they are under no particular compulsion to obey other sects or orders). Nonetheless, they will be under the occasional watch of Inquisitors. (It costs no points to become a Penitent, as the benefits of open psychic power use are outweighed by close Church scrutiny.)

Recognized Penitents can use their powers freely without fear of Church retribution (although they may suffer politically-trumped up charges and trials if their powers were not used for the good of the Church). The penalty for impersonating a Penitent is ritualized torture before a crowd under the close watch of theurges ready to prevent the psychic from using his powers to escape. From there, the impersonator is offered lifetime imprisonment, slavery at the hands of psychically-shielded Chainers, or a chance at reform — a trip to a Penitent monastery for treatment. Despite the rumors of cruelty among the Penitent confessors, most psychics choose reform.

Friends of reformed psychics claim that they return from their sabbaticals changed and scarred. They no longer laugh they way they used to and see sin waiting around every corner. The Church counters this by claiming that the psychic is no longer in the thrall of his own Dark Twin and is less dangerous to others, besides now being a Pancreator-fearing soul. It is true that the Penitent reform process usually purges the Urge, but it is also known to purge levels of Psi.

Psychic powers became the premier science of the Second Republic, the prestigious profession to which all geniuses turned their faculties. The central forum for this profession was the Phavian Institute, where the "mental sciences" of telepathy, psychokinesis, ESP and other phenomena were widely studied by many experts.

But the Fall changed all that.

Psychic powers, as with technology, were considered by the Church to be one of the causes of humanity's troubles. Unlike theurgy, psychic powers are intensely personal and

internal; one can develop one's own powers without the aid of a teacher or — more dangerous — a doctrine. In addition, the common folk who did not possess psychic powers resented those who did. A psychic "next step in evolution" movement made this worse, painting non-psychics as evolutionary footdraggers. Hence, the Phavian Institute was disbanded and psychics became the targets of Inquisitorial witchhunts. These hunts did not stop psychic powers from developing, but it drove some psychics underground. Others, those who were faithful, bought the Church line that their powers were sinful. Many anguished people, in the grip of their Urges, committed suicide rather than face sin. Others fell on the Church's mercy, begging aid and forgiveness. The Church accepted many of these repentant psychics and indoctrinated them with a code of behavior when using their powers. These became the Penitents.

Other psychics ran to the League for protection, hoping the republican sentiment would get them some mileage. It did. The League began a psychic guild and for years resisted the Church's protests. But the Church won out and the guild was disbanded, leaving psychics with no formal protection. While the Church can hassle League or house psychics, they cannot formally reprimand them. But psychics without the protection of guild membership or royal title must hide from the Inquisition. Thus the covens (see Chapter Eight: Gamemastering).

Paths: Psychic powers come in "paths", which means that a character chooses a path and must buy each level consecutively. A psychic with Sixth Sense cannot buy Darksense (level 2) unless she has first bought Sensitivity (level 1). Each path has a range of levels, generally from 1-10, although some do not have lowers levels (see Omen, below).

Most paths have more than one power per level. Only one representative power is given per level in the examples below. Also, the tenth levels are not revealed here, as they are far beyond the ken of beginning characters.

FarHand

The path of FarHand, or Psychokinesis, was one of the most intensively studied at the Phavian Institute, for many considered it the most "practical" category of psychic powers. FarHand deals with the manipulation of physical objects and energy fields through the application of pure will. The range for nearly all FarHand powers is sight, which cannot be extended without one of the Sixth Senses (like FarSight or Shared Sense). When a "physical" Strength or Dexterity rating is needed for a FarHand power, use Passion.

Unless otherwise noted in the power description, the duration on FarHand powers may not be extended; the psychic must make another activation roll to maintain the effect.

FarHand is a psychic power which quickly becomes obvious to even those ignorant of psychic powers. However, they will not necessarily be able to trace the phenomena back to the psychic. Most peasants will turn their ire against strangers first.

Lifting Hand

(Level 1, Extrovert + Focus, sight, temporary, 1W)

The first level of FarHand enables the psychic to generate a simple field of directional force which can either slowly lift a single object up (1 meter per turn) OR move it to one side (but not both — that requires another separate field). A maximum weight equal to 25 kg per level of the psychic's Wits may be lifted. (Additional mass can be bought at 10 kg per Wyrd point.) The only limit to how high an object can be lifted is the range of the power when activated. Once the duration is exceeded, the object will drop from whatever height it was raised to.

Throwing Hand

(Level 2, Passion + Focus, sight, temporary, 1W)

The psychic can perform simple manipulations of two such directional fields, enabling her to both lift AND propel an object with appreciable velocity and force. A maximum weight equal to 10 kg per level of the psychic's Wits may be thrown. (Additional mass can be bought at 5 kg per Wyrd point.) When aiming at a moving target (another person), the psychic must roll Passion + Throwing. Damage is determined by the object thrown (the gamemaster should declare a base damage for the object, using the weapon damages given in Chapter Six: Combat as a guideline) plus the victory dice gained on the throwing roll. Objects within sight can be thrown, but the range of the thrown object is usually only 10 meters.

Crushing Hand

(Level 3, Extrovert + Fight, sight, temporary, 1W)

This slightly more complex manipulation involves turning two or more directional forces against themselves, enabling the psychic to hold an object steady (when it is being pushed by normal physical forces from varying directions), or crush it altogether. To hold an object, use the grappling rules (Chapter Six: Combat), substituting the above roll. To punch a target with Crushing Hand, the above roll is used as a goal roll. The damage is 3 plus any victory dice gained from the activation roll. Wyrd points only have to be spent when the power is activated, not for every punch or grapple.

Dueling Hand

(Level 4, Extrovert + Melee or Shoot, sight, temporary, 1W)

Complex and precise manipulations of single objects are now possible, enabling the psychic to operate a machine or fight with melee weapons or firearms using only the mind.

A successful activation roll must be made to lift a weapon into the air, after which the weapon remains aloft under the mental control of the psychic for the duration of the power. However, she must make a successful Extrovert + Melee or Shoot roll to swing or fire the weapon at a target (although she does not have to spend more Wyrd).

FarArms

(Level 5, Extrovert + Focus, sight, temporary, 1W)

The psychic can use all the previous powers in combination to lift, throw, hold or manipulate a number of objects equal to his Wits rating.

FarWall

(Level 6, Extrovert + Stoic Mind, sight, temporary, 1W)

The simple directional force field can now be expanded and broadened into a force barrier, similar to that generated by energy shield technology. The intensity of the barrier, as well as its shape and position, can be modulated by the psychic to allow for air flow, letting friends in while keeping foes out, and directing attacks to the outside of the barrier.

The maximum armor rating for a FarWall is 10d + victory points; the minimum amount of damage which will activate the FarWall is equal to the psychic's Urge. (If she has no Urge, then 1 point is the minimum.) The gamemaster may require an additional Wyrd expenditure if the barrier is subjected to a prolonged barrage.

AirStride

(Level 7, Introvert + Focus, temporary, 1W)

The psychic focuses directional forces upon herself sufficient to lift her body off the ground and even cruise at a maximum velocity of 10 meters per turn + 5 meters for each victory point. The duration may be extended by 10 turns for each additional Wyrd point spent. Unlike other powers, the character can elect to spend this point anytime after the activation roll.

Demolishing Hand

(Level 8, Passion + Focus, sight, instant, 1W)

The psychic compresses a field of energy at a point on or near the target's body and explodes it, like coiling a spring and suddenly releasing it. The damage is equal to Wits + victory points. This is stun damage, like from a Stunner Gun, and ignores energy shields. If the target takes ANY damage (after figuring armor points), he must roll Endurance + Vigor. A failure means he is stunned that turn and the next; on a critical failure, he falls unconscious. If the damage taken is greater than the target's Endurance, a failure means the target is knocked unconscious. Stun damage heals completely after one span.

AirDance

(Level 9, Extrovert + Focus, sight, temporary, 1W)

The psychic can focus the forces of AirStride upon oth-ers, levitating a number of people equal to his Wits rating, and, with an additional Wyrd expenditure, send them in as many separate directions as his victory points (otherwise they will all move in a single direction as a fixed group). Unwilling targets may resist this power with a Dexterity + Dodge roll. The duration may be extended as with AirStride.

Omen

The Omen path seeks to expand normal time-bound human awareness to include perceptions of the past and possible futures, known in the Phavian Institute as Postcognition and Precognition, respectively. Knowledge of past events is a fairly straightforward matter — whatever happened, happened. Visions of the future are trickier, however, since they can only represent the possible results of actions in the present. Knowledge of future events can be used either to prevent them from occurring or to ensure that they will occur. In any case, the gamemaster is advised to keep careful notes and to be ready to improvise… a lot.

This path begins at level 6. There are no known powers below this level.

Shadows Gone By

(Level 6, Calm + Observe, sight, temporary, 1W)

Past Resonance allows the psychic to see, hear and feel what has happened in the past around a particular object. For instance, a knife used in a killing can be "read" to get a vision of the murderer, as well as the room where it took place, etc. Multiple items may not be selected. The psychic chooses the time period, but it can be accompanied with a request for a particular event ("Who used this knife to kill the marquis?"). How far she can see into the past depends on her successes: one year per success or centuries with a critical success. The psychic can see a past period of about 10 turns (30 seconds), but she can see more if she extends the duration of this power to prolonged (a "scene" will play itself out for her; cost: 1 extra Wyrd).

Shadows to Come

(Level 7, Calm + Observe, sight, temporary, 1W)

Future Resonance allows the psychic to see, hear and feel what will happen in the future around a particular object, place or person (the room a person will be in, who will be with them, etc.). These are shadows of the future, not what WILL happen. Multiple items may not be selected. The psychic chooses the time period, but it can be accompanied with a request for a particular event ("Where will the duke hold his birthday ball?"). How far she can see into the future depends on her successes: one month per success or years with a critical success. The psychic can see a future period of about 10 turns (30 seconds), but she can see more if she extends the duration of this power to prolonged (a "scene" will play itself out for her; cost: 1 extra Wyrd).

Voice from the Past

(Level 8, Wits + Focus, prolonged, 1W)

The psychic can channel the personality of someone who is dead. As in the film *Rashomon*, these ghosts of the past can sometimes be accepted as witnesses in certain murder trials. Ancient or alien personages may require a scholar on hand to overcome barriers posed by dead or unfamiliar languages. The ghost will speak through the psychic long enough to give her tale (gamemaster's discretion).

The Church claims that these are not departed people but figments of the psychic's twisted mind or demons parading as dead loved ones, but most people in the Known Worlds believe in ghosts anyway.

Oracle

(Level 9, Calm + Focus, 1W)

The psychic can foretell the future with accuracy — but cryptically. The psychic goes into a trance and says things which must then be interpreted (i.e., he speaks of events to come in metaphors, abstractions, or inconclusive sentence fragments). The gamemaster is the "voice" for these omens, and he should use this power to reveal the possible future for the characters in his drama. For example, a psychic player character uses Oracle to try to ascertain whether one of the other player characters will be heir to a Hawkwood barony on Leminkainen. The gamemaster knows that there is a ri-val who has not yet revealed himself, and this is a perfect moment to introduce him. So, the tremulous voice from the future declares: "Two will climb the mountain... but only will reach the peak."

Psyche

The path of Psyche refers to the old Phavian designation of Telepathy, the direct transference of thought and feeling from one mind to another. Originally the Institute focused its studies on the more passive and receptive side of telepathy, like Intuit and MindSight, but since the fall of the Second Republic, the aggressive potential of telepathy, illustrated by powers like HeadShackle and BrainBlast, has come to predominate.

Players should be reminded that their characters may try to block mental intrusions with an Ego or Faith + Stoic Mind roll (or Psi or Theurgy + Stoic Mind), whichever is higher.

Unless a bond is created, the range of these Psyche powers cannot be extended without Sixth Sense.

Intuit

(Level 1, Extrovert + Empathy, sight, temporary, 1W)

The psychic can read another's surface emotional state, whether she is angry or sad, happy or confused. Emotions are read directly from the target's mind, as opposed to aura reading, which can be subject to misinterpretation.

Emote

(Level 2, Passion + Charm or Impress, sight, instant, 1W)

The psychic can project emotions to another, to let them know how he feels (although he can fake emotions by rolling Passion + Knavery instead). The target simply senses the emotion but does not have to react in any particular way to it. The target of this power will know whose emotions he is sensing, although he may not know that his intuition is caused by a psychic power.

MindSight

(Level 3, Extrovert + Observe, sight, temporary, 1W)

MindSight allows the psychic to read another's surface thoughts. Note that surface thoughts are only what is occupying the target's attention at that moment, and rarely involve long-range plans, habitual behavior or detailed recollections. Language barriers can get in the way, as can differences in the psychology of alien races from beyond the Known Worlds.

A level 5 version of this power, MindSearch, allows the psychic to delve deeper, into the target's deepest thoughts and memories. The number of victory points should act as a guideline as to how deep or private are the memories which can be read.

MindSpeech

(Level 4, Extrovert + Charm, sight, temporary, 1W)

The psychic is able to project her thoughts into the mind of another. The psychic can choose to hide the source of these thoughts, but the target may become aware that something is happening if a thought seems too strange or unfamiliar to him. As with MindSight, language can be a barrier.

Heart's Command

(Level 5, Extrovert + Impress, sight, temporary, 1W)

The psychic can actually telepathically control another's emotions. Language is not a factor here, but differences in alien psychology can pose a problem, as is illustrated by the story of the psychic who, in attempting to ingratiate himself to a feral Vorox, accidentally triggered the predator's violent mating behavior.

HeadShackle

(Level 6, Extrovert + Charm or Impress, sight, temporary, 1W)

The psychic gains the ability to telepathically dominate the minds of others. Detailed commands may be projected, which the target will carry out to the best of her ability, but only as long as this power is actively used upon her (this requires one action per turn). Once again, language can be an obstacle.

BrainBlast

(Level 7, Passion + Impress, sight, prolonged, 1W)

BrainBlast instantly overloads all pain receptor sites in the target's brain, effectively "wounding" him without inflicting any physical injury. For each victory point on the psychic's roll, the target suffers a -1 wound penalty as if actually wounded (the Vitality rating itself is not affected); note that the penalty affects ALL rolls the target may make, and this lasts for the rest of the span.

Sympaticus

(Level 8, Extrovert + Empathy, sensory, prolonged, 1W)

The psychic can easily communicate with, or feel the emotions of, bonded targets, allowing the formation of a telepathic network among non-psychic characters (all information must flow through the psychic using this power, i.e., non-psychic targets may not communicate directly, except through normal channels). However, use of Sympaticus actually makes it harder to manipulate or control these targets (-4 on all rolls to do so).

Puppetry

(Level 9, Ego + Focus, touch, prolonged, 1W)

The psychic can telepathically project her will upon a target, dominating them completely and possessing them body and soul. The psychic's own body must remain inactive during the possession, but the gamemaster may allow actions to be taken with an additional expenditure of Wyrd points (one per action).

Sixth Sense

Known in the old Phavian Institute as Extra-Sensory Perception, this path seeks to cultivate modes of perception which are considered to be inherent in all sentient beings, but which are seldom or never consciously accessed.

Sensitivity

(Level 1, Perception + Observe, sensory, prolonged, 1W)

This power improves the physical senses, allowing the character to see in darker situations (but it does not confer IR or UV vision — he still cannot see in total darkness), hear better, and even smell or taste drugs or poisons in food and drink (at the gamemaster's discretion). If successful, the character gains +3 to his Perception. This bonus can help offset any negative Perception modifiers due to adverse conditions or darkness (see the Perception Modifier Chart in Chapter Six: Combat).

Darksense

(Level 2, Wits + Observe, sensory, prolonged, 1W)

Darksense allows the character to perceive when there is no light or when she is somehow blinded. She suffers none of the usual negative Perception modifiers for darkness and can use her Sixth Sense powers in the dark. Darksense manifests in a variety of ways, including sonarlike acuity of hearing, tactile hypersensitivity to ground vi-

brations or minute air currents, and using the character's own biomagnetic field as a kind of radar. Printed words or pictures may not be seen with Darksense.

Subtle Sight

(Level 3, Extrovert + Observe, sight, temporary, 1W)

The character can perceive the psychic auras of others. Auras can reveal general emotions and states of mind, whether someone is human or alien, and if he/she has psychic powers. Auras cannot reveal specific thoughts, although a very successful roll can supply quite a lot of useful information about the target; colors correspond to emotions, movement of the aura indicates general state of mind, and shapes within the aura can show what types of thoughts the target is thinking. See the Auras Chart.

Premonition

(Level 4, Extrovert + Observe, sensory, temporary, 1W)

The psychic can sense danger before it harms her. She must deliberately sense for this; it does not work automatically. Premonition will only warn the psychic that danger exists, not tell her exactly what is about to happen; the gamemaster may, however, allow her to sense what direction it will come from (when applicable) when three or more victory points have been rolled. Note that this power will only indicate immediate peril, such as a weapon aimed at the psychic, a critically overheated stardrive core, or a land mine the character is about to step on. Premonition does not reveal the existence of traitors, conspirators, or assassins who are merely stalking the character but who are not yet poised to strike.

When this power is active, the psychic adds +2 to her initiative rating.

FarSight

(Level 5, Extrovert + Observe, distance, prolonged, 1W)

Occasionally known by the old Phavian designation, "clairvoyance," FarSight allows the psychic to see a distant place. The goal roll to activate FarSight is modified according to the familiarity of the target location:

Easy (+4) — The psychic's own home.

Natural (+2) — The psychic's home town or neighborhood, her regular haunts, etc..

Standard — A place with which the psychic is personally familiar, i.e., anywhere he has been to and can consciously remember.

Hard (-2) — An unfamiliar place which the psychic knows about, e.g., famous public places on Byzantium Secundus or Holy Terra, or somewhere the psychic has studied through maps or detailed records.

Demanding (-4) — An unknown place with which the psychic has a personal link, e.g., where a friend is being held captive.

Auras Chart

General Types of Auras

Race/Condition	Aura Type
Human	Simple elongated ovals
Ur-Obun	Exaggerated egg-shapes, with the big end at the top
Ur-Ukar	Exaggerated egg-shapes, with the big end at the bottom
Vorox	Torn, raggedy edges
Vau	Sleek wedges, pointed at the head
Symbiot	Tiny filament-threads stretching out to infinity (which cannot be detected without a critical success)
The Changed	Folded or crimped around the altered body part
Unconscious	Pale, empty aura
Asleep	Pale, empty aura, with all color and activity concentrated in the center
Psychic/Theurge	Deeper, more three-dimensional

Colors

(seen with all successful rolls)

Color	Emotion
Red	Angry
Orange	Repelled, disgusted
Yellow	Happy
Green	Desirous
Blue	Sad
Violet	Satisfied
White	Loving, caring
Black	Afraid
Gray	Indicative of purely abstract thought

Motion

(seen only with three or more victory points)

Motion	State of Mind
Upward	Elated
Downward	Depressed
Inward	Introverted (directed toward self)
Outward	Extroverted (directed toward others)
Vertical spiral	Determined
Horizontal spiral	Confused
Quivering	Excited
Sloshing	Indifferent
Melting	Fatigued, tired

Shapes

(seen only with five or more victory points)

Shape	Thought
Spike	Hatred
Cloud	Doubt
Column	Certainty
Swirls	Whimsy
Veins	Nagging insistent thoughts
Rays	Strongly directed emotion
Hard outer edge	Suspicion, distrust

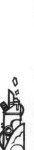

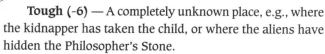

Tough (-6) — A completely unknown place, e.g., where the kidnapper has taken the child, or where the aliens have hidden the Philosopher's Stone.

FarSound

(Level 6, Extrovert + Observe, distance, prolonged, 1W)

Occasionally known by the old Phavian designation, "clairaudience," FarSound allows the psychic to hear a distant place. The same modifiers for FarSight apply.

(The Ur-Ukar supposedly have an additional power at this level: FarTouch.)

Shared Sense

(Level 7, Extrovert + Empathy, distance, prolonged, 1W)

This power opens a direct sensory conduit from a bonded target to the psychic, who can then see what the target sees, hear what he hears, and so on. Shared Sense allows the psychic to use her powers from a bonded target's perspective, treating the target's touch, sight and sensory ranges as her own. In other words, she can sense danger to the target with Premonitions, see from the target's eyes with Subtle Sight, etc..

Wyrd Sight

(Level 8, Introvert + Observe, sight, temporary, 1W)

The psychic can perceive normally invisible occult activity, such as theurgy rites, psychic powers, occult artifacts, etc.. This can be considered an extremely refined form of Subtle Sight, revealing things which do not register at the lower level. For instance, the aura of a psychic shows a brilliant scintillating white light in the forehead; a beam extending from this light to another person can indicate a telepathic connection or Shared Sense. Most theurgic activity appears to be enveloped in a large unflickering candle-flame, the top point of which stretches up to infinity.

Wyrd Sight does not automatically confer the aura-reading ability of Subtle Sight; each power operates within a different range of the astral spectrum. The gamemaster is urged to be creative when describing what a psychic sees with Wyrd Sight; keep in mind that individual auras are not being read, but rather all the broad occult forces at work in a given scene.

Senses Shock

(Level 9, Extrovert + Impress, touch, instant, 1W)

With Senses Shock the psychic can break down his target's natural adjustment of the intensity of sensory input, overloading the target's senses: mild light becomes blinding, whispers are screams, a massage becomes a pummeling, and so on. If activation is successful, the target is stunned and incapacitated for one turn per victory point on the activation roll (perhaps more if she is subjected to bright lights, loud sounds, a pummeling, etc.). If the target was a psychic using a Sixth Sense power, she may roll Introvert + Stoic Mind to resist being stunned.

Soma

The path of Soma (also called Prana Bindu) is the culmination of many ancient Urthish techniques of body control, and was one of the earliest established departments in the Phavian Institute. Since the Fall, the majority of this path's practitioners have found employment only as traveling medicine show freaks.

No ranges are listed for these powers, since they affect only the psychic herself. The maximum amount to which any trait may be raised is twice its natural rating.

Toughening

(Level 1, Introvert + Vigor, prolonged, 1W)

While this power is activated, the psychic may add 2 to his Endurance rating, plus another 1 per victory point. This does not add to Vitality, only Endurance.

Strengthening

(Level 2, Passion + Vigor, prolonged, 1W)

While this power is activated, the psychic may add 2 to her Strength rating, plus another 1 per victory point.

Quickening

(Level 3, Calm + Vigor, prolonged, 1W)

While this power is activated, the psychic may add 2 to his Dexterity rating, plus another 1 per victory point.

Hardening

(Level 4, Introvert + Stoic Body, prolonged, 1W)

This power actually hardens the skin to a steely consistency, providing an armor rating of 3 + 1d per victory point against hand-to-hand, melee and conventional firearm attacks, and 1 +1d per victory point against energy weapons. There is no Dexterity or Vigor penalty.

Sizing

(Level 5, Extrovert + Vigor, prolonged, 1W)

With Sizing, the psychic may physically become shorter or taller, broader or thinner. This does not affect physical characteristic ratings. The amount by which size may be changed is based on the psychic's victory points for the activation roll:

Victory Points	Height Increase	Height Decrease	Weight Increase	Weight Decrease
1	+10%	-10%	+20%	-10%
2	+20%	-20%	+40%	-20%
3	+30%	-30%	+60%	-30%
4	+40%	-40%	+75%	-40%
5	+45%	-45%	+90%	-45%
6	+50%	-50%	+100%	-50%

Masking

(Level 6, Extrovert + Charm, prolonged, 1W)

At this level, the psychic may physically change her facial features (bone structure, eye color, skin color and texture, hair length and color). One feature may be changed

with each victory point. With complementary rolls in Disguise and Acting, the psychic can mimic others.

Recovering

(Level 7, Introvert + Remedy, instant, 1W)

With this power, the psychic can regenerate one Vitality level per victory point.

Slowing

(Level 8, Calm + Focus, prolonged, 1W)

At this level, the psychic can slow down his bodily operations to an almost undetectable rate, feigning death and reducing his need for oxygen. The duration of this power can be increased at a cost of 1 Wyrd point per additional span.

Closing

(Level 9, Introvert + Vigor, prolonged, 1W)

Closing renders the psychic immune to adverse environmental effects, such as airborne drugs and toxins, conventional diseases, extreme weather, etc.. Closing does not render one immune to heat or cold in excess of freezing or boiling temperatures, corrosive atmospheres, explosive decompression or Symbiot invasion.

Sympathy

This path was little known to the Phavian Institute, perhaps because research on psychic groups was rare, as most psychics tended to work alone. With the rise of the psychic covens of the Dark Ages — a response to the Church's ban on psychic powers — this path became somewhat more prevalent. It is still largely unknown outside of the covens.

This path begins at level 3. There are no known powers below this level.

Bonding

(Level 3, Extrovert + Empathy, touch, perpetual, variable W)

A character can psychically bond with another person(s). This makes it easier to use psychic powers on that person later. The target of the bond must be willing, although he may be scared into accepting the bond (Impress) or fooled into it (Charm or Knavery). He may also be psychically forced to do so. It costs the psychic a number of Wyrd points equal to the target's Ego or Faith (whichever is higher) to bond him, and a full span must be spent in meditation (the target does not have to meditate, but he must be present during the meditation).

When using powers against Bonded targets, the Wyrd cost for extending range, duration or choosing multiple targets is one less, making it easier for the psychic to affect those Bonded to him at range or more than one of them at once. In addition, the psychic suffers no goal roll penalties for extending his range or number of targets.

A psychic bond can last for years, but it will slowly wear away if not reinforced through use.

Sanctum

(Level 4, Calm + Focus, sight, perpetual, 3 W)

The psychic may attune himself to a particular place so that his powers may be used easier in connection with that place. While the place may be anywhere (it does not have to be planetbound — it could be a stateroom on a spaceship, a cave on an asteroid, etc.), it can only be a spot 10 meters in diameter. When within that spot, the psychic gains a +3 goal roll bonus to activate any of his psychic powers. The psychic must meditate within that place for a full span before creating the Sanctum bond.

If the psychic also has the FarSight power, he is automatically alerted when someone enters his sanctum, as long as he is within the same solar system.

Totem

(Level 5, Wits + relevant skill, touch, perpetual, variable W)

The character can create a bond with an item, allowing him to use his powers easier in association with that item. Wyrd costs are one less, and all tasks are considered Natural (+2) — although this does not allow him to more easily use the item itself; a think machine may be just as baffling before a Totem Bond as after. In addition, the character gains such an affinity with the item that he always knows where it is anywhere within his sensory range. This does not confer any form of FarSight, it is simply a sense of the item's location. Wyrd points may be spent to extend this range for one span; this can only be done a number of times per week equal to the psychic's Perception rating. Also, he knows whenever the item is damaged (as long as it is within his affinity range).

The skill used to activate the bond depends on skill rolled to use the item: Melee for a sword, Vigor for a pair of boots, Observe for a book, etc.

The size of the item determines the Wyrd cost to bond it:

Size	Cost
XS	1
S	2
M	3
L	4
XL	5
H (huge, crate)	6
G (gigantic, rhinoceros)	7
I (immense, tank)	8
GA (gargantuan, building)	9
M (monumental, large building or starship)	10

The psychic must meditate while touching the object for a full span before activating the Totem bond.

Coven Brand

(Level 6, Ego + Impress, touch, perpetual, variable W)

A particular psychic is declared anathema, and has a sort of anti-bond placed upon him whereby it is harder for him to use his own powers against the psychic. This is usually performed by members of a psychic coven upon an outcast from their coven, to prevent him from easily working against them at a later date. This is mainly used by the Favyana rather than the Invisible Path, who punish most extreme transgressions against them with death instead of exile. It is only effective between the user of this power and the recipient.

This is cast just like Bonding (level 3, above) except that the recipient must accept the brand. When a branded psychic uses powers against the psychic(s) who branded him, the Wyrd cost for any of his powers is increased by one. In addition, the psychic suffers a -2 goal roll penalty on all activation rolls against him.

Mojo Bond

(Level 7, Extrovert + Impress, sight, temporary, 1W)

The psychic can form a bond with another person over a distance and against his will. To do so, he must have a sympathetic focus, an item that bears the target's psychic resonance, such as a well-worn item of his clothing, a lock of hair, fingernail clippings, etc. These items must have a relatively fresh connection to the target, having been on him within the past month.

The psychic does not need to meditate or spend more than 1 Wyrd point, but the duration of the Mojo Bond may not be extended — he has 10 turns in which to gain his advantage. Once successfully used, this power may not be re-used on the same target for the rest of the span, and a fresh sympathetic focus must be used.

Mojo Bond confers the same Wyrd cost bonus and goal modifiers as the level 3 Bond.

Sever Bond

(Level 8, Ego + Impress, tough, 2W)

The psychic can sever any type of bond between two psychics (including a Mojo Bond or a Coven Bond, below). The severing is permanent, although new bonds may be formed again using the same powers. Wyrd points may be spent to increase the targets if more than two people share the bond.

Coven Bond

(Level 9, Extrovert + Empathy, sight, temporary, variable W)

Two or more psychics who share a Bond (level 3) can merge their psyches into greater sympathy, allowing them to place Wyrd points into a collective pool from which any of them can draw upon at will for the duration of the span. The

amount of Wyrd spent at activation by each of the participants is the amount of the collective Wyrd pool; a psychic's Psi rating determines the maximum amount of Wyrd he may contribute. This pool exists for only one span, after which it disappears; the participants do not get any unspent Wyrd points back. While only one of the participants activates this power, the others may make complementary rolls to aid her and all may contribute Wyrd. This power is often used by covens performing group powers (see sidebar, below).

Note that this power is not confined to psychics alone; a theurge who shares a psychic bond may also contribute and draw Wyrd.

Vis Craft

Practically unknown to the researchers of the Phavian Institute, the power of energy control and manipulation is still rare in the 51st century. Vis (Latin for "energy") Crafters can manipulate material energy: kinetic, electric and fusion, and some can manipulate spiritual energies (Wyrd). One cannot work with such power, however, and remain unmoved — Vis Crafters tend to be excitable and passionate people, sometimes twitchy and nervous, unable to stay still for long. Also, just because a psychic can manipulate energy doesn't mean she fully understands it; this may require a Tech + Science (Physics) roll.

Vis Eye

(Level 1, Perception + Focus, sight, temporary, 1W)

The psychic can sense the use of energy around him (a foe's active energy shield, a laser sight trained on the psychic, a spy camera filming him) and discern the type of energy (electrical, fusion) and trace its source (although this may require a sustained roll if the source is well-hidden).

A level 3 version of this power allows the psychic to sense and discern spiritual energies, such as Wyrd, Symbiot Lifeforce or even the strange energy used by Anunnaki tech.

Vis Drain

(Level 2, Passion + Volt Redemption, touch, temporary, 1W)

The psychic can drain or cut off the flow of the power to or from various items, such as fusion cells or a building's power grid (this power is not transferred anywhere useful unless the character also uses the Vis Flow power, below). The amount of Wyrd points spent determines how much power can be drained from a source. The psychic can spend Wyrd to increase the duration to prolonged.

Wyrd	Power (equivalents)
1 (base)	1 fusion cell
2	10 fusion cells; enough energy to power a small room or skimmer
3	Enough energy to power a building or flitter
4	Enough energy to power a city block or agora-based fusion generator
5	Small-class starship (explorer, escort, raider)
6	Mid-class starship (frigate, galliot, assault lander, freighter)
7	Capital class starship (cruiser, dreadnought, luxury liner)
8	Capital city
9	Starbase
10	Terraforming engine; Symbiot World Egg

Note that the range on this power may not be increased. Instead, a level 4 version must be bought; its range is sight, which may be increased with Wyrd expenditure as per the normal rules.

Vis Flow

(Level 3, Passion + Volt Redemption, touch, instant, 1W)

The psychic can channel incoming energy to charge fusion cells, flashlights or starship engines. He must touch the item to be charged and the source of energy (a sparking live wire, a fusion charging plug, a Symbiot giving its Lifeforce). Mild shocks will not harm the psychic while this power is active, but he is not immune to energy attacks or severe power surges. It is possible to use this power when being attacked by lasers, blasters or higher levels of Vis Craft, but regardless of success on channeling the energy, the psychic will suffer any damage normally. (If an energy shield is used to absorb the damage, it also absorbs the energy — the psychic cannot transfer this energy.)

Generally, the transfer is power to power: a blaster bolt will charge one use by a blaster on a fusion cell, but this may mean two uses by a laser. The gamemaster should compare the different uses for fusion cells and the total charges allowed per weapon, and be conservative in allowing too many uses from this power.

There is a level 4 version of this power which allows the psychic to transfer spiritual energies, such as Wyrd, Symbiot Lifeforce and even Soul Shards to his own Wyrd. However, only energy directed at the psychic — such as through a psychic or theurgic power — may be transferred. The psychic is not a vampire — he cannot walk up to someone, grab him, and transfer Wyrd points. However, if the psychic is the recipient of the Laying on of Hands rite which heals two Vitality points, he could choose to channel these two points to his Wyrd rather than his Vitality.

Note that the range on these powers may not be increased. Instead, a level 5 version (Vis Flux) must be bought; it's range is sight, and may be increased with Wyrd expenditure as per the normal rules.

Vis Shock

(Level 4, Dexterity + Fight or Melee, touch, instant, 1W)

The psychic can transform her own bioelectrical field into a high voltage discharge with a hand-to-hand or melee

attack. This normally adds four dice to any damage roll. However, a character can also attempt to slowly slip under shields and hit the target once his fist or weapon is past the shield (suffer -2 to Initiative, withhold victory dice and hope the damage does not exceed the shield's impact threshold). Once the blow contacts a surface, the psychic can release the charge (four dice, ignore energy shields but not other armor).

The range on this power may not be increased.

Vis Shield

(Level 5, Endurance + Stoic Body, 10 hits, 1W)

The psychic may use his own bioelectrical energy to erect a personal energy shield around himself. This acts similar a standard energy shield; it allows 10 hits per power activation and the protection rating is 5/10. In addition, the field fluctuates at need, so the character can wear any form of armor he desires without compromising the field. Note that this field does not interfere with the Vis Flow power (above); attacks absorbed by this power can be transferred elsewhere.

Vis Bolt

(Level 6, Dexterity + Shoot, sight, instant, 1W)

The psychic can project energy at a target from a distance. The damage is equal to Endurance plus victory dice, plus one die for each extra Wyrd point spent (max = Psi rating). In addition, this damage can bleed through energy shields on damage dice results of 1 or 2.

Vis Vortex

(Level 7, Endurance + Vigor, touch, instant, 1W)

The psychic can generate power, which he can use to recharge fusion cells, power skimmers, etc. Use the chart given with the Vis Drain power, above, to determine the Wyrd point costs per power generated. The maximum amount of points the psychic may spend on Wyrd to generate power is equal to his Psi rating. The range and duration of this power may be increased normally.

Vis Storm

(Level 8, Passion + Vigor, sight, instant, 1W)

The psychic can unleash an energy surge on an area from a distance. The base radius from the shock point is 10 meters, and anyone standing within this radius is affected. The radius may be increased by 5 meters per extra Wyrd point spent. The damage is equal to Endurance plus victory dice, plus one die for each extra Wyrd point spent (max = Psi rating). In addition, this damage can bleed through energy shields on damage dice results of 1 or 2.

Primal Vis

(Level 9, Passion + Focus, sight, instant, 0W)

The psychic can tap into an invisible, universal spiritual power grid to replenish and/or add to his Wyrd points. This power may be used only once per span, but it can generate an amount of Wyrd equal to 1 plus the victory points

Group Psi Powers

Psychics rarely convene to cast powers together, but when they do, the Wyrd costs and goal penalties for extending range, duration or number of targets can be offset more easily. Use the following guidelines:

• The number of participating psychics is limited by the focal psychic's Psi rating.

• Each participating psychic must be Bonded to one another (see the Bonding power, in the Sympathy path).

• They must each know the power at the required level.

• Only one among them is chosen as the focal psychic, the one who makes the goal roll for activation. All others make complementary rolls. The victory points on these rolls may help offset the goal penalties levied for extending psychic powers, and even cause the goal number to exceed 20; use the Excessive Goal Numbers Chart in Chapter Two: Rules.

• All participants can donate as much or as little Wyrd to fuel the power as they desire. For instance, the focal psychic may spend 1 Wyrd to activate the power, while one of the participants spends 2 to extend the range and another participant spends 1 to add more targets. Such expenditures can be done in any combination desired. However, those participants who don't contribute their fare share of energy may be barred from future conventions.

Note that this collective Wyrd spending may only be done with the group power, unless a Coven Bond is activated (see Sympathy powers).

• Once all goal bonuses or penalties have been figured, and the proper amount of Wyrd pooled (but not spent yet), the focal psychic makes his goal roll.

Only the focal psychic's roll is used to determine the success or failure of the power itself. Participant failures do not adversely affect the focal psychic's activation, but any critical failure will automatically cause the power to fail (additional ill effects can be levied at the gamemaster's discretion).

gained on the activation roll. In times of dire need, however, the psychic may call on his Urge for aid: he gains an extra amount that span equal to his Urge rating. The psychic must roll to resist its awakening (Ego + Stoic Mind); failure means that the Urge is awake. Even if the psychic had no levels in Urge, he may elect to take one level to gain the Wyrd. Regardless, any Wyrd points replenished with the Urge's aid are also tallied into the Dark Twin's Wyrd pool with which it builds its psychic body (see level 4 Urge power Wyrd Drain).

Some Vis Crafters theorize that the source they are tap-

ping into is a grid that encompasses all of space-time and was erected by the Anunnaki, and that it is this grid which powers devices like Philosophers Stones and jumpgates.

Other Paths

Other paths are rumored to exist, though they are even more rare than those above: Visioning, which allows the psychic to project illusions of progressively greater believability; Cloaking, in which the psychic learns to conceal not only his physical presence, but his aura and thoughts as well; Turning, which enables the psychic to defend herself against psychic attacks and theurgic rites, often by reflecting the assault back upon the attacker. Training in the path of Turning and the higher levels of Cloaking is only available through organized covens like the Favyana or the Invisible Path. (Details on these powers and others can be found in various **Fading Suns** sourcebooks.)

Urge

This is the dark side of psionics. Urge has one main path, that of the Doppelganger, or Dark Twin. There are other paths, but they are rare and conditional.

Whenever a psychic fumbles a psychic power roll (or a Psi roll), her Urge stirs. For the next span, this dark twin may (or may not, gamemaster's discretion) actively take part in the psychic's life, in a manner dependent on the Urge level (see the list below). It may act in any way its level allows (using all lower level powers also) as many times as it wishes throughout the span.

We say "it" here, but it is really the character herself who is acting. Once she gains one or more Urge levels, the stress of her psychic powers has split her ego into two distinct personalities, one of which remains hidden in her unconscious. But with more power (Urge levels), this dark personality begins to grow, eventually becoming an entirely separate person.

Urge Powers

The Urge is awakened when a psychic fumbles a Psi roll or a roll to activate a psychic power. The Urge may then use any of the following powers up to its level at any time during that span. As the character's Jungian Shadow (or evil twin, if you will), the Urge seeks to break down the good and moral parts of the psychic's mind, often forcing her into situations where she must either act on her more negative impulses or break her own personal code of morality in order to succeed or even survive. Generally, an Urge will take whatever action it can to foul up the psychic's life, usually employing the psychic's most closely guarded secrets, repressed desires and rivalry among peers.

The awakened Urge is played by the gamemaster, who should remember that, while it may be fun to turn a

Resolving Urge/Hubris Conflicts

Psi/Urge and Theurgy/Hubris are unique resisted traits. Psi and Theurgy will come into conflict when a character tries to raise one trait past the level of his Urge or Hubris. For example, Eusebius has Psi 5 and an Urge 5 and wants to raise his Psi to 6; he must first tame a level of Urge.

Because the two traits have come into direct conflict, the character can choose to enter a combat of wills (for Psi) or attempt extreme humility (for Theurgy). A roleplaying event occurs: For psychics, they confront their Urge (the gamemaster plays the Urge) and must force, cajole or charm it into retreating; theurgists must gain recognition or pity from a stranger (not a fellow player character) by performing good works, selfless duty, etc. Only after the outside recognition of such sacrifice from another, will Hubris be put at bay.

These events need to be roleplayed, and their resolution is largely up to the gamemaster. However, a player can demand a roll if he feels a climax has been achieved without gamemaster recognition. Psychics: Wits + Stoic Mind, Charm, Impress or Knavery (whichever task is undertaken). Theurgists: Faith + Empathy, Vigor, Charm (whichever the gamemaster feels is most appropriate).

Success does not cause a reduction in Urge or Hubris levels, but does allow the character to raise his Psi or Theurgy by one level (if he pays the proper amount of experience points). This may mean that the traits are no longer symmetrically resisted (Eusebius will have Psi 6 and Urge 5 — totaling 11). Every time the character wishes to raise his Psi or Theurgy past the level of its opposite, this contest of wills must take place (even if he has already succeeded in a previous contest of wills).

However, neither Urge or Hubris takes regard of their resisted traits when they are raised — they simply rise to whatever level is called for (see the Gaining Urge chart). Raising Urge and Hubris does not require a contest of wills. Thus, it may be the case that Eusebius' Urge was raised to 6 before he even tries to raise his Psi.

Making a Deal With the Devil

A character may choose to use his Urge or Hubris levels instead of his Psi or Theurgy for any roll requiring Psi or Theurgy (such as when defending against occult powers). However, if the roll is successful, this deal with the devil will have consequences. In the case of Urge, the Dark Twin will awaken for the rest of the turn. In the case of Hubris, the ill effects spread or get worse, affecting a broader area (gamemaster's discretion). If the roll failed, there is no dire effect.

character's dark side against him, everything the Urge does should be in the interest of the overall drama. Don't let cruel fun with the Urge get in the way of the main plot.

Note: If a character does not want to perform the action the Urge demands, he can resist by spending a Wyrd point. This Wyrd point goes into the Doppelganger's pool (see Wyrd Drain) and no action is performed that turn. If this keeps up, the gamemaster may require a battle of wills between the psychic and his twin: the psychic rolls Calm + Stoic Mind or Focus, while the twin (using the psychic's traits) rolls Passion + Impress. If the psychic wins, the Urge is put back to sleep; if the Urge wins, the psychic may not resist its actions for the rest of the span.

Speak in Tongues

(Level 1, Extrovert + Knavery)

As the Dark Twin awakens, it gains the ability to speak. The psychic becomes prone to Freudian slips, especially dangerous ones which may reveal her powers. (e.g., "We cannot stand against them, my lord, due to your marital shortcomings — er, I mean, MARTIAL shortcomings!") For each victory point rolled, the Urge may change one word the psychic says; with a critical success, the Urge may reword an entire sentence uttered by the psychic.

Misdirection

(Level 2, Wits + Focus)

The Dark Twin begins to flex its psychic muscles, causing the character to accidentally use his powers on an unintended target. If the Urge rolled one to three victory points, the psychic's action is redirected toward a neutral target like an innocent bystander; for four to six victory points, the action is redirected toward a friendly target such as another player character. In the event of a critical success, the character must perform an action other than that selected, one that benefits the growing Doppelganger.

Voices

(Level 3, Perception + Knavery)

The psychic begins to hear voices, sometimes those of friends or nearby people, and may think they've actually said something to her — or what they said sounds different to her. (e.g., The noble lord says "kneel" and you think he said "steal.")

For each victory point, the Urge may change one word the psychic hears; with a critical success, the Urge may reword an entire sentence heard by the psychic. The gamemaster should feel free to get creative.

Wyrd Drain

(Level 4, Introvert + Vigor)

The Doppelganger now begins to collect the energy

Gaining Urge

Urge is gained through roleplaying. Certain acts or deeds undertaken by a character may cause her Urge to awaken, and from there to slowly grow if she keeps performing similar deeds. What determines if a deed is heinous enough to cause such a divide in the psyche? Breaking societal taboos can be an element, but personal codes and ethics also play a part. Even if the character is an outsider to society, the societal mores she grew up in and unconsciously absorbed still affect her innermost being, regardless of how she tries to deny this. Like it or not, we are social beings.

In the case of barbarians or characters raised by wolves and thus never exposed to any form of human society, the gamemaster should figure out his own criteria for awakening Urge.

Below is a general guideline for humans born and raised in the Known Worlds of the **Fading Suns**. It includes the taboo, the roll required to gain Urge from it (the character must fail this roll or else gain Urge) and the level(s) gained (gamemaster discretion).

Taboo	Roll	Levels
Refusing sacrament	Ego + Stoic Mind	1
Missing confession for more than one year	Ego + Focus	1
Suffering Inquisitorial torture	Calm + Stoic Mind	1 - 2
Suffering excommunication	Faith + Stoic Mind	2 - 3
Exposure to another psychic's Urge	Psi + Stoic Mind	1
Fumbling a psychic power roll	Psi + Stoic Mind or Focus	1
Exposure to alien occult powers	Human or Alien + Stoic Mind	1
Exposure to evil artifact	Human or Alien + Stoic Mind	1 - 3
Declaring a vendetta	Passion + Focus	1
Murder	Passion + Focus	1 - 2
Rape	Passion + Focus	1 - 2
Stealing	Wits + Focus	1
Rebellion against (house, Church, Emperor)	Wits + Focus	1

Losing Urge

Characters can learn to control themselves and dissolve their Dark Twin (or other Urges). But it is harder to close Pandora's Box than it is to open it; losing Urge levels requires a quest or great deed of some sort:

Deed	Roll	Levels
Pilgrimage	Faith + Vigor	1
Church mercy (becoming Penitent)	Faith + Focus	1 - 2
Performing Church mission	Faith + Focus	1
Exposure to Soul Shard	Psi + Stoic Mind or Focus	2 - 3
Exposure to Philosophers Stone	Psi + Stoic Mind or Focus	1
Selfless sacrifice	Passion + Empathy	1 - 2
Exposure to Second Republic Psi Clinic	Introvert + Stoic Mind or Focus	1 - 2

The gamemaster should feel free to create his own taboos or deeds.

needed to build its psychic body. The victory points on the Wyrd Drain roll represent the amount of Wyrd points instantly drained from the psychic. Keep a tally here — every point drained by Wyrd Drain builds into a pool which is later used against the psychic if his Dark Twin ever separates (write the Wyrd Drain pool on the back of the character sheet). The Doppelganger may only attempt one Wyrd Drain per span it is awake.

Visions

(Level 5, Perception + Knavery)

The psychic begins to see things that are not really there, but which are quite convincing at the moment they occur.

Visions cannot harm the character or anyone else, but can convince the character that he has been injured, or trick him into harming himself or someone else.

With one or two victory points, the Urge can induce hallucinations involving simple objects (e.g., making the psychic think her gun is not in her holster when it really is, or that it is when it really isn't, or making her think it is a banana instead); with three or four victory points, the Urge can do the same with multiple objects or a single person. With a five or six victory points, multiple people can be targeted in this way (e.g., the psychic sees a pursuing horde of snarling hungry feral Vorox behind the prince instead of his

155

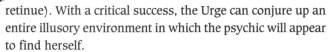

retinue). With a critical success, the Urge can conjure up an entire illusory environment in which the psychic will appear to find herself.

Urges

(Level 6, Passion + Empathy or Torture)

The Dark Twin takes a more active role in the psychic's internal life, causing her to feel emotions she does not necessarily want, like anger, hate, fear, etc.. Note that this is NOT permanent, lasting only for the span in which the Doppelganger is active. Each victory point becomes a negative penalty applied to any Spirit characteristic roll that the psychic may make either to hide these unwanted emotions or to resist acting upon them.

Dementia

(Level 7, Ego + Knavery)

As the Dark Twin's influence increases, the psychic develops a permanent neurosis or psychosis, such as intense paranoia, schizophrenia, the need to kill people in a serial fashion, etc. Each victory point represents the degree to which this mental illness is affecting the psychic at the moment: from one to two, the psychic may be annoying or disruptive; from three to four, the psychic is actually counterproductive to the task at hand; from five to six, the psychic is driven to destructive acts which can endanger friends and allies. With a critical success, the psychic may be driven to self-destructive acts.

Note that this IS permanent, and can only be gotten over therapeutically IF the psychic's Urge rating is reduced to lower than 7.

Outer Child

(Level 8, Extrovert + Focus)

The Doppelganger has grown strong enough to project its psychic body outside of the character, and goes out for occasional jaunts. This is only an illusory projection, and the Dark Twin is incapable of taking direct actions against other characters, other than simply appearing and speaking. With regard to the psychic character, however, this projection is as real and solid as anything else. Each victory point on this roll equals one level on the distance chart (see Range, above); this is how far away from the psychic herself that the Outer Child may actually project itself. When appearing in the psychic's presence, the victory points are used as a negative penalty against any other character's Perception roll to tell the difference between the real psychic and the Dark Twin.

Doppelganger

(Level 9, Extrovert + Vigor)

This is the true birth of the Doppelganger; the Dark Twin is finally realized and becomes a separate, physical being, able to run around the universe all it desires. It has exactly the same traits as the psychic (although the psychic's Urge 9 becomes Psi 9 for the Doppelganger), but its Wyrd rating is equal to the pool it has been developing out of the psychic's own mistakes (see Wyrd Drain, above). The victory points from this roll are used as a negative penalty against any other character's Perception roll to tell the difference between the real psychic and the Dark Twin.

The Doppelganger is permanent — losing Urge will not make it go away (although regaining Urge afterwards will build yet another Doppelganger). The Doppelganger is real and subject to all the things which will kill a living person.

Theurgy

Unlike psychic powers, theurgy rituals do not have paths; characters simply learn the individual rituals at their required levels and do not need to buy a lower level first.

Since theurgy is more restrictive in its use (requiring liturgy, gestures, prayer, etc..) and less flexible, it tends to have a bit more bang for its buck per level than psychic powers. It lasts longer also (average one span, but some are instant); see the power description for each ritual. Unlike psychics, theurgists may not extend the range and duration, or add more targets, by spending Wyrd points.

Components

Rituals have one or more of the following three components used during the casting (not duration) of the rite:

- **Liturgy (L):** Words must be spoken. Some rites call for long orations, others for a simple prayer.
- **Gestures (G):** Symbols and signs must be traced in the air or on the object of the ritual. This could be a simple cross or a complex rune.
- **Prayer (P):** The priest must meditate for the rite. This can be a short moment of concentration or an hours-long trance.

A ritual can be performed without its components, but the theurgist suffers a -3 penalty to his goal roll. (Thus, an Eskatonic priest can still use liturgical or gestural theurgy when bound and gagged.)

Vestments

Vestments can add to the goal roll of certain theurgy rites. Below are some vestments and the types of theurgy rites in which they are effective. When used in a rite in which it is effective, a vestment will add +1 to the goal roll. Extra vestments can be used for more bonuses; add +1 for every two additional vestments.

Official Church vestments, blessed and properly prepared, are made theurgically potent with the Sanctification or Consecration rites.

Vestment	Type of Rite
Miter (Rank 4+)	Wisdom (Divine Revelation, Tongues of Babel)
Crosier (Rank 3+)	Command, leadership (Devotional Liturgy, Exorcism)
Robes	Protection (Armor of the Pancreator)
Censor	Cleansing (Cleansing, Consecration)
Jumpgate cross	Morale, avert (Dispersing the Darkness, Fearsome Majesty)
Water	Healing (Laying on of Hands, Healing Hand of Saint Amalthea)
Rosary bead	Concentration, meditation (Righteous Assignation of Penance, Righteous Fervor)

Relics

Some holy relics or vestments can hold Wyrd or allow the wielder to perform a rite she has not learned. Anything can be a relic, as long as it was involved in some faithful task in the past (consecrating it for its theurgic task). Some effects are:

• **Wyrd Tabernacle:** The relic may act as a Wyrd pool, storing Wyrd points. These points may be extracted and used each roll by the wielder with a Faith + Focus roll; the maximum which may be used is equal to the victory points. Once these points have been used, the Tabernacle must be recharged with Wyrd from a willing sacrificer (one point per point expended). This requires a ceremony and a Theurgy + Focus roll; the maximum that may be stored during that ceremony is equal to the victory points. Such tabernacles are created with the 8th level Eskatonic rite of Investiture.

• **Saint's Lore:** The relic is invested with one or more theurgy rituals, usable by anyone wielding the relic. These relics are very rare, for the only known method of investing objects with ritual lore is by miracle; the object was invariably the former possession of a saint, whose deeds were so faithful and memorable that the object still remembers them and can repeat them. A Saint's Lore relic can be combined with a Wyrd Tabernacle. The required amount of Wyrd points for the rite must still be spent by the wielder. As an example, a finger bone of Saint Rasmussen might have Avert

Casting Multiple Rituals

A person can potentially be under the spell of multiple rites per turn. In other words, a Brother Battle could cast upon himself Soul's Vessel, Armor of the Pancreator, Liturgy of the Wrathful Host and Smiting Hand. However, each rite after the first costs one extra Wyrd point to cast. In addition, casting so many powers upon oneself is vain act; each extra rite increases the chance of gaining Hubris should a casting fail miserably.

Every time a theurgist fumbles a theurgy rite casting roll, he must roll Theurgy + Focus or else gain a level of Hubris. Casting multiple rites enacts penalties on this roll:

Rite	Penalty
First rite	None
Second rite	-2
Third rite	-4
Fourth rite	-6
Fifth rite	-8
Sixth rite	-10

Each rite thereafter adds an additional -2 penalty.

A theurgist may cancel any of his active rites anytime he chooses with but a gesture.

Rites targeted against a person's will provide an exception to this rule, such as the Avestite Sting of Conscience. If these rites are not successfully contested, they affect the target regardless of the number of rituals active upon him. They are not counted against a person's active rites and do not necessarily cost extra Wyrd points or add to the chance of gaining Hubris. If their effects contradict active rituals, they are deemed to take precedence and dampen the first rite (which still lasts for its duration, but may not take effect until the invasive rite's duration is over).

Some rites will compete and offset each other. For instance, a Brother Battle under the spell of Soul's Vessel adds three to any rolls involving athletic feats. If an Avestite casts Tortures of the Damned upon him, the Brother would still gain his +3 bonus, but it would be offset by the painful wound penalties enacted by the Avestite rite.

Evil (Level Three) and Devotion (Level One).

• **Article of Faith:** This type of relic can aid the faithful in their ritual tasks. Like a vestment, this relic adds to a character's goal roll when performing a ritual. It is specific to a certain ritual (such as rosary beads which aid Second Sight). To gain the bonus, the character must hold the article during performance of the rite. Such articles are created with the 8th level Sanctification rite.

Church Rituals

Each sect has its own rites, associated with its patron saint and Virtues. The cost for a character to learn another sect's rites is normally +1 Extra point per level or 3x current rating in experience points. Sometimes, a character does not even have to go to a member of that sect to learn the rite — a hoary old master within his own sect may know it, usually changed somewhat to more properly reflect his own sect's ceremonies. However, he must still pay the increased cost for this rare rite.

Below are some rites common to all sects; characters may learn these at regular cost:

The Prophet's Holy Blessing

(Level 1, Faith + Focus, G, touch, 1W)

By tracing the Church's symbol on a companion's forehead or in her general direction, a theurge may aid the target in a particular task, adding the victory points to the target's goal roll. The effect lasts until the target has made the roll for the particular task blessed. (If the rite is successful, the character will receive a minimum of at least one victory die, regardless of the number of successes rolled.)

The Devotional Liturgy

(Level 2, Extrovert + Oratory, L, sensory, prolonged, 1W)

Recitation of this passage from the Omega Gospels is the traditional way of boosting morale, usually before battle. The liturgy takes about fifteen minutes to read, and all true believers within earshot add the theurge's victory points to all rolls involving Faith or Calm for the next span. (The range of this effect is not extended by PA systems or long-distance communications.) Characters under the effect of the Liturgy may not Incite Passion or employ Steady Hand.

The Laying On of Hands

(Level 3, Calm + Remedy, P, touch, instant, 1W)

By calling upon Amalthea, Patron Saint of healing and compassion, disciple of the Prophet, the theurge may bring comfort to his injured comrades by touching their wounds. Each victory point heals one wound level.

The Prophet's Censure

(Level 4, Passion + Focus, LG, sight, 1W)

The theurge may give an enemy of the faith a small taste of divine displeasure by repeating the first two lines of the Prophet's Admonishment of the Unbelievers and making the sign of the barred jumpgate in the target's direction. The reverse of the Holy Blessing, Censure penalizes the target in a particular task, subtracting the theurge's victory points from the target's goal roll. The effect lasts until the target has made the roll for the particular task censured.

The Pulpit's Gift

(Level 5, Passion + Oratory, LG, sensory, one act, 1W)

Developed mainly for use by missionaries on new worlds, this rite increases the social influence of a theurge upon the people to whom she preaches. For the rest of the act, the theurge may add her victory points from this rite to any Charm or Impress rolls directed at a member of her new "flock."

Oath to the Saints

(Level 5, Faith + Oratory, LGP, sight, perpetual, 1W per person)

Inspired by the Oath of Fellowship pledged by Zebulon's eight disciples to one another in their time of worst trial, this rite allows a party to pledge themselves to each other under the patronage of a saint. This rite must be cast by an ordained priest not of the party (a witness before the Pancreator), although any theurges within the party may assist in the rite (see Group Rites, below). This is similar to the psychic power of Bonding, for it allows all members of the party bonuses when casting theurgy upon one another (+2 goal roll).

The particular saint whose name is invoked lends each member of the party a +1 goal roll bonus when performing certain tasks associated with that saint's Virtue:

Saint	Task
Paulus	Pathfinding, investigating mysteries
Lextius	Upholding a pledge, providing example to others
Amalthea	Aiding those in need, easing pain
Mantius	Defending the faithful (applies to defensive actions only), bettering oneself
Maya	Defending the innocent (applies to defensive and offensive actions), punishing the guilty
Horace	Research, lorekeeping
Hombor	Befriending others, selfless acts of charity
Ven Lohji	Meditation, artistic endeavors

Gamemasters should feel free to introduce lesser saints that player characters can pledge themselves to.

Betrayal by the party members of each other or their saint breaks the oath and brings bad consequences: all previous bonuses become penalties until the offender has redeemed himself by pilgrimage or other faithful deed. In addition, the offender's oathbreaking is stained on his soul and can be seen with Rending the Veil of Unreason rite.

The Tongues of Babel

(Level 6, Wits + Empathy, GP, prolonged, 1W)

Also common among missionaries, the Tongues of Babel enables a theurge to understand and speak almost any language he does not already understand. For some time before the rite, he must hear the language spoken frequently

by natives or other fluent speakers. The victory points for this roll provide bonuses for any roll involved in communicating in that language during that span, whether it be orating before a crowd or reading a moving sermon.

This rite does not confer the ability to read the language, unless it is normally written (or happens to be spelled out phonetically) in the Urthish alphabet; alien, Kurgan and most other barbarian or Lost World tongues do not use the Urthish alphabet.

The Righteous Assignation of Penance

(Level 7, Faith + Empathy, LP, 1W)

This rite is central to the Church's function in the Known Worlds, since this is how humanity learns, through confession, to make good its sins. In most cases, of course, the rite is no more than a ceremonial formality, but when the sins in question are of overwhelming enormity, or have occult implications beyond simple personal salvation, theurgic Assignation can prove to be the only way of navigating these dark mysteries.

The effect of the Righteous Assignation is primarily concerned with roleplaying rather than rules; most penances tend to be charitable donations, community or personal service, pilgrimages and quests. However, a penance which is successfully completed could result in a player character gaining a Blessing or removing a Curse, or the reduction of Urge or Hubris ratings for psychics and theurges. Note that, unless the gamemaster rules otherwise, this does not affect the regular expenditure of experience points, it merely incorporates it into the ongoing storyline. (i.e., Experience must still be spent for a Blessing gained through penance, and losing a Curse does not take points away from any other character rating.)

The subject of this rite must perform the penance assigned him by the ritecaster, or else suffer nightmares and bad luck — or worse (gain Hubris or lose Faith). Gamemaster's discretion.

Sanctification

(Level 7, Faith + Focus, GP, touch, perpetual, 2W)

The theurge sanctifies an object, turning it into a Vestment (see above). While this rite does not provide the occult protections that the level 1 Orthodoxy rite of Consecration does, it is permanent. Although vestment's may lose their sanctity over time and neglect, as long as they are well-cared for, they will continue to add bonuses to a theurge's rites. This rite may be cast a number of times per week equal to the theurge's Theurgy rating; it is not intended to allow priests to run vestment factories.

A 8th level version of this rite allows the theurge to create an Article of Faith; its bonuses to a particular rite are equal to the Wyrd spent upon activation.

Shield of Faith

(Level 8, Extrovert + Focus, GP, 1W)

Similar to the technological energy shield, this rite creates a hemispherical field with a three meter radius around the theurge, and moves as she moves. The Shield lasts for the rest of the span, and the radius can be extended with additional Wyrd points at a rate of one meter per point spent. The maximum armor rating for the Shield of Faith is 15 plus the theurge's victory points; the minimum amount of damage which will activate the Shield is the theurge's Hubris rating. (If she has no Hubris, then 1 point is the minimum.) The Shield can take a number of hits (see Energy Shields in Chapter Seven: Technology) equal to her Theurgy rating plus the victory points on the casting roll; an extra number of hits equal to her Theurgy rating may be gained with each additional Wyrd point spent.

Providential Deliverance

(Level 9, Faith + Focus, LGP, 1W)

This rite enables a theurge in an extremely dangerous situation to escape in some unlikely manner that may even border on the miraculous. A successful casting of Deliverance means that the gamemaster must orchestrate events in such a way as to allow the caster to make a clean getaway from the peril in which he finds himself. This does not mean that the impossible can happen, only the highly improbable; Deliverance can take such forms as a unknown assailant attacking someone who is about to kill the theurge, or a captor accidentally dropping his keys while visiting the theurge's dungeon cell. A famous example is the Hazat chaplain Father Constantius, who was on the verge of being dismembered by a horde of enraged Kurgan loyalists when a freak earthquake opened up the ground beneath him. The good father was dropped (with minimal injury) into a network of subterranean caverns, through which he was able to make his way back to Imperial territory.

Orthodox Rituals

Consecration

(Level 1, Faith + Focus, GP, touch, one act, 1W)

Consecration purifies an item from evil taint, effectively making a vestment out of it for the duration of one act. (After that act, the item returns to normal, unless a critical success was rolled, in which case the Consecration is permanent.) The Consecrated item resists being affected by psychic powers, Antinomy, Urge or Hubris; half of the casting victory points (rounded up) become a negative penalty for any of these powers attempting to target the item. Items of Tech Level 5+ are hard to consecrate; subtract one from the casting roll.

Light

(Level 2, Passion + Focus, G, prolonged, 1W)

This rite creates a glowing insubstantial sphere in the theurge's palm capable of casting enough light to read by in a three-meter radius. This radius is extended by one meter per victory point (at caster's choice).

An alternate version of this rite creates a tight searchlight-type beam which extends from the theurge's palm, which can be used to search darkened rooms or blind enemies of the Faith. The range for this beam is 10 meters plus two meters per victory point.

Armor of the Pancreator

(Level 3, Faith + Dodge, LG, prolonged, 1W)

A more exact equivalent of the energy shield, this theurgic force field protects the target by conforming itself to the target's body. Unlike Shield of Faith, the Armor of the Pancreator does not need to be centered on the theurge herself, but can be projected around another person. (The target must be declared when this rite is cast, and cannot be transferred to anyone else.) The Armor lasts for one span.

The maximum armor rating for the Armor of the Pancreator is 10 plus the theurge's victory points; the minimum damage which will activate the Armor is the theurge's Hubris rating. (If she has no Hubris, then 1 point is the minimum.) The Armor can take a number of hits (see Energy Shields in Chapter Seven: Technology) equal to the caster's Theurgy rating plus the victory points on the casting roll; an extra number of hits equal to her Theurgy rating may be gained with each additional Wyrd point spent. This rite cannot be used upon a target wearing armor thicker than leather (unless the target is unconscious or incapacitated), and does not activate if attempted.

Faithful Heart

(Level 4, Introvert + Stoic Mind, LP, prolonged, 1W)

This rite shields the soul and mind of a true believer against mental invasion or domination by psychics and their Urges, theurgists, alien telepaths or Antinomists. It can be cast by the theurge upon himself or another. The victory points for casting become a negative penalty on all mental attacks directed at the target.

Dispersal of Darkness

(Level 5, Passion + Impress, LG, temporary, 1W)

The theurge may act as a kind of physical repulsion field against certain servitors of evil, such as the husks of the dead (see Chapter Eight: Gamemastering), the Doppelgangers of psychics, those under malicious influence from a negative Ur-artifact, etc.. The number of successes represents the closest distance in meters to which an evil minion can approach the theurge. The duration may be extended by 10 turns for each extra Wyrd point spent (these points can be spent any time after activation).

Consecration of Land

(Level 6, Faith + Focus, GP, one act, 1W)

Usually a prerequisite when building a temple, this rite acts as the single-item Consecration above, but is applied to an area equal to the theurge's Extrovert rating x10 in square meters. Consecrated ground is impassable to the walking dead, and occult powers originating from unpenitent psychics, Antinomists or negative Ur-artifacts receive a penalty equal to the victory points from casting the Consecration. Note that this does not only apply to powers being used from within the Consecrated area, but also when the area is targeted from without. For example, an unpenitent psychic on the other side of town trying to search the inner temple with FarSight receives the same penalty.

After the act is over, the area returns to normal, unless a critical success was rolled, in which case the Consecration is permanent.

Blessing the Crops

(Level 7, Extrovert + Survival, LGP, 1W)

Growing from the traditional role of the priesthood in agrarian cultures, this rite enables a theurge to purify or enrich an amount of food equal to his Theurgy rating in kilograms. Crop Blessing will neutralize impurities and organic poisons, restore perishable foods within two days of their having spoiled, and, in the case of untainted foodstuffs, make them more nutritious and fulfilling by 50% (e.g.: a ten day supply of rations can be stretched out to fifteen days). This rite is very valuable on many worlds, where the fading suns fail to nourish crops.

Exorcism

(Level 8, Faith + Impress, LGP, sensory, 1W)

With this rite a theurge can drive out any dark power which is influencing or possessing the target (usually psychic or Antinomic domination and demonic possession, although the influence of Ur-artifacts and certain aliens can also be dispelled in this way). Exorcism can be a long and arduous process. It is a sustained action, and the exorcist needs to accumulate 25 victory points in order to rid the target of whatever is possessing or influencing him. He must spend the Wyrd point cost with every roll. If he runs out of Wyrd before accumulating 25 successes, the exorcism fails, and the theurge must start all over, losing all his accumulated successes.

To make things more difficult, the demon can contest the theurge's rolls with its vessel's Ego + Charm, Impress or Knavery (depending on the demon's personality and preference). Demons usually supernaturally enhance their vessel's characteristics and skills, thus making the task even harder for the exorcist.

In the case of psychic influence, the exorcist must accumulate victory points equal to the psychic's Psi rating. If the psychic is aware of the exorcism and the exorcist is in range, he can contest the rolls with whatever characteristic and skill is required for the power he is using on the target.

In the case of alien effects, the gamemaster should set a number which reflects the strength of the spiritual invasion (use the guidelines given for sustained actions in Chapter Two: Rules).

Sealing the Temple

(Level 9, Calm + Impress, LGP, prolonged, 1W)

In times of great trouble, Orthodox priests used this rite to protect their flock (and, in some unfortunate cases, protect themselves from their flock) by turning their temple into a temporary fortress. When ritually sealed in this way, a temple is considered to have a large energy shield surrounding it; the maximum armor rating is 20, the minimum damage which will activate the seal is the caster's Hubris rating (if he has no Hubris, then 1 point is the minimum), and it can take a number of hits equal to double the caster's Theurgy rating. (Additional hits can be purchased at a rate of one Wyrd point for a number of hits equal to the Theurgy rating.)

Brother Battle Rituals

Soul's Vessel

(Level 1, Passion + Stoic Body, P, prolonged, 1W)

One of the core teachings of Brother Battle is the perfection of the physical body as the instrument of action in the service of the Pancreator. This rite aids the theurge by adding three to the goal number of all non-combat rolls involving physical traits (running, jumping, lifting, etc.).

Rightfully Guided Hand

(Level 2, Faith + Fight, Shoot or Melee, LG, temporary, 1W)

By calling on the Pancreator to steady her hand when under fire, a theurge may add the victory points from casting this rite to the goal number of her combat skill rolls. Note that this may only be applied to the combat skill used to cast this rite (i.e., Fight, Shoot or Melee), usually the Brother's favored weapon. (If the rite is successful, the character will receive a minimum of at least one victory die, regardless of the number of successes rolled.)

Armor of the Pancreator

(Level 3, Faith + Dodge, LG, prolonged, 1W)

This rite is identical to the level 3 Orthodoxy rite, above, except that the Brother Battle version can be expanded to include bulkier armor which has been Sanctified or Consecrated.

Righteous Fervor

(Level 4, Passion + Vigor, L, one act, 1W)

Brothers Battle monks are renowned for their discipline and loyalty. The Rite of Righteous Fervor intensifies their

already legendary stoicism, allowing a Brother to resist all temptations, persuasions, fast talks, etc., that would sway him from his duty. During casting, the Brother declares his duty ("No harm shall come to the bishop under my watch," or "I shall safely deliver the writ to the Heirophant on Byzantium Secundus."). If the casting is successful, the Brother is immune to any mental or social obstacles which would hinder his duty (such as the orders of the bishop to step down from duty, the knavery of the Decados marquis, the lamentation of a peasant to get her trapped brother from under the fallen ox-cart, etc.). In addition, he receives +3 to his Perception to notice possible physical obstacles (cutpurses, Decados assassins sneaking through the crowd, etc.).

While the Brother Battle dedication is to be admired, it should be noted that fervored Brothers can become quite callous to pleas for help if they seem to hinder their duty. If they do refuse such pleas while fervored, they must confess their guilt within a week after the rite's effect has ended. Otherwise, they risk gaining Hubris.

Liturgy of the Wrathful Host

(Level 5, Passion + Charm, LP, sensory, prolonged, 1W)

This passage from the Omega Gospels is read to Brothers about to go into combat so that their hearts may be filled with the fire of their holy cause, whatever it may happen to be. For the next span, the victory points from the reading may be added to the goal number of all listeners' rolls involving Faith or Passion. The Liturgy takes about 10 minutes to read, and the range of this effect is not extended by PA systems or long-distance communications. Characters under the effect of the Liturgy may not Incite Passion or employ Steady Hand.

Smiting Hand

(Level 6, Faith + Vigor, LG, instant, 1W)

Using this rite to channel the force of the Holy Flame through his limbs, a Brother may strike down his foes with righteous power. The victory dice from casting this rite may be added to the Brother's fist, kick or melee weapon damage — in addition to normal damage from the weapon and the goal roll's victory dice. (If the rite is successful, the character will receive a minimum of at least one victory die, regardless of the number of successes rolled.)

Fearsome Majesty

(Level 7, Passion + Impress, LG, sight, prolonged, 1W)

This rite causes fear of the Pancreator to clutch the heart of the target. The target may take no action for that turn, and for the rest of the span suffers a penalty to all initiative and goal rolls equal to the victory points of the rite. The number of targets may be doubled with each additional Wyrd

point spent. This rite cannot be cast upon someone under the influence of the Prophet's Censure or Tortures of the Damned.

Oath of the Shieldmates

(Level 8, Extrovert + Empathy, LGP, sensory, prolonged, 1W)

Similar to the psychic power Sympaticus (see the Psyche path, above), this rite allows a Brother to band his comrades into an elite fighting unit. He can easily communicate with, or feel the emotions of, chosen targets, allowing the formation of a telepathic network among non-theurgic characters (all information must flow through the Brother who cast the rite, i.e., non-theurgic targets may not communicate directly, except through normal channels). However, use of this rite actually makes it harder to manipulate or control these targets (-4 on all rolls to do so). Not just any target can be chosen, however. It must be a shieldmate — someone who has pledged loyalty with the Brother to a common cause and has been subject to the Prophet's Holy Blessing ritual with him. This most often includes other Brothers, but boon traveling companions can be included as can those to whom the Brother owes duty or loyalty.

Salutation to Zakhayelos, Lord of Hosts

(Level 9, Passion + Impress, LGP, 1W)

This exceptionally rare and powerful rite, a closely guarded secret of the order, enables a theurge to contact and summon to the physical world one of the "bodiless powers of the Empyrean," the strong and warlike intelligence known as Zakhayelos. According to Eskatonic doctrine, Zakhayelos rules in the Fifth Emanation from the Celestial Sun, among the ranks of the Imperitories.

Zakhayelos is the pure embodiment of all the military virtues to which the order aspires: strength, courage, discipline, a perfect understanding of strategy and logistics. As with all of the Empyrean powers, Zakhayelos will almost never take direct physical actions, such as fighting alongside the troops, but, as a being of nearly limitless capabilities, can act in ways both grand and subtle to tip the scales of victory in the Brothers' favor. Zakhayelos has been known to aid the order with signs and omens that reveal enemy positions and tactics, or to bolster troops with substantial (but temporary) increases in characteristics, or to appear in the sky above Brother Battle armies, displaying its most fearsome form to the enemy. When taking a visible form, Zakhayelos will most often appear as a tall noble knight clad in shining, elaborately decorated armor, wielding a flaming sword and a mirrored shield emblazoned with the Church symbol.

Many outside the Church claim that such "angelic beings" are merely mass hallucinations called up from the

Church Cosmology

Humanity will be judged by the fate of the stars. A sun must burn to birth light. When your passion burns, you give off light. You are born in light but travel in darkness. Beware the dark between the stars. Bring a lantern to it.

—The Prophet's words, from the Omega Gospels

The Prophet preached about a Holy Flame, a Celestial Sun which mystically burns at the center of the universe, providing light and life for all souls. Since this is holy light, it cannot be perceived with gross (material) senses. The light of this ever-burning sun flows outward and touches everything — except the darkness emanating from the demons, whose shadows blot the light. Since this fire is mainly spirit, actions of the spirit nourish or damage it.

The Avestites take this flame very literally, especially the Prophet's words about burning out sin, which they attempt to do with flameguns. Less zealous priests claim that the Prophet was speaking metaphorically, that sin would be burnt out as darkness before a revealed light.

The material world is the reflection of the Holy Light. Evil stands between the Light and the material world, blocking the light which reaches mortal beings. This is why other points of light and reflections within the material world are so important, since they reflect the Light from other directions, not just directly from before. The virtues polish the soul to reflect the light, making the soul a beacon or lantern in the night of shadows. This holographic web of lights can thus be stronger in the material world than the direct ray of light itself, which is too often blocked by evil.

The Pancreator resides in the Empyrean, the seat of the Holy Flame. It is a place of pure spirit and light, nigh unimaginable to our sin and shadow-stained minds. It is from here that the light of the Holy Flame shines into all dimensions of existence. Some say that it is not above the world, but central to all worlds (although the idea of many worlds is still an argued tenet). Others say it is above all, that it's light is sent by the Pancreator downwards into the world of matter. This is called the Descent of Grace. When grace is accepted, the soul becomes a mirror, reflecting back the light of the Holy Flame. This is called the Luminous Return (the souls of the faithful return to the Empyrean with the light after death, and thus a bright soul is all-important to cast a powerful enough light back to heaven; if not, the soul may not reach all the way, falling off like weak light, getting lost in the darkness).

Each soul is meant to be a mirror for the light so that it can be reflected in all directions throughout the world(s). But sin blackens the soul. Enough sin will eventually shut out the holy light, leaving the sinful one's soul a black blotch of shadow — pure evil, the stuff of demons, who cloak themselves in fogs of shadow. Sin is like verdigris on the mirror of the soul. To remove the sin, the soul must be polished, and there are many methods for this, differing with each sect. In general, however, the eight major virtues represent the necessary steps to polishing the soul.

Certain sects (Eskatonics among them) believe that everyone is born with a spark of the Holy Flame. The purpose of the Church is to fan this flame into a fire. This is best done through exposure to the supreme Holy Flame through mystical illumination or meditation. Thus, certain faithful are not merely mirrors but beacons themselves. The Orthodox Church believes this idea may be heretical, that the best humans can hope for is to be reflectors, not generators, of divine light. The former tend to seek inward for grace, while the latter look to external actions for grace, although both honor meditation, for it is known that in contemplation, the Holy Flame can be glimpsed.

Astrology: In the Diaspora, the Church taught that the stars were material manifestations of the Holy Flame. It was natural for people to yearn for distant stars; the Diaspora was an extension of humanity's search for the Pancreator. A whole new field of astrology became popular in occult circles, categorizing stars by the quality of their energy. People born under certain constellations would thus behave in certain ways, as ordained by the qualities of the Holy Flame being projected from these stars on the night of a person's birth. Pilgrimages became popular to certain systems known for a particular energy quality, such as healing or insight.

Moons had particular qualities of their own, being reflectors of the Holy Flame. The light they gave off was an alchemical result of the sun's light and the moon's own energy. Occult powers could be gained from certain moonlight.

After the Fall, the Church ignored the "star as Holy Flame" doctrine (the Doctrine of the Embodied Flame) and spurned Church astrology. It taught instead that each person must be content with the sun he was born under. Emperor Alexius is attempting to revive the Embodied Flame doctrine to spur new discovery.

Geomancy: This obscure philosophy is still studied by the Eskatonic Order. Each planet's molten core is believed to be, like a star, a piece of the Holy Flame. The energy of this fire escapes to the surface in certain ways, creating magical sites and ley lines. It is believed that the terraforming architects of certain planets knew this geomantic science and built the worlds to take maximum advantage of it. The Eskatonics believe that Pentateuch is one such place, as is Byzantium Secundus. Holy Terra is special, for it is the cradle of humanity and is thus rich with natural ley line energy. Geomancers are desperate to find untouched, unterraformed worlds to investigate, hoping to prove their theories.

minds of believers by the theurge, and that they do not really exist. But they rarely make such claims in public.

Eskatonic Order Rituals

Celestial Alignment

(Level 1, Perception + Observe, P, perpetual, 1W)

One of the earliest rites developed by Eskatonic theurges was that of Celestial Alignment, which proved useful to explorers on new planets seeking Ur-artifacts or forgotten wisdom. This rite enables a theurge to keep perfect mental notation of all the movements of the surrounding solar system, as well as the constellations (as they appear to an observer on planetside). Thus the theurge, with but a glance at the sky, can reckon sidereal time and track his position, direction and motion as he travels across the planet.

The effect of this rite is permanent, but applies only to the planet upon which it was cast, and does not need to be recast if the theurge returns to that planet. Celestial Alignment has some application to interplanetary navigation (i.e., travel within a solar system), but not to interstellar travel or complex maneuvers like combat, docking or landing on a planet. The accuracy with which a theurge can figure his relative position in time and space is based on the victory points from casting the rite:

Victory Pts	Time	Position
1	+/- 10 minutes	+/- 10 kilometers
2	+/- 9 minutes	+/- 8 kilometers
3	+/- 7 minutes	+/- 6 kilometers
4	+/- 5 minutes	+/- 4 kilometers
5	+/- 3 minutes	+/- 2 kilometers
6	+/- 1 minute	+/- 1 kilometer
Critical	exact second	exact centimeter

Divine Revelation

(Level 2, Wits + Focus, P, 1W)

Developed from the common prayer for guidance, this rite guarantees the theurge some kind of significant insight into whatever problem is vexing her. The gamemaster should adjust the degree of insight according to the victory points: one would furnish only the slightest of clues, something which might not even seem important to the player; three provides a more substantial answer that will lead most characters to a solution; five or six will grant the theurge a clear indication to the exact nature of her dilemma and what needs to be done to alleviate it. With a critical success, profound leaps of logic are possible, where the gamemaster may opt to give the player information to which her character would not normally have access.

Rending the Veil of Unreason

(Level 3, Perception + Focus, P, sight, prolonged, 1W)

This rite grants the theurge the equivalent of the psychic power Subtle Sight, except that the auric image that the theurge actually perceives is based on the Eskatonic conception of the soul. Rending the Veil shows the actual "mirror" reflecting the light of the Celestial Sun, the Holy Flame of the spirit, centered on the heart region within the conventional aura. The size of the reflected Flame indicates the target's Faith rating; with a Faith of 10, the Flame is large and bright, filling the surface of the "mirror," while a Faith of 1 shows up as a candle flame seen at the end of a dark corridor. Because this "mirror" can be "tarnished" by sinful actions and intentions, the theurge may guess at the type and extent of the target's sinful ways by examining the condition of the target's "mirror."

Sin	"Tarnish"
Pride	Narrow vertical streaks
Greed	Broad horizontal streaks
Lust	Violet bubbles rising from bottom
Envy	Greenish streaks pointing inward from outer edges
Sloth	Thick bluish bubbles rolling down from the top
Wrath	Reddish streaks radiating from the center
Oathbreaking	Cracks; one for each oath broken, with size of crack equaling importance of oath

Besides this moral insight, the theurge may also read the aura as if using Subtle Sight, but the theurge needs victory points one greater than required for each level. General types may still be discerned with one victory point, but two is necessary to see colors, four to see motion and six to see shapes.

Second Sight

(Level 4, Perception + Focus, P, sight, prolonged, 1W)

This rite is the theurgic equivalent of the psychic power Wyrd Sight, but with more of an emphasis on the moral forces at work in the targeted viewing area. A theurge casting Second Sight may see a psychic's Urge, for example, as a dark fetal form in the psychic's brain (at lower levels) or as a fully formed shadow which moves independently of the psychic casting it. Second Sight reveals the presence of demonic influence, with their dark forms hovering in the air around a Antinomist, or coiled up in the body of someone who is possessed. Second Sight also shows the theurge details of any theurgic rite in effect, its type, target and caster.

Second Sight does not automatically confer the aura-reading ability of Rending the Veil of Unreason; each power operates within a different range of the astral spectrum. The gamemaster should be creative when describing what a theurge sees with Second Sight; keep in mind that individual auras are not being read, but rather all the broad occult forces at work in a given span.

Osseous Transmutation

(Level 5, Wits + Alchemy, LG, touch, perpetual, 1W)

By calling upon the transformative powers of his own indwelling portion of the Holy Flame, an Eskatonic priest can fossilize any object or body of substance less than or equal to his Theurgy rating times 20 in kilograms. (Additional mass can be bought at 10 kilograms per Wyrd point.) The transmuted object is composed of a gray chalky sandstone-like stuff, which is just strong enough to support a human's weight but brittle enough to crack or crumble with sharp impact. The effect is permanent. Ur-artifacts are not affected by this rite.

Living organic tissue cannot be affected with this rite. Even if it could, it would be considered an especially grave crime by the Order, since it would freeze the target's soul in the statue-like body and prevent the target's Luminous Return to the Empyrean. There are, of course, rumors of renegade priests who have somehow attained such ability.

All-Seeing Eye

(Level 6, Perception + Observe, LP, prolonged, 1W)

The equivalent of the psychic power FarSight, the Rite of the All-Seeing Eye allows the theurge to observe a place in which she is not actually present. Consult the description of FarSight to see how the casting roll should be modified according to the familiarity of the targeted place.

Refinement of Essence

(Level 7, Wits + Alchemy, LG, touch, perpetual, 1W)

A more specialized form of the Rite of Osseous Transmutation, the Rite of Refinement enables the theurge to cast out impurities or non-essential elements from an object or body of substance less than or equal to his Theurgy rating times 20 in kilograms. (Additional mass can be bought at 10 kilograms per Wyrd point.) Refinement may be used to purify fuel, strengthen building materials and detoxify food, water or the atmosphere of an enclosed and sealed space.

Unlike Transmutation, Refinement may be used on living beings for beneficial effects, but the same penalties apply and considerable discrimination and forethought are required; benign drugs and medicines, surgical implants, transplants or tissue grafts, and even undigested food will be forcibly expelled from the target's body. Cybernetic enhancements may break down or cause damage to their bearer.

Investiture

(Level 8, Calm + Focus, LGP, touch, perpetual, 1W)

The Rite of Investiture is used to create a Wyrd Tabernacle (see Relics, above) out of a targeted object. The maximum number of Wyrd points which the Invested Tabernacle may store is equal to the number of successes on the casting roll, and may be increased up to a maximum of 20

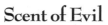

through repetition of the rite. Note that the Rite of Investiture does not actually bind any Wyrd points into the Tabernacle; this is a separate process involving a Theurgy + Focus roll, as described above under Wyrd Tabernacle.

Knowledge and Conversation of Tholumiyelos, Lord of Wisdom

(Level 9, Passion + Impress, LGP, 1W)

This exceptionally rare and powerful rite, a closely guarded secret of the order, enables a theurge to contact and summon to the physical world one of the "bodiless powers of the Empyrean," the clever and insightful intelligence known as Tholumiyelos. According to Eskatonic doctrine, which describes the Empyrean as being presided over by "luminous sentiences" occupying a hierarchy of concentric Emanations from the Celestial Sun, Tholumiyelos rules in the Eighth Emanation, among the ranks of the Archons.

Embodying the Eskatonic virtues of questing for secret lore and the cultivation of metaphysical understanding, Tholumiyelos rarely manifests in physical form, and prefers instead to converse with the theurge who summoned it. These conversations would be virtually impossible for outsiders to understand since they are highly ritualized and formulaic, being a kind of catechism or question-and-answer session with Tholumiyelos taking the part of the teacher and the theurge being the student. Tholumiyelos seldom answers a direct question (e.g., "Is the duchess poisoning my meals?"), but is more likely to ask the theurge questions which will lead him to his own answer (e.g., "How do you think the duchess feels about you, and what political necessities might impinge on your relationship?"). When taking a visual form, Tholumiyelos will appear as a elderly hermaphrodite with clear sparkling eyes, holding an ancient book in the right, or male, hand and a bubbling crucible in the left, or female, hand.

Temple Avesti Rituals

Knowing the False Heart

(Level 1, Perception + Empathy, G, sight, prolonged, 1W)

Essential to the Avestite pursuit of justice, this rite allows the theurge to act as a human lie detector. Since this rite focuses only on intentional dishonesty and deliberate untruthfulness, it is sometimes possible for the target to dissemble, hiding or twisting the truth with a contested roll of Wits or Calm + Charm. This roll can receive a negative modifier if the target is trying to hide a sin of his own, and a positive one if the target is protecting an innocent under suspicion. The Avestite may still detect half-truths with three or more victory points, and may guess their exact nature with a critical success. This rite affects only a single target.

Scent of Evil

(Level 2, Perception + Empathy, GP, sensory, prolonged, 1W)

Casting Scent of Evil enables a theurge to "sniff out" acts of Antinomy, the actions of a psychic's Urge and the presence of demons or alien artifacts with a negative influence. This rite only indicates the presence of such evil, but does not show the theurge exactly what is going on; some degree of precision is possible, however, with a more successful roll. One victory point, for example, merely signals evil's presence in a general area ("There is evil in this house!"); with three, a more specific area can be sensed ("Somebody in this room..."); five or six gives the theurge a sense of the type of evil present (i.e., Antinomic, Urge, alien, etc.). With a critical success, the evil's source can be pinpointed ("J'Accuse! Antinomy most foul!").

Sting of Conscience

(Level 3, Extrovert + Impress, LG, sight, prolonged, 1W)

This rite is usually accompanied by a verbal harangue from the theurge or another Avestite, the two combining to make the target feel incredibly guilty about some past sin or misdeed. If uncontested, the target will feel compelled to confess and make up for the transgression. The target may choose to contest with a roll of Calm + Stoic Mind.

When this rite is cast without the verbal accusations to guide it, there is no telling exactly what its effect may be. A relatively guiltless person may begin to obsess on some minor bit of mischief from childhood, while a truly sinful person may be driven to wildly self-destructive acts that could endanger everyone around him.

Torchbearing

(Level 4, Passion + Focus, G, touch, temporary, 1W)

With this rite the theurge can create a flame without using lighters, matches or flint and steel. After the first 10 turns, the fire will need fuel to burn like any other, but it can be kept burning without fuel by spending one Wyrd point for each extra five turns. Normally the flame can only be ignited at touch, but a 6th level version of this rite exists in which the flame can be created anywhere in sight.

Fault of the Soulless

(Level 5, Passion + Impress or relevant Tech Redemption, LG, sight, 1W)

Developed soon after the Fall, this rite targets a piece of high-tech and causes it to malfunction. Normally used against personal technology (blasters, comlinks, a single computer terminal, a robot of human size or smaller), this rite can be used to target larger machines with an additional Wyrd expenditure based on size and complexity (e.g., 2 points to disable a personal land vehicle, 5 points for a building's security system, and 50 points to take out a

starship. At the gamemaster's discretion, this can be adjusted by circumstances; for example, a theurge with sufficient tech knowledge may try to target only the starship's control systems for 7 points.)

The severity of the malfunction is based on the victory points: One would be simple mishaps taking only a few turns to correct, such as misfires, jams, etc.; three is more serious but repairable damage which cannot be corrected until the next span, like dead batteries, overheating motors, system crash, etc.; five or six means the machine is permanently ruined and unfixable, with broken chassis, cracked casings or wiped memories. With a critical success, spectacularly destructive effects may occur: fuel leakages, core meltdowns, smoke and sparks pouring out of the control panel while gears and springs drop out of the bottom of the console.

Fearsome Majesty

(Level 6, Passion + Impress, LG, sight, prolonged, 1W)

This rite is identical to the level 6 Brother Battle rite of the same name.

Inquisitory Commandment

(Level 7, Passion + Inquiry, L, sight, temporary, 1W)

Use of this rite is the theurgic version of a shot of truth serum; the target is compelled to answer all questions addressed to her. Questions must be answered fully, completely and honestly, without evasion or trickery. If the target chooses to contest the rite, the theurge's Faith rating is subtracted from the contesting roll (see Defending Against Occult Powers, above).

Tortures of the Damned

(Level 8, Passion + Impress, LG, sight, prolonged, 1W)

This rite has basically the same effect as the psychic power BrainBlast, incapacitating the target with unimaginable pain, except that this theurgic version floods the target's mind with images of Gehenne (hell). These visions may take the form of Orthodox and Avestite description, burning hellfire or numbing cold lasting (or at least seeming to last) for eternity, or may take a more personal form, the reliving of a traumatic event or seeing one's greatest fears come to pass, or some amalgamation of both. In either case, the target will be a pathetic, sobbing wreck for at least seven turns after the rite is discontinued. Due to the deep psychological nature of this experience, however, residual effects (such as dementia) may last for long afterward.

This rite may not be cast on a target suffering the effects of the psychic power BrainBlast.

Petition to Jachemuyelos, Lord of Judgment

(Level 9, Passion + Impress, LGP, 1W)

This exceptionally rare and powerful rite, a closely guarded secret of the sect, enables a theurge to contact and summon to the physical world one of the "bodiless powers of the Empyrean," the stern but fair arbiter of disputes known as Jachemuyelos. According to Eskatonic doctrine, Jachemuyelos rules in the Fourth Emanation from the Celestial Sun, among the ranks of the Dominions.

Odd as it may seem to outsiders, the guidance of Jachemuyelos is what keeps the more fervent and overzealous inquisitors in check; this is not an entity of blind wrath and damnation, but a truly objective intelligence with a perfect comprehension of the balance between retribution and repentance. Only the most malevolent enemy of life and faith will ever see the harsh and vengeful aspect of Jachemuyelos, which is only spoken of in euphemistic whispers. All interactions with Jachemuyelos must be worded in rigid and precise legalese, as a counselor approaches a judge. The visible aspect of Jachemuyelos is that of an older man with a long beard and stately judicial robes, holding the scales of Justice in one hand and the gavel of Order in the other.

Sanctuary Aeon Rituals

Cleansing

(Level 1, Faith + Focus, LGP, touch, prolonged, 1W)

Similar to the Orthodox Rite of Consecration, Cleansing may be used to target people as well as objects, purifying them from evil taint or influence. The Cleansed person resists being affected by psychic powers, Antinomy, Urge or Hubris; half of the casting victory points (rounded up) become a negative penalty for any of these powers attempting to affect the target. This rite has also proven effective in treating wounds when no antiseptic is available. Some Amaltheans perform this rite daily as part of their regular devotional ceremonies. A Cleansed person participating in a rite acts as a vestment (+1 to the rite roll), but the target must have some knowledge of theurgy, if not actual ability, in order to really participate. ("Hand me that crosier," does not count.)

Hearth

(Level 2, Passion + Focus, LG, touch, prolonged, 1W)

Favored by missionaries on uncivilized worlds, this rite creates what appears to be a campfire, generating enough light to see in a 10 meter radius, and enough heat to boil water or cook food. Unlike the Avesti rite Torchbearing, however, the flame created is not a natural fire; it is not hot enough to fire pottery or smelt ore, and cannot be used to start other fires or ignite flammable materials. No fuel is needed, but a cleared space must be prepared for the rite. Hearth lasts for one span per Wyrd point.

Calming

(Level 3, Calm + Charm, G, sight, prolonged, 1W)

Considered something of a joke by outsiders, the Calming rite disperses the negative energies of rage, hate, fear

FADING SUNS

Group Rites

Religion is a group activity; so are its rituals. While theurgy is usually cast by a single priest, many priests can band together to increase the effectiveness of their rites.

When one or more priests joins together in a rite, use the following guidelines:

• One theurgist is designated the rite leader while all others are participants. Theurgists can only actively participate in rituals they each already know. Thus, if two priests join in casting a Prophet's Holy Blessing rite, each must already have learned the rite.

• There is no limit to the number of theurges who can join in a single rite. However, gamemasters should use common sense before packing a room full of theurges — such spiritual experts are not common in the first place, and when two or more get together there is no guarantee that they will know the same rites.

• Members of different sects can sometimes learn the same ritual. However, methods of casting may differ from sect to sect. If a rite has participants of multiple sects (even if it's just one Amalthean among two Eskatonics), reduce all participants' goal numbers by one.

• Group rites can extend the range and/or number of targets that the rite may affect. Choose only ONE of the following options before resolving the casting roll:

The number of targets which the rite affects can be doubled with each participant. If two priests cast a rite which is normally effective only against a single target, it can now affect two targets. If three priests are involved, it can affect three targets. If the rite normally affects five people, 10 can be affected with one additional rite participant, 20 with a third, and so on. The Wyrd cost increases by one per extra target added.

OR

The range of the rite can be increased with each participant in the rite. Refer to the Distance listing in the Psychic Powers Chart: each participant raises the rite by one level. For example, a "touch" ranged rite may be raised to "sight" with the addition of one participant, or to one kilometer with three participants, and so on. The Wyrd cost increases by one per distance level gained.

If the ritecasters desire to increase the range AND the number of targets, then EACH rite participant (including the rite leader) must spend one additional Wyrd point.

• The rite participants can donate as much or as

continued...

...continued

little Wyrd to fuel the power as they desire. For instance, the rite leader may spend 1 Wyrd to activate the power, while one of the participants spends 2 to extend the range. Such expenditures can be done in any combination desired. However, those participants who don't contribute their fare share of energy may be reprimanded later.

• Each participant makes her casting roll and applies any victory points to the rite leader's goal number (as per normal complementary skill rolls). This may raise the rite leader's goal number above 20; use the Excessive Goal Numbers Chart in Chapter Two: Rules.

Only the rite leader's roll is used to determine the success or failure of the rite itself. Participant failures do not adversely affect the rite leader's casting, but any critical failure will automatically cause the rite to fail (additional ill effects can be levied at the gamemaster's discretion).

and even less negative (but sometimes equally destructive) simple excitement. This rite has prevented many confrontations from escalating to violence, which accounts for the Amaltheans' reputation as diplomats. In addition, Calming may be effective for targets who are psychically manipulated or possessed by demons; while it does not actually cure or prevent these conditions, it may aid the target by, for instance, silencing the possessed so that the Exorcism may continue undisrupted. Add the victory points to any Calm rolls the target needs to make.

Knowing Heart

(Level 4, Perception + Empathy, P, sight, temporary, 1W)

This rite combines the effects of the psychic abilities Intuit and MindSight, in that it allows the theurge to observe the internal workings of the target's psyche, both emotional and intellectual. The same restrictions for MindSight apply here, in that only the current state of mind may be read (or felt); subconscious or deeply buried feelings, thoughts or intentions are not disclosed by the Knowing Heart, but may, if the gamemaster allows, be probed for with a critical success.

Fruitful Multiplication

(Level 5, Faith + Vigor or Sleight of Hand, LP, touch, perpetual, 1W)

Most often used to help feed famine areas, this rite increases the mass of a single targeted substance (such as food, water, cloth, building materials, breathable air, etc.) by a factor equal to the victory points. This rite will not replicate manufactured items, only basic materials. Attempting

168

to use this rite on money or precious metals is grounds for excommunication.

Restoration

(Level 5, Faith + Stoic Mind, LGP, touch, instant, 1W)

By invoking the compassion of Saint Amalthea, a theurge can restore a body's spiritual humours to their proper balance: diseases can be cured and poisons expelled. Damage from these ills is not healed but the cause of the problem is removed, allowing patients to recover normally. In the case of disease, the patient's own immune system wins over the virus, while poisons are expelled from the body, leaving evidence which may be analyzed by investigators attempting to trace the poisoner. Additionally, emotional turbulence can be soothed; the symptoms of neuroses or psychoses are abated, and a theurge may use this rite to aid therapy for such afflictions; the victory points on the activation roll become goal bonuses for the therapist or patient to work toward recovery.

Manna from Heaven

(Level 6, Faith + Focus, LP, 1W)

Casting this rite creates a sufficient amount of food to feed 10 adults for one day per point of Wyrd spent. The quality and variety of food created is dependent on the victory points: 5 or 6 yields fully prepared meals, 3 or 4 a simple but hearty assortment of meats, vegetables, etc., and 1 yielding a chewy dense substance somewhere between jerky and old bread.

Healing Hand of Saint Amalthea

(Level 7, Calm + Physick, LGP, touch, instant, 1W)

By meditating upon Saint Amalthea and reciting all the names of the Pancreator from the Compassionate Truths, the theurge may not only heal back one Vitality point per victory point (as in the Church level 3 Rite Laying On of Hands, above), but may also reattach severed limbs and remove deeply embedded shrapnel, diseased organs or insidious parasites. At the gamemaster's discretion, the newly dead may be revived with a critical success.

Sanctuary

(Level 8, Faith + Charm, LGP, prolonged, 1W)

Perhaps the foundation of Sanctuary Aeon's political survival through the ages, this rite acts as a powerful "damper field" preventing any violent or harmful actions. Affecting either a large room or a 10 meter radius around the theurge, any roll made within the Sanctuary using Fight, Melee or Shoot only succeeds on a 1, and any other malevolent or overly aggressive action, such as psychic attack, will be contested by the rite's roll.

Invitation to Hamomeyelos, Lord of Mercy

(Level 9, Passion + Impress, LGP, 1W)

This exceptionally rare and powerful rite, a closely guarded secret of the order, enables a theurge to contact and summon to the physical world one of the "bodiless powers of the Empyrean," the compassionate and beneficent intelligence known as Hamomeyelos. According to Eskatonic doctrine, Hamomeyelos rules in the Sixth Emanation from the Celestial Sun, among the ranks of the Virtues.

Hamomeyelos has never revealed itself directly to anyone, but always manifests in a tangible physical form under the guise of a good Samaritan, a kindly stranger, a timely messenger, or any manner of helpful or generous locals, passersby, wandering mendicants or even forgotten acquaintances. Regardless of the type of manifestation, Hamomeyelos will always be in a position to make available to the theurge and her party whatever safety, sustenance or support is necessary (not necessarily what is requested, but what is truly required.)

Hubris

The dark side of theurgy. Hubris has many levels of sin; those given below are the most common.

Whenever a theurge fumbles a theurgy rite roll (or a Theurgy roll), her Hubris — overweening pride before the Pancreator — grows. Unlike Urge, Hubris is with a character always — the effects lasts until the character has lost the level of Hubris which empowers them (unless stated otherwise in the description). Hubris comes in many forms, but the levels listed below are the most common.

Hubris is not a split personality or a dark entity growing in the character; it is the character's own human fallibility before the divine. Lack of humility leads to overweening pride at one's ability to call forth miraculous powers, powers which are supposed to be the Pancreator's gift, not the character's own will exerting itself. Extreme Hubris can lead to a loss of faith.

Hubris Powers

Unlike Urge powers, which represent specific actions taken by the Dark Twin, the powers of Hubris represent the changing relationship between the theurge and the Pancreator — which is to say, between the theurge and the universe at large. Most are permanent, or always in effect, once that level has been reached, while others (like levels 2 and 4) require specific circumstances to become active. No rolls need be made, since the exact manifestation of each power is largely left to the imagination of the gamemaster.

Avert Beast

(Level 1)

Animals fear the theurge: dogs bark at his passing, birds take flight, cats hiss and spit, horses rear and throw their riders, oxen bolt from their harnesses, etc.. "Skittish as a Terran cart-mule," is a private joke among rural priests, whose Hubris seems to be kept in check by this "early warning" effect; among the urban Church fathers, Hubris is less likely to be noticed, since they have less direct contact with the natural world.

Guilty Soul

(Level 2)

The theurge becomes prone to Freudian slips which reveal her sin — her soul wishes to speak out so that she may recognize her sin and gain humility and thus forgiveness for it. Normally, public knowledge of this sin can endanger her career, so she keeps it hidden from others, but her Guilty Soul will speak out at the most inappropriate times and say embarrassing things. Like Urge effects, the power only lasts for a span when the character fumbles a theurgy rite, a Theurgy characteristic roll or a Faith roll (or rolls a critical success on an Ego roll).

Blemishes

(Level 3)

The theurge's pride before the Pancreator soon grows until it cannot cure itself through speaking, so it shows itself physically. Blemishes (warts, splotches, marks, etc.) appear on the theurge's face (or hands), signs that he has stepped over the boundaries of the Church. Unlike theurgic stigmas, Blemishes are recognized by the faithful as ominous taints. Some observers of fashion note that the Avestite preference for long robes with concealing hoods and veils dates back to an unusually corrupt period in their history.

Flagellation

(Level 4)

If the Guilty Soul (above) is left unchecked, it can grow too large for the dark recesses of the theurge's heart, building pressures which could cause it to burst from mere words into actual deeds. The theurge's guilt eats away at her and she begins to perform unintended actions — sometimes dangerous — designed to reveal her guilt. Like Urge effects, the power only lasts for a span when the character fumbles a theurgy rite, a Theurgy characteristic roll or a Faith roll (or rolls a critical success on an Ego roll).

Dolorous Stroke

(Level 5)

As the sin of spiritual pride increases, it is accompanied by disdain for the real, the mundane and the physical; the soul is twisted between these extremes, and it twists the body along with it. A process begun with Blemishes (above) is completed as the theurge suffers some crippling afflic-

Gaining Hubris

Hubris is gained through roleplaying. Certain acts or deeds undertaken by a character may cause her Hubris to grow, and from there to slowly build if she keeps performing similar deeds. What are such prideful acts? Breaking Church taboos. As a practitioner of theurgy, the character has agreed to certain precepts of her religion, and believes heartily in these precepts. If it was ever revealed that she did not believe, she would lose Faith and perhaps her theurgic powers. Breaking the rules of the religion have consequences.

Below is a general guideline for members of the Universal Church of the Known Worlds of the **Fading Suns**. Certain barbarians and aliens have different religions, and thus different precepts. The chart includes the taboo and the roll required to gain Hubris from it (the character must fail this roll or else gain Hubris).

Taboo	Roll	Levels
Refusing sacrament	Ego + Stoic Mind	1
Missing confession for more than one month	Ego + Focus	1
Suffering Inquisitorial torture	Calm + Stoic Mind	1 - 2
Suffering excommunication	Faith + Stoic Mind	2 - 3
Fumbling a theurgy rite	Theurgy + Focus	1
Exposure to alien occult powers	Faith + Stoic Mind	1
Exposure to evil artifact	Faith + Stoic Mind	1 - 3
Declaring a vendetta	Passion + Focus	1
Murder	Passion + Focus	1 - 2
Rape	Passion + Focus	1 - 2
Stealing	Wits + Focus	1
Inventing proscribed tech	Ego + Focus	1
Rebellion against sect	Faith + Focus	1
Starting your own sect	Faith + Focus	1 - 3

Losing Hubris

Characters can learn humility. But it is tough to regain squandered Grace; losing Hubris levels requires a quest or great deed of some sort:

Deed	Roll	Levels
Pilgrimage	Faith + Vigor	1
Church mercy (absolution for sins)	Faith + Focus	1 - 2
Forsaking Theurgy*	Faith + Focus	3
Performing a Church mission	Faith + Focus	1
Exposure to a Soul Shard	Human or Alien + Stoic Mind or Focus	1 - 2
Exposure to a Philosopher's Stone	Human or Alien + Stoic Mind or Focus	1
Selfless sacrifice	Passion + Empathy	1 - 2
Exposure to relic (once per relic)	Faith + Focus	1
Converting new faithful (heathens, heretics)	Faith + Empathy	1 - 2
Converting other sects or orders	Faith + Charm or Impress	1
Renewing the faith of one who had lost it	Faith + Empathy	1 - 3

* lose one Theurgy level; character must not practice for at least a year, or lost Hubris will be regained (but not lost Theurgy level).

tion, such as painful arthritis (sometimes bending a hand into a claw), a bent back, lame leg, etc.. This effect is permanent (unless the Hubris level is decreased), and may often involve the loss of one or more points from Body characteristics.

Faithless

(Level 6)

Inflated self-importance eclipses the place of the Pancreator in the theurge's heart, and guilt and sin spill out of his own form into the world around him. The theurge's Hubris is too great for him to bear alone, and it begins to taint others. His sermons, no matter how well or passionately delivered, cause others to feel a deep unease and a resultant loss of faith. They may desert his sect or even the Church itself, and in extreme cases (those who were already depressed), may commit suicide.

Waste Land
(Level 7)

As the secret sin grows, spreading from person to person, it begins to settle in the inanimate world as well. The theurge's overweening Hubris begins to taint the earth itself. The local land becomes barren: Crops will not grow, animals will not birth and their milk and meat go bad on the hoof. If the theurge leaves and never returns, the land may begin to recover, but it is a long and slow process which can only be accelerated with cleansing rites and blessings.

Plague
(Level 8)

As the faith of the people falters and the land is drained of its vitality, the theurge's sin is manifested in the bodies of those around her. A plague is delivered onto the local populace and she is its source. She does not suffer from the disease herself, but others around may catch it from her.

Dead World
(Level 9)

Standing at the brink of damnation, the theurge's insufferable pride is swollen to encompass his entire planet. The Pancreator has cursed the world on which he preaches. The planet he is on when he gains this level of Hubris becomes a wasteland — the entire planet dies. Only when he is healed of his Hubris (all of it) or is dead, will the planet live again. Priests whisper that this was the fate long ago of the planet Nowhere, the reason why so much of the planet — said in Second Republic texts to be lush — is now desert and windblown wastes.

Miracles

Random acts of grace can occur and do, according to many eyewitnesses of miracles. The Church, however, does not always agree with common accounts, and appears to have much narrower criteria for identifying miracles than the average peasant. This has lead many secular scholars to wonder just how often the Pancreator takes a personal hand in the lives of humanity, and how many miraculous occurrences are lost to history, because it was politically inexpedient for the Church to recognize them as such.

In play, any character may pray for a miracle. The gamemaster should put as much emphasis on roleplaying the prayer as possible. Have the praying character's player recite her prayer aloud for the group. Note exactly what is being asked for, and why. If the player is only seeking to further her or her group's interests, without regard for the greater good they might do with divine aid, a miracle is not called for. This is a wild card that characters can call on at times, although it may very well not work — few get a personal answer from the Pancreator. The roll is Faith; no skill is added and no theurgic training is needed as one cannot conduct a miracle into existence the way one casts a rite. One Wyrd point is spent. If the character has no Wyrd points, he can still pray for a miracle, but if it is granted, he cannot naturally regain Wyrd for one week.

Below are some general guidelines for miracles based on the successes:

Successes	Miracle
1 – 3	Simple fortuitous events which could just as easily happen without divine intervention, but are especially beneficial for the characters: finding a needed item or bit of information; bumping into the very person who can help out the party; timely intercession by parents, mentors, lieges, etc..
4 – 5	Less likely events: a runaway vehicle collides with an assassin; an attacking beast is calmed or frightened away by a certain color worn by a character; an Amalthean punches out an evildoer; the check clears the bureaucratic red tape in time to save the orphanage, etc..
6 – 7	Extreme longshots which are not impossible but highly improbable: lightning strikes an attacker; all shots in a close firefight miss the characters, etc..
8	Minor impossibilities: a broken machine runs one last time; a Reeve gives away his riches to charity; a disinterested passerby decides to trust the characters without being fast-talked or duped, etc..
9	Strange unexplainable events: omens, visions and revelations; voices from the sky; a mysterious stranger who saves the day then vanishes, etc..
10	Deeply profound, soul-stirring events: mass visions; parting seas; new constellations in the heavens; an Avestite judge shows clemency, etc..
Critical	Totally undeniable impossibilities: raising the dead; halting the sun; surviving the vacuum of space, etc..

Antinomy

Lurking in the shadows cast by dying stars across a crumbling empire, awaiting the return of a hollow darkened universe, poisoning the ears of high and low with greed, rage and fear, the dark lords of pain engineer the collapse of civilization. Antinomy and trafficking with malefic spirits can be traced back to the prehistory of Ancient Urth and other racial homeworlds, but appeared to have undergone a renaissance with the extinction of Sathraism. Much early Orthodox history contains detailed accounts of the practices and behavior of captured antinomists, but little has been gleaned of their beliefs or occult techniques.

One document intercepted by Avesti Inquisitors and translated by Eskatonic monks appears to be a round chant purporting to describe the hierarchy of all creation. It is written in an ancient dialect of Kurgan, a fact of which the Hazat never fail to remind Brother Battle troops in their border wars. Beginning with a brief recapitulation of Eskatonic cosmogony, the chant describes the Celestial Sun with Its layered Emanations, called Sefiros or "spheres" by the order; each Emanation, through the action of its residing intelligences or "Empyrean angels," reflects the Holy Flame outward until it is buried deep in the Tenth Emanation, or material world. From there the chant proceeds into a heresy long since purged from the Eskatonic Order; beyond the Tenth Sefiros lie ten more planes of existence cut off from the Holy Flame, dark empty shells of the Sefiros called Qlippoth in the chant.

The progression of Qlippoth twists through nonspace so that the outermost Emanation converges upon a central point, named by old heretics the Infernos Prime, an inconceivably dense orb of black devouring fire, the opposite of the Celestial Sun. Inhabiting the Qlippoth are the hollowed vessels of consciousness known as demons, who yearn to break through ancient barriers confining them to the Qlippoth and consume the never-ending bounty and grace of the Ce-

lestial Sun. Since their natural portals to the Sefiros were closed off by a great race in some primordial eon, they must enter the material plane through the heart of a human or other sentient, which can open its own doorways to heaven or hell.

Antinomists work in secret to open the way for the demons, using powers granted to them by their attunement to the Qlippoth, by spreading anger, hatred, mistrust and any manner of corruption which can drive the Holy Flame from within and eat away enough of the soul to receive demonic possession. A gamemaster wishing to use a Antinomist as an antagonist may create Qlippothic equivalents of most of the above occult powers, more intrusive, soul-rending and painful versions, with each level corresponding inversely to the Qlippoth through which the power of the Infernos Prime is accessed. (i.e., a first level power derives from the Ninth Qlippoth, a second from the Eighth, etc.) Practitioners of Antinomy are often plagued by their Fealty ties to a dark lord, which create effects similar to Urge and Hubris. Be sure that the antinomist never takes center stage for too long, however, as their kind prefer to watch from the wings as mastermind manipulators.

Chapter 6: Combat

Combat is an intense activity. Lives hang in the balance. Emotions run high, and arguments ensue — not only among the combatants but the players playing them. For this reason, gamemasters and players in roleplaying games often want detailed rules for fighting. Such rules provide an objective judgment on the results, helping to prevent arguments.

In addition, getting down and dirty into the small — often excruciating — details of fighting can be fun. For this reason, **Fading Suns** provides a simple, fair system for resolving combats between characters and includes some optional rules for those who wish to get into even more detail (and complication).

Gamemasters should be familiar with the rules described in Chapter Two: Rules, and it helps if players also know these rules. New rules useful for resolving fights are introduced below. These rules add extra complications to the game for the purpose of simulating fighting. They should be considered optional. The gamemaster is free to ignore whatever complications he feels slow down the drama.

Initiative

When more than one character acts in the same turn, an initiative rating is used to determine who acts first. Each character's rating is equal to the skill he is using, and the character with the highest rating acts first. For multiple actions, whichever skill is used first determines that character's initiative. For example, Tobo is swinging an ax ; his Melee skill is 6, so his initiative is also 6.

In the case of ties, characters compare their Wits characteristics. If Wits scores tie, the actions are considered to be simultaneous.

In addition, certain actions can add or subtract from a character's initiative rating. For example, Tobo performs a

Martial Hold, which subtracts one from his initiative. His Fight skill is 5, so his initiative is 4 for that turn.

Note also that multiple action penalties and wound penalties are applied to initiative ratings in addition to goal rolls.

Actions

In **Fading Suns**, a character's activity in combat is divided into actions: punching, kicking, grappling or shooting a gun. Actions may or may not have a positive or negative modifier to initiative, goal number, damage dice and a special effect (such as target knockdown). There are four basic offensive actions that anyone can perform regardless of training: Fist, Kick, Grapple and Charge. Any character can also perform a Dodge.

Specialized actions may require a special skill before they can be performed, such as Martial Arts or Fencing. Players should determine which actions they plan to perform frequently in combat and write them down on the character sheet. This includes the traits for the particular weapons their characters carry and any Martial Arts or Fencing actions they may have learned.

Fist: A punch, slap or strike with the hand or arm.

Kick: A strike or sweep with the leg or foot.

Grapple: Wrestling. This can be a hand, arm or head lock, or a full body grapple. The intent can be to hold an opponent down, to disable him or to injure him. If the attacker succeeds in a goal roll against his target, he has grabbed him (this roll can be resisted with a dodge). He then rolls Strength + Vigor versus the target's Strength + Vigor. If successful, the target is grappled and cannot move or dodge. The attacker can choose to deliver his grapple damage immediately and once per turn thereafter. All the actions above are considered part of one grapple action — there is no multiple action penalty — but no other actions can be

Multiple Actions

A character may perform up to three different actions in a single turn. However, if more than one action is taken, all actions will suffer a penalty:

Two actions: Both actions are considered Demanding (-4).

Three actions: All three actions are considered Tough (-6).

In addition, no character can perform more than one of the same action per turn (except for firing or throwing ranged weapons, such as guns, bows or darts). A character *can* fire a ranged weapon up to three times in a turn, as long as the weapon's rate of fire allows it. A character cannot swing his sword twice at a foe in a single turn, although he may swing his sword and dodge his foe's riposte.

Strength Bonus

Don't forget that characters with high Strengths will receive a bonus to their hand-to-hand or melee damage. See Strength in Chapter Four: Traits.

General Modifiers

Combat is not always simple. It seems there's always something getting in the way, whether it is a foggy alley or a freshly waxed floor to slip a fencer up. Below are some modifiers to use in addition to the more general bonuses and penalties given in Chapter Two: Rules.

Perception Modifiers

Perception modifier	Condition
-2	Moonlit darkness
-4	Fog or smoke
-6	Near or total darkness
+2	Well-lit
-2	Extremely bright light
-4	Blindingly bright light
+2	Utterly silent
-2	Loud noise
-4	Extremely loud noise

Physical Obstacles

Dexterity modifier	Obstacle/Condition
-2	Slippery floor
-2	Performing a Fight or Melee attack from the ground
+2	Performing a Fight or Melee attack against a target on the ground
-2	Attacking from partial cover (behind a crate)
-4	Attacking from full cover (behind a wall)

performed in the same turn as a grapple.

Note that the target must perform an action to gain the Strength + Vigor resistance roll; he can "abort" to resist if he has already take an action that turn (see Dodge, below) or choose not to resist, in which case the grappler's victory points on his initial goal roll are used to determine damage.

Each turn after the first, the target can try to break the hold with another Strength + Vigor contest. This is the only combat action a grappled character can take in a turn. However, the attacker gains a bonus to his roll each turn after the first that he holds his opponent:

Turn	Attacker Bonus
Second	+2
Third	+4
Fourth	+6
Fifth	+8
Sixth +	+10

Charge: Ramming into an opponent with the intent to knock him down and injure him. If successful, both attacker and target go down. Add one die of momentum damage per three meters run. The next turn, the attacker may attempt to grapple the opponent; he gains a +2 bonus to his initiative and goal roll as long as he can act before his opponent stands up again. But a Charge attack is not for wimps: The attacker also suffers any momentum damage rolled against his target.

It takes two actions to stand up. Thus, someone could conceivably be knocked down and stand up again by the end of the turn, although only if he had planned on taking three actions (and thus applying the penalty to all his rolls that turn). No roll is required to stand up.

If the character performs no other action than a Charge that turn, he may move up to his full running distance (see Vigor, in Chapter Four).

Dodge: The character leaps out of the way of an oncoming attack, deftly sidesteps a sword, or leaps to the ground to avoid a hail of bullets. This action can also include blocking an opponent's fist or kick by deftly redirecting its force with a slight tap. Trained fighters will want to complement their attacks with a good defense — thus they should learn both Fight and Dodge skills.

When dodging an attack, roll Dexterity + Dodge. If the dodger has more successes than his attacker, he has completely avoided the attack. Otherwise the number of successes is subtracted from the opponent's successes before figuring out victory points. For example, Cardanzo is fighting a Chainer mercenary. The Chainer kicks Cardanzo, who dodges the blow. Cardanzo rolls his Dexterity + Dodge and gets 10 successes. But the Chainer got 12 successes on his roll. The Chainer hits with two successes total (12 - 10 dodge successes). That means the Chainer gets no extra victory dice to add to his kick damage.

A character can choose to dodge at any time during the turn. However, it requires one action and should be declared at the start of the turn with any other actions, and it will suffer the multiple action penalty. If a character chooses to dodge after he has performed an action without taking the multiple action penalty, he can still do so — but he loses all further actions that turn, and his dodge will suffer the multiple action penalty. This is called "abort to a dodge" or simply, "aborting." In addition, he can only perform one action the next turn at a -4 penalty (as if he were performing two actions). A character cannot abort to a dodge if he has already performed three actions.

For example, Cardanzo is surprised in an alley by his Chainer foe's comrades. He punches one of them, hoping it will convince the others to halt their attack. It doesn't, and one of them swings a flail at him. Cardanzo decides to abort to a dodge. However, this is his second action in the same turn, and he did not take a penalty on his previous action (he originally didn't intend to perform another action). He can still dodge this turn, but his dodge suffers the penalty for performing two actions (-4), and he can only take one action during his next turn (instead of three), which will suffer a -4 penalty.

Initiative does not matter when dodging — the character simply responds to what comes at him. In addition, the dodge applies to all attacks made against the character that turn, unless he has aborted, in which case those attacks that occurred before he aborted are not affected.

A character gains some advantage versus ranged attacks when hiding behind cover:

Cover	Dodge bonus
Lying down	+1
Behind partial cover (a crate)	+2
Behind full cover (a wall)	+4

Martial Arts

It is one thing to throw a punch at someone, but another thing entirely to throw a punch after spending weeks — or years — training for it. By applying thought to body mechanics in a systematic way, the martial artist gains a significant edge in combat over his opponents. Martial Arts actions are mostly variations on Fist, Kick, Grapple and Dodge, but with more finesse and power. They are rated by the Fight skill level required to learn them. For example: Martial Hold is 4, meaning that a character must know Fight 4 to learn it. Each action must be bought seperately (buying the level 5 Claw Fist does not give the character the level 5 Tornado Kick or any other actions of lower levels). However, martial actions do not have to be learned in order (a character can buy Martial Hold without having to buy Martial Kick).

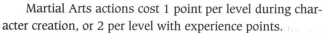

Combat Summary

Step One: Initiative

A character's initiative rating = skill used that action, plus or minus any initiative modifiers.

Step Two: Goal Roll

1. Add characteristic + skill = natural goal number

2. Add or subtract modifiers = modified goal number

3. Roll modified goal number or less on a d20.

Option: "Accent" the roll (see Chapter Two: Rules). Accenting must be declared before the die is rolled.

4. Compare results to:

- 1 = automatic success (no matter how low the goal number is, a character always succeeds on a "1." If his goal was 1, he succeeds but does not critical)
- Less than modified goal number = success (number of successes equals the amount rolled on the d20. If the roll was 8, then the character has 8 successes)
- Modified goal number = critical success (double victory points)
- 19 = automatic failure (no matter how high the goal number is, a character always fails on a "19")
- 20 = critical failure or fumble: something very bad happens, determined by the gamemaster (no matter how high the target number is, a character always fails on a "20")

Step Three: Damage Roll

1. Determine damage dice:

- Compare goal successes to the Victory Chart: each victory point equals one extra damage die.

Successes	Dice
1–2	0
3-5	+1
6-8	+2
9-11	+3
12-14	+4
15-17	+5
18	+6

Critical success = Dice x2

- Add the weapon's damage dice to the victory dice.

2. Roll d6 damage dice. Each d6 that rolls 1, 2, 4 or 4 = one point of damage

3. The total amount of damage points are applied to the target's armor. Target rolls d6 armor dice; rolls of 1, 2, 3 or 4 = one armor point. Each armor point subtracts one from the total number of damage points; remaining points are subtracted from the target's Vitality.

Multiple Actions

Repeat steps 1 – 3 for 2nd and 4th actions. Once actions are complete, begin a new turn.

Martial Arts actions cost 1 point per level during character creation, or 2 per level with experience points.

Styles

Martial Arts actions vary greatly depending on the style they come from, although in strict rules terms, a throw is a throw, regardless of whether it is performed by an aikidoka or judoist. In **Fading Suns**, style is mainly a matter of atmosphere. While styles do flavor and modify certain actions, they are mainly used to enhance roleplaying — characters don't just pull their Martial Arts actions out of nowhere; someone had to teach them. In the Known Worlds, martial stylists proudly advertise their affiliations and engage in fierce rivalries with other stylists. Grand tournaments are held to determine whose style is best. But, in the end, it is usually not the style that determines the outcome of a fight, but the fighter herself.

Below is a list of the more famous martial styles. Others exist, but teachers are rarer.

Shaidan: A no-nonsense power form similar to ancient Urth karate. The Grand Master of this style is Duke Enrico de Aragon, a Hazat noble. He has spread the popularity of this art far and wide, and it is now considered the art of choice for people of class and distinction. Honor is highly valued and underhanded fighting tactics are frowned upon — such maneuvers are for peasants, not noble lords.

Shaidan stylists may learn Fist actions at one level lower than the action's required level. However, kicks and grapples are considered somewhat uncouth and are not as widely practiced. Kicks and grapples cost one extra experience point to learn.

Koto: A tricky art using misdirection to deliver unexpected blows onto an opponent. Named after a mythological trickster bird from the folklore of the planet Aylon, the current Grand Master of this style is Baron Jamal al-Malik, a student of Count Rumi al-Malik. Jamal inherited the title after the mysterious disapearance of his master. The art is steeped in weird mystical philosophies involving riddles and deconstructive ontology. Count Rumi's students teach the art to anyone who proves worthy, and are said to teach even serfs (a crime on some worlds).

Mantok: Named for Mantius, the Prophet's disciple (also known as the Soldier) whose purview is Protection. This is the Brother Battle martial fighting style, taught only to members of that order. There are harsh penalties for teaching its secrets to outsiders. At low levels, it is a powerful style utilizing strength and body mechanics prowess. At the higher levels, internal, or Wyrd, power is utilized to perform amazing feats with little effort.

Brother Battle monks who practice Mantok can buy any martial action for one less experience point than the usual cost.

Iron Heel: An art practiced by the Muster. It is a down-and-dirty commando art which recognizes the necessity of incapacitating an opponent over the need for honor. Kicks and holds are specialized in, the former for their reach, the latter for their ability to hold an opponent long enough to cuff him.

Muster stylists may learn Kick and Grapple (Hold) actions at one level lower than the action's required level. However, internal mastery actions are rarely practiced; add two to the experience point cost of any action of Level 7 or above.

Jox Kai Von (Jox Boxing): A nasty and dirty Ur-Ukar art with no-holds barred — eye gouges, groin punches, ear pulls, etc.. It is a close-in fighting style, and thus relies on few kicks. Although the Grand Master is an Ur-Ukar, this art is popular among the Decados as a sport against freemen and serfs (they rarely use it against fellow nobles).

Jox stylists may learn Grapple (Hold) actions at one level lower than the action's required level. However, kicks cost two extra experience points to master.

Graa: Because this style relies on a Vorox's six limbs, non-Vorox may not learn Graa. Vorox physiques allow for special techniques, and a few Vorox have taken advantage of this and raised their techniques to a martial form. This art is rare among the Vorox, as it is practiced by only a small percentage of civilized Vorox.

Martial Arts Actions

Refer to the Martial Arts Actions Chart for specific rules effects.

Martial Fist (Level 1): A punch, slap or strike with the hand or arm using advanced techniques. Throwing a martial punch is not just a matter of thrusting the arm outward; it also involves foot stance and torso movement. In many styles, power is generated in the torso rather than with the arm. There are many types of martial punches with many names, from Shaidan's Royal Palm, Koto's Jagor Strikes the Amenta (named after alien beasts) to Mantok's Step Forward, Deliver the Sermon.

Martial Kick (Level 2): A strike or sweep with the leg or foot using advanced techniques. Training in Martial Kick also implies a certain amount of limberness and flexibility in the legs. Different styles have different kicks, from high kicks to the head to low kicks to the shin. Styles vary from Shaidan's Peasant Heel, Koto's Step to Sky, to Mantok's Bend Knee, Turn the Page.

Head Butt (Level 3): Exactly what it sounds like. Not a charge, but a close-up blow from the attacker's head. This may hurt the attacker in addition to his opponent, and thus is only for the tough and (fool)hardy. The attacker will take the full damage of any blow that deals more damage than his Endurance (armor will protect him but not an energy shield).

Most people can butt their heads against a foe, but without training in this action, they will take the full damage they deal to their target, regardless of their Endurance.

There are no head butts in Shaidan style, but Koto has Wisdom Meets Folly and Mantok teaches Bow to Pray, Greet the Beloved.

Martial Hold (Level 3): A Grapple is brute strength versus brute strength, but a Martial Hold uses body mechanics to more easily fell an opponent. This can either be a wrestling maneuver or a simple wrist grab and lock, depending on the style. It relies on leverage and effective holds rather than raw strength to immobilize opponents.

The stylist rolls Dexterity + Fight to first grasp his target (this can be resisted with a dodge). If successful, he rolls Dexterity + Fight again, but he can add the victory points from his previous roll to this roll. This roll is contested by the target's Strength + Vigor roll. If the stylist is successful, the target is grappled. The attacker can then choose to deliver the grapple damage (3d) per turn. The normal attacker bonus for successive turns of grappling applies (see Grapple, above).

In addition, characters who learn this action can choose to resist Grapples or Martial Holds with their Dexterity + Dodge rather than Strength + Vigor.

Some names for different hold maneuvers are Shaidan's Bid Thee Kneel, Koto's Throw the Net to Catch the Fish, or Mantok's Grasp Hand, Bow to Pray.

Block (Level 4): An advanced dodge, the stylist can twist to avoid blows or redirect the force of the blow with his limbs. Resolve a Block just like a Dodge, but if the stylist's roll is successful, add three successes for resisting attacks. Thus, this action does not improve a character chances of meeting an attack, but if he does, he is better at deflecting it.

Confuse Foe (Level 4 and 7): The character performs all sorts of crazy, distracting tricks to overcome his foe's concentration, from mimicking drunken stumbles to pretending a greater enemy is standing behind the opponent. The character rolls Wits + Knavery; each victory point subtracts from the opponent's dodge or block roll for the character's next attack (in that turn or the next). A Level 7 version of this action allows a block action along with the confusion action (with no multiple action penalty).

Shaidan has no such confusion tactics, although Koto practioners are perhaps the best at them. They have many manuevers for this, from Monkey Steals the Peach to Jolo Bird Squawks (named after a particularly annoying Aylon bird's cries). Mantok even has Step to Side, Speak in Tongues.

Disengage (Level 4): The character knows how to best slip out of grabs or holds. He gains a +3 bonus on his Strength + Vigor roll to resist grapple actions. Shaidan calls this Ending the Tryst, while Koto artists call it Water Escapes the Net. Mantok has Step Back, Resist Temptation.

Martial Throw (Level 4): The stylist grabs his oppo-

179

nent and throws him. Not all styles utilize throws; those that do usually rely on leverage rather than strength.

This is resolved like a Martial Hold (above), but instead of grappling a target, the stylist throws him one meter per success, up to a maximum distance equal to his Strength. The damage is 3d plus 1d per three meters thrown. If the target was Charging the stylist, the stylist gains a +1 bonus to his second roll per meter the target has run.

This could be Koto's Fling the Monkey or Mantok's Grasp Hand, Send Gift to Heaven.

Rooting (Level 4): The character can sink and center himself, making it much harder for opponents to topple him. He gains a +3 on any roll to resist being knocked over in combat, although he may not move in the same turn he roots. Once a character successfully roots, he does not have to keep rolling until he is uprooted.

Of the many names for this action in different styles, there is Shaidan's Astride the Throne, Koto's Sage Stays Home, and Mantok's Remain Still, Reach to Heaven.

Claw Fist (Level 5): A more lethal punch than Martial Fist, its name comes from the most common variant of this action, which involves a raking or piercing strike to a vital area. This could be Shaidan's Sword Fist, Koto's Royal Vorox Decrees, or Mantok's Close Palm, Reach the Heart.

Drop and Kick (Level 5): The character drops low and kicks, hopefully gaining surprise by hitting his opponent from an unexpected angle. This enacts a -2 initiative penalty on the attacker's next action. Of the many names for this action, Shaidan has Diegn to Speak, Koto has Bow to Offer Tithes, and Mantok has Bend Down, Step Through Door.

Tornado Kick (Level 5): A spinning back kick. The stylists spins in a circle, striking his opponent with his outthrust leg, which has gained immense momentum from the spinning. This could be Koto's Weathervane Predicts the Storm or Mantok's Raise Foot, Spin the Prayer Wheel.

Sure Fist (Level 6): A punch that trades speed for increased accuracy. This could be Shaidan's Noble Decree, Koto's Tortoise Wins the Race, or Mantok's Spread Palm, Speak the Truth.

Leaping Kick (Level 6): The stylist leaps through the air to connect with his opponent while airborne. Iron Hand stylists have been known to knock interfering nobles from their mounts with their leaping kicks. This could be Koto's Prophet Walks on Clouds or Mantok's Leap Forward, Embrace the Sun.

Choke Hold (Level 6): A grappling action designed to render an opponent unconscious either by cutting off his air (choking) or through system shock.

After three turns of successful grappling (or if the target becomes stunned by grappling damage), the attacker rolls Strength + Vigor versus his target's Endurance + Vigor. If successful, the target falls unconscious for a number of turns equal to the attacker's Strength.

Various different Choke Hold maneuvers include Koto's Singing the Lullaby or Mantok's Clasp Neck, Wring Out the Robes.

Bear Hug (Level 7): A crushing grab. The character wraps both arms around his opponent and squeezes. This is considered a grapple, but the target does not get a resistance roll (unless he elects to dodge). For each successive turn, the character can keep squeezing his target and inflicting damage; he does not have to reroll the goal but he must reroll the damage. His target must make a resisted Strength + Vigor roll to escape the hold.

In Koto, this action is called Vorox Greets a Friend, and Mantok calls it Extend Arms, Embrace the Pilgrim.

Iron Body (Level 7): The character has practised many painful excercises which have hardened his bones. When he blocks a hand-to-hand attack (not weapon attack), his opponent may be injured. When making a block action, the number of victory dice gained on the roll act as damage dice against the character's attacker. Otherwise, the block action is resolved normally to resist attacks.

Shaidan calls this practice Golden Armor. Koto calls it Ascorbite Lends His Hide. In Mantok, it is known as Cross Arms, Don the Robe.

Speed Fist (Level 7): A quick punch designed to land a blow before an opponent can defend against it. Add three to the successes to resist an opponent's dodge (these successes do not affect damage). This could be Shaidan's Cannon Fist, Koto's Snake Surprises the Sleeper, or Mantok's Thrust Hand, Pluck the Coal.

Trip Kick (Level 7): A low kick designed to knock an opponent off his feet, usually by hooking the ankle around the opponent's ankle or by throwing the opponent off balance through misdirection and toppling him with a kick.

Compare the goal roll to the target's Dexterity + Vigor roll. If the attacker is successful, the target is knocked down. (It takes two actions to stand up again.)

This could be Koto's Monkey Tail Plays While Hands Surrender or Mantok's Step Forward, Sweep the Floor.

Throw Group (Level 7): The character must first learn Martial Throw (see above). The stylist defends against multiple attackers by throwing them, using their own momentums against them. This is a defensive action, and only opponent's attempting to engage the stylist in a hand-to-hand attack may be thrown.

The stylist's Dexterity + Fight roll is contested against each attacker's goal roll (attackers cannot dodge this roll since they have committed themselves to an offensive action). The stylist can throw each opponent against whom he has the most successes. (One meter per success up to a maximum of the stylist's Strength; 1d damage per three meters thrown.)

Each turn he performs this action, he can throw a maximum number of people equal to his Fight rating. A Throw Group action is the only action a character can perform in the turn, since he is in effect performing many multiple actions.

This has various names, from Koto's Fools Follow Fools, All Will Follow to Mantok's Lower Arms, Call the Faithful to Prayer.

Block and Strike (Level 8): At this level the stylist has mastered two separate maneuvers so well that he can perform them as one. The stylist first performs a Block against an opponent's attack. If she is successful, she then rolls a Martial Fist or Martial Kick attack — and she suffers no multiple action penalty. The combination of Block and Strike is considered to be one action.

Slide Kick (Level 8): The character slides under his foe to kick her feet, hopefully knocking her down. Of course, the character also winds up on the ground, but is prepared to take advantage of the situation. He may get up and perform another action in the next turn without suffering a multiple action penalty. The attacker compares his goal roll successes +3 against an opponent's Dex + Vigor (or Acrobatics) successes; if the attacker has the most, the opponent is knocked down.

Koto calls this Old Lady Falls and Gets Up, while in Mantok it is known as Drop to Ground, Scrub the Floor.

Power Fist (Level 9): An extremely powerful punch utilizing internal power — subtle body mechanics combined with breathing. The stylist can choose to spend Wyrd points immediately before rolling and gain extra dice of damage (if the roll succeeds). The cost is one Wyrd point per die of damage, up to a maximum of three. This is often accompanied by a shout.

This esoteric action is known by various names, from Shaidan's Imperial Decree, Koto's Comet Strikes the World, to Mantok's Stretch Spine, Speak the Word.

Shaidan stylists do not get their Fist cost bonus with this action; they must purchase it as a Level 9 action.

Vital Strike (Level 10): A strike to a vital point on the opponent's body. Knowledge of this action implies some knowledge of anatomy. The stylist can make a complementary Perception + Physick roll (this does not require a separate action), but the victory points add to the Vital Strike damage dice instead of the goal roll. This, combined with the Vital Strike roll's own victory dice and 3d of damage, can produce a truly lethal blow.

Some of this deadly blow's names are Shaidan's Shadow Strike, Koto's Mantis Injects the Poison, or Mantok's Wave Hand, Put Out the Light.

Graa (Vorox Martial Art) Actions

Banga ("Charge", Level 3): Do not stand in the way of a charging Vorox. This action allows the Graa stylist to take full advantage of his superior bulk and six limbs to become a veritable speeding train.

Drox ("Second Hand", Level 5): The Vorox has trained himself to use one of his extra limbs to perform one extra action per turn without suffering the multiple action penalty. This extra action must involve use of one of the Vorox's other limbs — a fist to punch, a foot to kick, a hand to grasp the bucking carriage, etc.. The character can also use this martial ability with melee weapons or ranged weapons. The prospective second-hand fencer or gunslinger must have Melee or Shoot skill at level 5.

Throx ("Third Hand", Level 9): The character must first learn Drox before he can learn Throx. The Vorox has trained himself to use another of his extra limbs to perform a total of two extra actions per turn without suffering the multiple action penalty. Each of these extra actions must involve use of one of the Vorox's other limbs — a fist to punch, two arms to grasp the rope while the other fires a gun, etc.. The character can also use this martial ability with melee weapons or ranged weapons. The prospective second- and third- hand fencer or gunslinger must have Melee or Shoot skill at level 9.

Fencing

Fencing is the art of the blade. Fencing duels are the preferred method of resolving disputes of honor among the nobles of the Known Worlds. A noble who doesn't know how to handle a sword may find himself dishonored or dead.

Fencing actions are trained tricks of the trade. Anyone can thrust with a blade, but only those who have carefully practiced will gain special benefit from it. Fencing actions are rated by the Melee skill level required to learn them. For example: Disarm is 5, meaning that a character must know Melee 5 to learn it. Each action must be bought seperately (buying the level 5 Feint does not give the character the level 5 Disarm or any other actions of lower levels). However, fencing actions do not have to be learned in order (a character can buy Disarm without having to buy Slash).

Fencing actions cost 1 point per level during character creation, or 2 per level with experience points.

Fencing Actions

Refer to the Fencing Actions Chart for specific rules.

Parry (Level 1): Perhaps the most basic and important action in fencing — the ability to deflect an opponent's blade with one's own.

Thrust (Level 2): A forward thrust with the point of the blade. Although best performed with a thin blade, such as a rapier, a broadsword thrust can still be devastating. Thrusting allows the fencer extra reach.

Slash (Level 3): A sideways, downward or upward swing of the blade. Unlike thrusting, slashing has a larger contact area (the edge of the blade rather than the point), but not as much reach. In addition, it is hard not to telegraph (reveal) a slash before it hits, perhaps giving an opponent time to react.

Counter Parry (Level 3): When the character's attack is confronted by a parry, she can counter the parry by swiftly rotating her blade, gaining a better chance of getting past the parry. A successful Wits + Melee roll means that a parrying opponent loses the +2 bonus to her goal. The attacker does not suffer a multiple action penalty for this roll.

Fancy Footwork (Level 4): The character dances and dodges, twists and turns, doing everything possible to confuse her opponent. Every victory point on a Dexterity + Vigor roll reduces her opponent's goal on any melee attacks by one. This footwork constitutes one action; characters performing it with any other action (except dodge, block or parry) will suffer the multiple action penalty.

Flat of Blade (Level 4): A slap with the flat of the blade rather than the edge, meant to hurt an opponent rather than kill him. However, this can be an insulting gesture and many nobles may become enraged if repeatedly slapped this way, causing them to lose their composure and poise, perhaps even driving them to reckless and poorly defended actions — "Exactly the point," say the dastards who employ this maneuver.

Draw and Strike (Level 4): Normally, drawing a sword from its sheath or picking it up from the ground takes one action. But a fencer with this training can whip out his sword or kick it up from the ground, catch it and strike in a single motion—handy if one is being hunted by assassins.

Compound Attack (Level 5): The character goes through an elaborate pattern designed to set her opponent up for her next attack. While this turn's attack has a -1 to the goal number, whatever fencing maneuver she makes next turn is at +2.

Disarm (Level 5): The fencer can use his blade to knock an opponent's blade from his hand and send it flying through the air or skittering across the floor a distance of one meter per victory point.

The fencer rolls Dexterity + Melee (the target can dodge this roll). If successful, he rolls Dexterity + Melee again but adds the victory points from his previous roll. These successes are then contested by the target's Strength + Melee roll. Optionally, the fencer can choose to substitute Strength (rather than Dexterity) for this second roll.

Gracious fencers will allow their opponent to then fetch

their blade before continuing the duel, a lesson in humility. Cads will take full advantage of a weaponless foe.

Feint (Level 5): The fencer fakes a move (such as a thrust to heart) but then swiftly changes it (a thrust to the leg), throwing off an opponent's defense. This action adds three successes to contest dodges only. A Feint will only work twice against a single opponent per engagement.

Stop Thrust (Level 5): When done properly, a stop thrust attack will prevent an opponent from landing his attack. In reality, the character's often lands just moments before the opponent's attack. While that may be all the character needs to win the duel, this is not always the case.

Off-hand (Level 6): The fencer has trained to fight with a weapon in both hands. He suffers no penalties for using a weapon in his off-hand. He can thus switch hands if one arm tires or he wishes to throw off an opponent — "But I thought you were right-handed!" "Ho, sir! I fight equally well with either hand." Or he can use an off-hand defensive weapon to parry with, such as a main-gauche or dagger.

Parry/Riposte (Level 6): The fencer's reactions are good enough to parry and then swiftly return a strike. This is treated as one action. The fencer must allow his opponent the first attack, which he parries and then returns. If his opponent elects not to attack or misses, the fencer may strike at the end of the action.

Wall of Steel (Level 6): The character can parry up to three attacks in a turn without a negative modifier, though he can do nothing but parry. The character must have already purchased the Parry maneuver before buying this one.

Cloak (Level 7): The fencer can use a cloak in her off-hand with which to parry or disarm her opponent. In addition, on a successful parry, she may try to Disarm her opponent without taking an extra action — the effort is so swift it takes place as the opponent tries to withdraw his blade (the character must first learn Disarm, level 5). This action is popular among nobles who are subject to ruffian assault while traveling incognito. The fencer must first learn Off-hand (Level 6).

Florentine (Level 7): With this action, the character can use two blades — one for attacking and one for defending. He can take two actions, an attack and a parry, without negative modifiers. Taking a third action would require that all his actions for the turn have the normal -6 modifier. The character does not have to know the Off-hand action to fight Florentine, but if he does not, any other actions he takes with an off-hand weapon will suffer a -4 penalty.

Athletic Strike (Level 8): The fencer — in the swashbuckling tradition — can swing from a chandelier, slide down a banister, leap from a window, etc. — and still strike his opponent in the same action! He suffers no multiple action penalties for doing so. This feat plus the strike must be the only actions performed in the turn. Gamemaster discretion.

Pierce (Level 9): The fencer's precision is amazing — she can slip her blade between the joints of an opponent's armor. Her attacks ignore armor (except energy shields). If the opponent is wearing armor with no joints or openings of any kind which would allow the point of a blade through, then this maneuver must contend with that armor. However, such a situation is very rare and is usually encountered only with ceramsteel battle suits, designed to be environmentally sealed.

Double Strike (Level 10): The fencer can strike with his blade and quickly follow it up with a strike from his off-hand (a dagger, sword, punch, etc.). This is considered to be a single action. Both attacks are rolled separately. The fencer must first learn Off-hand (Level 6).

Shields

Old-fashioned wooden or metal shields are not that uncommon a defense on the battlefields of **Fading Suns** fiefs, and small bucklers can occasionally be seen in the hands of an expert fencer. However, characters must still spend some time learning to use them.

Shield Actions

Shield Parry: While a successful Dexterity + Melee roll allows any shield-bearer to apply the shield's armor rating against an attack, trained users can add their victory dice to the shield's defense dice. Parrying with a shield takes one action.

Shield Attack: The character can ram his shield into a target and inflict the shield's damage dice on him. Especially vicious warriors use razor-edged shields to make attackers think twice about engaging them or in case their main weapon is disarmed. This is an uncouth attack and is rarely practiced by nobles.

Attack & Parry: The character can perform an attack and parry with his shield in one turn without suffering multiple action penalties.

Guns

The gun is the great equalizer. Unlike martial arts or fencing, anybody can pick up a gun and deliver a killing blow. It is perhaps lucky for most that, in the Known Worlds, guns are not easily available to everybody. Gunsmiths charge exorbitant prices for their goods and their steady customers — rich nobles and wealthy guildmembers — support this practice, preferring to keep such tools in the hands of the upper classes. The outrageous cost for ammunition can also be blamed on this class bias. Much like medieval Japanese peasants who were not allowed to carry swords — such an honor being reserved for samurai — the average **Fading Suns** peasant is not permitted to carry firearms, and most simply cannot afford one. While there is a steady blackmarket

need for cheap, readily available guns, people get what they pay for. The lack of technical know-how ensures that these cheap knockoffs often fall to pieces after firing a few shots.

Gun actions are rated by the Shoot skill level required to learn them. For example: Quick Draw is 5, meaning that a character must know Shoot 5 to learn it. Most gun actions, however, can be performed by all but the most inept. If no level is listed for the action, it can be performed by anyone — it does not have to be bought as a learned action. However, all actions assume a minimum Shoot rating of at least 3. If, for some reason, a character has less Shoot skill than that, he cannot perform the action for the benefits listed.

Refer to the Gun Actions Chart for specific rules effects. See Chapter Seven: Technology for further details on guns.

Firearms Actions

Reload: A character can reload a clip or a revolver speedloader in one action. If she is using a revolver and doesn't have a speedloader, she can load three bullets per action. If she is using a bolt-action or a lever-action rifle, she can reload one bullet per action. A lever-action rifle can be recocked and fired in the same turn if the character learns the Recock action (below).

Aim: A character can take time to draw a bead on a target before he fires. For each turn he spends, he can add +1 to his goal roll. The maximum he can add this way is 3. However, if he has a sight, he can employ that also. Sights add up to 3 (depending on the quality of the sight), but one turn must be spent per +1 added. For example, the famous sniper known as the Black Mantis sits on a rooftop, aiming his rifle at the Hawkwood baron. He has a +3 quality sight, and takes the full time to aim: it takes him six turns before he gets his full +6 bonus (+3 for his natural ability, +3 for the sight).

Three-round burst: If a character is using a weapon capable of automatic fire, he can try a three-round burst. This has a bit more control than other autofire options and helps preserve bullets.

Six-round burst: If a character is using a weapon capable of automatic fire, he can try a six-round burst. This has a less control than a three-round burst, but it's more exact than emptying the entire clip. The hail of bullets is more damaging also.

Empty clip: Sometimes, you just want it to rain bullets. If a character is using a weapon capable of automatic fire, he can empty his entire clip of ammo by aiming his gun in a direction and holding down the trigger until it is empty. The gun bucks like a beast in heat and it's hard to aim at a particular target, but it's also hard to dodge so many bullets.

Spread: If a character is using a weapon capable of automatic fire, she can spread the arc of her fire over an area to hit more than one target. She can spread her fire up to five meters in a circle around her (she must spin in place for anything more than 3 meters). For each meter spread, she suffers a -1 penalty to her goal roll (up to a maximum of 10). She makes one roll with the total penalties applied; the successes on this roll are contested against anyone in the targeted area who is dodging. Anyone who is in or enters the area must dodge or get hit. Spreading fire empties the clip.

Hipshot: The character takes a quick shot without taking time to aim — he just trusts his aiming instincts. This can only be performed for the initiative benefits during the first shot of combat, as the gun is drawn, and only applies to handguns. At the gamemaster's discretion, a carbine or other light rifle may be used.

Snapshot (Level 4): A character can get off a swift shot at the same time he leaps to the ground, or he can jump from behind the corner, shoot, and leap back behind cover before the guards' bullets turn him into swiss cheese. In other words, a snapshot can be performed with a dodge in the same action for no penalty. However, no other actions may be taken in same turn.

Quick Reload (Level 5): The character can reload a clip, fusion cel or revolver speed-loader and fire the gun in the same turn without suffering a multiple action penalty.

Quick Draw (Level 5): The character has practiced pulling his gun out of his holster and firing often enough that he can do it in one swift motion. This is considered to be one action, and no multiple action penalties are levied.

Off-Hand Shot (Level 6): The character suffers no penalties for firing a gun in his off-hand.

Recock (Level 6): The character is so smooth with certain rifles, carbines or shotguns that she can recock and fire it in the same action. If the gun is a lever-action rifle or carbine, she can recock the gun by twirling it in one hand to engage the lever. If she has a pump-action shotgun, she snaps it forward and back in one hand quickly enough to engage the pump. All are handy skills for lawmen (and outlaws) on the frontier worlds.

Leap and Shoot (Level 7): The character can leap one meter in any direction and shoot at a target without suffer-

---

Optional Rule: Deadlier Guns

Gamemasters and players who want firearms to have a more realistic (i.e. more lethal) effect in their dramas can elect to use this rule: the victory points gained on slug gun and energy weapon attacks convert directly into damage POINTS, not dice. For those weapons which leak through energy shields, six-sided dice should be rolled; results of 1 or 2 are leaks.

ing adverse penalties for the movement (although other environmental factors — noise, opponent activity, etc. — may cause penalties).

Roll and Shoot (Level 8): The character can roll across the ground and shoot at a target without suffering adverse penalties for the movement (although other environmental factors — noise, opponent activity, etc. — may cause penalties). The character can cover up to three meters in any direction.

Two Guns (Level 8): The character must first learn the Off-Hand Shot action. He can fire two shots - one from a handgun or submachinegun in the right hand, the other from a gun in the left hand. He suffers no multiple action penalties for these shots. A Level 9 version of this action allows the character to fire an assault rifle or shotgun in each hand (Str 4 or higher required).

Instinct Shot (Level 9): The character can take a single shot at an unseen target and have a good chance of hitting it. This is not a psychic power, but relies instead on instinctual cues — the villain walking in the rafters above makes just enough noise to give his location away, or the character senses the slowly-opening hidden door behind the bar and the gunman hiding there. If there are no conceivable clues, no bonuses can be gained from this action.

Movement

Characters don't usually stay still during combat — they move around, testing new footing, trying to get an advantage on their opponent. Once a character has engaged another, movement tends to be in a small area around the place of engagement, until the engagement is over. A combat may be made up of two characters moving in close, trading blows, and then breaking off to circle from a distance before moving in to strike again (see the excellent duel at the end of *Rob Roy*).

During an action, a character may move one meter in any direction without penalty. He may also choose to take an entire turn to move, in which case he may move up to his full running speed (see Vigor, in Chapter Four: Traits). If he chooses to run as one of his multiple actions, he may move one meter per level of Vigor, but he will incur the multiple action penalty penalty to all his actions that turn.

For example, Alustro wants to dodge a sword thrust, run to the bar, and pick up the shotgun there — all in the same turn. First off, all his actions will suffer a -6 multiple action penalty (three actions). For example's sake, let's just say he dodged well enough to avoid damage. He now runs to the bar (four meters away, well within his Vigor rating of 5). He must now pick up the shotgun. The gamemaster decides that — since Alustro is really pushing it, and since the shotgun is under the counter out of easy reach — Alustro

will have to make a Dexterity + Vigor roll to get it this turn. This roll suffers the -6 penalty. Sadly, Alustro fails the roll and ends the turn groping over the counter for the shotgun as his enemies close in.

Alustro would suffer the same penalty if he wanted to dodge, move three meters, pick up the shotgun, and then move two more meters (5 meters maximum for his Vigor rating).

Knocked Down

It takes two actions to stand up. Thus, someone could conceivably be knocked down and stand up again by the end of the turn, although only if he had planned on taking three actions (and thus applying the penalty to all his rolls that turn). Otherwise, he'll have to wait until the next turn to get to his feet. No roll is required to stand up.

Damage

With the exception of stunners, there is no differentiation between quality of damage in **Fading Suns** — no "stun" damage as opposed to "lethal" damage. The character's own Vitality levels are the measure of mild or lethal wounds. Some people can take a blow to the head and shrug it off, while others may be laid up in bed for months afterwards. It all depends on how much Vitality they have. When trying to knock someone out, it is best to use weapons which do enough damage to exceed the target's Endurance without killing him.

Anytime a character takes more damage from a single blow than his Endurance, he is stunned and will lose all further actions for that turn. If he already acted, he loses his next turn's actions. For example, Priam gets shot in the arm, taking five points of damage. His Endurance is 4, which is less than the damage. Priam is stunned and cannot retaliate this turn.

Knocked Unconscious

An assailant may wish to render her target unconscious rather than kill him outright. The attacker must declare that this is her aim, and her roll is a Demanding task (-4), because it calls for aiming a blow at the head or shoulders. The damage done (after subtracting the target's armor) must exceed the target's Endurance levels. If so, the target must make an Endurance + Vigor roll or else fall unconscious. Even if he succeeds, he may be stunned (see above).

After a number of turns equal to the amount of damage taken have passed, the unconscious character can make an Endurance + Vigor roll each turn until he awakens, unless he rolled a critical failure to resist unconsciousness, in which case, he may not awaken for at least one hour.

Fire

If you stick your hand in a fire, you're going to get burned. The heat and size of the flame determines the damage a character takes — a person holding his hand over a candle may get burned, but it's nothing compared to someone thrown into a bonfire (the fate of many so-called "witches" in the Known Worlds). Fire damage is not rolled — wounds (damage points) are applied directly against a character's armor. A character who is exposed to a flame without any protection (bare skin) suffers the full wound effects. Burns are extremely painful; even if a character's vital levels are not affected, he will be in pain unless treated with anti-burn herbs or ointment.

Flame	Damage Points
Candle	1
Torch	3
Bonfire	4 - 6
Chemical fire	5

Falling

If a character leaps from enough buildings, horses, or banisters, he's going to get hurt. Gravity teaches harsh lessons to those who test it. The distance a character falls determines how hurt she may get, although the surface she hits may affect this damage. Falling damage is not rolled — wounds (damage points) are applied directly against a character's armor. A character who hits ground without any protection suffers the full wound effects. Only padded armor will fully protect against falling damage — cloth, leathers, synthsilk, etc.. Metal or hard plastic armor will only provide half their normal protection rating (round up). For example, plate armor will provide 5d.

Distance (in meters)	Damage Points
2	1
4	2
8	3
10	4
12	5
16	6
20	7
24	8
every +4 meters	+1
Surface	**Damage**
Sharp rocks, spikes	+2d
Soft (mattress)	-3 damage points
Water	-4 damage points

Disease

Plagues are not unknown on many worlds, especially with the reappearance of many viruses long-thought destroyed. Alien microorganisms wiped out by human terraforming are back. A recent plague on Icon is said to have been caused by such alien viruses, although it is whispered that secret chemical weapons experiments were actually at fault. Medical science is not what it was during the Second Republic; disease identification and curing is now largely in the hands of Sanctuary Aeon, although they possess few advanced resources.

Diseases come in an enormous variety — too great to list here. If the gamemaster wants to introduce them into the game, she must create her own traits for the illness. It can add a degree of realism to the game to have player characters deal with non-combat illness, but it can also rob the game of grandeur if it goes too far. Player characters should not be especially immune to disease — if they insist on investigating a plague quarantine area for Ur-artifacts, they may bring back more than artifacts. But disease is rarely healed in one night — or even one month — so gamemasters should avoid slowing the pace of the game by inflicting debilitating diseases on player characters. On the other hand, a quest to find a cure for a weird alien disease could add some excitement and dramatic tension to a game that may otherwise be slowing down.

Basic Fight Actions Chart

Action	Roll	Init	Goal	DMG	Effect
Fist	Dx+Fight			2	
Kick	Dx+Fight	-1		3	
Grapple	Dx+Fight	-2		2	If successful, roll Str + Vigor vs target's Str + Vigor. If successful, target is grappled; attack can choose to deliver grapple DMG per turn
Charge	Dx+Fight	-3		3+	If successful, attacker and target knocked down. Add 1d DMG/3m run
Dodge	Dx+Dodge				Subtract successes from opponent's successes

Martial Arts Actions Chart

Action	LVL	Roll	Init	Goal	DMG	Effect
Martial Fist	1	Dx+Fight			3	
Martial Kick	2	Dx+Fight	-1		4	
Martial Hold	3	Dx+Fight	-1		3	If successful, roll Dx + Fight (+victory pts) vs target's Str + Vigor. If successful, target is grappled; attacker can choose to deliver grapple DMG per turn.
Head Butt	3	Dx+Fight	-2	+1	4	Attacker takes DMG exceeding his Endurance
Block	4	Dx+Fight				As Dodge. If successful, add three successes to resist attacks.
Confuse Foe	4	Wits+Knavery				-1 per victory point to opponent's block, dodge or parry for attacker's next action
Disengage	4	Dx+Dodge	-1	+1		+3 to resist grapples
Martial Throw	4	Dx+Fight	-2		3	If successful, roll Dx + Fight (+victory pts) vs target's Str + Vigor. If successful, target is thrown 1m/success, up to Str. Add 1d DMG/3m thrown
Rooting	4	Dx+Fight				+3 to resist being knocked over
Claw Fist	5	Dx+Fight			4	
Drop & Kick	5	Dx+Fight		+2	4	-2 Init next action
Tornado Kick	5	Dx+Fight	-1		5	
Sure Fist	6	Dx+Fight	-2	+2	3	
Leaping Kick	6	Dx+Fight	-2	-1	6	
Choke Hold	6	Dx+Fight	-3	-1	4	After three turns of grappling, roll Str+Vigor vs target's End+Vigor. If successful, target falls unconscious
Bear Hug	7	Dx+Fight	-2	-1	4	Can roll DMG each turn until target escapes
Iron Body	7	by block				Attacking opponent takes 1 DMG per victory pt from defender's blocking roll
Speed Fist	7	Dx+Fight	+2		3	+3 successes against dodges and blocks
Trip Kick	7	Dx+Fight	-2	-1	4	Roll vs. target's Dx+Vigor. If successful, target is knocked down.
Throw Group	7	Dx+Fight	-2		3	Roll vs. target's attack roll. If successful, throw target 1m/success, up to Str. Add 1d DMG/3 m thrown. Can throw one attacker per Fight rating.
Block & Strike	8	Dx+Fight		+2/0	–/3 or 4	Block opponent's attack. If successful, roll Martial Fist or Kick attack with no multiple action penalty.
Slide Kick	8	Dx+Fight	-2	-1	5	Compare attacker successes +3 vs target's Dx+Vigor roll; if target loses, he is knocked down

187

continued next page...

Action	LVL	Roll	Init	Goal	DMG	Effect
Power Fist	9	Dx+Fight		-1	5	Option: Spend Wyrd to add DMG (cost = 1W per 1d, up to 3 max.)
Vital Strike	10	Dx+Fight	-3	-2	3	Roll complementary Per+Physick; add victory dice to DMG

Graa (Vorox Martial Arts)

Action	LVL	Roll	Init	Goal	DMG	Effect
Banga (Charge)	3	Dx+Fight	-3		3+	If successful, attacker and target knocked down. Add 2d DMG/3 m run
Drox	5	Dx+Fight	-2			Allows a second action (using another limb) with no multiple action penalty
Throx	9	Dx+Fight	-3			Allows a third action (using another limb) with no multiple action penalty

Fencing Actions Chart

Note: Weapon determines the base damage.

Action	LVL	Roll	Init	Goal	DMG	Effect
Parry	1	Dx+Melee		+2		Roll victory dice +weapon DMG as armor
Thrust	2	Dx+Melee	+2			
Slash	3	Dx+Melee	-2		+1	
Counter Parry	3	Wits + Melee				Eliminates opponent's +2 parry bonus
Fancy Footwork	4	Dx + Vigor				Opponent's goal is reduced by 1 per victory pt
Flat of blade	4	Dx+Melee			-3d	No victory dice are added
Draw & Strike	4	Dx+Melee	-2			Draw sword and strike in same action
Compound Attack	5	Dx + Melee		-1		Next turn's goal is at +2
Disarm	5	Dx+Melee	-2	-1		If successful, roll Dx+Melee (+ victory points) vs. target's Str+Melee. If successful, target drops blade, which can be thrown 1m/victory point
Feint	5	Dx+Melee	-2	-1		Add 3 successes against dodges only
Stop Thrust	5	Dx + Melee	+3	-2		Reduce opponent's goal by 2
Off-hand	6	Dx+Melee				Suffer no penalties for off-hand weapons
Parry/Riposte	6	Dx+Melee		+2/-1		Parry opponent's attack. If successful, roll attack with no multiple action penalty
Wall of Steel	6	Dx + Melee				Can make three parries
Cloak	7	Dx+Melee		0/-1		Parry opponent's attack with a cloak in the off-hand (armor = victory points +3; goal = 8 + Str). If successful, attacker can attempt to Disarm opponent with no multiple action penalty
Florentine	7	Dx + Melee				One attack and one parry without multiple action penalties
Athletic Strike	8	Dx+Melee	-3	-2		Perform athletic feat (swing from chandelier) in same action with no multiple action penalty
Pierce	9	Dx+Melee	-2	-3		Ignore target's physical armor (not energy shields)
Double Strike	10	Dx+Melee	-1	-1		Attack with primary and off-hand weapon in same action (roll both attacks separately)

Shield Actions Chart

Action	LVL	Roll	Init	Goal	DMG	Effect
Shield Parry	1	Dx+Melee				Roll victory dice +shield defense dice as armor
Shield Attack	2	Dx+Melee	-1			Ram shield into target; inflict shield DMG
Attack & Parry	3	Dx+Melee				Character parries with shield and attacks in same turn without suffering multiple action penalties.

Firearms Actions Chart

Note: Weapon determines the base damage.

Action	LVL	Roll	Init	Goal	DMG	Effect
Aim		Dx+Shoot	-3	+1/turn		Maximum bonus is 3 (more if a sight is used)
Hipshot		Dx+Shoot	+2	-1		Only for first shot of combat with a handgun
3-round burst		Dx+Shoot			+1	
6-round burst		Dx+Shoot	-1	-1	+3	
Empty clip		Dx+Shoot	-1	-2	+5	+3 successes against dodges only
Spread		Dx+Shoot	-2	-1/m	+4	Spread up to 5m, anyone in targeted area must dodge or get hit
Snapshot	4	Dx+Shoot	+1	-2		Can be performed with a dodge for no penalty (no other actions may be taken in same turn)
Quick Reload	5	None				Reload clip and fire; no multiple action penalty
Quick draw	5	Dx+Shoot	-2	-1		Draw gun and fire in same action
Off-Hand Shot	6	None				Suffer no penalties for off-hand handgun
Recock	6	Dx+Shoot	-2	-1		Recock rifle or shotgun and fire in same action
Leap & Shoot	7	Dx+Shoot	-1	-1		Leap 1 meter in any direction
Roll & Shoot	8	Dx+Shoot	-2	-1		Roll up to 3 meters in any direction
Two Gun	8	Dx+Shoot	0/-1			One shot from each handgun; no multiple action penalty
Instinct Shot	9	Dx+Shoot	+1	-1		Fire at unseen target

Weapons Charts

Key: DMG = number of d6 rolled, STR = Strength required to wield the weapon (otherwise -2 goal roll), RNG = Range in meters (Short Range/Long Range; any distance past long is Extreme), Rate = the maximum number of actions allowed with this weapon per turn, SIZ = XS (extra small), S (small), M (medium), L (large), XL (extra large), Cost = in firebirds (plus one load of ammunition) (A damage roll can also be made using a d20, if no six-sided dice are available. The goal number is 13 or less. Additionally, blasters leak through shields on roll results of 1, 2, 3, 4 or 5, while flameguns leak on results of 1, 2 or 3.)

Melee Weapons

Weapon	Roll	Init	Goal	DMG	STR	SIZ	Cost
Knife	Dx+Melee			3	1	S	2
Dirk	Dx+Melee			4	2	M	4
Main gauche*	Dx+Melee			3	2	M	4
Rapier	Dx+Melee			5	3	L	10
Broadsword	Dx+Melee			6	4	L	15
Scimitar/Katana	Dx+Melee			6	3	L	20
Two-handed sword	Dx+Melee	+1		8	6	XL	30
Glankesh Vorox sword	Dx+Melee			6	4	L	25 (15 for Vorox)
Axe	Dx+Melee			7	5	L	5
Spear	Dx+Melee	+1		5	3	XL	1
Staff	Dx+Melee	+1		4	3	XL	1 crest
Club	Dx+Melee			4	2	L	1 wing
Mace	Dx+Melee			5	3	L	10
Flail	Dx+Melee			4	4	L	4
Whip	Dx+Melee	+1	-1	3	4	XL	3
Suresnake Whip	Dx+Melee	+1	+3**	3	4	XL	100
Garrote***	Dx+Melee	-1	-1	3	3	XS	5

* When parrying, armor value is 5 + victory points

** Against one chosen target, who must not leave sight for over three turns or bonus is lost

*** Must first make successful grapple (-6 goal unless target is unaware of attacker), then roll garrote damage plus victory dice per turn

Energy Melee Weapons

Weapon	Roll	Init	Goal	DMG	STR	SIZ	Cost
Shocker*				+3d			+30
Frap Stick**	Dx+Melee	-1		6/3	5	L	15

* Electrified melee weapon; use weapon's traits

** Second damage listed is if the stick is used as a club

Artifact Melee Weapons

Weapon	Roll	Init	Goal	DMG	STR	SIZ	Cost
Wireblade*	Dx+Melee			8	2	L	10,000+ (10)
Flux Sword**	Dx+Melee		+1	7	3	L	15,000+ (10)
Mist Sword**	Dx+Melee		+1	7	3	L	30,000+ (10)

* Ignores physical armor (not energy shields)

** Flux and Mist Swords can leak through energy shields. Roll damage normally, but those dice which roll 1 or 2 ignore shields.

Thrown Weapons

Weapon	Roll	Goal	DMG*	STR	RNG	Rate	SIZ	Cost
Knife	Dx+Throwing		3	3	5/10	2**	S	2
Star	Dx+Throwing		2	2	5/10	2**	XS	2
Dart	Dx+Throwing		2	2	5/10	2**	XS	2
Rock	Dx+Vigor***		1-2	1-3	5/10	2**	XS-L	NA

* A character may add his Strength damage bonus.

** The rate assumes that the character is holding extra weapons in his off-hand and is quickly drawing from this stack with his throwing hand (loading does not require an extra action). A character can hold in his hand and throw more than one star or dart in the same action; maximum of three stars each. For each extra star/dart thrown in the same action, subtract one from the goal roll: It takes an entire action to "load" multiple stars or darts into one hand.

*** If Throwing skill is used instead of Vigor, add one to the goal roll.

Bows and Crossbows

Weapon	Roll	Goal	DMG	STR	RNG	Rate	SIZ	Cost
Hunting Bow	Dx+Archery		4	4*	20/30	3	M	5 (1 wing/arrow)
Long Bow	Dx+Archery		6	6*	40/60	2	L	10 (1 wing/arrow)
Target Bow	Dx+Archery		3	3*	30/40	2	M	7 (1 wing/arrow)
Hand Crossbow**	Dx+Shoot		3	2(3)	10/20	1	S	7 (3 wings/bolt)
Med Crossbow**	Dx+Shoot		6	3(6)	20/30	1	M	10 (1 crest/bolt)
Hvy Crossbow**	Dx+Shoot		8	3(8)	20/30	1	L	15 (1 crest/bolt)

* -1 goal for every level of Strength required above the character's own

** Number in parentheses is the Strength required to recock the bow. It takes two actions to reload a crossbow. If the character does not have the required Strength to draw the bow, it takes an entire turn to reload the bow — unless the bow has a crank or tool to aid him.

Slug Guns

Gun	Roll	Goal	DMG	RNG	Shots	Rate	SIZ	Cost
Derringer (.32)	Dx+Shoot	-1	3	5/10	4	2	XS	50 (5 slugs/firebird)
Lt Revolver (.32)	Dx+Shoot		4	10/20	6	3	S	100 (5 slugs/firebird)
Lt Autofeed (.32)	Dx+Shoot		4	10/20	13	3	S	150 (5 slugs/firebird)
Med Revolver (.40)	Dx+Shoot		5	20/30	6	3	S	200 (3 slugs/firebird)
Med Autofeed (.40)	Dx+Shoot		5	20/30	10	3	S	250 (3 slugs/firebird)
Hvy Revolver (.47)	Dx+Shoot		6	30/40	6	3	M	250 (1 slug/firebird)
Hvy Autofeed (.47)	Dx+Shoot		6	30/40	8	3	M	300 (1 slug/firebird)
Imperial Rifle (.40)	Dx+Shoot		6	40/60	10	2	XL	200 (3 slugs/firebird)
Assault Rifle (10 mm)	Dx+Shoot		7	40/60	30	3(A)	XL	500 (2 firebirds/slug)
Sniper Rifle (13 mm)	Dx+Shoot		8	50/70	5	2	XL	700 (3 firebirds/slug)
SMG (.40)	Dx+Shoot		5	30/40	20	3(A)	L	350 (3 slugs/firebird)
Shotgun — shot	Dx+Shoot		8*	20/30	7	2	L	300 (2 loads/firebird)
Shotgun — slug (.47)	Dx+Shoot		7	30/40	7	2	L	300 (1 slug/firebird)

(A) = Gun is capable of autofire

* -1 damage per 5 meters from the target

Range Penalties

Range	Penalty (goal roll)
Short Range	none
Long Range	-2
Extreme Range	-4

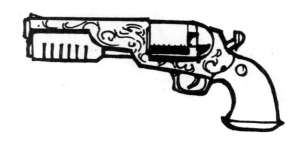

Energy Guns

Gun	Roll	Goal	DMG	RNG	Shots	Rate	SIZ	Cost
Palm Laser	Dx+Shoot		3	5/10	7	2	XS	200 (10/cel)
Laser Pistol	Dx+Shoot	+1	5	10/20	15	2	S	300 (10/cel)
Laser Rifle	Dx+Shoot	+1	7	30/40	23	2	XL	500 (10/cel)
Assault Laser	Dx+Shoot	+1	8	20/30	20	2	XL	700 (10/cel)
Blaster Pistol*	Dx+Shoot		7	10/20	10	1	S	700 (10/cel)
Blaster Rifle*	Dx+Shoot		9	20/30	15	1	XL	1000 (10/cel)
Blaster Shotgun*	Dx+Shoot	+2	9	10/20	8	1	L	1200 (10/cel)
Screecher (Sonic)**	Dx+Shoot	+1	5	10/20	15	1	S	300 (10/cel)
Flamegun***	Dx+Shoot	+2	5/3	10/20	10	1	L	150 (5/canister)
Stunner†	Dx+Shoot	+1	4 (S)	10/20	15	2	S	300 (10/cel)
Neural Disruptor††	Dx+Shoot	-3	5	10/20	6	1	S	3000 (10/cel)

* Blasters can leak through energy shields. Roll damage normally, but those dice which roll 1 or 2 ignore shields. Blaster shotgun: -1 damage per 5 meters from the target.

** Halve damage for targets with hearing protection (characters with their hands over their ears get this benefit).

*** Flameguns can deliver heat damage which ignores all armor. Roll damage normally, but those dice which roll 1 ignore armor (including shields). The second amount listed is the continuous damage due to the burning Ka plant oil sprayed over the target. Roll this damage (do not add victory dice) each turn after the first. If no damage is rolled in any turn, the flames go out.

† If a target takes ANY damage from a Stunner, roll Endurance + Vigor. If the roll fails, target is stunned for that turn (losing any actions not taken) and the next. If the roll is a critical failure, target falls unconscious. If damage taken is greater than the target's Endurance, roll as above, but failure means target is knocked unconscious. Stunner damage heals completely after one span; mark it with an "S" on the character sheet.

†† If damage exceeds target's Endurance (or Psi, whichever is higher), he is unconscious. Armor does not protect against this damage (except Psi Cloaks). Psychics may roll Psi + Stoic Mind vs. the attacker's successes.

Heavy Weapons

Gun	Roll	Goal	DMG	RNG	Shots	Rate	SIZ	Cost
Lt Machinegun (10mm)	Dx+Shoot		7	50/70	50	3(A)	XL	750 (2 firebirds/slug)
Grenade Launcher	Dx+Shoot	+1	V*	15/25	1	1	L	500 (65/grenade)
Rocketeer	Dx+Shoot	-2	9	20/30	5	1	XL	400 (25/grenade)
Missile Launcher	Dx+Shoot	+1	V**	75/100	1	1	XL	800 (100/missile)

* The damage varies based on what sort of grenade is used

** The damage these missiles do varies based on what kind they are. High Explosive missiles do 18 dice of damage in the same way as a grenade. Armor piercing shapes only do 13 dice of damage, and only effect one target, but armor only gets half of its protection dice.

Armor Chart

Key: Defense = number of d6 rolled (results of 1, 2, 3 or 4 = one armor point), Dex = penalty to user's Dexterity trait, Vigor = penalty to user's Vigor skill

Armor	Defense	Str	Dex	Vigor	Cost
Padded clothing (e)	1				1 wing
Heavy cloth (e)	2				1 crest
Polymer Knit (e)	2 (6 vs. slugs)				200 firebirds
Spacesuit	3				100
Leather jerkin	4				5
Synthsilk (e)	4				300
Studded leather	5				8 (15 for plastic studs)
Half plate	6		-1		30
Plastic	6				60
Scale mail	7		-1	-1	13
Plastic	7		-1		20
Stiffsynth	7		-1		500
Chain mail	8		-1	-2	20
Plastic mesh	8		-1		50
Armor mesh spacesuit	8		-1		500
Plate	10		-2	-2	40
Plastic	10		-1	-1	80
Ceramsteel	14		-5*	-5*	1000
Adept Robes**	14	+2	+1		NA
Flame retardant	+3 vs fire only				+50
Frictionless Gel ***	+6		-2		500
Psi Cloak	10d				3000

(e) = armor can be worn with an energy shield

* Penalties do not apply if suit is powered

** If not powered, use ceramsteel penalties

*** Can be worn over any type of armor; modifiers are cumulative. Defense is halved against energy weapons.

Shields

Armor	Roll	Defense	DMG*	SIZ	Cost
Buckler	Dx+Melee	4	3	M	7 (12 for plastic)
Large shield	Dx+Melee	8	6	L-XL	15 (20 for plastic)
Bullet-proofing		+4 vs slugs			x2 normal cost
Razor-edge			+3		+15 firebirds

* When shield is used for attack (rammed into a target); see Shield Actions Chart.

Energy Shields

Key: Protection = the first number is the minimum amount of damage required to activate the shield/ the second number is the maximum amount of damage the shield can block, Hits = number of activations per fusion cel

Shield	Protection	Hits	Cost
Standard	5/10	10	500
Dueling*	5/10	15	700+
Assault**	5/15	20	3000
Battle***	5/20	30	5000

* Concealable

** Very rare. Can be worn with leather, plastic or most metal armors (except plate) since its field has a wider radius.

*** Extremely rare. Can be worn with metal plate or ceramsteel armor since its field has a wider radius.

Example of Play

Every rule needed to play **Fading Suns** has been described. All that remains is to put it all together into an example of just how the game is played. First, we present a dramatic version of events, how a storyteller or fiction writer would describe the happenings within the game. This is followed by a rules explanation of everything that occurs. The actual game is a mix of both, with descriptions and dialogue provided by the gamemaster and players alike, helped along by the result of dice rolls.

The Dramatic Version

The dank cavern stank of rot and death, but Erian steeled herself against it and forged ahead. Behind her, Alustro coughed, trying to withhold his supper, but followed nonetheless. Onggangerak seemed little affected, although somewhat spooked by the strange carvings on the wall, scrawled figures resembling the hieroglyphics of the Anunnaki.

Erian fusion torch lit the way ahead and revealed a door at the end of the long corridor. "It is here!" she yelled to others, quickening her pace. She tromped up to the ancient seal and ran her hands on its bas relief sculptured gargoyle head. "The legend is true! Everything the old man said — it is all here."

"Wait!" said Alustro. "He spoke of traps also!"

Erian's hand withdrew from the door, but it was too late — the sculpture slid back into a recess and a loud clanking noise from somewhere beyond the walls rumbled through the corridor. In second, the door hissed open, and fresh air flooded the corridor.

"Jungle," Ong said. "I smell jungle. It leads outside."

"That cannot be!" Erian said. "It is supposed to be a vault! An ancient —"

She stopped speaking as she saw into the massive room revealed to them beyond the doorway. A great Ur chamber supported by huge, carved pillars spread out before them. In the center of the room, a ray of light fell from above, and a rope dangled from the hole in the ceiling. Past the light, they heard movement and the cocking of rifles.

"Throw down your weapons, Li Halan!" a voice yelled from the darkness.

"Boss Shavlack!" Erian yelled in disgust. "You stole our map! You honorless scoundrel!"

"I'm not going to argue with you, Erian," the voice replied. "Shoot them!"

Gunfire erupted from various points in the dark room and bullets spackled the wall around the three adventurers. Erian's energy shield sparked as it activated, and Ong grunted as a bullet penetrated his thigh. Alustro ran forward into the room to take cover behind the closest pillar, seemingly protected by grace, as no bullets hit him.

Erian, ignoring the gunfire, drew her sword and marched resolutely forward, searching the gloom for the Scraver thief who had beat her to the find of the century. Ong roared and charged forward on all sixes, immediately outdistancing Erian and disappearing into the darkness. Screams and yells of displaced gunners echoed through the chamber, and men ran toward the rope, jockeying with one another to be the first up it

and away from the maddened beast.

Abandoned by his men, the Scraver causally sauntered from the shadows, his hands raised and empty. "Okay, okay. We'll split the loot 50-50."

Erian placed the tip of her blade on his throat. "We will do no such thing. This is the property of the Emperor now, and I claim it in his name."

The Scraver grimaced and looked genuinely dangerous

flesh as if drawn by a magnet. Skin began to seal, leaving a ragged scar, but no wound. Ong smiled at the priest and nodded his thanks, and then padded over to the rope.

He stood at his full height, still almost meeting the guildsman eye-to-eye even though the man had climbed one third the distance to the top. "Don't think about sabotaging our ship. It is well guarded by others of our company."

The Scraver swallowed and only nodded, and then hur-

for a moment, but then smiled and shrugged his shoulders. "Well, that's that then. I guess I should just get out of your way." He sidled over to the rope, where the last of his men was just reaching the top, and began to shimmy up it.

Alustro, meanwhile, approached Ong, who limped into the light, and examined his wounded leg. "It's not too bad, but let me see if I can help." He prayed for a moment and placed his hand on the huge leg. A dim glow encompassed the wound and the slug slowly coaxed its way from the torn

riedly climbed the rest of the way up, leaving a fresh, pungent scent from beneath his tunic.

"This is too easy," Erian said. "Why did he give up? He has something. Ong, follow him and search him."

The Vorox nodded and vaulted up the rope using all six limbs, disappearing through the hole at the top in one third the time it took the Scraver. Outside, a yell and the sound of

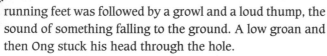

running feet was followed by a growl and a loud thump, the sound of something falling to the ground. A low groan and then Ong stuck his head through the hole.

"I can find nothing on his person, my lady."

Erian wrinkled her brow. "Then why did he desert the place simply because his offense failed?"

A rumble shook the room and the floor began to shift. In the center of the room was a great circular mosaic that was now revealed as a moving disk. It slid to the side, bearing Erian and Alustro with it, revealing a hole into darkness. From the gloom below, a tentative movement flickered. Then, a clawed tentacle shot out and latched itself to a pillar, and began pulling up the weight of… something big.

"By the Pancreator," Alustro whispered. "What is it?"

"Run, Alustro!" Erian cried. "Run!"

The priest ran toward the corridor they came from, followed by Erian, who spared one last look back before gasping and running with all her might. The scaled thing that pulled itself from the pit was nothing from this world — or if it was, it was better kept trapped below. They had freed it, but God knew how they'd chain it again…

The Rules Version

Chris gets his group of players together for another session of his **Fading Suns** epic. Tonight is another chapter in the ongoing saga of Lady Erian Li Halan and her entourage of adventurers. In the previous session, the group had split up, with Erian, Alustro and Onggangerak searching a cavern for an ancient chamber rumored to hold treasure, while the other player characters stayed to guard their spaceship.

The scene begins with Erian, played by Andrew, leading her group in a search. Alustro is played by Bill, while Jane plays Onggangerak (Ong for short). The first portion of gameplay involves the gamemaster setting the scene, describing its environment by appealing to the players' senses: sight, sound and even smell. He builds the atmosphere by adding mention of the spooky images seen on the walls, carvings made by alien races untold eons ago.

When Erian reaches the door, Andrew tells Chris that she examines the sculpture. Chris has him make a Perception + Search roll. Erian's Perception is 5 and her Search is 3, for a goal number of 8. He must roll this or less on a d20. He rolls a "9" — he just misses. Because he failed the roll, Erian missed noticing the inset around the carving, implying that it moves. To keep the action moving, Chris tells them that the sculpture recedes into the wall, opening the door.

He then describes the room, and yells out a taunt from the Scraver NPC. Andrew and his group refuse to give in to their rival's demands, and guns start firing.

There are five gunmen hidden throughout the room. Chris decides that two fire on Erian, two fire at Ong, while only one fires at Alustro. The gunmen all have Shoot skills of 7, and thus their initiatives are 7 each. He then asks the players what they intend to do.

Andrew says that Erian will draw her sword and walk forward, hoping her energy shield will defeat any gunfire that hits. She wants to find the Scraver and make him pay. Jane says that Ong will yell an intimidating roar and charge into the room, attacking the first gunman he sees. Bill, knowing that Alustro is no match for firearms, says Alustro will dive for cover. Chris tells him that the closest cover is a pillar in the room — he'll have to run into the gunfire to hide behind it. Bill shrugs and accepts the terms.

The only character doing anything active to compete with the gunmen's fire is Ong — his roar may affect their aim. This is an Extrovert + Impress roll; his Impress skill is 6 — the gunmen have the higher initiative and will fire first.

Chris adds their Dexterity (5) + Shoot (7) traits to get goals of 12. First, he rolls the two shots at Erian, with results of 11 and 6 — both hits. He then rolls damage: they are firing assault rifles, which inflict seven dice. One shot gets to add three victory dice (for 11 successes) and the other can add two (for 6 successes), for a total of 10 and 9 six-sided dice (damage is rolled on six-sided dice, looking for results from 1–4). He rolls the first: 3, 4, 2, 6, 1, 1, 4, 5, 3, 6, 2 = 7 damage points.

Erian has an energy shield which activates whenever it takes 5 or more points of damage — the first shot activates the shield, absorbing all damage. Erian is unaffected.

The second shot rolls: 6, 5, 2, 3, 1, 4, 2, 3, 5 = 6 points. Again, the shield activates, stopping all the damage. Andrew marks off two "hits" on his character sheet, representing the lower power remaining in his shield's battery (he can stop a total of 10 hits before changing batteries).

Chris now rolls for the two shots against Ong: 16 and 3. One fails but one hits. This one does 8 dice (+1 victory die for 3 successes): 3, 5, 4, 1, 2, 6, 3, 4 = 6 damage points. Ong does not have a shield, but he does have a suit of plastic chainmail armor. This gives him 8 defense dice: 1, 6, 5, 6, 3, 2, 6, 5 = only 4 points are halted, which means that 2 points still get through and are inflicted onto his Vitality.

Finally, Chris rolls for the gunman targeting Alustro. He allows Alustro a Dexterity + Dodge roll and a +2 bonus for running to cover; normally, he might allow more of a bonus, but since Alustro must run through the gunfire to hide, he only awards a small modifier. Bill adds Alustro's Dexterity (5) + Dodge (4) and bonus (+2) for a goal of 11. He rolls a "5." Now, Chris rolls for the gunman and gets a "3" — Alustro's successes are subtracted from the roll, leaving no successes — the shot misses.

Now, Ong gets to make his yell. He's trying to cow the gunmen, and Jane hopes his charge will only add to the effect. He totals his Extrovert (4) + Impress (6) for a goal of 10. Chris rules that the charge is worth some extra effect, since folklore tells many tales of the berserker rage of a wounded Vorox; he allows a +2 bonus, giving Jane a 12 goal. He rolls "12" exactly — a critical hit.

Chris chuckles and describes how the gunmen, completely freaked out by the Vorox's charge, immediately disperse and all run for the rope, screaming and yelling while shoving one another aside to be the first out of the room.

Faced with no allies, the Scraver gives up. While Erian speaks with him, Bill says that Alustro will try to heal Ong's wound with a theurgy rite: the Laying on of Hands. He totals his Calm (6) + Remedy (7) for a goal of 13, and rolls a "7" — two victory points, and thus two wound levels healed. Ong is restored to his full Vitality. Chris reminds Bill to mark off a Wyrd point on Alustro's character sheet, the cost of casting the theurgy rite.

Jane realizes that the Scraver may try to mess with their ship, and decides that Ong will try to scare him from considering it. After Jane says Ong's dialogue and Chris finds it sufficiently tough, Chris tells Jane to roll his Extrovert + Impress again, but this time it is contested by the Scravers own Wits + Impress — he's used to making threats himself.

Jane rolls a "6" — an okay roll. Chris totals the Scraver's Wits (7) and Impress (6) for a goal of 13. However, he rolls a "20" — a critical failure.

Chris invents something sufficiently embarrassing for the Scraver and the NPC exits the scene.

Andrew suspects something's up, though, and has Erian order Ong to search the Scraver. Chris deems that no roll to climb the ladder is needed (it would only slow down the action), but tells Jane that he needs to make a Perception + Observe or Search to frisk the weasel. He totals Ong's Perception (7) + Observe (7) for a goal of 14, and rolls a "7." Chris says that, besides trinkets, there is nothing notable on the Scraver's person.

The cliffhanger for the scene, however, needs no roll. When Andrew, speaking for Erian, says the appropriate dialogue, that's Chris's cue to introduce the true villain of the scene — the Thing That Must Not Awaken. Too bad all the fighting and yelling woke it up.

He describes only the barest beginnings of the creature's arrival, making sure to impress upon the players that this is something beyond their ability to fight — they're going to have to use wits against it. Asking for reactions, he is glad that his players are smart enough to evacuate their characters before he is forced to do nasty things to them…

Chapter 7:
Technology

"Will you shut up?!" Julia screamed. "I'm working here!"
She squinted again and bent forward to solder the two dangling wires.

"I'm just saying that if it's a fuse, connecting wires isn't going to solve anything," Cardanzo coolly replied, leaning through the cockpit hatch.

Julia turned around and gave him an evil stare. "Don't you think I would have checked the fuses? This is my ship, damn it! Nobody talks to me that way!"

"Calm down, both of you," Erian Li Halan said, looking into the tight room from over Cardanzo's shoulder. "How long is it going to be, Julia?"

Julia's eyes rolled. "I would have had it done five minutes ago if it wasn't for this hull rat and his suggestions."

"One of which prevented you from igniting the fusion reserves, thank you," Cardanzo said.

"Enough!" Erian yelled. "Just get us going again! My brother's fleet will be here any minute. If the ship is still dead in space, we will be too."

"Fine!" Julia said, touching the two wires together. A spark exploded and the ship lurched forward, spinning wildly out of control. Julia slid across the floor and her head stuck an overhanging console. The world went dark and she slumped into unconsciousness.

"Great!" Erian cried. "The engines are online again!"

"Uh…" Cardanzo said, looking at the prostrate Julia. "Who's going to fly this thing?"

There are a number of reasons why technology is rare in the Known Worlds. Perhaps the greatest cause is the Church. After the misery of the Fall, the Church zealously readopted their old, Diaspora-era doctrine of antitechnology. Church inquisitors are always on the look out for what they deem to be dangerous innovations, and they routinely proscribe certain "forbidden" tech, policing this with martial search-and-destroy missions.

Woe be it to those wily Engineers who are vain enough to believe that their secret labs are safe from the law of the Pancreator's army. When Inquisitors find a secret lab or research outfit, they send their troops in and blow the place to smithereens. Usually, the culprits behind the forbidden tech are first given the chance to surrender and recant, but since this usually involves a "cleansing" session (torture), most renegade scientists attempt to flee the scene of the crime. Some even escape — but they spend the rest of their lives looking over their shoulders, waiting for the tread of the Inquisitors' boots.

In addition, many groups (especially the guilds, but the houses as well) jealously guard their own tech advances, going so far as to assassinate anyone else who discovers them. Technology is power, and he who has the edge wins. At least, this was the case during the Emperor Wars. Now that Alexius is in charge, he is attempting to consolidate technology under the office of the Emperor. Most houses have agreed — in principle, at least. But everyone knows each group still has its own secret labs, developing new and old tech for the next bid at the Emperor's throne.

Another stumbling blocks on the way to high-technology is data. Most hi-tech information was lost after the Fall. Some of it was intentionally destroyed while other data was simply buried and has yet to be rediscovered. As the Known Worlds culture was rebuilt, it rebuilt around new computer languages, and the old knowledge stored on old operating systems was lost or is now irretrievable. In additions, computers were often the first targets in any war.

In the martial atmosphere of the empire, so soon after the Emperor Wars, current tech research concentrates on wartime advances and limits the study of non-war applications. War tech is usually more advanced than the common everyday tools of life. While a militia man on a backworld may have a laser, his wife still cleans the shirts on the rocks by

Tech Level Chart

Tech Level	Era	Item
0	Stone age	Flint dagger
1	Medieval	Swords, wagons
2	Renaissance	Gunpowder
3	Victorian	Electricity
4	Mid-20th century/ **Fading Suns** era	Aircraft, early computers
5	Diaspora	Spacecraft, ceramsteel
6	Early 2nd Republic	Advanced starships, advanced computers
7	Second Republic	Shields, robots (early A.I.)
8	Vautech/ Late 2nd Republic	Terraforming, adv. A.I.
9	Lesser Urtech	Soul Shard
10	Urtech	Jumpgate

Quality Chart

Each item is rated for quality (+3 to -3, with 0 as the base). This is a bonus or penalty the gamemaster can use in any way he or she sees fit. While it should not be used to add or subtract to combat goal rolls or damage, it can modify Tech Redemption rolls when trying to repair the item, or Lore rolls when trying to figure out something about the item's history or place in culture (a cheap gun can be placed as a street culture artifact, while an elegant gun can be considered upper class). The modifier can also be applied to victory points collected in sustained rolls (for instance, a premium Second Republic jumpdrive may only require 6 victory points to get back online, rather than the usual 9).

In addition, the quality of a product also affects its price.

Quality	Manufacture	Price Adjustment
+3	Premium (2nd Republic)	+30%
+2	Master guildwork	+20%
+1	Superior artisanship	+10%
0	Standard	base price
-1	Poor workmanship	-10%
-2	Unreliable	-20%
-3	Disrepair	-30%

the stream, hanging them out to dry and dreaming of the luxurious washing machines of the rich merchant families.

Finally, the difficulty of interstellar communication slows the spread of new tech (and thus progress). All these factors (and more) make innovation and new research a challenge.

Interface/Coding

Most people in **Fading Suns** can interface with tech but not code it. In other words, they are users, not programmers. The higher the tech, the more coding is required to make or repair it. From Tech Level 4 and up, coding becomes more and more prevalent, which means one person cannot necessarily make or even operate the item by himself.

A character's personal Tech characteristic as a user matches the levels given in the Tech Level Chart. In other words, most freemen (with a base Tech 3) interface tech in the Victorian era; they expect (depending on how smart or experienced they are) common tech to act like early Industrial Revolution devices. Serfs, on the other hand, have a base 2, and expect carts and dirty forges. Artisans are usually a little better, trained up to at least 4.

As a general guideline, it requires a Tech characteristic two levels higher than the Era to code (not just interface) tech of that era. In other words, while Tech 8 is terraforming level, it requires Tech 10 to actually code (invent, reprogram) terraforming technology. In other words, only the best of the best can do so. By this scale, no one in the Known Worlds can code Urtech (the technology left behind by the jumpgate makers).

Code here is defined as an ability to understand the technology thoroughly: its theory, practice and all that goes into its making. Of course, a serf with a Tech 2 and a Blacksmithing skill can still make a sword (even though his coding is stone age), but he cannot invent damascing or the elaborate process that goes into making a Japanese samurai sword. He can only make it the way he was taught.

When a character uses unfamiliar tech, compare the character's Tech against the item's Tech Level; if the item's level is higher, then character will suffer a negative modifier to his goal roll equal to the difference between his characteristic and the item's level. For example: Janus is trying to figure out a strange Second Republic artifact of Tech Level 8; his Tech characteristic is 5. His roll suffers a -3 penalty (8 - 5).

The converse of this is not true: A character with Tech 8 using a Tech 1 sword does not gain a +7 bonus.

The actual process of invention can be simulated with a sustained action. The inventor rolls Tech + relevant Tech Redemption skill (multiple skills may be needed for complementary rolls) and totals his victory points. The total victory points required depends on the goal: the more unique, new or unusual the device, the higher the total. There may be three levels of victory: a barely functional prototype might only require 7 victory points, a fully functional model might be 11 v.p., while an expert model might be 17 v.p. Beginning the process with a known model may allow the inven-

tor a bonus on his goal rolls. Likewise, inventing a device using technology the inventor is unfamiliar with may cause penalties.

The amount of time between rolls varies; it may be days for the first three rolls, then weeks between the next three, and perhaps even years between all successive rolls — invention does not always come easy or immediately.

Note: An inventor may only invent tech level functions two levels below his level of understanding (see the Tech Level Chart).

Money

The basic unit of commerce since Alexius took the throne is the "firebird" (so called because it bears his phoenix crest on one side and his portrait on the other). This unit is broken into quarters ("wings") and halves ("crests"). Firebirds are minted only on Byzantium Secundus using a unique metal called prismium requiring Second Republic tech to forge (this tech is heavily protected by the Imperial Eye, making it extremely hard to counterfeit). Its value is actually equal to the coin it represents — one coin holds about one firebird in value in its metal alone.

Throughout the book, costs for items are given in firebirds (1/4, 1/2 or whole). When converting from modern, twentieth century U.S. currency, figure that one firebird is worth roughly ten dollars. A crest is worth about five dollars, and a wing is worth about one dollar.

There is no central stock exchange for the Known Worlds. The Empire tries to set a fixed firebird rate for certain items, such as military construction contracts, but outside of Byzantium Secundus or Tethys, merchants and manufacturers can charge whatever they think they can get away with.

The advantage the League has over local guilds is that they can set their own fixed rates across the Known Worlds, providing interstellar travelers some stable spending base — as long as they trade with League merchants. On certain worlds, they will even lower their prices somewhat to compete with local prices. However, since they are interstellar and depend on repeat business, they rely instead on more expensive but dependable goods. Travelers cannot be sure what they are buying when they buy local.

The cost listed for items in most **Fading Suns** sourcebooks represents this fixed rate set by the League, although costs will fluctuate somewhat with local supply and demand.

Rogue Coinage

The farther one gets from Byzantium Secundus, the more varied the coinage one encounters. While, strictly speaking, alternate coinage to the firebird is illegal (Alexius has declared his firebirds to be the only legal tender throughout the empire), they are often accepted anyway. However,

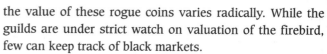

Goods and Services

Below is a list of various goods and services and the usual costs for them (in talons). While serfs and poor freemen tend to barter for most of their needs, outsiders will be charged money for them. The actual cost will vary with local conditions: a flood driving folks from their homes may fill up the nearby inns, raising costs for room and board in the region. The costs in cities may be more than in hamlets or villages, representing the increased costs of importing goods and the unscrupulous raising of prices to match the higher incomes of city residents. In addition, some items may only be available on high-tech worlds or cities (soda-pop, for instance, is rare on Malignatius). Some items have three listings: cheap/moderate/fine.

Gear/Tools

Item	Talon cost
Plain clothing	3/6/12
Candle	1/2/3
Lantern	5
Rope	5/8/12
Timepiece	
Mechanical	2
Electronic	5
Waterproof	+2

Food

Item	Talon cost
Ale	1
Beer	1/2/3
Hard liquor	2/4/6
Wine	3/6/12
Soda-pop	2
Snack	1/2/3
Breakfast	1/3/6
Lunch	2/4/8
Dinner	2/6/12
Travel rations	1/2/4

Lodging

Item	Talon cost
Table in main room	2
Shared bedroom	5
Private room	10
Add meals	3/6/10
Stable one small beast	4
Stable one large beast	8
Care for beast	2
Park small craft	2
Park large craft	4
Maintenance for craft	10

the value of these rogue coins varies radically. While the guilds are under strict watch on valuation of the firebird, few can keep track of black markets.

While rogue coinages vary, their uses are usually very similar. They can be broken down into two different types: Talons (purely local lucre, from a single fief or city) and house coins (usable only within that house's fiefs).

Talons come in many varieties, from the Madoc Coral (made of rare coral found only on that world, requiring special skills to carve properly) to the Tethys Matriarch (gold coins with the profile of Baroness Felicity Hawkwood, found only in one fief in the distant Grampas Mountains). While their value varies radically, they are considered the lowest class of coinage acceptable for trade. The Reeves call these coins "talons," since you can usually exchange one firebird for eight of them (the firebird depicts a phoenix with eight talons). One wing will yield two talons and one crest will yield four talons.

Among the varied house coinages are "mantises" (House Decados coins, with its crest stamped upon them), "claws" (the Hazat), "crosses" (Li Halan) and "sparklers" (al-Malik). "Black lions" were once minted by House Hawkwood, but they now support Alexius' demand for one firebird. Most house coins are now valued similarly to talons (eight house coins are equal in value to one firebird).

Wages

There are many ways to earn money; some possible jobs that player characters might hire themselves out for (or hire others to perform for them) are listed below. The prices assume trained or professional labor; jobs for untrained workers (hiring bully boys or ditch diggers off the street) pay much less.

Job	Pay
Aide de camp*	10 per week, more for danger pay
Assassin	50 per job, more for danger pay
Athletic trainer	10 per month
Author (successful)	100 per year
Author (moderately successful)	20 per year
Beast trainer	10 per month
Bounty hunter	25 – 500, depending on target
Bodyguard	10 per month, more for danger pay
Butler	5 – 15 per month
Carpenter	3 per month
Chauffeur	5 per month
Chef	5 – 10 per month
Courtesan	5 per session, 25 per month
Doctor (Physick)	10 per visit

Driver	1 per job
Duelist stand-in	10 per duel, more if to the death
Enforcer	10 per job, more for danger pay
Etiquette instructor	10 per month
Executioner	3 per job
Gambler	Portion of winnings
Informer	1 – 5 per topic
Investigator	5 – 15 per job
Laborer	1 per job
Lady-in-waiting	5 – 10 per month
Magic lantern shower	5 per show plus portion of ticket sales
Mechanic	5 – 10 per item repaired
Medic	5 per visit
Noble hanger-on	10 per month
Parish priest	5 – 10 per month
Pet/Toy	1 – 10 per month
Performer (high class)	10 per performance
Performer (low class)	1 – 5 per performance
Pirate	Portion of any bounty
Researcher	5 per month, or 2 per topic
Rumor-monger	1 per topic
Salesman	Portion of profits
Seamstress/Costumer	1 – 10 per outfit
Security consultant	5 per month
Security guard	5 per month
Seneschal	10 - 15 per month
Soldier	5 – 10 per battle
Starpilot	20 per jump
Starship navigator	10 per jump
Starship engineer	15 per jump
Starship gunner	5 per jump
Starship marine	5 – 10 per jump
Think machine programmer	5 – 10 per task
Torturer	5 – 10 per job
Town crier	3 per month
Vermin catcher	3 per month

* An open task situation: character is expected to perform whatever duty his patron requires, from escorting his children to the fair to exploring lost star systems.

Equipment

Life in the **Fading Suns** universe is diversified. From one dwelling to the next, family lifestyles can differ greatly. While there is little to separate a serf's existence from that of a pauper in the Middle Ages, for those with a little money, the entire world can change. In **Fading Suns**, the difference between living in a hovel with a hay stack for your bedding and living in an air-conditioned apartment with a waterbed is the amount of money you can spend.

Sadly, this discrepancy goes far beyond mere dwellings. For most serfs, anything even close to advanced medical care is legendary, the stuff of kings. Poultices and home remedies are the rule, surgery and antiseptic are the exception.

Below are a few examples of what **Fading Suns** characters might be able to afford to add to their accouterments, depending on how successful they are. The costs listed are averages on the open market; better designed or manufactured versions will be more expensive. These are only mere samplings of the vast amount of gear available in the Known Worlds. If a piece of equipment is not listed here, the gamemaster should feel free to come up with it on her own.

Weaponry

Refer to the weapon charts in Chapter Six: Combat for detailed traits for the weapons listed below.

Melee Weapons

Melee weapons saw a resurgence after the Fall, since energy shields are common among the nobility and those who can afford them. However, the needs of internal starship combat also helped promote their return. The ranged weapons necessary to penetrate space marine armor risk damaging a ship if they hit a key component. Thus marines and pirates have turned to melee weapons when onboard ships. The nobility's adoption of a dueling culture only adds to excuses for carrying melee weapons.

Knife: The only thing most peasants are allowed by law to carry is a knife, but this can be anything from a turkey carver to a mammoth survival knife. Smaller knives may deliver less damage; larger knives are considered to be dirks. Cost: 2 firebirds.

Spring Knife: The spring knife has the same traits as any other knife, but the blade stays concealed in the hilt until its user presses a button and brings it into play. Some of these are exceptionally well concealed, being worked into belt buckles and jewelry, but these are even more expensive than the normal ones. Needless to say, possession of one of these is a crime in many cities — these aren't tools. Cost: 5 firebirds.

Dirk: A large knife or short sword, depending on the manufacture. Similar to the Scottish knife from which it gets its name, this could also be a Gurka kukri or Roman gladius. Cost: 4 firebirds.

Rapier: The most popular melee weapon in the Known Worlds. It is elegant and light, perfect for fencing. The common rapier resembles a renaissance blade with a cup or swept hilt guard. Noble rapiers are usually engraved with fine decorations, and often have precious gems set into the pommels. Rapiers are popular among those who have the finesse to slide the blade under an energy shield's impact threshold (purposefully doing less damage by withholding victory

203

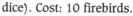

dice). Cost: 10 firebirds.

Broadsword: A heavy sword favored by certain soldiers. This could be a Viking broadsword, a Norman conqueror's sword or just about any broad, straight sword from history. Cost: 15 firebirds.

Scimitar/Katana: A curved sword with either two edges or one. This could be an Arabian sword, a pirate cutlass or even a samurai katana. Scimitars are popular among the Kurgan barbarians. Cost: 20 firebirds.

Two-handed Sword: The biggest, baddest sword around. This mammoth sword could be any huge blade, but is mainly modeled after the Scottish claymore. Two-handed swords are popular among those who do not have the finesse to slide a blade under an energy shield's impact threshold but who might deliver enough damage to exceeds its protection threshold. Cost: 30 firebirds.

Glankesh Sword: A deadly crescent blade resembling a Chinese deerhook sword. These blades of superior craftsmanship are made by the Vorox, originally invented to make up for their lack of claws (feral Vorox spurn these swords). While they are one-handed swords, Vorox warriors usually use one in each of their four-fighting hands. The crescent shape allows them to create a circle of death around their bodies as they slash the swords about with all arms.

These swords are forged from high-quality alloys found in abundance on Vorox. They are almost sacred to some Vorox warriors, who painstakingly engrave them with sigils of victory and hang "trophies" from the handles (enemy's teeth, hair, etc.). They don't like it when someone touches their Glankesh without permission. Cost: 15 firebirds for Vorox, 25 firebirds for non-Vorox

Axe: This could be a battle axe or a simple woodcutter's tool. This is the kind of heavy weapon often snatched up by peasants trying to defend their farms from strangers. Cost: 5 firebirds.

Staff: The ol' standby for merry men everywhere, this could be Little John's quarterstaff, a Japanese monk's bo staff, or just about any long stick (a short stick is considered to be a club). Cost: 1/3/5.

Spear: An old favorite, spears have made a comeback on many worlds. They are considered primitive by even most peasants, but the increasing need on some backworlds to supplement crops with hunting means that they are used anyway. Cost: 1 firebirds.

Club: Used by peasants and Zen masters alike, a club is an equal-opportunity weapon, because anyone can pick up a stick and beat someone with it. This could be a short tree branch found in the woods or a polished hate stick. Cost: 1/3/5 talons.

Mace: A metal ball or long-handled hammer. Basically, a very mean club, meant for hurting. This could be an or-

nate Inquisitor's "prod" or a blacksmith's hammer. Cost: 10 firebirds.

Flail: Two long sticks connected by a chain. This could be the standard medieval weapon or the more modern nunchaku. A flail wielder with five or more levels in Melee skill can purchase a special combat action called Flail Parry/Disarm. This acts just like the fencing action Cloak (level 7). Cost: 4 firebirds.

Whip: Whips come in all shapes and sizes, from bull whips to slaver whips. The above traits assume a simple leather whip. If metal is added to the end of the lash, add one die of damage. High-tech synthetic whips are known at Tech Level 6+, and these usually have a base of 4 dice of damage and require only STR 3 to wield. Cost: 3 firebirds.

Whip users can learn the fencing action Disarm (Level 5), but this must be learned separately for blades and whips. In addition, there is another action available:

Snare (Level Six): The whip user can wrap his whip about a target's limb or neck and yank the target off his feet. The whipper rolls Dexterity + Melee to first snare his target (this can be resisted with a dodge). If successful, he rolls Dexterity + Melee again, but he can add the victory points from his previous roll to this roll. This roll is contested by the target's Strength + Vigor roll. If the whipper is successful, the target is yanked off his feet. It takes two actions to escape a snare, although no roll is required.

Suresnake Whip (TL7): This can be any of the whip types listed above, but a special tracking wire has been threaded throughout the length of the whip. The tip of the lash holds a nanite computer which can home in on a chosen target; the tip must first be aimed at the target then "locked down" on that target with a flick of a switch in the handle (this takes one action). As long as the target does not disappear from the computer's sight for more than three turns, the whip gains a +3 goal roll bonus to hit its chosen target. These whips are popular among the Chainers, who use them to keep "special" cargo in line. Cost: 100 firebirds.

Garrote: A favorite assassin's weapon, garrotes have been used to strangle people throughout the centuries. Different models have been manufactured at different Tech Levels. A garrote user must first grapple his target around the neck (a Tough task, -6, unless the target is unaware of the attacker). If successful, he may roll the garrote's damage plus his victory dice once per turn. The victim can try to break the hold using the normal grapple rules.

Primitive versions are made from metal wire, but more advanced models can be made from unbreakable synthetic plastics. At Tech Level 4 and above, garrotes can be hidden in increasingly clever places, from a line drawn forth from a wristwatch to a line that shoots out of a pen to wrap around its target from a distance (see Suresnake Whip, above; range is 2 meters, add 100 to the cost). Cost: 5 firebirds.

Energy Melee Weapons

Shocker (TL5): Any knife, sword, mace or even whip can be turned into a Shocker; it simply means that the weapon is rigged to release an electrical charge whenever it hits a target. Once the target has been struck, add three dice of damage (this is considered energy weapon damage, so metal armors suffer a -1 from their protection values against it). Models vary, however, and some may only deliver one or two extra dice of damage. A fusion cell is required (it lasts for 25 turns). Cost: +30 to normal weapon cost.

Vibrating Blade (TL5): A sword or dagger is modified with an electrical apparatus so that, when a switch is flicked, the blade vibrates minutely but very quickly. A vibrating blade does no extra damage but it will cut through energy shields easier: add one to the minimum damage required to activate the shield and subtract one from the shield's maximum armor rating. For example, a standard shield would be 6/9 against a vibrating blade.

When the vibration is inactive, the sword is not as firm (it jiggles a little in its mounting), delivering one less die of damage. A humming sound always accompanies an active vibrating blade. Activation requires a fusion cell, which can last for 25 turns. Switching the blade on and off does not require an action. Cost: +100 to normal weapon cost.

Frap Stick (TL4): This is a simple stick with an electric tip (similar to an anti-shark stick). It is often used by thugs to slowly slip under shields and tap the target once the tip is past the shield (suffer -2 to Initiative, withhold victory dice and hope the damage does not exceed the shield's impact threshold). Once the tip contacts a surface, a charge is released (damage 6, ignore energy shields but not other armor). Cost: 15 firebirds.

Artifact Melee Weapons

Wireblade (TL8): A monomolecular blade, the height of Second Republic weapon technology. A wireblade can slice through even ceramsteel, and is popular among the very few space marine boarding parties who can afford to have one. When activated, the monofilament blade slides out of the handle and is surrounded by a corona of faint light (the only way to see the blade with the naked eye). Wireblades can be deadly to their users if they get careless, for the blades will cut through flesh with no hindrance, as if slicing through air. A fusion cell powers the light and lasts for 30 turns. If the cell runs dry with the blade extended, things could get tricky — there is no easy way to see the blade, and people may walk into it accidentally. Cost: 10,000+ firebirds.

Flux Sword (TL8): An energy sword. Flux swords — like most Second Republic energy tech — were developed from stolen Vautech. At the flick of a switch, a sword-shaped force field is created which instantly fills with plasma. Any-

thing which comes into contact with this blade-shaped field can get severely damaged, similar to being hit by a blaster. Like blasters, Flux Swords can leak through energy shields. Roll damage normally, but those dice which roll 1 or 2 ignore shields. These swords are powered by a fusion cell, which lasts for 30 turns. Flux Swords are rarely made today; the tech know-how is arcane. Cost: 15,000+ firebirds.

Mist Sword (TL8): A Flux Sword which is psychically attuned to the wielder. The wielder must have some Psi (at least one level). This attunement process is a sustained action whereby 20 victory points on successive Psi + Focus rolls must be collected. Once these points have been achieved, the Mist Sword is considered "bonded" to the character — she can use psychic powers on it easier. It is not alive and has no mind to be read, but FarHand powers costs one less Wyrd to use at range with the sword, and duration extension costs one less.

Bonded Mist Swords can become channels for psychic energy: The attuned wielder can spend Wyrd points to increase his goal rolls or his damage dice (one Wyrd point per +1 goal or +1 damage dice). The maximum amount of Wyrd which may be spent to channel energy is equal to the character's Psi rating.

These are among the rarest of Second Republic artifacts. Only a few were developed by a coven of psychics before the Fall, and none are known to have been made since then. Cost: 30,000+ firebirds.

Thrown Weapons

Knife: Throwing knives are not like normal kitchen implements; they are usually specially balanced to fly through the air and to hit a target with the blade rather than the pommel. They can also act as small knives if a melee is required. Cost: 2 firebirds.

Star: A small disk with serrated edges designed to be thrown quickly at targets. This can include any variety of shuriken ("throwing stars"). Cost: 2 firebirds each.

Dart: A pointed needle with small feathers or wings (like an arrow) designed for accuracy in throwing. These are not the common variety darts found in bars, but are larger and more deadly versions of the same. A favorite of assassins when the point is dipped in poison. Cost: 2 firebirds each.

Bows

Bows are a standard weapon among the poor and low-tech denizens of the Known Worlds, used for hunting or target practice at local carnivals and tourneys.

Bow damage is 1d for every 15 lbs. of pull. For example, a 60 lb. pull bow will deliver four dice of damage. Additionally, certain types of arrowheads may modify the damage or goal roll.

Hunting Bow: A 60 lb. pull bow designed to be drawn

Drawing a Bow

The required Strength to draw a bow (or recock a crossbow) is 1 Strength level per 15 lbs. of pull.

Strength	Pull
1	15
2	30
3	45
4	60
5	75
6	90
7	105
8	120
9	135
10	150

If a character does not have the required Strength to fire a particular bow (crossbows excluded), he will suffer a penalty to his goal roll: Subtract one for every level of Strength required above the character's own. For instance, someone with Strength 3 could draw a bow of 45 lb. pull or less with no penalty. But that same person trying to draw a 90 lb. bow would suffer a -3 penalty.

and fired quickly (as the deer bolts from the woods or the bird takes flight). It is smaller than other bows since it must be carried through sometimes thick underbrush. The rarer recurve bows have the same traits as a hunting bow; they are designed to be fired from horseback. Cost: 5 firebirds.

Long Bow (Military Bow): A 90 lb. pull bow designed for warfare, to fling arrows over long distances — usually over battlements or onto armies across the field. It is as tall or taller than most people. This is based off the English longbow but could just as easily be a Japanese bow. Cost: 10 firebirds.

Target Bow: A 45 lb. pull bow designed for target shooting at tourneys or carnivals rather than for killing. It is larger than a hunting bow but not as large as a long bow. Cost: 7 firebirds.

Arrows: Arrowheads come in many different varieties (see below), but the shafts are usually pretty similar for most bows, although some are longer and shorter and some have real feathers while others have plastic feathers. Cost: 1/4 bird (1 wing) each.

Arrowheads

There are a variety of special arrowheads designed for special jobs. Here is a sampling:

• **Jags:** Sharp heads with jagged edges. They deliver no extra damage when entering a target, but will deliver one die of damage (ignore armor) when removed from the wound, as its jagged hooks catch in the flesh. Minor sur-

gery is required to remove the head without causing damage (roll Dexterity + Physick). Cost: +1 firebird.

- **Streamers:** Arrowheads streamlined to fly faster and more accurately. Add one to the goal roll, but subtract one die from the damage. Cost: +1 firebird.

- **Boomers (TL5):** Truly nasty arrowheads that explode upon *entering* the target. They are "smart," designed to explode only after the head has pierced armor (or energy shields) and entered flesh. In other words, if the arrow inflicted as least one wound point on the target, roll an extra three dice of damage and ignore armor (including shields). However, subtract two from the goal roll due to the bulkiness of this arrowhead. Cost: +5 firebirds.

Crossbows

Crossbows are less common among the peasantry than traditional bows, but they are found among low-tech militia and noble guards.

Assuming the character has enough Strength to handle the pull of the crossbow, it takes two actions to recock and load the bow. He does not have to roll to recock a bow; he simply needs to spend time doing it. If he wants to fire and reload in the same turn, he must perform his full three actions doing so, and his shot will suffer from the multiple action penalty (-6). If the character does not have the required Strength to draw the bow, it takes an entire turn to reload the bow — unless the bow has a crank or he has a tool to aid him.

Hand Crossbow: A small, hand-held 45 lb. pull bow. Some models may be strapped to the wrist and fired with a flick of the wrist (just don't scratch your nose the wrong way). The bolts are smaller than usual and so must be specially manufactured. Cost: 7 firebirds for the bow, three 1/4 birds (3 wings) per bolt.

Medium Crossbow: A 90 lb. pull bow which is the standard for most low-tech but important guardsmen. Cost: 10 firebirds.

Heavy Crossbow: A 120 lb. pull used for warfare. This monster can pound through shields, but usually takes longer to reload than lighter bows. Cost: 15 firebirds.

Bolts: Standard size for most crossbows. Cost: 1/2 bird (1 crest) per bolt.

Slug Guns

Bullet-firing guns are not exactly rare in the Known Worlds, but they are outlawed among the peasantry. Thus, the majority of the Known Worlds population is forbidden to handle a gun, leaving the sport up to freemen and nobles. And a sport it is, for the nobles demand that their guns be elegant and a nice accessory to their outfits. The slug guns of the Empire are designed for looks and functionality. Noble slug guns tend to resemble Renaissance dueling pistols but act like advanced twentieth century firearms. While many guns are still factory manufactured, nobles insist that theirs be handmade by master craftsmen. This takes longer, of course, but usually creates a superior gun. The profession of weaponsmith to royalty is an important and lucrative one.

There are two different types of pistols listed below: revolvers and autofeed guns. A revolver holds its ammunition in a rotating cylinder; each pull of the trigger cocks the hammer and fires a bullet. Another pull fires again by recocking and rotating the cylinder where the next bullet is in line with the hammer; the gun can also be manually recocked by pulling down the hammer with the thumb. Bullets are loaded into the cylinder one by one or with a speedloader (a cylinderlike device which itself must be loaded one by one but which can be carried preloaded). Autofeed guns carry ammunition in spring-loaded clips or magazines. When the gun fires, another bullet is automatically fed into the chamber for the next shot (manually engaging the slide will also load a bullet into the chamber). Autofeed guns can jam — a bullet can get caught between the clip and the chamber. Until the jam is cleared, the gun will not fire (clearing a jam takes one action). Revolvers do not jam.

High-tech plastic models are available for most guns which can evade low-tech detection devices (TL 5 devices and below only detect for metal), but add 25 firebirds to the cost.

Derringer: A palm-sized gun designed to be hidden in a boot or other concealed but easy to reach spot. This gun can be either a revolver (2 shots) or autofeed (5 shots). Cost: 50 firebirds.

Light Revolver: These small pistols are popular as civilian sidearms. One model is the Mitchau .32 Protector, manufactured by the Mitchau family under the patronage of House Hazat. Cost: 100 firebirds.

Light Autofeed: Equivalent of a twentieth century .32 automatic or a Walther PPK. The most well-known in the Empire is the Mitchau .32 Rumbler. Cost: 150 firebirds.

Medium Revolver: Much like a twentieth century .38 special. The Mitchau .40 Thunderer is popular. Cost: 200 firebirds.

Medium Autofeed: Think of a 9mm Browning or similar twentieth century pistol. The Known Worlds equivalent is the Mitchau .40 Ripper. Cost: 250 firebirds.

Heavy Revolver: Like the twentieth century .44 magnum, these heavy guns can bring down large animals. The most popular Known Worlds models is the Sumpter .47 Ulik (named after a vicious Malignatian mammal), manufactured by the Sumpter family under the patronage of House al-Malik. Cost: 250 firebirds.

Heavy Autofeed: Similar to a .455 Desert Eagle or other heavy twentieth century pistol, the Known Worlds equivalent is the Sumpter .47 Urthquake. Cost: 300 firebirds.

Imperial Rifle: Alexius' generals are trying to standard-

ize the Empire's weaponry. The standard armored trooper is given this cheap but well-manufactured assembly-line rifle. Nearly a dozen guilds and an equal number of Imperial armories are making these cheap, low-quality rifles. The rifles are now finding their way into the black markets of every planet where there is an Imperial military base. Cost: 200 firebirds.

Assault Rifle: Think of any number of twentieth century assault rifles, from an M-16 to an AK-47. There are many Known Worlds models, such as the Masseri 10mm Stomper or the Van Gelder Thracker (named after an astonishingly quick reptile from Vorox). All assault rifles are autofeed guns, and most of them are capable of autofire. Cost: 500 firebirds.

Sniper Rifle: These sleek and accurate rifles come in many varieties with many add-ons (sights, silencers) and some can break down to be carried in a suitcase for assembly at the sight of the intended kill. Most sniper rifles use bolt action (each shot must be chambered manually). The Radir family handcrafts the most sought after sniper rifles, under the patronage of House Decados. Cost: 700 firebirds.

Submachine Gun: A fully-automatic gun similar to twentieth century Uzis or Macs. The Jahnisak Muffler Gun is perhaps the most widely-used in the Known Worlds, although the Lank Stinger is better manufactured but more expensive. Cost: 350 firebirds.

Shotgun: Like twentieth century models, shotguns throw an arc of pellets or a single slug. Most Known Worlds models are pump loaded, but there are automatics and two-shot double barrels. Best known is the Dreskel Boomer, manufactured by Ariman Dreskel under exclusive contract to the Scravers. Cost: 300 firebirds.

Silencer: Attached to a slug gun, a silencer muffles at least some of the noise made by a shot. Silencers vary just as much as any other technological artifact in the Known Worlds; some completely deaden the noise and make a gun more accurate, while others barely do anything and burn out after only a few uses. An average silencer requires anyone not near the shot (in the same room or within 20 meters) to make a Perception + Shoot roll to hear the gunshot and know what it is. These are illegal on most planets. Cost: 5 firebirds.

Ammunition

There are a variety of slug calibers and types of slugs, from slappers (riot ammo) to needlers (armor-piercing) to blast capsules (explosive).

Slappers (TL5): Meant for use against rioting crowds, slappers knock people down but don't damage them as much as most slugs. The slug is made of a viscous plastic which balloons out as it flies through the air, impacting the target on a wider area but with little penetration. The target feels

like he's just been walloped by a good Vorox left-hook. Do not add victory dice to slapper slugs. A target's armor dice only generate armor points on rolls of 1, 2 or 3. Cost: +3 firebirds each.

Needler (TL5): An armor-piercing bullet. When rolling damage, those dice which roll 1 ignore armor (except energy shields). Cost: +3 firebirds each.

Sunder Slugs (TL6): Ceramsteel fragments in a gel medium, encased in steel. Add one die of damage and halve the target's armor defense dice (except energy shields). Cost: +3 firebirds each.

Vorox Claws (TL5): An expanding bullet which opens into a five-claw blossom upon impact. Increase damage by two dice. Cost: +2 firebirds each.

Blast Capsules (TL6): Blast capsules have a special charge of stored plasma which is released upon impact. Add three to the damage. As with a blaster, these capsules can leak through energy shields, although not as effectively (only on damage rolls of 1). These cannot be made in calibers below .40. Cost: +6 firebirds each.

Costs: Standard ammunition costs depend upon the availability of the ammo and caliber (size). The cost of clips or magazines to hold the ammo is usually 1/10th the cost of the gun.

Caliber	Cost
Light (.32 caliber)	1 wing/slug (5 per firebird)
Medium (.40 caliber)	1 crest/slug (3 per firebird)
Heavy (.47 caliber)	1 firebird/slug
Assault Rifle (10mm)	2 firebirds/slug
Rifle (13mm)	3 firebirds/slug
Submachinegun (.40)	1 crest/slug (3 per firebird)
Shotgun (10 gage)	1 crest/slug (2 per firebird)

Energy Guns

Most energy guns came from Vautech filtered through Second Republic manufacturers. At the height of the Second Republic, some of these weapons were even improved beyond the Vau's own level of design, but that was a long time ago. Most of these are still manufactured, but they are very expensive, well out of the range of most buyers.

Fusion cells are required for most of these guns (except for Flameguns and Rocketeers).

Palm Laser (TL6): A derringer-sized laser, used for self-defense when it is not possible to carry a larger gun. The Martech Midget is the most popular model, manufactured by Martech, a sub-guild of the Engineers. Like all lasers, this gun suffers a -2 penalty to its damage dice when shooting through thick fog or smoke, or anything which could scatter or defuse the coherent beam. Cost: 200 firebirds.

Laser Pistol (TL6): About the size of a medium autofeed slug gun, the Martech Gold (so called because it emits a yellow beam) is the standard laser handgun of the Known Worlds. Lasers suffer a -2 penalty to their damage dice when shooting through thick fog or smoke, or anything which could scatter or defuse the coherent beam. Cost: 300 firebirds.

Laser Rifle (TL6): The Martech Indigo is the most popular laser rifle model, about the size of a sniper rifle. Lasers suffer a -2 penalty to their damage dice when shooting through thick fog or smoke, or anything which could scatter or defuse the coherent beam. Cost: 500 firebirds.

Assault Laser (TL6): The Varsten Blacklight carbine competes with the Martech Red for popularity. The Varsten rifles are being manufactured by House Decados, and the Martech guild is not happy about this, especially since certain royal troops seem to prefer Varsten lasers. Lasers suffer a -2 penalty to their damage dice when shooting through thick fog or smoke, or anything which could scatter or defuse the coherent beam. Cost: 700 firebirds.

Blaster Pistol (TL7): These marvels of technology generate plasma from fusion cells using a mysterious transference chamber stolen from Vau weaponry. Only a few people in the Known Worlds understand these things, and they are usually master weaponsmiths for the guilds, revealing their secrets only to loyal apprentices after years of study.

When the trigger is engaged, a force field forms about the plasma and is violently ejected down the barrel. It begins exploding once it exits the barrel, leaking through the field. Once it hits a physical object (the target, hopefully), the field disintegrates, loosing the full force of the plasma.

Blasters can leak through energy shields. Roll damage normally, but those dice which roll 1 or 2 ignore shields. However, these guns are dangerous; they have been known to blow up when treated badly.

The only reliable blaster pistol that nobles trust is the Alembic, manufactured by the Supreme Order of Engineers under various contracts. Cost: 700 firebirds.

Blaster Rifle (TL7): A more dangerous version of the above, but the best-known model is the Crucible. Blasters can leak through energy shields. Roll damage normally, but those dice which roll 1 or 2 ignore shields. Cost: 1000 firebirds.

Blaster Shotgun (TL7): An awesomely deadly weapon, firing a scattering discharge of plasma balls with one pull of the trigger. The Volcano is the model feared by anyone with an ounce of sense. Blasters can leak through energy shields. Roll damage normally, but those dice which roll 1 or 2 ignore shields. Cost: 1200 firebirds.

Screecher (TL6): A sonic gun, emitting a concussive force and a high-pitched squeal which damages hearing. Halve the damage for targets with hearing protection (characters with their hands over their ears get this benefit). Various models are known. Cost: 300 firebirds.

Flamegun (TL5): A popular weapon among Avestites, flameguns hold canisters of Ka-plant oil (an alien plant na-

tive to Pyre). With the pull of a trigger, this highly combustible oil is sprayed past a spark at the tip of the barrel, igniting into a flume of burning and smoking oil. The Ka oil is kept cool by refrigerants in the canisters powered by fusion cells (considered to last for 10 shots, until the canister is empty), but after even two firings, the oil heats up enough to send billows of black and awful smelling smoke pluming out of the barrel. It is this smell which often reveals the impending presence of the Inquisition.

Flameguns can deliver heat damage which ignores all armor. Roll damage normally, but those dice which roll 1 ignore armor. The second amount listed on the weapon chart in Chapter Six is the continuous damage due to the burning Ka plant oil sprayed over the target. Roll this damage (do not add victory dice) each turn after the first. If no damage is rolled in any turn, the flames go out.

Cost: 150 firebirds for the gun, 5 firebirds per canister (which is refillable and rechargeable for 2 firebirds).

Stunner (TL6): Stunners emit a concussive force field which causes nervous system shock, effectively stunning a target or knocking her unconscious. If a target takes ANY damage from a Stunner, she must roll Endurance + Vigor. If successful, there is no further effect, but if the roll fails, she is stunned for that turn (losing any actions not taken) and the next. If she fumbles the roll, she falls unconscious. If the damage taken is greater than the character's Endurance, she rolls as above, but failure means she is knocked unconscious.

Stunner damage is healed differently than other damage; after one span, stunner damage is healed entirely (mark stunner damage with an "S" rather an a checkmark on the Vitality levels). However, it is system shock damage, and is cumulative with other damage taken: If a character who has suffered stunner damage takes other damage which takes her below zero Vitality, she dies.

These were Second Republic riot police weapons. Due to the constant lawsuits brought against police by stunner victims, it became illegal to manufacture stunners with too much power. It is rumored that the Engineers have developed a more powerful version which can easily render a target unconscious. The most popular regular stunner is the Arbogast Sleeper. Cost: 300 firebirds.

Neural Disrupter (TL8): These small palm guns fire a nearly invisible and slightly erratic stream of energy which causes destruction to nerve cells and brain matter. If damage exceeds Endurance (or Psi, whichever is higher), the target is unconscious. If damage exceeds Vitality, the target is dead. Armor does not protect against this damage (although a Psi Cloak does).

Psychics may defend against neural disrupter attacks. To deflect the energy stream, roll Psi + Stoic Mind contested against the attacker's successes.

The Neural Disrupter had only just begun production

as a prototype when the Fall of the Second Republic came to pass. Very few of these weapons are known to exist. Cost: 3000

Heavy Weapons

Characters are more likely to encounter (and want) heavy weapons than they will most of the other tools of warcraft. This category includes weapons larger than the standard rifle but which can be carried into battle by one person. Most of these weapons utilize larger power cells, bigger magazines or different kinds of ammunition, and many require a crew to operate them effectively. The most primitive are slug throwers which have a higher rate of fire than do their smaller brethren. The most sophisticated are giant blaster cannons, web missiles and high-powered wave guns.

Light Machinegun (TL5): Manufactured by the Jahnisak weaponsmiths, this is one of the more common support weapons currently available, having found users on all sides of the Emperor Wars. Small and not especially effective, it does continue the Jahnisak reputation for ruggedness and reliability. Cost: 750 firebirds.

Grenade Launcher (TL5): This relatively cheap weapon is often used for squad support. A little bigger than a shotgun, it fires specially designed grenades (also made by the Dreskel family and costing somewhat more than a standard grenade). While extremely accurate at short range, it loses something the farther away the target is. Cost: 500 firebirds, 65 per grenade.

Rocketeer (TL5): A hand-held rocket launcher a little bit larger than a shotgun. The most famous model, the Nightstorm, is well-loved by the Muster, for it helped them win the Battle of Barga Gully on Sutek during the Emperor Wars, a decisive conflict. The standard load is a miniature but powerful grenade (radius of 3 meters) in a clip of five. Cost: 400 firebirds for the launcher, 25 per grenade.

Missile Launcher (TL4): Missiles fill a number of different roles in the **Fading Suns**, being used against land, sea and air vehicles; fortifications; spacecraft; and people. The standard missile launcher (a Dreskel bazooka) is a point and shoot weapon. It takes an entire turn to reload a missile launcher; soldiers usually have teams of two: one to load, one to fire. Technicians have developed a wide array of warheads for them as well, including high explosive charges, armor-piercing shapes, incendiary devices, non-lethal shockers, and energy blasts. Cost: 800 (standard missiles cost 100 each).

Explosives

The wide variety of explosives is countless, from kitchen-made pipe bombs to devastating planet bombs. Below is a favorite of player characters who to like to throw things at enemies.

Grenades (TL4+): These come in all sizes and shapes, but their common feature is that they damage people and things in a wide area from where they explode. Each grenade is rated for the number of meters its radius encompasses and the damage it delivers at ground zero. The standard radius for a hand grenade is five meters, but this can increase with tech levels above 4. Standard damage is 12 dice (this can also increase at higher tech levels). A character tossing a grenade does not get to add his victory points to the damage — the grenade does all the work; all the character has to do is get it to its destination. However, anyone standing in the radius will suffer the damage rolled (after subtracting armor). One point is subtracted from the grenade's damage for each meter away from its point of explosion.

For example, Cardanzo is standing in a room when someone tosses a grenade in and shuts the door. The grenade lands two meters from Cardanzo and explodes. The grenade damage is rolled: seven damage points. Two points are subtracted for distance (two meters from the grenade), so Cardanzo takes five points of damage.

Grenades usually have timers set to count once the pin has been pulled or the button activated. The standard time is a little less than three seconds; a grenade thrown at the start of a turn will go off at the end of that turn. If the grenade was thrown at the end of a turn, it might go off in the middle of the next turn

Cost: 50 firebirds each.

Wire Grenade (TL4): A grenade that unspools a monofilament wire in all directions. The damage is the same as a regular grenade (12d), but the armor defense dice of anyone in the radius is halved. Radius is 3 meters. Cost: 80 firebirds

Blast Pellet (TL6): A mini plasma pellet which explodes upon impact. Blast pellets come in various sizes, from ball-bearing sized (3 dice damage) to small rubber ball sized (6 dice damage). The explosion will affect anyone in a one meter radius around its point of impact. As with most plasma weapons, blast pellets can leak through energy shields (on a damage dice roll of 1 or 2). Cost: 20-30 firebirds each (depending on size).

Plasma Grenade (TL6): A plasma grenade, larger than a blast pellet. These devastating weapons do 18 dice of damage, which can leak through energy shields (on a damage dice roll of 1 or 2). Radius is 6 meters. Cost: 100 firebirds.

Demolition Rig (TL4+): While any fool with a pipe bomb can blow something up, true experts prefer more exact equipment, the kind of stuff they can measure out to do just what they want it to — no more, no less. The demolition rig can come with any of a variety of explosives, including nitroglycerin, plastique or Ukar demo cream. It also usually features a number of different detonators, including fuses, timers and remote detonators.

Characters with a demo rig generally have about 100 damage dice worth of explosives as well as 20 detonators. The rig allows them to place and shape charges, focusing the damage in a specific direction if they make a Tech + Demolition roll. This means the explosives will only do half their damage in the direction the demo expert does not want it to go. Cost: 200 firebirds.

Armor

Everyone needs a little protection from time to time, especially when traveling off-world. Naturally, most of the protective gear available comes in the form of heavily padded clothing or leathers enhanced with metals and plastics.

See the Armor Chart in Chapter Six: Combat for the traits of the armors listed below. The Tech Level is the lowest at which the armor is manufactured; higher tech level versions may be made of lighter materials.

An armor's defense value is rated as a number of six-sided dice (results of 1, 2, 3 or 4 = one armor point). Metal armors subtract one die from their defense against energy weapons.

Characters can sometimes wear two types of armor. Padded clothing, heavy clothing, leather, synthsilk and polymer knits can be combined. Add their protection dice together and subtract -2 from Dexterity and Vigor (in addition to existing penalties). For example, Cardanzo is wearing a synthsilk jumpsuit under a suit of stolen leather Decados guard armor. The total protection is 8d (the synthsilk's 4d plus the leather's 4d), but he suffers a -2 penalty to both his Dexterity and Vigor.

Such a combination of clothing is not very comfortable, as it is usually tight and hot. Gamemasters may want to levy additional Vigor penalties if a character spends too much time under two outfits to reflect heat fatigue or rashes.

Metal armors assume an underlayer of leather or cloth, and thus cannot be worn over or under an additional layer of armor. Stiffsynth is generally too tight to be worn over another layer, and it expands too much to be worn under another layer.

Padded Clothing: Clothing two layers thick — a jacket or thick sweatshirt. Not usually intended to be used as armor, it will nonetheless prevent some damage. This is the most protection a serf can be expected to wear. Padded clothing can be worn with an energy shield. Cost: A few talons at most.

Heavy Clothing: A heavier and stiffer fabric than padded clothing, sometimes designed as fashionable armor where thick leathers or metals would be too "barbaric." This can include light leather, but not heavy or thick leather. High-fashion designs can cost much more than a few wings, depending on who is tailoring the outfit. Heavy clothing can

be worn with an energy shield. Cost: Negligible to quite a few firebirds for fashionable clothing.

Spacesuit: A standard spacesuit is designed to resist common tears but does not stand up well against swords or gunshots. It is airtight when completely assembled (gloves, boots, helmet). Cost: 100 firebirds.

Leather Jerkin: Popular among many as an elegant armor, leather is often worn when heavier armors would be too "brutish." In fact, Brute-hide leather is a fine, supple material that is heavy enough to work well as armor. Most guards wear leather in addition to whatever other armor they might have. Cost: 5 firebirds.

Studded Leather: Studded leather is a simple, inexpensive alternative to heavier metal armors. It adds a degree of extra protection to a leather jerkin without too much added discomfort. However, as with most metal armors, the defense dice suffer -1d against energy weapons. Some of the more expensive forms of studded leather use hard plastic instead of metal. Where plastics are used, there are no penalties against energy weapons. Many factions of the Church use studded leather jerkins as the armor of choice for their journeymen. Cost: 8 firebirds for metal, 15 firebirds for plastic.

Scale Mail: Overlapping metal scales in a variety of shapes and sizes bolted to a leather jerkin. Common among low-tech militias but disfavored by those who can afford better. Cost: 13 firebirds for metal, 20 for plastic.

Chain Mail: Woven layers of metal links. Higher tech versions are known using lightweight but strong plastics (no Dex penalty). Common among low-tech but well-equipped militias. Cost: 20 firebirds for metal, 50 firebirds for plastic.

Half Plate (metal): Conquistador-style chest plate with light vambraces and greaves. Usually worn only by commanding officers, but also the armor of choice for Brother Battle priests. Often decorated or enameled with fanciful designs or depictions of animals. Plastic versions are available at Tech Level 5 and above. Cost: 30 firebirds for metal, 60 firebirds for plastic.

Plate: Medieval style, bulky metal armor. Used by well-equipped troops on many worlds when energy shields are unaffordable or unavailable. Plate composed of moderately flexible lightweight plastics (TL5 and above) is rarer than metal plate, and thus used mainly by commanding officers. Cost: 40 firebirds for metal, 80 firebirds for plastic.

Synthsilk: One of the finest inconspicuous armors, synthsilk is comfortable and lightweight. Used for construction and utility worker uniforms during the Second Republic, it comes in a variety of colors, but is quite expensive. Most of the synthsilk made today is manufactured using precariously maintained Second Republic textile mills. Synthsilk was first designed and used in the Diaspora era.

Later improvements allowed for thinner, lighter materials until, by the time of the Second Republic, the fabric was as light as cotton and just as comfortable to wear. Synthsilk can be worn with an energy shield. Cost: 300 firebirds.

Stiffsynth: Heavy, leatherlike material, stiffsynth even looks like leather until it is struck. Upon impact, stiffsynth hardens temporarily into an inflexible shell, and then softens a second later.

Stiffsynth was originally used as protective gear by Second Republic athletes during vigorous sporting events. Stiffsynth suits are passed down from generation to generation. The secret of their manufacture has been lost (except perhaps among a few secret guilds). Most existing suits still bear the insignias of various sporting teams. It is stretchable and can fit just about anyone of the same relative height it was originally manufactured for. Cost: 500 firebirds.

Polymer Knit: A plastic and cloth weave highly resistant to bullets. Very rare — the tech know-how to make polymer knit (such as Kevlar) was lost after the Fall, since it was rarely made during the later Second Republic time of energy shields and guns. Polymer Knit can be worn with an energy shield. Cost: 200 firebirds.

Ceramsteel: This heavy duty, thick-formed armor is designed to withstand amazing impacts. It is composed of the high-tech ceramics and metal combination used to make starship hulls. Most suits are lacquered or painted by the owner to represent their house, sect or guild affiliation.

Unless powered by a cell pack, this armor is simply too heavy to lift without a substantial penalty to mobility. Once powered, however, the armor seems remarkably light. Cost: 1000 firebirds.

Adept Robes (Cassock Superior): The legendary powered armor of the Brother Battle order. It is an enhanced ceramsteel suit that boosts its wearer's abilities and provides an array of extras: 30 minutes of life support, built in range-finders, 10x binoculars, radio sending and receiving, and protection from skin-contact poisons and dangerous levels of radiation. Some models even provide hoverpacks, leg servos for faster running and incredible leaps, built in weapons (flamers) and more. These suits cannot be bought with firebirds; they must be earned by Brother Battle monks.

Frictionless Gel (TL7): This amazing substance was first created during the Second Republic for use as a frictionless oil in advanced engines. However, someone early on realized its potential as a toy, and began marketing it as a "slimy fun gel for slick, slippery play." It is applied to a surface (such as a piston or gear or human skin); after an hour of drying, its dried surface becomes frictionless. Obviously, this can avoid a lot of kinetic damage, but if misapplied, can lead to pratfalls. Gamemasters and players are encouraged to get creative with the possibilities. The effects only last for a day before the substance dries out completely.

Frictionless gel can be smeared over any type of armor; modifiers are cumulative. Cost: 500 for enough to cover an average sized human.

Psi Cloak (TL8): A Psi Cloak defends against mental powers and neural disrupters. It isn't so much a physical cloak as an energy aura around the wearer. The aura is not visible to the naked eye, but will is revealed in the ultraviolet or infrared spectrum (as a shimmering haze around the wearer). Most occult perception powers (Subtle Sight, Second Sight, etc.) will also perceive the cloak.

Physically, the cloak is like a dueling shield core, and can be concealed in a casing, such as a belt buckle, brooch or wristwatch. It requires a fusion cell and will take 10 hits (just like a shield) before shutting down. Some rarer models are known which can take more hits or defend with more dice. These are no longer manufactured and are highly sought by everyone. Cost: 3,000

Shields

Buckler: Bucklers are small shields, held in the off-hand and used to parry or block hand to hand or melee blows. The Tech Level of the buckler determines what materials it can be manufactured from: TL 1 (wood and leather), TL 2 (metal), TL 4 (plastic), TL 5+ (lightweight plastics). Cost: 7 firebirds (12 for plastic).

Large Shield: A larger and usually heavier version of a buckler. They come in many shapes: round, kite, square, etc. The Tech Level determines the manufacture (see Buckler). Cost: 15 firebirds (20 for plastic).

Energy Shields

Energy shields are not uncommon in the Known Worlds. Anyone involved in dangerous work has one. Dangerous work can be anything from adventuring into Unknown Space, spying on enemy installations, or even being a diplomat to a rival house or sect.

Although churned out by the millions during the Second Republic, the theories used to develop energy shields are now lost, but the maintenance of the technology is fairly common, since they are found all around among nobles, Church priests, guildsmembers and military forces. Peasants and yeoman would love to have them, but they're not *that* common.

Shields are impact and energy activated, meaning that they automatically turn on when their field (usually an inch around the body) is compromised by a kinetic or energetic force of a certain magnitude. The magnitude threshold is determined by the shield.

A shield is rated by the minimum amount of damage it takes to activate it and the maximum amount it will block. In other words, attacks with damage below the minimum amount of damage rating (the impact threshold) will not

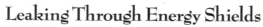

Leaking Through Energy Shields

Some weapons are more effective against energy shields than others. Flux swords, blasters and flameguns can deliver damage which will "leak" through an activated energy shield. Each of these weapons leaks on varying d6 roll results: blasters and flux swords leak on rolls of 1 or 2; flameguns on rolls of 1. When rolling damage dice, each die that rolls these numbers ignores energy shields — the damage "leaks" through the shield. Dice which roll above the numbers, but are still successful, deliver normal damage.

For example, Cardanzo fires his blaster pistol at a foe with a standard energy shield. Assuming he barely hits and gets no victory dice, he has seven damage dice (the base blaster pistol damage). He rolls: 3, 2, 6, 4, 4, 1, 2. This is a total of 6 points of damage. However, before this is applied against his foe, Cardanzo's player makes a note that three of those dice rolled 2 or below — 3 points which ignore energy shields. Now, he applies his total 6 points of damage, but this activates his foe's shield. Normally, the foe would take no damage at all, but in this case he takes the 3 points which leak through.

Cardanzo fires again and gets five victory dice. He rolls his 12 dice of damage: 3, 2, 4, 6, 2, 2, 4, 1, 3, 3, 1, 4 — 11 points of damage, five of which "leak" through shields. This damage is enough to activate and exceed his foe's shield by 1 point. Normally, the foe would take just this 1 point of damage. However, 5 points also leak through, and so the thug takes 6 points of damage.

activate the shield, but any attack with damage over the minimum will activate the shield. Attacks with damage over the maximum rating will inflict however much damage exceeds that rating.

Example: Erian Li Halan has a 5/10 shield. Any attacks doing 5 or more points of damage will activate the shield, which will block damage from 5 points up to 10; damage over 10 will be inflicted on Erian. So, Erian will take damage from attacks doing 1, 2, 3, 4 or 11, 12+ points of damage.

Because of the preponderance of shields (designed to defend against firearms and energy weapons), a dueling culture has arisen, where swords are the main method of attack. The skill in fighting then is to nick an opponent light enough not to activate his shield, but strong enough and often enough to harm or kill him.

Shield cores are small devices which can be placed in many different receptacles (which must be designed for this purpose). Nobles prefer gilded brooches or amulets, while soldiers prefer belt buckles. Cores are bulky and obvious to all who know what to look for, although some models (dueling shields) are concealable in a small piece of jewelry or wrist watch.

Shields have fusion cells which require occasional recharging. Since they are only activated when field integrity is breached, they are rated by number of hits they can take. Each time a shield blocks damage, mark it; when it takes more hits than it has, its battery is dead and the field is shut down.

The drawback to a shield is that the field only maintains integrity within an inch or so of the body. Thick clothing or armor may destroy that integrity, causing the field to shut down. These things were designed by Second Republicans for sport and play, to accompany fashionable clothing; the know-how to adjust the field range has been lost. Assault and battle shields are exceptions.

Shields are designed to activate for direct impacts in a small area — a bullet, sword point or even an axe blade, for instance. The force field only hardens at the point(s) of impact. When confronted with a broad-area impact (or energy dispersal), the shield may burn out. The player should roll 13 or less on one d20 (or 1, 2, 3 or 4 on a d6). If the roll succeeds, the shield works (and will continue to work) as normal. If it fails, the shield will work for this impact only and then burn out for one turn per point blocked. If the roll is a critical failure, the shield burns out immediately (battery dead) and will not even block this impact.

For example, Erian, pursued by thugs, jumps off a tall building, confident that her shield will protect her (such leaps were a common sport during the Second Republic, when medical tech was superb). When she hits the ground, she takes 8 points of damage. The shield perceives a broad area impact, one which it was not designed to function against. It marshals all its resources into a broad-area force field. Erian's player rolls a 14 (she needed 13 or less). The shield works, blocking the damage, but burns out for 8 turns (one for each point of damage absorbed).

Also, when confronted with multiple small impacts from many directions ("et tu, Brute?"), the shield may fail. In this case, it is not the impact but the number of impact points (attacks) which matter: If the number of attacks from different directions exceeds the minimum rating, roll for shield failure as above. This applies to autofire bursts of six rounds or more, which sorely test a shield's ability to compensate.

Energy shields are very expensive. A standard shield costs 500 firebirds, while a dueling shield costs anywhere from 700 to 1000 (depending on just how concealable it is). Assault shields are minimum 3000 firebirds and battle shields are almost never found below 5000 firebirds.

Shield Damper: It makes sense that someone would eventually figure out the best way to disable an energy shield. The most common method is a shield damper, a device which

sets up a field disturbance on the same vibrational frequency as most energy shields. Since shields were developed from stolen Vautech, few people really understand why and how they work. The frequency is normally invisible to most current tech devices designed to measure energy fields.

When activated, the damper will shut down all energy shields in its area of affect. Different models have different areas (minimum 10 meters, maximum 50 meters). However, the larger the area, the more energy used. Generally, a damper will work for one span, but less if it covers a larger area. After the time is up, it burns out, and exchanging batteries will not make it work again; only a repair session with high-tech tools will do so.

Shield dampers are extremely rare and quite illegal — no noble likes to think they can be assassinated by any common thug with a shield damper. Nonetheless, they are sought out by nobles to use against their rivals. Using a damper on a starship can cause damage to the stardrives or even jumpdrives — penalties for doing so usually involve being tossed from an airlock.

Costs vary, but the average is no less than 1000 firebirds.

Medical Gear

Medical supplies are a necessity for most adventurers. The availability of quality medicine is good for those with money, as there are apothecaries on all of the Known Worlds. But the better the medical care, the rarer and more expensive it is.

Physick's Kit (TL2): This is a collection of standard low-tech first aid supplies: bandages, alcohol, herb poultices to staunch bleeding, ointment to relieve pain, animal gut or cloth thread for stitching wounds. It allows for minimal first aid and some minor surgery and is found among healers to the poor on most of the Known Worlds. Sometimes, such bags can be complemented with higher tech equipment, if the bearer is lucky enough to afford, barter or steal it. Cost: 10.

MedPac (TL3): A standardized first aid MedicalPackage, found among military troops, in starship lockers, and carried by most medics. The white plastic box contains sterilized gauze, alcohol, medical tape and a burn ointment designed to numb pain rather than to actually heal the damage caused by a burn. Generally, this is a better quality and more compact version of a Physick's Kit. Add 50 firebirds to the cost and this kit will include an Elixir injector with five doses (see below). Cost: 20.

Expedition MedPac (TL5): These stainless steel, airtight canisters contain enough cotton gauze and tape to keep a small army well bandaged. They also contain antiseptics, burn ointments and real medicines. Among the special equipment is a collection of anti-venoms for virtually every form of poisonous animal venom found on the planet of manu-

Energy

The Second Republic standardized its power needs for most consumer devices into the fusion cel. These rechargeable batteries come in various sizes, depending on their intended use, but they can all be recharged at a standard fusion power station. The Merchant League has kept some of the old fusion stations running, and there is one to be found on nearly every agora on every planet in the Known Worlds. However, prices for its use vary, depending largely on the demand and how well-maintained the station is. Some stations are gleaming, spotless paeans to Second Republic durability, while others are still running only on spit and gum, and occasional explosions are not unknown.

Fusion Cel (TL6): This was the standard battery used by most Second Republic tech, and is still used in Alexius' time. They come in all shapes and sizes, from canisters for blaster pistols to tiny discs for video watchbands. They can be recharged at any fusion charging station, which usually have adapters for any size cel. Cost: 10 firebirds each (average 3 firebirds to recharge a cel).

facture (the kits can be purchased for particular worlds) and five water purification tablets. The tablets are designed to treat as much as 50 gallons of water each, and are essential for off-world travelers. Also included in the kit is a 100-count supply of antihistamine tablets, more than enough to allow most people time to adjust to new environments.

At one time, the Expedition MedPac was considered essential for space travel. In addition to what is carried within the pack today, there were also immunization injections for virtually every planet. These days, the immunizations are far too expensive and far too unstable to add into the standard packages. Tech Level 5. Cost: 100.

Surgery Kit (TL5): This collection of surgery supplies includes pain killers in both pill and injection form (10 doses each), stainless steel surgical tools, a cauterizer laser (instantly staunches bleeding, 10 charges), a stitcher (automatically sews wounds, with eight pre-threaded needles for sutures), and three inflatable bone splints (small, medium, large). This collection also includes everything found in the MedPac.

These kits were once the standard for high-risk planetary exploration. But it is too high-tech to be common anymore. Cost: 200.

NanoTech MedPac (TL7): These high-tech MedPacs are a rarity and are normally only available to the highly influential. Some of the finest nano (miniaturized) robot technology available is used in the production of these medical miracle kits. If there is a medical crisis, this kit has the nanite

for the job. From major burns to blood infusions, from shattered bones to nerve-cell reparation, this is the finest medical assistance that money can buy. Even optical nerves can be rebuilt with a NanoTech MedPac. For instance, nanite Bone Weavers (miniature robots programmed to re-set fractured or broken bones by attaching themselves to the bones and aiding the body to regulate healing) are extremely delicate and complex to manufacture, but when used properly can reknit a broken bone in a matter of hours.

However, it does not come with an instruction book and can only safely be administered by a qualified surgeon (roll Tech + Physick). The label on the airtight briefcase clearly explains that NanoTech (the original Second Republic manufacturer) will not accept responsibility for deformity or injury caused by the improper use of the MedPac.

The healing time for wounds treated with a NanoTech MedPak is reduced to one quarter of the normal time. Once the wounds are healed, the nanites will eventually exit the body through the patient's waste. Surgeons often keep nanite patients under watch until all the nanites have been recovered, although reclaiming the robots in working condition once they've made their journey is rare.

NanoTech Corporation was once the very pinnacle of medical emergency technology manufacturers. The company is long gone now, as is the easy availability of their equipment. The al-Malik have continued to fund the manufacture of these kits today, but very few outside of a noble house can afford one. Many of the finest and most expensive surgeons have access to these kits, but the cost to their patients is exorbitant. Replacements for the items in the kit are expensive. Cost: 1000.

Elixir (TL7): Tissue regenerative serum. One standard dose (administered through an Elixir injector) is enough to heal 5d6 of Vitality points lost to wounds. Some batches are more potent than others, delivering more dice of healing, while other batches are worse, delivering less dice.

Elixir was the original Second Republic name for this popular tissue regenerative serum. No one is really sure how it works anymore, and those who do know keep the secret to themselves, making big money off its manufacture. Immensely popular among the elite, factories on many worlds churn gallons of Elixir out — some batches not as good as others. The desperate need of Elixir on the Kurgan and Symbiot fronts have bumped prices up recently. Cost: 25 for the injector, 10 per dose.

Drugs and Poison

The Known Worlds are full of assassins with poison-dripping knives, alien beasts with venomous fangs, soldiers with chemical bombs, or merchants dealing in illicit substances. Drugs and poisons come in many varieties; some samples are listed below.

As a general rule, poisons are contested with Endurance + Vigor rolls. Complementary Physick rolls may be helpful if the right materials (antitoxins, herbs, etc.) are available. Most poisons cause direct damage to the victim's Vitality. Some, however, affect motor skills (Dexterity or any skill paired to Dexterity, such as Fight) or muscle strength. Specially engineered poisons or some plants may affect Wits or Perception, while others may cause victims to enter rages (Inciting Passion) or to become listless and disinterested in activity (enhancing Calm and Introvert). The latter kind are often taken willingly as popular relaxation drugs.

Theurgy can intervene where medical science is unavailable: the Refinement of Essence rite will expel poisons, as will a critical success on a Laying On of Hands rite. The Amalthean rite, Restoration, will purge these substances with a simple success. See *Theurgy* in Chapter Five: Occult for more details.

The gamemaster should feel free to get creative with drugs and poisons.

Selchakah: Among House Decados' most popular — and equally contraband — exports is the Severan opiate poppy, which produces *selchakah*: an extremely addictive narcotic which is illegal outside Decados holdings. Users proclaim that the bliss and joy delivered by selchakah is unequaled in this world. The extremes addicts will go to obtain more of the drug are likewise unequaled — murder and high treason are not unknown tactics. It is rumored that the Decados intentionally addict nobles and high-ranking Church or League members to the drug, constrict their supply, and then dole out the desperately desired drug only in return for secrets. Cost: 3 – 7 firebirds per dose (at least at the start; the price inevitably rises with the user's demand).

Vorox Poison: The poison from a Vorox's claws is a slow-acting paralytic. Some have adapted it for use as blade venom or to coat darts with — or even as a food additive; this requires a Wits + Arts (Culinary) roll to hide the smell. If the coated weapon inflicts damage (or if the target ingests it), the target is poisoned and suffers a cumulative -1 penalty per turn on all physical actions; when a number of turns equal to the target's Vitality rating is reached, the target is unable to take any physical actions for the rest of the span. A coated weapon may only make one attack before the poison is dissipated enough to be inert. Cost: 20 firebirds per does (enough to coat a dirk).

Plox Blade Venom: An Ukari poison. This sticky, clear paste (made from ground *boca'ti* seeds and oils) causes paralysis when exposed to the blood. Whenever a blade coated with plox inflicts damage on a target (after armor or energy shields are considered), he must roll Endurance + Vigor for three successive turns to resist its effects. If any roll fails, the victim succumbs to mild paralysis, falls to the ground and is able to make only minute movements for the next 10

turns. After 10 turns have passed, the victim can move again, but he suffers a penalty of -4 to all actions for the rest of the span.

Plox requires either the skill Alchemy or Lore (poisons) to manufacture (in addition to raw boca'ti seeds, found only in certain subterranean tunnels on Kordeth and Aylon). One dose (enough to coat a dirk) cost 25 firebirds and will remain on the blade for three strikes (after which it has dissipated enough to be inert). The blade must then be cleaned with a strong solvent; otherwise, it may stick to its sheath (two actions to draw).

Grixi: A more deadly Ukari poison, Grixi is made from distilled solka blood (odd, albino apelike creatures from Kordeth) mixed with various Kordeth herbs. It is a greenish, slick paste that causes excessive bleeding in wounds. Whenever a blade coated with grixi inflicts damage on a target (after armor or energy shields are considered), it adds one to the damage and continues to inflict one point of blood loss damage every turn thereafter until the flow is staunched, or until five turns have passed (whichever comes first).

The problem is that traditional methods cannot stop the blood flow — the clotting process is impaired. Elixir will seal the wound, as will the theurgy rite Laying On of Hands. This poison is hated especially by nobles if for no other reason than that it soils finery with excessive bleeding.

One dose (enough to coat a dirk) cost 50 firebirds and

remains on the blade for two strikes (after which it has dissipated enough to be inert).

Communications

Squawker (TL4): This radio, or "Squawker" as it is sometimes called, is the finest long-range radio currently manufactured. It is used by Muster guildmembers to coordinate their mercenary and slaver activities, so it's got to be reliable. Lightweight and durable, the Squawker is capable of receiving and transmitting on over 200 channels (although, in Alexius's time, there's not an awful lot of chatter on most of these bands), and has an effective range of 25 kilometers. The two most common models either strap onto a belt or fix to a helmet. A more expensive model (Tech Level 5), costing 30 additional firebirds, can be worn around the wrist.

The Squawker is powered by a fusion cell which must be recharged after 24 hours of continuous use. Cost: 50 firebirds.

Whisper Pin (TL5): This miniature radio can be hidden in just about any inconspicuous object, from a lapel button to an earring. It usually comes in two pieces: a transmitter worn somewhere near the owner's throat (lapel or ear) and a receiver hidden in the owner's ear. The transmitter is programmed to hear only the owner's voice and can pick up and transmit even a slight whisper from him, and sends a

signal on a special tight band with a range of 10 kilometers. The receiver must be worn in the ear since it only releases faint vibrations, which the owner must be trained to interpret. House Decados controls the technology on these useful spy radios and is very picky about who they sell them to, but each house, sect or guild which uses them has its own vibration code by which they send messages to their spies.

The Whisper Pin is powered by a tiny fusion cell which must be recharged after 5 hours of continuous use. Cost: 100 firebirds.

Starlight LRCD (TL5): The Starlight Long Range Communication Device is a heavy but portable military field radio designed for protected planet-to-starship communication in adverse conditions. The briefcase sized radio is encased in a ceramsteel carrying unit and is powered by a standard, rechargeable fusion cell. Starlight LRCD's are expensive to manufacture, and are licensed exclusively by the Imperial Navy to various houses. The high cost of the LRCD reflects the fact that the technology is not only rare but amazingly useful. LRCD's send messages in a series of tachyon pulses, allowing for extremely short response times. Cost: 300 firebirds.

Light

Lanterns and Candles: The only reliable light sources available to most serfs are the medieval standbys of lanterns, candles and torches. Some worlds have advanced fossil fuel mining, allowing for networks of gas lamps on streets and in homes, but most folks must be content with wax or animal fat candles (which can stink horribly). Torches provide a lot of light but tend to burn out too quickly to be useful for anything but short-term work. Lantern craftsmen are somewhat in vogue, called upon by the rich to design beautiful glasses and lenses for a wide variety of handheld or mounted lanterns. The costs are anywhere from a few talons to a few firebirds (see the Costs of Goods sidebar, earlier in this chapter).

Fusion Torch (TL5): The standard light source for Second Republic citizens, a fusion torch is available in all sizes, from a pen-light to a hand-held searchlight. It is powered by a standardized fusion cell which will last for 10 hours of continuous use (24 hours or even a week for higher tech level models). Generally, the size determines how far one can cast light, but high-tech models with advanced lenses and bulbs are known in all sizes. Cost: 5 firebirds per tech level.

Tools

Mech Tools: A standard kit of wrenches, screwdrivers, hammer, and other tools necessary for handling most minor mechanical tasks. Without these tools, some jobs may be impossible (you cannot turn a Phillips-head screw with your fingers). Cost: 5 firebirds.

Volt Tools: A standard kit with a soldering iron and solder, volt meter, wire cutters, wire, tape and other tools to aid in electrical repair work. Without these tools, fixing faulty wiring may be impossible (although a little spit and gum may hold those wires together long enough to make it through the jumpgate). Cost: 7 firebirds.

Hi-Tech Tools: There is no standard kit for working with high-tech devices; each device has its own arcane requirements. Characters who want to repair tech will want to collect tools as they find them. Such tools include a fusion siphon for preventing explosions when working with fusion cells or blasters, a field emitter and meter for calibrating energy weapons, spectrum goggles for seeing energy leaks, or just about any other tool imaginable. These things are specialty items and usually cost anywhere from 5 to 10 firebirds apiece.

Security Systems

Wellesley Lock (TL4): A bulky, metal lock with protection against prying. Small spring-loaded steel plates make it difficult for a thief to break into these locks with his picks (-2 Lockpicking). The Wellesley steel used in manufacturing these locks makes them tough enough to discourage most efforts with anything short of a welding torch. Wellesley Forges is best known these days for the metals its smiths forge and sell, from weapons manufacture to starship repairs, but they got their start making fine locks for valuables. Most locks encountered in the Known Worlds are of this make. What most people don't know is that the Scravers secretly design these locks and know all the tricks to disable them. Costs vary.

Magna-Lock (TL5): Magna-Locks are heavy, durable locks that, when activated, are capable of resisting almost any force. These ceramsteel devices come in a variety of shapes and sizes, and all require a power source. Magna-Locks were first used during the Diaspora Era. These locks are strong enough to resist 2,000 pounds of pressure, and are still used on most spacecrafts. They cannot be picked with physical picks, but require a Scrambler Pad or similar device. Cost: 50+ firebirds.

Gen-Lock (TL6): Gen-Locks are the very finest security locks available. Created during the Second Republic, the locks are specifically designed to scan the genetic code of anyone requesting entry into a building. The entire person is examined on a molecular level by a scanning laser. If one of its preprogrammed genetic code files is not met, the entrance remains barred. If anyone attempts forced entry, the Gen-Lock immediately sends out a piercing alarm.

Gen-Locks have been around since the height of the Second Republic. Very few people can afford to have these extremely expensive locks throughout an entire household.

Most are simply placed in certain key locations and are used to guard valuables. Cost: 1000+ firebirds.

Thieves' Keys (TL3): For as long as locksmiths have been making locks, thieves have been doing their best to open them. This series of carefully crafted picks and prods is essential for most thieves. A proper set of Thieves' Keys can allow a skilled lock pick access into virtually any home that does not rely on powered locks. Cost: 5 firebirds (more at higher tech levels).

Scrambler Pad (TL6): Scrambler pads are small boxes with a number of attachments for fitting into powered locks. These devices are designed specifically for forcing entry into high-security buildings. The Scravers are responsible for the first Scrambler Pads, but their popularity has led to several models being designed and sold by various manufacturers. Cost: 100 firebirds.

VS Perimeter Guards (TL6): Visual Security Manufacturing (VSM) is long since gone but its legacy lives on. Technically, VS Perimeter Guards are used as early warning systems. The four small floating orbs are supposed to be set in a perimeter around a camp and programmed to monitor the area. In reality, the dull spheres are often used for industrial spying. Each orb is only a few inches in diameter, and a skilled technician can use them to scout out entire buildings with little fear of being spotted. Costs: 200 per orb.

Restraints

Muster Chains (TL6): These handcuffs are the finest personal restraints in the Known World. They are lightweight, remarkably durable, and come complete with a pain-inducing shocker. The shocker is activated with a remote control device (which also controls the locks) and causes no real damage, but will drop almost anyone unfortunate enough to be wearing the chains to the ground, writhing in pain. Since the cuffs are made of a ceramsteel alloy, nothing found to date can break Muster Chains without also damaging the wearer. The locks are incredibly sophisticated and can only be opened with the proper code sent by a companion remote control unit (only a cuff's particular unit can open the cuffs). Any non-Muster guildmember caught possessing these chains is likely to end up on the auction block. Muster Chains are usually not sold, but a few have found their way to the black market. Cost: 300 firebirds.

Wet Jackets (TL7): These silvery sheets of hard metal expand when activated to cover an opponent and then contract to bind him. These nanotech devices are no longer manufactured, but are still fairly common (many were made during the Second Republic and they are almost indestructible). Each jacket is attuned to a specific control device, which is small enough to fit into a pocket. Wet Jackets were originally designed to peacefully restrain aliens resisting removal to reservations. Cost: 600 firebirds.

Think Machines

Computers were once so commonplace even a child could use one. This is no longer the case. These high-technology machines are largely proscribed by the Church, although they are allowed in approved libraries and for necessary uses, such as plotting jump coordinates. Nowadays, those who use computers — called think machines by most people — must be ever-watchful for roving Inquisitors.

Using a computer requires a Tech + Think Machine roll. Especially user-friendly machines may allow a Wits + Think Machine roll.

Computers are extremely expensive, beginning at 500 firebirds for the clunkiest models. All starships have think machines as a necessity, and Drive Starship skill allows a pilot minimal use of the computer, but only for piloting tasks.

At low tech levels (4 or 5), computers are not much different than those used in the late 20th century, although they may be more or less advanced. At Tech Level 6, different substances can be used, such as the superior silicon-like substances found on Shaprut or other worlds. At Tech Level 7, truly advanced or wondrous materials can be introduced, such as Pygmallium, necessary for artificial intelligence neural networks. In addition, as the Tech Level increases, different methods of information storage and retrieval may be used. Some advanced computers store their data through coherent light or sound, rather than magnetic scribblings. These advanced methods require advanced understanding of their workings — one of the many reasons data from the Second Republic is so hard to retrieve. Once a light or sound think machine has broken down or been corrupted, many do not know how to retrieve the raw data that may still be stored within the machine or on disks.

Most think machines store removable data on laser disks (or crystals), which come in a variety of sizes and require a variety of media to read them. There are three main standards — or sizes — to most Diaspora and Second Republic-era disks: mini, standard and mega. The mini is a tiny disk meant to fit into wristwatch style think machines (30 firebirds); the standard is the most common size, a bit smaller than a late-20th century compact disk but capable of holding more memory (20 firebirds); and the mega is a large cassette which holds an immense amount of memory (40 fireibrds). There are other disk standards, but they tend to be unique to rarer think machine systems.

Some think machines can link up with other machines to share data or programs. Such networking is rare in modern times, but is known, especially among the Engineers or Reeves. Usually, models produced by the same guild will network with each other, but not necessarily with the machines of a competing guild. Almost all Second Republic computers can network with other computers of the same era.

All think machines require a power source. Most built during or after the Second Republic use fusion cells. One cell will power a think machine for about 1 week worth of continuous use. Certain high-tech cities on Byzantium Secundus, Leagueheim and Criticorum still maintain a fusion power grid which a think machine can plug into.

Accountant (TL4): Accountancy engines were once an integral part of Republic businesses, but the average modern merchant considers them to be far more useful as paperweights. Detailed programs integrate a host of factors, including depreciation of goods, loss of income from funds that could have been gathering interest in Republic banks, opportunity costs, and shortcuts in long-since defunct tax codes. Users that can silence these babbling subroutines, however, will be able to keep track of their business with double-entry bookkeeping and a basic adding machine. The Reeves have the current patent on this type of machine, although their reprogrammed versions are very difficult to use. Only desktop models are known, which store data on internal drives or standard discs.

Users can a +2 bonus to any math-based or mercantile skill. Most programs run on Constantinople or Suprema. Cost: 600.

Mapper (TL5): Learning the proper use of this laptop machine takes a little bit of work, but the rewards are worth it. Travelers venturing over long distances, either on foot or by vehicle, can input details they encounter along the way into a personalized mapper think machine. The result is a slowly growing map of the planet the travelers are exploring. Some machines require the user to take snapshots of the stars to help figure their position; others contain preprogrammed disks (standard size) with maps of many of the more popular worlds. The most sophisticated come with a light pen that can be used to detail the streets and byways of urban areas.

This machine greatly magnifies an entourage's ability to learn the geography of a new planet or town (+2 to skills involving navigation). However, the machine is not without its risks. A failed roll on a Tech + Think Machine roll can result in a poorly constructed map or a woefully lost group of travelers.

Most mappers are programmed in either Turing or Suprema. Cost: 700.

Facial Scanner (TL5): This simple hand-held device makes social intercourse much easier. It can store the images of over a thousand human and alien faces, recording not only the identity of an individual, but also notations that the user wishes to remember. For instance, if a merchant runs into a noble and his entourage, the scanner can retrieve the noble's name, his proper title, notes on his proficiencies and weaknesses at fencing, records or his last three affairs, the identity of his bodyguard, and highlighted notes on which archbishop's name one should never repeat in his presence.

The device is stored in a small satchel that is worn over the shoulder. It is equipped with a discrete lens for observing, a microphone for recording, an earphone for advising, and a rechargeable solar battery pack. Noble families have also been known to hand them down from generation to generation. In game terms, this allows the gamemaster to feed a great deal of information to players who prefer intrigue-oriented plots. Cost: 700

Tracker (TL5): This device was once common on many fringe worlds. Upon arrival, a bounty hunter or law enforcement official could obtain a few data files on escaped criminals and wanted renegades. The tracker would retain information on fingerprints, footprints, height and weight, scent, and distinguishing characteristics. The tracker can also be programmed in the field (Turing or Suprema).

If the user can converse with an individual for at least two minutes, the machine will note and store all relevant details about that person. As a result, the user can later use Tech + Think Machine rolls as a complementary roll to any tracking rolls involving that individual. Cost: 700.

Journal (TL6): The wealthy were once able to indulge their egotism by extensively and tediously documenting all details of their lives. As a result, there are a variety of think machines that are constructed to chronicle all aspects of an expedition or all the minor details in the life of an adventurer. A journal is a multimedia think machine that records written text, visuals, sounds, scientific data, and other sensory data. The information is organized and retrievable in formats that can be edited either for academic purposes or personal pleasure. The most expensive versions of this device uses high-quality disks that are less prone to decay. The Academy Interatta is slowly building a library of journal entries to document their expeditions (or, more precisely, the expeditions that survive and return with their sanity intact). Most are programmed in Turing. Cost: 1000.

Hierarchy (TL7): A hierarchy wrist computer is intended to be the ultimate in personal data management. The user can recite any information that comes to mind and even store small segments of visual information. The trick is in retrieving the information later. If the user is curious about anything he has previously encountered, he can ask the hierarchy a few simple questions, and theoretically, the artificial intelligence within the device will organize it in a format accessible to the user. There's even a small video screen for magic lantern displays. The memory is seemingly limitless, but the tech is old enough and delicate enough to eventually lose information.

When it works, the user can roll Tech + Think Machine as a complementary roll to any knowledge-based skill roll. When it doesn't work, the same roll is required to retrieve

anything at all. An annoying version of this is the Rhetorical Hierarchy, a think machine that will respond to any question with another question that may help clarify the problem.

The usual programming language is Turing. Cost: 1500.

Library (TL7): In a world where scientific knowledge is rare, this is one of the most valuable of think machines. Library devices are designed to interface and download with practically any repository of data (they can read most programming languages). Much of the tech relies on translators to incorporate the data into the proper format, artificial intelligence circuits to organize it, search engines to retrieve it, protocol circuits to negotiate access, and anti-viral programs to stave off contamination. If everything works properly, this personal solar-powered device, about the size of a paperback book, will retrieve the information verbally specified by the user. If something goes wrong, random files within the machine will be corrupted. Cost: 2000

Advisor (TL8): This is a crude artificial intelligence that can offer advice on any number of subjects. It does far more than store and retrieve information. It interprets, extrapolates, compares and contrasts, and even offers personal opinion. It is, for all intents and purposes, a sentient think machine. This is balanced by its temperamental nature, the random short circuits in its Pygmallium circuitry matrix, and its

occasional psychological quirks. Each advisor develops its own personality, which can consist of anything from a fictional archetype to an officious mediator.

Unfortunately, a malfunctioning advisor can be a pain. It might say that it does not want to reveal an answer (for the user's own good, of course) or engage in frustrating demands for more information in exchange. (*"Quid pro quo, citizen. Quid pro quo!"*) Like a wide variety of surviving TL8 devices, it is despised by its owners almost as much as the Inquisition. This has reduced its price considerably. With the pragmatism of the modern age, many devotees of tech state that they would rather follow their own advice.

Using an Advisor is normally a Tech + Think Machine roll, but rolls of Wits + Debate are not uncommon with recalcitrant models. Cost: 3000

Programming Computers

There is a wide array of unique programming languages still used, especially for those who want to encrypt their data — breaking the code requires understanding the language. The skill Think Machine is used to interface with computers, while the Science (Think Machines) is used to program them.

Think machines are notorious for their difficult operating systems and programming languages. Each programming language must be learned separately; programming

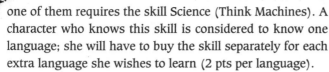

one of them requires the skill Science (Think Machines). A character who knows this skill is considered to know one language; she will have to buy the skill separately for each extra language she wishes to learn (2 pts per language).

Turing: This is the premiere high-tech coding language of the Empire, an artificial language constructed by the Engineers. Since only members of that guild are familiar with this language, computers that are completely reprogrammed by them can only be fully accessed by their members. Most incarnations are effectively TL6.

Constantinople: The Reeves Guild has developed its own language as well, although it is used mainly to store records and financial data. Since only a handful of these bureaucrats have the knowledge to construct data systems, they've done a shockingly poor job. Any system using Constantinople is five times more difficult than it needs to be, and only other members of the Reeves guild can decode these arcane operating systems. Consider this TL5.

Lex V.V: The Church has sanctioned and developed this cumbersome programming language. Take the crude raw data language of the First Republic, translate it into Latin, require a system of declensions for different situations, and you'll be decoding the Tetragrammaton in no time. The first version of Lex was TL4; this one is TL5.

Ië: This programming language of the Ur-Obun was developed completely independently of human society. It reflects the cultural preferences of that race, and humans find it annoying at an almost instinctual level. TL5

Link: Golems (robots) have their own various computer languages within their data matrixes. Link is a meta-language that applies to most of them. Explorers who find ancient golems have a better chance of kick-starting them if they understand it. TL5 to TL7

Suprema: This is the original form of Turing, present in many TL5 computers. Its raw data format makes it easy to translate into other languages. Add +2 to any Think Machine roll that involves Suprema. The Church is notorious for capturing these machines and modifying them to allegedly work better under Lex V.V.

Vehicles

It is not uncommon for the serf taking his goods to market in a beast-drawn cart to look up and see his lord flying overhead in a skimmer. The serf knows that there is no way she will ever be able to afford anything better and accepts that as the way things are. Characters, on the other hand, almost never accept such discrepancies, and the following section covers many of the vehicles they may find themselves in — or under.

Vehicle Traits

Fading Suns rates vehicles for a number of different factors. Speed rates the vehicle's top level, though how fast it gets to that point (or how quickly it can stop from there) depends on the vehicle's quality. Armor shows how much protection it provides both its own internal machinery and its occupants. Fuel lists what powers the craft, while Range refers to how far it can go on a full tank, fusion cell or before its team has to rest. The Cargo trait details just how heavy a load a vehicle can carry. The People rating show how many people are needed to drive the craft and how many can ride in it under normal conditions.

Drive Rolls

Characters with the appropriate Drive skill do not need to make rolls to handle normal driving conditions. Gamemasters should only force them to make rolls when they try to do something special (jump over a herd of brutes) or something unexpected happens to them (someone has cut the air brakes on their skimmer). Failed Drive rolls can mean anything from losing a race to going off the road to running into a mountain. Complementary skills include local Lores. Knowing the terrain will always help.

Sample Drive Roll Modifiers

Penalty	Condition
-1	Bad Road (ground craft only)
-2	Inclement Weather
-3	Pedestrian in Road
-3	Hairpin Turn
-4	Unexpected Obstacle
-4	Sudden terrain change (skimmers only)
-5	Cut Off

Chases

The success of characters in catching or escaping other people is primarily determined by the quality of their own vehicle. The faster it is, the more likely they are to win a chase. The only time gamemasters need to worry about more details is when both the pursued and the pursuer's vehicles are similar. In this case the gamemaster will want to establish the number of victory points a side will need to accumulate on a sustained Wits + Drive rolls in order to win the chase (usually 10 more than the other side). The roll should be modified by various conditions: darkness helps the pursued while having a transmitting bug in the escaping vehicle helps the pursuer.

Collisions

When the gamemaster decides that the character's vehicle runs into something, he has to decide just how much damage both the vehicle and the occupants take. In a head-on collision, damage equals one die of damage for every 10 km/hr of speed for both vehicles as well as one die for each of their armor dice. In a rear-end collision, the gamemaster should subtract the lead vehicle's speed and armor dice from

the rear vehicle's speed and armor dice and then roll the damage as above. Finally, in a side collision, or when the vehicle runs into a stationary object, she should roll based solely on the speed of the impacting vehicle and the armor dice of what it is running into.

The damage applies to both the vehicle and the occupants (though the gamemaster might want to roll the damage separately or have each player roll it for their characters). The vehicle's armor also protects both the vehicle and its occupants, and the occupants' armor also protects them. Shields work normally, but seat belts and air bags are not common features in **Fading Suns**.

Attacking Vehicles

When attacking a vehicle, characters have the option of aiming for the vehicle or the occupants. Occupants get to treat the vehicle as cover, usually reducing the goal number by four or six. If the vehicle is moving, then the attacker should have another -2 penalty, and if his vehicle is moving, then that should provide yet another -2. Misses have no effect on the occupant or the vehicle, except to break out a window if the gamemaster likes.

If attacking the vehicle itself, any damage the characters do over the vehicles armor takes away from its Vitality. As the vehicle takes more damage, its driver will have a harder and harder time keeping it under control, as represented by the listed subtractions. Gamemasters should feel free to get descriptive with just what this damage is (broken axle, cracked engine, floor disintegrates, etc.). When the last level of Vitality gets marked off, the vehicle no longer functions (the engine is destroyed, both axles fall off, it blows up, etc.) and is probably not redeemable. Gamemasters should feel free to apply damage which exceeds both the vehicle's Armor and Vitality to its occupants.

Characters can also target specific parts of the vehicle to attack. For instance, aiming for the repulsor pads of a skimmer might have a -4 target number, but the gamemaster can rule that any damage to it will reduce the skimmer's speed, and that damaging all four will bring it to the ground. The most commonly targeted vehicle parts are the tires on ground craft. Hitting the tire on a moving vehicle is a tough task (-6), and it has 2d armor. If penetrated, the tire deflates or, if enough damage was done, blows up. The driver has to make an immediate Dexterity + Drive roll to stay in control, and this and all future rolls are at -3. A ground craft can continue driving with all its tires blown out, but it will be at -12 to any drive rolls, and will suffer permanent damage. Its top speed will be 10% of what it normally is.

Beast Craft

The most common vehicles in the Known Worlds are powered by the muscles of beasts, slaves and serfs. These include brute carts, carriages, and Li Halan rickshaws. On poorer planets, even nobles use these vehicles more than any others.

The common form of transportation for most serfs is the wagon or cart — a four-wheeled wooden box drawn by an animal (usually a Brute, but horses and oxen are also common). Most wagons are actually very well manufactured, but they are hardly works of art. On many planets, wagons function as roving homes. More durable models are known, as are those with collapsible roofs, which allow the wagoneer to travel in the roughest terrains or through truly nasty weather with little or no fear. Most are designed such that only a severe catastrophe will capsize the wagon and its passengers. They are usually built from local resources, primarily wood with some metal for reinforcement. An average wagon can carry six comfortably, along with their possessions and ample food supplies. Brutes for pulling the wagons are sold separately, some assembly required.

Wagons have been a staple on many of the more remote worlds for a long time. Having learned from their ancestors' hubris, many cathedrals created local laws minimizing the use of mechanized flight and ground transportation — for serfs at least; most freeman suffer under no such law. Tech Levels 1-4. Cost vary.

Brute Cart

Speed	Armor	Fuel	RNG	Cargo	People
6 km/hr*	2d	Feed	50 km	1 ton	1/12

* Brutes can only maintain this pace for a short time. Usually the cart travels at half that speed.

Vitality Levels: Ruin/-8/-6/-4/-2/0/0/0/0 (Brutes have their own Vitality levels)

Weapons: None

Tech Level: 1

Firebird Cost: 10

This rugged cart appears anywhere brutes are found, and is a preferred means for getting crops to market. Most serfs who own one built it themselves or inherited it from their parents. They yoke a team of two to eight brutes to the cart and away they go. The above traits are for an unloaded cart with a two-brute team. Extra brutes will not increase the carts speed (brutes can only run so fast), but they will increase the amount of cargo they can pull.

Landcraft

These vehicles appear most frequently on planets with good road systems — a distinct minority of the Known Worlds. They may be powered by the wind, steam, fossil fuels, electricity, fusion cells or solar power, and use either wheels, tracks or skis for movement. The guilds use more of these vehicles than does anyone else, relying on them to move goods and people from place to place. Nobles prefer skimmers, which cost more and carry less.

Scraver Open-Back Scrounger

Speed	Armor	Fuel	RNG	Cargo	People
90 km/hr	5d	Gas	600 km	500 kgs	1/9

Vitality Levels: Ruin/-8/-6/-4/-2/0/0/0/0/0/0/0

Weapons: None

Tech Level: 4

Firebird Cost: 3000

The Scravers developed this vehicle ostensibly for artifact hunts in areas where roads are bad, but have found it very useful in smuggling goods along back roads. It features a sturdy cab which can seat up to three people, an open cargo area in back, oversized tires for off-road driving and large, side-mounted gas tanks. These are the most dangerous part of the vehicle, for they risk blowing up if punctured. Critics say this is actually a positive feature, for it gives Scravers an easy way to destroy the evidence.

Skimmers

Most popular among the nobility and rich League members, skimmers travel at heights of up to 250 meters and at speeds of several hundred kilometers per hour. While they zip over all kinds of terrain, drivers still need to be careful because sudden terrain changes can send a skimmer plummeting. For this reason pilots rarely fly them high over cities, for fear that the streets and buildings may acts as canyons. Most people in skimmers prefer to follow roads, and only the cockiest will speed over unfamiliar terrain.

Hoverbike

Speed	Armor	Fuel	RNG	Cargo	People
250 km/hr	2d	Fusion	450 km	20 kgs	1/1

Vitality Levels: Ruin/-8/-6/-4/-2/0/0/0/0/0

Weapons: None

Tech Level: 5

Firebird Cost: 9,000

Young nobles are the biggest fans of hoverbikes, racing one another wherever they meet. Peasants are the biggest enemies of the hoverbikes, often run down by racing nobles. In any case, these small, fast craft are fairly rare, rarely having been produced since the Second Republic. They provide very little armor, for their pilots sit on them, not in them. Most of their parts also have very little protection.

Hoverpack

Speed	Armor	Fuel	RNG	Cargo	People
120 km/hr	2d	Fusion	75 km	–	1/0

Vitality Levels: Ruin/-8/-6/-4/-2/0/0

Weapons: None

Tech Level: 6

Firebird Cost: 7,000

These extremely rare devices have not been manufactured since the time of the Second Republic. They feature extremely small hover engines, marvels of miniaturization

the likes of which have never been equaled, and a fuel cell protected by the engine. The hoverpack straps on to a user's back like a backpack, and she controls it via two levers. The one on the right controls up/down movement while the one on the left controls left/right movement. A button on the right determines acceleration while the one on the left handles braking.

Hoverpacks take a lot of getting used to, and have their own special Drive skill: Drive Hoverpack. Controlling one without any training can be next to impossible, but a lot of fun to watch.

Flitters

A custom flitter is the surest sign that a noble has made it. These expensive flying machines make jaunts around a planet take no time at all, and these are the machines peasants think of when they hear about nobles traveling around their fiefs. While this category includes everything from propeller-driven biplanes to custom antigrav yachts, most people think of the grand noble air yacht when they think of these vehicles.

Air Yacht

Speed	Armor	Fuel	RNG	Cargo	People
750 km/hr	8d	Fusion	3K km	2 tons	2/12

Vitality Levels: Ruin/-8/-6/-4/-2/0/0/0/0/0/0/0
Weapons: None
Tech Level: 6
Firebird Cost: 25,000

The air yacht is a true luxury flitter, capable of flying at high speeds or hovering imperiously off the ground. Its crew consists of a pilot and co-pilot, both of whom need the Drive Aircraft skill. While one person can pilot it in a crisis, two are always recommended. It can seat 12 passengers in extreme comfort, and more if needed. Of course, an air yacht's traits hardly reflect its true value. Its primary purpose is to impress other nobles, and to this end its owner will customize it in a dozen different ways — reentry ability, gold trim, retractable roof, arboretum, in-air torture chamber, etc.

Hoppers

The guilds' answer to the flitters, hoppers are far more utilitarian than are flitters. Most consist of little more than engine, wings, fuel tanks and as much open cargo room as possible. They reach altitudes of almost 20 km, and pilots have been known to transfer cargo from space landers to hoppers high above the prying eyes of customs officials. Very few nobles would agree to ride in one of these dirty, oil-streaked monstrosities, but members of the League swear by them — maybe because the nobles won't get in them.

Wagon of Paulus

Speed	Armor	Fuel	RNG	Cargo	People
500 km/hr	10d	Fusion	5K km	20 tons	1/20

Vitality Levels: Ruin/-8/-6/-4/-2/0/0/0/0/0/0/0/0/0
Weapons: None
Tech Level: 5
Firebird Cost: 15,000

The price given above is for a used Wagon of Paulus, because new ones, while occasionally made, are rarely for sale. Most of the wagons date back to the Second Republic, when they were known by a variety of names. The guilds found it useful to rename the entire class after Paulus, the saint of travelers, and these hoppers have proven themselves almost miraculously reliable. While the Wagons of Paulus may have built up centuries of grime, they have continued to run no matter what. The most vulnerable machinery tends to be their life support, especially worrisome for merchants who use these to ferry goods down from orbit.

War Vehicles

The Emperor Wars saw all kinds of war vehicles come into use, ranging from steam-powered self-propelled guns to fusion-powered assault hovercraft. Armored battles became all the rage during the 4970s, but proved far too expensive. Instead, armored units served primarily as infantry support, though a few nobles (especially among the Hazat) preferred to lead their troops from a tank at the front of the battle.

These vehicles are far too difficult for most individuals to own or maintain. Some mercenary groups own their own, but most are the property of houses or guilds. Of course, the Church has its own collection of war vehicles, as does the Brother Battle order. (Future **Fading Suns** sourcebooks will more fully detail war vehicles.)

With the decline of transportation technology, many nobles have taken to sending their troops into battle on animal back. Horses have made an especially significant comeback, and nobles from all the royal houses claim to be the best mounted warriors in the Known Worlds. Other animals have also come into common use, with the Pheriza lizards being an example.

Warhorse

A well-trained warhorse is a marvel to behold. A horse without such training is a danger to its rider and everyone around. Characters attempting to bring a horse without such training into a fight should have to make a Dexterity + Ride roll every turn to keep it from trying to bolt or throw her. On the other hand, a character with a warhorse may maneuver normally, and only needs to make such rolls if she or the horse is hit, or if she tries to do something special. Most warhorses are not trained to attack.

Most warhorses are the extremely large and powerful Destriers, but other (smaller) horses can be used as well. The statistics below are for a standard Aragon Destrier.

Firebird cost: 5,000 (only noble characters can begin

225

play with a warhorse; they need not spend Benefice points for this)

Body: Strength 12 (+3 DMG bonus), Dexterity 6, Endurance 8

Mind: Wits 4, Perception 6, Tech 0

Natural Skills: Dodge 5, Fight 3, Observe 3, Vigor 6

Weapons: Hooves 7 DMG, -1 goal and initiative, Bite 5 DMG

Vitality: -10/-8/-6/-4/-2/0/0/0/0/0/0/0/0

Pherizas ("Spitters")

Pherizas are native to Kish and serve as the preferred mounts and burden beasts for desert travel. These eight foot long greenish-brown lizards possess suckerlike pods on their toes that allow them quick travel through sand or even along walls and ceilings (only the strongest can bear riders while walking slowly up walls). Their sturdy frames, legendary stamina, tolerance for heat and infrequent need for water enable them to survive for weeks at a time in the deep desert. They have been domesticated by the Li Halan and are now bred for both stamina and speed. Some of these have found their way to other desert environments, such as Pyre, where they thrive even near the famous Burning Desert.

Called "Spitters," wild pherizas have sacs along their inner jawline containing a caustic acid. They can spit this liquid up to 10 meters, covering an area about the size of a human. They use this acid to wound prey and to break down any tough hide it may have so they can reach the meat beneath. Pherizas live to be about 40, breeding between the ages of 10 and 30, when they lay two to six eggs each year. Those who have been domesticated have the caustic sacs removed, which must also be done to newborns sometime after their first year of life. The main danger unaltered pherizas pose is to those unfamiliar with them. The lizards are notoriously cranky, spitting at anyone who disturbs them when they are resting or feeding or doing nothing at all, but just feeling out of sorts. It is not unheard of for some altered pherizas to grow back their caustic sacs and those who deal with the creatures on a daily basis walk slowly and talk softly around them... just in case.

Firebird cost: 3,000

Body: Strength 13, Dexterity 6, Endurance 10

Mind: Wits 2, Perception 2, Tech 0

Natural Skills: Fight 4, Vigor 4

Weapons: Caustic acid spit. Pheriza acid causes 3 DMG, burning through clothing, skin or armor where it hits (ignore shields also). Roll Dexterity + Fight, Range 5/10.

Vitality: -10/-8/-6/-4/0/0/0/0/0/0/0/0/0

Cybernetics

Cybernetics in **Fading Suns** is the science of installing tech inside the human body. This can be desirable for any number of reasons, ranging from altruistic motives for enhancing the human body to deviant urges of cyberfetishism and criminal tendencies. The simplest of cybertech might be little more than a plastic device grafted onto human flesh or a small smuggling compartment hidden inside a human body. The most elaborate coordinate a number of high-tech devices and may involve the installation of a valuable think machine.

Cybernetic devices are often surgically attached to a character and do not usually come off without further surgery. They can include a whole gamut of technological sophistication, from a clunky and obvious vision enhancement lens attached to a character's eye socket to sleek synthetic eyes which can pass for organic ones, or from noisy and bulky mechanical limbs to cyberlimbs sheathed in synthflesh or actual flesh and blood. Second Republic-era cybernetics can still be found, and are by far the most advanced and expensive. Later cybertech is somewhat clunky but usually reliable.

A cybernetic implant or device must be purchased during character creation with Extra points, or during gameplay with the character's money and time (characters must also spend experience points for devices that enhance characteristics or Vitality; see below). A character who possesses cybernetic implants has a stigma attached to him, and may even be killed on sight in some places. It is perhaps best to hide these devices from others.

Cybernetic devices allow a character to begin the game with traits over 8, and he may even exceed the human maximum of 10.

A list of cybernetic devices is given below, along with a method for players and gamemasters to build their own devices.

Building Cyberdevices

When building cyberdevices, there are a number of questions to be asked:

• What Does the Device Do (its Function)?

Does the device allow the user to pick up radio transmissions and increase his hand-eye coordination? Or does it simply slice bread? Part of answering this question involves figuring out what features the device has; features are chosen at each stage listed below.

Features are the abilities and powers a cybernetic device lends its user. These effects vary from the enhancement of characteristics (boosted Strength or Dexterity) to expanded sensory organs (radio hearing, hypersensitive touch or smell) to the ability to conceal the device and more. Some features are considered Afflictions: they subtract from the Extra point cost of a device. (If a device has more Afflictions than positive traits, it provides the character Extra points just like any Affliction.)

Each feature is listed with its effect or power, its cost (in firebirds and Extra points) and Incompatibility modifiers (see *How Compatible with the Body and Mind is it?* below).

Armor (2 pts per die): Armor must cover at least half the body, such as the torso or all limbs (its distribution is up to the player). The cost is two Extra points per die of armor. As with any cybernetic device, the armor is Obvious unless bought otherwise; Hidden armor may take the form of a metal sheath around the character's bones, while Incognito armor may be synthetic muscles — obvious to those who touch the cyborg's skin or view it closely. Firebird cost: 100 per die. Incompatibility +1 per die.

Chemical Pump (1 pt): The character has a chemical reservoir and pump or injector that introduces a chemical into his bloodstream when triggered. It takes three actions to load the reservoir; once loaded, it takes only one action to trigger the injector. The reservoir can hold up to ten injections worth (+1 pt per +10 injection capacity). If the device also has Automatic Activation, the injector automatically triggers whenever the cyborg needs the drug. For instance, a Chemical Pump with the Elixir regenerative serum and Automatic Activation will inject a dose of Elixir whenever its user loses Vitality (the cyborg can manually deactivate this function if he does not want to be healed immediately). Firebird cost: 300 for the basic pump and reservoir, 100 per extra capacity. Incompatibility +2

CyberLung (varies): This device allows the bearer to breathe a different medium (water, methane, etc.) than his native one (oxygen).

Cost	Effect
4	**Water:** Character can extract oxygen from water and breathe underwater as he does in air. If this is not Concealed, then some sort of gills or venting system is obvious. This assumes fresh water or salt water; if the liquid is a soup largely composed of chemicals other than hydrogen and oxygen, the character must buy Gaseous, below. Firebird cost: 700. Incompatibility +2
7	**Gaseous (TL6):** Character can breath in one gaseous medium (methane, nitrogen, ammonia, chlorine, florine, sulfur, carbon dioxide, bromine, radon, liquid halogen, etc.). This does not make the character immune to any acidic or allergic effect the chemical/gas may have on her skin; it simply allows her to breathe the medium rather than asphyxiate in it. Firebird cost: 1500. Incompatibility +3
10	**Vacuum (TL7):** Character can either recycle his own oxygen (or other medium he is capable of breathing) or he has an extra supply. In the absence of oxygen, he can still breathe for a number of hours equal to his Vigor. This does not allow a character to survive decompression, only to exist in it without a constant supply of oxygen. Once the character has left the vacuum (or other airless medium), he must "recharge" the oxygen in his cells by spending a number of hours breathing it equal to the number of hours spent in vacuum. Firebird cost: 3000. Incompatibility +5

Cybersenses (varies): The device allows the character to either perceive in a visual spectrum normally invisible to the organic eye, hear in a range normally inaudible, touch with increased sensitivity or taste normally undetected chemicals in foods.

Cost	Effect
1	**Magnifier/Telescope:** Character can perceive objects as if through a telescope (or binoculars), seeing faraway objects as if they were near, or picking out small details of close objects. When combined with a think machine, the exact range of objects can be determined. The base cost is for a 10x telescope. It costs one Extra point per extra 10x magnification. Firebird cost: 300. Incompatibility +1
2	**Ultraviolet:** Character can see into the ultraviolet spectrum, seeing as well at night as he can during the day. Firebird cost: 500. Incompatibility +2
3	**Infrared:** Character can see into the infrared spectrum, seeing the heat signatures of people or things even in the dark. Firebird cost: 700. Incompatibility +3
6	**X-Ray (TL6):** Character can see through or past objects (except lead) and examine their internal workings. Firebird cost: 1000. Incompatibility +5
3	**Camera:** Character can take photographs from whatever perspective the device sees (eyes, a finger camera, etc.). Firebird cost: 500. Incompatibility +1
4	**Video:** Character can record video footage from whatever perspective the device sees (eyes, a finger camera, etc.). One hour of video can be recorded (each extra point spent doubles this time). The media is almost always a mini data crystal. Firebird cost: 1000, +100 for each recording time increase. Incompatibility +2
1	**Higher pitch:** Character can hear sounds in a higher pitch than normal, picking up dog whistles or the eerie whine of approaching gravcraft or Landers (atmosphere capable starships). Firebird cost: 300. Incompatibility +1
1	**Lower pitch:** Character can hear sounds in a lower pitch than normal, picking up deep rumblings which may signify approaching land vehicles or imminent earthquakes. Firebird cost: 300. Incompatibility +1
2	**Radio:** Character can hear radio transmissions on most bands or frequencies. Firebird cost: 300. Incompatibility +2
3	**Spy radio:** Character can hear radio transmissions on protected or prohibited bands, such as those used by noble houses, League merchants or even pirates. However, most of these transmissions are encoded, so the character must know how to decode them. Firebird cost: 500. Incompatibility +2
3	**Tape recorder:** Character can record sounds heard (including radio receptions received). One hour of video can be recorded (each extra point spent doubles this time). The media is almost always a mini data crystal. Firebird cost: 700, +50 for each recording time increase. Incompatibility +2
1	**Hypersmell:** The character can discern people or things by scent alone; roll Perception + Observe, adding bonuses or penalties depending on familiarity or unfamiliarity with a scent. The character can attempt to track someone's pas-

sage by his scent trail; roll Perception + Tracking. If the prey passes through water or a crowded area with conflicting smells, penalties may be applied to the roll. Firebird cost: 300. Incompatibility +1

1   **Hypertouch:** The character can determine what a touched object's surface is made out of through touch alone; roll Perception + Observe, with certain Lores being complementary. He may even be able to detect involuntary emotional responses in people when touching them (increased pulse rate, flushed skin, etc.); roll Perception + Empathy. Firebird cost: 300. Incompatibility +1

1   **Hypertaste:** Character can determine the chemical content of objects when tasting them, perhaps even identifying poisons. Roll Perception + appropriate Lore (cuisine or poison). Firebird cost: 300. Incompatibility +1

Efficient Organ (1 pt): The character replaces one of his natural organs with a more efficient cyberorgan (replaced limbs should use the Extra Limb feature, below). While the new organ has no dramatic game effects, it generally works better: a stronger heart leads to less fatigue, cybereyes don't suffer eye strain, etc. Special powers like infrared vision or the ability to breath underwater must be bought with Cybersenses or CyberLung, while dramatically improved eyesight or endurance should be bought with the Enhanced Characteristics feature. Some people may need such cyber transplants to replace damaged or injured organs or limbs. Note: Brains cannot be replaced (although mad scientists keep trying), but they can be implanted with think machines that boost their capacities (see Think Machine, below). Firebird cost: 300-1000 depending on the complexity of the organ.

Energy Shield (varies): An energy shield can be implanted on or within a person's body. Energy shields cannot be Self-Powered, they must be Battery-Powered (although a cyborg with Power Generation can recharge batteries).

Cost	Shield Type	TL	Hits	Firebirds	Incompatibility
7	Standard	7	10	750	+3
9	Dueling	7	15	1000	+3
18	Assault	8	20	4500	+5
30	Battle	8	30	7500	+5

Enhanced Characteristics (2 pts per +1): The device enhances a character's natural characteristic. Through this device, a character can exceed his normal racial maximum score for that characteristic, possibly even beginning gameplay with a score over 10. The exceptions to this rule are Tech, and the spirit characteristics Ego, Faith, Self and Other, none of which can be raised through cybernetics. While certain cybernetics can modify behavior (affecting Passion or Cal, Extrovert or Introvert), they cannot change overall attitudes, such as one's Faith. Neither can they impart an understanding of scientific paradigms (Tech). It is conceivable that a device may be able to enhance a character's Psi (gamemaster's discretion), but no known cybernetic device

228

(save perhaps an Anunnaki artifact or Church relic surgically attached to a character) can raise Theurgy characteristics. Firebird cost: 300 per trait bonus. Incompatibility +1 per trait bonus.

Some devices may only modify one aspect of a characteristic, such as sight or hearing for Perception or hand-eye coordination for Dexterity (applicable when shooting guns but not when walking tightropes). Partial characteristic enhancement costs 1 pt per +1. Firebird cost: 200 per bonus. Incompatibility +1 per trait bonus.

A character must spend experience points to integrate the enhanced characteristic or suffer from incompatibility (he has the feature CyberNut until he spends the proper amount of experience points). The cost is 3x the characteristic bonus. For example, Jahn the Charioteer has a natural Dexterity of 4. Through cybernetics, he boosts it by three, for a total Dexterity of 7. He must first spend nine experience points before he can use the boosted abilities.

Enhanced Reflexes (1 pt per +1 Init): The character's reflexes and reaction timing have been boosted cybernetically. Perhaps his body is sheathed in a network of wires capable of transmitting signals from the brain quicker, or his nerves were replaced with more efficient, synthetic nerves. Each point spent adds one to the character's Initiative rating. Firebird cost: 200 per bonus. Incompatibility +1 per bonus.

Enhanced Vitality (2 pts per +1): The character is harder to kill. Usually, increased Vitality implies increased size and mass, but this is not necessarily the case with cybernetics — a device may simply aid the redundancy of the character's organs, toughen his immune system, generate copious amounts of flesh to replace lost tissue, etc. Firebird cost: 500 per bonus. Experience point cost: 2 per increase. Incompatibility +1 per bonus.

Extra Limb (3 per limb): The character has an extra arm, leg or tentacle which operates as effectively as the others. Each extra leg adds +3 to the character's base running distance. Firebird cost: 500 per limb. Incompatibility +2 per limb.

Flesh Cavity (1 pt): Many devices rely on hollowing a cavity in a person's body in which to hide a weapon, camera or think machine. The cost for such hidden compartments is included in the Hidden or Incognito features. However, some people use cavities for smuggling small amounts of cargo. Such a space usually requires removing an organ or replacing it with a smaller cyberorgan. A flesh cavity can hold one Medium sized item, two Small items, or three Extra-small items. Firebird cost: 300. Incompatibility +1.

Flight (TL7, 5 pts): A personal hoverpack allows the character to fly through the power of antigravity. The character must learn the Fly skill, and even taking off — let alone maneuvering through the air — requires a Dexterity + Fly roll. Failure does not necessarily mean the character falls, but it can mean she is flung off-course for a turn or two. These are not generally designed for combat use. Flight speed is five meters per turn + one meter per success on a Dexterity + Fly roll. Firebird cost: 3000. Incompatibility +3

Lights (varies): A lantern or flashbulb. For 1 pt, the user can illuminate a three meter radius area or 10 meters forward in a one meter wide arc. Double this area and distance with each extra point spent. Firebird cost: 200 per level. Incompatibility +1

Flash (2 pts): The user can produce a flash of bright light to temporarily blind anyone who sees it; they are blinded for three turns (plus three turns for each extra point spent, up to 12 turns maximum). They may contest with a Perception + Vigor roll to close their eyes in time; each victory point subtracts one turn from the duration of blindness. Blind targets suffer a -6 penalty to all actions involving sight. Firebird cost: 300. Incompatibility +1

Movement Boost (varies): Cybernetics can enhance a character's natural movement capabilities, either allowing her to run faster, jump higher or swim like a fish. Firebird cost: 300 per level. Incompatibility +1 per movement affected.

Running (x2 distance per 2 pts): The character has powerful muscles in his legs or perhaps wheels with rocket-assist. Double the running distance per point spent. No more than three levels can be spent on this feature for bipeds. Quadrupeds can spend up to five levels.

Jumping (x2 distance per 3 pts): The character has powerful muscles or springs in his legs or his leap is rocket-assisted. Double the jumping distance per point spent. No more than five levels can be spent on this feature.

Swimming (x2 distance per 3 pts): The character has a streamlined body with a fin or flippers. Double the jumping distance per point spent. No more than three levels can be spent on this feature.

Pain Desensitivity (3 pts): The character is not distracted by pain, although he is still aware of damage to himself. His pain receptors still work, but he is no longer tormented by the pain. Perhaps electrode patches are placed at key points on his body to short-circuit his pain sense, or his nerves have been rewired, or his brain's pain sensory center has been fiddled with. The character ignores any wound penalties suffered by losing vital levels of Vitality, and is not affected by occult powers or other methods of causing pain. Firebird cost: 500. Incompatibility +2

Think Machine (varies): A computer capable of a number of functions. Base cost: 1 pt. Firebird cost: 1000 for the computer, +300 per tech level. Incompatibility +1

Data Interface (1 pt per extra language): The computer can interface with another computer, read the data on that computer and copy it into its own data banks. However, each computer operates on a programming language and can only

229

interface with another computer that operates on the languages it knows (see The Electronic Tower of Babel sidebar). At TL5, computers must interface through plug-in wires; at TL6, they can interface through remote radio connection. Firebird cost: +300 per extra language. Incompatibility +1

Skill Programs (1 pt per 2 skill levels): A host of learned skills can be gained through programs without going through a long training process; just slip in the Drive Starship program crystal and off you go. Physical natural skill programs (Fight, Sneak, Vigor, etc.) require a Neural Interface (see below). No program can provide more than 10 levels of a particular skill. Characters who wish to rely on buying skill programs instead of learning a skill naturally should be warned that the Inquisition often erases any such "unnatural data" they discover. Firebird cost: +100 per skill level of the program. Incompatibility +2

Neural Interface (TL6, 3 pts): The computer is hooked into the user's nervous system, allowing it to use physical skills programs (Fight, Sneak, Vigor, etc.). Firebird cost: +500. Incompatibility +1

Multitasking (TL6, 1 pt per program): Some think machines can run more than one program at once. Only those programs which are in current memory can be run simultaneously. Without this extra memory, a character may only run one program at a time and must change chips for each new skill. Firebird cost: +500 per extra program capacity. Incompatibility +1

Advisor (TL7, varies): An artificial intelligence that can answer questions put to it on subjects with which it is familiar. The AI possess a Wits trait and a number of Lores or Sciences, and must roll Wits + relevant area of knowledge when answering questions or giving advice. The cost for the Wits rating is 1 pt per 2 levels; the cost is the same for skills. Firebird cost: +1000 plus 200 per Wits rating and 50 per skill rating. Incompatibility +3

Tool Implant (1 pt): Characters can install tools and other utilitarian or common objects into their bodies, such as a fingertip with hinges back to reveal a screwdriver, or a electric drill that pops up out of a cavity. The placement and effect of the tool should be approved by the gamemaster. If the tool has a Benefice cost, add it to the 1 Extra point required to adapt it to the body. Firebird cost: x1.5 normal tool cost. Incompatibility +1 per tool implanted.

Toxic Immunity (2 pts per immunity): A special organ protects the character from harmful poisons. The user chooses to which poison(s) he is immune; this can include cyanide, Xaos gas, the plague, Vorox poison, alcohol or whatever. Usually, the organ's filter must be replaced after 10 uses, depending on the deadliness of the poison. Firebird cost: 1000 for the organ, 500 per extra immunity applied to that organ, and 50 firebirds per replacement filter. Incompatibility +1 per immunity.

Weaponry (varies): Some folks like to wield or graft swords or guns to their bodies, replace their teeth with metal fangs and even place electroshock pads on their hands (what a handshake!). Most such weapons must be custom made or at least modified. Design what you want the weapon to do (a sword that slides from a sheath in the arm, a flux sword hidden in the user's palm, or a derringer hidden in the thumb), and use the following guidelines to build the weapon:

Damage (varies): Use the weapons given in the Weapons Chart (see Chapter Six: Combat) for examples of damage capability: knives do from 2 – 3 dice, swords from 4 –7, etc. Use those examples as a basis for firebird costs also (x2 for cyberfitting). Incompatibility +2 per material weapon, +3 per energy weapon

Cost	Damage type
1 per die	Muscle-powered (fist, knife, club)
1 per die	Kinetic (bullet)
2 per die	Energy* (blaster, flame)
1 per die	Stun (see Stunner gun for effects)

* Damage leaks through energy shields on d6 rolls of 1 or 2.

Range (varies): If the weapon can be used at range (guns, crossbows), there is a cost depending on its effectiveness over distance. A spring mechanism to hurl a knife or sword from a concealed sheath or a mini-rocket attached to the weapon can turn a melee weapon into a missile weapon. The actual range should be decided upon, but it is unlikely that a spring-loaded knife would have better than 5/10 range. (If the weapon is simply thrown by the user, such as a shuriken or grenade, the range is 5/10 and there is no Incompatibility.) Incompatibility +1

Cost	Ranges
0	5/10
1	10/20
2	30/40
3	40/60
4	50/70

Area of Effect (1 pt per 1 meter radius): The weapon affects anyone within its area of effect, such as a net or a grenade. Instead of aiming the weapon at a person, it is aimed at a place, such as the ground beneath the person. Only one goal roll is required; if successful, all persons within the weapon's area of effect (measured from the weapon's location, not its thrower or user) are hit (unless they successfully dodge). Common sense should be used when building such weapons: nets are unwieldy at more than 3 meters radius. For explosions, the maximum area of effect is equal to its damage in meters; one point is subtracted from the damage for each meter away from its point of impact.

Entangle (varies): Some weapons (nets, taffy guns) aren't designed so much for damage as for catching enemies. An entangling weapon is rated for its Strength; the cost is 1 pt for Strength 8, +1 pt per +2 Str. Once an entangling attack

successfully hits, the target must contest his Strength + Vigor against the weapon's Strength or else be confined by the weapon.

Ammunition (varies): Weapons that don't project slugs or darts or plasma bolts require no ammunition or batteries, but guns, bows and crossbows require ammunition. Cyberweapons generally use the same types of ammunition (slugs, arrows or bolts) as normal weapons; simply choose what type is used. Does the cybergun fire the same ammo as a Med Revolver or an Assault Rifle? Use the guidelines from the Weapons Chart (see Chapter Six: Combat) for ammunition Extras and firebird costs. The same applies to throwing knives, shuriken and other disposable weapons.

Load capacity: The weapon has a set load of shots it can fire before reloading. The default (0 pts) is 10 uses before requiring a reload, 1 pt for 20 uses, +1 pt for five uses, +2 pts for only one use. A cybernetic weapon requiring energy rather than physical ammunition —such as a blaster — uses standard fusion cels with the same capacities as listed above; it cannot be Self-Powered (although a Power Generator can recharge its fusion cels).

Autofire (3 pts): The weapon can unleash bursts of ammunition with one action. The weapon can perform any of the standard autofire actions: 3-round burst, 6-round burst, empty clip or spread.

• How is it Attached?

Most cyberdevices are implanted or grafted to their users surgically, and cannot be removed without further surgery or causing damage to the user. (See the Implantation sidebar.) Some devices are tied so integrally to a user that damage to the device also damages the user.

Removable (3 pts): The cybernetic device can be removed without surgery. It takes at least one turn to detach or reattach it. Firebird cost: 500.

Omnisocket (1 pt socket, 3 pts per device): A universal socket or mount for attaching Removable cybernetic devices. This allows a device to be removed and another put in its place. Each device must have the Removable feature (3 pts) and be fitted to latch onto the socket (0 pts, 50 firebirds per device). The Omnisocket itself costs 300 firebirds. Incompatibility +1

Organic (+2 pts): The device is so closely tied into the character's body (nervous system, musculature, etc.) that repairing it requires not only the proper Tech Redemption skill but Physick also. In addition, when the device is damaged, the character loses one or more Vitality points (depending on the nature of the injury; gamemaster discretion).

Burns Flesh (+5 pts): The character's cybernetics "burn" organic tissue, costing him one Vitality point each turn it is used. This is not necessarily a literal burning; it can be a loss of vital body fluids or tissue through bleeding or grinding by the device's gears, etc.

Implantation

Actually hooking up with cybertech can be difficult. Just having the firebirds to afford it isn't enough. After acquiring the proper tech, the prospective user has to find a cybersurgeon or cybertech engineer who can install it. Many low-tech surgeons keep a low profile, trying to compensate for the amount of risk they live with by inflating their prices and allying with sub-legal fixers who act as intermediaries. High-tech surgeons affiliate with powerful and wealthy patrons who can offer them protection, and their employers may require favors or compensation before they allow surgeons in their retinue to perform freelance work.

Furthermore, any installation (after character creation) is a gamble. Critical failure on a surgery roll can result in slow physiological degradation, psychological maladjustment, or technological breakdowns at crucial moments. The capability of any cybernetic implant is limited by the skill of the surgeon, quality of the device, and wisdom of the user. Caveat emptor.

Implanting cybertech requires the cybersurgeon to make a sustained Tech + Physick roll; the number of victory points needed varies with the complexity of the device and its position in the body. Installing a knife onto the stump of someone's arm may only require three or four victory points, while a concealed think machine in the brain may require as many as 32 victory points — a critical failure at any time during the process may lead to severe consequences.

The costs for surgery vary depending on the quality of the surgeon and the local legal conditions. On some worlds, Inquisitors routinely patrol the streets searching for illegal flesh chop shops. More cosmopolitan worlds, however, may have walk-in cyber clinics. Use the following guidelines for figuring surgery costs:

Device Complexity	Fee
Per feature in the device	+10%
Implant Location	**Fee**
External	300
Internal (implanted into bones, veins, skull, etc.)	600
Vitals (brain, heart, nervous system)	1000
Surgery Conditions	**Fee**
Illicit chop shop	Standard
Guild hospital	+10%
Palace hospital	+20%
Filthy/poor chop shop	-10%
Site suffers routine Inquisitorial scrutiny	x2 cost
Surgeon	**Fee**
Famous	+20%
Infamous	-20-50%
Per Physick rating above 3	+10%

Example: A Centurion Knife (see Devices, below) with two features (Incognito and Tool Implant) is implanted by an average surgeon (Physick skill 3). The base cost for an external implant (it's going into a flesh cavity on the surface of his arm) is 300. He adds +20% for the two features and 5 firebirds for the spring-loaded knife, for a total of 365 firebirds.

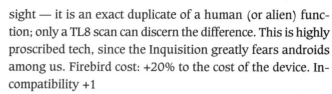

• How is it Powered?

Unless the device is a simple mechanical tool, like a screwdriver on a fingertip or a spring-mounted knife sheath in the arm, it needs power. But power isn't always free — the device either needs to generate its own energy or draw from batteries. Choose one of the features listed below:

Battery-Powered (TL5, varies): The device requires electrical (TL5) or fusion (TL6+) juice to operate. For +2 points, it can be used 10 times before requiring a recharge (at any electrical outlet or fusion charging station). +1 points allows 15 uses, while the default (0 pts) allows 20 uses. Features which only draw mild amounts of power (flashlights, radios, etc.) can operate for 24 hours, or one hour for 1 pt. Devices with the Battery-Powered and Automatic features use up power once per turn, so a 10-use device will run out of power 10 turns later. Firebird cost: 10 per fusion cel (3 per recharge)

Self-Powered (TL6, 1 pt): The device uses a fusion generator that can handle all of its needs, or else runs on the energy or muscle power of the body. Firebird cost: +25% the cost of the device. Incompatibility +1

Power Generator (TL7, 2 – 3 pts): The device uses streamlined fusion which generates more power than is needed for the device itself. Excess power can be used to charge fusion cels or power devices connected to it by a wire (such as a flashlight or radio). For 2 pts, 10 charges worth can be generated per day (10 blaster shots or energy shield hits); 3 pts allows 20 charges per day. Firebird cost: 3000 firebirds. Incompatibility +2

• What Does it Look Like (its Form) and What is it Made of (its Materials)?

Form follows function, but how well it does so varies. First, how noticeable is the device?

Obvious (0 pts): The cybernetic device is obvious to anyone who sees the user — he is revealed as a cyborg. Incompatibility +1

Unsightly (+1 pt): The device is ugly, no two ways about it. Whenever the device is noticed, the character suffers a -2 Extrovert penalty, in addition to the usual bad reactions cyberdevices illicit. Incompatibility +1

Messy (+1 pt): The device leaks fluids, steam, sparks or is noisy. In other words, it is a messy device, leaving pollution behind, often causing people to get rather annoyed at the owner of the device. Incompatibility +1

Incognito (1 pt): The device is noticeable with scrutiny or once the device is activated. Incompatibility +1

Hidden (TL6, 2 pts): The device is not obvious to onlookers, and is either hidden in a covered cavity or underneath a sheath of flesh. Firebird cost: +10% to the cost of the device. Incompatibility +1

Simulacra (TL8, 3 pts): The device is hidden in plain sight — it is an exact duplicate of a human (or alien) function; only a TL8 scan can discern the difference. This is highly proscribed tech, since the Inquisition greatly fears androids among us. Firebird cost: +20% to the cost of the device. Incompatibility +1

Second, what materials went into its construction?

Metal (0 pts): At lower tech levels, most devices are made of any number of metals, from aluminum and copper to stainless steel. Those with electrical functions may have rubber in their manufacture. While metals are sturdy, and rust is rarely a problem for the alloys used, they are usually heavier than more advanced materials. In addition, they conduct electricity too well; subtract one defense die against volt-oriented weapons (shockers, frap sticks) or attacks (lightning, etc.).

Plastic (TL6, 0 pts): At higher tech levels, sturdy plastics can be substituted for metals and stand in for complex functions, such as small gears and moving parts; the advantage is that they are lighter and less sensitive to electrical attacks. Firebird cost: +10% to the cost of the device

Ceramsteel (TL6, 1 pts): The strongest known substance. Even though ceramsteel smelting exists at TL5, it is rather crude, used for starship and tank plating rather than cybernetic implants. At TL6, manufacturing methods allow for the finer details necessary for cybernetics. Ceramsteel devices are considered +1 Quality (see below) regardless of workmanship. Firebird cost: +50% to the cost of the device. Incompatibility +1

Synthflesh (TL6, 0 pts): Grown in vats, synthflesh mimics human skin well. It is not alive, but looks and feels like flesh (although close scrutiny reveals its false nature). Synthflesh alchemists can also make versions to mimic the skins of certain alien races. Synthflesh is mainly used in small patches to cover up body cavities or implant jacks. Firebird cost: +5% to the cost of the device, 20 firebirds for replacement patches.

Synthlife (TL8, 4 pts): This substance perfectly mimics human flesh (it is always considered Simulacra; the cost for this is already included), and even regenerates when wounded. Like synthflesh, it is still a form of rubber, but a smart form, one which is programmed to replicate flesh exactly (even mimicking a blush when the user is embarrassed). Only TL8 scans or laboratory tests reveal that it is not actual flesh. This substance is highly proscribed by the Church. Firebird cost: +30% to the cost of the device. Incompatibility +2

Nanotech (TL8, 3 pts): An advanced science involving microscopic robots, nanotech can perform amazing feats and go unnoticed (it is always considered Hidden; the cost for this is already included). However, due to the massive datas purges of the Dark Ages, much lore about nanotech is lost. Controlling the little techo bugs once unleashed is not al-

ways easy. Still, they are efficient and tiny. Firebird cost: x2 normal cost of the device. Incompatibility +2

• How Well is it Made (its Quality)?

Unless otherwise specified, cybernetics must be maintained (cleaned) on a regular basis (at least once per week). When cybernetics break down, a technician must repair them (using Tech + relevant Tech Redemption skill).

Automaintenance (TL6, 3 pts): The device is capable of self-repair and maintenance, routinely lubricating itself or sending little nanotechnicians out to repair breakages (TL8). An Automaintenance device must be of standard or better workmanship. Firebird cost: 500. Incompatibility +2

Quality effects how easy it is to repair a device. The higher the quality, the easier the repairs (and the harder it is to damage the device in the first place). Quality modifiers should be used to modify Tech Redemption rolls and should be taken into consideration in case the user rolls a critical failure — the repercussions to the device will be less for higher quality devices. Most cybertech is of standard, solid workmanship.

Superior (1 pt): The device is well made; either add +1 to the repair roll's goal number or subtract one from the victory points required on sustained rolls for more intensive modifications. Firebird cost: +10% to the cost of the device.

Master Guildwork (2 pts): The device is an example of trained workmanship; either add +2 to the repair roll's goal number or subtract two from the victory points required on sustained rolls for more intensive modifications. Firebird cost: +20% to the cost of the device.

Premium (TL6, 3 pts): These devices are extremely durable and don't break or malfunction easily. They are equated with Second Republic-era tech. Either add +3 to the repair roll's goal number or subtract three from the victory points required on sustained rolls for more intensive modifications. Firebird cost: +30% to the cost of the device.

Poor (+1 pt): The device is poorly made or has a flaw in its manufacture; either subtract -1 from the repair roll's goal number or add one to the victory points required on sustained rolls for more intensive modifications. Firebird cost: -10% from the cost of the device.

Shoddy (+2 pts): The device is badly made or has many flaws in its manufacture; either subtract -2 from the repair roll's goal number or add two to the victory points required on sustained rolls for more intensive modifications. Firebird cost: -20% from the cost of the device.

Primitive/Delicate (+3 pts): The device is in disrepair or is extremely delicate; whenever the user fumbles a roll involving the device, the device malfunctions and must be repaired. The nature of the malfunction is up to the gamemaster, but it requires skilled maintenance. In addition, either subtract -3 from the repair roll's goal number or add three to the victory points required on sustained rolls

for more intensive modifications. Firebird cost: -30% from the cost of the device.

Expert Tech (+2 pts): The device is so complex that only an expert can repair it. This expert must have the proper Tech Redemption skill equal to the tech level of the device. For example, a mechanical cyberdevice of TL6 which requires Expert Tech maintenance can only be repaired by a technician with a Mech Redemption skill of 6 or higher.

• How Does it Work?

Most cyberdevices must be switched on or activated manually each turn it is used, by a shrug of the shoulders, a flick of the wrist or a mental command.

Automatic Activation (2 pts): The device pretty much runs on its own and requires little supervision by the character. Complex devices, such as cameras and think machines, require this trait to be self-operating. Otherwise, the player must state that his camera is taking pictures or his think machine is computing a problem. With the Automatic Activation trait, a camera will always be shooting video footage or a think machine is always online, unless a character consciously switches it off. Firebird cost: 300. Incompatibility +1

How easy is it to use? Most devices can be wielded with no bonuses or penalties, although a skill roll may be required in some instances. Some devices require their users to learn a unique skill particular to that device's use.

Skill Use (+2 pts): Using the device is somewhat complicated and requires that the character receive some training. The character must purchase a learned skill named after the cyberdevice, and this skill is only used to operate the device, paired when rolling with whatever characteristic is appropriate at the time.

Easy (1 pt per +1 goal): The device is either especially easy to use or actively aids the user in its use, such as a whip with a tracking sensor or a think machine with artificial intelligence and its own skill sets. Firebird cost: +10% to the cost of the device per goal bonus.

Unwieldy (+1 per -1 goal): The device is bulky, awkward or poorly built and actually hinders the user. Firebird cost: -5% to the cost of the device per goal bonus.

Unpredictable (+1 pt): The device sometimes acts in ways not counted on by its user. This could be caused by a variety of reasons: shoddy workmanship, an unfinished prototype, corrupted memory structures (in the case of nanotech), etc. Anytime the character rolls a critical failure when using the device, it begins to act up in unpredictable ways. This usually lasts for a number of turns (or hours) equal to the character's Ego score, but if the device has been misused or unmaintenanced, the effects may last longer. Firebird cost: -10% from the cost of the device.

• How Compatible with the Body and

Mind is it?

Cybernetics, needlessly to say, are not natural. Not everyone adjusts well to having a machine in his body. Sometimes, the implantee's mind and body are simply unable to integrate the excess foreign elements and will physically and psychologically reject them. Some people even go psycho (see the CyberNut feature below). A character can only possess so many cybernetic devices before his mind or body rejects them. The higher his Ego trait, the higher the rejection threshold.

Each feature in a cybernetic device is rated for its Incompatibility. Cyborgs should add the Incompatibility modifiers from all their devices; the total a character is allowed depends on her Ego trait, as listed in the chart below. Johanna the Scraver with an Ego of 3 can possess up to 11 Incompatibility modifiers (in any combination of devices).

Incompatibility	Ego trait
1-5	1
6-8	2
9-11	3
12-14	4
15-17	5
18-20	6
21*-23	7
24-26	8
27-29	9

* Cyborgs with more than 20 Incompatibility modifiers (64% loss of original physical form) are considered "soul dead" by fanatical members of the Church

CyberNut (+4 pts): Regardless of his Ego trait's level, the character is unprepared to integrate his cybernetics into his self. In time of great stress to the character, the gamemaster may require a Tech + Focus roll to prevent the character from "freaking out." A failure on the roll means that the character loses his iron grip over the wayward elements composing his self. Roll 1d20 to determine which of the following options occurs:

Roll	Result
1 – 13	Character develops a temporary neurosis based on the situation or the cybernetics. This usually lasts only for one span or act at the longest.
14 – 16	Character develops a permanent psychosis based on the situation or the cybernetics. This can be cured with long-term psychological counseling, but that is a rare skill in the Known Worlds. Religious counseling may also help, depending on the character's beliefs and the quality of the counseling.
17 – 19	Character loses control over the cybernetics — they begin working on their own. This lasts a number of turns equal to the character's Other rating.

20   Character goes berserk, attacking whatever is at hand — friend or foe alike. This lasts a number of turns equal to the character's Other rating.

CyberNut is not a feature of the device itself; it is the character's personal reaction to the device.

Proscribed (+2 pts): While all cybernetics is considered sinful by most Church officials, some devices are especially bad and are considered proscribed tech: Inquisitors usually burn first and ask questions later. Firebird cost: +10% to the cost of the device (the seller risks his life peddling such a device).

· What is the Tech Level of the Device?

The feature with the highest tech level determines a device's overall tech level. Below is a list of suggested guidelines to use when building devices.

Tech Lvl	Device
5	The lowest tech level at which cybernetics can be made is TL5. Most tech made at this level is obvious or incognito at best and cannot be hidden or made to perfectly replicate human functions. Power is confined to electrical energy stored in batteries. Materials include metals and basic polymers.
6	Hidden devices, standard fusion power, synthflesh, advanced polymers, ceramsteel
7	Field manipulation (energy shields), artificial intelligence (Pygmallium), advanced fusion power
8	Simulacra devices (synthlife), nanotechnology, advanced artificial intelligence (nearly indistinguishable from human sentience)

Tech Level (1 pt per +1 tech level): Some devices may be made with a higher tech level than required: a TL8 camera if far more advanced than a TL5 version. In general, the higher the tech level, the smaller, more durable and efficient the device. It costs 1 pt and 200 firebirds per tech level higher than the minimum required.

· How Much Does it Cost?

Total the Extras points of all the devices features; this is the cost to begin gameplay with that device. If a character seeks the device during gameplay, total the firebird cost of all the features and the surgery costs (see the Implantation sidebar); this is the cost to purchase the device from a dealer and have it implanted into the character. It is not necessary to spend experience points when buying cybernetics in gameplay — except for devices with the Enhanced Characteristics or Enhanced Vitality features).

Devices

Centurion Knife (2 pts)

TL5

Features: Incognito, Tool Implant (spring-loaded blade)

Incompatibility: 2

Firebird cost: 365 (5 spring-loaded blade, 360 surgery)

Centurions and Vipers are the best examples of simple holdout cybernetic weapons. The Centurion stores a 20 cm blade in the forearm along the ulna. Upon activation, the blade springs up through the palm, where it can be grasped by a simple hilt. The blade is not actually attached to the character; it is simply stored in the cavity. Roll Dex + Melee, DMG 4

Viper Sword Arm (6 pts)

TL5

Features: Incognito, Weaponry (sword)

Incompatibility: 3

Firebird cost: 740 (20 blade, 720 surgery)

An extendible fencing sword surgically attached to the character in the forearm along the ulna (hence, it cannot be disarmed). Once the telescopic blade is extended and locked in position (which takes one action), the fencer has an elegant blade at his disposal. Installing the blade back into the compartment takes one turn, although it is wise to clean it with alcohol first. Careless practitioners of this art will require daily maintenance to prevent disease and infection. Roll Dex + Melee, DMG 5

Arm Harpoon (4 pts)

TL5

Features: Incognito, Weaponry (harpoon)

Incompatibility: 3

Firebird cost: 725 (5 harpoon, 720 surgery)

The Arm Harpoon is similar to the Centurion save that it is used as a missile weapon. A groove in the forearm is concealed by a layer of fake skin (synthflesh for TL6 version), and specially modified steel rods can be loaded into the device. The internal mechanism can, upon activation, launch the projectile through the palm of the hand up to 30 feet. Up to five of these arm harpoons can be stored in the forearm at a time. Roll Dex + Shoot, DMG 3, RNG 10/20, Shots 5

Jonah (7 pts)

TL5

Features: Incognito, Tool Implant (winch), Weaponry (harpoon)

Incompatibility: 4

Firebird cost: 745 (20 winch and line, 5 harpoon, 720 surgery)

A slightly more expensive version of the Arm Harpoon involves a cable attachment and an internal pulley mechanism. Citizens on water-worlds refer to these as Jonahs, since they're popular among fishermen. The internal winch is capable of pulling up to 100 kilograms. To capture a person with the Jonah, the Jonah user must first hit his target (Dexterity + Shoot) and then win a contest of his Strength + Vigor versus the target's Strength + Vigor; the Jonah user

may add the victory points from his goal roll to his Strength + Vigor roll. Roll Dex + Shoot, DMG 4, RNG 10/20, Shots 5

Aqua-Lung (3pts)

TL6

Features: CyberLung (Water), Organic, Self-Powered
Incompatibility: 3
Firebird cost: 1655 (875 gills, 780 for the surgery)

Artificial gills that can extract oxygen from water. More advanced version are known that hide the gills (+2 pts Hidden, +1 Incompatibility, +150 firebirds).

Engineer's Eye (6 pts)

TL6

Features: Cybersenses (Magnifier/Telescope, IR Vision), +1 Perception (sight), Self-Powered
Incompatibility: 6
Firebird cost: 2340 (1500 eye, 840 for the surgery)

These devices are popular with many guild Engineers, who are often seen scrutinizing people through the large lens. They look like monocles studded with wires and small lights attached over the left (or right) eye socket.

Ether Ear (3 pts)

TL6

Features: Cybersense (Radio), Hidden, Self-Powered, Skill Use
Incompatibility: 4
Firebird cost: 1245 (405 for the ear, 840 for the surgery)

A radio concealed in the character's inner ear. The character must learn a special skill (Ether Ear learned skill) for receiving transmissions, or else he may not get the band or frequency he wants (he gets the Charioteer muzak meant for the local market instead of the Charioteer pilot chatter).

Use of the radio is not necessarily obvious to other people, although the Ether Ear skill can help in concealing any of the radio listener's telling behavior when tuning in to transmissions.

Goliath Skin (10 pts)

TL6

Features: +3 Strength, +2 Endurance, Organic, Self-powered
Incompatibility: 6
Firebird cost: 2715 (1875 skin, 840 surgery)

This device is a sheath of synthetic muscles surgically implanted into the owner, replacing many of his natural muscles. The model detailed above only replaces muscles involved in lifting (biceps, triceps, deltoids, hamstrings and quads, etc.). Other models are known which are strong enough to protect the owner from damage or pain (Armor). The above model does not conceal the muscles; they are bulkier than natural muscles and have a metallic sheen and ribbing, instantly recognizable as cybernetic.

Lithe Wire (5 pts)

TL6

Features: +3 Dexterity, Organic, Self-Powered

Incompatibility: 4

Firebird cost: 2425 (1125 lithe wire, 1300 surgery)

This device is a network of synthetic nerves cabling over and inside the owner's body, connected to hubs up and down the spine and augmenting the nervous system. It allows for superb motor control, including manual and fine dexterity. These cables are not concealed although they are durable enough (encased in flexible metal sheaths).

Oxy-Lung (9 pts)

TL7

Features: CyberLung (Vacuum), Organic, Hidden, Self-Powered, Proscribed

Incompatibility: 7

Firebird cost: 5250 (4350 lung, 900 surgery)

The Oxy-Lung is a device that allows humans to survive for long periods without an outside oxygen source, such as in deep space. One lung is replaced with an efficient recycling system that allows the body to convert carbon dioxide back into oxygen. However, the user must still have a spacesuit to protect the body from a vacuum.

Second Brain (11 pts)

TL6

Features: +2 Wits, Think Machine (Data Interface w/ Suprema, Skill Programs, Multitasking 3), Hidden, Self-Powered

Incompatibility: 10

Firebird cost: 5515 (3915 computer, 1600 surgery)

A computer that is surgically hidden in the owner's skull. It can be accessed for maintenance by removing a flap of synthflesh and bone at the base of the skull. Programs can be loaded by slipping chips into a socket usually placed behind the left ear (again, hidden beneath synthflesh).

Programs (6 pts)

Skills: Lore (choose a subject) 4, Lore (choose a second subject) 4, Think Machine 4

Firebird cost: 1200

Spy Eye (6 pts)

TL6

Features: Cybersenses (Magnify/Telescope, Video), Hidden, Self-Powered, Skill Use

Incompatibility: 5

Firebird cost: 2655 (1755 eye, 900 surgery)

A video camera hidden in a synthetic eye. The character's natural eye (right or left) has been removed and replaced with this device, which resembles his original eye. The recording medium is a standard mini data crystal. These crystals were developed in the Second Republic for wristwatch entertainment cameras and music players and lend themselves perfectly for hidden surveillance. The basic model can record video up to one hour in length before changing crystals (which cost about 30 firebirds each). The crystal is usually housed in a small cavity behind the left or right ear underneath a flap of synthflesh.

The character must learn a special skill (Spy Eye learned skill) for taping with this camera, or else he may not get the picture he wants (the target will be out of frame, the image overexposed, etc.).

Use of the camera is not necessarily obvious to other people, although the Spy Eye skill can help in concealing any of the videotaper's telling behavior.

Stimusim (3 pts)

TL6

Features: +2 Perception, Cybersenses (Hypertouch), Organic, Incognito, Self-Powered, Proscribed

Incompatibility: 5

Firebird cost: 2715 (1215 stim, 1500 surgery)

Cyberfetishism and xenophilia were not unknown during the height of the Second Republic. Xenophiles who wanted to try to understand alien culture would pay handsomely to augment their human body with simulations of alien physiognomy. This rather expensive version of synthflesh demonstrates the somewhat decadent and perverse impulses of cyberfetishists. Stimusim replicates the sensitivity of flesh covering reproductive organs, both human and otherwise. Layers can be placed over any part of the body, although weaving the nerve network required is a meticulous process. With this implant, almost any part of the body can be used for pleasure in the same manner as a sexual organ (although with no extra reproductive capabilities). This is particularly useful for xenophiles who, for whatever reason, seek congress with alien life forms using unusual techniques. The Church, for obvious reasons, does not care for the idea.

X-Eyes (4 pts)

TL7

Features: Cybersenses (X-Ray Vision), Organic, Incognito, Self-Powered, Skill Use

Incompatibility: 7

Firebird cost: 2150 (1250 eyes, 900 surgery)

This costly enhancement is detested by both law enforcement officials and would-be criminals. It allows the user to see through layers of solid matter, both organic and inorganic. The simplest use (at TL6) involves modified x-rays, although this often results in a variety of cancers in the flesh and olfactory centers. More progressive variants reflect the history of passive scanning devices — TL7 X-Eyes can see through TL7 shielding, and so on.

Adjusting to X-Eyes can be an extremely tedious process. In fact, learning the fine points of operation is a skill in itself. Proficient users can effectively see in the dark, learn

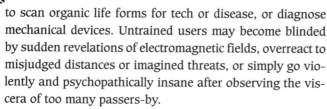

to scan organic life forms for tech or disease, or diagnose mechanical devices. Untrained users may become blinded by sudden revelations of electromagnetic fields, overreact to misjudged distances or imagined threats, or simply go violently and psychopathically insane after observing the viscera of too many passers-by.

It is impossible to fully conceal X-Eyes when they are activated. Unlike the Engineer's Eye, this device resembles a normal human pair of eyes when it is not in use. When activated, however, X-Eyes emit a dim, red glow. Usually, a cyborg who needs to use this device surreptitiously either wears dark sunglasses or places a hand over her eyes.

Starships

Starships are built to last, and many of the ships plying the jumpgates in Alexius's time were actually built during the Second Republic — or even during the Diaspora in some cases. It takes a core of dedicated technicians to keep them running, but since League trade, noble power and Church influence all rely on space travel, these techies are well-paid. If they were to slack off on their jobs, vital information may not make it to its destination in time or important shipments may arrive too late to be of use. Most important shipboard positions are taken by hired guildsmembers; freemen or serfs make up the bulk of the crew complement.

The technical details of most starships are unknown to most people; all Known Worlders usually know about ships is that they go up and out through a jumpgate and sometimes come back again. More advanced knowledge is usually confined to specialties: a ship pilot may know little about the engine or its needs, and a captain may not know how to fly the thing if the pilot has a seizure.

What is known by all is that these things can be broken fairly easily — a stray shot from a slug gun or blaster could foul up the life support system or blow a hole in a bulkhead. No matter how good the technician, it may take days to fix such problems, by which time all on board could be dead. Everyone is expected to be on their best behavior on a starship. Of course, this rule is rarely heeded by villains and player characters. Gamemasters must handle these situations as best they see fit.

Jumpgates

Jumpgates are giant, hoop-shaped artifacts in space, most of them as large or larger than a moon. They are the devices which allow travel between the stars. A starship must have a jumpdrive to use them, and the workings of these complex engines is a closely guarded secret by the guilds.

Each system in the Known Worlds has one working jumpgate through which all traffic must pass. A ship preparing to jump sends system coordinates to the gate, which

opens a passage in space to that system. The ship then enters the hoop and exits from another jumpgate in the desired system. Making a jump requires a jumpkey, a small metal cylinder invented during the Second Republic which holds complex, pre-programmed coordinates. Each key usually holds coordinates for one destination, although keys with multiple jumproutes are known. Without the proper coordinates, a jumpgate will not open; anyone passing through its hoop will not leave the system.

The Known Worlds are formed by the jumpweb — the known routes between jumpgates in systems. If one of these routes were to be lost or a system's gate sealed, that world would be cut off from the rest of space-faring civilization. Most worlds host multiple jumproutes (Byzantium Secundus has nine from its jumpgate), but some have only one known route (Nowhere), making them vulnerable to jumproute loss.

When a ship approaches a jumpgate, the jumpkey to the desired location is inserted into a computer panel, which relays the information to the jumpgate in a series of light transmissions. If the coordinates are correct, the gate opens. The singular nature of each jumpkey makes them valued commodities. The measure of a Charioteer is often the number of jumpkeys she carries. Jumpkeys are a favorite booty of pirates, always seeking new jumproads to plunder.

Only the Charioteers know how to make these keys, and they guard the tech fanatically. A "Chauki stride" in the vacuum of space (i.e., being thrown out of an airlock) is the usual fate of those who try to bootleg jumpkeys, threatening Charioteer hegemony over the jumproads.

The cost of a jumpkey varies radically, since they are not for sale. They are given to Charioteers who earn them by working their way up the ranks of the guild. Assume that a Charioteer character has one jumpkey for each rank he attains past the first (he gets his first jumpkey when he becomes a Chief). These keys hold one jump coordinate each (such as Byzantium Secundus to Pyre).

Nonetheless, the black market does support a trade in these goods, whether stolen or bootlegged. It would be a lucky day to find a common, single route key (Byzantium Secundus to Criticorum) for only 3000 firebirds. Jumpkey traders can smell a client's desperation from leagues away, and will jack their prices up accordingly. There is obviously no guarantee that a black market key will work or even get the buyer to the promised destination.

Without a jumpkey, it may take hours or days to program the proper jump coordinates into the ship's Think Machine (a task requiring 18 victory points on a sustained Tech + Think Machine roll, with the Jumproads Lore being complementary). This assumes the rough coordinates are known; most ships do not keep libraries of this data as the Charioteers are highly protective of it, since such lore is their bread and butter. They are the exclusive manufacturers of

Astronomical Units

Space is vast. For ease of calculation, stellar distances in **Fading Suns** are measured in AU (astronomical units), rather than using an unwieldy amount of miles or kilometers (1 AU is about 150 million kilometers). Most jumpgates are anywhere from 70 to 100 AU distant from their system's sun, while most habitable planets are within 1 to 3 AU of the sun (Earth is 1 AU). That leaves a lot of space to traverse to get from one system to another, but when you add in starbases, other planets and even asteroid fields, systems are rarely empty.

new jumpkeys, and do not appreciate illegal keys or data files.

Jumpgate Reset

Using a jumpgate to leave a system is considered an active jump; arriving in another system is considered a passive jump. It takes a jumpgate a varying time to reset itself after an active jump. No active jumps can be made while the gate resets itself, although ships can exit from the jumpgate at anytime (passive jumps). For this reason, fleets tend to jump together, synchronized to go through the gate at once, rather than spread out in a long line. The Second Republic engineers solved the problem of gate resetting, but it requires a special key in addition to the destination jumpkey. These keys are especially rare and held only by a few. Certain Charioteers or Engineers travel from system to system selling the use of their reset keys, and most ships of the Imperial Fleet have them. Some Inquisitors also have them, to the dismay of those trying to escape their fury.

To figure out how long it will take for a gate to reset for another active jump, roll 1d20 and compare the results to the chart below:

Roll	Jumpgate Reset Time
1-5	1 minute
6-10	10 minutes
11-14	30 minutes
15-17	1 hour
18-19	1 day
20	1 week

Pursuit

It is not easy to determine the location to which a previous ship may have jumped. This requires experience with jumpgates and their routes (a successful Tech + Jumproads Lore roll). Obviously, if a jumpgate only provides one road out (as is the case with Nowhere, which leads only to Stigmata), it is easy to figure where a previous ship went.

Starship Design Worksheet

1. Choose Ship Class

This determines:
- Size rating
- Grade (lander, atmosphere, void)
- Engines (Slow, standard, fast)
- Maximum allowed shields, turrets and gundeck hardpoints
- Minimum crew requirements

2. Purchase Hull

Size rating x10,000 in firebirds

3. Purchase Shields

3000 firebirds per shield (do not exceed the ship's maximum allowance)

4. Armament

- Place weapons in gundecks and/or turrets (do not exceed maximum allowed hardpoints); hardpoint costs per weapon are listed in the Armament Chart.
- Purchase armaments and/or turrets; see prices listed with armament descriptions.

5. Purchase Sensors

See prices listed with sensor descriptions.

6. Hire Crew and/or Marines

See wages listed with crew descriptions.
- Must fill ship class's minimum requirements.
- Extra crew, marines and/or passengers can be hired/brought aboard, up to the ship's size rating +1.
- 1 – 5 extra people allowed per 10 metric tons of cargo space converted to staterooms/bunkrooms.

7. Cargo Space

- Base allowance: ship rating x10 in metric tons.
- Convert gundeck hardpoints: 10 metric tons per hardpoint
- Convert Vitality: 10 metric tons per level (mark this as cargo on the Vitality circles)

8. Supplies

- Determine base supplies: 10x size rating in days, -2 per person aboard.
- Cost: 1 firebird per person per week
- Convert cargo space for more supplies: 10 people per day per metric ton

9. Vitality = size rating x 10

10. Other Systems

- Upgrade think machines; see programs and costs in think machine descriptions.
- Purchase escape pods (one allowed per size rating above 3): 3000 firebirds per 3-man pod.

Starship Traits
Class

The hull type of the ship, which also determines it general size and function. The most common classes and their sizes are listed in the Ship Classes sidebar. Each noble house owns a secret manufacturing technique for a series of unique hulls in most starship classes. Thus, a Hawkwood ship is designed differently than a Decados — although privateered booty ships seized in combat from either faction may show up in either fleet, repainted with their current owners' colors.

Ships hulls are listed by their grades, which determine whether or not they can enter an atmosphere. Landers are streamlined and can land on planets (preferably at a spaceport) without difficulty. Atmosphere grade hulls are streamlined to enter the upper atmospheres of planets only; they cannot land on planets and must either dock in orbit or at a spacestation. Void grade hulls are not streamlined and may not enter an atmosphere in any way; they cannot obtain orbit and must dock at a spacestation.

The firebird cost for a ship hull is usually 10,000x its size rating. Ship systems — shields, armaments, sensors, fuel, supplies — must be bought separately. Costs for these are given below.

Speed

Rather than keep track of a ship's exact movements per turn over vast regions of space, **Fading Suns** tracks five stages of velocity: full stop (the ship is not moving at all), quarter thrust (one quarter the ship's maximum acceleration), half thrust, three-quarter thrust and full thrust (the ship's maximum acceleration). Movement at any of these rates may involve a modifier to initiative and piloting rolls when attempting quick maneuvers or hotshot tactics, or when attempting to pursue a ship or escape pursuit. The Speed Chart lists these modifiers. (See also *Spaceship Combat*, below).

These velocities are relative to the ship's engines — a fast engine has more velocity at full thrust than a standard engine.

Ships travel forward on vectors opposite from their direction of thrust. Most hull designs place engines in the rear of the ship, sending the ship forward with its nose pointing to the fore. In space, once an object starts moving, it doesn't stop until something stops it. This allows a ship to spin and rotate freely as it continues to travel along its vector — once initial thrust is applied, the ship no longer has to face in any particular direction (unless it wants to go faster along its direction of travel, in which cases its engines must face opposite its vector again). To change vector, the ship must rotate so that its engines face opposite the new direction, and

then apply thrust. To decelerate, the ship must turn around — face its engines toward its direction of travel — and apply thrust, countering its momentum until the ship comes to a full stop.

It takes one turn to accelerate or decelerate to the next higher or lower thrust; this is considered an action for the pilot, although he does not need to make a roll. To switch from acceleration to deceleration, or vice versa, the pilot must turn the ship around; this takes one turn, during which the pilot cannot change speeds.

These amazing acceleration speeds are made possible by artificial gravity created by stolen Vau repulsor technology. Gravity is normally maintained by repulsor pads in the ceilings of a ship, exerting a constant downward pressure on the passengers, just enough to mimic a comfortable level of gravity.

The only real limitation on speed is a ship's shields — a ship must have enough shields to protect it from space dust and debris when traveling at extreme speeds. See *Shields*, below.

Shields

Space is not a complete void — it's full of dust and other particles, some larger and harder than others. Starships are protected from space debris (and enemy weapons) by energy shields — industrial versions of the personal energy shield. While all hulls have a degree of armor, it cannot easily withstand weaponry or asteroid collisions (and boarding marines have torches to cut through it). Shields, however, can stand up to all sorts of beatings.

Like personal shields, shipboard shields activate their fields upon sensing impact with kinetic energy or matter. The problem is that, the faster the ship goes, the more debris it encounters, and thus the more shields it needs to protect against this onslaught. The larger the ship, the greater the area needing protection. Larger ships tend to move more slowly when engaged in combat than smaller ships, since their shields cannot protect them at high speeds. Ships that travel faster than their shields can protect against will begin tearing apart, pounded by debris.

Ships are rated by the number of shields they have available at various speeds. In general, all are available whenever is ship is at a full stop, but as it begins accelerating, more and more banks are activated by debris, and are thus unable to protect against weapons fire. This works inverse to the ship's velocity: At quarter thrust, three-quarters of the ship's shields are available, half of them at half thrust, one quarter of them at three-quarter thrust, and none at full thrust (the last bank is busy protecting against space debris). Note, however, that a ship with 6 shields at full stop has only 4 at 1/4 thrust, 2 at 1/2 thrust, 1 at 3/4 thrust, and none at full thrust.

Ship Class Chart

Shields, Turrets and HP (Gundeck Hardpoints) are the MAXIMUM that may be placed on a particular hull; they must each be bought separately.

Crew is the MINIMUM required to man the ship without suffering penalties. Military ships of the line often need double the required complement. P = Pilot, N= Navigator, Bc = Bridge Crew, E = Engineer. Note: In addition to the minimums listed, each gun must have a gunner (or think machine program) to fire it.

Ship Class	Size Rating	Dimensions*	Grade	Engines	Shields	Turrets	HP	Crew
Shuttle	1	10 x 5 x 7	Lander	Fast	2/2	—	2	P
Explorer	3	30 x 10 x 7	Lander	Fast	2/2	1 Small	3	P, E
Raider	4	35 x 12 x 10	Lander	Fast	2/2	1 Small	10	P, E
Escort	4	40 x 13 x 10	Lander	Fast	2/2	1 Small	15	P, E
Frigate	6	60 x 20 x 15	Atmosphere	Fast	4/4	1 Med (2)	30	P, N, E x2
Galliot	7	70 x 23 x 17	Atmosphere	Fast	4/4	1 Med (1)	20	P, N, E x2
Fast Freighter**	8	65 x 33 x 25	Void	Fast	4/4	1 Small	3	P, N, E
Small Freighter**	10	90 x 38 x 30	Void	Standard	6/6	1 Small	6	P, N, E x2
Assault Lander	10	100 x 33 x 25	Lander	Fast	8/8	1 Med (2)	20	P, N, Bc, E x3
Destroyer	10	100 x 33 x 25	Atmosphere	Fast	8/8	2 Med (2)	50	P, N, Bc x2, E x5
Cruiser	14	140 x 47 x 35	Void	Standard	9/9	2 Large	75	P x2, N x2, Bc x3, E x8
Large Freighter**	15	150 x 40 x 38	Void	Standard	6/6	1 Small	6	P, N, E x3
Luxury Liner***	15	140 x 50 x 38	Void	Slow	6/6	1 Small	6	P, N, Bc, E x2
Dreadnought	25	250 x 80 x 62	Void	Standard	12/12	3 Large	105	P x2, N x2, Bc x5, E x10

* Internal dimensions: length x width x height. Ship dimensions can vary from builder to builder — some ships are wider or taller than they are long. In general, the length is 10 meters per size rating, while the width averages a third of the ship's length. The height is usually one quarter of the length. Most ships are designed with 10 meter-high ceilings; freighters are an exception, as they often have large cargo bays.

** Most space is taken up by one or more cargo pods, standardized shipping crates which are usually pre-packaged at the pick-up point. Fast freighters usually have only one pod, while a large freighter may have five small pods or two larger pods, or any combination of sizes. Freighters and luxury liners are almost always accompanied by escort ships to defend them from pirates.

*** Most space is taken by passenger stateroom and dining halls.

Since shields are distributed evenly around a ship, the ship only gains half its available shields against a single attacker in one turn, although the other half can defend from another attack as long as is directed to the other side of the ship. Shields are thus listed by the flank they protect (left or right).

Each shield blocks one shot from a shipboard gun per turn (regardless of how much damage that shot actually does). Certain weapons can leak through shields, just as a hand-held blaster does against personal shields. On damage die results of 1 or 2, the damage ignores shields and is inflicted directly on the ship's Vitality.

Cost: 3,000 firebirds per shield.

Armament

The ship's weaponry. Each hull has a certain number of hardpoints which it can mount weaponry upon; the larger the ship, the more guns it can carry. However, these guns must be distributed evenly throughout the ship, and thus not all may be able to fire at the same target in a single turn. Figure that a ship can fire half its gundeck armaments at any targets off one side of the ship in one turn, although it

Speed Chart

Thrust	Engine speed*			Combat modifier	Pursuit modifier
	Slow	Standard	Fast		
Full stop	NA	NA	NA	NA	NA
1/4 thrust	1%	1%	2%	+1	-1
Half thrust	2%	2%	4%	0	0
3/4 thrust	3%	4%	6%	-1	+1
Full thrust	4%	6%	8%	-2	+2

* Percentage of lightspeed, based on ship class

Distance Traveled

Speed	AUs/24 hrs	Jumpgate*	Total Trip**
1% lightspeed	1.73	40 days	80 days
2% lightspeed	3.46	20 days	40 days
3% lightspeed	5.19	14 days	28 days
4% lightspeed	6.92	10 days	20 days
6% lightspeed	10.38	7 days	14 days
8% lightspeed	13.85	5 days	10 days

* Distance to jumpgate (average 69 AU)

** Planet to jumpgate to planet

can fire the other half at targets on the other side of the ship. Turret-mounted guns can fire in any direction, but only once per turn.

Note that ships smaller than cruisers cannot mount heavy weapons, and only frigate class and above can mount medium guns.

See the Armament Chart for more details.

Direct Fire

Blaster: A gun that fires a hot ball of plasma energy encased in an energy field. The field explodes upon impact with an object, releasing the plasma energy. Blasters, like shipboard lasers, can leak through energy shields. Cost: 2000 for light, 3000 medium, 4000 heavy.

EM Pulse Gun: A gun designed solely to burn-out a shield. Whenever an EM Pulse Gun hits a shield, the shield is burned-out for one turn and cannot defend against weapon fire. It is a rare weapon, but effective when combined with slug guns. Cost: 3000 firebirds.

Gatling Laser: A small, short range gun with a rotating barrel that allows it to recharge — and thus fire — more quickly than other shipboard weaponry. It can only fire at adjacent targets, such as indirect ordnance, boarding marines or grappled ships. Cost: 3000 firebirds.

Grappling Gun: A gun that fires grapples which magnetically lock onto an enemy hull. The cable then retracts, pulling the two ships together (the smaller ship is drawn to the larger). Cost: 1000 firebirds.

Gremlin Gun: A gun which causes havoc with a target ship's electrical systems. A successful hit ignores shields and levies a -3 penalty on all that ship's actions for four turns. Cost: 3000 firebirds.

Heat Blaster: A gun that fires a sheath of super-hot flame. Normally, shields cannot protect against this weapon, but some angles of fire will activate shields nonetheless. This is represented by a -3 goal penalty to hit a shielded ship with the gun. Cost: 3000 firebirds.

Laser: A gun firing an intense beam of coherent light. Lasers, like blasters, can leak through energy shields. Cost: 2000 for light, 3000 for medium, 4000 for heavy.

Meson Cannon: Perhaps the most feared of starship weaponry, the awesome meson cannon easily tears through shields and anything else in its path. Only cruisers can mount the light cannon, and only dreadnoughts can mount the larger, spinal mount meson cannon. Cost: 10,000 for light, 20,000 for heavy.

Slug Gun: A gun that lobs a large mass of heavy metal or explosive at an enemy ship. Slug guns are not very effective against shields, but they are devastating to unshielded targets. Cost: 2000 for light, 3000 for medium, 4000 for heavy.

Spacecraft Armament Chart

Roll: Dexterity + Warfare (Gunnery)

DMG: Roll the number of dice listed plus the gunner's victory points on a Dexterity + Warfare (Gunnery) roll.

Direct Fire

Weapon	Goal	Dmg	HP*	Effect
Lt Slug Gun		4	2	Cannot leak through shields
Md Slug Gun		5	3	Cannot leak through shields
Hvy Slug Gun		6	4	Cannot leak through shields
Gatling Laser		1	3	Short range weapon; cannot leak through shields
Lt Laser	+2	2	2	Leaks through a shield on DMG rolls of 1, 2 or 3
Med Laser	+2	3	3	Leaks through a shield on DMG rolls of 1, 2 or 3
Hvy Laser	+2	4	4	Leaks through a shield on DMG rolls of 1, 2 or 3
Lt Blaster		3	2	Leaks through a shield on DMG rolls of 1, 2 or 3
Med Blaster		4	3	Leaks through a shield on DMG rolls of 1, 2 or 3
Hvy Blaster		5	4	Leaks through a shield on DMG rolls of 1, 2 or 3
Heat Blaster	-3 vs shields	3	3	A hit ignores shields
Lt Meson Cannon		5	4	Overpowers shields: each shield stops only 1 DMG pt
Hvy Meson Cannon		11-20†	20	Overpowers shields: each shield stops only 1 DMG pt
Grappling Gun		special	1	Ignores shields, grapples targeted ship
EM Pulse Gun		2	3	Burns-out shield for 1 turn
Gremlin Gun		special	3	Ignores shields, target ship suffers -3 penalty to all rolls for four turns
Tractor Beam		special	4	Decelerates target ship by quarter speed per turn.

* Hardpoints: This is the number of hardpoints the gun takes up on a ship; see the Ship Class Chart for the number of hardpoints a hull can bear.

Indirect Fire

Weapon	Goal*	Dmg	HP	Effect
Rocket**	7	2	2	Ignores shields, travels for 4 turns, -2 to evade
Missile**	8	4	3	Ignores shields, travels for 6 turns
Torpedo**	9	6	4	Ignores shields, travels for 8 turns

* Goal number is determined by ordnance type, not gunner skill.

** Indirect fire ordnance may be shot down by any weapon except indirect fire ordnance. At least 3 victory points on Dx + Warfare (Gunnery) roll must be scored to destroy the ordnance. Alternatively, crack pilots can try to evade ordnance by outrunning or outmaneuvering it. This requires a sustained Wits + Drive Spacecraft roll; if 15 or more successes are scored within four turns, the ordnance has been successfully evaded.

† Roll a d20 and add 10 to any results of 10 or less, for a total range of 11-20.

Tractor Beam: A gun that creates a field around its target, absorbing its momentum and slowing the ship down. An extremely rare piece of Second Republic technology, it is especially loved by Inquisitors who police the spacelanes. Once a ship has been caught by the beam, it cannot escape except by maneuvering between the beam-emitting ship and a stellar object (moon, planet). Cost: 15,000 firebirds

Indirect Fire

Rocket: The smallest indirect fire ordnance, a rocket is also the fastest (-2 on evasion rolls) but it loses its lock on a target easier (-3 goal). Rockets slip right past shields without activating them. Cost: 2000 for the launcher, 200 per rocket.

Missile: The standard ordnance, missiles suffer a -2 goal penalty but ignore shields. Cost: 3000 for the launcher, 300 per missile.

Torpedo: The largest ordnance, a torpedo can really tear an enemy ship apart. -1 goal penalty, ignore shields. Cost: 4000 for launcher, 500 per torpedo.

Turrets

A turret mount costs for than a gundeck mount. Add the following costs to the weapon price:

Turret size	Guns allowed	Cost
Small	One Light gun	2000
Medium	One Medium gun	4000
Medium	Two Light guns	5000
Medium	Two Medium guns	6000
Large	Three Light guns	7000
Large	Three Medium guns	10,000
Large	Three Heavy guns	12,000

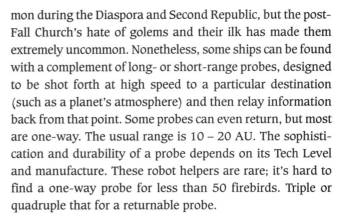

Sensors

Sensors are rated on a scale of 1-10 (representing astronomical units) and by type. Sensors require little attention except when trying to discover details, such as whether that ship exiting the jumpgate is a frigate or a scout ship, and if it's a Church or League ship. This fine observation requires a Tech + Science (Sensors) roll. However, subtract one from the roll for each AU (astronomical unit) distant the ship is. Sensors cannot detect anything useful past their ranges (one AU per rating).

Active transmissions are handled differently; as long as the receiving ship is within range (see *Transmissions*, below), it can gain whatever details are transmitted.

Ships have one or more of the following sensor arrays:

Radar (TL4): The most common type of sensors, using active radio wave transmissions. Radar cannot be rated higher than 5 (planetary signals and space debris interfere with the range). Cost is 500 firebirds plus 200 per rating.

Laser radar (TL5): Light-based radar, sending active light transmissions. While more information can be conveyed than with radar, it can be blocked or confused by debris, gas clouds, or other obstructions. Cannot be rated higher than 5. Cost is 750 firebirds plus 200 per rating.

Densometer (TL5): Measures the density of surrounding space. Cannot be rated higher than 5. Cost is 750 firebirds plus 200 per rating.

Infrared (TL5): Reads the infrared spectrum for heat sources such as spaceship engines. Cannot be rated higher than 7. Cost is 1000 firebirds plus 200 per rating.

EMS (TL6): Sensors which read a wide array of the electromagnetic spectrum. Cannot be rated higher than 8. Cost is 3000 firebirds plus 200 per rating.

Neutrinos (TL7): The standard sensor array of the Second Republic, using neutrino beam transmissions. Rating can go up to 10. Cost is 5000 firebirds plus 500 per rating.

Psi sensors (TL8): Extremely rare, these psionic devices scan space for neural activity. They can be rated up to 10, but can only read people, not ships. These sensors do not require psychics to operate them. These are used as backup sensors only; a ship with Psi sensors alone would not be able to read large, lifeless space debris. Cost is 30,000 firebirds plus 200 per rating.

Transmissions

Sending information is easier than passively receiving it. The range is potentially unlimited, although in actuality signals are broken up over distance, making them effectively unreadable at extreme ranges. Assume a ship has a transmitter similar to its sensor, but the AU range at which it can send viable signals is 5x its sensor range (level 5 Radar can transmit radio messages up to 25 AU away).

Probes (TL5+): Robotic probes were somewhat common during the Diaspora and Second Republic, but the post-Fall Church's hate of golems and their ilk has made them extremely uncommon. Nonetheless, some ships can be found with a complement of long- or short-range probes, designed to be shot forth at high speed to a particular destination (such as a planet's atmosphere) and then relay information back from that point. Some probes can even return, but most are one-way. The usual range is 10 – 20 AU. The sophistication and durability of a probe depends on its Tech Level and manufacture. These robot helpers are rare; it's hard to find a one-way probe for less than 50 firebirds. Triple or quadruple that for a returnable probe.

Buoy (TL5+): Stationary buoys can be placed at various points in a solar system to quickly relay information to a ship designed to receive its coded message. Since this form of transmission is one way (from buoy to ship), it is meant to travel farther than most two-way sensors. The usually range is 25 AU, but a chain of buoys can be linked to send information farther. Such "guard posts" (most buoys scan within a 3 AU region) are favored by those noble houses who can afford to lace their planetary systems with them (they are often destroyed by malcontents, pirates or rivals), and are especially favored by pirate-hunting Inquisitors. The average buoy costs 300 firebirds.

Emergency Signals: All ships can emit an emergency signal, an interplanetary call for help. This signal gives little information beyond the location of the troubled ship. The range is usually 25 AU.

Note: Such science fiction standbys as life scanners are unknown in the Known Worlds, although Symbiots are rumored to be able to detect life at long ranges. In addition, very little about a planet's atmosphere can be detected without a sample of that atmosphere — which usually requires entering the atmosphere.

Crew

Each ship class rates the minimum crew needed to fully operate the ship (see Ship Class sidebar, above). Besides the minimum, a ship can bunk a captain and a number of people equal to its size rating +1; this total allowed crew complement can include extra crew, marines and/or passengers. A ship also includes bunk space for one gunner per gun it mounts.

This complement assumes that the officers — the captain, pilot, navigator and engineer — each have private bunks, while all others share double (or triple) bunks. Extra room for passengers can be made by transforming officer bunks. In addition, if a gun is run by a think machine program instead of a gunner, the empty gunner's bunk space can be taken by a passenger or marine.

Crewmembers tend to be hired for certain tasks, and while some can cross-over to perform other tasks, most know

only their own field of expertise. The typical shipboard positions are:

Captain: All military ships have a captain — almost always a noble — presiding over the vessel's missions. Non-military vessels may or may not have a captain in addition to the positions listed below — League merchant vessels are often captained by their pilots.

Pilot: All ships must have a pilot. This position is almost always taken by a Charioteer guildmember, although some factions use Charioteer-trained pilots who aren't actual guildmembers. Every ship must have a pilot. A pilot can double for a navigator but he must take two actions to both fly the ship and use the sensors in the same turn. Wage: 20 per jump.

Navigator: The navigator mans the sensors and helps the pilot plot a course through the ever-revolving stellar bodies within a solar system. This task is often performed by the pilot on smaller ships. Navigators can usually fly the ship in emergencies. Wage: 10 per jump.

Bridge crew: Larger ships need a complement of crewmen on the bridge to run all the functions. Some may be guildmembers, but most will be freemen or serfs from the captain's fiefs. Some bridge crew may be able to fly the ship for short stints in emergencies. Wage: 3 per jump.

Chief Engineer: A post usually filled by a member of the Engineer's guild. Wage: 15 per jump.

Assistant engineers: Smaller ships need only one engineer, but larger ones need assistants. Only the most wealthy vessels can man these posts with Engineer guildsmembers. Wage: 5 per jump.

Gunner: The guys who actually aim and fire the guns, whether turret or deck-mounted. Wage: 5 per jump.

Miscellaneous: Different ships have different needs. A cruiser might need a chef to feed its huge amount of crewmen, while a luxury liner needs pursers and butlers to attend the needs of its wealthy passengers. Military ships need jet jockeys to operate their maneuver jets. Most ships also have a number of swabbies, crew whose job it is to fill in the blanks: scrub the floors, peel the potatoes, or fill in for an injured or sick crewman. Wages vary between 1 – 3 firebirds per jump.

Spacesuits

Not every captain can afford to outfit his entire crew with spacesuits. When a hull breach occurs, that section is sealed off from others by airlocks which can be opened manually. Crewmembers within the compromised section must rely on "vac bags," sealed environment bags that allow little freedom of movement; their air supply comes from hoses hooked to the central life support piping. Vac bags don't stand up well to combat.

Important crewmembers (captain, guildsmembers) get spacesuits, which provide freedom of movement and some protection from a boarding marine's sword. Cost: 100 firebirds.

Marines

Ships often have a number of marines aboard to repel invaders or to board enemy ships. Usually, only military ships or escorts have marines, although luxury liners may have a small complement. A ship's marines and/or marauder complement is counted towards the ship's total allowed crew complement (see Crew, above).

Ships attempting boarding combat fly close to their target ship and fire grapple guns. Once these hit, they retract and draw the two ships together. Then, marines are released into space along the tether lines to cut their way into the enemy hull (or enter a hole created by weapons fire). Once in the enemy ship, they are usually met by defending marines, and must fight sword to sword to gain the bridge, where they can force the captain's surrender.

Some ships carry marauders, specially trained and equipped boarders. Marauders wear jet-propelled, powered-armor spacesuits that allow them to propel through space to another ship without needing a grapple cable to slide along (although they must still be within range of boarding; see *Spaceship Combat*, below.)

Wages for marines vary between 5 – 10 firebirds per jump, depending on how good they are. Double or triple this fee for marauders.

Passengers

Each ship lists the number of passengers (in addition to crew and marines) the ship was designed to comfortably allow. Military ships allow for little room than that necessary to carry their crew complements. Any positions from the total allowed crew complement not filled by crew or marines are left open for passengers.

Cargo

A ship is rated by the amount of metric tons it can haul. Most ship hull designs allow for some cargo space in addition to their ship systems (usually size rating x10 in metric tons); ships that need more will have to convert space from ship systems (gundecks, engineering, etc.) to cargo space. Each gundeck hardpoint converted allows 10 metric tons of cargo space. Interior bulkheads and exterior hull can also be removed to allow for more room: each Vitality point converted to cargo equals 10 metric tons of space. This Vitality is not subtracted from the ship's total, but is marked as cargo — any hits taken to those levels will also destroy the cargo hauled.

If necessary, cargo space can be converted into staterooms or bunkrooms for extra passengers. Figure that 10 metric tons of space can make one stateroom, which can hold one or two people comfortably (a total of five can

squeeze in if necessary).

Most cargo-carrying freighters use an industrial cargo pod shipping system that dates back to the Second Republic and which has been maintained by the Merchant League. Cargo pods come in all shapes and sizes and are designed to clamp to a freighter's hull. Certain freighters hulls are no more than skeletons designed to carry multiple pods. There are smaller freighter, however, that don't use cargo pods, but instead have huge internal cargo bays.

Supplies

How much food, water, air, etc., the ship normally contains. Almost all ports have merchants who deal specifically in reprovisioning ship stores. Most ships can carry 10x their size ratings in days, -2 per crewmember, passenger or marine. (A Decados dreadnought with a size rating of 25 and total complement of 111 people can carry enough supplies to provision the crew for 28 days.) More supplies can be stored by taking up cargo space; figure that enough to provision 10 people for one day can be fitted into one metric ton of space.

Costs are generally one firebird per person per week. (444 firebirds for the Decados dreadnought's crew for 28 days, or four weeks.) Certain passengers may cost more, especially if they insist on their own staterooms and caviar with every meal.

Vitality

The amount of damage a ship can take before it becomes an empty hulk floating through space. A ship's Vitality is equal to its size rating x10.

Unlike characters, ships do not heal by themselves; any Vitality damage must be repaired by a technician. The cost for repairing hull damage is usually 100x the ship's size rating per Vitality point. For example, the cost to repair one Vitality level of damage on an al-Malik explorer (size rating 3) is 300 firebirds.

However, loss of the last five "vital" levels (those that levy penalties) signifies engine damage, limiting a ship's ability to power all system continuously (the penalties apply to ALL ship systems rolls, including gunnery). In addition, the generators refuse to recharge, limiting the ship's fuel supply and thus its maximum travel range.

Normally, a ship's fusion generators handle most power needs on a ship. Since a ship only needs to engage its thrust when accelerating — it will maintain its speed until thrust is applied to slow it down — fusion generators can recharge between thrusts. If a ship suffers damage to its "vital" levels, it progressively loses the ability to generate sufficient fuel. If this happens, the engines must be repaired and recharged at a starbase or spaceport. The cost is usually 10% of the ship's base hull cost per "vital" level repaired.

When the -2 Vitality level is lost, a ship only has enough fuel remaining to travel 150 AU (one trip from a planet to jumpgate to planet again). If the -4 level is lost, this distance is halved (75 AU), and so on until at -10, the ship only has enough fuel to take it 10 AUs. Emergency power for life support, radio transmissions and minimal shield coverage (enough to protect the ship from debris but not weapons) will last for a number of days equal to the ship's rating x5, -1 per person aboard. (A disabled explorer unable to ignite its thrust engines can keep its three-man crew alive for 12 days.)

Note that a disabled ship will continue to travel along its vector at its former speed until stopped. The pilot can call on emergency power to perform maneuvers — such as pointing the ship toward a planet — at the cost of one day of life support per maneuver.

Other Ship Systems
Think Machines

Each spacecraft requires a think machine. Most ships are assumed to have think machines capable of handling all their standard requirements; getting them to do anymore than that, however, is problematical. Below is a list of some extra programs available.

Gunnery: There are a variety of think machine programs which can aid under-manned ships, taking over gunnery positions. These automatic tracking systems usually have a goal of 7, making them worse than most living gunners but better than an empty turret. AI gunners usually have more dice, but are proscribed by the Church. The cost for the hookups is 500 firebirds per gun, plus 3000 for the software to run them all.

Autopilot: The ship can pilot itself. It must be given a destination to which it will plot the best course. Giving it extra parameters helps (i.e., you need to get there faster rather than safer). Some autopilots have emergency landing routines whereby they will choose the destination themselves (the closest, safest landing or orbit). The cost is for the hookups is 500 plus 5000 for the software (Drive Spacecraft goal of 9).

Combat pilot: A more advanced autopilot, this program can take over tight maneuvering. It is best for defensive maneuvers, but performs relatively well in offensive situations also. Most programs have a goal of 7 for dodging enemy fire. Add 3000 to the cost of the autopilot software.

Mapping: The computer can map and remember multiple star systems, storing many details on these systems. It costs about 3000 firebirds for a mapping program and about 500 firebirds per preprogrammed system. Proscribed routes (for worlds such as Stigmata or Vau) are more expensive, and hard to find.

Data Analysis: The computer can analyze various situations. It must have the requisite skill program (usually a

Lore), which costs anywhere from 50 to 300 firebirds. Most data analysis machines have a goal of 7. The usefulness of the analysis depends on the number of successes rolled.

Jumproutes: The computer has preprogrammed jumproutes within its memory. Beware, however, for the Charioteers consider this illegal. They will destroy such memory and usually the machine with it, if not the ship's crew also. While it is harder to steal jumproute data than a jumpkey, it takes longer to access the data. Most routes are available on the black market. Costs vary with the route, but the most common (Byzantium Secundus to Criticorum) still costs 3000 firebirds.

Escape Pods

Well-maintained ships usually have a complement of escape pods for a full crew and passenger load, but with less well-maintained ships this is not always the case. There are few manufacturers of life boats left in the Known Worlds, leaving many ships in the predicament of having less escape pods than needed, or none at all. Most military ships have a full complement, as do most noble ships, but it is not uncommon for a freighter to only have enough room in its escape pods for half its crew. Some crews have taken to bolting landers to their ships to serve as life boats instead.

Escape pods are usually built in three man increments, ranging from three-man escape pods to 18-man escape pods. These pods usually hold enough food for a full passenger load for two weeks, in addition to tents, a small handgun and an emergency beacon. This beacon has a range of about 25 AU and activates as soon as the escape pod is jettisoned from the mother ship. Most escape pods travel at 5% of the speed of light. They usually have a range of about 10 AU. Escape pods cannot be fitted with a jumpdrive.

An escape pod can be jettisoned within one combat turn after everyone has boarded. The escape pod, equipped with an emergency landing autopilot, then locates the nearest habitable area (it usually has radar sensors rated at 5), usually another ship or a planet. The crew of the pod may refuse certain destination choices, such as an enemy ship. The escape pod's computers look for the most basic life requirements, meaning that the planet it decides upon may be just marginally habitable. These computers, of course, are prone to failure. Some have been know to fly straight into a sun or crash into another ship.

Cost: 3000 per three-person capacity. A ship may carry one pod per size rating above 3.

Spaceship Combat

Starship combat can get quite complicated, especially when tracking each ship's position and speed in relation to one another. **Fading Suns** provides a very simple rules resolution system for such combat. Players wishing for more detail (hit locations, exact positioning, internal systems dam-

age) should consult the **Noble Armada** starship miniatures combat game, also available from Holistic Design. It provides a hex-by-hex yet easy-to-play combat system for fleet engagements.

Combat between spaceships in **Fading Suns** is handled, for the most part, like combat between characters, only on a larger scale.

Pursuit

Pursuit can only take place between ships which can detect each other with their sensors. Pursuit is treated as a sustained action. Each pilot rolls Wits + Drive Spacecraft (adding or subtracting the ship's tactical modifier and any speed modifier) and must accumulate a number of victory points in a series of sustained rolls. Whoever collects the required victory points first is the winner: the pursuer closes on his prey and combat begins, or the prey outdistances his pursuer, leaving sensor range. The amount of victory points depends on the situation; the usual amount is 10. As a general rule, the number should be no less than the pursuing ship's Sensors rating.

The amount of victory points can be adjusted by various factors: if the pursuer is close to the prey when the chase begins, he may have to accumulate less points than his prey; a chase through an asteroid field may increase the amount the pursuer must roll (in addition to requiring Dexterity + Drive Spacecraft rolls to avoid colliding with an asteroid); and a run through a nebula may interfere with both ships' sensors, dramatically decreasing the amount the prey needs to escape. In addition, the gamemaster may want to award faster ships a bonus to each roll they make.

A Good Engineer: Sometimes, a ship needs to give all she's got to escape a battle or to start one. The ship's engineer can temporarily tweak his engines to give his ship the extra oomph it needs. Each turn, roll Tech + High Tech Redemption and add the victory points to the ship's pursuit victory point total (see Pursuit). However, this is dangerous, for it strains the engines past their safe operating limit. If a critical failure is rolled, the engines shut down. The ship immediately begins to drift. The engines will remain down for at least one hour.

Combat

Once a ship has closed within fighting range of its prey, it may fire its guns.

There are a number of things to take into account for combat:

Initiative: A ship's initiative depends on its pilot's Drive Spacecraft skill.

Ship speed: A ship's tactical speed affects its combat and pursuit capabilities. Ships must state how fast they are traveling: full thrust, three-quarter thrust, half thrust or quarter thrust. See the *Speed Chart*, above, for a list of modi-

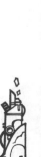

Al-Malik *Odyssey* Class Explorer

A popular vessel among Questing Knights and scavengers alike, the *Odyssey* class explorer is also used by itinerant nobles who have fierce wanderlusts and small entourages.

Size rating: 3 (30 meters long, 10 wide, 7 high)

Grade: Lander

Engines: Fast

Shields:

Speed	Left/Right
Full thrust	0/0
3/4 thrust	1/1
Half thrust	1/1
1/4 thrust	2/2
Full stop	2/2

Armament: 1 Lt Laser, 1 Grapple Gun

Sensors: EMS 5

Crew: 4 (captain, pilot, navigator/gunner, engineer)

Marines: 0

Passengers: 3

Cargo: 30 metric tons

Vitality: -10/-8/-6/-4/-2/0/0/0/0/0/0/0/0/0/0/0/0/0/0/0/0/0/0/0/0/0/0

Cost: 49,000 firebirds

fiers and rules.

There are a number of actions that can be taken by pilots and crewmen. Unless otherwise noted, each of these takes one action; performing more than one action per turn levies a multiple action penalty.

Dodge: A pilot can maneuver his ship to avoid enemy fire. Roll Dexterity + Drive Spacecraft and contest the number of successes against all goal rolls targeted against the ship, just as with a hand-to-hand combat Dodge. This takes one action to perform; if the pilots performs other actions in the same turn (such as maneuvering around that asteroid), he suffers the multiple action penalties for all his actions that turn.

Firing Guns: A pilot or gunner can fire one of the ship's guns. Roll Dexterity + Warfare (Gunnery) and add the victory dice to the weapon's damage. This takes one action to perform; if the gunner performs other actions in the same turn, she suffers the multiple action penalties for all her actions that turn.

Shields may block weapon damage (see *Shields*, above). Any shots that get past shields do damage directly to the ship's Vitality.

Approaching to Board: A ship that desires to board another must first approach within range of its grapple guns. Unless the target ship allows this to happen, this requires a sustained and contested roll between the two pilots. The amount of victory points required is 6; if the boarding ship wins, it is in range to fire grapple cables. If the cables miss, the target ship can try to disengage (see below).

Once grappled, a ship can launch boarders. They take one turn to traverse space and breach a ship's hull, after which they are inside the ship and will travel towards the bridge unless halted by defenders. Combat between boarders is handled with the **Fading Suns** combat rules given in Chapter Six: Combat.

Disengage: At anytime in the combat, a ship can attempt to disengage and escape. This is a sustained and contested action between the ship and any ships attacking it. Roll Wits + Drive Spacecraft; the number of victory points required is 10. Local obstacles (asteroids, nebulas) can provide bonuses on the disengaging ship's roll. Once a ship has successfully disengaged, it has escaped and no further pursuit rolls need be made. At the gamemaster's discretion, this may require the ship to land on a moon or planet.

Example of Space Combat

Andy's character is a Charioteer merchant who plies the spacelanes in his Free Trader selling contraband goods to shady customers (actually, the ship belongs to his guild — if he breaks it, he'll have to pay a fine). His partner in crime is played by Bernie, who acts as gunner on their small ship. They are traveling to the planet Madoc with particularly sen-

sitive cargo — think machines with Second Republic history texts. As they approach the planet, their sensors immediately alert them to the Inquisition frigate lying in wait behind the moon.

Gamemaster: "You are hailed by Inquisitor Drelig of the Church ship the 'Rack.' He demands that you come to a full stop and prepare to be boarded so that he may examine your cargo."

Andy: "No way! I'm getting out of here. If I can get to Madoc, can I lose them?"

Gamemaster: "Depends on how well you fly. Let's see, since you're not too far from the planet, you'll need to collect 6 victory points to reach it. Once there, you can lose them in the atmosphere. However, if they get 6 V.P. first, they can start firing on you."

Andy: "I'm going for it!"

Bernie: "Are you nuts? We should just let them do what they want and hope for mercy!"

Andy: "Yeah, right! They'll lock us up and brand us for trading heretical stuff — Republican propaganda, they call it. I'm still traveling at full thrust. How fast are they going?"

Gamemaster: "They accelerated to quarter thrust from a full stop as soon as they saw you."

Andy: "Good. That means they've got a penalty on their pursuit rolls, right?"

Gamemaster: (Checking the Speed Chart.) "Yeah, -1."

Andy: (His character's Wits 5 + Drive Spacecraft 8 give him a natural goal of 13. Adding his +2 full thrust pursuit modifier gives him a modified goal of 15. He rolls and gets five successes.) "One victory point!"

Gamemaster: (Rolls for the Inquisition frigate pilot: a Wits of 7 and a Drive Spacecraft skill of 7 gives him a 14 goal; even with the -1 penalty, he gets 10 successes.) "Looks like they did better — they got three V.P. Their ominous frigate gains on you as you make your mad dash to the water world."

Andy: "Argh. I'm not giving up yet." (Rolls again and gets two V.P.) "That gives me three victory points so far."

Gamemaster: "They accelerate to half thrust in their attempt to intercept you." (There's no pursuit penalty for that speed, but the pilot does suffer a -4 multiple action penalty for accelerating and pursuing in the same turn. The roll result is 9 — 3 victory points, for a sustained total of 6 V.P.) "Tsk, tsk. Their pilot pulls a quick maneuver and slips in front of your ship. You are engaged."

Andy: "They're not getting me without a fight!"

Gamemaster: "All right, you've got a Drive Spacecraft skill of 8, but you suffer a -2 initiative penalty for your speed. Their pilot's skill is 7, with no modifier for speed. They've got the initiative. Their right broadside unleashes all guns — four Heat Blasters."

Andy: "I'm dodging that!" (Rolls his Dexterity 7 + Drive

League *Free Trader* Class Freighter

Built from a converted League *Courier* class escort, the Free Trader class freighter is the favored starship of entrepreneurial Charioteers who travel the merchant lanes buying low and selling high with little overhead. One drawback, however, is that its cargo hold is interior to the ship, precluding the merchant from hauling preloaded cargo pods.

Size rating: 4 (35 meters long, 15 wide, 13 high)
Grade: Lander
Engines: Fast
Shields:

Speed	Left/Right
Full thrust	0/0
3/4 thrust	1/1
Half thrust	1/1
1/4 thrust	2/2
Full stop	2/2

Armament: 1 Lt Laser (turret), 1 Grapple Gun
Sensors: Laser radar 5
Crew: 5 (captain, pilot, navigator, gunner, engineer)
Marines: 0
Passengers: 3
Cargo: 330 metric tons
Vitality: -10/-8/-6/-4/-2/{0/0/0/0/0/0/0/0/0/0/0/0/0/0}/0/0/0/0/0/0/0/0/0/0/0/0/0/0/0/0/0/0/0/0/0
(The last 14 pts of Vitality before penalties represent cargo space; damage also applies to cargo)
Cost: 58,750 firebirds

Characters and Scale

Ships have Vitality, shields and weapons. However, these traits are on a much larger scale than similar character traits. In most instances, a character's weapon will be incapable of harming a spacecraft, or do so little damage as not to matter. When dealing with character scale situations (characters at the spaceport shooting a docked ship with their blasters), figure that each point of ship Vitality is worth five points of character damage (this is not necessarily true inside the ship). In addition, starship weapons do their normal damage x5 when directed against characters. For instance, a Light Laser, which normally does 2 dice of damage, will do 10 dice against characters (plus any victory dice gained by the gun operator).

Spacecraft 8 , -2 for traveling full thrust, for a modified goal of 13, and gets 11 successes.)

Gamemaster: (The Inquisition gunners only have goals of 10; thanks to Andy's 11 successes, they'll only succeed on rolls of "1" — always a success, no matter the odds. The roll results are 3, 5, 15, 7 = no hits.) "Gouts of flame burp from the gundeck but miss your ship."

Bernie: "My turn!" (Rolls his character's Dexterity 5 + Warfare (Gunnery) 3 and gets 6 successes, or two victory points.) "Got him!"

Gamemaster: "Their pilot attempts to dodge your fire. He gets five successes. Since this is a contested roll, that leaves you with one success: no victory dice to add to your damage. At half thrust, they've got two shields available on the flank facing you. Only one is required to completely stop your laser, but you may leak through it on rolls of 1 or 2."

Bernie: "Good enough." (Rolls Light Laser damage of 2 on six-sided dice and gets results of 3 and 4 = two damage points, none of which leaks through the shield.) "We can't touch these guys! They way outgun us!"

Andy: "Forget fighting! I'm going to disengage."

Gamemaster: "Okay, turn two. You attempt to disengage but they attempt to stop you — and they keep firing at the same time. They've got initiative, so the guns fire first. (Rolls for the Inquisition gunners, who have goals of 10 or less. Heat Blasters suffer a penalty against shields, but since Andy and Bernie's ship is traveling full thrust, it has no shields available for defense. The roll results are 3, 15, 11, 13. Only one hits, with one victory point. Even if there was a shield available, the Heat Blaster would ignore it; the damage is applied directly to the ship's Vitality. The gamemaster rolls 3 six-sided dice + 1 victory die, with results of 2, 4, 6, 1 = three points of damage.) "A sheath of flame engulfs your small ship, melting metal and popping rivets. A heat wave washes over you before your life support adjusts for the increased temperature."

Andy: "We won't last long with that." (He rolls, adding his +2 escape modifier for traveling full speed. His goal is now 15 or less and he rolls that number exactly — a critical success with 10 victory points.) "Yes!"

Gamemaster: "Don't celebrate yet — unlike pursuit, this one's a contested roll." (Rolls for the Inquisition pilot and fails.) "Damn! He didn't anticipate your sudden slip to the right, and went left instead. You shoot past them and into the atmosphere of Madoc. Their sensors can't pick you out among the flitters and wildlife flying around the planet, so you escape."

Bernie: "We were lucky — this time."

Passage Costs

Characters who do not own spacecraft or who do not work on one must pay for passage. Cost varies with the type of ship, the accommodations accepted and the length of the journey. Most ships do not allow passengers to carry weapons on board; they will confiscate them at the beginning of a journey and keep them in a weapons locker until arrival.

Tramp freighter: The worst accommodations available — crammed into a cargo box with a bunch of other passengers. Most people stake out a corner or imaginary square; on long journeys, territorial squabbles and fights are not unknown. There is little or no privacy under these conditions (blankets hung from the rafters at best). Sometimes, passengers share the space with cargo and are considered responsible for any damage to that cargo. This can be especially uncomfortable if the cargo is live animals. Bare rations are provided. The cost for this type of travel is usually 20 firebirds per person per jump, more if a lot of personal effects come along.

Transport: Better than a tramp freighter, the transport option is still not grand. While the passenger gets a room, he has to share it with nine other people. Most people get bunks, but at least three people get the floor (or hammocks). Unappetizing food staples are served in a common mess. The cost is usually 50 firebirds per person per jump.

Stateroom: A passenger shares a room with at least one other person. The room is not spacious, but it is far better than sharing the same size room with eight other people. Good meals are served in a cabin with the ship's crew. The cost is usually 100 firebirds per person per jump.

Luxury Liner: The best kind of travel. A spacious, comfortable stateroom is shared with no one (except, of course, those the passenger invites). Meals are either shared with the ship's officers in their dining room, or are served in the room itself, freshly cooked (well, as fresh as space food can get). Minor entertainments are usually available, in the form of magic lantern shows or live plays. The cost is usually 300

firebirds per person per jump, but this can be much higher for higher quality liners.

Alien Artifacts

The universe is full of the remains of earlier civilizations, both human and alien. Some of these are truly unique and even magical. Psychics swear that occult power seeps from certain structures found in ruins, while the Church whispers about demonic or angelic powers.

Gargoyles

These brutish beasts are found in ruins throughout the Known Worlds and beyond, and are always associated with the artifacts of the Anunnaki. They come in many forms, most notably statuary or bas relief, but their images adorn many Ur ruins. They are known to be efficacious against evil occult effects, and are now often placed on buildings or on the prows of starships to defend against evil influence. Sensitive psychics and theurgists all aver to a Gargoyle's power. Indeed, no ship with a Gargoyle prow has yet encountered a Void Kraken.

They are rare but still common enough to be found occasionally, sparking a fight for ownership between emperor, nobles, priests and merchants. They can be sold for many firebirds to just about anybody, but those who don't get it will hold a grudge against the seller — a good way to make enemies.

Scholars disagree about the purpose of these Gargoyles. Some claim they are depictions of the Anunnaki themselves. Others say they are but images from the Anunnaki's fancy. Some claim they are images of horrors which the Anunnaki fought, while others say they are guardians against even worse horrors.

Characters with some form of mystical vision (Wyrd Sight, Second Sight) can tell that Gargoyles are not merely stone or alloy; they exude a mysterious, unreadable aura. They also hamper the actions of Urge and Hubris, although to a varying degree; some Gargoyles are more efficacious than others. The most legendary Gargoyle, found in the wastes of Nowhere, is said to generate omens to certain individuals, and people come from all over on pilgrimage to it, despite the dangers of the nearby Stigmata system.

The power of a Gargoyle is rated from 1–10. It will completely dampen Urge or Hubris levels equal or lower than its rating; dark twins will be put back to sleep and Hubris effects will not reveal themselves.

Gamemasters should feel free to create other mysterious effects for certain Gargoyles; each is unique.

Soul Shards

These psychic crystal shards are powerful artifacts. They were studied extensively by Second Republic scientists of the Phavian Institute and were deemed to be not alien-made artifacts but elements. Arguments ensued over how such elements were created: Are they naturally occurring, or do they require an alchemical process using Preadamite superscience? Evidence exists for both arguments, although the evidence for the former only occurs near Ur ruins.

These crystals are highly sought after by not only psychics but the Church, which seeks to hide them.

Soul Shards act as Wyrd batteries just like a Wyrd Tabernacle (see Relics in Chapter Five: Occult), although the limit to Wyrd storage depends on the size of the crystal: A hand-held shard can hold up to 20, while a menhir can hold over 100.

In addition, each shard can be attuned to one psychic path (see Mist Sword, above, for the procedure) and will boost any use of powers in that path. A hand-held shard will add one to goal rolls, while a menhir may add six.

Finally, Soul Shards are known to be helpful in healing psychological wounds or neuroses. They can aid in balancing an imbalanced personality, but such uses have no firm rules. The gamemaster should feel free to create rules for particular situations.

Philosophers Stones

The most powerful of all Preadamite artifacts is a Philosophers Stone. This is a catch-all term for a class of powerful items which come in many shapes and sizes but universally allow their wielders to break the laws of reality. Each stone is unique and they are all greatly sought after. Gamemasters should use Philosophers Stones in whatever way they see fit, realizing that they are neither strictly technological nor purely occult but something transcending both paradigms.

Each stone should be allowed one power, but this can be an incredible one. As an example, the most sought after stone yet was found by Vladimir I. It allowed any ship it was placed on to jump between stars without the use of a jumpgate — a never-before known phenomenon. The stone was instrumental in allowing Vladimir to create the office of the emperor. It was hidden by him before his coronation and has yet to be discovered again.

Philosopher's Stones are worth any price; rumors exist of crafty peasants lucky enough to uncover one in some forsaken alien ruin who have attained peerage (noble status) by gifting it to a lord with the power to grant such boons. But most people believe that anyone finding such a treasure would be killed as others rush to seize it.

Chapter 8: Gamemastering

For many people, gamemastering is the most enjoyable aspect of roleplaying. Players get to explore all the peculiarities of one character, but a gamemaster gets the entire universe. He can twist it any way he wants, developing the way people and organizations interact, their hopes and fears, and their successes and failures. At the same time the gamemaster becomes the center of attention, gets to stimulate new ideas in his friends, and ensures that they have a good time.

The gamemaster's main task is to come up with new dramas for the players. The dramas are highpoints in the characters' lives; those moments of excitement that stand out for them. Secondly (but not always), he creates the epic in which the characters adventure. The epic is an overlying structure which unites the individual dramas. Finally the gamemaster arbitrates conflict between the players, seeing to it that their characters deal with each other equitably.

This is not nearly as difficult as it may appear. Many times the players will influence the drama or the epic to the point that all the gamemaster has to do is react to them. Other times the gamemaster will get to take center stage, throwing the characters into some unforeseen land of adventure. The Known Worlds of the **Fading Suns** are filled with thrills; gamemasters should have little trouble keeping the players' interest.

Andrew's Maxims

Andrew has always had this conceit that he knows how to run games, so he insisted on sprinkling some of his own basic rules throughout this chapter. Sometimes he explains them and sometimes he leaves them open to interpretation. Feel free to treat these maxims as you would any sprinkles — avoid them, sneer at them, or enjoy them.

Andrew's #1 Maxim:
Always err on the side of fun.

How to Gamemaster

The most basic part of being a gamemaster is arbitrating between the players and everything else in the universe. The players each control one character; the gamemaster controls everyone and everything else. This ranges from the lowest peasant to the very laws of physics. The universe is as she sees it. If she decides that the Earth's sun has gone nova, then so be it. Maybe the characters will find a way to stop the process (not likely), but this only happens if the gamemaster decides such a thing is possible.

Gamemasters should familiarize themselves with the information in this book, but they should not feel bound by it. Feel free to change both the rules and the setting. While we at Holistic Design believe that both work extremely well, we have no way of knowing what every player wants out of the game. **Fading Suns** is a framework for your dramas, and you should never feel confined by it.

Andrew's Maxim: Let the characters
affect the dice at least as much as the
dice affect the characters

On the other side of the coin are those players who are going to want the gamemaster to follow every rule to the letter. The easiest way to deal with these players is with a shovel, but some people frown on that. Instead, gamemasters will want to keep two concepts in mind: fairness and consistency. Players will enjoy the game more if the gamemaster at least appears to be fair. If something has worked for one player, it should work for another. If the villain gets to fire his blaster while hanging out an airlock in space, then so should the characters.

Consistency should maintain a place of importance in the game, but gamemasters should never become a slave to it. Just because long-range shots have always been a -2 task

does not mean a gamemaster cannot make it more or less difficult. The gamemaster will probably need to give a good reason for her decision, and should listen seriously to the players' input, but in the end it is her choice.

Andrew's Maxim: The game is yours; treat it accordingly.

Dramas

Dramas, whether done as part of an epic or as stand-alone adventures, usually share a number of qualities. The gamemaster sets up a beginning that gets the players interested, lets their actions guide it through the middle (with some twists provided by the gamemaster), and then ends it with an exciting conclusion that answers many questions (but often raises more).

The Beginning

Since it is almost impossible for gamemasters to predict what their players are going to do, the beginning of a drama is the most crucial part. This is the only area a gamemaster can actually script and have a lot of confidence that the players will follow his path. At some point the characters will begin taking the game in weird directions, but with some preparation the gamemaster can ensure that she will be ready for most of the surprises the players spring on her.

Getting the basic idea will often bring other factors into place. Some gamemasters come up with a fun setting — the hidden Asher monastery on Vril-Ya or the gleaming spires of Leagueheim. Others develop a neat villain like the deranged Abbot Judas of the Asher monastery or Luken Emmanualson, the psychic jester who seeks to tear the League apart. There are some gamemasters who prefer to begin with a specific event, like a series of mysterious murders in an isolated monastery or a pirate attack on a Charioteer ship. Finally, some gamemasters concentrate on a specific object like a lost tome of heretical knowledge or a diamond which symbolizes a noble family's power.

The inspiration for these ideas can come from books, movies, songs and other media (science fiction related or not), conversations, or even just from taking a look at the players' character sheets. These should be scanned anyway to see if the players made mistakes or if their characters have something that would make a drama too easy or difficult, but a player who has taken the Bad Reputation Affliction has just given the gamemaster a wealth of possible dramas.

No matter where the basic idea originates, gamemasters should take care that it fulfills two major functions — it should promote conflict, and it should allow the players to affect it. An Edenlike world may be intriguing, but if it has nothing for the characters to do, then the gamemaster had better start throwing in some snakes.

Andrew's Maxim: Try the setting first. Most of the great science fiction works (e.g., Foundation, Dune and Ringworld) stressed their setting to a high degree. The setting is often the most engrossing part; take full advantage of it. It certainly can provide more areas for drama than anything else .

Some gamemasters get caught up in trying to figure out when the drama should begin. If the characters have to stop a conspiracy to kill the Emperor, does the drama start at the beginning of the conspiracy? Does it start when the assassin lands on Byzantium Secundus? Does it start when the assassin enters the school disk depository from which she will shoot her magic bullet? The best way to handle this is to have the drama begin at the point when the characters will face the most exciting challenge while still having a chance to effect the ending. If the characters are all soldiers, then they probably should get involved late in the conspiracy. If they like intrigue and research, they should begin earlier.

Other factors the gamemaster will want to keep in mind are what kind of tension he wants to build. For instance, are the characters under extreme time pressure? Do they have 10 minutes to find and defuse the bomb before the spaceliner is destroyed? Or do their actions determine the pressure? After all, the Li Halan and the Hazat won't go to war if the characters don't reveal how the Hazat betrayed its rivals to the Emperor.

Andrew's Maxim: Can't stop with just one. Once you have a basic idea for a drama (the characters have to rescue an alien prince), combine it with another (a character's hated cousin, a Scraver, is smuggling lethal chemicals off-planet) for twice the fun. This is a traditional device in books and movies (meshing plots and subplots) that works equally well for roleplaying.

The Hook

Most dramas, especially the first ones in an epic, require hooks to help involve the characters. This brings the characters together and gives them a common cause. For instance, the characters could meet at the constable's office when they all come in to report a missing loved one. This gives them an immediate interest in working together.

Some classic ways to bring the characters together include:

• Having the characters know each other before the game begins. If they are old friends, relatives or acquaintances,

they will have immediate reason to team up.

• Having the characters share a common interest. If all the characters have some kind of tie to the Scravers, then any major incident involving that guild (like one of its warehouses blowing up) can immediately attract the characters.

• Giving the characters a common enemy. When the Avestite priest has his underlings investigate all the characters, they will have to team up to keep the Inquisition off their tales.

• Placing the characters under orders. Almost everyone in the Known Worlds has an overlord. These lords have their own interests which may be completely antithetical to the characters'. The characters may not know why their masters have ordered them to work together, and they might not like the reason when they find out — but by then it will be too late.

• Giving the characters no other choice. Who knows why Duke Li Halan has declared them outlaws? They never even met each other before. If they want to stay alive long enough to discover why they have been set up, they are going to have to pool all their resources.

Conflict

The saying that conflict is the soul of drama is almost as old as drama itself. It applies just as well to roleplaying games as it does to fiction or the stage. The more the characters have to strive and struggle, the more the players will enjoy the game. That doesn't mean that toil and sweat should fill every second of the characters' existences; however, the players should get the feeling that they must overcome obstacles to achieve their desires. The tougher the barrier, the more satisfaction players get from seeing it crumble.

Gamemasters looking to add more conflict to their dramas can use some standard literary devices to help them out. What follow are a few of the classic ones. Gamemasters can get ideas here before setting up the drama, though they will probably find that other conflicts develop without any planning.

Person vs. person (One of the characters is chasing a rogue Inquisitor)

Person vs. machine (The characters have to defeat Second Republic automatic defenses to get the vaccine required to save a village)

Person vs. society (One of the characters is trying to increase the acceptance of the Ur-Obun)

Person vs. nature (The characters are trapped in the badlands of Pandemonium and must make their way to safety on foot)

Person vs. the supernatural (Demons plague one of the characters)

Person vs. self (A character must expunge that part of her which attracts demons)

Theme

A theme is a unifying concept that ties a story together. For instance, one of the main themes of **Fading Suns** is the seeking. What the characters look for or find does not matter nearly as much as does the quest itself. This theme appears in everything from the average peasant's attempts to rebuild his life following the Emperor Wars to the League trying to create a new republic, the Church looking to form a theocracy, and the Emperor's efforts to change space. None of these forces may ever achieve their goals; instead, the way they conduct themselves as they follow their goal takes center stage.

As soon as a gamemaster chooses a theme he wants to follow, drama ideas will start leaping out at him. Do the characters encounter someone on a quest? Do they have to start one of their own? Will quests start competing with each other — one character having to obtain an item and another having to return it to its original owners?

The theme does an excellent job of setting an overall structure for the gamemaster. It lets him tie everything together easily and, whenever he is at a loss as to what should happen next, he can look to the theme for guidance. Also, if he opts to have some sort of moral attached to the drama, he can weave it into the theme.

The theme can also appear as a question: "Why do people commit evil acts?" It can show up as a sentence: "Evil comes from greed." It can even be a single word: "Evil." All of these are areas open to the players and gamemasters for them to explore in their game.

What follow are some samples of themes gamemasters might want to include in their dramas. This is by no means an exhaustive list; the best dramas gamemasters create will probably spring from themes of their own devising. Some gamemasters like to tie their themes into the theme inspiring the entire epic, while others like to mix them up a bit more.

• What sort of leader do people need? Questions about leadership can arise between the nobles and guilds, within a city, on a ship or even among the characters. Put the characters in situations where a leader is necessary (only one person can speak for the group, someone has to make tactical decisions, etc.) and see what happens.

• The ends do not justify the means. The gamemaster can present the players with an admirable goal (rescuing an orphanage, salvaging a lost ship) and then give them a number of different routes. If the characters follow the easier but more destructive route, their goal becomes more and more flawed. If they follow the harder but more commendable path, their goal has some surprising rewards.

• The ends justify the means. You can't make an omelet without breaking eggs. If this is the lesson the gamemaster wants to get across, then he needs to set up a goal which

will redeem the characters for their actions.

• Morality. The Known Worlds harbor many moral systems, a number of which consider themselves the only legitimate one. The characters get to see these moral codes in action, and decide for themselves if one is better than any other.

• What causes people to hate one another? The characters find themselves in the middle of an ancient feud. The only way out is to find out why the feud started and hope to resolve it (something which may very well be impossible).

• Things are never as they seem. Conspiracies abound. The person you believe is your worst enemy may actually have your best interests at heart. The person you think you can trust will do anything to hurt you.

• Exploration. Continually put the characters in a position to discover new things. This game is centered around the characters' journeys to strange new places and the many odd things they find there.

Mood

The mood is the overall feel the dramas impart. If the characters discover a lost world, full of both hope and danger, the gamemaster might well want a mood of excitement and anticipation. He helps enforce this mood by keeping events running at a rapid pace, throwing in new events whenever things seem to be slowing down and giving the characters new challenges every time they overcome an old one.

A gamemaster running a drama centered around conspiracies on Byzantium Secundus, however, will probably strive more for a mood of nervous paranoia. He will concentrate more on the buildup to an event than on the event itself. Players will have plenty of time to decide what their characters will do, but they will remain unsure as to whether or not they are doing the right thing. Additionally, they can never be sure that the other characters are not conspiring to stab them in the back.

Different dramas utilize different moods. The gamemaster might well want to concentrate on games where the characters do not have much opportunity to effect great change on their surroundings. This is often true in horror-oriented dramas where the characters may not be able to destroy their nemeses but can try to blunt any evil impact. Here the gamemaster wants to create a mood of uncertainty and tension, making the players wonder whether their characters will even survive. Some other moods are described below.

• Excitement. This is often the mood of space opera, where the characters go flying across the Known Worlds, battling evil and making the universe safe for everyone. The players should never know what's going to happen next, but they should definitely be looking forward to it.

• Horror. Again the gamemaster needs to ensure that

the players will not know what is going to happen next, but they are going to dread it a lot more. Players should feel anxious and worried, never really knowing if they can deal with the problem at hand — or if something worse will follow it.

• Romance. Conflict still exists, but the players will have more hope. They will aim for more, realizing that their actions have a direct effect on the things they care about. Much of this will come about in the gamemaster's descriptions — colors are more vibrant, textures sharper and life is interesting.

• Uncertainty. This is especially important when conspiracies are at the heart of the game. The players will never know if what is happening is for good or ill. They will seek out as much information as they can, but the more they uncover, the less certain they should become. All their old prejudices may be dispelled, but the truth will not take their place.

The Middle

Once the gamemaster and players have gotten the drama off and running, most things should fall into place. At this point, the gamemaster's main role is to feed information to the players so that they stay interested without learning too much. This is where he changes the goals on the players, introducing the fact that the initial goal was just a ploy to get the characters involved in the drama. This is also the point where fun plot twists show up ("What do you mean you're the duke's daughter?"), allies become enemies (and vice versa), and whole new factors get thrown in ("The Vau are landing!").

Andrew's Maxim: Suspense, suspense, suspense — then up the suspense some more. Suspense comes from having almost all the information. The players should have enough to know something of what is going on and care about what they don't know.

When Things Bog Down

Sometimes gamemasters may notice the game slowing down and the excitement draining out of the players. It may happen because the characters have reached an impasse and are unable to decide what to do next. It may happen because they have explored the wrong paths and are now far away from their goals. It may be that they have gone in a direction where the gamemaster has no idea what should happen next. It may be that everyone is just plain tired. That's when it's time to shove a submachine gun in the door and spray the room with bullets.

That's an old mystery writer's trick for when the writer has no idea what to do next, and it appears in innumerable

books and movies. The writer does not have to explain why it happened until later, but it certainly shakes everyone up. When a gamemaster pulls this same trick, whether she does it with a submachine gun, a psychic assault or an alien power, even she does not have to know why it happened. She has plenty of time to work up an excuse later. For now it is enough that the game gets moving again.

Gamemasters can do other things to get the game moving. One of the reasons to have a theme and mood is so the gamemaster can refer to it when she is at a loss for ideas. When the game slows, the theme or mood should provide some ideas to get things moving. If worst comes to worst, take a break.

Andrew's Maxim: When in doubt, blame a conspiracy.

The End

The ending really has two parts. The first is the climax, where the major questions get answered and the main conflict is resolved (for better or for worse). The second part is the resolution, also known as the debriefing or denouement. Here the players come to as complete an understanding as they can about the drama, the next drama is often set up and the players clean up loose ends. Record keeping, like assigning and spending experience, is often handled here.

Andrew's Maxim: Try to have a picture of the end when you start. Just don't expect to ever see it.

The Climax

This will probably be the most exciting part of the game. At this stage the characters either defuse the bomb or blow up. As gamemaster, you need to make sure that the characters have had an opportunity to succeed. Feel free to let them fail if they mess up, but at least try to make sure the players feel that their actions could have made a difference.

One interesting aspect of player psychology is that if they feel the end of a drama is fast approaching, they are more likely to have their characters act heroically. It is almost as if they want to make sure their character will be remembered once the game is over. This means the gamemaster should try to accomplish at least two things: 1) give the players clues that the drama is coming to a close, and 2) give the characters the chance to be heroes.

Time clues are usually the easiest ways to let players know the drama is almost over. If the game usually ends at midnight and that time is fast approaching, players should get the hint. Gamemasters might also want to pick up the pace at the end of the drama, rushing players' decisions as events get more hectic. The more excited the gamemaster

seems, the more excited the players will be.

There are many ways the gamemaster can let the characters act heroically. They can become martyrs, throwing themselves on grenades to save the others. They can push their characters to the extreme, using up every last point of Wyrd they ever had. They can become philanthropists, sacrificing all the firebirds they sweated and slaved over to help a village meet its debts. They can even become models of virtue, risking everything to rescue some lost child (they don't have to realize he's really a demon in disguise). Give them the opportunity to become heroes and they may well rise to the occasion.

Andrew's Maxim: The characters should always have a chance to survive.

The Resolution

Here the characters get their rewards or punishments and try to wrap up loose ends. The excitement level here should be way down from the climax. Now the characters need to regroup, not charge back into action. The most tension the players should feel will come from the question of how much experience their characters will get.

This stage is very important, and gamemasters should set aside time for it even if it does not get played out immediately after the climax concludes. Let the players figure out what their characters plan to do next, let them do some shopping for new equipment if they are someplace that can happen, assign out experience points and let them spend whatever they can, and let the players discuss what to do next. Of course, the next drama will undoubtedly make all their plans useless, but for now they can dream.

The Epic

Some **Fading Suns** dramas are one-shot affairs, played out with no intention of follow up. Other dramas, however, make up a continuing epic. In an epic, the players take on the roles of the same characters for drama after drama. The characters grow with experience and change in ways the players want to see them develop. Players get to see what kind of effect their characters have on the Known Worlds, and they can make long-range plans as well. Gamemasters get to develop storylines which run for more than one drama, introduce recurring characters, and build up pressure as the players learn more about the Known Worlds.

There are two main kinds of epics, both defined by when the gamemaster and players want to end them. The first kind is the terminating epic, in which the gamemaster has a definite end in mind for the players. The second is the infinite epic, in which the game can continue for as long as the gamemaster and players like. While all epics share certain characteristics, gamemasters will want to plan differently

for each of these. Of course, there is no reason the players and gamemaster could not continue a terminating epic past its grand finale or decide to end an infinite one, but they can deal with these spur of the moment changes when they happen.

Terminating Epics

This kind of epic most resembles stories from books, movies and theater. The characters need to accomplish some goal, and the gamemaster creates the conflicts which may block them. These goals can range from the most grand (relight the suns, end the Symbiot threat) to the most personal (rescue a character's family from the Chainers, become a duke). The players might not even know the goal when the epic begins, but discover it as the conflict unfolds.

For instance, at the beginning of the game, the characters know that someone has kidnapped people close to them. The characters go to the local authorities (where they get little cooperation) but meet each other. They decide to take matters into their own hands and rescue their loved ones, but they also discover a secretive cult trying to discredit the local government. In battling the cult for a number of dramas, they soon discover that one of the royal houses (hopefully one of which a character is a member) is behind the sect. As they investigate the royal house, they find that demons have begun possessing the nobles. Now they discover what the goal of the entire epic has always been — stop the demonic threat to the Known Worlds and save the royal house from destruction.

When they finally defeat the demons for the last time (or the demons eat their souls — always give players the chance to fail), they gain a great deal of recognition for their efforts, obtain their just rewards, and the characters retire from this crazy life of adventure.

The gamemaster's main responsibility all along has been to feed the characters challenges that whet their appetites for further adventure. The players have had a great deal of an impact on how the story resolved, and no doubt threw in innumerable twists of their own, but the gamemaster was the main guide all along.

The difficulties with this kind of epic lie in the amount of preparation most gamemasters will need to put into it. The idea for the epic may hit the gamemaster at any time, but she has to take time to work out the individual steps that take the players from beginning to end. She also has to work with the players so that any individual goals their characters might have do not clash too strongly with the main thrust of the epic.

The main strength of this kind of epic is that the characters' actions do not take the gamemaster by surprise too often. Whenever the game starts to drift, the gamemaster can quickly put it back on line. While a number of unrelated (or seemingly unrelated) dramas may occur as the epic continues, most will somehow tie into the overarching storyline. For instance, if one character's main goal is to defeat the baron who murdered her father and usurped his barony, she can still go help the Engineers find a traitor in their midst, thus furthering the career of the Engineer character in the group. It might serve their goal by gaining them new allies, but then again, it may not. Still, most stories will relate to the characters' quest for justice.

Additionally, terminating epics come in handy when the gamemaster and players know the epic will have to end at some definite date — the end of classes, when the next gamemaster is ready to run her game or when this gamemaster jets off to India. The players may not fulfill all their characters' goals, but they should have a heck of a time racing against the clock as they try.

Infinite Epics

Infinite epics never need to end. They can run for years, with players cycling through as need be and even gamemasters switching off on occasion. The gamemaster might have an overarching storyline in mind, like having the characters protect an infant who might turn out to be the messiah, but for the most part the infinite epic is more like improvisational theater than a novel. No one knows exactly what route it will take or where it will end up.

The main difficulty with this kind of epic is the amount of thinking on her feet the gamemaster will have to do. Players have all sorts of things they want their characters to do, and the gamemaster will have to stay on her toes to keep up with them, weaving the characters' goals in with whatever storyline she has developed.

The main advantage of this kind of epic is that not only will the gamemaster have to do less before-game preparation, but dramas she never would have thought of will spring out of her interaction with the players. The gamemaster and players will get to explore aspects of the **Fading Suns** and their own characters that would never have otherwise occurred.

For instance, if the gamemaster has set up a drama where the characters have to stop a rogue mercenary group from destroying a small town, she may find that the characters have no intention of training the town to defend itself. Instead they plan to hire the mercenaries to help them raid a House Hawkwood research installation they discovered during a previous drama. She quickly discovers that the players do not trust the Hawkwoods. She now has to decide what the Hawkwoods really are up to, and how the characters' actions will affect the house. She may decide the players are right not to trust the Hawkwoods or else show how their fears have been baseless and perhaps manipulated by a minor house's warlock. In any case, the epic has progressed in a far different direction than anyone had planned.

This also allows the players to shape the game to their

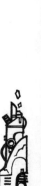

liking and gives them greater control over how their characters develop. For instance, if a player creates a Charioteer, then she may well dream of seeing her character eventually become a consul or even the dean. While this might not be possible in the terminating epic, in an infinite epic, anything goes. She can work tirelessly to advance the guild's interests, make friends at all ranks of the League, and still help her closest friends, the other characters.

Indeed, a major reason groups with members as varied as a Brother Battle, a psychic al-Malik, a pious Scraver and a rogue alien work together is that they can each help the others further their ambitions. This sort of alliance gives each character a group of competent friends who will go to great lengths to assist one another. There is little chance that the al-Malik will ever seek power in the Brother Battle order, so the characters know they have reason to trust one another. The more they work together, the more likely they are to risk their own status to help the others.

Andrew's Maxim: Leave unfinished business — don't resolve everything at once.

Mixing the Two

Gamemasters and players may well want to mix the terminating and infinite epics together. For instance, if one player will only be able to stay in the game for a month, then he and the gamemaster can work out a specific goal for his character, like tracking down his long-lost brother. The gamemaster comes up with a reason why all the characters will want to help (that long-lost brother has a map to a Second Republic armory tattooed on his back), and for as long as the player is with the group, they work on that one goal. The player's last drama with the group centers around actually rescuing that brother from the Inquisition or watching him (and the tattoo) fry.

Also, never be afraid to change from one kind of epic to another. If the gamemaster and players are both enjoying a terminating epic too much to ever want it to end, just add on another layer of conspiracy for the characters to unpeel. If the gamemaster suddenly gets transferred to the Philippines, then she can work up a climactic end to the epic based on whatever kind of dramas the group was last involved in.

Memorable Characters

There is no way that the gamemaster can develop the characters under his control to the extent that the players can develop theirs. After all, they only have to concentrate on one while the gamemaster has everyone else in the universe to worry about. Still, memorable gamemaster characters are a necessity in roleplaying games. They stimulate players to further develop their own characters, allow

gamemasters to come up with new dramas almost effortlessly and make the game sessions where they appear unforgettable.

This is true whether the gamemaster's characters work with or against the players' characters. Gamemasters often spend most of their time developing archvillains and their assistants, but players remember their allies at least as well as they do their enemies. The whispering information broker who gives characters clues in the weirdest places can leave as lasting an impression as the deadly Decados assassin who follows their every move.

Andrew's Maxim: Make the little things count. Gamemasters rarely have time to create every aspect of every character in the game, and players would not remember everything anyway. Instead, gamemasters should give each at least one memorable feature — a handlebar mustache, slight lisp, long hair, penchant for dark suits, or a habit of flipping a coin in the air.

The Friends

The most important thing to remember about the allies characters acquire is that they should never solve the characters' problems for them. They should provide the characters with just enough information or assistance that the characters can take care of their own difficulties. The last thing the gamemaster wants is for the players to feel that their characters are inconsequential or that they can do as they please and then call in the duke to get them out of their difficulties.

Gamemasters may have a hard time doing this if a player has made that relationship a central aspect of her character. If one of the players has spent the points to make her character the son of the archbishop of Delphi, then she should legitimately expect the archbishop to help her out against the Inquisition. The gamemaster has to decide just how much impact he wants this ally to have on the game, and then come up for a reason why he can do no more. He might be under pressure from the Inquisition as well, or he might want to teach his son a lesson, or he might even suspect that his son might be a heretic and that the Inquisition would be the best thing for him.

Of course, the gamemaster should feel free to require that the characters constantly solve their allies' problems if they want them to remain friends. This method is an excellent story hook, and can be used again and again. If one of the characters knows a secret weapons dealer, then that dealer should come to the characters for help when one of his sales gets him in trouble with the Charioteers. Then the characters can discover that a Charioteer is trying to squeeze

all the other guilds off the planet and figure out what they want to do about it. Just hope they act before the Charioteer reveals that he is a Symbiot bent on destroying the whole world.

The same ally should not keep running to them for help, however. Mix it up and keep these allies in minor roles. Of course, the gamemaster should still strive to make these associates memorable. Try and build their relationships with the characters to the extent that the players want to help them and go out of their way to make their lives easier. For instance, if the players become close enough to a priest who gives them blessings, they might want to start a drama where they try to get the priest promoted to bishop. This would mean revealing his competitor's role in a crime ring, but that shouldn't be too hard, should it?

There are many ways to make these allies sympathetic. Have them seek out the characters when the players have no idea what to do next and offer some key help. Have them socialize with the characters. If a Scraver needs to pass information on to them, then he can invite them to dinner at his house, have them meet his family, present them with a lavish spread and then tell them what they need to know. This kind of roleplaying may take only 15 minutes, but it leaves the players with a much higher estimation of this contact. That way, when the Scraver comes crawling to them dressed only in tatters and tells them that his house has burned down and his family has disappeared, the characters will do anything to help.

The Foes

Somebody competing with the characters for lost artifacts can be an adequate villain. Make him an Ur-Obun and he gets a little more engaging. Add in his role in discrediting the troupe's young noble, and the guy becomes even more exciting. Now have his ultimate goal be the destruction of another character's home planet, and you have an archvillain worth battling. Some sample antagonists follow this section; gamemasters should feel free to include them in their dramas as they are or change them to suit their needs.

Villains come in all sizes, from the interstellar menace of evil dukes to the local hassle of a corrupt sheriff. No matter how big they get, they all have the same goal in life — to make the characters' lives as interesting as possible. To this end the gamemaster should give them whatever tools they need to get in the characters' way and should change their tactics over time. After all, if the characters get experience, then why shouldn't their enemies?

> *Andrew's Maxim: Add justification for better villains. No one thinks of himself as evil. Even the most psychotic serial killers can justify their actions to themselves. Your villains should be the same way.*

> *There is a reason they act the way they do, and knowing it will allow the gamemaster to roleplay these characters with even greater certainty.*

The Archvillain

Someone in the game is going to provide the characters with more trouble than anyone else. This might not be the most powerful villain in the game, but she will be the most memorable. Her plots and schemes will leave the characters in fits and the players talking about them for years. Archvillains range from tyrannical dictators to zealot revolutionaries, from inflexible Inquisitors to hedonistic demon worshippers, but most share certain characteristics.

First of all, they have goals both lofty and base. A duke may dream of ruling the Known Worlds only to be brought down when he tries to carry off a peasant woman he lusts after. A sect leader may be only days away from becoming elected patriarch only to throw it all away for revenge against a childhood nemesis. For all their might, they have intense (though well-hidden) flaws.

Secondly, they believe they can only trust themselves, and in the end often find they can trust no one at all. No matter how many loyal henchmen they may surround themselves with, they watch each for the first sign of treachery. When it happens, they leap on it with relish, glad to have been proven right about everyone else in the world.

This brings up a final trait of many archvillains: They would rather be dead than wrong. They have very strong views on themselves and the universe and will go to extremes to avoid having to give them up. Even when a particular point of view handicaps them, like the belief that all peasants are inferior, they would prefer to continue underestimating their lower-class opponents rather than face up to their mistakes. Gamemasters can get a better grasp on her archvillains by determining what their particular prejudices are. When characters discover what an archvillain's weaknesses are, they can (and should) make use of them.

The Henchman

A classic addition to villains both fictional and real, the henchman renders his overlord invaluable assistance. He has his master's wishes at heart and fulfills all orders to the best of his ability. He may not have the most expertise (those with the most ability become villains in their own right), but he makes up for it with dedication and a desire to serve.

Characters will encounter several different kinds of henchmen over the course of their dramas. Some, like guards and low-level cultists, will have only passing impact. Others, like assassins or chauffeurs, may provide a brief obstacle on a number of different occasions. The best, like the villain's main bodyguard or psychic advisor, will furnish drama ideas of their own, and defeating them may even

261

become a major element of the epic.

Whatever their level of skill, henchmen share certain qualities. They have a great deal of loyalty to their patrons, and characters will not have much success turning them against the villain. On the other hand, henchmen do not have much experience thinking for themselves, and players can have fun putting them in conundrums that their original orders do not cover. Then again, the characters could just punch them out.

The Freelancer

Jabba the Hut had Boba Fett, Hitler had Rommel and Elmer Fudd had his sarcastic hunting dog. These are all cases of archvillains relying on talented but not necessarily obedient underlings. The villains need these agents because their own servitors do not necessarily have what it takes to defeat the characters. Their henchmen may be loyal, but devotion won't beat a bunch of well-played characters.

That's why the villain calls in the specialist; that fabled freelancer with the talent to succeed at what the villain's best have failed. The freelancer has no special loyalty to the villain and usually works for him out of mercenary interests or because she is somehow indebted to him. Freelancers can show up once or in drama after drama, perhaps continuing a vendetta with the characters after they have defeated the villain. In fact, turning the freelancer against the villain is a great way to defeat both. When the great Ur-Ukar assassin Vannanna Esin finds out that Duke Markana Decados funds anti-alien hate groups, she may well make him her next target. She may also decide that a contract is a contract and kill the characters first. Whatever a freelancer may be, she is not predictable.

Tweaking the Game

There are as many ways to play **Fading Suns** as there are people playing it. This book contains only the basic ingredients. The most important elements are the gamemaster's and players' own imaginations. They should feel free to play this game in whatever way they most enjoy. What follow are a few variations on playing out the dramas. Gamemasters should only use the ones they want to and ignore the rest. None of these are necessary, but they can add spice to any epic.

The Milieu

The universe of the **Fading Suns** is a huge place, but there is no reason for gamemasters to feel overwhelmed. The very vastness of space provides the gamemaster plenty of opportunities to personalize the game and give it her own stamp. She can introduce her own alien races, planets, noble houses, technologies, characters, monsters and whatever else she can come up with. While Holistic Design plans to detail a number of the major planets and factions, most of the others will be left up to the gamemaster to do with as she

pleases.

Even when Holistic Design does publish a book about Byzantium Secundus or anything else, gamemasters should not feel obligated to obey every word of it. Everything Holistic Design publishes should be considered recommendations, not the final word. The game was designed for gamemasters and players, and they should do whatever they want to it.

Not only should they change around the **Fading Suns** setting, but they should feel free to use the system for other games, the setting with their own rule systems, or even create whole new settings for the game. Science fiction has more possibilities than any other genre, and anything that might ever happen is open to the gamemaster. She should use whatever she wants to and ignore anything else.

Backstory

While characters appear to begin the game fresh and with no baggage from the past, they really have many years of history behind them. Players and gamemasters can take this into account by running a backstory session. This is an abbreviated session of pure roleplaying (no dice rolling allowed), where a gamemaster and player discuss important aspects of the character's past. For instance, how did the character feel when the Li Halan killed her parents during a raid? What was her response to seeing the Vau for the first time? How does she feel about the nobility? The Church? The League?

This session should be more player-directed than any other session. The gamemaster should come up with complications and issues for the player to deal with, but the main advantage of this kind of game is that it gives the player a much better feel for his character. This backstory may very well have an impact on the game at some later point as well, and players may want to refer to it when thinking about what their characters should do next.

The Big Picture

Most character groups will include a number of relatively influential individuals, but there will always be someone out there who is more powerful. Players often forget this and begin to think that their characters act in a vacuum, and that their characters' actions have little impact on the universe. One way to shake them up is to have them do a grand-scope one shot.

Here the players take on the role of characters other than their own, and powerful ones at that. For instance, if the players' five main characters have destroyed a cathedral on a Decados planet and begun raiding off-planet shipping while trying to find a missing relic, then the gamemaster can call a convocation of affected parties. This would include a powerful Decados duke, the Emperor's ambassador to the Decados, the planet's archbishop, a Charioteer consul, and the god-king of the Hironem, a local alien race.

The gamemaster needs to determine what goals each of these characters has, what their traits and powers are, and what they know about each other as well as the situation. The gamemaster then briefs each player who takes on the role of one of these powerful individuals, and the player then takes the role of that character during the convocation.

This drama should only last one game session, but the players will have a chance to see the matter from a number of new viewpoints. There is always the risk that they might cop out and vote to give their old characters 10,000 firebirds (in which case the gamemaster should feel free to use those firebirds against the characters later), but most players will have little problem getting into character. They may well decide to have their old characters hunted down, in which case the gamemaster should have little trouble coming up with the next drama.

Andrew's Final Maxim: Always err on the side of fun.

Antagonists

The following villains are only a brief sample of those the characters might encounter across the Known Worlds. After all, the Empire is a big place, even if most people never meet anyone outside their own community. Gamemasters should feel free to change these antagonists in any way they want to make them better fit their game.

Known Worlders
Minor

These antagonists are best used for a few stories or as recurring minor characters. Their schemes are unlikely to trouble the characters for too long, but should be very annoying in the short term. They can appear anywhere the gamemaster likes and are easily changed between house, sect and guild affiliations.

Lady Rene Gooddale Hawkwood

While a serf would murder his entire family for the chance to be a noble, nobles do not always find their lives that worth living. Those who encounter such ennui find other ways to occupy their time. Religion, drugs, suicide — these are fine for some nobles, but Rene contemplated all of them and found them lacking. Instead, she decided to become a pirate.

To the eternal shame of her family and house, she sold many of her ancestral lands in order to afford a small frigate. She hired a small crew and took off in the dead of night, leaving her nagging husband behind. Since then she has raided the space lanes incessantly, and her own house has put a price on her head.

Race: Human
Quote: "Excitement, adventure, glory… am I doing this right?"
Description: An attractive woman in her early 30s, Rene no longer wears the clothes of a noble but has yet to adjust to a pirate's rough garb. As a result, her wardrobe is a mish mash, and appears disconcerting to both groups.
Age: 32
Equipment: Scimitar, blaster pistol, leather jerkin, standard shield
Entourage: 20-40 competent pirates
Body: Strength 6, Dexterity 7, Endurance 6
Mind: Wits 5, Perception 4, Tech 5
Spirit: Extrovert 5, Introvert 2, Passion 4, Calm 1, Faith 1, Ego 3
Natural Skills: Charm 5, Dodge 6, Fight 6, Impress 6, Melee 8, Observe 5, Shoot 7, Sneak 5, Vigor 6
Learned Skills: Disguise 1, Drive Spacecraft 3, Etiquette 3, Gambling 1, Knavery 2, Lore (Nobility) 2, Performance (Singing) 3, Read Urthish, Redemption (High-Tech) 1, Search 3, Social (Leadership) 2, Social (Oratory) 1, Think Machine 1, Warfare (Gunnery) 2, Warfare (Military Tactics) 1
Fencing Actions: Parry, Slash, Draw & Strike, Disarm, Off-hand
Wyrd: 4
Vitality: -10/-8/-6/-4/-2/0/0/0/0/0/0

Father Boris Spitteri

A prominent pastor on Grail, Spitteri has spent years ministering to Grail's underclass, getting to know their ways and means. Well, the means are the more important part, for Spitteri serves thieves, pirates and the like financially as well as spiritually. He has become a major part of the world's extensive fencing network, and can unload stolen goods in no time flat.

If he were just a fence for stolen goods, he might not be

so bad, but he has extended his aim. He has begun telling his contacts exactly what items he wants — primarily religious relics. Should the characters own such, they may well become targets of his low-life friends.

Race: Human

Quote: "Only a sinful soul could make an accusation like that."

Description: Tall and muscular, Spitteri make an intimidating priest. He avoids violence, but looks like he would have no problem should it come to that.

Age: Early 40s

Equipment: Energy shield, Expedition MedPac

Entourage: Spitteri has two novitiates who help him with everything, and they are at least as big as he is. Additionally, he can call on numerous underworld figures should he find himself in trouble.

Body: Strength 8, Dexterity 7, Endurance 8

Mind: Wits 5, Perception 6, Tech 4

Spirit: Extrovert 6, Introvert 2, Passion 5, Calm 2, Faith 3, Ego 3

Natural Skills: Charm 4, Dodge 5, Fight 6, Impress 9, Melee 5, Observe 5, Shoot 4, Sneak 4, Vigor 7

Learned Skills: Bureaucracy 5, Etiquette 1, Inquiry 4, Knavery 5, Lore (Underworld) 5, Lore (Relics) 3, Read Latin, Read Urthish, Search 2, Social (Acting) 3, Social (Oratory) 2, Streetwise 7, Torture 1

Wyrd: 5

Vitality: -10/-8/-6/-4/-2/0/0/0/0/0/0/0/0

Chief Chongho Sook

Characters will rarely encounter Chongho handling his own plots and schemes, but they will run into him nonetheless. Chongho provides muscle for those who need it, muscle capable of handling the most sordid affairs. Need a witness permanently silenced or a Reeve advocate scared off? Chongho is your man.

His childhood gave no appearances of leading in such a direction. His parents hired laborers for the Muster and assigned them to appropriate positions. Chongho became a Muster member at eight, running errands for them and other guild members. He became fascinated by the swaggering guild mercenaries before deciding to emulate them. He found that in order to succeed, he had to be bigger and meaner than the rest, and that he is.

Race: Human

Quote: "My employer requests that you die."

Description: 6'6" of solid muscle, Chongho looks like he can batter his way through a brick wall — and he can. As skilled with his bare hands as he is with weapons, he lets nothing get between him and the completion of a job. He has also learned that looking shocking is often half the job.

Age: Late 20s

Equipment: Two-handed sword, laser pistol, assault

laser, chainmail, squawker, expedition MedPac, Muster chains, torture kit

Entourage: Whatever thugs his bosses hire for him to work with.

Body: Strength 8, Dexterity 9, Endurance 8

Mind: Wits 6, Perception 8, Tech 7

Spirit: Extrovert 2, Introvert 4, Passion 3, Calm 3, Faith 1, Ego 4

Natural Skills: Charm 4, Dodge 8, Fight 9, Impress 9, Melee 9, Observe 8, Shoot 9, Sneak 6, Vigor 9

Learned Skills: Drive Landcraft 3, Etiquette 1, Gambling 2, Knavery 1, Read Urthish, Remedy 3, Ride 3, Social (Leadership) 3, Stoic Body 3, Stoic Mind 8, Streetwise 5, Torture 4

Fencing Actions: Parry, Thrust, Slash, Draw & Strike, Athletic Strike, Pierce

Firearm Actions: Snapshot, Quick Draw

Martial Arts: Martial Fist, Martial Kick, Martial Hold, Claw Fist, Leaping Kick, Choke Hold, Trip Kick, Throw Group

Wyrd: 3

Vitality: -10/-8/-6/-4/-2/0/0/0/0/0/0/0/0

Major

These villains can shape entire epics. Meeting them face to face should only occur after a number of other stories which lead up to it. Characters would be wise to avoid attracting their attention as long as possible, and have some powerful allies whenever they finally do. Much of what they are doing is up to the gamemaster to decide. Is Brother Lazio crazy, a pawn of someone else or something far worse? Does Duchess Salandra work for herself, the Decados, the Engineers or something else? Gamemasters should use these characters as they see fit.

Duchess Salandra Decados

Salandra's earliest tutors, servants and slaves whispered nervously to each other about how anyone could be such a perfect Decados. To them, Salandra's nature was the culmi-

nation of centuries of Decados' decadence, treachery and madness. Her greatest pleasure came from hurting others, be they her playmates, servants, siblings or parents. By the time she was eight her parents had had enough, and they secretly shipped her off to the Supreme Order of Engineers for discipline.

When Salandra returned seven years later, she no longer went out of her way to hurt others. At least, she was never caught doing so — not even when her parents died a month after her return. She immediately took the reins of the family's planet, scaring off Duke Silen Decados when he tried to claim the world. Her rise through the family has been swift and effective, and no one, not even the Emperor, can claim to have control over a more effective network of spies and assassins than she. That she acquiesced so readily to Alexius' victory surprised many. That she has been so busy ever since has scared them even more.

Rumors run rampant about her plans and connections. Whether she wants power for some unknown purpose, or just for its own sake, no one knows. That she lusts after power goes without question, and no one doubts that she would go to extreme measures for it. Many Decados believe she would sell them out without a second's thought if it advanced her cause, and some whisper that despite her family's opposition to Alexius, she and the Emperor have been occasional lovers. Such talk sends good Hawkwoods into paroxysms of horror.

Race: Human (?)

Rank/Class: Duchess

Quote: "Kill him."

Description: Salandra's appearance varies from day to day. She is usually a tall, androgynous woman, but this can change within hours. Even her cybernetic implants are so well-hidden that they offer no permanent means of recognition. Duchess Salandra's motives should be well beyond the characters' initial understanding. Her plots are so deep that only the most dedicated digging should get to the heart of them.

Entourage: Some of the leading experts in their field. An Engineer cosmetic surgeon goes with her everywhere, and perfects her look whenever the whim seizes either of them. Her bodyguards can kill with a single motion and her technicians can fix (or destroy) anything.

Body: Strength 8, Dexterity 11, Endurance 9

Mind: Wits 9, Perception 12, Tech 9

Spirit: Extrovert 5, Introvert 5, Passion 5, Calm 5, Faith 1, Ego 9

Natural skills: Charm 10, Dodge 9, Fight 9, Impress 10, Melee 9, Observe 10, Shoot 8, Sneak 10, Vigor 8

Learned skills: Academia 8, Acrobatics 6, Alchemy 3, Arts (Rhetoric) 5, Bureaucracy 8, Disguise 10, Drive Spacecraft 4, Empathy 5, Focus 9, Inquiry 8, Knavery 9, Lockpick 5,

Physick 4, Read Latin, Read Urthish, Read Urthtech, Search 7, Social (Debate) 6, Leadership 8, Spacesuit 4, Stoic Body 6, Stoic Mind 8, Streetwise 7, Think Machine 5, Torture 9

Blessing: Ambidextrous

Occult: Psi 7, Urge 2

Powers: Sensitivity (Bonding), Psyche (Intuit, Emote, MindSight, MindSpeech, Heart's Command, Head Shackle, Brain Blast), Sixth Sense (Sensitivity, Darksense, Subtle Sight, Premonition, Far Sight), Soma (Toughening, Strengthening, Quickening)/ Urge (Speak in Tongues, Misdirection)

Wyrd: 8

Equipment: Poisons, private spaceship, shield damper

Weapons: Tranquilizer gun (with various poisoned darts), vibrating rapier (when turned on, energy shields are only half as effective), dagger with poison jets (Salandra can press a button to release poisons when she hits her foe).

Martial Arts: Martial Fist, Martial Kick, Martial Hold, Block, Claw Fist, Choke Hold

Fencing: Parry, Thrust, Slash, Draw & Strike, Disarm, Feint, Parry Riposte, Pierce

Armor: Dueling shield, synthsilk

Cybernetics: Ether Ear, Second Brain (Internal Think Machine), Lithe Wire (TL 8, concealed)

Vitality: -10/-8/-6/-4/-2/0/0/0/0/0/0/0/0/0/0

Brother Lazio Urtana

Brother Lazio walked out of the Malignatius wilderness one day and began preaching. Nobody knew where he came from and nobody knew his allegiance, but they listened anyway. In a time of unending war, his words of imminent apocalypse and severe, divine justice found a ready audience. His fiery sermons caught the crowd's attention at once and his doctrine has spread like wildfire around the world. Before the local authorities could react, it had anchored itself firmly into the planet's culture and no one has tried to uproot it yet.

While Brother Lazio has yet to attract inquisitorial attention, his followers are moving out to other planets. Anyone who looks closely at his "theology" realizes that it is a strident indictment of the Emperor and the Church, but no one has raised this point yet. At least, no one has raised it and lived.

Brother Lazio has also incorporated himself deep into Malignatius life. His followers have spread through guilds, Decados fiefs and even other parishes. Some of the planet's Reeves joke that he gets more firebirds from every deal on the planet then they do. As his coffers grow, so do fears of what he might use that money to fund. At least one Questing Knight has tried to find out, only to never be seen from again.

Race: Human

Rank/Class: Novitiate

Quote: "Your sins will rain down fire upon your heads, and your homes will be as blast furnaces if you continue to turn your face from God!"

Description: A middle-aged, bearded man with fire in his eyes. He alternates between wearing the best, most respectable clothing available and the simplest, ugliest robes. Reform-minded characters might be initially attracted to Brother Lazio, but they will soon realize that he only wants to replace the current structure with an even more oppressive theocracy, with him at the top.

Entourage: Brother Lazio has thousands of committed followers and is constantly surrounded. Any skills he might need are at his command.

Body: Strength 4, Dexterity 4, Endurance 8

Mind: Wits 8, Perception 7, Tech 3

Spirit: Extrovert 9, Introvert 1, Passion 7, Calm 3, Faith 7, Ego 3

Natural skills: Charm 10, Dodge 4, Fight 3, Impress 10, Melee 3, Observe 6, Shoot 3, Sneak 3, Vigor 5

Learned skills: Empathy 8, Focus 2, Lore (Business) 5, Lore (Theology) 5, Physick 3, Social (Debate 8, Leadership 8, Oratory 10), Stoic Body 3, Stoic Mind 6

Wyrd: 7

Vitality: -10/-8/-6/-4/-2/0/0/0/0/0/0/0/0

Hasaline akir Vetenant

Hasaline's father, a leading Ukari chieftain, had high hopes that his race could learn to live with humans. To prove his point he sent his two children, Hasaline and her younger brother Jekail, to a Church school to learn to be "more human." The children stayed at the school after his death, and after an Avestite became headmaster of the school. Soon almost all the old teachers had left, replaced by his Avestite brothers. Then Jekail was accused of heresy.

Older students seized the child from his bed in the middle of the night and took him to the lowest cellars of the school.

Hasaline's attempts to reach her brother were met with sticks, and by the end of the night she was a beaten mass, with blood streaming from every part of her body. She was shipped home the next day and never saw her brother again.

The Vetenant clan had lost a great deal of power by this time, and no official investigation was ever carried out. Hasaline has never spoken of the incident again, and joined the ranks of Ukari diplomats. Her early schooling has proven invaluable, and she is second-in-command to the Ukari delegation on Byzantium Secundus. Now she has begun the task of making humanity pay.

She has taken every opportunity to spread dissension and chaos. She and her agents encourage riots, sabotage charity efforts, spread rumors about Questing Knights, and promote the belief that the Emperor is anti-Church. She would like nothing better than to see the Emperor Wars erupt again in all their fury.

Race: Ur-Ukar

Rank/Class: Diplomat

Quote: "Ever so pleasant to meet you. I hope you don't find my species unsettling. Good. Oh yes, I certainly find the Decados more unsettling as well."

Description: Tall and regal. She has less tattoos than many of her people and looks a little more human. She favors human dress, wearing traditional Ukari garb only on special occasions. Hasaline will do everything in her power to appear as a friend to all humans. She constantly praises human culture and practices, all the while striving to turn human against human.

Entourage: A scattering of official bodyguards, but Hasaline associates with no close friends. Her only real friends are being hunted by the Imperial Eye as alien terrorists.

Body: Strength 6, Dexterity 6, Endurance 7

Mind: Wits 8, Perception 7, Tech 6

Spirit: Extrovert 4, Introvert 6, Passion 5, Calm 5, Faith 2, Ego 7

Natural skills: Charm 9, Dodge 4, Fight 6, Impress 7, Melee 4, Observe 8, Shoot 4, Sneak 6, Vigor 6

Learned skills: Academia 5, Alchemy 3, Arts (Rhetoric) 8, Bureaucracy 8, Empathy 5, Etiquette 7, Inquiry 7, Knavery 7, Lore (Humanity 7, Theology 3), Read Urthish, Read Ukarish, Read Latin, Social (Debate 7, Leadership 3, Oratory 7), Stoic Body 3, Stoic Mind 5, Torture 6

Powers: Psi 5, Urge 3

Powers: FarHand (Lifting Hand, Throwing Hand, Crushing Hand, Dueling Hand), Psyche (Intuit, Emote, MindSight)/ Urge (Speak in Tongues, Misdirection, Voices)

Wyrd: 9

Vitality: -10/-8/-6/-4/-2/0/0/0/0/0/0/0/0

Barbarians

Brutal and uncouth, these outworlders lust after the riches of the Empire. Barbarians can be from any number of non-Empire worlds, including those from recently rediscovered Lost Worlds, allied a millennium ago with the Known Worlds but lost after the Fall. They can be Viking types, Mongol types, or Islamic types getting in the way of a holy crusade. How "uncivilized" they are is often a subjective opinion.

The Kurgans

The major current barbarian conflict in the Known Worlds is the Kurgan Conflict on one of the Hazat borders. It is waged against the Kurga Caliphate for rights to a Lost World discovered recently. The citizenry of the world itself is split on ownership issues: some aid the Caliphate, some rebel and aid the Empire. This conflict has devolved into a series of costly and difficult guerrilla-type skirmishes, a situation which has proven extremely profitable for the Muster. Any player characters who are shanghaied by the Chainers will most likely find themselves in the middle of this war.

Many recently mustered-out soldiers and mercs will probably have seen battle in this conflict, and might know some of the Kurgan language and ways due to exposure to the Kurga-influenced natives on the embattled world. Some face charges of heresy for saying that the Kurgan Caliph (who is both political and religious leader to his people) follows a variant interpretation of the same Prophetic teachings as the Orthodox Church. Others have met with unfortunate accidents after repeating the rumor that the Caliphate is harboring a survivor of the old House Chauki lineage.

Zulaykha Turakina

Once the most sought-after courtesan in the Caliphal court, Zulaykha Turakina was exiled from Kurgan space when her beauty caused the Caliph's nephew to undertake rash actions. Although embittered, she is still devoted to the Caliph and will do anything to regain his favor. To this end she makes her way to the court of the Phoenix Emperor, keeping ears, eyes and hands open for any information or items she can use to buy her way back into the presence of the Caliph.

Race: Human

Rank/Class: High Courtesan

Quote: "Never in all of my years have I been experiencing a lovemaking so passionate, and yet so consummately skilled, as yours, O my lord!" (or, "O my lady!" as circumstance demands…)

Description: Very tall for a Kurgan (183 cm), Zulaykha is taller than most Known Worlds females and many males, a fact she emphasizes with high heels and hairstyles seemingly conceived by late Republican architects. Though slender, her body is taut with well-trained muscle softened by ripe curves only partly attributable to cosmetic surgery.

Her real hair is wavy black with a reddish tint and, when unbound, falls to her ankles. Olive-complexioned, her face combines the finest features of all the various human racial types, especially favoring the Asian, though her almond-shaped eyes are naturally green. The poet Rustam is quoted as saying that her broad pearly smile could melt the polar caps of Malignatius, but is occasionally marred by a bitter scowl — usually reserved for enemies and servants — that once caused a Vorox to soil himself.

Roleplaying: All people are your playthings, worshipping your beauty, vying for your glance, craving your touch. And why not — for are you not the most desirable creature in all the universe? Associate only with the richest and most powerful, but know the value of winning over their underlings as well.

Entourage: Besides an ever-present train of suitors, admirers and entrepreneurs, La Turakina travels with five slaves. Four are female — two clothiers, a hairdresser and a cosmetologist — and, though said to be as lovely as Zulaykha herself, only their dark eyes may be seen peering coyly through their long veiled gowns. The fifth is a huge (2m) musclebound albino eunuch with a shaven head and an enormous scimitar. All five are deaf-mutes, communicating only with their mistress through complex hand-signs and body language.

Body: Strength 4, Dexterity 7, Endurance 6

Mind: Wits 5, Perception 6, Tech 4

Spirit: Extrovert 7, Introvert 1, Passion 6, Calm 4, Faith 4, Ego 5

Natural skills: Charm 8, Dodge 6, Melee 5, Observe 6, Sneak 4, Vigor 7

Learned skills: Arts (Fashion) 7, Disguise 5, Empathy 6, Etiquette 8, Inquiry 4, Knavery 7, Lockpicking 2, Perfor-

mance (Dance) 8, Read/Speak Barbarian (Kurgan), Remedy 4, Ride 5, Sleight of Hand 3, Social (Acting) 6, Speak Urthish, Torture 3

Blessings: Beautiful (+2 Charm), Casanova (+2 Passion when seducing others)

Curses: Prideful (-3 Calm when insulted), Vain (-1 Perception when flattered)

Benefices: Retinue

Afflictions: Barbarian (Kurgan)

Equipment: Elaborate wardrobe, aphrodisiacs

Weapons: Twin stilettos (with bejeweled ornamental handles — worn as hairpins)

Fencing: Thrust, Draw & Strike, Feint

Cybernetics: Pheromone Enhancer (+3 Charm vs. humans of any gender/preference, +2 vs. humanoid aliens like Obun and Ukar, +1 vs. most mammalian lifeforms, including Vorox)

Vitality: -10/-8/-6/-4/-2/0/0/0/0/0/0

The Vuldrok Raiders

A loose and undisciplined alliance of minor star nations, the Vuldrok claim they threw off the hated rule of the Second Republic a millennia ago to become free nations, battling for glory and riches, aided by their gods. The Vuldrok of Hargard — a planet with jumproutes leading to Leminkainen — claim they were once a Hawkwood protectorate, but that the house abandoned them during a famine caused by a millirice blight. Hawkwood representatives have since tried to explain that the planned shipments of famine aid were interrupted by the collapse and near-extinction of their house, but old resentments harbored through centuries of starvation are hard to quell. The Vuldrok have pirated some Hawkwood ships which they use to plunder outlying Hawkwood holdings. Plunder is a greater motivation to the Raiders than personal revenge; they want loot and when they don't get it, they will retreat back home.

Ragnald the Red

The son of a minor thane, Ragnald lost his ancestral lands when he supported the losing side in a civil war on Frost, a Vuldrok planet beyond the borders of the Known Worlds. Escaping with a handful of his most loyal warriors, he spent the next years raiding independant worlds near Vuldrok space, making his way eventually to Leminkainen during the middle years of the Emperor Wars. In poor shape after battling Decados fleets, Hawkwood ships could put up little fight. Ragnald landed on the world and stuffed his ship's hold with stolen riches, fleeing just before reinforcements from Ravenna could arive. He settled on Hargard and took a wife, who gave him many sons. But this life now bores him, and he feels the urge to raid again. He has gathered his warriors and intends an extended trip into the Known Worlds, this time aiming for Byzantium Secundus.

Race: Human

Rank/Class: Warrior-Thane of Hargard

Quote: "If someone attempted to steal our god's treasures, we would form a shield wall and fight to the end!"

Description: A tall, powerfully built man, Ragnald dresses in battle gear and furs, and carries a flux sword inscribed by a Vitki Runecaster so that it has twice as many charges per fusion cel. He wears protective amulets around his neck, and beneath his furs, reflective scales of armor shine through. His beard has begun to gray.

Body: Strength 8, Dexterity 4, Endurance 7

Mind: Wits 3, Perception 3, Tech 2

Spirit: Extrovert 6, Introvert 2, Passion 5, Calm 2, Faith 2, Ego 5

Natural skills: Charm 2, Fight 8, Impress 5, Melee 7, Shoot 6, Sneak 1, Vigor 6

Learned skills: Beast Lore 3, Gambling 1, Leadership 4, Lore (Jumproads) 2, Social (Oratory) 3, Read Vuldrok, Speak Vuldrokish, Speak Urthish, Survival 5, Warfare (Naval Tactics) 3

Curse: Vengeful (+3 pts: -3 Calm when honor insulted)

Benefices: Riches (5 pts), Barbarian (Vuldrok)

Equipment: Dueling energy shield

Weapons: Flux sword (60 turns of activation per cel), knife, laser pistol

Fencing: Disarm, Off-hand

Armor: Chainmail

Vitality: -10/-8/-6/-4/-2-/0/0/0/0/0/0/0

Psychic Covens

These secret organizations lurk everywhere in the Known Worlds, harboring outlaw psychics, pagan priests and sorcerers. They are the favorite bugaboo in many peasant conspiracy theories, believed to be the hands behind many disasters, such as cows giving curdled milk or the assassination of Vladimir I. In actuality, most of them are simply mutual survival and support networks for those blessed/cursed with occult powers. Some of them, however, really are up to their necks in conspiracies.

Covens come in all sizes and shapes. Most of them are merely local organizations, bound to the planet they exist on. But some of them are interstellar, true guilds of sorts, gathering wayward occultists from across Human Space (and elsewhere, it is rumored). Some of these major occult covens are detailed below, although many others exist.

The Favyana

This widespread coven acts as a support group for psychics, working to make psychic powers accepted. They provide teaching and advice on how to hide, but ask aid in return — members may get a phone call in the night, requiring them to leave their house, homeland and even planet to perform some secret duty. The Favyana maintain a general attitude of benevolence toward all sentient life, but conflicts with the Church have, in the past, taken on a somewhat vicious edge.

The coven's name is a kind of homage to the Phavian Institute, which flourished during the Second Republic as the finest school for paranormal research and psychic training. While the Favyana have nothing that approaches the facilities enjoyed by their predecessors, they are still the best resource available to psychic player characters wishing to increase their powers.

Mama Rahveloon

Mama Rahveloon has worked for House Juandaastas for most of her life, usually as part of the entourage of their well-traveled daughter Margrita. When traveling, Raveloon seeks out psychics in trouble and often arranges for their passage to the Juandaastas homeworld, where she runs a Favyana halfway-house under the guise of a midwifery school.

Race: Human

Rank/Class: Midwife to House Juandaasta

Quote: "There, there, my dearie. Have a sip of this and tell me what is troubling you."

Description: A short matronly woman with olive skin and an open smile, dressed like a cross between Aunt Jemima and Carmen Miranda

Body: Strength 4, Dexterity 5, Endurance 7

Mind: Wits 4, Perception 7, Tech 4

Spirit: Extrovert 8, Introvert 2, Passion 6, Calm 3, Faith 5, Ego 3

Natural skills: Charm 7, Dodge 5, Impress 5, Observe 7, Sneak 5

Learned skills: Arts (Dance) 3, Disguise 3, Empathy 8, Etiquette 5, Focus 7, Lore (Juandaasta Folk) 8, Physick 7, Social (Acting) 4, Speak Urthish, Speak Juandaasta Dialect, Speak Obunish, Stoic Body 7, Stoic Mind 6, Streetwise 4

Blessing: Compassionate (+2 Passion when helping others)

Benefices: Passage Contract (4 pts)

Occult: Psi 8

Powers: Sixth Sense (Sensitivity, Darksense, Subtle Sight, Premonition, FarSight, FarSound, Shared Sense, Wyrd Sight), Psyche (Intuit, Emote, MindSight, MindSpeech, Heart's Command, MindSearch), Sympathy (Bonding, Sanctum, Totem, Coven Brand)

Equipment: Enough extra clothing and make-up to disguise refugees.

Weapons: Sharpened decorative comb (1 DMG)

Vitality: -10/-8/-6/-4/-2/-0/0/0/0/0/0/0

The Invisible Path

This not-so-nice mob of psychics believe they are evolutionarily superior to non-psychics and seek to control the universe. Extremely secret and tightly organized into small cells of only a few members each, the Invisible Path is nevertheless limited in its accomplishments by bitter infighting and factionalism. Ultraconservatives consider normal humans (and aliens without psychic power) to be no better than animals, while moderates seek a peaceful coexistence with non-psychics (once they learn their place, of course). Rank in the Invisible Path is determined by one's level of psychic power, and conflicts are often resolved by psychic duels.

Some believe that the Invisible Path has infiltrated the Imperial Eye and thus endangers the Emperor.

Gablante

Hiding behind the demeanor of a peaceful Obun priest of Voavenlohji — the Church path of the Prophet's eighth disciple — is the cynical and hateful Gablante. Sick and tired of seeing his psychically superior people belittled by humans, he decided a long time ago to join a terrorist cell on Velisimil, with the intent to shut down that system's jumpgate. Just before joining his comrades on the appointed day of their strike, a premonition warned him away. His cell-mates were slaughtered by Imperial Eye assassins. He was the sole survivor of their idealistic crusade.

What sickened him worse was the reaction of his fellow Obun: while they did not condone the violence done to the rebels, they clucked endlessly about their "shameful, conflict-ridden ideology." Pushed too far, Gablante realized that most of his own kind had become trapped by a once beautiful philosophy that now ensured their eventual, evolutionary demise.

He sought out the rumored Invisible Path, and after years of proving himself (and slaying any of his superiors who stood in his way), he now leads coven operations across the Known Worlds, attempting to destroy the Empire's infrastructure so that psychics on a dozen worlds can rise up and seize the reigns of power unopposed by interstellar reinforcements.

Race: Ur-Obun

Rank/Class: Canon (Chief Enforcer in Invisible Path)

Quote: "Turn the other cheek? Only to better unbalance your foe!"

Description: A brown-skinned Obun in priestly robes with a well-read and annotated edition of the Omega Gospels. He has perfected the art of the innocent smile.

Body: Strength 6, Dexterity 10, Endurance 5

Mind: Wits 8, Perception 6, Tech 5

Spirit: Extrovert 5, Introvert 5, Passion 7, Calm 2, Faith 1, Ego 8

Natural Skills: Charm 7, Dodge 6, Fight 8, Impress 6, Observe 7, Shoot 5, Sneak 5, Vigor 4

Learned Skills: Focus 6, Inquiry 5, Knavery 8, Lockpick 3, Remedy 2, Search 6, Speak Obunish, Speak Urthish, Stoic Body 6, Stoic Mind 8, Streetwise 4, Survival 3, Torture 2

Blessing: Shrewd (+2 Wits against attempts to fast-talk)

Benefices: Passage Contract (6 pts)

Occult: Psi 8

Powers: Sixth Sense (Sensitivity, Darksense, Subtle Sight), Soma (Toughening, Strengthening, Quickening, Hardening, Sizing, Masking, Recovering, Slowing), (Vis Craft (Vis Eye, Vis Drain, Vis Flow)

Equipment: Lockpick tools, false credentials

Weapons: Obun stunner gun, palm laser, knife

Vitality: -10/-8/-6/-4/-2/-/0/0/0/0/0

Cyberevolutionaries

During the Second Republic, cybernetics became more than a mere fetish for certain forward-looking citizens; they saw in the melding of man and machine a key to the next step in evolution. Some even declared that the Anunnaki were not dead, that the Philosophers Stones and jumpgates *were* the Anunnaki, a race so melded to its technology that no trace remained of its organic beginnings. Although most scoffed at the preposterous claims of these fanatics, their numbers steadily increased in the latter days of the Republic. "Cyber-evolution" became more than a fad — it was a marketing slogan applied to any cool new technology meant to make interfacing with life easier.

After the Fall and the Church's fierce reprisal against technology — especially those who dared to place it inside their bodies for any but dire medical reasons — certain cyber fanatics refused to simply give in and refute their cherished progressive ideology, which promised, they believed, an escape for all sentients bound into the miserable cycle of merely organic life. Thus began the Cyberevolutionaries, a coven of sorts for the cybernetically-enhanced. (Members alternatively emphasize the cybeRevolution and the cyberEvolution.)

Cyberevolutionaries are not pure technosophists, however, for they spurn robots and AI golems — mere machines are not enough. The promise of transcendence comes only

with the melding of life and machine.

Baronet Andros Harmonic

A prominent member of the Cyberevolutionaries, Andros lives openly with his philosophy and cyberdevices. The fact that his family is one of the more powerful on Criticorum goes a long way toward protecting him from reprisal. Nonetheless, he has become the target of hateful serfs or freemen who blame "lousy tech-lovers" for all their problems. This does not prevent him from speaking out on the wonders of cybernetics and its potential to aid all races.

Rumors of his involvement in less peaceful pursuits, such as the firebombing of Church cathedrals and libraries (places in turn rumored to hold records on suspected criminals) are unproven as yet. He always has a good alibi (or at least someone prominent willing to cover for him).

(The traits in parentheses are cybernetically-enhanced.)

Race: (more than) Human

Rank/Class: al-Malik baronet

Quote: "Greetings! (shakes hands) You see — a hand like any other! Little did you suspect the wires and diodes beneath. Cybernetics, my friend, is the answer."

Description: A pale, thin noble who gets too little exercise and sunlight, preferring to stay in darkened rooms interacting with magic lantern holo-partners (virtual reality programs). His unshaven face embarrasses his family members, but his value to the house's technology interests keeps him well in its graces.

Body: Strength 3, Dexterity 6 (9), Endurance 3

Mind: Wits 6 (8), Perception 4, Tech 8

Spirit: Extrovert 2, Introvert 6, Passion 3, Calm 1, Faith 1, Ego 7

Natural skills: Observe 5

Learned skills: Etiquette 3, Physick 3, Read Urthish and Urthech, Science (Cybernetics), Speak Urthish, Speak Graceful Tongue, Stoic Body 2, Streetwise 4

Blessing: Gracious (+2 Extrovert with guests)

Benefices: Gossip Network (4 pts)

Cybernetics: Lithe Wire, Second Brain, Stimusim

Equipment: Tool kit in richly embroidered belt-pack.

Weapons: Palm laser

Vitality: -10/-8/-6/-4/-2/-/0/0/0

The Changed
(Genetically Engineered)

Humans have been tampering with their genetic makeup for millennia, but the practice became especially common during the Second Republic. During this time, corporations and other groups created entire races of genetically altered beings, fine-tuning them for use on uninhabited planets; for use as slaves, warriors and workers; and just for fun. During the decline of the Republic, the Changed became a popular scapegoat as people saw their universe crumble about them. Millions were killed in the ensuing havoc, and most of the rest have been in hiding ever since.

Almost every one of the Changed can be considered part of a secret society, because being revealed as such often leads to death at the hands of the government or scared citizens. While none of the larger sects specifically preach against the Changed, many of the smaller sects do. Even the larger sects see the Changed as something unnatural, perhaps contrary to the Pancreator's will. Thus the changed do their best to stay hidden, quietly remaining in contact with one another in order to keep tabs on whomever is after them now.

Of course, their enemies believe that the Changed are one of the most successful conspiracies, with an eventual goal of subjugating all humanity. These opponents believe the Changed are united under a ruling body, sometimes called The Circle of the Change, which includes incredibly powerful mutants. Few educated people believe in The Circle, but it is a popular bogeyman amongst the peasantry.

The Animalized

During the Second Republic, genetic engineering got… well, out of hand. Scientists experimented on many non-sentient earth animals and alien races, creating all sorts of recreational playmates or sporting targets. However, some scientists didn't know when to stop, and began experimenting with sentient races (almost all of them unwilling victims). The results were whole new races of animal/alien/human combinations, capable of breeding. As soon as the government found out, the experiments were covered up and the new races banned. In other words, they were to be exterminated. But, as is to be expected, some of them escaped. The lucky ones led their pursuers on mad chases across the stars before finding sanctuary with some odd interest group or other. Enough of them escaped to create a serious ethical issue for the Republic. News of the government's attempted genocide spread like wildfire, and rights to life for what were being called the Animalized were quickly ushered into law. Since the Fall, however, these laws have been ignored.

The Animalized are now few in number, but they have bred and spread across the Known Worlds. They have won the rights of similar sovereign races in the Known Worlds, which means they are "free" only in word, but rarely practice. They are second class citizens whose very existence is considered blasphemous to many. Their close ties to their animal instincts also make them dangerous, as not a few have reverted to their non-sentient and hungry origins in the midst of a human populace.

Alien Beasts

In the process of colonizing the Known Worlds, humanity encountered several other intelligent races. They also ran across other creatures. Some of these were easily controlled, while some were judged far too dangerous to be allowed continued existence. A few were simply too strange to comprehend. Humanity's indomitable will has proven unhealthy to human and alien beast alike in several cases.

Each world, although similar in political structure and metaculture, has its own array of unique flora and fauna. "Standard" lifeforms, such as horses or other beasts of burden, can vary greatly. The genetic stock was radically altered during the Second Republic, creating all sorts of specialized creatures. After the Fall, the noble families seized the rights to certain stocks, breeding them for profit on their worlds. Thus, Aragon destriers (from the Hazat's homeworld of Aragon) are well-known as the best warhorses throughout the Known Worlds; Severan stallions (from the Decados homeworld of Severus) are known to be the smartest; and Qalim (racehorses bred by the al-Malik) are known to be the fastest. The Muster specializes in transporting animals (and people) across the stars, and often ferries these prize stallions from world to world for famous races and contests.

Below are some examples of strange creatures encountered on the planets of the Empire. Most are located on specific planets and are seldom seen elsewhere, while a few tend to pop up in the strangest places. The traits given below represent an "average" member of the species. Traits may be higher for exceptional members of the species or lower for younger members of the race.

Animals and non-sentient aliens do not have Spirit characteristics. Beast Lore skill is used when interacting with non-sentients, and Xenobiology may come in handy.

Amen'ta ("Hull Rats")

Amen'ta were long thought to be myths created by Diaspora merchants until the day they appeared on Criticorum (then capitol of human space). They were first encountered on their native Severus, where their large numbers and feral nature were kept in check by larger and far more vicious predators. They evolved as scavengers preying upon left-over kills, but most of Severus' prey species have thick, armored hides. To obtain their food, most predators evolved into bloodsuckers rather than develop the claws needed to rend their kills. The Amen'ta evolved steel-sharp teeth to gnaw through the left-over kills' hides and reach the meat beneath.

The first human expedition to the planet did not take the cautions of the natives seriously until after the Amen'ta vermin destroyed their Lander. When a relief ship finally arrived, little was left of the scouting mission. They had been picked off one-by-one by predators and their remains devoured by Amen'ta. But the new expedition failed to learn from the failure of the first, and the Amen'ta infiltrated the starship and took off with the expedition to seed the planets of the Known Worlds.

have shown two organs seemingly unique to these creatures. The first of these organs is a gland, the Slumber, which releases a powerful hormone that sends the creatures into hibernation. While hibernating, the Amen'ta require almost no oxygen and no source of nutrients. This gland has become a popular "wonder pill" recently, tauted by certain unscrupulous merchants as a cure-all. However, if taken in too great a quantity, it can cause severe narcolepsy.

The second organ, a secondary brain, is a miracle of evolution. While in the hibernation cycle, this small brain sends commands to the body on a genetic level, forcing metabolic changes that allow the creature to adapt to virtually any environment. This organ helps the Amen'ta develop immunities to virtually every poison used to destroy them. Worst of all, the immunities are passed on to future generations of Amen'ta. This organ was popular among Second Republic genetic engineers, who are said to have synthesized human versions of the organ allowing for vast adaptability. But that was long ago, and if anyone still knows how, they aren't telling.

Perhaps the most devastating aspect of the Amen'tas' ability to adapt is the overwhelming hunger the creatures feel when they awaken. The biological changes in the animals' genetic make-up requires substantial energy, and they normally lose all of their stored reserves by the time they come out of hibernation. Anything available at the time they awaken is fair game, and ship and crew alike are often in danger when the Amen'ta stowaways revive.

Quote: "Used to be you could find a ship where the damned Amen'ta hadn't managed to eat most of the insulation. These days, it don't seem possible."

Description: The Amen'ta are like no other vermin. They are less than a foot in length with heavy black fur and hard, scaly skin. More like small armadillos than actual rats, the Amen'ta bear sharp claws and chisel-like teeth which are almost as strong as steel, a result of their native environment on Severus. The pack mentality of these Hull Rats has made them something of a menace. These creatures are naturally cautious and almost impossibly quiet.

Body: Strength 1, Dexterity 3, Endurance 1
Mind: Wits 2, Perception 5, Tech 0
Natural Skills: Dodge 6, Fight 3, Observe 5, Sneak 8
Weapons: Claws (1 DMG), Teeth (2 DMG), Gnaw (given enough time, Amen'ta can gnaw through anything except a force field or ceramsteel)
Armor: 1
Vitality: -3/-1/0/0

Vrasht Bugs

Vrasht Bugs have recently been discovered in the areas of Pandemonium that have lost their terraforming. Unscrupulous people have exported them elsewhere for their own twisted schemes. They are notoriously dangerous and ag-

Amen'ta find places to hide within the nooks and crannies of ships, usually deep within the pipes and insulation. They can enter a state of deep hibernation during which their bodies adapt to their new environment. A week after their entry onto the ship, the creatures awaken with a voracious appetite, and begin devouring anything they can find. All too often, they find power cables and circuitry to gnaw on. While their attempts to digest power cables fail, the resulting loss of energy or control of ship systems quickly proves more than simply inconvenient. Attempts to flush them out with poison or gas often result in their disappearance for a week, after which they reappear and start their voracious scavenging all over again.

Amen'ta must be found while they are hibernating; otherwise, they may damage a ship beyond repair. A subguild of the Scravers has developed to specialize in flushing ships of these vermin, although they are not always successful. Nonetheless, the dirty job is necessary and pays well, in passage contracts if not in hard cash. (Scravers are sometimes referred to as Hull Rats due to their amazing adaptive skills, although never to their faces. Also, the title of "Severan rat" applies equally to Amen'ta and Decados nobles.)

Much to the chagrin of Known Worlders, the Amen'ta have proven remarkably adaptable. Virtually every planet has had a few of these creatures that have been accidentally deposited by visiting ships. Unfortunately, the nasty little mongrels reproduce at a terrifying rate. From time to time, waves of Amen'ta flood through an area, building warrens in the most impossible locations and devouring the local flora and fauna (who usually have little defense against their sharp teeth and numbers) with wild abandon. In rare cases, small outposts and towns have been forced to evacuate their homes as a result of Amen'ta infestation.

Life Cycle: The Amen'tas' ability to adapt is a powerful bonus to their survival. Autopsies of the Hull Rats' bodies

gressive to a fault. To date, they have caused hundreds of deaths.

Quote: "Do you seek an exquisitely painful death? Then place your hand by the stinger of the Vrasht Bug."

Description: When in their pupa stage, Vrasht Bugs look surprisingly like snakes, complete with fangs and forked tongues, but are only a few inches in length. In the adult stage (one month after birth), Vrasht Bugs develop segmented bodies and eight pairs of legs. A ninth pair of legs extends further than the others, and terminates in a set of lobsterlike pinchers used for grabbing prey. A tenth set of legs terminates in two barbed stingers, complete with a powerful neurotoxin. In adult form, these creatures are over two feet in length. The name of these insects comes from the hissing sound they make when aggravated.

Body: Strength 1, Dexterity 4, Endurance 4
Mind: Wits 1, Perception 3, Tech 0
Natural skills: Dodge 4, Fight 2, Sneak 5
Weapons: Pincers (1 DMG/turn. Once an attack is successful, the pincers will not release unless they are pried away or broken.), Stingers (2 DMG. If damage penetrates armor, neurotoxin is released, causing paralysis and intense pain. The victim must roll Endurance + Stoic Body or be paralyzed for three turns. The effect of multiple stings is cumulative, however, and more than three stings will completely paralyze motor functions, including breathing.)

An anti-venom for Vrasht Bug stings is known, but it is rare and expensive, requiring a long synthesis. It is said that certain individuals on Pandemonium have some of this anti-venom but will only part with it in return for dangerous and possibly illegal favors.

Armor: 2
Vitality: -3/-1/0/0/0/0

Brutes

It only took the colonizers of Byzantium Secundus a few months to figure out how to remove the native Brutes' defensive glands. Afterward, they learned that Brutes are very easily trained to perform as both wagon beasts and farm animals. Initially, the animals were easily startled, which resulted in some very foul musk attacks and several disastrous stampedes. But surgery and several generations of captive and docile lives have led to an almost perfect work animal. The rare wild Brutes should be avoided at all cost, however, as they are responsible for a number of accidental sprayings in any given year.

The demand for Brutes has begun to exceed the supply. As a result of rising demand and a substantial increase in the cost of removing the glands from the Brutes, several farmers have begun shipping their livestock with an occasional unaltered Brute in the herd. The results have been nothing short of disastrous.

Quote: "They may be ugly, but you won't find a better farm animal."

Description: Not all of the life forms encountered by humans are vicious. The Brutes are a perfect example of this fact. Brutes have low-slung bodies, capable of pulling as much as a ton of weight with little effort. These slow-witted creatures stand on four legs and are roughly six feet tall at the shoulder, with wide legs and equally wide feet. They have short necks and thick shoulders, allowing them little peripheral vision. But they are not defenseless from behind. The Brutes have a natural defense not unlike that of an Urth skunk. Whenever the animal is frightened, pungent musk is emitted from special glands. This musk is so powerful that most people struck by the odor are immediately overcome, and often regurgitate their last meal.

Body: Strength 10, Dexterity 3, Endurance 9
Mind: Wits 1, Perception 2, Tech 0
Natural skills: Vigor 4
Weapons: Musk Glands
Vitality: -10/-8/-6/-4/-2/0/0/0/0/0/0/0/0/0/0

Weird Monstrosities

Power is down. The ship lies heavy in the starry void. Urthtech sigils scroll across the oracle panel: "All systems dead. All systems dead."

Captain Shatari stares at the bridge door. Funny, how the ship seems so much louder now. Engines gone, the constant reassuring whir of the life support now replaced by the creaking of metal fatigue and the moans of dead crewmen. The door is her only protection from the husks, her former friends and crew.

Lieutenant Davies, critically wounded at the colony, was the first affected. Blood maddened and inhumanly strong, he slashed a swath through the med-team. The team who, each in turn, became night-crackers themselves. In twelve hours, the entire crew was gone. She had barricaded herself on the bridge. That was two days ago.

From what she remembered of the folk lore, husks quickly lost all reasoning capacity. She doubted that any of them could still remember how to override her door lock. Still, life support was down. She had about a day's worth of breathable air. Did they need to breathe? No matter. Without life support they would freeze solid in a few more days. She smiles weakly at the thought. The smile fades.

Three choices left: Stay on the bridge and slowly suffocate like a trapped hull-rat. Go out and let them kill her, maybe take a few down with her, maybe become one of them herself. (At least she wouldn't be alone anymore.) Or — she slowly unhooks the clasp on her blaster holster.

A quick prayer, for herself and her damned crew. Not their fault, not really. "Prophet forgive me..."

The shot echoes maddeningly through the halls of the death ship. The husks bay mournfully in inarticulate reply.

The incandescent glow of the oracle panel plays across her body. "All systems dead. All systems dead."

There are a host of monstrosities spreading throughout the empire. Born under strange and alien suns, they are the spawn of Second Republic super science and of newly reawakening magic. None of the monstrosities listed here may be used as player characters.

Husks (Zombies)

Husks. Scarecrows. Night-crackers. These are but a few of the names serfs give to the walking dead. Husks are clinically dead but animated creatures who quickly become host to all manner of carrion. These zombies are known haunt the badlands, the most desolate, rural areas on many worlds. They rarely plague urban areas. Most city dwellers think of them as folk stories.

A "zombie plague" first erupts among those on the verge of death — soldiers dying of sword wounds, terminally ill patients in Church hospices, or peasants dying of malnutrition. These near-dead suddenly discover a new hunger for life. Possessed by an unnatural strength and bloodlust, they can carve their way through a rural population in no time. Each person they kill also becomes a husk.

When husks first appeared, the serfs prayed for deliverance — this was a sign of the end times. Some scientific heretics in the Engineers guild scoff at this, believing that the phenomenon has a rational cause. They have yet to find one.

Newborn night-crackers possess exceptional strength and resilience. They also retain all their mental faculties. This does not last long, however. The initial burst of energy quickly fades; within a week they become mentally and physically lethargic. They still present a threat, however, because they remain hungry for flesh and are difficult to kill. Many of them possess a low, feral cunning. There are stories of some husks who retain their intelligence for longer periods, although even the most degenerate of these creatures may occasionally form a coherent sentence.

Most serfs believe that husks are the souls of the vengeful dead. Aliens are not known to become husks, although zombies will attack aliens and humans alike.

Traits: Newborn husks (night-crackers) have above average Body characteristics: add +2 to the newly-dead's Body characteristics, which may now exceed 10. They have varying, but rapidly diminishing mental capabilities.

Older "scarecrows" suffer fading capabilities. They have above average Body characteristics except Dexterity, which fades away: Subtract one Dexterity level per week after death, with a minimum Dexterity of 1. Scarecrows suffer the same fate with their mental capacities: Subtract one from all Mind characteristic per week after death, with a minimum of one level in each characteristic. Despite their lethargy, even old scarecrows can move quickly for short bursts to feed flesh-

eating lust.

Spirit characteristics and learned skills fade the same way Dexterity and Mind characteristics do, but there is no minimum score — husks may eventually have zero Spirit characteristics and zero in formerly known skills. Humans with a Faith of seven or more do not become zombies.

All husks ignore wound penalties and gain five extra levels of Vitality. However, they do not heal naturally; when they lose a level of Vitality, it does not come back. Despite the folk-lore, head wounds have no more effect than any other wound. Even a decapitated husk remains dangerous.

All husks gain a Scary reputation (+2 Impress) and lose whatever occult characteristics and powers (including Wyrd) they may have possessed.

Peasant Night-cracker

Everything fades away like the sun setting for the last time. This husk didn't have much, just a small farm house, a few animals and a wife. Then there was the accident. Andros was careless with the bailer. A slip, a sudden race of red and blackness. He died, but *it* is alive. Now it hungers for life. It feels the pulse in every one of its neighbors and friends. They have what it once took for granted… life.

Quote: "Please no run away! It not my fault I changed! Me still your husband…"

Description: A straw man, a broken parody of what

once was, this newly born night-cracker is a pallid, be-draggled shadow of its former self. Still wearing the clothes it was seen in last, this husk is an eternally receding portrait of a once-living human. All its living hopes, dreams and fears mingle with a ravenous insanity. Husks grow only leaner and hungrier with the passage of years.

Race: Human
Body: Strength 8, Dexterity 6 (fading), Endurance 6
Mind: (all fading) Wits 2, Perception 2, Tech 2
Spirit: (fading) Ego 3
Natural skills: Fight 6, Melee 4, Observe 4, Sneak 7, Vigor 8
Learned skills: Beast Lore 4, Blacksmithing 3, Knavery 4, Regional Lore 4, Survival 6, Tracking 4
Curses: Scary (+2 Impress)
Weapons: Medium autofeed slug gun (stolen from murdered constable)
Armor: Leather blacksmith's apron (3d)
Vitality: 0/0/0/0/0/0/0/0/0/0/0/0/0/0/0

Demons

Demons are dark presences that block out the light of the Pancreator. Serfs blame demons for everything from earthquakes to spoiled milk and impotence. Most people are aware of the deepening shadows on their planet; they believe in monsters, aliens and hidden covens. Still, most cannot fully bring themselves to believe in the reality of demons. They are real to the Church, however. Church Inquisitors have documented instances of demonic possession on numerous occasions (some secretly claim there has been an increase since Alexius's coronation). The Eskatonic Order is highly concerned with demon lore and claims to know the names and offices of certain "demon sultans."

Demons only manifest in the material world through possession. Thus, all that is factually known of them comes either the utterances of their receptacles or the mystical visions of priests (which have little to back them up but the priest's own reputation). Some educated folk believe that if demons do exist, they are extra-dimensional aliens or powerful psychics parading as demons. Many serfs believe that there is an infernal hierarchy much akin to that of the human nobility, although this may merely be a projection of their personal prejudices.

Likely targets of possession are murderers, the truly innocent, and willing (though often duped) Antinomists. The Eskatonics say that there are nine circles of demonic power, based on how many "emanations" the demon is removed from its "primeval" source in the infernal realms. The Church maintains that evil is reflected from a prime source, as though through a series of mirrors. Each reflection grows progressively weaker. Thus, a demon of the "ninth emanation" is considered of the lowest order, the least powerful of the infernal hosts.

Possessed victims gain potent powers, called Qlippoth. The number of powers gained depends on the emanation of the possessing demon; the lower the emanation (the closer to the source of evil), the more power provided. One Qlippoth is given at the ninth emanation, another at the eighth, another at seven, and so on, until nine Qlippoths are gained at the first emanation. Thus, a demon of the ninth emanation may provide one Qlippoth, while a demon of the seventh emanation has three.

Darkling energies fuel these powers. Qlippoth increase in strength with each step the demon takes towards the primary source of evil. Through Qlippoth, the possessed may ignore the dualistic balance between the Spirit characteristics. For instance, a possessed person may have a Passion 5 and a Calm 6. This is not healthy, however, for it represents a fracture in the psyche goaded into further disharmony by the alien presence. If the person ever escapes possession, it may still take time to regain control over her emotions.

Demonic receptacles (victims of possession) each gain one Infernal stigma for each Qlippoth. Each Infernal stigma makes its victim less human in appearance, ranging from the lowest level of unobtrusive but bizarre stigmas such as mismatched pupils to high level extreme deformities such as scales or lizard eyes. Because of these stigmas, only the weakest (or the most clever) demons can withstand much scrutiny among humans.

It is interesting to note that, while demons can control all the thoughts and actions of their receptacles, they cannot use the receptacle's own occult powers (Psi and Theurgy). They must use Qlippoth instead.

Demons sometimes leave their hosts of their own accord, once their work is done or for other, unknown, reasons. Theurgic exorcisms rites can also drive them out of a host. It is extremely rare, but some instances have been known where demons are tricked out of their hosts through wit alone, but playing mind games with demons is extremely dangerous.

Possessed Priest

Even a minor demon is able to cause great mischief. Lower order demons typically possesses humans to spread carnage or misinformation. A holy person possessed by such a creature may preach false sermons, corrupt his parish or go on a killing spree before the demon returns to the nether regions which spawned it. Demons can stay longest in areas of great brutality.

Quote: "Bless you, my flock. Have I ever related the parable of the corrupt patriarch and the three harlots?"

Description: A receptacle for a lower order demon, this possessed priest is able to pass for human. Even so, his parish may notice he is haggard, and "smells funny."

Rank: Priest (Eighth Emanation demon)
Body: Strength 13, Dexterity 6, Endurance 10

Mind: Wits 4, Perception 4, Tech 4

Spirit: Extrovert 8, Introvert 1, Passion 9, Calm 1, Faith 1, Ego 7

Natural skills: Charm 5, Dodge 5, Fight 8, Impress 7, Melee 5, Sneak 5, Vigor 7

Learned skills: Academia 5, Bureaucracy 5, Debate 5, Empathy 3, Etiquette 3, Folk Lore 5, Oratory 7, Read Latin

Benefices: Ordained 7

Qlippoth: 8 – 9 (Enhanced characteristics and skills)

Wyrd: 5

Weapons: Wireblade

Armor: Heavy clothing

Vitality: -10/-8/-6/-4/-2/0/0/0/0/0/0/0/0/0/0

Golems

In a society that barely tolerates technology of any sort, the idea of a mechanical human is blasphemous. Golems rob humans of their sacred place in the cosmos, diminishing and mocking the works of the Pancreator. After the Fall, the Church destroyed artificially intelligent robots (AI, or "smart robots") outright, with little consideration for any sentience they may have displayed. Their antirobot dogma does not necessarily spread to the many non-intelligent robots throughout the empire.

AI robot brains are a cephalic matrix built from a rare element known as Pygmallium. This element simulates the neural pathways of the human brain to a remarkable degree. Smart robots are just as prone to emotions, both good and bad, as humans. A golem may be a benign creature, or a remorseless killer. Most golems have a pre-programmed desire to serve humans. A "behavioral repressor" is the only known way to enforce a golem's servitude, but the golems resent it. (For them, it is similar to electroshock therapy.)

During the Second Republic, robots came in many shapes and performed a wide range of functions (combat, explora-

tion, recreation, research, etc.). Since the Fall, Church Inquisitors have watched robots and their makers very carefully. They are rare now, but not unknown. Some golems are highly mechanical in appearance, while others (those built during the later Second Republic) are almost perfect duplicates of human beings.

Primitive robots are possible at as low as Tech Level 4, although these are little more than toys. At Tech Levels 5 and 6, robots become increasingly sophisticated, but are still not truly sentient. Most robots built currently by the Engineers are at this level. At Tech Level 7 artificial intelligence is possible, although few in the modern empire are able to create such technology. Golems at this level may be vastly intelligent, and may even have some rudimentary emotions. Robots built during the later Second Republic, and by the greatest human roboticists of the present, may reach this level. Advanced AI is only possible at Tech Level 8, or above. Some robots built during the final days before the Fall are of this generation. Advanced AI robots are vastly intelligent, and display a wide range of complex emotions, and are sometimes indistinguishable from humans. AI robots of any kind are very rare.

Because of their superior design and engineering, Second Republic robots are virtually immortal if they avoid destruction and receive regular maintenance. If these robots have an agenda it is unknown.

Modern robots are built by a few eccentric Engineer geniuses in hidden labs. Such work is highly expensive (and often illegal). These Engineers have a near religious fervor for their work.

Both the Ur-Obun and Sanctuary Aeon have shown some public sympathy for the remaining golems. Both groups believe that owning one is akin to slavery, and destroying one is murder.

Golems often have cybernetic features (see Cybernetics).

Traits (Tech 7 AI): Variable Body, high Mind. Robots may reach, or exceed 10 in any Body and Mind Characteristics. Tech 7 robots have rudimentary emotions (Spirit characteristics), but do not always master them. Some of them are a bit "twitchy."

Traits (Tech 8 AI): Variable Body, high Mind. Advanced AI robots have Spirit characteristics. Tech 8 constructs have more emotional mastery than their Tech 7 "children."

Note: Robots are usually programmed with a Tech characteristic one or two levels below their own level of manufacture. This is to discourage golems from procreating. Golem procreation is punishable by death. Humans who create golems may be fined, jailed or executed. Certain houses, sects and guilds may legally own robots by obtaining an Imperial license.

The Protector

Made by an entrepreneurial Engineer, the Protector was sold to the highest bidder as a bodyguard. Programmed to protect its new master's safety above all other concerns, the golem may appear brusque to others.

Quote: "You are not permitted here. Leave, or be destroyed."

Description: A clinking, clanking pile of calamitous junk. Pulsing turbines, whirring gears and the smell of burning oil. Black iron plate steel encases its clockwork interior. Two faces, back to back, spin into place as the occasion warrants it. A smiling, vaguely benign face with blinking saucer-plate eyes beams at the world when all is safe. When its master is endangered, however, the golem's head spins in its iron hood, replaced by a fearsome gargoyle's mask. The protector has several menacing weapons built into armatures on its body.

TL 6

Body: Strength 15, Dexterity 7, Endurance 15
Mind: Wits 5, Perception 7, Tech 5
Natural skills: Dodge 5, Fight 8, Impress 8, Melee 8, Shoot 8, Vigor 8
Learned skills: Drive Landcraft 5, Etiquette 3, Remedy 3
Curses: Gullible (-2 Wits when money is involved)
Benefices: Oath of Fealty 3
Cybernetic Features: Automaintenance, Battery Powered, Cybersenses (Telescope, Radio)
Weapons: (all built in) Blaster rifle, flamer, stunner
Armor: 6+ 6d
Vitality: -8/-6/-2/0/0/0/0/0/0/0/0/0/0/0/0/0/0

Symbiots

Occasionally, a Symbiot sneaks through the barricade at Stigmata to run amok throughout the Known Worlds. These insurgents usually disguise as humans until they reach their chosen destination.

Some posit that Symbiots are not all mindless, that a cabal of sentients rules over their chaotic culture on Chernobog, lusting for the Known Worlds' tech and prosperity. Others agree, but conjecture that the Symbiots attack humans from fear and misunderstanding, and that dialogue — not war — is called for. These few compassionate ones are usually scorned and ostracized — if not stoned — by their communities, who begin to suspect them of being Symbiots themselves.

Symbiot Terrorist

Poor Jenner. He was once a noted official on Absolution, beloved by the populace for his negotiating ability with the local lords. That was before the Symbiots arrived. Now, Jenner is something else, not human anymore. A Symbiot parasite has fully taken over his body and uses Jenner's memories and personality to fool humans. He appears human at first, but when he assumes his war form and thorns sprout from his limbs, nobody is fooled.

This Symbiot has managed to slip into the garrison on Stigmata, and from there he has entered the rest of the Known Worlds. He could be encountered on just about any planet. He is a recent conversion victim, not a natural born Symbiot. He has been sent to the Known Worlds to cause trouble. Like many Symbiots, he has a psychic connection to the Lifeweb, and must roll to Remain Calm when traveling in areas where it has been damaged. This includes excessively terraformed planets (almost all worlds).

Thank the Pancreator that he is not a breeder, but only a warrior. He cannot plant Symbiot spores in others.

Race: Symbiot
Quote: "What are you staring at? I am human too."
Description: In his human form, he appears as a somewhat plump but otherwise unremarkable yeoman. Once he takes his war form, thorns sprout from his limbs and back. He can assume different forms for short periods of time by spending Wyrd.
Body: Strength 7, Dexterity 9, Endurance 8
Mind: Wits 4, Perception 8, Tech 3
Spirit: Extrovert 8, Introvert 1, Passion 9, Calm 1, Faith 1, Ego 7
Natural skills: Charm 1, Dodge 5, Fight 8, Impress 7, Melee 2, Sneak 7, Vigor 8
Learned skills: Speak Urthish
Powers: Symbiot shapeshifting. Assume he has all levels of the Soma Psychic Path but no actual Psi or Urge rating.
Wyrd: 7
Weapons: Thorns (Dx+Fight, 4 DMG, anyone attempting to grapple him automatically suffers damage)
Armor: Thorns 5d
Vitality: -10/-8/-6/-4/-2/0/0/0/0/0/0/0/0

Option: Passion Play Roleplaying

Fading Suns is called a futuristic passion play, for it is a story about the sufferings and triumphs of humankind in a medieval-space setting millennia from now. Historical passion plays were about the sufferings of Jesus, while morality plays displayed the triumphs of Christian virtue over sin. **Fading Suns** uses the term passion play in a somewhat new sense: as a morality play of the future concerning the lives of the player characters, whether they be heroes or villains. It is a sort of reenchantment of science fiction, mixing medieval mythic with millennial marvels.

In addition to using the term as a description of its setting, **Fading Suns** allows for an optional mode of play called Passion Play roleplaying. Not all **Fading Suns** games need use this as an element, but it can make for some powerful

roleplaying experiences.

A Passion Play roleplaying drama or epic is meant to go over-the-top and play up the medieval stageplay elements to the hilt. The characters are thrust into a universe where their every action and decision has momentous consequences for good or ill. They may not be aware at first of their pivotal roles or the ramifications of their deeds, but it eventually comes clear through the intervention of strange coincidence or even the appearance of Empyrean angels or demons to guide, warn or harass the destined characters.

In short, the drama or epic becomes like a tale told by future generations, where the characters are mythologized as heroes, saints or villains and their deeds are teaching-lessons or examples for all — much like the lives of the Prophet and his disciples are viewed by Known Worlders. They were perhaps relatively normal people before their deeds were elevated well beyond realistic proportions. In Passion Play roleplaying, the player character's deeds are treated just as importantly. However, nobody within the game world treats the characters as such, for they go about their lives as most do in a world of cloudy meaning, but future generations see things differently, reading into the actions of even minor NPCs the characters meet the work of providence.

At the end of a game session, the gamemaster and players review the recent events and weave a morality play from them, deciding the meaning of what may have been random or spontaneous choices during gameplay, but which are now examples of destiny in action.

For instance, in a game session one night, all the player characters did was to go to the noble ball and participate in minor intrigue and gossiping. However, once the session is over, and they review the events, they see that one of the character's discussions with Princess Amiko Li Halan wasn't merely about gardening — it was a metaphor or even parable about rulership itself. Amiko's hints about invading insects in the flowerbeds are foreshadowed warnings about enemies in the court — obvious to future tellers of the tale, but perhaps not to the characters.

As both players and gamemasters get more comfortable with this mode of gameplay, they can integrate it into actual play, introducing comments on events from the passion play perspective, and even change events to more fully play-up the theme.

Intentionality

One of the key concepts to Passion Play roleplaying is that the theme of an epic or drama is not simply a gamemaster tool for unifying story elements — it is a metaphysical principle, a mandate from heaven, that colors the physical (and supernatural) universe of the drama. It doesn't just tie-up loose plots or determine the behavior of NPCs — it changes the nature of random chance in the universe, bending the probabilities towards completion of the theme.

In short, it allows the gamemaster — and players — to cheat a little bit with the dice, all within the bounds of a simple rule: When player characters or NPCs perform actions that aid the fruition of the theme, they gain a simple bonus (+1 or +2, sometimes more) to their die rolls. Likewise, actions that hinder it may receive penalties on die rolls.

This "intentionality" of the universe is not perfect. It represents probable outcomes, greater forces which push the likely outcome of an event toward a desired end, but not a predestined end. Other forces work at odds to tilt the balance in other directions — whether through simple statistical odds stacked in favor of another outcome, or by the work of demons blocking the light of the Empyrean.

This is not about fate so much as destiny — player characters have free will in all their choices; it's just that some of their choices will be easier to accomplish than others. Morality and ethics are useless concepts without choice, and thus choice is also a vital element of Passion Play roleplaying. It differs from a tragedy play in this one vital aspect, for Oedipus had no choice but to do the things he did — he was dragged along by the tragic fate spelled out in prophecy. The heroes and villains in a Passion Play epic always have the choice to do good or evil — or the self-serving good which inevitably leads to evil.

The Grand Theme

This rule-bending theme is called the Grand Theme, for it supersedes and encompasses all the lesser themes within a drama or epic. It is the only one that actually changes the dice-rolling odds.

The Grand Theme may apply to the universe at large — in which case, everyone struggles for or against its theme — or it applies to the player characters alone. While the latter is more genuine for a passion or morality play, the tragedies and triumphs of the player characters are meant to mirror the struggles of humanity at large. Although only the player characters may have been singled out as agents of Heaven's Will (only they gain or suffer the roll modifiers), they do so as an example to all.

Not all subjects are worthy of such a theme. Some timeless classics are suggested here:

Triumph over Evil: The goal of the player characters is to win out over evil. This foe takes many forms, from oily and sanctimonious villains to the riled-up village mob — or even demons possessing the innocent. Goal bonuses for combating or sniffing out evil should only be given not when true evil is confronted, but when good is defended. And the question must be asked: How far can the player characters themselves go toward the dark side in defense of the good?

Triumph of Evil: Heaven grows more distant with every day, and evil is winning out. It is perhaps a foregone conclusion or even the ultimate intention of Heaven. The conflict is in seeing how long the player characters can re-

sist evil's allure. Do they give in and become tyrants or killers, or do they fight for their own integrity to the bitter end? This is the test put to them; how well they succeed determines the myth-cycles they inspire — stories of valiant courage and sacrifice or of supreme, world-shattering evil.

Restoration of Balance: The goal is not to whup ass on evil or to praise pious men — it is to maintain harmony and balance in a universe all too prone to chaos and dissolution. The good and the bad both have their day, but the ultimate good is not to deny the bad, but to understand it and suffer it as necessary and with virtue. Sometimes, this involves conflict with one extreme or the other — maybe an evil dark lord needs to be destroyed to return balance, but it could also be a fanatic priest and his army of paladins who imposes too harsh a regime on his "sinful" subjects.

Redemption: Like healing the Fisher King in the Arthurian saga, this theme can involve healing others' wounds (physical, psychological or spiritual) or redeeming oneself of past crimes or regretful actions — or both. Maybe one of the player characters killed one man too many in his past, and now seeks to atone for it. It won't be easy, and a supreme self-sacrifice might be required in the end. Indeed, redemption is not possible without sacrifice — whether it's the player characters willingness to brave dangers in search of the grail or a single character's refusal of fame and fortune in service to another's life.

Seeking: The Grand Theme of **Fading Suns** itself, this does not have to be every gamemasters' theme. This one concerns discovery and seeking enlightenment, wisdom, understanding or personal growth. Through discovery, we change ourselves and the world around us. It reveals that we aren't islands unto ourselves, that there is a greater world out there, one with many wonders to experience. The conflict comes when this urge outwards is stifled by lesser needs or the small minds of petty men. Too many want to keep others from experiencing what they are afraid to see themselves. The status quo must be maintained, and those who would introduce new ideas or prove that the world is round must be stopped.

The Fall: The universe is a misbegotten thing, a failed experiment removed from God. As in extreme Gnostic myths, a Demiurge has built a cage for the souls of men, trapping them from the Truth of God. That cage is this universe. The goal here is for the player characters to realize it and then turn all their wills towards escape. Can they break through to a greater reality? And if so, do they desert those left behind, still living in ignorance of the Truth? This theme has been popularized in novels by Philip K. Dick or in movies such as "The Matrix."

Transcendence: The goal is progress, evolution, the Next Step forward. It is opposed by the footdraggers and regressives, people who not only want the present to return to the past but to prevent all change. They prefer a static, unmoving universe, or the "good old ways" of ignorance. To make this a true Passion Play, it's not only the rulers and Inquisitors who fight against progress — they are joined (or ruled) by demons, entities hateful of change or fearful of humans achieving their evolutionary potential.

Revealing the Grand Theme

Players should not be aware of their epic's grand theme or intention at first — they must learn of it as they go, as their trials and tribulations reveal more and more of the secret hand(s) guiding their lives. When gamemasters fudge rolls by adding intentionality bonuses or penalties, they should not spell out the reason behind the modifier. Chock it up to "unknown forces" or "unseen complications." After a while, the players will put 2 and 2 together and perceive the workings behind the stage — the deus ex machina in the play.

They should be helped to this realization by clues within the drama: Street signs seem to repeat the same name or books opened randomly reveal the same message, although reworded or in different form. Dialogue overheard between strangers eerily echoes meaningful events in the drama. Depending on just how obvious or supernatural the gamemaster wants to get, even stranger coincidences can occur, from the appearance of long-lost relatives just as their names are mentioned to the timely reopening of a jumpgate long sealed.

In addition, certain dice rolls have greater meaning than usual: a critical hit is not simply an over-and-above achievement, it becomes a key moment in the mythology of the character that rolled it — it is the Moment of Triumph over Baron Vail, or the Winning of the Bride. Upon rolling such an unexpected result, the gamemaster then interprets it with far more fanfare than a normal critical result would receive. Such an event becomes a pivotal moment in the drama, around which other events are hinged, for it represents a supreme connection to the theme (for or against, depending on the roll). Future generations of children around the fireside will beg their parents to tell them once more the tale of Adept Gregory's Masterful Blow or Captain Julia's Great Escape.

The flip side of this, however, is that critical failures become just as mythic. The character's gun doesn't just jam on a fumble, it becomes the story of Erian's Failure at the Cave, or Alustro's Fall from Grace.

Gamemasters should beware, however, not to punish (or reward) characters too much for random dice rolling. In the end, it is their actions and roleplaying choices that are important — dice rolling simply embellishes the tale. Dice provide a game's unexpected moments of glory or tragedy, its surprise and shock value, but they do not substitute for actual roleplaying.

Chapter 9: Planets

Brother Alustro stood amid the smoking crops and tried to shut his ears to the weeping of the serfs around him. Fumes choked him, and he tugged his robes over his nose and mouth. On the far horizon, dim specks in the distant sky, the raiders shot through the upper atmosphere on their way back to whatever world they had come from, their work done.

Although chemical bombings were rare these days after Alexius' ascension, it seemed that not everyone had learned the terrible lessons of the Emperor Wars. Few had seen first-hand the tragedy such high-tech solutions to petty vendettas wrought on the innocent.

Alustro held back tears at the sight of an old woman collapsed onto her knees, praying. She, like most here, had lived her entire life in these fields. It was all she knew. Only those connected to the noble houses, guilds or Church had the freedom and resources to travel the Known Worlds. As she muttered her prayers, Alustro wondered how many interstellar travelers had maintained during their worst trials a faith as strong as this woman's simple belief. She prayed even though the situation was hopeless. Nothing could now grow from these fields — the chemical bombs had ensured that.

Alustro turned away; he was already late returning to his liege and her ship. As he stepped through the wilting grains, he gasped as a sudden torrent of rain lashed down on him. There had been no heavy clouds in the sky, but now rain poured down, its golden sheen sparkling in the full light of the sun. The steam unleashed by the wave rose from the fields like a curtain, temporarily leaving Alustro disoriented and unsure of his path.

Then it was gone. The sun baked the moisture from the air in seconds and no sign of it remained. Except... the grain was now brighter and stood taller, as if a burden was lifted

from it. The poisons so recently unleashed now floated harmlessly through the upper atmosphere, spread so thin they were barely noticeable.

Alustro looked at the women. She stood and gathered her scythe, and then began to work.

"By the Pancreator," Alustro whispered, "the suns cannot fade forever with such faith alive in the world...."

The Known Worlds

Refer to the map of the Known Worlds to determine the jumproads between certain planets. Below are simple sketches about the planets in the Empire and along the border; gamemasters should feel free to create their own details about these worlds.

Absolution

This world has been compromised by the Symbiots. It is outside of the Stigmata Garrison's direct influence, and the people of Absolution have been abandoned by the Known Worlds. Do people still even exist on this planet? Or are they all Symbiots now? Travel to Absolution (and to all compromised worlds) is forbidden. Any ship caught trying to enter the Known Worlds from these planets is destroyed by the Stigmata Garrison.

Apshai

A joint human and Vau world. Apshai has many citizens of the Empire living upon it, and the Vau rarely leave the one continent they forbid humans to enter, where the G'nesh also live (see Chapter One: The Universe). Human colonization of Apshai was allowed during the Second Republic, a secondary result of years of diplomatic negotiations concerning an affair long since forgotten (surely the Vau remember, but they do not speak of the incident). Empire spies are sent here to observe the Vau, but they are

never allowed close enough to see anything of worth. A "mission to Apshai" is equivalent to a vacation or retirement.

Artemis

Home to the head Sanctuary Aeon monastery, Artemis is a holy world with strict immigration policies. While nobles and guildmembers live on Artemis, they must follow Church law, which imposes strict behavioral rules. Every law is designed to minimize conflict, including such penalties as exile to far continents if the two parties cannot govern their relationships with each other. Despite the seemingly harsh rules, the best medical technology in the Empire is found here. The sick and dying who can afford the journey to Artemis for healing usually return whole again (although with a samaritan penance they must perform as payment).

Aragon

The Hazat homeworld has both benefited and suffered from its proximity to Leagueheim and Byzantium Secundus. Both have brought a great deal of wealth to Aragon, but the Hazat nobles have also spent a lot of their money on those worlds. The Hazat and the wealthiest of their subjects are undeniably well off. The poorest live in squalor. The wealthiest parts of the planet, like the capital and its unparalleled military academy, are second to none. The poorest are among the most dangerous and inhospitable in the Known Worlds.

Aylon

Ruled now by the al-Malik, Aylon was once owned by the Ur-Ukar. It is famed for being the first planet the Prophet set foot upon after his miraculous vision (gained on the now-lost world of Yathrib, beyond Aylon's jumpgate). Pilgrims come from all over annually to see the spot where the Prophet first preached. The rest of the planet is taken up by large reserves, and the al-Malik make a lot of money catering to the interests of off-world hunters and recreationalists.

Bannockburn

The headquarters of the Muster, who coordinate their efforts against both the Symbiots and the Vuldrok raiders from this planet. It is also the homeworld of the Gannok, devilishly clever tricksters with a penchant for invention and high-tech jury-rigging. Most of the inhabited sections of the planet are rugged and craggy highlands with broad moors. Strange Ur ruins can be found in various places, most long since stripped of their valuable artifacts.

Byzantium Secundus

While the capital of the Known Worlds suffered some damage during the Emperor Wars, it no longer bears any signs of the strife. Indeed, Emperor Alexius has embarked on an ambitious building plan, and even more construction is turning what was once known as the "Concrete Capital" back into its old gray, metal-covered self. Every major faction in the Known Worlds (as well as the Vau) maintains a presence on this rainy world, and all have interests at stake on a daily basis. For more information, see the sourcebook **Byzantium Secundus**.

Cadavus

One of the poorer worlds in the Empire, Cadavus fell into Decados' hands during the Emperor Wars. The Decados are only the most recent rulers of the planet; almost every faction of note in the past 2000 years has had an interest in it at one point or another. While the planet has little in the way of industry, mining or agriculture now, it still remains a center for a number of religious groups, whose monasteries maintain records dating back to the beginning of space exploration.

Cadiz

Ruled by the Decados, the great cities of Cadiz are legendary. Second Republic diplomats chose this world as their base for negotiations with the Vau, and the cosmopolitan fervor which gripped the planet caused the rise of many towering metropoli. But the Vau refused to come to Cadiz, and instead demanded that the diplomats come to them on Vril-Ya. The cities are now teeming with the poor and restless, who crowd into apartments once reserved for the rich. Cadiz also holds the only reservation reserved for the indigenous Hironem aliens.

Chernobog

The Symbiot homeworld. Little is known of Chernobog, for the last humans to set foot upon the world never returned. The jumpgate to Chernobog from Stigmata is blockaded; no one is allowed in or out, although the occasional Symbiot force breaks through nonetheless. It is said that the planet is a steamy jungle teeming with Symbiot lifeforms of all kinds, fighting each other tooth and claw for dominance.

Criticorum

No al-Malik would ever deny this planet's value, nor would they deny the extreme problems it has caused the house. Once considered for the capital of the Second Republic, it has jumproutes to seven other worlds, and travelers from Byzantium Secundus, the Church worlds, the al-Malik planets, the Decados hegemony, the Li Halan worlds and Kordeth regularly stop there. The League has also established a substantial presence here, and the guilds maintain a number of vehicle and weapons plants. As a result, the world hosts legions of ambitious schemers and spies from around the Known Worlds. Intrigues here may lack the subtlety of those on Byzantium Secundus, but they are at least as common.

Daishan

Compromised in the Symbiot War, Daishan was scorched by the Stigmata Garrison. Symbiots cannot grow anything on scorched worlds, but neither can humans. The world is

still off-limits, guarded at its jumpgate by a small fleet of Imperial troops. The Imperial Eye is rumored to have sent an expedition to the planet to ascertain the strength of any remaining Symbiot presence. Tales about what the expedition brought back have spread throughout the Known Worlds, but they vary widely: some say nothing was found but an empty wasteland, while others tell campside horror stories about the warped and twisted troops who returned to their Imperial masters, now hungry for human flesh. Strangely, Imperial and Church forces seem to encourage the worst of these stories.

Delphi

The homeworld of House Hawkwood, Delphi has suffered its share of setbacks, but even with the devastation of the Emperor Wars, the Hawkwoods are stronger now than they have been for some time. Imperial support is behind them. Delphi is where the leaders of the house meet to plan the next victories to raise them above all other families — or so they fervently believe.

De Moley

An inhospitable and barren planet, De Moley has little atmosphere (about as much as Mars). Terraforming was incomplete when the Second Republic collapsed. Nonetheless, De Moley is home to the prime Brother Battle monastery. Visitors must negotiate the treacherous paths up the high crags to reach the monastery, since the howling winds are too much for most flitters to handle. The valleys between the high mountains are calmer, hosting the atmosphere domes in which a small populace lives, helping to reap De Moley's resources. A hard life is all the peasants of De Moley know. Those few who escape from this world are valued for their hardiness.

Grail

Ruled by House Keddah (a minor house), Grail's vast forests and mountains are home to the Etyri, a sentient avian race. Grail is where the Prophet was healed by Amalthea of the darkness which had infected his soul on a Lost World beyond the border. The planet's name comes from the symbol for the Amaltheans, and there is a Sanctuary Aeon monastery on the planet at the site of the Prophet's healing.

Gwynneth

Gwynneth has suffered of late from the Vuldrok Raiders' invasions. It is believed to be only a matter of time before the Vuldrok set up a permanent base in the forested wilderness, hidden from easy scrutiny. The Hawkwood rulers voice fears that the long-defiant pagan peoples living in the woods would welcome the Raiders. Muster mercenaries, hired by a Hawkwood lord, have recently come from Bannockburn to defend the planet from further assault, but they seem to concentrate instead on keeping the local popu-

lace in line. The Hawkwoods have allowed Vuldrok ambassadors to pass through their space to Byzantium Secundus in the hopes that Alexius will act once he meets the uncouth barbarians face-to-face.

Hargard (Vuldrok)

A number of Lost Worlds exist past the Hawkwood jumpgates, ruled by a loose confederation of barbarians with jumpdrive capability. Not much is known about the worlds except that their natives are uncouth and savage, occasionally raiding the Known Worlds for plunder. The world immediately past Leminkainen's jumpgate is called Hargard, and is the source of recent barbarian raids. The Hawkwoods are currently hiring mercenaries to take the raiding back to the Vuldrok.

Hira (Kurga)

This world is off the map (it can be reached through Vera Cruz's jumpgate). It is a Lost World being fought over by the Hazat and the Kurga Caliphate (a barbarian regime beyond the Lost World). The world actually has many names, depending on who you talk to (a native, a Hazat soldier, or a Kurgan); whomever wins it will surely rename it anyway.

Holy Terra (Urth)

The capital of the Church and the cradle of humanity. The planet is overcrowded; teeming masses of the faithful squeeze into the cities that dot the globe. This is partly because vast regions are given over to wilderness and allowed to exist in their natural, unterraformed states as an example of the Pancreator's bounty. Permits to visit these wildernesses are allowed, but overstaying one's allotted time is a crime, prompting manhunts for any recalcitrant hermits. Immigration is strictly controlled by the Church, and those born on Holy Terra are given special consideration over foreigners. It is the prime planet for pilgrimages, however, as holy sites important to human history are found on every continent.

The Patriarchal Seat (some say "throne") is always situated here, usually near the birthplace of the reigning Patriarch. If the Patriarch was born elsewhere, he chooses the seat's new location based on rather complex readings of ancient texts and affinities for local saints. Most, however, simply inherit their predecessor's seat, which has been in Rio Brasilia for the last century. The Church's grand archives are spread throughout the world.

The planet Mars hosts one of the most popular pilgrimage sites: the alleged birthplace of the Prophet. Little is actually known of Zebulon's early years, and many worlds during the Second Republic claimed his natal spot (Sutek, Grail, Malignatius). During the Dark Ages, however, the Patriarch declared Mars the one and only true site of Zebulon's birth.

Icon

The Li Halan hold Icon sacred, for it is where they announced their conversion to Orthodoxy. The planet was originally valued for its Ur ruins, but those ruins have been scoured inch by inch since, and there are few mysteries left. The Li Halan consider Icon to be a bulwark against the dangerous ideas coming out of Manitou, and they often pester the Inquisitorial Synod with requests for cleansings (with the result that the synod rarely bothers with Icon, a fact which the residents are glad of).

Istakhr

Istakhr boasts not only one of the greatest bazaars in the Known Worlds (the Istakhr Market), but some of the most stupendous buildings. The al-Malik rulers have used much of their wealth to build pleasure palaces for themselves, awe-inspiring cathedrals and even museums open to their serfs. The vast amounts of wealth floating around this largely desert world have attracted all sorts of people to Istakhr, from the most ambitious to the most unscrupulous.

Iver

A newly-discovered world with a jumproute leading to Pandemonium, Iver is an interdicted planet. In its years of isolation from the Known Worlds, its inhabitants developed a heretical version of Church scripture; until they recant, the Inquisition attempts to block anyone from coming or going to Iver. The world's existence is not even common knowledge in the Known Worlds yet. This suits the Hazat just fine, for the house is trying to claim the world before its own rulers can prove their claim to the ancient Chauki lineage — and thus the lands of the Hazat.

Kish

Homeworld of the Li Halan, Kish is an extremely conservative desert planet. It has changed little throughout the devastation of the Emperor Wars, and the residents consider the relative chaos of surrounding worlds to be proof that the Li Halan are the only rulers worthy of the title. Outsiders claim that there are more peasant uprisings on Kish than the Li Halan admit to.

Kordeth (Ukar)

Now owned jointly by the al-Malik and Merchant League, Kordeth was once a proud if fractious world. Homeworld of the Ur-Ukar and capitol of their former empire, it is still an autonomous region for Ukari although it is monitored heavily by the Church. The planet's surface is rocky and without arable soil, covered with craggy gullies and sharp cliffs. Life exists only in the vast underground tunnels that comb the planet. Here grow thousands of mosses and fungi, and indigenous predators and prey — both insect and mammal — crawl in the darkness.

Leagueheim

No other planet in the Empire can claim to have as many

technological wonders as Leagueheim. No other planet can claim to have politics as vicious as Leagueheim, either. With several hundred guilds represented on the planet, anything can — and does — happen. Here anything that can make someone a firebird is legal and already being done. Still, discretion is the key word here. No one wants the Inquisition ruining the fun.

Leminkainen

A Hawkwood-ruled border world which suffered heavily from the barbarian invasions of the past. It was occupied for a time by barbarians, and their descendants still live here, maintaining what they claim is a sovereign nation. The Hawkwoods say the barbarians are deluded, and only live separately from others because the Hawkwoods allow it. Still, the forests are full of pagans who openly ignore the Church missionaries attempting to save their souls.

Madoc

This aquatic world is a rich resource for the League. The vast majority of the surface is covered by water, and the marine life is varied and wondrous, producing many delicacies. However, this cuisine is hard to ship off-world, so the rich who desire it must come to Madoc. The amphibian Oro'ym live in its oceans, long believed extinct until they revealed themselves once more. While they now live in primitive squalor, scientists believe their ancestors once traveled the stars with the Anunnaki. Madoc is one of the rare worlds which required little terraforming, and is said to hold many undespoiled secrets beneath its waves.

Malignatius

Once a Li Halan planet, the Decados seized this arctic-and-tundra world early in the Emperor Wars and have held it ever since. It still bears the mark of its former rulers, and religious fervor regularly sweeps the world. Since the Decados took over, however, the Orthodox view has become diluted. New sects crop up on a regular basis, and even different members of the same group find themselves battling over dogma. Newcomers often find themselves caught up in this factional fighting against their will.

Manitou

A joint human-Vau protectorate, Manitou is home to some of the few psychic covens which dare to operate openly. The Vau do not allow the Inquisition to enter the system, and so criminals and outcasts from across the Known Worlds desperately seek to find their way here. The Vau either do not care or have planned it this way, using the world as a viewing glass into the underbelly of human culture. The human government is run by a local guild, although it has strong ties to the League and claims fealty to the new Emperor.

Midian

A Li Halan world, famed as the birthplace of Patriarch Palamedes, founder of the Universal Church. It was the Prophet's preaching here that converted Palamedes, heir to vast lands then owned by House Alecto. The planet's religious heritage is pounded into the hearts and minds of all the residents, many of whom nonetheless abandoned the Orthodoxy during the Emperor Wars to join the multitude of new sects springing up on the planet, much to the horror of the devout Li Halan.

Nowhere

A barren wasteland where sits the Gargoyle of Nowhere, an ancient statue said to deliver omens to those who come seeking it. The Stigmata Garrison Commander suspects that Symbiots have compromised the world, although there is no proof in the sand-blown deserts. Pilgrims who go to Nowhere may not be allowed back into Known Worlds, and nomadic caravans of such refugees roam the world, eking out a living in the sands. It is said that Nowhere once had lush forests and that many secrets lie hidden in its wastes.

Pandemonium

See the Appendix for details on this frontier world.

Pentateuch

Terraformed by the legendary Doramos, Pentateuch is considered by many to be a magical planet, the ultimate wedding of magic and technology. There seems strong evidence that Doramos deliberately designed the terraforming to create ley lines and energy centers, although most of these are little understood today, for Doramos left no records of his secrets. The Eskatonic Order claims the cathedral and rulership of this world, although the planet is a frequent target for Inquisitorial scrutiny.

Pyre

Home to the famous Burning Desert, a hot-house hell that proved unterraformable, this world is claimed by Temple Avesti, which is allowed to rule it in the name of the Patriarch. The sect's main monastery lies in the harsh desert, but there is little tech to aid the monks in surviving the heat. Most are forced to relocate to the milder habitats by the sea. The planet is considered Inquisitor central, but most Avestite Inquisitors leave the system to look for sin elsewhere, never suspecting it might reside on their homeworld. As a matter of fact, at least one secret laboratory operates on the southern continent, far from the eyes and attention of the monks, who do not have the facilities to monitor all space traffic to and from the world.

Rampart

This frontier world was once owned by the League but was seized by the Li Halan during the Emperor Wars. The independent guild that once ran the planet is still powerful, but choking under the reforms of the Li Halan governor, who seeks to clean up what she perceives as social decay and moral licentiousness. The Li Halan are attempting to

285

enforce onto the frontier-minded residents of Rampart the sort of social laws they expect on their other, better-behaved worlds. But the rigid caste structure they impose is resisted by the residents, and the call for a major uprising is spreading despite the best efforts of Li Halan information police.

Ravenna

A Hawkwood world, and the birthplanet of Emperor Alexius. While the planet is safe from Vuldrok so far, it is between two worlds which have suffered harassment. The people are used to a quiet existence and pastoral pastimes, from falconry to beastback hunting. Many outsiders believe they are in denial about the threat to their world and way of life, drinking bitters as their other worlds are plundered. Others believe that, should Ravenna be attacked, Alexius will finally make a serious move against the barbarians.

Severus

Very few humans lived on this jungle planet before the collapse of the Second Republic. Then its Decados owners opened it up to refugees from the major trouble spots, if those refugees would pledge allegiance to the house. Those who made the pledge may well have regretted their decision, because Severus is a most inhospitable world. Its native species and indigenous sentients (the primitive Ascorbites) have evolved tough, almost metallic skin and sharp teeth to break through skin to the sweet blood within. Severan hull rats are probably the most famous of these, and they now infest ships throughout the Known Worlds (see Chapter Eight: Gamemastering). They use their sharp teeth to gnaw through anything in search of nourishment.

Shaprut

This mineral-rich planet has avoided much of the intrahuman strife that has plagued other worlds, but it has suffered occasional raids from Symbiots. These few attacks have been used by local lords as further justification to keep the ungulate Shantor, Shaprut's native race, on their reservations, where they are supposedly safe from contamination — and well out of sight of humans. Most of these Shantor return the favor to their lords by serving as slaves in the mines.

Stigmata

Stigmata is the hotly-contested world that forms a bulwark against the Symbiots, and is home to the powerful Imperial Stigmata Garrison, the best collection of troops in the Known Worlds (next to the Imperial Guard). Little is known about the Symbiot-claimed worlds beyond Stigmata, since those who have gone out have not been allowed to return, despite their radio claims of being whole and uncorrupted by what they saw. Before they can deliver full reports, their ships are destroyed to prevent organic infection from entering Human Space. Those legionnaires who have survived their tours of duty here are shaken and hollow men, scarred by what they have seen on the battlefields of Stigmata.

Sutek

The first humans to fly through a jumpgate found themselves in this star system, and humans have been here ever since. Its cities have sprung up on the ruins of its older municipalities, and inhabitants regularly find artifacts dating back to the earliest days of the First Republic. Most of the valuable items disappeared years ago, but rumors still crop up about major hidden troves of antique treasures.

Tethys

An Imperial world, once run by an independent guild but now owned by the Emperor. This is one of the oldest worlds in Human Space, and was stripped of its resources long ago. It now survives by attracting renowned craftsmen and manufacturers, promising land and low noble status in return for a cut of their profits. The Mitchau family of weaponsmiths has recently relocated here from Aragon to take advantage of these benefits. One of the remote continents on a nearby planet in the system is said to be used by the Imperial Guard for training and war games; entry onto this planet is closely guarded.

Ungavorox (Vorox)

The homeworld of the Vorox is a vicious environment composing many conflicting biomes. The planet breeds some of the fiercest and most dangerous predators in the Empire, many of them poisonous with toxins even most assassins dare not use lest they be turned against them. Amid this chaos of competition, the Vorox reign. While not as big as some Voroxian predators, they learned early on to use teamwork to take down their prey and defend themselves from their own predators — on this world, no one is above the food chain. The planet is owned by Li Halan, who are careful only to allow civilized Vorox off-world.

Vau

A closed world; nobody is allowed into Vau Space without diplomatic permission. They rarely kill invaders, though. They simply snatch them up with their plasma-nets and deposit them back on their side of the border. Repeated attempts to enter, however, may be met with deadly force. This said, black-market trade does take place between the nations, but mainly in Human Space, on worlds such as Manitou or Vril-Ya. Vau is home to the mandarins who venture into Human Space on missions for their leaders. It is rumored that one of the Vau leaders is placed on this world, sent from one of the many Vau worlds beyond the planet's border.

Vera Cruz

Long known as one of the most beautiful planets in space, this Hazat world bears the stamp of the great terraformer Doramos, whose wife is said to have come from

here. Some of the wealthiest people in the Empire used to come here to escape their concerns and worries, but the recent military buildup for the war over Hira has somewhat marred its peaceful demeanor. Still, many older Hazat retire here (or get retired here), and they still do their best to keep their hands in the intrigues which plague the Known Worlds.

Velisimil (Obun)

The homeworld of the Ur-Obun, officially owned by House Hawkwood. The Obun have a degree of sovereignty envious to other races, and still maintain their ancient culture of wisdom. The architecture of the planet is like nowhere else in the Known Worlds, with graceful spires reaching beyond the clouds, beautiful fountains miles high, perfect gardens and wide promenades. Human malcontents attempting to find a black underbelly to Obun culture have so far been unsuccessful.

Vril-Ya

The Vau ambassadorial world. Humans are allowed here to discuss matters of state, but they must stay on the single island reserved for their use. Certain lower-caste Vau run a secretive black-market, selling Vau tech items to those who can afford them and are discreet enough not to bring the deal to the attention of the mandarins. They rarely deal openly, using alien go-betweens instead, such as Hironem or other minor races.

The Lost Worlds

At its height, the Second Republic spanned far more planets than does the Empire. A number of these have disappeared from public records. Their jumpgates sometimes operate, but no one knows how to reach them. They still exist, circling their isolated suns, separated from the rest of humanity by ignorance alone.

These worlds range the spectrum from those that have declined to caveman levels to those rumored to have kept their Republic-era technology — and improved upon it. Some people suspect that a few planets deliberately eliminated any outside knowledge of themselves, and have agents in the Known Worlds dedicated to protecting their solitude.

The Emperor has let it be known that he will handsomely reward anyone who brings word of a rediscovered world. The houses seek the added power and prestige that comes with ruling more planets, the guilds want to expand their trade routes, and the sects yearn to add the souls of those poor heathens to their ranks. Of course, everyone wants to uncover whatever Philosophers Stones and other artifacts an unknown world might be hiding.

Still, most of the people who have gone searching for hidden planets have done it for their own reasons. Some have been looking for a new place to live, having either voluntarily left their old home or been thrown off it. Others

have sought abandoned treasures and lost knowledge. The bard Arletra wrote her acclaimed epic "Vladimir Unforgotten" while on a quest for her family's ancestral world of Principia.

Discovering such a world is exceptionally difficult. The easiest way is via research, sifting through what few records remain from the Second Republic, looking for references to forgotten planets. These records rarely provide information on jumproutes to those worlds, however. Finding a key to a lost jumproute is guaranteed to bring a character lots of money and trouble.

Planet Design Process

Too many science fiction stories diminish the importance of individual planets in their settings. A living, breathing world becomes the backdrop for one adventure, before the cast moves on to the next world. But gamemasters in **Fading Suns** should treat each planet as a highly complex entity, with almost endless possibilities for adventure. Few people roam freely among the stars in **Fading Suns**, and most never leave their home planet. Characters will, of course, travel between planets, but an entire epic may occur on a single planet, or a small number of worlds.

A planet design process is provided here to aid gamemasters in designing worlds. Below are details on the categories, or traits, given to planets in **Fading Suns**. For an example of a pre-designed world, see the Appendix for details on Pandemonium.

Name

Planet names vary widely throughout the Empire. Some worlds bear the names of historic places or mythical people (Delphi, Artemis). Others are descriptive of the planet's nature or function (Pandemonium, Nowhere, Pyre). Many earlier planets received Sathraist names from the earliest gatejumpers.

There are usually two names for a planet: the name chosen by the first discoverer and the more modern, Imperial name. Locals often have their own name for their planet and maintain it against force of custom in the rest of the Empire. (Holy Terra is still called by its original name, Urth, by many who live there.) A planet may have many names, gathered over the centuries. These names may be human, alien or a mix of both. Often the reason behind a planet's name is obscure. Many aliens resent the idea that their planet was "discovered" by humans and tenaciously hang on to their planet's original name. Such an issue may become a rallying point for disaffected aliens tired of human rule. In some cases a planet's name may vary among various parties, though every planet has one "official" name used by the Imperial stellar cartographers on Byzantium Secundus.

Ruler

Decide which House, Church sect or guild controls the planet. While most planets have a mix of interests represented, usually one group manages to scramble to the top. Sometimes there may be more than one ruling group. These may be close allies or bitter rivals. Ironically cooperation is often more likely between coalitions of differing power structures (i.e., a noble house and a trade guild) than between members of the same umbrella group (i.e., Brother Battle and Temple Avesti). Some rare planets are ruled by none of the major powers within the Known Worlds, and those worlds in barbarian space (outside of the Known Worlds map) are ruled by a variety of powers. Alien worlds, lost remnants of the Second Republic and some autonomous fringe worlds are often independent of Imperial interests.

The nature of the ruling group affects all aspects of life on that planet, but the reverse of this is also true. Rulers sent by one of the three main interests often find themselves transformed by local customs. Many strange hybrid groups have appeared over the centuries, and do not always tow their parent group's ideological line.

Most planets are ruled by nobility, although title alone does not necessarily confer power. Often a hollow dukedom may be a mere facade for the Church or guild interests who really pull the strings. Even a strong noble cannot rule peacefully without the approval of these two groups. Few populations on any planet will follow a noble who has been declared "Godless" by the Church, and only the most powerful nobles may rule without material support from the guilds. Many local power consortiums, whether noble, Church or guild oriented, are despotic and unresponsive to the needs of the people. As a result, many planets must contend with sporadic (and sometimes successful) revolts. The Empire usually considers these to be purely internal matters and leaves the local authorities to deal with them as they see fit. Major regional conflicts may rage for years, even centuries, without direct Imperial intervention.

Cathedral

Almost every human inhabited planet has a cathedral on it. The gamemaster should decide which sect, or sects, hold the most influence here. The three most common holders of a planet's "Holy See", or diocese, are Urth Orthodox, the Eskatonic Order and Temple Avesti. Brother Battle holds sees on a few embattled border worlds such as Stigmata and planets bordering Vau space. All other Church sects hold sees on few, or no, planets. The see is important, even if the Church is not the ruling group on the planet. Both the nobility and the guilds must defer to the Church on many issues. A planet's see is a sought after prize on any world, and often the subject of intense competition between sects.

The diocese on a planet is best represented by the main cathedral on the world, an often-grand structure usually situated in the planet's capitol city. Many worlds compete to build the greatest monuments to the glory of the Pancreator, de-

Typical Garrison

Level	Planet	Troops	Weaponry
1	Destitute, pacifist	Serf militia	Melee
2	Poor	Mercenaries	Slug guns
3	Unimportant	Enlisted Army	Artillery
4	Average	Local Navy	Small fleet
5	Minor house	Local Royal Guard	Frigates
6	Holy, proscribed	Patriarchal Guard	Church fleet
7	Trade nexus	House Navy / Muster mercs	Destroyers
8	Wartime, border world	House Marines	Brother Battle, Cruisers
9	Major house homeworld	House High Command	Flagship & fleet
10	Byzantium II	Imperial Guard	Dreadnought

spite admonitions against hubris by some priests. Despite strong Church dogma governing the architectural conventions of early cathedrals, many modern cathedrals have a strong local flavor. Some cathedrals borrow heavily from Second Republic — or even alien — designs. Most cathedrals have all the conventional architectural elements familiar to medieval churches (transepts, flying buttresses, stained glass, etc.), and most of the cathedrals built during the Dark Ages and the early days of the Empire are seven sided in recognition of the seven disciples of the Prophet and of the seven great virtues. (There were actually eight disciples, although Orthodox doctrine tends to ignore the Ur-Obun disciple. Some cathedrals, especially those catering to Ur-Obun worshippers, are eight sided.) All cathedrals have an ornate lantern — called an "Orb" — behind and above their altars to represent the Celestial Sun. This lantern is always lit. It must never go out. The best cathedrals use everlights (Second Republic fusion lights which require little maintenance), but most cathedrals use electric or oil lamps. If the light were to ever go out, cleansing and purification ceremonies must be performed.

An ominous phenomenon has occurred in a few cathedrals: the lights of the Orbs have dimmed for no apparent reason. These cathedrals have become potent symbols of the fading suns themselves, places of pilgrimage to those faithful who pray to be forgiven before the dimming of the Holy Flame.

Cathedrals also have banks of candles along the walls, to represent the suns of the Known Worlds (forty of them now, but a new candle is added with news of each rediscovered planet). Those candles representing Church worlds are the largest with the most ornate holders; Holy Terra is represented by the best candle of all.

Agora

The agora is the planet's main marketplace, and the gamemaster should decide which guild(s) run it. Competition for controlling interest in the agora is every bit as fierce

as that for the cathedral, but usually more orderly. The major guilds are interdependent and usually handle their differences in a "peaceful manner." They usually realize that a wide range of guilds need to work together to create a viable economy for their products. Few guilds seek to prevent others from setting up shop in the agora, though all seek the top position.

The guild, or individuals, who control the agora have all sorts of trade advantages and may control many of the trade rules by which it operates, in addition to tax levies above and beyond those taxes or tithes imposed by a ruling house or Church sect. The agora's size and ownership tends to affect the general level of technology on the planet (see below); planets with an Engineer-run agora generally have the highest technology levels. The Charioteers run the agora on almost half of the worlds in the Empire, with the Scravers a close second, but they are continuously tested for signs of incompetence by the Reeves.

While there are, of course, many marketplaces on a planet, there is only one main agora. The agora is usually in the capitol city, near the spaceport. An agora's name is usually descriptive of the main product sold there, and may reflect the nature of the guild who runs it. The "Block" on Bannockburn, the Muster homeworld, for example, sells human services, including slaves. The "Arcanum" on Icon (run by a Charioteer/Engineer consortium) deals in rare and exotic artifacts. Most agoras are simply called "the Agora."

Garrison

The gamemaster should rate the planet's standing military on a scale of 1 to 10. Noble homeworlds and other important planets tend to have the highest ratings, while minor baronies have the lowest. The garrison's rating should reflect its overall strength and take into account a number of factors such as size, preparedness, morale and technological sophistication. While the garrison is officially there to guard against outside threats, it all too commonly becomes a tool of oppression. Planetary armies often become

the private police of the corrupt nobles, merchant princes and ambitious clergy who run the planet.

A suggested scale to determine a garrison's strength is given below. The naval fleets and ships listed refer to starships, not aquatic ships.

Capital

As with planet names, capitals may range widely in nature and origin. Capital names are more independent of the whims of the stellar cartographers on Byzantium Secundus and often have a wholly local flavor. Some even retain their original alien or Second Republic names.

The capital is the area where the characters are likely to spend the most time when they are planetside. The gamemaster should be as detailed as possible when designing one, asking many questions: Is the capital a destitute border city, or a thriving center of culture and wealth? Is it a new city constructed by Imperial settlers, or built over older Second Republic (or even alien) remains?

The Second Republic technicians built things to last, and there are many still functional Second Republic buildings and infrastructures evident throughout the Empire. During the Empire's current expansion, many such sites are being modified or built over, however.

The gamemaster should also consider the overall mood of the city. A capital city may be light and airy or dark and oppressive. Most architecture in the Empire is large and looming, and the fading suns make most planets darker (and cooler) in nature.

The capital is usually the largest and most modern city on the planet. Capitals may vary in population from anywhere between a few tens of thousands to those dwarfing the size of the largest twentieth century metropoli. Most, however, have a population of about one to three million. Life in the Empire is increasingly agrarian and large cities are becoming less common.

Planetary capitals are the center of the planet's cultural and mercantile institutions and are rife with intrigue. They are usually home to the planet's spaceport, cathedral and main agora, as well as the Empire's governing institutions. The emperor, Church and guilds maintain an embassy in every planetary capital. Despite, or perhaps because of this fact, citizens on the rest of the planet often view the capital with suspicion..

Jumps

The number of jumps the planet is away from the Imperial homeworld, Byzantium Secundus. The number of known planets has shrunk precipitously since the days of the Second Republic. Few planets in Human Space are farther than six jumps from each other. Records indicate that during the height of the Second Republic it took as many as 20 jumps to reach the most distant planets. The Vau's known uni-

verse is said to be even greater.

The number of jumps between two planets does not necessarily connote how close they are to each other in physical distance. The planet Pentateuch, for example, is only one jump from Byzantium Secundus, but it is thousands of light years from Byzantium II in real space. Conversely, the planet Delphi is two jumps away from Byzantium Secundus, yet it is half as far away in galactic distance from Byzantium II as is Pentateuch.

Most consider Byzantium Secundus to be the secular sun of the Empire, and most astro-navigational terminology reflects this ideal (although some clergy draw their starcharts in relationship to Holy Terra, rather than Byzantium Secundus). As a ship jumps away from Byzantium Secundus, it is said to jump "nightside." Jumps that bring the ship closer to Imperial center are "dayside" jumps. A jump that brings the ship neither closer nor farther from Byzantium Secundus is called a "parallel" jump.

Imperial power usually fades with each consecutive jump nightside, just as the influence of earthly empires fades on the fringes of their territory. This does not mean that nightside planets are necessarily more lawless (though this is often the case), but that law and custom are more influenced by local power centers. Such local power centers rarely affect planets more than one jump away from themselves, however. Known planets beyond the borders of the Empire are known as the "tenebrous worlds." Most people consider these worlds barbaric, regardless of their level of cultural or technological sophistication.

Adjacent Worlds

The term "adjacent worlds" applies to worlds directly connected to the planet by one jump. The gamemaster should refer to the Known Worlds star chart to determine the planet's surrounding worlds, and record the planet's status as dayside, nightside or parallel to Byzantium Secundus. Thus, an adjacent world that is a jump farther away from Byzantium Secundus is on the nightside of that planet. Serfs are especially suspicious of anyone from a world more nightside than their own.

Adjacent worlds may or may not have a fair amount of influence over each other. Two adjacent worlds may be friendly, neutral or openly at war with each other. The gamemaster should consider how each planet interacts with its neighbors. Local spheres of influence may coalesce around several worlds in a jumpgate community. These neighborhoods may share a number of common cultural elements (dialect, dress, custom) born of centuries of interaction. They may also have mutual defense pacts. Unfortunately, however, most worlds have closed themselves off from each other since the Fall. Residents of these worlds view other worlds suspiciously, like isolated medieval towns.

Extensive knowledge of any world more than one jump away is usually hard to obtain. Planets which are three or more jumps away are truly exotic. Even adjacent worlds may know little about each other. The concept of space travel is no longer new. It no longer fires the public imagination as it once did, even during the latter days of the Second Republic. Most people do not even care about what is happening on other planets. Indeed, peasants in some isolated communities do not even believe that other planets exist. Others believe the most fanciful of stories about other worlds. For example, serfs may believe the gossip that all people from Manitou have three eyes, or that everyone from Byzantium Secundus is over three meters tall. Many peasants never even see an off-worlder during their entire lives.

Solar System

The gamemaster should determine how many other planets there are in the solar system and their order from the sun. Each planet's distance from the sun in astronomical units (see *Starships*, in Chapter Seven: Technology) should also be determined. This gives pilots a way to figure the travel times between a system's worlds and its jumpgate. In addition, any important moons should be put in parenthesis following their hosts (not all satellites need be listed).

Most habitable planets are within one to three AUs from the sun, although Second Republic terraforming and pressure-dome tech often allowed colonies on outer worlds. Most of these are no longer functional, however, but they may still be available for exploration.

For an example, here is Holy Terra's solar system: Mercury 1 (0.387 AU), Venus 2 (0.723 AU), Earth (1 AU; the Moon), Mars (1.524 AU; Phobos, Deimos), Ceres asteroids (2.76 – 2.80 AU), Jupiter (5.203 AU; Io, Europa, Ganymede, Callisto), Saturn (9.539 AU; Titan, rings), Uranus (19.182 AU; Titania, Miranda), Neptune (30.058 AU; Triton, Nereid), Pluto (39.44 AU; Charon)

A planet's solar neighbors are, in many ways, more real to it than worlds on the other side of a jumpgate. The Anunnaki usually constructed their jumpgates beyond the most distant planet possible from any inhabitable planets. Alien ruins from other spacefaring races await on uninhabited planets in some solar systems, and rumors of still functioning space colonies abound. Modern organizations also build and maintain off-world bases for a number of reasons, such as commerce, research or defense. These are rare, however, for they are costly to maintain.

The gamemaster should also decide if the solar system or any of the planets are odd or significant in any way. Examples of such oddities may include a binary star system (such as that in the Gwynneth system), wobbling planetary orbits or asteroid belts. The gamemaster may also wish to note if Void Krakens are rumored to exist within the solar

system. The main planet may also have one or more orbiting space stations. These often house the planet's naval garrison and other planetary power groups. These stations range greatly in size and nature. Some are stripped down, utilitarian military or research facilities, while others are well appointed, even opulent, vacation or business spots. As is the case with interplanetary bases, these are expensive and not all planets have them.

Tech

A planet's tech level refers to the most advanced technology with which the planet's artisans can interface (see the Tech Level Chart in Chapter Seven: Technology). Only a planet's upper echelons have access to this level of technology, however. The vast majority of the Empire's population live in a Victorian-era level of technology (level 3), although a sizable minority of serfs live in medieval conditions (level 2) or even below. Some human settlements are reverting to near barbarism. This is especially common on the poorest, or "pariah," planets. The highest tech level generally available to most citizens is 4, while powerful local groups may have access to 5 or, in rare cases, 6. Empire planets with a rating of 6 are exceedingly rare, though a few may even approach 7 in some areas of technology. (There may be even higher technology in hidden research complexes.) Most planets in the Empire have a top rating of 5.

A planet's tech level is a major factor in all facets of life on the planet. It decides what sort of medical care is available on the planet. Do the citizens drive a car to work, or ride a cart? (Most people ride carts.) Technology also affects people's entertainment, methods of communication and almost every other aspect of their lives. Just because a planet has a high level of technology does not mean that technology is common throughout the planet, however. As a rule, most people live one or two levels below the optimum. This is for a number of reasons. The economy is generally stagnant and the mass production quantities are not nearly sufficient to reach the vast majority of people. Furthermore, powerful interest groups such as the nobles, the Church and the guilds monopolize the best technology for themselves, although certain egalitarian or enterprising traders wish to make technology more freely available to the populace at large. They are especially common among the Charioteers, although they have sympathizers in almost every League organization. The other powers watch these groups carefully. Most people see technology as "sinful," although those in power are accorded special exceptions to this rule.

Human Population

The number of humans living on the world. On most Imperial worlds, humans constitute the vast majority of the population. Most planets have a human population of no more than one billion. Most planets average from 400 to 800 million people, while some have as few as a hundred thousand. Mining colonies have a few thousand, and some known planets (Vau worlds) have a human population of one. No one is sure of the real human population numbers on Stigmata anymore. Imperial giants such as Leagueheim and Holy Terra boast populations of as high as four billion. Byzantium Secundus tops the chart with six billion people to oil its bureaucratic machinery. These three giants are followed by Delphi, Severus and Criticorum at over two billion each. Kish, Aragon and Istakhr round out the top ten list of planets. The current population trend on most planets is downward.

Although many aliens may think otherwise, humans vary greatly from planet to planet. Almost three thousand years of space travel, genetic manipulation and inbreeding has created a vast panoply of human genotypes. Cultural differences vary even more widely, not only from world to world, but from hamlet to hamlet. At the same time many smaller population groups have become increasingly isolated by the receding tide of the Second Republic. As population groups diminish, inbreeding occurs. Genetic "misfits" such as hunchbacks, dwarves and "village idiots" are becoming far more common. Such inbreeding is not just relegated to the lower social strata, however. Many serfs believe that they can detect a Decados or Hawkwood "look."

Alien Population

Humans are top dog on most planets and they don't let the alien population forget it. Aliens are tightly monitored and controlled. To be an alien in the Empire is to be a second-class citizen, and brutality is far more common than most would care to admit. Except for a few rare planets, aliens are also in the minority. The Empire is dominant throughout all of Human Space, and is not afraid of pushing its weight around. Still, it rarely attacks planets outright before checking for Vau involvement (the lessons of first contact die hard.) If Vau are nowhere evident, however, the Empire is fairly blasé about claiming new worlds. This does not mean that it is careless, however. Some alien worlds are a can of worms the Empire wishes that it never opened. Chernobog is a prime example here. Nevertheless, Alexius has managed to instill a new sense of manifest destiny among his subjects. The Empire is currently in an expansionist phase.

The average alien to human ratio on most worlds is 1 to 500, or .2%. Worlds with a significant number of aliens keep most of them on reservations— out of sight, out of mind. Aliens on Empire-controlled planets never reach more than fifteen percent of the population, except on a few alien homeworlds. On some more progressive worlds (Byzantium Secundus, Leagueheim and others) aliens may have a fair amount of freedom and autonomy. A few aliens may even gain a degree of fortune and personal power. Some use this

influence to better the lot of their fellow aliens, while others hoard and misuse it.

Many humans in the Empire are oppressed and desperate. The plight of most aliens is far worse. Sometimes desperate groups of humans and aliens band together for mutual survival, and strong friendships have grown from these alliances. All too often, however, desperate humans kick the aliens down even further to make themselves feel better about their own lot. Human institutions do not slaughter aliens very often anymore, as they did during the Diaspora. Indeed, there are laws to protect aliens, although they are rarely enforced. A few reformers in groups such as Sanctuary Aeon, the Charioteers and, most importantly, House Hawkwood, support these laws. Most serfs view aliens with a great deal of superstition; some clever aliens use this fact to great advantage.

Resources

Resources are the notable and valuable natural attributes of the planet. These may include anything from common items such as minerals to rare alien and Second Republic artifacts. Food is an increasingly rare commodity because of the Fading Suns effect and the declining level of technology. Crops fail frequently on most planets and famine is not uncommon. Some planets are far more productive than others, and occasionally these planets throw open their granaries to help their less fortunate neighbors, but the vast majority hoard what little food they have left. The Church receives a crop tithe of five to ten percent on many worlds, thus insuring against famine. Unfortunately, much of the food disappears before it can help famine victims, as it usually ends up on the black market to feed the appetites of the well-heeled from all backgrounds. There is a thriving black market on almost all worlds.

Some items, such as Philosophers Stones and strategic materials, are available on only a few worlds — or on a single planet. A planet with a lock on a very rare, sought-after item or material guards its treasures jealously. The planets Manitou, Leminkainen and Absolution are the only known natural sources of "Pygmallium" (Shaprut depleted its once-rich mines long ago). This natural element is the only material known that can create the delicate cephalic matrix of artificial intelligence robots (see Golems, in Chapter Eight: Gamemastering). Pygmallium is so uncommon that only a few tons of the material have been mined over the last thousand years. "Rare as Pygmallium" is a common phrase among the Engineers. There are strategic caches of the material on the three largest worlds, and sale of it is restricted. Other items such as alien or Second Republic artifacts are even more valuable.

Exports

Many of the backworlds of the Empire run on the barter system. There is an official currency (the "firebird") and several house or local currencies, but many on-planet transactions are still carried out through barter. Planet-to-planet transactions require currency or credit. Exporting materials between worlds is very expensive due to taxes and shipping expenses (guilds must have their take). Unfortunately, almost anything shipped between worlds is also worth stealing. Pirate ships are relatively common. Few planets export food, simply because it is too expensive for little return. Most exports are in the form of quality manufactured goods. Rich off-worlders spend small fortunes to collect the goods of every planet. Because of this fact, artists may flourish on even the most destitute worlds, if they find the right patrons. The Ur-Obun are a prime example of this sort of success story.

Unfortunately, some unscrupulous traders are not above preying upon desperation. Some famine-stricken worlds are so desperate that they trade extremely valuable resources for just a paltry sum of food. These worlds may attempt to find better buyers, but are often lashed back into line by the Scravers.

The guilds conduct the vast majority of trade between worlds, but all major power groups maintain their own merchant fleets. There is also a thriving black market providing not only trade in illicit goods, but also in legitimate wares. Many merchants become freebooters to escape the onerous taxes levied by the state. The Empire is on the lookout for smuggling, however, and guards the jumpgates to prevent it. This sentry duty is very expensive, however, and not consistent. Most jumpgates are not directly guarded, though some have remote satellites that track the comings and goings of ships through the gate. Well-armed cruisers guard the gates near the most important worlds on a full time basis, making smuggling a risky business. Getting an illegal item through several jumps is difficult, though smugglers may improve their odds through bribery. Many worlds are less strict than others about enforcing Imperial law.

Landscape

A planet's physical characteristics. Although most Empire worlds were terraformed during the Second Republic to resemble Urth, this resemblance is often superficial at best. Alien flora and fauna, long ago considered extinct, are reasserting themselves on many worlds. Additionally, the descendants of Second Republic genetic creations populate many of these worlds: Dinosaurs (or their alien equivalents) were cloned for entertainment purposes on some worlds during the Second Republic. These ancient monstrosities survived their creators' fall and now prey on their makers' grandchildren in the wilds of some planets. This strange mix of alien, Terran and genetically mixed creatures combines to form bizarre and complex ecosystems.

Most species of flora and fauna were catalogued during

the Second Republic, but many of these records have since disappeared. Strange creatures are often mistaken for aliens or demons by most of the population. The line between odd — but natural — creatures and the supernatural is greatly blurred in the minds of most. There are too few scientists conducting the pure research necessary to enlighten people as to which is which. Along with the many bizarre strains of flora and fauna rampant on many worlds, there are also many new strains of viruses which are immune to even the best medicines. Pestilence, as well as famine, has reared its ugly head throughout much of the Empire.

There are also environmental factors on most planets over which the terraformers had little or no control: major topographical features, binary suns or strange atmospheric idiosyncrasies. These challenges often defied even the superscience of Second Republic terraforming architects.

Habitable worlds that are mostly desert, glacier or tropical jungle exist, but such worlds are the exception, not the rule. Most worlds have environmental regions and ecosystems every bit as diverse as those on Urth. The gamemaster should create as much detail as possible when designing a world's environment. Such factors as precipitation, climate and geological factors may combine to create breathtaking vistas and eerie, alien landscapes. Is the world mostly ocean, or is water scarce? Is the planet a new one, or a very old one orbiting a dying red sun? Although there is a habitable planet in every known solar system with a jumpgate, some of them are just barely so (some are not habitable by humans, but may host alien life.) A planet's biosphere strongly affects the culture that lives there. The gamemaster should consider how a nomadic desert culture may differ from a farming culture in a more temperate zone.

Most habitable planets have a gravity close to that of Urth. One of the first tasks of the terraformers was to equalize gravity throughout the Second Republic. But some planets proved trickier than others when it came to installing and running gravity engines, and maintaining terraformed gravity is not an easy task in the current Dark Age. Thus, certain planets in the Known Worlds have gravities varying from anywhere between one-third to four times normal Urth gravity. Low gravity worlds have thinner atmospheres, while on high gravity planets, humans must live in specially pressurized complexes. The vast majority of populated Imperial worlds are still 80% to 120% Urth gravity.

Perhaps the greatest environmental factor on planets throughout the Empire is the Fading Suns phenomenon. Suns that have shined steadily for billions of years are abruptly (at least in galactic terms) dying. This phenomenon greatly affects the planets that circle them. Natural systems forged over eons are rapidly unraveling as planetary biospheres contend with unprecedented changes to their development. Temperatures are plummeting on most worlds. Although the

temperature drop was barely noticeable at first, it has accelerated greatly in recent generations. Climatic patterns are disrupted on many worlds as hitherto unknown weather patterns emerge. Planetary atmospheres are stormier than ever before, and the mean temperature on most worlds has dropped by five to ten degrees over the last three centuries. Many worlds have witnessed new periods of glaciation since the fading suns phenomenon was first observed during the Second Republic. Strangely, a few worlds have grown blisteringly hot as their suns become prematurely hotter. On some planets lush forests have degenerated into wastelands in a single generation. The fading phenomenon varies greatly in effect on many worlds. On some planets it has wrought untold devastation, while other planets are only beginning to feel its effects.

Humanity is more at nature's mercy than at any time since the First Republic. Due to humanity's diminishing technology and increasingly agrarian lifestyle, the caprices of nature affect everyone. The up side of this coin is that environmental degradation is less of a problem on many worlds than in the past. Many consider this cold comfort. During the Second Republic humanity gained great control over the natural environment. Humanity's undisputed mastery over terraforming extended to control over weather systems and even such natural phenomena as volcanism and earthquakes. The Second Republic terraforming machines still churn on most worlds, but they are showing signs of strain. The planet Pandemonium (see Appendix) is an example of what can happen when the machines finally seize up. Most citizens of the Empire believe that it was humanity's hubris in such matters that lead to the Fall in the first place. Since the Fall, nature has again become a frightening, almost malevolent force to many. Even the very ground now seems reluctant to nourish humanity on many worlds as crop failures become more common.

History

Human history on an Imperial world may stretch back millennia, centuries or mere months in the case of newly-discovered planets. Human history on most worlds stretches no further back than the Diaspora. In general, the Empire consists of the earliest human settled planets, especially those immediately surrounding Holy Terra. Human civilization spread out from Urth, following the path of the jumpgates. Thus, the planets nearest to Holy Terra are generally older in terms of human history than those farther away. This is not always the case, however, since jumpgates to some planets were overlooked during earlier waves of expansion. Human history on a planet may stretch back to the First or Second Republics, or it may be more recent. Not every world has an alien history, but those that do may stretch back thousands of years or more.

The gamemaster should also consider the planet's Anunnaki origins. All known worlds have jumpgates, and thus have some footing in the most ancient past. Few other scraps of Anunnaki history exist, however, and those that do are considered top secret by the Empire's security apparatus. Historians who dig too deeply into such matters may well disappear.

Since the Fall, much of humanity's history has been shrouded by the mists of time. The Church is, by tradition and law, the primary repository of much of the past's knowledge. Most history is replete with a highly theological spin. Few secular scholars have the access to the knowledge necessary to refute Church doctrine on most points. The study of history outside the Church is considered a frivolous, if not dangerous, pursuit on most worlds. Some nobles with "too much time on their hands" may study history, but usually within the context of Church doctrine. They, of course, have their own strict interpretation of their house's history. Many nobles can recite their lineage back to the Diaspora age or earlier. The guilds also usually follow Church teachings on history, though many secretly depart with Church dogma on the true nature of the Second Republic. Humanity has lost much of its history because of earlier civilizations' overdependence on computers as an archival medium. The Church, at least, has learned from these past mistakes and keeps hard copies of all of its historical records. The art of computer-designed, illuminated manuscripts is currently enjoying a great renaissance. Copies of these documents are displayed in cathedral reliquaries throughout the Empire.

Naturally the planet with the oldest human history is Holy Terra. Every serf knows that it is the cradle of human civilization, in accordance with Church teachings. Almost everyone within the Empire believes certain "irrefutable truths" of human history. Urth history stretches back to humanity's earliest origins, though any knowledge prior to the First Republic is highly conjectural.

Some alien cultures have histories that stretch back just as far, if not further. Ancient alien ruins are common on a few worlds. Most human historians consider alien history irrelevant in the great scheme of things. Nevertheless, the Empire frowns upon research into these areas. Alien history is taboo and historians (both human and alien) must gain special dispensation from either the local Church or nobility to pursue such studies. The Ur-Obun have the most open and accessible of alien histories, and share much of it with those few humans interested in learning. Humans know virtually nothing of Vau or Symbiot history.

The vast majority of people are only dimly aware of humanity's great past. Few have any detailed knowledge stretching back more than a few generations on their own planet. Public schooling varies greatly from planet to planet, and rarely deals with off-world matters in anything but the

most basic manner. Most citizens believe that the only history of import relates to matters on Byzantium Secundus, Holy Terra and their own planet. The history of neighboring planets (those one jump away) may, or may not, be studied, but usually becomes distorted by local political concerns.

The Church teaches that all human members of the Empire are brothers and sisters in the eyes of the Pancreator, but this rarely prevents local prejudices from gaining dominance. The vagaries of inter-planetary history are far too arcane for all but the most adept scholars. The gamemaster should make only certain basic tenets of local and Imperial history available to the characters unless they have the appropriate Lore skill to know more. In some cases, such lore may directly contravene Church doctrine. Certain areas of inquiry are heretical and, thus, strictly forbidden. The Church generally considers the Second Republic to be a time of great decadence and wickedness, a latter day Sodom and Gomorra. Conversely, the Church usually lauds Diaspora history and before as belonging to a mythic "Golden Age."

Present Conflicts

If most in the Empire are ignorant of history, they are all too aware of the current conflicts that wrack their own world. Many of these conflicts, unfortunately, arise from just this lack of historical perspective. Local despots bend both ancient history and current events to their own political agendas. Conflicts on a planet may spring from any number of sources. The Church, nobility and guilds are all involved in internal and external conflicts for control of local power and resources. House may battle house or Church sect may battle trade guild for dominance. Usually this conflict is peaceful, but no less intense.

Conflict may also spring from local power struggles. Just because the Empire consists of many planets does not mean that each planet is unified along political and social lines. Occasionally wars flare between differing countries, continents or social groups on the same planet. These battles may be for ideological purposes, for control of rapidly dwindling resources or because of stupid prejudices. Many planets are little more unified than twentieth century Urth was.

Other conflicts may come from the outside. Barbarians and pirates may plague the planet. Alien forces, such as the Symbiots, may beleaguer the planet from within, or local aliens on reservations may conduct open or covert attacks on the local human population (or vice-versa). Barbarians harry many border worlds, while some daring corsairs may even stage raids near such central worlds as Byzantium Secundus. There are also occasional wars between neighboring planets. Wars may take place between inhabited planets in the same solar system or between those separated by jumpgates. The cost of such conflicts is prohibitive, however, and the Empire quashes such interplanetary conflicts if they get out of hand. The Pax Byzantium has generally kept the peace between neighboring planets since the beginning of Alexius' reign.

Some planets are so beset from without that they are, for all practical purposes, quarantined by the Empire at large. Bulwark planets such as Stigmata (the center of the Symbiot front), Apshai and Vril-Ya (both Vau worlds) are forbidden to most in the Empire without the appropriate security clearance. Local jurisdictions may declare martial law for any number of reasons, and natives from these planets are rarely allowed to leave. Both the Empire at large and local interests have an interest in controlling access through the jumpgates. In theory, legal access from world to world is tightly controlled and entails a good deal of red tape. This is especially true for those in the lower strata of society. Many serfs are not only legally restricted to their own planet, but many may not even leave their own province or village. The authorities rarely enforce this restriction, however, since few people have either the resources, or inclination to travel. (The authorities do enforce borders if there is a "security issue" at stake.) There is a great deal of fear in the Empire. Most conflicts raise the tenor of this fear so that few people wish to leave the safety of their communities.

Secrets

Every planet, whether in Human Space or without, has secrets known to only a few. Players may purchase secret knowledge about a certain planet (or group of planets) through Benefice points at the beginning of the game. These secrets may be of any kind. Church secrets may involve anything from internecine bickering between sects, to the location of a sacred relic. Guild and noble secrets may include the secret machinations of the Decados duke, or inside information on the price of millirice and secret technologies. Planetary secrets are those concerning the planet itself. These secrets may have to do with its strange flora and fauna, non-aligned humans (such as covens) and the planet's Anunnaki origins. Alien secrets involve almost everything else. The gamemaster should be specific in naming her category: secrets about the local nobility may be labeled Decados, Hazat or Imperial secrets. Any of the above categories may have one, or many, secrets.

The Benefice cost for a given secret depends on its magnitude and usefulness. A potentially powerful secret about the existence of a potent Philosophers Stone becomes somewhat academic if there is no clue whatsoever to its whereabouts. Such a secret may only cost one Benefice point, while a reference to the same relic paired with a cryptic, but still usable map may cost two or three points. The exact location of a hitherto undiscovered jumpgate would cost 5 Benefice points, but rest assured that someone else knows about it also. The gamemaster is the final authority on how much secrets cost.

Appendix: Pandemonium

This chapter presents a detailed look at one of the planets of the Known Worlds — Pandemonium, once a backwater world but now a nexus for important secrets affecting noble houses, Church sects and League guilds. This chapter is intended for gamemasters only and should not be read by players — they will only spoil their fun by knowing some of the secrets revealed herein.

History

Grange was once the breadbasket of the Second Republic. The planet was modified by a terraforming genius named Gilgar to yield fertile crops year round. Cargo ships constantly plied the jumproads to and from Grange to bring its bounty to all the worlds of the Republic.

It took more than 25 years for Gilgar to transform the original environment of Grange from a perpetual sandstorm into a planet with rich soil and plentiful water. The task was not easy, but Gilgar was a driven man. Why he chose to transform a desert into a garden paradise is unknown, although vanity surely had a lot to do with it. Gilgar was the only apprentice to Doramos, the legendary architect of Pentateuch. Grange was to be his masterpiece. Like many works of art, it had to be lost for many years before it could be appreciated.

During the riots of the Fall, disgruntled terrorists managed a never-before conceived feat: they damaged the main jumpgate leading to Grange. Shipments had to reroute through lesser gates, but in the confusion of the succession, many of these gates were lost. Fanatics destroyed computers and jumpkeys, and some planets deliberately shut themselves off from the madness going on around them. When

Pandemonium Traits

Ruler: House Decados (Count Enis Sharn)
Cathedral: Orthodox
Agora: The Bazaar (Scravers)
Garrison: 4
Capitol: The Hub
Jumps: 4
Adjacent worlds: Rampart and Apshai (Dayside), Iver (Nightside)
Solar System: Barloom 1 (.465 AU), Sheen 2 (.801 AU), Luck 3 (1.7 AU), Pandemonium 4 (2.78 AU; Flaxom, Floxom, Everlight), Farcry 5 (44.23 AU), Shiver 6 (67.777 AU), Jumpgate (77.3 AU), 2nd Jumpgate (123.5 AU)

Of the three small moons around Pandemonium, Flaxom and Floxom have irregular orbits and Everlight has a stable orbit. But Everlight's stable orbit has begun to slowly deteriorate due to malfunctioning of the terraforming engines.

Tech: 5
Human population: 500,000 (estimated)
Alien population: 100+
Resources: Ores, Ur artifacts
Exports: Refined ore, Ur artifacts, slaves
Landscape: Post-terraforming cataclysms shake the planet, causing a riotous profusion of many biomes. Vast plains of farmland still exist, but they are mostly deserted. While badlands nomads still roam the cataclysmic terrain, most of the populace huddles around or within the walls of the Hub.

the dust cleared and the blood spilt by revolution had dried, whole worlds were gone, unreachable through the vastness of space, their jump coordinates lost in the great data purges. Grange was one such world.

One hundred years ago, Grange was rediscovered. Complicated diplomatic dealings with the Vau on Apshai involved an exchange of gifts. The Vau gave Count Vano Juandaastas a jumpkey that would open the jumpgate from Apshai to the lost world of Grange. The Vau seemed to have no interest in the world, though they had known for centuries how to reach it. The count immediately went to investigate this grand find.

He discovered a peaceful and stable world. The farmers of Grange continued on after the Fall in a virtual paradise. Famine was a myth, and the predatory beasts of the field had been penned in the mountainous southern hemisphere long ago. Occasionally, population explosions would lead to conflict and wars, but these would eventually die out when the population was once again steady. Slowly, however, technology regressed. The planet had few technicians to begin with, and those it did have were practical rather than theoretical. But high tech was not missed. The people retained a practical knowledge of everything they needed, including medicine and crop planting methods.

Count Vano Juandaastas was overjoyed. He believed he had found a world that would allow his family to once again rise to prominence. But among the Grange populace was a small but respected family proud of its Second Republic heritage and its family name: al-Malik.

Over the next decades, Grange was torn by conflict as Juandaastas fought with al-Malik over rulership of Grange. By the year 4951, the al-Malik won and forced all Juandaastas off the planet. Baron Afil al-Malik rushed to Grange with a boon from the family head to rule the planet. He had an ulterior motive in mind. A psychic he encountered in a brothel on Istakhr swore to him that there was something important on Grange, but could not say what. Afil meant to find that something. He spent a substantial amount of his money searching for hidden treasures on every continent of Grange and on the surrounding worlds. Years went by, and finally he had to admit that he'd been had. Nearly destitute and embarrassed in the eyes of his family, Afil turned to an old friend and business associate for help.

Count Enis Sharn of House Decados was willing to aid his old friend, even though both families where embroiled in the Emperor Wars' bitter give and take of land and power. Secret negotiations with Duke Hakim al-Malik put the world in Decados hands without any bloodshed. Although the amount Sharn paid for the rights to the world and the system was not quite as much as Afil might have wished, the transaction did manage to save him from financial ruin.

Historians and pundits to this day wonder what was exchanged in secret, what powerful favor or relic could possibly be worth ownership of an entire world. Certainly, Pandemonium would have been very hard to maintain for the al-Malik, for it lies three jumps from their closest world. But why sell to the Decados? Why not award the planet to the Emperor, who the duke was even then allying with? Some who claim to know state that the exchange was a preventative measure: Pandemonium was given in return for the Decados giving up all claim to the legendary lost world of Yathrib, which, once found, would mean immeasurable wealth to the al-Malik for its pilgrimage value alone — Yathrib is the world where the Prophet received his vision of the Holy Flame.

Regardless the reason for the planet's new ownership, in 4981 Count Sharn set about trying to glean any possible truth about the wealth hidden on the planet. But the League beat him to it. Entirely by accident, a second jumpgate was discovered beyond the fringe of the solar system by the Charioteers. Never before had two jumpgates been discovered in the same system. However, the new jumpgate was not operational, and in fact seemed incomplete, as if work on it had been abandoned before it was finished. The League had hit the jackpot — this incomplete gate could tell them more about the workings of existing jumpgates than any before. The problem, of course, came down to ownership. The Decados claim it, because it is near Grange, but the League say it is theirs because it sits outside the system and is thus covered under the ancient laws of salvage discovery (laws lobbied long and hard for by Scravers). Both parties have taken their claim to the Emperor and await his decision. As of 4999, Alexius has still avoided ruling on the issue.

But just as this wondrous Ur-artifact was discovered, disaster struck on Grange. The great terraforming engines that maintained the nearly-perfect atmosphere began to malfunction. On the other side of the planet — far away from the safe haven of the Hub, the capitol city and by far the most technologically advanced location on the planet — the first signs of the cataclysms appeared.

Three small outposts, with populations of only a few hundred each, were destroyed as the ground heaved beneath them. The people in the area were never found, but the remains of the various outposts can still be seen, poking out from a vast sandy plain, or resting atop a newly formed mountain. Before long, another of the great engines stopped functioning, and hundreds of people were forced to leave the settlements their ancestors had built as violent storms and savage earthquakes brought their communities to ruin.

Count Enis Sharn immediately sent for qualified technicians to ensure that the engines beneath the Hub continued to function properly, and sent messengers to all of the outposts he could locate, warning that only the capitol was safe from the massive devastation. In less than a year's time, the Hub was overflowing with immigrants from all points

on the globe, and the ravaging storms had claimed most of the world. Despite Sharn's warnings, many stayed in their settlements. They have not been heard from since.

True to the Count's warnings, only the Hub remained stable. If not for the ruler of the planet, many of the citizens would surely have perished. Many feared that even the capitol would fall, but the Supreme Order of Engineers have managed to keep the area stable, and the dread felt by most of the refugees has calmed. News of the planet's troubles spread far and wide, and universally, Grange earned a new name: Pandemonium.

Since then, new jumpgate coordinates have been gleaned from the dysfunctional gate, allowing a jumproad to be opened from the working jumpgate to the long lost world of Iver. This world is unequivocally claimed by the Decados, since it can only be opened through their jumpgate. However, the bounty of this new world is the source of dangerous conflicts — the rulers of Iver are descendants of House Chauki, once overthrown and eliminated by the Hazat. Their very existence threatens the Hazat's legitimate ownership of Chauki lands, should they try to make a claim upon them. Hazat now crawl the spaceways and streets of Pandemonium, seeking to prevent any Chauki from leaving Iver for the Known Worlds.

Pandemonium has an embarrassment of new discoveries and conflicts, leading many to coin the adage: "Beware a Vau bearing gifts."

Present Conflicts

The recent discovery of Iver has caused a substantial increase in the population of the already overcrowded planet. Other noble houses have made their presence known on Pandemonium, and the Church has nearly tripled its representatives here. The Charioteers are staying busy, as fortune seekers and others pay for passage to Pandemonium in search of wealth, power or simple confirmation of their faith. The rumors of lost Ur artifacts have only increased the influx of newcomers. It is not at all uncommon for a group of treasure hunters to come from a dozen different planets, each seeking to make a fortune.

With so many new people mixing into the chaos of so many relocated natives, the Hub has become an almost lawless arena. Rules and regulations once held immutable are now ignored with no fear of retaliation. The town guards are as corrupt as anyone else on Pandemonium. Although a few will still take the time to arrest anyone they actually see committing a crime (especially if that crime is in the northwestern wealthy district), most will look the other way in exchange for financial compensation. There is little the Decados can do about the matter. Despite their willingness to stay and fight for a profitable resolution of the jumpgate

argument, their finances are not infinite. Most of the assets available to Count Enis Sharn are tied up in a dozen expensive programs, and what little remains in addition is used to make sure that Manse Sharn remains inviolate.

The new money flowing into Pandemonium's economy has not helped matters. In an area where money can purchase almost anything, including temporary loyalty, whoever spends the most, rules. Despite the legal claims of the Decados, several other houses are in the process of moving into the area, seeking news of Iver or the mysterious second jumpgate, plundering the planet's natural resources or establishing connections to use later, when the matter of who owns the second jumpgate is resolved.

There are also numerous small-time operators in the Hub. These individuals and organizations are unscrupulous and hungry. Several roving groups make their living by assaulting those foolish enough to walk alone. Once they have taken everything of value from their victim, they turn him over to the Chainers in exchange for a few firebirds. Gambling outfits and prostitution rings are abundant, as are those dealing in stolen weapons and contraband of every imaginable sort. A dozen fences work the Bazaar, dealing in both properties and secrets. While it is often hard to know whose information is accurate, these rumor brokers tend to be fairly honest: Those who cheat their customers usually do not live long. Possibly the heaviest trade in the Bazaar comes in the form of mercenary work for hire. In the teeming chaos of the Hub, a person who knows how to kill is a valuable commodity.

The Hub

The Hub once housed some 100,000 people. These days, virtually the entire remaining population of Pandemonium calls the capitol home. While others are rumored to still survive in the Badlands, no one has heard from them. Half a million people have been forced to move from everything they once called their own. The people have to take meager comfort in the only remaining city the planet can provide. Many claim that House Decados is responsible for the cataclysms, that the constant scouring for hidden treasures caused the destruction of the great engines buried far beneath the ground — or that they attempted to activate the second jumpgate, causing a magnetic disturbance that effects celestial phenomena the system over. The count does not acknowledge this rumor. Instead, the ruler of Pandemonium does his best to accommodate a population that far exceeds the available resources.

The once-tranquil Hub has expanded into a miasmic pool of chaos. All along the edges of the long-established homes and buildings of the city, small collections of people have built their own, crude structures. These hovels are seldom strong enough to actually be called buildings, but they are all that most can afford. The prosperous farming communities are gone, destroyed by the violent weather and dangerous upheavals that have devoured most of Pandemonium. Instead, small farms have been set up within the city, walled off and guarded from starving peasants.

The once-proud memorial gardens dedicated to Gilgar have been replaced by a massive collection of tents and lean-tos. Where the people of the Hub used to come to contemplate life or to picnic with loved ones, the scavengers of Pandemonium now gather to sell their wares to anyone who can afford their price. The Bazaar is run by the Scravers, but many independent operators move about the area, selling food and stolen goods, or simply seeking prey weak enough to kill for a meal.

With the terraforming in most parts of the world gone, many have come to take advantage of the rich metals that are easily claimed from the ruined land. Heavy industry has taken away even the last vestiges of the parks, replacing the lush greenery with massive factories for refining the ores and smelting them into ingots easily transported off-planet. Even as the citizens of Pandemonium try to cope with the changes in their life, the Decados and others are making the most of the situation. Many of the guilds building new factories in the Hub employ armed security forces to evict anyone who tries to find shelter within their buildings. Few in Pandemonium are happy about the new industrial age that the cataclysms have brought.

Even as the world falls apart, strange life forms, unseen for almost a thousand years, are returning to the turbulence beyond the Hub. The preserves where these creatures were held are gone. Odd creatures that do not fit into the world Gilgar envisioned have seemingly returned from the grave, and even in the Hub native plants that were once deemed harmless have begun to grow with almost virulent speed. Swarms of violent creatures roam the Badlands, often stalking into the capital city in search of food or shelter from the unpredictable tremors that rock the planet.

For 25 miles in any direction from the center of the Hub (where the starport is located), the air is normally calm and life goes on. Beyond this distance, the world lies in ruin. Large parts of what were once suburbs of the Hub are now outside the area of protection. While the cataclysms have not destroyed these suburbs, they are in constant danger. Harsh storms blow through the area, and poison gasses waft across the land, causing violent coughing fits and occasionally even killing the weak. Once-sturdy buildings are now crumbling into ruin, and the roads are cracked and blistered. Only the most destitute souls live in these suburbs, and there is little they will not do for a chance to move into "the Circle," where the solitary terraforming engine guarantees safety from the rapidly encroaching Badlands. Violence and murder are commonplace in the area, and few dare walk

past the visible line of demarcation. There are rumors that the Chainers are using the areas just outside the Circle as a fresh source of new slaves. The desperate and often half-starved people in the area are easy pickings for the Muster, and few except their families notice when refugees are taken.

Graaf, "King of Thieves"

The small operators in the Bazaar — indeed, in all of the Hub — must answer to one man when it comes to their conflicts. That man is Graaf, a secretive figure, often heard of and seldom seen. Some claim that Graaf is actually an alien, one with powerful connections on several planets. Most scoff at the notion, feeling that an alien could not hope to hold the sort of power that Graaf maintains. Despite his title as the "king of thieves" Graaf tends to act as the unofficial mayor of the Hub. It is said that everyone of import in the Bazaar owes their status to Graaf. An equally strong statement is that everyone answers to Graaf for the crimes they commit. Some whisper that Graaf is actually a member of the Imperial Eye, the Emperor's intelligence agency. All that is really certain about the mysterious figure behind the criminal activities in the Hub is that those who cross him seldom live long enough to brag about their deeds.

The Cathedral in the Badlands

The Orthodox Church has recently come to Pandemonium, offering guidance to the people of a world in turmoil. A great cathedral is under construction in the Badlands. The purpose of this structure is simple enough: The people of Pandemonium realize that the Pancreator is still with them, offering his aid in their time of greatest need. While incomplete, the cathedral stands as a testament to the Church's dedication to life. The cathedral is an inspiration to many, and it is not uncommon for pilgrimages to leave the Hub and wander across a substantial part of the Badlands in order to reach the site where surely the Pancreator's miracles can be seen. Despite the tumultuous upheavals and violent storms, the cathedral still stands unharmed. Surely this is evidence of the Pancreator's will for all to survive. Others point to the recent surge in artifacts appearing in the Hub since cathedral construction began. They whisper that the cathedral construction may hide a Church archaeological dig for Ur or Second Republic artifacts thrust up from the ground by the cataclysms.

Diplomatic Immunity

"Diplomatic Immunity" is a sample drama for **Fading Suns**. It takes place on Pandemonium, and assumes that the player characters have found their way to this world for whatever reason and have either already met each other or encounter each other in the first act.

Pandemonium attracts not only the downtrodden, desperate for any opportunity to better themselves, but also the powerful, seeking more power in its wreckage. The characters may come from either of these groups, but their main encounters during "Diplomatic Immunity" come from both. While they serve a powerful Hazat noble and interact with Pandemonium's leading families, they also get to see the lives of some of the planet's most wretched inhabitants.

Don Marchenko Catilla Arronto Justus, a Hazat count, has just arrived on Pandemonium (perhaps on the same spaceship the characters were on) as a representative of his house. His position is only temporary; however, for his main role is to assess what threat (and opportunities) the newly discovered planet of Iver represents. To this end, he intends to meet with those who have gone to Iver and perhaps sponsor some expeditions of his own.

Unfortunately, more than a few people prefer that he never get the chance to do this. The characters encounter some of these people immediately after Don Marchenko disembarks, and get to meet more and more as the week continues. Someone wants Marchenko dead — perhaps more than one person. Some people merely dislike him, while others wish that he were dead. The players have the fun task of both finding out who the latter are and protecting Marchenko from them.

Do not expect this drama to detail every way to handle what the players want their characters to do. The only thing you can expect from players is that they will not do what you expect them to. "Diplomatic Immunity" details a series of events occurring over a period of days. Characters might persuade Marchenko to do different things, but he is strong-willed and unlikely to change his plans without good reason. As long as the characters work for him, they need to follow his orders.

Riot

Sometimes Pandemonium gets hot. Okay, Pandemonium is usually hot. Fine, have it your way — Pandemonium sweats like it was sitting in the middle of the holy flame itself. The small space liner "Ryko's Trust" landed during one of these sweltering hot days, one of many oppressively warm days in a long string of such days. The heat has helped aggravate conditions on this overcrowded

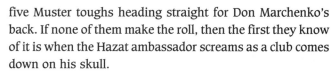

planet, and tempers have risen as high as the temperature.

This is especially true in the spaceport, where the various guilds have begun bitterly clashing over issues of territory and employees. The Muster and the Scravers have butted heads repeatedly, with both groups wanting greater control over the loading and unloading of spaceships. While the Reeves and Charioteers could usually bring such tensions under control, outside forces now prevent that.

Unloading "Ryko's Trust" just became the center of this dispute, and things do not look good. A small crew of Scraver stevedores shows up and begins unloading the ship, only to have a Muster crew show up, waving papers to prove the ship's owner hired them in advance. As the ship's passengers watch, both sides of the argument begin attracting supporters, and tempers flare.

It does not really matter who throws the first punch, only that it does get thrown. Within seconds, the entire docking area erupts in violence, with 100 guild members fighting, running and causing as much havoc as possible. The characters might just want to get themselves into cover. They each have the chance to make one Dex + Dodge roll to get to safety behind crates and other cargo. Any who succeed are immediately safe. Any who fail take 3D damage every turn until they make it to cover. They can continue trying to Dodge to safety, and any comrades who want to help them can do so with a Dex + Fight roll.

Of course, the tumult of the riot is not the only danger. The characters also get a Perception + Observe roll to spot

five Muster toughs heading straight for Don Marchenko's back. If none of them make the roll, then the first they know of it is when the Hazat ambassador screams as a club comes down on his skull.

Stopping this attack should not prove especially difficult, but finding out who planned it is. The five thugs believe Don Marchenko is the ship's owner (he is not) who double-crossed them by first hiring them and then allowing Scravers to do the work. This belief stems from a video conference held nine days ago, in which a figure bearing striking similarities to Don Marchenko did hire the Muster to unload the ship. This was, in fact, the assassin using video compositing to make it appear that Don Marchenko was behind everything. Of course, Don Marchenko was on "Ryko's Trust," in the Rampart solar system, at that time, and could not have made any such call. The assassin also set up a high quality squawker near the docking area. When the Muster bearers appeared, she insulted the Scravers viciously, egging the bearers on to violence. The incident embarrasses the Muster severely, but they still have their suspicions.

Don Marchenko's Plans

Don Marchenko intends to make his moves slowly and surely. His primary responsibility is to ensure that Iver's House Chauki can in no way threaten the Hazat. He intends to discredit any claims it might have to being the original House Chauki, or, failing that, find some way to neutralize it. This can mean violence, getting the Church to excommunicate it, or, if possible, shutting down the jumpgate yet again.

He intends to begin his trip to Pandemonium with the social necessities — visiting Count Enis Sharn, undertaking a pilgrimage to the Cathedral and making the acquaintance of the planet's leading figures. Then he hopes to start tracking down those individuals who have had any contact with Iver. This list includes Enis Sharn's agents, the few Church missionaries who have traveled to Iver, smugglers who have managed to start small trade routes between there and Pandemonium, and the technicians who first reactivated the jump route.

The day after the riot, he intends to visit Count Sharn in the early afternoon to gather information on Iver. Count Sharn will not tell him much, but will direct him toward several Hub merchants who traffic in Iver relics. Don Marchenko hopes to visit them the following day to get the names of smugglers who trade goods out in the badlands.

His unspoken hope is that he can prove that the rulers of Iver usurped the real House Chauki on their planet, thereby giving the Hazat some claim to their world. He would like to visit Iver himself, but knows that in his condition, such a trip would pose innumerable difficulties. Perhaps a team of intrepid explorers could do it for him.

Getting the Players Involved

Gamemasters should have little trouble finding ways to work the characters into this drama. Pandemonium's spaceport is one of the planet's busiest areas, and everyone has reason to be here. All the guilds conduct heavy business on its premises, the noble houses oversee their investments, and priests come out to minister to space crews, bless ships and watch cargo for signs of heretical material — or choose the best for themselves.

If the characters do not have permanent ties to Pandemonium, they might very well arrive on "Ryko's Trust" themselves. Perhaps they work for the ship or Don Marchenko hired them before arriving on the planet. If they have no such ties, then Don Marchenko will seek to hire them if they play any role in fighting off the Muster thugs. He offers housing in a nice villa (a serious luxury on Pandemonium) as well as standard salaries. Even if the characters refuse to accept this position, the assassins have seen them associating with Don Marchenko and may target them as well.

Fanaticism

After a relaxing night at Don Marchenko's Pandemonium villa, Don Marchenko and his new friends prepare to visit Count Enis Sharn. The stable master outfits enough horses for everyone as this is Marchenko's preferred mode of travel. Even characters without the ride skill can travel this way — as long as nothing happens to upset the animals. The first half of the one-hour ride is pleasant enough, but then the characters get Perception + Observe rolls to hear a commotion from around the corner.

Any characters who make the roll have one turn to prepare before Friar Mizraim Reuss and his devoted followers turn that corner. These are 50 anti-tech fanatics in the harshest sense, carrying clubs, torches and rocks with which to destroy any technology they may encounter. These vigilantes do not have to target the characters. Don Marchenko carries no obvious tech objects, and they will leave him alone. The characters, on the other hand …

Anyone who has any obvious items (and any aliens) finds himself on the receiving end of a volley of rocks (five per turn, hit on a 9 or less, and do a base 2D damage). Anyone with obvious cybernetics gets picked out for special attention, and five club-wielding nuts come after her. These guys should not prove too difficult to disperse, but they should add to the characters' paranoia. The assassins have nothing to do with Friar Mizraim and his followers, but the characters have no way to know this. This red herring should keep them quite worried.

Sniper

When the characters and Don Marchenko finally get to Enis Sharn's manor, the planet's owner will actually greet them himself. He has long hoped to talk to this famed warrior, and will put up with whatever bizarre entourage he brings with him. He also apologizes for the commotion that Don Marchenko has encountered (the spaceport riot, the religious fanatics), but stresses that Pandemonium is going through uncertain times.

After a pleasant afternoon with the Count (during which time enterprising characters can learn much about the planet), the horses get saddled and again the team rides off. It's another hour getting back to the villa through the dusky streets of the Hub. The group is only 15 minutes from home when Marchenko's horse rears as if shot and begins bucking wildly. A sniper, knowing that a noble would have a shield, shot a crossbow dart into his horse. The dart, coated with a painful (though not lethal) poison, has driven the beast into a frenzy. Though Marchenko is a skilled rider, he has little hope of maintaining his seating against this fury. The characters have two turns to resolve the situation before the beast pitches Marchenko to the ground. While the actual unseating will probably not get through his shield

MacDougall

(9D damage), the resulting trampling from his maddened horse will. This trampling does 5D damage every turn until characters rein the beast in.

Characters who want to control the horse at any point need to accumulate 10 victory dice on a Dexterity + Beast Lore roll. If they want to drive it off, they need to accumulate three successes on a Strength + Impress role. Marchenko would prefer that they brought it under control one way or another and absolutely detests seeing animals harmed. Characters should have to decide between tracking down the sniper (located in a four-story building just off the main road to the villa) and protecting Marchenko and the horse. The sniper has set up his ambush spot well, ensuring rapid access to the roof from which he hops from building to building until he reaches a dark ladder several blocks away. Once there he clambers to the ground and rushes to join his cronies at a nearby barber shop.

The Physick

The episode shakes Marchenko up badly, and once back at the villa he sends the houseboy for a local physick. While the local physick has served his community for most of his life, cutting hair and amputating limbs, he is not the gentleman who appears in response to Marchenko's summons. The physick and his family are currently bound and gagged in their own house, watched over by several thugs. In his place comes Bitash the sniper, dressed in the physick's robes. He tends Marchenko as best he can, and he may well convince any characters who monitor his work of his legitimacy. If they ask any of the villa's servants about the physick, they all assert to never having seen him before, though he looks like the old physick. If questioned, he says that the local physick was away on a call when the houseboy showed up requiring aid.

Before leaving, he gives Marchenko a drink of a warm herbal tea to help him sleep. He has already prepared the herbs with a slow-acting poison — one that should not take effect until well into the night. Barring character intervention, he takes a one firebird fee and heads back to the barbershop to gather his band and disappear into the Hub.

Don Marchenko goes to sleep within 30 minutes of drinking the tea, and the poison begins working shortly thereafter. By the time he wakes, fiery pain tearing through his belly, he has less than an hour to live. Healing him requires 10 victory levels on Wits + Physick rolls as well as possession of at least a Physick's Kit (which the villa has). Each roll takes 10 minutes, so characters can take six rolls over the next hour to save him. If they seek out the local physick, they find him at home with a police guard. If the characters convince the guards to let them talk to the physick (five-firebird bribe), then they immediately notice that this is not the one who worked on Marchenko. The real physick tells of being held captive, though he does not know why or

by whom. He will rush to help Marchenko, but will only have thirty minutes (three rolls), and his Wits + Physicks goal is 12.

Theurgy can help Don Marchenko as well. While Laying on Hands or Cleansing will not rid his body of the poison, each successful use allows him to live another 30 minutes and reduces his agonizing pain. Restoration or the Healing Hand of Saint Amalthea completely rids Marchenko of the poison and makes him feel better than he has in years.

The Assault

If the characters manage to save Marchenko, then Bitash (the sniper and fake physick) is getting frustrated. He will make one more attempt the next night. He takes his time approaching the villa. He has hired a dozen thugs to charge the front door as a distraction. When the thugs begin mixing it up with the characters, he intends to sneak in the villa and kill Marchenko himself. He hopes to sneak up on Marchenko (who will still be bed bound following his recovery from the poison) and slit his throat with a vibrating dagger, which Bitash has coated with poison just in case.

Normally Marchenko could handle the assassin alone, but barring some miraculous healing, the poison has left him with one point of Vitality and a —10 on all his rolls. Characters who are vigilant for danger from any source besides the thugs can make Perception + Observe rolls contested with Bitash's Dex + Sneak to notice him. Of course, if anyone is waiting in Marchenko's bedroom, they automatically see Bitash, who comes through the door (or window, if there is a guard at the door).

This is Bitash's final attempt on Marchenko. If he fails this time, he will try to seek out his patron for further instructions, only to discover that he cannot find her. If he succeeds, then he disappears for a while, staying on the outskirts of the Hub for a year. If he gets caught, he has no intention of being killed (or killing himself), and will trade money (up to 400 firebirds) and information for his freedom.

So Who Did It?

This drama tends to assume that the Kurgan spy Zulaykha Turakina (see Chapter 8: Gamemastering) is the main force behind the assassination attempts. The courtesan has begun assembling a decent ring of informants and operatives through Hazat space, and word of Don Marchenko's quest did not take long to reach her. She feared that the Hazat might end up with another world whose resources could turn against the caliphate, and took steps to neutralize this threat. Zulaykha Turakina flees the planet before characters figure out who was behind everything, and may well reappear to haunt them again later (or hire them — who knows which way loyalties might change?).

However, this is not the only possibility. The Iver

Chauki's would want to hinder his mission if they knew about it. Early in Don Marchenko's career, he became involved in a number of serious atrocities on Byzantium Secundus, and those families effected by his actions may want revenge. Psychics upset at Don Marchenko's harsh role in shutting down the dervishes later in his career might also target him for retribution. The opposite side of this is the fact that religious fanatics might see his association with psychic as a high sin and target him as a lesson to others. Additionally, his own servants might want to kill him since the Don has a notorious history of seducing their spouses. Finally, the assassins might not even have a grudge against Don Marchenko. Instead, they may hope killing him serves as an embarrassment to Count Sharn and helps prove to Decados leaders that he cannot control the planet. The gamemaster can take whatever approach most fits his style.

What Next?

If the characters seek out the lady who hired Bitash, they should have very little luck. He has no idea how she found him, but she proved herself well informed, cultivated and wealthy. She did not speak, instead communicating with him via an old, hand-held think machine when they met at Hazred's Tavern (a notorious bar catering to the underworld). Unless the gamemaster wants them to encounter her, she has left the planet — probably to crop up later to bedevil the characters.

Marchenko is not overly concerned. He knows many people want him dead, and stopping one will not end all the threats against him. If the gamemaster likes, Marchenko can offer the characters permanent positions as his entourage, give them jobs gathering information on other worlds, or thank them for their help and send them on their way. If they continue working for him, they may have to escort him through the Badlands as he gets involved in politics at the Cathedral, make contacts with the Hub's criminal element (perhaps meeting Graaf himself), or help keep other houses from making deals with Iver.

Personalities:
Don Marchenko

Born into the wealthy Justus branch of the Hazat, Don Marchenko Catilla Arronto Justus proved that a privileged childhood did not exclude one from the sacrifices of war. He commanded house legions while still young, and helped lead the Hazat invasion of Byzantium Secundus early in the Emperor Wars. He helped form the Hazat dervishes, their psychic commandos who proved so effective. When the Emperor Wars ended, the Church brought a great deal of pressure to bear to disband these units, and the task fell to Don Marchenko. More than a few dervishes bitterly objected to being discarded after having risked their lives repeatedly.

The objections turned violent, and Don Marchenko found himself forced to battle several of his own former companions. He lost his left arm during their fights, and spends the next year recuperating. He still suffers nightmares from this time and has trouble sleeping.

He has finally decided he is too old to take personal action, and hopes to serve his house as a diplomat. He has helped push the Church to call a Crusade against the Kurgans and now is in charge of Hazat relations with Iver. His traits represent his age — he used to be a lot more physically capable.

Race: Human

Quote: "I do believe we can work things out."

Description: His 5'8" frame stands ramrod straight, and his military bearing screams out at anyone who sees him. His white hair is cut close to his head and his mustache is well trimmed. He wears elegant clothes, but not especially gaudy ones. He does nothing to hide the fact that he has one arm and does not intend to replace it with a cybernetic one.

Age: Late 60s (he has stopped taking rejuvenation drugs but still looks 10 years younger)

Equipment: Dueling shield, rapier, excellent clothing, wrist squawker, enough money to buy anything else he pleases

Entourage: Don Marchenko has left his old servants behind on Vera Cruz, intending to recruit locals. If the characters do not stay on with him, he will hire others. His villa has five servants: a head butler, a cook, a maid, a stable master and a serving boy. The stable master also takes care of landscaping what little land the villa has.

Body: Strength 7, Dexterity 7, Endurance 5

Mind: Wits 9, Perception 9, Tech 6

Spirit: Extrovert 6, Introvert 4, Passion 5, Calm 5, Faith 3, Ego 5

Natural Skills: Charm 9, Dodge 8, Fight 8, Impress 9, Melee 8, Observe 9, Shoot 8, Sneak 6, Vigor 7

Learned Skills: Beast Lore 5, Empathy 3, Etiquette 9, Focus 9, Inquiry 8, Lore (Psychics) 5, Lore (Nobility) 7, Read Latin, Read Urthish, Remedy 5, Ride 7, Social (Leadership) 10, Social (Oratory) 5, Search 6, Stoic Body 8, Stoic Mind 8, Survival 8, Think Machine 2, Warfare (Military Tactics) 9,

Fencing Actions: Parry, Thrust, Slash, Draw & Strike, Athletic Strike

Martial Arts: Martial Kick, Leaping Kick, Choke Hold

Psi 6

Psychic Paths: Soma (Toughening, Strengthening, Quickening, Hardening), Far Hand (Lifting Hand, Throwing Hand, Crushing Hand)

Stigma: When he uses his psychic powers, his right hand temporarily develops an extra pinky

Wyrd: 8

Vitality: -10/-8/-6/-4/-2/0/0/0/0/0

Bitash the Sniper

One of Pandemonium's better assassins, Bitash can use guns or poisons equally well. He was hired by a cloaked woman who gave him 500 firebirds, a photograph of Marchenko, and a schedule of his planned activities. He knows nothing beyond that and has no idea how the woman found out about him. Bitash understands the consequences of his actions and knows that Count Enis Sharn will have him killed if he gets turned over to the authorities. He will do everything he can to keep that from happening, cooperating with anyone who captures him to the best of his abilities. He knows very little about who hired him, and does not even realize she has already left the planet.

Quote: "I don't know anything!"

Age: Early 30s

Equipment: Crossbow, heavy revolver, standard shield, three grenades, vibrating dagger

Body: Strength 5, Dexterity 7, Endurance 6

Mind: Wits 5, Perception 7, Tech 6

Spirit: Extrovert 2, Introvert 4, Passion 3, Calm 5, Faith 1, Ego 4

Natural Skills: Charm 4, Dodge 6, Fight 6, Impress 5, Melee 7, Observe 7, Shoot 8, Sneak 7, Vigor 5

Learned Skills: Crossbow 8, Inquiry 3, Knavery 6, Lockpicking 6, Lore (The Hub) 5, Lore (Poisons) 7, Physick 1, Read Urthish, Remedy 5, Search 3, Social (Acting) 4, Streetwise 7, Warfare (Demolitions) 3

Wyrd: 5

Vitality: -10/-8/-6/-4/-2/0/0/0/0/0/0

Thugs

A number of rather common street thugs appear in this drama, ranging from Muster bearers to religious fanatics to common ruffians. These are not the bravest of individuals, and will usually try to break off a fight if they take four or more points of damage. The following traits can work for all of them.

Race: Human

Quote: "Get 'em"

Description: Local toughs. Poorly dressed and educated.

Equipment: Large clubs (bearer's poles, 2x4s, maces), heavy clothing (2D armor)

Body: Strength 5, Dexterity 5, Endurance 5

Mind: Wits 4, Perception 4, Tech 4

Spirit: Extrovert 3, Introvert 1, Passion 3, Calm 1, Faith 3, Ego 1

Natural Skills: Charm 3, Dodge 4, Fight 4, Impress 4, Melee 5, Observe 3, Shoot 3, Sneak 3, Vigor 4

Wyrd: 3

Vitality: -10/-8/-6/-4/-2/0/0/0/0/0

Index

Upcoming Products

Holistic Design has a host of **Fading Suns** products in print and more planned for release in the coming months. Be on the lookout for:

Gamemasters Screen & Complete Pandemonium

A screen sturdy enough to halt the charge of a rampaging Vorox, including all the Second Edition rulebook charts and tables a gamemaster needs. It also comes bundled with the "Complete Pandemonium" book, providing new **Fading Suns** gamemasters with ample adventures to inflict on their players.

Legions of the Empire

This book brings out the Known Worlds' most dangerous people and places with a bang, allowing gamemasters to put players in the middle of the bloodiest conflicts against the most feared warriors — including the Symbiot-fighting Stigmata Garrison! New weaponry and war tech provides numerous excuses to blow things up.

Star Crusade

It had to happen — the jumpgates to the barbarian worlds have opened and Questing Knights, adventurers, seekers and scoundrels of all stripes now risk life and limb to exploit the riches of these new worlds. The Hawkwoods aim to take back what is theirs from the Vuldrok Raiders, while the Hazat seek to overthrow a rival star-empire with the aid of the Church. The player characters must carve out their own fates amid these struggles. "Star Crusade" is a vast new campaign setting for the **Fading Suns** universe.

War in the Heavens: Hegemony

The second in the epic trilogy begun with "Lifeweb," this book takes the characters into Vau space for the first major emissary with the enigmatic, high-tech aliens in years. But what do the Vau want with the players characters? A sourcebook and adventure book revealing tantalizing details about this strange race. Events here lead into the mysteries of the Anunnaki in the final book of the trilogy: "Pantheon."

Available Products

These **Fading Suns** books and games are available now!

The Sinful Stars: Tales of the Fading Suns

The world of the **Fading Suns** is revealed in the tales of its people: priests, nobles, guildsmembers, aliens and peasants. This short story anthology reveals: The quest of an Ukar for an ancient relic of his race's mythology - a crown that can bend time itself; a priest finds absolution from his tortured sins in the storms of Pentateuch, the Planet of Mysteries; a low-ranking noblewoman dares a joust of words with the cunning Decados to find the truth behind her betrothed husband's death; a scientist studying nanotech ressurects an evil from the time of the Second Republic. These stories and more show the tumultuous fate of humankind four millenia from now. # 234, ISBN 1-888906-14-6, $15.95

Fading Suns Players Companion

A valuable expansion to the **Fading Suns** rules, this big book includes new Blessings and Curses, Benefices and Afflictions, skills, occult powers, weapons, equipment and valuable rules expansions. In addition, there are new character roles: Knightly order, Church sects, new religions, guilds, military units, long-awaited details on sentient alien races and the genetically engineered Changed. A must for players and gamemasters! #229, ISBN 1-888906-07-3, $25.00

Lords of the Known Worlds

Nobles are the unquestioned rulers of the universe. Few are privy to their lifestyles and secrets, and the great unwashed understand little of the perks (and problems) associated with rulership. There are taxes to collect, wars to wage, and rivals to crush. Indeed, as any noble would tell you, the sacrifices they endure more than justify their opulent lifestyles. Not just anybody can be such a martyr; it takes blood privilege. A privilege the nobility protects at all costs, even if it requires deadly duels or declarations of war. #226, ISBN 1-888906-11-1, $18.00

Priests of the Celestial Sun

The nobles may rule the secular lives of the Known Worlders, but the Church guards their souls — and in so doing, dictates to the nobility. Few lords dare to defy the will of the Patriarch and his bishops. But the Church's rock is not as stable as it once was — new sects and orders have appeared in the wake of the Emperor Wars, shifting the populace's loyalties and reawakening ancient heresies. While the Church stands united against the powers of the Emperor, the Royal Houses and the Merchant League, they feud within their cathedrals, vying for dominion over the faithful. #228, ISBN 1-888906-06-5, $18.95

Merchants of the Jumpweb

The nobles and the Church may vie for the leadership and minds of the Known Worlders, but the merchants own the stars. Without their high-tech savvy or the loans from their coffers, travel and commerce could not take place. This book details the histories and modus operandi of the Merchant League guilds, from the weird Engineers to the stately Reeves. #231, ISBN 1-888906-09-X, $20.00

Byzantium Secundus

There is no more important or intrigue-laden world than Byzantium Secundus, throneworld of the Empire. Here the fates of millions are determined and the destiny of humanity is in the hands of the royal ambassadors, Church priests, merchant princes, alien envoys and underground conspiracy groups — all vying for the emperor's attention and favor. Includes new character roles for the Imperial Eye — the emperor's intergalactic spies. #275, ISBN 1-888906-02-2, $18.00

Weird Places

Explore some of the varied sites of the **Fading Suns** universe: Roam the strange fields of Pentateuch, a planet terraformed with occult laws. Discover a secret lost world hiding a powerful artifact sought by all. Shop the stalls of the eclectic Istakhr Market, where everything is for sale. Or dock at Barter, a traveling marketplace in space. Ship out to Bannockburn to halt a deadly Symbiot excursion, or search the haunted chapel of Manitou for lost lore. # 227, ISBN: 1-888906-05-7, $12.95

Hawkwood Fiefs: Imperial Survey Vol. 1

The Emperor has sent his Questing Knights across the Known Worlds to bring back word on the state of his empire. Ever the canny propagandist, he has published their reports in affordable gazetteers for his citizens to read. The first report reveals the Hawkwood Fiefs: Delphi, Ravenna, Gwynneth and Leminkainen. #236, ISBN 1-888906-15-4, $6.95

Forbidden Lore: Technology

The weird world of **Fading Suns** technology is revealed, from starships to ominous psychic artifacts. But beware: the Church claims that such items can endanger the soul, and the Inquisitor's flameguns are ever ready to burn those who dare to use such proscribed and sinful tech. Includes enough equipment lists to choke a Vorox. # 225, ISBN: 1-888906-03-0, $15.00

The Dark Between the Stars

The Anunnaki left behind many strange devices and their ancient secrets lie buried on many worlds, secrets which can bring salvation — or destruction. But other entities lurk in the void, tempting human and alien alike to enact schemes against the civilized order. An occult book, detailing psychic covens, Sathraists, Antinomists and the many entities and forces involved in the supernatural universe. #230, ISBN 1-888906-08-1, $17.95

War in the Heavens: Lifeweb

The first in an epic trilogy, "Lifeweb" details the Symbiots, explaining who and what they are, from their beginnings on Chernobog to their modern starfaring empire, carving worlds from human space. Also included is an adventure pitting the player characters against the Symbiots, with the fate of the Empire at stake. #235, ISBN 1-888906-12-X, $20.00

Children of the Gods: Obun & Ukar

One of the earliest sentient alien races humanity discovered was the Ur-Obun — peaceful and wise philosophers. Soon after, humanity met their cousins, the Ur-Ukar — vicious and cruel warriors with a starfaring empire of their own. Humanity has played the two against each other ever since. This book details the histories, cultures and unique powers (theurgic and psychic) of these two races. #232, ISBN 1-888906-10-3, $12.95

Sinners & Saints

Here is a rogues gallery of people and creatures from the Known Worlds and beyond: noble rivals, well-meaning (and not so well-meaning) priests, space pirates, deadly mercenaries, assassins, alien animals (pets and predators), bizarre creatures and more. Each has a story to tell and will lead player characters into intrigue and adventure. Each comes on its own sheet for ease of use by both players and gamemasters. # 233, ISBN 1-888906-11-1, $16.95

Letters of Marque: Starship Deckplans

A collection of deckplan maps for use with **Fading Suns** roleplaying or the **Noble Armada** miniatures game — it has also been approved for use with **Traveller**®! In fact, it can be used with just about any science fiction game. Five starships are featured (including an al-Malik explorer and League escort), each depicted on 25mm scale maps — perfect for detailed boarding actions or roleplaying game firefights from corridor to corridor, stateroom to engine room. #501, ISBN 1-888906-51-0, $14.95

Noble Armada Starship Miniatures Game

A starship miniatures game of broadsides and boarding actions in the **Fading Suns** universe. Royal houses vie against rival fleets and pirates for supremacy of the Known Worlds. Command frigates, destroyers or dreadnoughts to carve a fiefdom from the stars! Let loose all guns against your enemies and loot their crippled ships! Includes 32 plastic starship miniatures. #500, ISBN 1-888906-50-2, $55.00

Go to www.fadingsuns.com for product updates.

Look for these products in your local gaming store or order direct from HDi. Send list of products with check or money order, plus postage fee*, to: Product Orders, 5295 Hwy 78, D-337, Stone Mountain, GA 30087.

* $4.00 per order under $50.00. Expect 2-3 weeks delivery time. International orders: postage fee is 25% ot total purchase or $10.00, whichever is greater. Expect 4-8 weeks ship time.

HOLISTIC

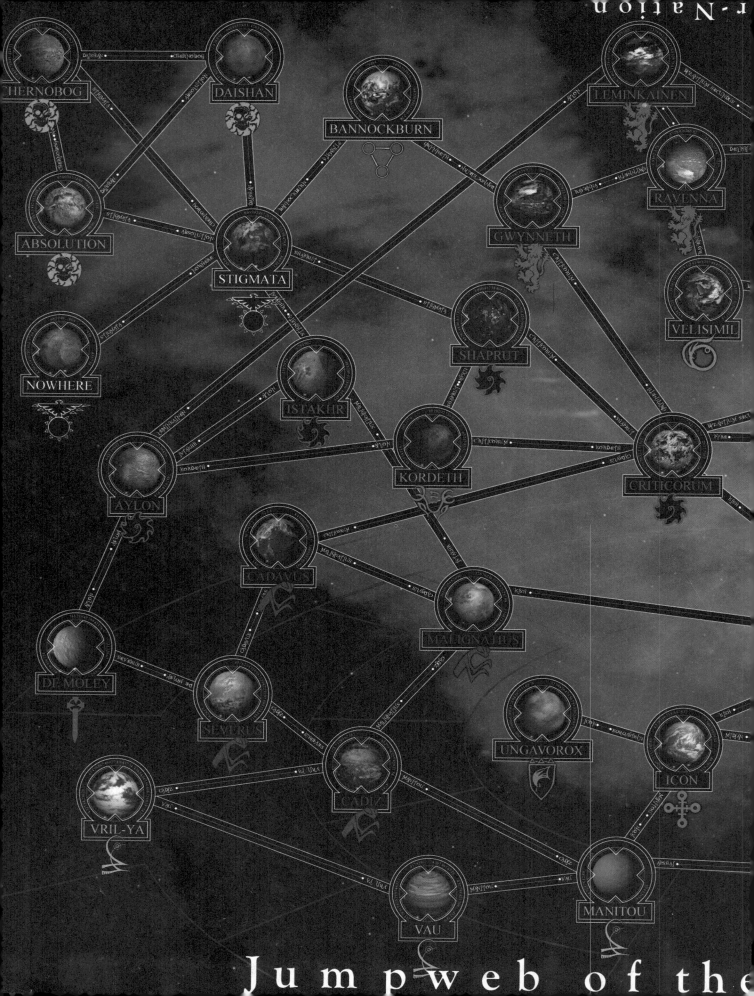

CHERNOBOG

DAISHAN

BANNOCKBURN

LEMINKAINEN

ABSOLUTION

STIGMATA

GWYNNETH

RAVENNA

VELISIMIL

NOWHERE

SHAPRUT

ISTAKHR

KORDETH

CRITICORUM

AYLON

CADAVUS

MALIGNATIUS

DE MOLEY

SEVERUS

UNGAVOROX

ICON

VRIL-YA

CADIZ

VAU

MANITOU